Encyclopedia of Transcendentalism

Encyclopedia of Transcendentalism

TIFFANY K. WAYNE

Facts On File
An imprint of Infobase Publishing

Encyclopedia of Transcendentalism

Copyright © 2006 by Tiffany K. Wayne

All rights reserved. No part of this book may be reproduced or utilized in any form
or by any means, electronic or mechanical, including photocopying, recording, or
by any information storage or retrieval systems, without permission in writing from
the publisher. For information contact:

Facts On File, Inc.
An imprint of Infobase Publishing
132 West 31st Street
New York NY 10001

Library of Congress Cataloging-in-Publication Data
Wayne, Tiffany K., 1968–
Encyclopedia of Transcendentalism / Tiffany K. Wayne.
p. cm.
Includes bibliographical references and index.
ISBN 0-8160-5626-9 (hardcover: alk. paper)
1. American literature—19th century—Encyclopedias. 2. Transcendentalism
(New England)—Encyclopedias. 3. United States—Intellectual life—1783–1865—
Encyclopedias. 4. American literature—New England—Encyclopedias. 5. New
England—Intellectual life—Encyclopedias. I. Title.
PS217.T7.W39 2005
810.9'384—dc22 2005008384

Facts On File books are available at special discounts when purchased in bulk
quantities for businesses, associations, institutions, or sales promotions. Please call
our Special Sales Department in New York at (212) 967-8800 or (800) 322-8755.

You can find Facts On File on the World Wide Web at http://www.factsonfile.com

Text design by Joan M. Toro
Cover design by Cathy Rincon

Printed in the United States of America

VB Hermitage 10 9 8 7 6 5 4 3 2 1

This book is printed on acid-free paper.

CONTENTS

INTRODUCTION

Encyclopedia of Transcendentalism is a complete A–Z guide to the American Transcendentalist movement of the 19th century. Entries address the philosophical, theological, political, and literary aspects of the movement through identification of the major figures, books, essays, sermons, poems, newspapers, clubs, and organizations from its origins in the first decades of the 19th century to the activities of a second generation of thinkers and activists after the Civil War.

Transcendentalism has suffered a problem of definition from its own time to ours. Contemporary Charles Dickens visited Boston and observed that he had been led to believe that "whatever was unintelligible was certainly Transcendental." Even Nathaniel Hawthorne, whose literary and social ties to the movement mean that he is often identified as a Transcendentalist himself, remarked that Transcendentalism was surely "a monster—whose features cannot be defined." Ralph Waldo Emerson, the leading spokesperson of the movement, offered only the simple definition of Transcendentalism as "Idealism as it appeared in 1842" and an emphasis in all things "on the power of Thought and Will, on inspiration, on miracle, on individual culture."

This volume also resists a single definition of Transcendentalism. From the entries here, the reader may instead grasp a sense of the movement as a set of ideas emerging at a specific historical moment and eventually reaching out to engage a range of issues of the time—literary, theological, and political. Encompassing a variety of ideas and individuals throughout the 19th century, Tran-

scendentalism at its core was a tendency toward new literary explorations, a belief in progress and renewal, and a spiritual quest for self-development and self-knowledge.

OVERVIEW OF TRANSCENDENTALISM

Although influenced by and helping to shape an overall shift in American culture toward a focus on the individual, American Transcendentalism began as a crisis of faith, as a reaction against Boston Unitarianism. In exploring the role of the individual in a theological sense, Transcendentalism ultimately rejected the need for biblical Christianity, replacing belief in the God of the Bible with belief in the divinity of humanity. While Unitarianism, influenced by Enlightenment thought of the 18th century, preached that the Bible could be studied rationally, just as any other text, Transcendentalism went even further than Unitarianism to the belief that one need only look *inward* to one's own personal subjective beliefs and definition of truth to form spiritual and moral beliefs.

Unitarianism had an impact on the development and course of Transcendentalism beyond the theological issues, however. Unitarians believed in perfecting individual character as humanity's destiny on Earth and promoted the connection between a healthy spiritual life and intellectual life. Some Transcendentalists maintained their Unitarian connections, but others found that their formal ties with Unitarianism were strained. Transcendentalists shared Unitarian beliefs in the divinity of nature and in humanity's free will and innate goodness, but Transcendentalists had moved from a Unitarian focus on a benevolent God and a divine Christ to urging individuals to look within, as Emerson explained in his 1838 Divinity School Address: "to go alone . . . to be a divine man." Transcendentalists began to speak of man's inward nature as a guide to spiritual truth and of the idea of the "Over-Soul" as the guiding force of the universe. This was a secularization of the idea of a "unified" God, beyond the biblical God to the idea of the universe as one giant soul, encompassing God, humans, and nature working together toward truth and perfection.

Transcendentalism was more than a theological break between generations, however, emerging as a distinct philosophical, literary, and social reform movement itself. While some individuals—notably Ralph Waldo Emerson, George Ripley, Theodore Parker, James Freeman Clarke, as well as many others—were Unitarian ministers who became prominent Transcendentalist lecturers, critics, and writers, others, such as Margaret Fuller and Henry David Thoreau, came to Transcendentalism not through Unitarianism but through literary and philosophical interest in exploring new forms and questions. As detailed in the entries in this volume, Transcendentalism was influenced not only by Puritan Calvinism and Enlightenment thought but also by other religious-spiritual movements of the time, such as Quakerism (with its emphasis on the "inner light" and social justice), and by German philosophers such as Johann Wolfgang von Goethe and Immanuel Kant (from whom the term *transcendental* was adapted), as well as by the leading figures of English romanticism, such as Samuel Taylor Coleridge.

Transcendentalism was ultimately, then, not a new or separate system of thought but a synthesis of these various traditions and approaches. The core of Transcendentalist thought emphasized both the religious and the secular or humanist aspects of the philosophy. The mandates to "know thyself" and to act according to one's own subjective understanding of truth (one's intuition) were direct intellectual challenges to Enlightenment rationalism and to institutional authority and even biblical revelation as guides and sources of truth. Transcendentalism suggested instead that the individual was the spiritual and moral center of the universe and that the mind, not the scriptures, held the keys to a moral life.

The year 1836 has been identified as the "annus mirabilis," or miraculous year, of the Transcendentalist movement. In 1836 the Transcendental Club was formed to bring together individuals interested in discussing the new ideas. Also in 1836 several key figures published Transcendentalist manifestos on a variety of themes related to nature, philosophy, individualism, and debates within Unitarianism, including Ralph Waldo Emerson's *Nature.* Throughout the remainder of the century the Transcendentalists met, discussed, lectured, experimented with social reform and newspaper publishing, established clubs and schools, and wrote poetry, fiction, literary criticism, and philosophical treatises.

KEY CONCEPTS OF MOVEMENT

Transcendentalism was a set of ideas promoting a new understanding of the individual, his or her relationship to nature and society and the universe, and the importance of self-development. Self-knowledge was the key to education for the Transcendentalists in their focus on the individual as the source of and route to all knowledge. They rejected contemporary social mores that were anti-individualistic or encouraged social conformity, emphasizing instead "self-reliance" and self-expression as their primary values.

Transcendentalists believed that the natural or physical world had meaning only as a reflection of the divine. Humans could experience divinity directly through nature, a spiritual practice in which no mediation, such as through the churches, was needed. As part of the natural world, the human mind itself was divine, and therefore one must pay attention to understanding one's own thoughts, feelings, and emotions as reflective of universal truths. As Emerson said of the times, it was as if "the mind had become aware of itself." In more modern terms, this was a philosophy of subjectivity, privileging the intuitive and the individual over rational thought or formal learning. In other words, the Transcendentalists believed that there were universal truths governing the world, but that these truths were not contained in texts or in tradition, rather that individuals reached the universal truths in different ways through their own minds and experiences.

The paradox of Transcendentalism is how this philosophy of the self translated into a social conscience, for the mid-19th century was also the age of reform, as Americans looked for new solutions, philosophically, spiritually, and socially, to the problems brought by extreme changes in their society, such as industrialization, urbanization, immigration, and westward expansion. Despite traditional understandings of Transcendentalism as primarily a literary-philosophical impulse, many individual Transcendentalists made names for themselves as social reformers. This volume pays particular attention to those reformers whose political and social consciences were informed by their commitments to self-culture, to progress, and to the life of the mind, such as George Ripley with the utopian community at Brook Farm, Bronson Alcott and Elizabeth Palmer Peabody with education reform, Margaret Fuller with women's rights, and Theodore Parker and Henry David Thoreau with antislavery, just to name a few.

Transcendentalists were no different from many of their contemporaries in that they possessed the optimistic spirit of the time and believed that human society could be changed. On the principles of self-reliance and nonconformity, many resisted joining reform organizations which they feared stifled individual thought and were too narrowly focused on one issue at the expense of addressing the interrelatedness of problems. In addition, most reform associations proposed political solutions for what were, according to Transcendentalists, spiritual problems. However, even while retaining different philosophical approaches to reform, many Transcendentalists did lend their voices and their time to the most significant reform causes of their time, such as education, labor rights, women's rights, and the abolition of slavery. In fact, Transcendentalist philosophical concerns, such as the commitments to individual freedom, self-development, and social progress, helped shape the issues and focus of those reform efforts. Attention to social reform as a main issue for Transcendentalists helps illuminate the wider cultural engagement and significance of Transcendentalism and also brings in a variety of individuals not always associated directly with the literary aspects of the movement, but who were, in fact, engaging Transcendentalist themes and concerns.

A NOTE ON THIS VOLUME

In addition to providing a source of information on individual Transcendentalists and their literary and cultural activities, the overall goal of the *Encyclopedia of Transcendentalism* is to illuminate the broader cultural context and wide-ranging impact of American Transcendentalism in its own time. In terms of the literary emphasis of the movement, this volume is unique in bringing together all of the major, as well as some lesser-known but significant, books, essays, lectures, and poems of the wide circle of writers and thinkers associated with Transcendentalism. This volume also pays attention to the intellectual influences on American Transcendentalism, from ancient philosophy, both eastern and western, to Enlightenment principles, to the continental European thinkers and writers of their own time. While providing an overview of the importance of these ideas and thinkers, the emphasis in these entries remains on the Transcendentalist use of and interpretation of such traditions and ideas as they fit in with and informed their own 19th-century concerns. The effect is to look beyond the handful of traditionally identified significant Transcendentalist figures and their published works, to include a larger number of individual participants as well as a broader definition of "literary" or cultural work. The volume thus includes entries on a range of more obscure written and oral efforts, as well as some unpublished works.

Entries are alphabetically arranged, and cross-referenced entries are indicated with SMALL CAPITAL LETTERS. The end-of-entry bibliographies provide the most relevant and most recent references consulted for the information provided in that entry or for general further reading. Not all of the individuals covered in this volume have had biographies written or have had their works published in modern editions, but the appendix provides a more thorough resource for further study, including lists of major works by Transcendentalist figures. Readers should keep in mind that the nature of the movement meant that some of the most significant contributions by some figures were not full-length texts, but the numerous articles and editorials submitted to a range of periodicals, as well as sermons, lectures, and even "conversations," many of which remained unpublished. Any list of "major" works and contributions is therefore only a partial overview of the activities of the Transcendentalists as a whole.

The bibliography at the back of the book also includes a listing of anthologies or collections of Transcendentalist writings and lists of major essays, editions of books, or even unpublished journals and letters by each major writer. The list of secondary sources is not comprehensive, as the literature on Transcendentalism is vast; only the most recent, most useful, or most significant texts are included. Finally, a chronology of events, people, organizations, and publications is included. Transcendentalism emerged as a separate movement in the 1830s and is traditionally understood as peaking by the 1850s, but the chronology helps place that period of intense activity in the context of what came before, as far as intellectual influences, and what came after. In fact, one of the goals of this volume is to emphasize the wider context of Transcendentalist activity especially after the Civil War, with continued interest in forming clubs and organizations and participating in lectures, schools, and publications, by major original figures as well as a new generation of thinkers and writers interested in continuing to apply Transcendentalist ideals to social problems and philosophical questions through the end of the 19th century. As Henry James characterized the New England spirit during the time of the Transcendentalists in his novel *The Bostonians,* it was "the age of plain living and high thinking, of pure ideals and earnest effort, of moral passion and noble experiment."

abolitionism

Many Transcendentalists were connected to abolitionism—the movement to end slavery in the United States—through their participation in Boston reform activities in the 1830s, '40s, and '50s. Although Transcendentalist philosophy in general emphasized a belief in the universal nature of societal reform rather than political action focused on a single issue and favored acting as individuals rather than joining organizations, the antislavery activities of individual Transcendentalists included writing essays and poems, giving lectures, attending abolitionist conventions, and writing and editing abolitionist newspapers. Even if some Transcendentalists criticized or avoided the political strategies of reform organizations, most supported the goal of ending American slavery.

One of the earliest commentaries against slavery from within the Unitarian-Transcendentalist community was the Reverend William Ellery CHANNING's 1835 essay *Slavery*. A few years later, in 1840 and 1841, several Transcendentalists attended Boston's CHARDON STREET AND BIBLE CONVENTIONS to discuss the issue. Chardon Street, however, exemplified the split between some Transcendentalist intellectuals and more radical abolitionist reformers over the best strategy for ending slavery. As residents of Boston, many Transcendentalists, including Ralph Waldo EMERSON, were drawn more directly into the antislavery cause during the 1854 capture and trial of Anthony BURNS, in which Boston's white community

was forced to take a stand on the FUGITIVE SLAVE LAW of 1850. Several of the Transcendentalists came to Burns's defense and participated in public riots and speeches against what antislavery Bostonians called the "kidnapping" of Burns.

In the 1850s Emerson in particular emerged as an outspoken public figure in the abolitionist cause. He delivered his "FUGITIVE SLAVE LAW ADDRESS" on several occasions in the 1850s, celebrated the Emancipation Proclamation in his poem, "BOSTON HYMN," and, in 1855, delivered his most coherent views on the issue in the lecture, "AMERICAN SLAVERY." The abolitionist commitments of the Transcendentalists were most evident in their response to the crusade of John BROWN. Throughout 1859, a group of men known as the SECRET SIX, most of them with ties to Boston's Transcendentalist community, raised money for Brown's attack on slavery that culminated in the unsuccessful raid at Harpers Ferry, Virginia.

Other highly visible abolitionists with Transcendentalist ties included Amos Bronson ALCOTT, the founder of the utopian experiment at FRUITLANDS which boycotted the use of slave-produced southern goods; Lydia Maria CHILD, author of *An Appeal in Favor of that Class of Americans Called Africans* (1833) and editor of the *National Anti-Slavery Standard*; Thomas Wentworth HIGGINSON, a member of the Secret Six who eventually led one of the first black regiments during the Civil War; Unitarian minister Theodore PARKER, who became a chairman of the Boston Vigilance Committee intended to protect fugitive slaves in the 1850s; and

Henry David THOREAU, who had lectured on "SLAVERY IN MASSACHUSETTS" in 1854 and who, more than anyone else, publicly supported John Brown in the months following the antislavery martyr's capture, trial, and execution, in a series of late 1859 addresses that included "A PLEA FOR CAPTAIN JOHN BROWN," "Martyrdom of John Brown," and "The Last Days of John Brown."

Bibliography

Gougeon, Len. *Virtue's Hero: Emerson, Antislavery, and Reform.* Athens: University of Georgia, 1990.

Renehan, Edward J., Jr. *The Secret Six: The True Tale of the Men Who Conspired with John Brown.* New York: Crown, 1995.

"Address at the Woman's Rights Convention"
Ralph Waldo Emerson
(1855)

Ralph Waldo EMERSON's only public lecture on the nineteenth-century movement for WOMEN'S RIGHTS was given at the Woman's Rights Convention in Boston on September 20, 1855. Other Transcendentalists such as Amos Bronson ALCOTT, Margaret FULLER, Thomas Wentworth HIGGINSON, and Theodore PARKER were outspoken advocates of woman's advancement, but Emerson had limited involvement with most organized reform efforts out of principle. He believed that organizations stifled individual action and that the best reform efforts began at the personal level of moral conscience. Throughout the early 1850s, however, he was perceived by women's rights activists as sympathetic to their cause and was asked to speak at earlier conventions by many of his Boston colleagues. He was hesitant until finally agreeing to the request by Paulina Wright DAVIS to appear at the 1855 convention.

Even though he had not publicly addressed the issue before this date, the issue of women's rights, in particular the nature of female genius, had engaged him in his private journals and correspondences with such powerful female figures as his aunt, Mary Moody EMERSON, and fellow Transcendentalist Margaret Fuller. His wife Lidian

EMERSON was also a supporter of the cause. From such relationships with intellectual women it is evident that Ralph Waldo Emerson believed that while female genius was possible and should be encouraged, the social responsibilities of marriage and motherhood limited participation in intellectual and professional life for most women.

Still, in inviting him to speak, his colleagues and admirers in the organized women's rights movement hoped that Emerson could at least articulate his philosophical views on female genius and woman's right to individuality, theoretical foundations that would bolster their demands for specific rights. In the 1855 convention speech he did emphasize women's moral superiority and positive influence on men, but he hoped that "the best women" would not seek power through such corrupt avenues as politics and business. His position on women's advancement, therefore, was ultimately quite traditional rather than radical, and some women's rights advocates came away from his address unsure about his position. Transcendentalist colleague Caroline DALL (who had also helped arrange his appearance at the convention) wrote to Emerson honestly that the newspaper reports of the event left interested readers confused as to "whether you were for us or against us." Emerson did not speak at another woman's rights convention, but his 1855 speech was reprinted in whole or in part in various women's rights periodicals through the end of the century. The somewhat revised address appears in collections of Emerson's works simply as "Woman."

Bibliography

Garvey, T. Gregory, ed. *The Emerson Dilemma: Essays on Emerson and Social Reform.* Athens: University of Georgia, 2001.

Adirondack Club

In August 1858 a group of Boston intellectuals, including the Transcendentalist Ralph Waldo EMERSON, embarked on a wilderness expedition to Follensby Pond in the remote Adirondack mountains of New York State. The two-week-long camping trip was organized by artist William Stillman as an activity for the SATURDAY CLUB, a Boston-Cambridge literary society whose members included Emerson, the Harvard scientist Louis AGASSIZ, the editor James Russell LOWELL, and others. The most detailed accounts of the Adirondacks expedition are found in a poem by Emerson, "THE ADIRONDACS," and in a painting and a later published account—both entitled *Philosophers' Camp*—by the club's organizer, Stillman. Stillman's painting is now held by the Concord Free Public Library.

The men of the Adirondack Club were accompanied by hired guides and, besides Emerson the philosopher-poet, included several scientists who used the trip to gather botanical and animal specimens. Stillman portrayed the coexistence of utilitarian and philosophical aspects of the trip in his painting that shows a thoughtful Emerson reflecting on the surrounding trees while other members of the camp are busily engaged in various duties related to outdoor living, such as target shooting, or scientific pursuits, such as collecting and dissecting fish.

The members of the Adirondack Club were so enamored of the wilderness in which they found themselves that they made tentative plans to purchase land and build a permanent site at Follensby Pond. In his poem Emerson alludes to this plan of securing a spot for the next generation, their sons, to come and enjoy the wilderness: "We trode on air, contemned the distant town, / Its timorous ways, big trifles, and we planned / That we should build, hard-by, a spacious lodge / And how we should come hither with our sons, / Hereafter,—willing they, and more adroit." The club did, in fact, purchase some land at a site they called Ampersand Pond, but the plan to return with their sons never materialized, and they eventually lost the title to the land due to unpaid back taxes.

Emerson's poem is not only a literary reflection on the experience, but also a detailed account of the trip that discusses the various activities of club members. In addition to Emerson's poem, Stillman's 1893 account of the "Philosophers' Camp" for *Century Magazine* provides the most thorough details on the men's activities. Significantly, the publication of his essay was followed by passage of a New York statute preserving and protecting the wilderness of the Adirondacks.

Bibliography

Burkholder, Robert E. "(Re)Visiting 'The Adirondacs': Emerson's Confrontation with Wild Nature." Paper presented, Massachusetts Historical Society, April 2003.

"The Adirondacs"
Ralph Waldo Emerson
(1867)

Transcendentalist Ralph Waldo EMERSON was inspired to write the poem "The Adirondacs" after his August 1858 wilderness expedition to the New York mountains with members of the ADIRONDACK CLUB, including Louis AGASSIZ, Samuel WARD, John Holmes (brother of Oliver Wendell HOLMES), and several other prominent Bostonians. Published in his collection MAY-DAY AND OTHER PIECES in 1867, the 343-line blank verse poem—subtitled *A Journal. Dedicated to My Fellow-Travellers in August, 1858*—was both a record of their trip and a reflection on the meaning of one man's interaction with the natural world.

The poem provides detailed information on the physical landscape and natural history of the area, acknowledging the unnatural intrusion of the philosophers and scientists into the pristine forest. Emerson the poet does not uncritically glorify nature's lessons for humanity, however, but instead comes away from the experience in fact celebrating the triumph of humankind and technology over the untamed wilderness. Emerson not only reconciles but also celebrates the coexistence of humankind (of technology and capitalism, even) and nature. This theme is explicitly underscored with the poem's final stanza celebrating the laying of the Transatlantic Cable, news of which reached Emerson and his party while at the "Philosophers' Camp." The triumph of technology rather than the communion with nature at the camp itself is in some ways the central event of the poem. The news of the Cable—"This feat of wit, this triumph of mankind"—is explicitly contrasted with earlier lines in which Emerson acknowledged the lack of communication represented by the wilderness: "No courier waits, no letter came or went."

In the end, the nature expedition has taught Emerson more about civilization than about the wild, and in comparing what each has to offer, Emerson chooses civilization: "We flee away from cities, but we bring / The best of cities with us, these learned classifiers, / Men knowing what they seek, armed eyes of experts / We praise the guide, we praise the forest life: / But will we sacrifice our dear-bought lore / Of books and arts and trained experiment, / Or count the Sioux a match for Agassiz? / O no, not we!" In seeing nature first for what it offered mankind in the way of advancing scientific knowledge, and, in fact, as something which humanity can even improve upon, Emerson presents a view of the wilderness that is quite different from the later writings of Henry David THOREAU, such as the essays in THE MAINE WOODS and WALDEN, which are more often cited as representative of Transcendentalist ecological thought.

Bibliography

Burkholder, Robert E. "(Re)Visiting 'The Adirondacs': Emerson's Confrontation with Wild Nature." Paper presented, Massachusetts Historical Society, April 2003.

Aesthetic Papers
Elizabeth Palmer Peabody
(1849)

Elizabeth Palmer PEABODY edited and published the literary journal *Aesthetic Papers* in May 1849 as a forum for the New England Transcendentalists. By the end of the 1840s individual Transcendentalists had published in various other journals, and, as a group, they had experimented with creating their own journals, including THE WESTERN MESSENGER (1835–41) and the Boston DIAL (1840–44). By the time she decided to start another paper, Elizabeth Peabody had established herself as the publishing center for Transcendentalism in Boston. Her bookstore at 13 West Street provided access to foreign books, served as a meeting center, and published other volumes such as the *Dial* and Amos Bronson ALCOTT's RECORD OF A SCHOOL. It is not surprising then that Peabody, already a promoter and publisher of many of the first important Transcendentalist works, sought to contribute to the movement's literary production as well by establishing a new periodical.

In general, the collection of essays appearing in *Aesthetic Papers* provides a sampling of the most important themes for the Transcendentalists during this time period of the late 1840s—whether it be the continued emphasis on German thought and literature as an important influence, an eclecticism that sought to bring together the best of several strains of thought into a usable philosophy, or practical reform interests. Although Peabody intended to include writers and thinkers from a variety of philosophical perspectives, the majority of contributors were Transcendentalists. Others who might have been expected to participate, had *Aesthetic Papers* gone on to produce other volumes, were absent from the collection, such as Peabody's friend Bronson Alcott or Margaret FULLER, who was in Italy at the time.

The volume began with Peabody's introductory essay explaining her definition of "The Word 'Aesthetic,'" and included two other essays by Peabody ("The Dorian Measure, with a Modern Application" and "Language") and contributions by seven other individual writers. The table of contents shows an essay by Samuel Gray WARD on "Criticism," John DWIGHT on "Music," an 1838 lecture by Ralph Waldo EMERSON on "War," Parke GODWIN on "Organization," Sampson REED on "Genius," J. J. G. Wilkinson on "Correspondence," a short story by Nathaniel HAWTHORNE entitled "Main Street," S. H. Perkins on the "Abuse of Representative Government," followed by Henry David THOREAU's 1847 lecture "Resistance to Civil Government" (appearing here for the first time in print, the piece that would later be titled "CIVIL DISOBEDIENCE" and become perhaps the most famous essay by a Transcendentalist), and an anonymous piece by "An English Resident" on "Vegetation about Salem, Mass." Transcendentalist poetry was also well represented in the issue. Published anonymously and interspersed between various essays were poems by Peabody, Ellen Sturgis HOOPER, Thomas Wentworth HIGGINSON, his sister Louisa Higginson, and Ann Sargent Gage.

Aesthetic Papers provides some of the best insight into Elizabeth Palmer Peabody's early thought especially, since she served as editor and contributed both introductory material and two other essays. Peabody's essays examined the idea of art, of criticism, and of EDUCATION, all themes that she sought to explore in her choices for the other pieces in the volume. In "The Dorian Measure" she brought her interests in educational reform together with a call for funding for classical education in the public schools. In her introductory piece she defined an "aesthetic" of art that de-emphasized specific critical elements in favor of universal themes and divinely inspired ideals. Most of the essays in *Aesthetic Papers* followed this theme of cultural unity and agreed with Peabody's approach to criticism. However, a few others explored different themes, including, most notably, Thoreau's "Resistance to Civil Government," which promotes individual conscience over social unity.

In the original prospectus to *Aesthetic Papers*, Peabody had no particular plan for the number of volumes to be published. Ultimately, there was not sufficient subscriber interest to warrant publication of a second volume, but Elizabeth Peabody and the other writers would continue to expand the themes addressed in *Aesthetic Papers* into other forums, and several of the essays, including those of Peabody, were reprinted in other journals and collections.

Bibliography

Gohdes, Clarence L. F. *The Periodicals of American Transcendentalism.* Durham, N.C.: Duke University Press, 1931.

Ronda, Bruce A. *Elizabeth Palmer Peabody: A Reformer on Her Own Terms.* Cambridge, Mass.: Harvard University Press, 1999.

"After the Death of John Brown"   *See* "A PLEA FOR CAPTAIN JOHN BROWN."

Agassiz, Jean Louis
(1807–1873)

Jean Louis Agassiz was a Harvard professor who influenced the Transcendentalists through his work as a naturalist and scientist. A native of Switzerland, Agassiz first visited the United States as a lecturer at a time when he was widely regarded as a premier natural historian, zoologist, and geologist. Agassiz was well known for his study of glaciers and his contribution to formulating a theory of the Ice Age when he was recruited by Harvard, where he spent the rest of his professional career. In Boston and Cambridge Agassiz was introduced to the intellectual and literary elite of the area, including many of the Transcendentalists. He lectured regularly in the area and was one of the original members of the SATURDAY CLUB, a dinner and conversation group founded in 1854. Other members included Ralph Waldo EMERSON and James Russell LOWELL, but Agassiz's steady presence and prominent voice at the Saturday Club led some to refer to the group as "Agassiz's Club." He was also a member of the ADIRONDACK CLUB, a group of Saturday Club members who embarked on a two-week camping trip into the Adirondack wilderness in 1858, a trip that inspired Emerson's poem, "THE ADIRONDACS." While Emerson was the expedition's poet-philosopher, Agassiz was the naturalist who used the excursion to gather botanical specimens for his research.

Once at Harvard, Louis Agassiz set about gathering extensive animal specimens and established the most significant zoological collection in America. In 1847 either Agassiz or his assistant, James Elliot CABOT, began communicating with Henry David THOREAU, who eventually catalogued and collected several CONCORD, MASSACHUSETTS, area specimens and shipped them to Agassiz. According to Thoreau's letters, in one shipment he included "1 larger land tortois, and 5 muddy tortoises, all from the pond by my house . . . one black snake, alive, and one dormouse caught last night in my cellar." There is even evidence of Thoreau sending a fox, which Agassiz kept in his yard. Such exchanges lasted for only a few weeks, however, after which time Thoreau's correspondence no longer mentioned assisting Agassiz, perhaps because Thoreau realized, as Agassiz stated elsewhere, that science needed "many more specimens than most naturalists would care for."

In fact, it is surprising that Thoreau participated at all, as Agassiz's scientific goals would seem to have been in conflict with Thoreau's intent on preserving the wilderness, as well as his Transcendentalist philosophy. In his own work at this time, Thoreau was moving away from collecting actual objects and refining his trademark interest in observing and recording information about plants and animals in their natural habitats and in exploring the interrelatedness, both physically and spiritually, of species and of the natural world with the human world. While Agassiz's work resulted in the presentation of his classifications in his 1848 textbook, *Principles of Zoology,* and in the creation of his Museum of Comparative Zoology at Harvard, as early as 1843, well before working with Agassiz, Thoreau commented in his journal, "I hate museums, there is nothing so weighs upon the spirits. They are catacombs of Nature. They are preserved death."

Louis Agassiz exerted a substantial amount of influence over American science and culture in general, not only through his teaching and experiments but also as an educational reformer, as founder of the zoology museum, and as a promoter of science as a profession by offering specialized training at Harvard. Agassiz was also instrumental in the founding of such scientific research and educational organizations as the Smithsonian Institution and the American Association for the Advancement of Science. All of these activities ultimately legitimated professional scientific activities over the naturalist and natural history approach of "amateurs" such as Thoreau. Although pursuing different professional and scientific goals from Transcendentalism, the philosophy in general corresponded with Agassiz's belief in a spiritual approach to understanding the natural world. Even as he promoted scientific knowledge, Agassiz did not accept all of the prevailing scientific theories of his day. In particular, he strongly rejected the ideas of Charles DARWIN as put forth in *The Origin of Species* (1859) and instead retained a strict creationist view of both the animal and human worlds long after other scientists, including his own students, as well as the Transcendentalists, accepted the premises of evolution in some form.

Bibliography

Bolles, Edmund Blair. *The Ice Finders: How a Poet, a Professor, and a Politician Discovered the Ice Age.* Washington, D.C.: Counterpoint, 1999.

Walls, Laura Dassow. *Seeing New Worlds: Henry David Thoreau and Nineteenth-Century Natural Science.* Madison: University of Wisconsin Press, 1995.

Alcott, Abigail May
(1800–1877)

Abigail "Abba" May Alcott was the wife of Transcendentalist Amos Bronson ALCOTT and the mother of popular novelist Louisa May ALCOTT. Abba May came from a prominent family who were members of Boston's first Unitarian church, King's Chapel. Her brother, Samuel Joseph MAY, became a Unitarian minister and a member of the TRANSCENDENTAL CLUB. In 1830 she married Bronson Alcott and subsequently gave birth to four daughters. Abba Alcott was a tireless advocate of slaves as well as women and the poor in her social reform work in Boston. She was involved in ABOLITIONISM as a member of the Female Antislavery Society, and she and her husband once visited the radical abolitionist William Lloyd GARRISON in jail. Throughout the 1840s and 1850s Abba May Alcott also worked hard to support her family through periods of financial difficulty due to Bronson Alcott's inability to find regular paid work. At one time she operated a clearinghouse for collecting and distributing clothing and food to the poor and for connecting immigrant laborers with employers. Her work with the poor and immigrant populations fueled her reform spirit for improving the lives of others, including blacks who, due to racism, received little or no assistance from other agencies who helped Irish and German immigrants. Abba resigned her position in 1850, exhausted by the long hours and low pay, and briefly operated an employment service for placing women as domestic workers. In 1851 she described her own life and priorities in a letter to her brother, Samuel J. May: "My life is one of daily protest against the oppression and abuses of Society."

Louisa May Alcott memorialized her mother, alternately, as the kind and gentle "Marmee" in one of the 19th century's best-selling novels, *LITTLE WOMEN* (1868), and, later, as the overworked and underappreciated "Hope Lamb," the fictional wife of the inconsiderate and abusive male utopian reformer in "TRANSCENDENTAL WILD OATS," her satirical account of Bronson Alcott's social experiment at FRUITLANDS. Abigail May Alcott did not entirely fit either of these characterizations, however, as she was a reformer and social critic in her own right, although a less visible and public one than either her husband or famous daughter.

Bibliography

Barton, Cynthia. *Transcendental Wife: The Life of Abigail May Alcott.* Lanham, Md.: University Press of America, 1996.

Dahlstrand, Frederick. *Amos Bronson Alcott: An Intellectual Biography.* East Brunswick, N.J.: Associated University Presses, 1982.

Alcott, Amos Bronson
(1799–1888)

Philosopher, poet, teacher, reformer, and writer Amos Bronson Alcott was one of the central figures of American Transcendentalism and a living example of the belief in self-culture, in that he had no formal education or profession but, instead, dedicated his life to the pursuit of knowledge and reform of self and society. His most important activities as a Transcendentalist were as the founder of the communitarian experiment at FRUITLANDS, a poet and essayist, a lecturer and leader of CONVERSATIONS, and an educator who founded several progressive schools for both children and adults, culminating with his CONCORD SCHOOL OF PHILOSOPHY AND LITERATURE during the last decade of his life.

Alcott was interested in the human learning process and looked to children for lessons about adult spiritual life. He was inspired by the ideas of the Swiss educational theorist Johann PESTALOZZI, whom he read in the pages of the *American Journal of Education,* where his own first published work— accounts of his early teaching experiences—would appear. The publication of a book on the subject, *Observations on the Principles and Methods of Infant Instruction,* led to offers to establish schools based on his methods in Pennsylvania. Although his efforts there were ultimately unsuccessful, it was in Pennsylvania that he and his wife Abigail May (ALCOTT) had their first two daughters, Anna in 1831 and Louisa May ALCOTT in 1832. Now a father, he focused his observations on his own children and on the implementation of his educational theories.

Alcott's views were also influenced by European ROMANTICISM, particularly his reading of Samuel Taylor COLERIDGE's *Aids to Reflection* (1825). Romanticism strengthened Alcott's belief in the innate goodness and spiritual lessons of childhood. He taught his own children at home and kept detailed journals of his methods. Eventually he returned to Boston where he opened his TEMPLE SCHOOL in September 1834, with Elizabeth Palmer PEABODY as his assistant. Peabody's carefully recorded classroom notes were published as RECORD OF A SCHOOL (1835). The book generated some concerns about Alcott's teaching methods, particularly his challenges to orthodox religious views. His supplemental Saturday classes on Jesus' teachings lessened such concerns until these sessions were made public as well with the 1836 publication of CONVERSATIONS WITH CHILDREN ON THE GOSPELS. Attacks in the religious papers accused Alcott of blasphemy and of assuming an ability to teach spiritual lessons without himself having any theological training. Alcott's Transcendentalist friends resented the clergymen who attempted to control religious knowledge, and James Freeman CLARKE and Ralph Waldo EMERSON, among others, publicly defended Alcott. Worried parents still took their children out of the Temple School, forcing its closure.

Bronson Alcott thus found allies within the emerging Transcendentalist community of ministers and writers disaffected with Unitarianism and seeking new routes to a spiritual life. In September 1836 he attended, along with Orestes BROWNSON, Clarke, Emerson, Frederic Henry HEDGE, and George RIPLEY, the first meeting of the TRANSCENDENTAL CLUB. That same year Alcott's *Conversations with Children* appeared and included a separate introduction titled "The Doctrine and Discipline of Human Culture" that situated Alcott's views within the "new thought" of Transcendentalism. Alcott embraced the idea of dependence on the individual soul rather than institutions for real social and moral reform, and he refused to accept any further employment that went against this core belief.

Writing offered the possibility of such independence, and in 1840 he published a series of 50 "ORPHIC SAYINGS" in the first volume (July 1840) of the Transcendentalist journal, the DIAL, and 50 more of them in the January 1841 issue. These obscure and mystical prophecies were caricatured by the popular press and became the focus of ridicule not only of Bronson Alcott but of the *Dial* and the Transcendentalist movement as a whole. In the face of criticism, Alcott took a break from public writing and turned his attentions to social reform activities around him. In spring 1842 he traveled to England, with Emerson's financial sponsorship, to meet with reformers there who had been intrigued by his methods and had even founded a school in his honor, ALCOTT HOUSE. Alcott met Henry Wright and Charles LANE, who accompanied him back to the United States with plans for their own utopian community, which they established at Fruitlands in June 1843. Louisa May Alcott was only 10 years old at the time she lived at Fruitlands, but thirty years later she published a fictionalized account of her father's experiment in the short story "TRANSCENDENTAL WILD OATS." By the time the story appeared, Louisa May Alcott had a best-selling novel, LITTLE WOMEN, and had become the main financial support of her family.

Discouraged by criticisms of his teaching and writing, Alcott next turned to CONVERSATION as a mode of interacting with an audience. In late 1848 he held his first series of Boston Conversations on spiritual and moral regeneration through educational reform. He did not seek to promote a specific viewpoint or issue but instead encouraged the natural flow of ideas between participants. Alcott's relative success with his Conversations led him to organize such venues in other cities. In 1868 he published another book, TABLETS, which was a collection of Transcendentalist meditations and perspectives on daily life. His work on this book and the success of his conversations, as well as the issue of slavery and the reality of the Civil War, renewed his interest in spiritual reform and regeneration. After the war he joined with many younger Transcendentalist colleagues as members of the FREE RELIGIOUS ASSOCIATION, an organization devoted to drawing together spiritual beliefs and lessons from a variety of world and historical religions.

Alcott continued to lecture and facilitate conversations as he traveled throughout the western states. He visited Saint Louis on more than one occasion where he met with the Philosophical Club and eventually published an essay on "Genesis" (in 1867) and a series of "Philosophemes" (modeled on his earlier "Orphic Sayings" in the *Dial*) in the JOURNAL OF SPECULATIVE PHILOSOPHY, edited by his friend William Torrey HARRIS. For Alcott, these activities were a continuation of his Transcendentalist interests since the 1830s, but he increasingly found his beliefs at odds with this

new generation of philosophers. The Saint Louis group were followers of HEGELIAN philosophy, which required too much logic and structure for Alcott's emphasis on spiritual intuition, and the free religious advocates were too dependent on new scientific theories rather than spiritual solutions for social and moral problems. Still, throughout the 1870s he found progressive audiences open to his ideas and his stories about his famous New England friends. In 1872 he published another book, CONCORD DAYS, a diary-like account of life and thought in CONCORD, MASSACHUSETTS, and in 1877 he published TABLE-TALK, a collection of his spiritual reflections and philosophical sayings, a format he had developed with his earlier "Orphic Sayings" and "Philosophemes."

Alcott translated his gift for speaking, his interest in the philosophical themes of an earlier Transcendentalist generation, and his longtime idea for establishing an "academy" into the Concord School of Philosophy and Literature, which met every summer between 1879 and Alcott's death in 1888. At the Concord School Alcott brought together philosophers from the western states with the Concord Transcendentalists in a forum committed to his own mission of spiritual renewal. During the period of the Concord School, Alcott published his last books, the 1881 autobiographical poem of his early life, NEW CONNECTICUT and the 1882 SONNETS AND CANZONETS.

Bronson Alcott's literacy legacy to American Transcendentalism is mixed. He was a prolific writer but was ridiculed and caricatured by contemporaries for his obscure writing style, and he produced no widely read or lasting body of work. In rejecting established forms and conventions Alcott was like others among the Transcendentalists, though others managed to find more success with their written work. He was best known for his "Conversations" and his social experiments, but as his biographer Frederick Dahlstrand laments, unlike his fellow Transcendentalist reformers such as Margaret FULLER or Henry David THOREAU, Alcott "lacked the expressive power to make his rebellion a revolution." Ultimately, his position as a Transcendentalist social reformer highlights the practical side of the movement and is an example of the commitment to translating ideals into meaningful social and personal change.

Bibliography

Dahlstrand, Frederick. *Amos Bronson Alcott: An Intellectual Biography*. East Brunswick, N.J.: Associated University Presses, 1982.

Alcott, Louisa May
(1823–1888)

Louisa May Alcott, one of the most well-known authors of the 19th century, was the daughter of Transcendentalist poet, teacher, and reformer Amos Bronson ALCOTT and his wife Abigail May ALCOTT. Louisa May Alcott never identified as a follower of the philosophy. Her childhood, however, was spent alongside many of the Transcendentalists as friends and neighbors, and her literary work was influenced by Transcendentalist ideas as well as social reform experiments. She was only 10 years old in 1843 when her father cofounded—and moved the family—to the utopian community at FRUITLANDS. After the collapse of the Fruitlands experiment in 1844, the Alcott family moved to CONCORD, MASSACHUSETTS, where, at one time, they lived across the street from Ralph Waldo EMERSON and his family. Alcott's first book, *Flower Fables* (1855), was a collection of stories she told to children as a schoolteacher in Concord. The book was dedicated to Emerson's young daughter, Ellen EMERSON, who had copied Alcott's stories down in a notebook and shown them to her parents, who encouraged their publication. Alcott had proved her ability to write for children and later turned to her own childhood for writing material with great success. *Little Women,* her 1868 best-selling novel, was a semiautobiographical tale of the loving relationships and economic struggles within a family of four daughters, like her own.

Louisa May Alcott never attended school but was taught at home with her sisters by their father, an educational reformer and experimentalist. She read widely in the classics as well as in contemporary works by Thomas CARLYLE, George SAND, and the writings of the Transcendentalists themselves, such as Ralph Waldo Emerson and Margaret FULLER. Alcott admired and looked up to Emerson, and he allowed Louisa to browse his library where she first encountered the authors that most engaged the Transcendentalists, such as German idealist philosopher Johann Wolfgang von GOETHE.

The Alcott family moved regularly and was never financially stable due to Bronson Alcott's pursuit of idealistic philosophizing and social reform projects rather than regular paid employment. Although the Fruitlands experiment was short-lived, the period was an especially difficult time for her family, both financially and in terms of the physical strains endured by her mother in her support of the community. Bronson Alcott and cofounder Charles LANE were philosophically opposed to the use of animals, even as labor on the farm, but as Abby Alcott and, later, Louisa May would note, they were not against depending on the back-breaking labor of women. Louisa May Alcott eventually became one of the most outspoken critics of the experiment and of Transcendental philosophy in general with her satirical fictionalized account of Fruitlands in "TRANSCENDENTAL WILD OATS," a short story originally published in 1873.

Louisa May sought out a career as a writer in order to support their "pathetic family," as she later characterized them. She wrote her first stories while still a teenager and began publishing regularly while in her twenties. She herself never married and thus pursued writing full time. The success of her novels, especially *Little Women,* established her as a best-selling children's writer, and she would indeed become the main financial support of her family throughout her adulthood. *Little Women* was followed in 1871 with *Little Men,* which also drew upon incidents from her own life, particularly the portrayal of her father's educational philosophy as he had promoted it at TEMPLE SCHOOL, now represented as the school at Plumfield in the novel. *Little Men* also made references to Alcott's childhood reminiscences of Henry David THOREAU in the character of Mr. Hyde, and to other aspects of life in Concord.

Louisa May Alcott's childhood as the daughter of Bronson Alcott and especially her relationship with and respect for Ralph Waldo Emerson closely linked her to Transcendentalism, and her published writings as well as her journals and letters reflect that she absorbed and shared many of the philosophical ideals of the Transcendentalists, including themes such as self-reliance, reform, and nature. She regularly visited the pulpits of popular Unitarian-Transcendentalist ministers, such as Cyrus BARTOL, Octavius Brooks FROTHINGHAM, and, one of her favorites, Theodore PARKER, though she never joined any church. Her most thoroughly autobiographical novel, WORK: A STORY OF EXPERIENCE (1873), includes a character based on Theodore Parker, and she wrote the introduction to an 1881 edition of Parker's sermons. In the 1870s and 1880s she aided her father in housing and entertaining lecturers and attendees at his CONCORD SCHOOL OF PHILOSOPHY AND LITERATURE, although she remained skeptical and somewhat critical of philosophical exercises when there were very real social issues to be solved; she wrote in her diary during the period of the Concord School, "Why discuss the unknowable, till our poor are fed & the wicked saved?"

Louisa May Alcott had been born on her father's birthday in 1823, and she died on March 6, 1888, just two days after her father's death. The two are buried at Sleepy Hollow Cemetery in Concord. Transcendentalist and Alcott family friend Ednah Dow CHENEY immediately memorialized her with an 1889 biography and edition of her papers, *Louisa May Alcott, Her Life, Letters, and Journals.*

Bibliography

Stern, Madeleine B. *Louisa May Alcott.* New York: Random House, 1996.

Alcott House

In 1838 the English Transcendentalist and educational reformer James Pierrepont GREAVES established Alcott House just outside of London. The boarding school for children was founded on the educational principles of Johann Heinrich PESTALOZZI as adapted by Transcendentalist Amos Bronson ALCOTT at his TEMPLE SCHOOL in the United States. Greaves had corresponded with Alcott and read of his methods in RECORD OF A SCHOOL. In 1842

Bronson Alcott traveled to England and was taken to the school by another leading English Transcendentalist, Charles LANE, and the Alcott House principal Henry Wright. During Alcott's visit in the summer of 1842 he found Alcott House to be the center of conversations not only about educational reform but also health, diet, marriage, religion, and political reform. Based on the belief that social ills and disease were extensions or manifestations of physical or bodily ills, the reformers at Alcott House emphasized good physical and mental health as part of the overall educational program. All of the children boarding at Alcott House maintained a strict vegetarian diet and were required to engage in daily physical exercises. It was at Alcott House in England that Bronson Alcott, Charles Lane, and Henry Wright first discussed their plans for a communitarian experiment in harmonious living, a plan that would culminate in the creation of FRUITLANDS back in Massachusetts the following year.

Bibliography

Dahlstrand, Frederick. *Amos Bronson Alcott: An Intellectual Biography.* East Brunswick, N.J.: Associated University Presses, 1982.

Allston, Washington
(1799–1843)

The Transcendentalists praised landscape painter Washington Allston as America's only internationally recognized Romantic artist. Allston himself was not a Transcendentalist, but he was at the center of intellectual life in Cambridge, Massachusetts, and promoted the ideals and sensibilities of European ROMANTICISM through his art. His place in a transatlantic Transcendentalist community was secured by his attendance at Harvard, his close friendship with English romantic writer Samuel Taylor COLERIDGE (of whom he painted a portrait in 1814), and his marriage to Ann Channing, the sister of the Unitarian minister William Ellery CHANNING.

Washington Allston lived in Cambridge where he regularly gave talks at his home on art and aesthetics and mentored artists such as Ednah Dow CHENEY, Horatio GREENOUGH, and Sophia Peabody

HAWTHORNE. His idealist perspective on art influenced the art criticism articulated by both Ralph Waldo EMERSON and Margaret FULLER. In April 1839 Harding's Gallery in Boston hosted a tremendously popular exhibit of Allston's work. Many of the Transcendentalists attended the exhibit, and some, like Margaret Fuller, made multiple visits during the two-months-long show. Fuller published her "Record of Impressions Produced by the Exhibition of Mr. Allston's Pictures in the Summer of 1839" in the first issue (July 1840) of the new Transcendentalist periodical, the DIAL. Allston's "pictures" inspired two poems in that issue, as well: Samuel Gray WARD's "To W. Allston, On Seeing His 'Bride,'" and Fuller's "To Allston's Picture, 'The Bride.'" Elizabeth Palmer PEABODY's article, "Last Evening with Allston," was published several years later. For the Transcendentalists, Allston's work displayed the Romantic ideal of portraying landscapes in the ideal state, as organic wholes from which humans can derive moral lessons; or, as Emerson would write in his essay, "ART," "the painter should give the suggestion of a fairer creation than we know."

Washington Allston was also a poet who wrote several sonnets, including a eulogy of his friend Coleridge with a "Sonnet on the Late S. T. Coleridge." Many of his poems were published in his 1850 collection of *Lectures on Art, and Poems.*

Bibliography

Bjelajac, David. *Washington Allston, Secret Societies, and the Alchemy of Anglo-American Painting.* New York: Cambridge University Press, 1997.

"American Literature, Its Position in the Present Time, and Its Prospects for the Future"   *See* PAPERS ON LITERATURE AND ART.

"The American Scholar"
Ralph Waldo Emerson
(1837)

On August 31, 1837, Ralph Waldo EMERSON delivered a commencement address to Harvard's Phi Beta Kappa society, a speech that eventually became known as "The American Scholar." Emerson's audience that day included not only the graduates but many of the faculty, including his own former influential professors such as Edward EVERETT and Andrews NORTON, literary and reform colleagues such as James Russell LOWELL and Wendell PHILLIPS, and other luminaries such as U.S. Supreme Court justice Joseph Story. Immediately published as *An Oration, Delivered before the Phi Beta Kappa Society, at Cambridge, August 31, 1837,* the lecture was first titled "The American Scholar" when it appeared in Emerson's 1849 collection, NATURE: *Addresses and Lectures.*

Emerson's main theme in the speech was to urge Americans to break from European tradition and dependency on "the mind of the Past" and to look around at the present unique circumstances of America for intellectual inspiration. Placing the "American Scholar" in the specific context of American political, social, and economic institutions—democracy and capitalism—Emerson argued "Life is our dictionary" and "the way to learn grammar" was to talk with working men and women about their lives. He posited that, here in the everyday is where true knowledge and inspiration could be found as, indeed, "Colleges and books only copy the language which the field and the work-yard made."

While not going so far in terms of democratizing American culture by placing Harvard scholars in the same class as men of the "trades and manufactures," some of Emerson's own teachers, such as Edward Everett, for example, had previously made similar arguments about breaking from the European tradition and promoting American culture. The theme was one which in 1837 particularly engaged Emerson as a Transcendentalist as intellectual culture at that time still emphasized ideas to be drawn from European thinkers and had not done much toward applying those ideas to development of American thought and culture. At the time of his speech many of his Transcendentalist colleagues were hard at work on translations of French and German philosophers for George RIPLEY's SPECIMENS OF FOREIGN STANDARD LITERATURE series, and most of them had published journal articles on the European figures most influential for the movement, from Samuel Taylor COLERIDGE to Immanuel

KANT to Johann Wolfgang von GOETHE. Of course, American Transcendentalism itself relied heavily upon ideas from these thinkers, and Emerson as well was influenced by and dedicated many hours to studying these same European writers. All of his REPRESENTATIVE MEN (1850) were ancient Greek or European, but this was not because Emerson did not wish to celebrate original American genius— he just believed that America had not yet matured enough to produce any.

"The American Scholar" is most forceful, however, as a call not just to an elevation of American literary culture in general, which Emerson was increasingly discouraged at not finding, but to the development of the American *individual* as thinker and scholar. He sought for his fellow Americans freedom not just from a European-dominated education but from the institution of education itself. In this speech Emerson articulated the idea of "Man Thinking," a state of being rather than a profession, and urged his listeners to aspire not solely to be "bookworms," members of a "book-learned class," but to think and process what they read as it relates to their own lives; to engage in "creative reading, as well as creative writing." Even more radical, he urged them to break from reliance not only on European thought, but on books in general, from too much studying: "Books are for the scholar's idle times." He urged his listeners or readers, particularly that group of Harvard students at the original 1837 address, to rely upon themselves as the true source of knowledge and to read to learn about themselves, reminding them that "Cicero, Locke, and Bacon were only young men in libraries when they wrote these books." Emerson thus criticized the very institution at which he spoke as well as some of the men in attendance when he critiqued the continuing "past utterance of genius" that passed for higher education, but which unfortunately taught young men to "look backward and not forward."

Emerson thus used the word *scholar* to mean not just a "student" but a true intellectual, an original thinker. The scholar—man thinking—was a theme Emerson continued to follow in lectures and essays in the coming years. "The American Scholar" quickly became one of Emerson's most influential and lasting statements on American intellectual culture and the life of the mind. Oliver

Wendell HOLMES—who had also attended the original oration—referred to it nearly 50 years later in his biography *Ralph Waldo Emerson* (1884) as "our Intellectual Declaration of Independence."

Bibliography
Sacks, Kenneth. *Understanding Emerson: "The American Scholar" and His Struggle for Self-Reliance.* Princeton, N.J.: Princeton University Press, 2003.

"American Slavery"
Ralph Waldo Emerson
(1855)

Transcendentalist Ralph Waldo EMERSON delivered his "American Slavery" address in January 1855 as a response to the outcome of the Boston trial of alleged fugitive slave Anthony BURNS. Earlier in his career, Emerson had emphasized individual conscience as a reform strategy and had been reserved in making public statements on the issue of slavery, but events of the 1850s, including the Burns case, galvanized him, like many other northerners, to become more directly involved in public ABOLITIONISM and to raise a collective voice against the political and economic system of southern slavery. Emerson's speech was also representative of the extent to which slavery, and therefore its counterpart, freedom, had come to be the dominant metaphors through which all Americans discussed the political, social, and cultural destiny of the nation.

Emerson's "American Slavery" address was never published in his lifetime, but a transcription of the speech appeared in the newspaper the following day. The address was presented as part of a public lecture series on the issue organized by members of the Boston Vigilance Committee, a radical group of abolitionists working against the enactment of the FUGITIVE SLAVE LAW. Despite the radical nature of that group as organizers, the speaker series was in fact intended to be a public debate and included other speakers representing at least moderate pro-slavery arguments. Emerson addressed the passage of the Fugitive Slave Law directly, commenting how, "in 1850, the American Congress passed a statute which ordained that justice and mercy should be subject to fine and imprisonment, and that there existed no higher law in the universe than the Constitution and this paper statute which uprooted the foundations of rectitude and denied the existence of God."

The speech addressed not only political but philosophical concerns about slavery and its effect on the American character: "We sit here, the third generation in the humiliation of our forefathers, when they made an evil contract with the slave-holders at the formation of the government. We have added to that the new stringencies of the fugitive law of 1850." And he warned that this issue affected not just the south but the north as well, since "a high state of general health cannot long co-exist with a mortal disease in any part." "American Slavery" affects America as a whole, not just politically, in terms of sectional tensions, but psychically as well since "it staggers our faith in human progress."

Emerson's solution was, as usual, to look to individuals to pursue the "higher law." When, unfortunately, "the public fails in its duty . . . the American government and courts are false to their trust . . . [and] the government is forced into all manner of false and ridiculous attitudes," the solution is for "private men to take its place." Emerson's outrage was tempered somewhat by his reserved proposal for how to end slavery. In "American Slavery" Emerson supported the controversial strategy adapted by the British of compensating slaveholders for their lost property by purchasing former slaves: "Was there ever any contribution levied that was so enthusiastically paid as this will be?" Ralph Waldo Emerson's "American Slavery" address was delivered on multiple occasions to receptive audiences and stands out as one of his clearest efforts to understand his own opposition to slavery within a larger Transcendentalist framework.

Bibliography

Gougeon, Len. *Virtue's Hero: Emerson, Antislavery, and Reform.* Athens: University of Georgia Press, 1990.

Von Frank, Albert J. *The Trials of Anthony Burns: Freedom and Slavery in Emerson's Boston.* Cambridge, Mass.: Harvard University Press, 1998.

American Social Science Association

Founded in 1865 by Franklin Benjamin SANBORN, the American Social Science Association (or ASSA) included many Transcendentalist social reformers among its founders, officers, and members, including, most notably, Caroline DALL, Samuel Gridley Howe, Thomas Wentworth HIGGINSON, and the abolitionists William Lloyd GARRISON and Wendell PHILLIPS. Others were interested in the work and some, including Amos Bronson ALCOTT and Elizabeth Palmer PEABODY, became honorary members. From its founding in 1865 to his retirement in 1898, Franklin Sanborn was the driving force behind the ASSA, which he organized at the end of the Civil War in Boston as an association "whose object shall be the discussion of those questions relating to the Sanitary Condition of the People, the Relief, Employment, and Education of the Poor, the Prevention of Crime, the Amelioration of the Criminal Law, the Discipline of Prisons, the Remedial Treatment of the Insane, and those numerous matters of statistical and philanthropic interest which are included under the general head of 'Social Science.'" The ASSA established four primary departments of concern—Education, Health, Jurisprudence, and Finance—which were modeled after the British National Association for the Promotion of Social Science. The main activities of the American Social Science Association were inviting inquiry and discussion through the presentation of papers at annual meetings and the publication of its annual report in the form of *The Journal of Social Science*, edited by Sanborn.

Like other post–Civil War social reform organizations, the ASSA signaled a shift from the romantic individualism and scholarly eclecticism of the earlier generation of Transcendentalism to the increasing professionalization of the social science disciplines during the last half of the 19th century. The ASSA, in fact, played a part in the organization of separate disciplines such as history, political science, and sociology, with its emphasis on the application of moral principles and philosophical ideals to social and economic problems. The independent and genteel model of intellectual life represented by members of the ASSA was ultimately replaced by those disciplines, as formal academic training and specialization came to define professional as well as intellectual authority.

As the personification of the ASSA, Franklin Sanborn represented this bridge between the two generations and between the intellectual commitments of Transcendentalism and the later-century social sciences. Sanborn had intellectual and personal ties to Transcendentalism as an early admirer of Ralph Waldo EMERSON, as a CONCORD, MASSACHUSETTS, schoolteacher and a later historian and biographer of the Transcendentalists. Sanborn was also an abolitionist and social reformer who sought to combine the Transcendentalist emphasis on individual development with social and community-based solutions offered by professional reformers. Because of Sanborn, then, the ASSA looked to new solutions offered by scientific study and the organizational strength of bureaucratic institutions, but with philosophical ideals informed by Emersonian IDEALISM. In Sanborn's understanding, as in Transcendentalism, there was no separation between the concerns of scientists and philosophers, or between the work of improving society and the intellectual work of improving oneself.

By the 1890s, the ASSA began to lose influence as America faced new social problems brought on by new waves of urbanization, industrialization, and immigration and as professional social scientists were increasingly university trained and government sponsored to address these problems. The ASSA was disbanded by 1909, as throughout the previous decade its work had been replaced by some of the very organizations it inspired and gave rise to, such as the American Economic Association, the American Historical Association, and, most significantly, the founding of the American Political Science Association in 1903. The creation of these organizations signaled the shift toward professional specialization and divided the membership and purpose of what had been a unified reform vision of Sanborn's generation.

Bibliography

Haskell, Thomas L. *The Emergence of Professional Social Science: The American Social Science Association and the Nineteenth-Century Crisis of Authority.* Urbana: University of Illinois Press, 1977.

American Union of Associationists

The American Union of Associationists (AUA) was formed in 1846 as a national-level umbrella organization for individuals, as well as local and re-gional groups, interested in implementing the principles of French utopian socialist Charles Fourier in the United States. Headquartered in New York, the AUA had direct ties to the Transcendentalist-inspired utopian community at BROOK FARM in Massachusetts. Members were also actively involved in a variety of reform movements, and delegates and groups attended antislavery conventions, labor meetings, and an international peace convention.

When Brook Farm dissolved in 1847, the AUA took over publication of its official paper, *THE HARBINGER*. Annual conventions of the AUA were the primary planning sites for Fourierist communities—also called PHALANXES—in the United States. The national organization also directly oversaw the operation of some phalanxes. The creation of the American Union of Associationists was an important step in vocalizing a commitment to Fourierist philosophy and publicizing the creation of phalanxes. According to historian Carl Guarneri, however, the establishment of the AUA in 1846 was ultimately too late to secure the long-term success of FOURIERISM in the United States. By 1846 many of the most significant phalanx communities had already been established, several had already failed, leadership was already established and spread out regionally, and popular support and funding had quickly faded by the time the AUA was even founded to start promoting such efforts. Even the effort to maintain an official newspaper to keep Fourier's ideas before the public was split by internal divisions. The AUA was represented first through *The Harbinger* and then briefly through William Henry CHANNING's *SPIRIT OF THE AGE*, both of which ceased publication by 1850. The American Union of Associationists itself was therefore an ultimately short-lived organization, with its final annual convention held in 1851.

Bibliography

Guarneri, Carl. *The Utopian Alternative: Fourierism in Nineteenth Century America.* Ithaca, N.Y.: Cornell University Press, 1991.

American Unitarian Association (AUA)

Founded in May 1825, the American Unitarian Association, or AUA, was the formal break between

Unitarians and Congregationalists in the United States and was formed out of a commitment to organize a new denomination under a unified mission and project a consistent statement on church beliefs and theology. Prior to the establishment of the AUA, "liberal Christians" (as they were then called), including Andrews NORTON, William Ellery CHANNING, and others, were interested in ways to organize the clergy, but when the AUA was proposed, Channing, at least, rejected the idea as too divisive. In its early years the AUA attempted to avoid the consolidation of power by having membership open to individuals only, not to churches or congregations. UNITARIANISM began in the United States in 1805 and was the theological perspective taught at HARVARD DIVINITY SCHOOL throughout the early 19th century. The establishment of the AUA was the culmination of at least a decade of intense debates, regional divisions, and conflict within Unitarianism, including the theological controversy that led to the emergence of the Transcendentalist movement.

Even though the Transcendentalists ultimately pushed even liberal Unitarianism to its extremes, and many Transcendentalists eventually broke from any organized religious affiliation at all, few prominent conservative Unitarians spoke out publicly against the Transcendentalist challenge through the height of the controversy in the late 1830s. The most notable and extreme criticism came from Andrews Norton, who condemned the writings of Ralph Waldo EMERSON and George RIPLEY, who in 1838 was still a member of the AUA. Although these most radical figures broke their ties with Unitarianism and with organized religion in general, other Transcendentalists who were Unitarian ministers continued to preach and enjoy the fellowship of other Unitarians.

Theodore PARKER continued to preach and identify as a Unitarian minister and was a member of the AUA as well throughout the 1830s. After the controversy over his South Boston sermon, published as A DISCOURSE ON THE TRANSIENT AND PERMANENT IN CHRISTIANITY (1842), Parker was alienated from his Unitarian colleagues, however, who ceased sharing the pulpit with him. Parker ignored such attempts to distance him from Unitarianism, however, and continued to attend local conferences and annual meetings of the AUA. Such radicals as Parker, the earlier MIRACLES CON-

TROVERSY, and the increased public presence of the Transcendentalists in general exposed Unitarianism to criticism that questioned its Christian foundations, forcing the AUA to reign in the potential for radical interpretations by declaring that Unitarianism was united in accepting the "teachings of Christ . . . as infallible truth from God." In regards to any question about the divinity of Christ and the nature of the miracles he performed, the AUA also issued a statement that "the Divine authority of the Gospel, as founded on a special and miraculous imposition of God, is the basis of the Action of the Association." Transcendentalism, then, which grew out of the liberal religious environment that Unitarianism fostered in the early 19th century, was in turn responsible for the turn to conservatism by the official organization of the AUA.

Other Transcendentalists active in Unitarian affairs included James Freeman CLARKE, who served as secretary of the AUA at one point, and Frederic Henry HEDGE, who served as president of the organization between 1859 and 1863. Ironically, given his conservatism as head of the AUA, Hedge, through his early reviews of the writings of Samuel Taylor COLERIDGE and his primary role in creating the TRANSCENDENTAL CLUB, is often credited as one of the earliest instigators of Transcendentalist thought and criticism that caused a split within Unitarianism in the early 1830s. Hedge remained one of the few Transcendental Christians who retained ties to the organized church and, during his tenure as president of the AUA, he sought to bring together the moderately liberal and the more radical or unorthodox elements of the denomination.

During its first few decades, the main work of the AUA was in sponsoring missionaries and in publishing series of tracts and reprints of sermons by Unitarian ministers. Some of these tracts were written by ministers associated with Transcendentalism, such as Convers FRANCIS, and in 1875 the AUA published an edition of the works of the Reverend William Ellery Channing. The main paper of the AUA was the CHRISTIAN REGISTER, which it began publishing in 1826. In 1861 the AUA merged with the Universalist churches to form the Unitarian Universalist Association, which is still in existence to this day.

Bibliography

Wright, Conrad Edick, ed. *American Unitarianism: 1805–1865*. Boston: Massachusetts Historical Society and Northeastern University Press, 1989.

antinomianism

Antinomianism literally means "anti-law" and is the belief that Christians are not bound by human laws, particularly the laws dictating behavior in the Old Testament. Antinomian thought was present in the early Christian church but was fully expressed in certain sects during the Protestant Reformation of the 16th century. A distinctly American tradition of antinomianism began with the 17th-century controversy within New England PURITANISM created by the case of Anne HUTCHINSON. Hutchinson was put on trial and eventually banished from the Massachusetts colony for speaking against Puritan ministers, whom she charged with preaching a religion of good works, rather than God's pure grace, as the route to salvation. Two centuries later, the 19th-century Transcendentalists were an outgrowth of UNITARIANISM's rejection of the Calvinist thought of Puritans and, in coming to terms with New England's Puritan religious and cultural past, were particularly interested in the antinomian tradition of religious dissent as an alternative American tradition.

In his 1841 essay on "NEW ENGLAND REFORMERS," Ralph Waldo EMERSON made the historical connection between Puritan dissenters and cultural and religious reformers of his own time, noting that "Others assailed particular vocations, as that of the lawyer, that of the merchant, of the manufacturer, of the clergyman, of the scholar. Others attacked the institution of marriage, as the fountain of social evils. Others devoted themselves to the worrying of churches and meetings for public worship; and the fertile forms of antinomianism among the elder puritans, seemed to have their match in the plenty of the new harvest of reform." In his 1842 essay on "THE TRANSCENDENTALIST," Emerson made the connection with his own movement when he wrote that "In action, he (the transcendentalist) easily incurs the charge of antinomianism by his avowal that he, who has the Lawgiver, may with safety not only neglect, but even contravene every written commandment."

Other Transcendentalist reformers were more interested in Anne Hutchinson as an individual, not just the larger movement of theological dissent she represented for Emerson. In her 1897 *TRANSCENDENTALISM IN NEW ENGLAND*, feminist Caroline DALL identified Hutchinson by name as the historical starting point of American Transcendentalism and 19th-century Transcendentalism as "rank antinomianism" in its purest sense.

Bibliography

Lang, Amy Schrager. *Prophetic Woman: Anne Hutchinson and the Problem of Dissent in the Literature of New England*. Berkeley: University of California Press, 1987.

antislavery   *See* ABOLITIONISM.

"Art"
Ralph Waldo Emerson
(1844)

Ralph Waldo EMERSON's essay on "Art" originated as part of an 1836–37 lecture series and was first published as the final piece in his 1841 collection of *ESSAYS: FIRST SERIES*. The lecture series as a whole dealt with the general subject of the philosophy of history and was the earliest presentation of some of the core Transcendentalist ideas Emerson would later develop in other important essays, such as "HISTORY," "SELF-RELIANCE," "SPIRITUAL LAWS," and "THE OVER-SOUL." "Art" is one of Emerson's shortest essays in the *First Series* collection and deals with the topic of creativity. He opens the essay with the belief that all activity of the human soul is artistic or creative process: "Because the soul is progressive, it never quite repeats itself, but in every act attempts the production of a new and fairer whole."

Emerson defined "Art" not as a specific product or process but as "the need to create." More broadly, he defined it as "the conscious utterance of thought, by speech or action, to any end." Emerson emphasized the "conscious utterance" of creativity and compared this human endeavor to nature, which acted unconsciously: "Relative to themselves, the bee, the bird, the beaver, have no art, for what they do, they do instinctively." However, even his own distinctions between conscious and unconscious acts are not fixed, for nature does not act only relative to itself but in the presence of and in relationship to humanity and to the universe at large. He expanded his statement about nature to reconsider that "those things which are said to be done by Nature, are indeed done by Divine Art." When seeking to answer the questions of what is art and who creates it, Emerson identified the creation of the world itself as the ultimate artistic expression.

Humans as well are part of "the universal soul" that creates art in nature, and therefore humans do not act independently in their creativity either, since "to make anything useful or beautiful, the individual must be submitted to the universal mind." Emerson describes this larger force as "a gigantic hand" guiding the artist and the resulting best or representative art of any given time as that which "denote(s) the height of the human soul in that hour." Emerson argues that the best art, that which has affected him most, whether it be sculpture or painting or music, is that which "itself pierced directly to the simple and true; that it was familiar and sincere; that it was the old, eternal fact I had met already in so many forms." Emerson provides not only a spiritual look at humanity itself as art but a substantial commentary on art in the 19th century. He offers up an alternative aesthetic to the classical ideal of "imitation" in favor of a new ideal of inspiration, inspired by ROMANTICISM of the early 19th century. The aim of the artist is not to copy other great works but to provide new representations, to "give the suggestion of a fairer creation than we know." Even in more realistic endeavours such as portraiture, the artist can only offer a representation of the living person, "he must inscribe the character, and not the features, and must esteem the man who sits to him as himself only an imperfect picture or likeness of the aspiring original within." Although "works of highest art" are "universally intelligible," there are some cultural guidelines that must be followed in order for art to reach beyond the artist to a wider audience and influence. Art must have an element of the familiar in order to speak to an individual, and

so "the artist must employ the symbols in use in his day and nation, to convey his enlarged sense to his fellow-men. Thus the new in art is always formed out of the old."

Although throughout the essay Emerson gave many examples from classical and European art, he concludes with a search for a particularly American aesthetic, as "it is in vain that we look for genius to reiterate its miracles in the old arts." Although any art might inspire, Americans "must find beauty and holiness in new and necessary facts, in the field and road-side, in the shop and mill." Indeed, the American experiment itself, "a steamboat bridging the Atlantic between Old and New England," is an act of creation, "a step of man into harmony with nature." For Emerson, of course, Life itself is Art, the ultimate creative act. Even after applying his perspective to all the familiar artistic forms—portraiture, sculpture, painting, architecture, music—Emerson concludes that "There is higher work for Art than the arts." "The sweetest music . . . is in the human voice." "A great man is a new statue. . . . A beautiful woman is a picture which drives all beholders nobly mad. Life may be lyric or epic, as well as a poem or a romance." An original poem on "Art" accompanied the essay in subsequent editions of Emerson's collection and was later included in his 1867 volume of poetry, MAY-DAY AND OTHER PIECES.

At Home and Abroad   *See* "THINGS AND THOUGHTS IN EUROPE."

Atlantic Monthly
(1857–)

The *Atlantic Monthly: A Magazine of Literature, Art, and Politics* was founded in Boston in 1857 and served as the premier site of New England cultural commentary and thus, throughout the 19th century, featured many essays by and about the Transcendentalists. In addition to nearly every major writer and thinker of the period, most Boston-area intellectuals associated with Transcendentalism were published in the *Atlantic Monthly* at some point: Amos Bronson ALCOTT, Ralph Waldo EMERSON,

Henry David THOREAU, Theodore PARKER, George RIPLEY, Cyrus BARTOL, James Freeman CLARKE, Caroline DALL, Octavius Brooks FROTHINGHAM, Frederic Henry HEDGE, Elizabeth Palmer PEABODY, and Franklin Benjamin SANBORN. Its first editor was Emerson's associate and friend James Russell LOWELL, and its first publisher was Phillips, Sampson, and Company, the house then also publishing works by Emerson. In fact, the first issue of November 1857 included several pieces by Emerson including the essay "Society and Solitude" and the poems "BRAHMA" and "DAYS." The first two years of the paper were thus devoted almost entirely to New England literary culture until another publisher, Ticknor and Fields, purchased the magazine in 1859 and began to publish more widely in current affairs and included reviews and serializations of its own forthcoming works. The *Atlantic Monthly* continues today and remains an eclectic intellectual magazine that publishes writing on a variety of themes, including history, art, science, religion, and current affairs, as well as retaining its literary interests through book reviews, short fiction, and poetry.

Bibliography

Sedgwick, Ellery. *The Atlantic Monthly, 1857–1909: Yankee Humanism at High Tide and Ebb.* Amherst: University of Massachusetts Press, 1994.

"Autumnal Tints"
Henry David Thoreau
(1862)

Henry David THOREAU's "Autumnal Tints" was first published in the *ATLANTIC MONTHLY* in October 1862, just a few months after his death. Thoreau had delivered "Autumnal Tints" as a lecture several years earlier in 1859, and he spent the last months of his life revising several lectures and essays for publication; "WALKING" and "WILD APPLES" also appeared in the *Atlantic Monthly* in late 1862. In "Autumnal Tints" Thoreau sought to illuminate for the reader the deeper significance of the many colors of fall that might otherwise be missed with only a superficial viewing. As a naturalist-observer, Thoreau describes the actual physical characteristics of the leaves, but he also, as a philosopher, describes their meaning, the lessons learned from nature. In a Transcendentalist reading of "Autumnal Tints," the reader does not merely learn about the leaves but becomes the leaves themselves, their physical and spiritual journeys analogous. He states this interpretation clearly in alerting the reader that every leaf "stands there to express some thought or mood of ours." The leaves and the trees that bear them become "teachers" and "preachers . . . ministering to many generations of men," and, as seen in their many colors as the seasons change, the leaves have much to teach about life as well as death.

The changes from green to brown that leaves undergo in the fall are not cause for despair, Thoreau assures us, but, rather, "the emblem of a successful life concluded by a death not premature." Fall is preparation for renewal and awakening of the senses, represented by the many colors or "tints" which Thoreau describes. The colors of autumn are not just browns and golds, but reds, and even purples: "For beautiful variety no crop can be compared with this. . . . The ground is all parti-colored with them." Nature, in Thoreau's eyes, is not chaos but purpose and "beautiful variety." Thoreau compares nature's variety to the diversity found within human society, seeing that "every tree is a living liberty-pole on which a thousand bright flags are waving" and celebrating these "flags of all her nations." Fall is not death, but "the great harvest of the year," when the trees provide "a leaf's thickness to the depth of the soil" in preparation for new growth, "for future corn-fields and forests."

Bibliography

Hoag, Ronald Wesley. "Thoreau's Later Natural History Writings." In *The Cambridge Companion to Henry David Thoreau,* ed. Joel Myerson. New York: Cambridge University Press, 1995.

Walls, Laura Dassow. *Seeing New Worlds: Henry David Thoreau and Nineteenth-Century Natural Science.* Madison: University of Wisconsin Press, 1995.

B

"Bacchus"
Ralph Waldo Emerson
(1846)

"Bacchus" is considered one of Ralph Waldo EMER-SON's best works in his 1846 collection POEMS and is an example of his interest during this time period in Persian literature and ideas. In particular, it invokes images from Emerson's own translations of the poet Hafiz and from his readings of Sa'di (the subject of the 1842 poem "SAADI"). The primary theme of the poem "Bacchus" is, as in much of Emerson's other work, the relationship of the poet to his art. Even though Bacchus, the Roman god of wine and revelry, celebrates physical pleasure, the speaker in the poem resists such a sensual experience of his surroundings and seeks instead a Transcendentalist or mystic self-identification with the images he presents in his art. The poem opens with an appeal to "Bring me wine, but wine which never grew / In the belly of the grape." The poem instead seeks to find spiritual meaning out of the basic needs of the body: "Water and bread, / Food which needs no transmuting, / Rainbow-flowering, wisdom-fruiting, / Wine which is already man, / Food which teach and reason can."

Bacchus was also representative of Emerson himself, and his poem serves as commentary on the role of the poet. The wine itself so celebrated by Bacchus serves in the last section of the poem as a symbol of inspiration for writing: "Pour, Bacchus! The remembering wine; /Retrieve the loss of me and mine! / . . . A dazzling memory revive; / . . . And write my old adventures with the pen." Emer-son would invoke Bacchus again for assistance in writing poetry several decades later in his essay on "Poetry and Imagination," published in the 1876 collection, LETTERS AND SOCIAL AIMS: "O celestial Bacchus! Drive them mad,—this multitude of vagabonds, hungry for eloquence, hungry for poetry, starving for symbols, perishing for want of electricity."

Bacon, Delia
(1811–1859)

Delia Bacon briefly stirred the interest of Boston intellectuals, including several Transcendentalists, with her controversial theory questioning William SHAKESPEARE's authorship of several plays. Bacon's theory was that Francis Bacon, Walter Raleigh, and others had hidden their own subversive political views in plays such as *King Lear* and *Julius Caesar* and attributed the works to William Shakespeare in order to avoid persecution. Delia Bacon was raised and educated in Connecticut, where she taught at a girl's school in New Haven and wrote historical fiction. In the early 1850s she traveled throughout New England, presenting lectures on a view of history that detailed not solely political events but a more comprehensive view of the past through an examination of culture, literature, and daily life. She befriended Caroline DALL—who was attracted to this idea of history and with whom Bacon had corresponded as early as 1850—and Elizabeth Palmer PEABODY, both of whom introduced her into

Boston intellectual and social circles. Dall took over control of Bacon's lecturing schedule and promotion in Boston, and Peabody worked to find a publisher for Bacon's proposed book project on the Shakespeare theory.

In 1852 Bacon met Ralph Waldo EMERSON and, the following year, Nathaniel HAWTHORNE. Neither of these men wholeheartedly accepted Bacon's thesis, but, intrigued by her originality of thought and forcefulness of argument, they agreed to help her find a publisher. With a letter of support from Emerson, Bacon was able secure financial sponsorship to travel to England to conduct research for her project. Emerson continued to help her while abroad, writing letters of introduction for her to meet Thomas CARLYLE. Luckily for Bacon, Nathaniel Hawthorne was then residing in England as U.S. consul in Liverpool and agreed to personally pay for the printing of her book, *The Philosophy of the Plays of Shakespeare Unfolded,* published in 1857 with an introduction by Hawthorne. Bacon suffered a mental breakdown in the wake of negative reviews of the book, and she died in an asylum in September 1859. Hawthorne remembered her efforts and detailed his personal interactions with her in an essay entitled "Recollections of a Gifted Woman," published in the *ATLANTIC MONTHLY* in 1863.

Although none of the Transcendentalists felt that Delia Bacon's theory could be substantiated, Shakespeare was a particularly intriguing figure during the 19th century and several others wrote about him—from Emerson's selection of Shakespeare as "The Poet" in his *REPRESENTATIVE MEN* (1850) to Caroline Dall's 1885 publication of *What We Really Know About Shakespeare,* which included a chapter on Delia Bacon.

Bibliography

Deese, Helen. "A New England Women's Network: Elizabeth Palmer Peabody, Caroline Healey Dall, and Delia S. Bacon," *Legacy* 8:2 (1991): 77–91.

Bancroft, George
(1800–1891)

George Bancroft was a contemporary of the early Transcendentalists and shared with them an inter-est in German literature and philosophy of the 1820s and 1830s. At Harvard, Bancroft studied under such Unitarian luminaries as Andrews NORTON and Edward EVERETT. After graduation he spent time at the University of Göttingen in Germany where he met Johann Wolfgang von GOETHE, the idealist philosopher who was one of the premiere inspirers of American Transcendentalism. Bancroft subsequently published several articles and translations of German writers such as Goethe and Friedrich SCHILLER in journals such as the *NORTH AMERICAN REVIEW* and the *American Quarterly Review*. He also contributed translations to a volume edited by John Sullivan DWIGHT and published as part of George RIPLEY's *SPECIMENS OF FOREIGN STANDARD LITERATURE* series. His former adviser, Andrews Norton, was one of the strongest critics of Transcendentalism and warned Bancroft of becoming too immersed in the German thought which had influenced the movement. Despite his own contributions in bringing German writers to the attention of American intellectuals and his shared philosophical and moral reform viewpoints (for example, his interest in educational reform and philosophy led him to many of the same conclusions and approaches advocated by Amos Bronson ALCOTT), Bancroft never called himself a Transcendentalist. Bancroft is primarily known as a historian, and his most significant literary contribution was his 10-volume *History of the United States,* published between 1834 and 1875. This comprehensive work was praised by his 19th-century contemporaries, including some of the Transcendentalists, and is still an important reference volume today.

Bibliography

Handlin, Lillian. *George Bancroft: The Intellectual as Democrat.* New York: Harper and Row, 1984.

Bartol, Cyrus Augustus
(1813–1900)

Cyrus Bartol was a prominent Boston Unitarian minister who was a personal friend and mentor to many Transcendentalists but was more conservative than many radicals within the movement. He graduated from HARVARD DIVINITY SCHOOL along with other Transcendentalists such as James Freeman CLARKE, Christopher Pearse CRANCH, and John Sullivan DWIGHT. During his years at Harvard Bartol was introduced to the ideas of the emerging Transcendentalist controversy within UNITARIANISM. He attended lectures of Ralph Waldo EMERSON, notes of which he recorded in his journal, and became intrigued by the educational and spiritual philosophy of Amos Bronson ALCOTT, who would become a lifelong friend and mentor. He was a founding member of the TRANSCENDENTAL CLUB, which began in 1836, and, indeed, several of the meetings were held at his home.

As an ordained Unitarian minister Bartol was involved in most of the public controversies surrounding Transcendentalism in the 1830s and 1840s. In most matters he proved more conservative than his Transcendentalist friends. He critiqued the individualistic and un-Christian excesses of specific works by both Emerson and Theodore PARKER, but, still, Bartol defended the two radicals from censure in the wake of, first, Emerson's 1838 "DIVINITY SCHOOL ADDRESS" and then Parker's 1842 *A DISCOURSE ON THE TRANSIENT AND PERMANENT IN CHRISTIANITY*. When a movement was under way to remove Parker from the pulpit in light of his radical views, Bartol stood by his friend and declared that he would leave the pulpit in solidarity. However, as Parker remained a preacher and continued to promote a Transcendentalist version of Unitarian Christianity in his sermons, Bartol grew increasingly critical. He never accepted Parker's insistence on a personal religion that denied the existence of God as the creator, but he still admired Parker's adherence to his own beliefs, stating after his friend's death in 1860, "I must affirm his position a false one, however the man was true."

Bartol's own writings spoke both to and against some of the core Transcendentalist tenets, leading early historians of the movement confused over whether or not he should be considered a Transcendentalist. In his 1850 collection of sermons, *Discourses on the Christian Spirit and Life,* he defended the divinity of Christ, which the Transcendentalists had denied in favor of understanding Jesus purely as a human role model. Bartol was responding directly to an Emersonian emphasis on

the historical rather than divine importance of Jesus Christ when he declared that Jesus "is not, in the phrase of the day, a 'representative man,' but representative of deity. . . . He transcends all our transcendentalism."

The influence of Transcendentalism on Bartol's thought was even more evident in his travel and nature writings than in his theological beliefs. After a European tour he published *Pictures of Europe, Framed in Ideas* (1855), which shows the influence not only of Transcendentalism but of SWEDENBORGIAN themes as well in its impressions of the language and metaphors of nature as spiritual lessons. The book received praise as a classic of travel writing, and one reviewer of the time went so far as to call it "an international version" of Henry David THOREAU's *A WEEK ON THE CONCORD AND MERRIMACK RIVERS.*

In the latter half of the century, Cyrus Bartol returned to the radicalism of Transcendentalism in his search for personal religious freedom and increasingly moved away from the organized Unitarian church. He was instrumental in the founding of the FREE RELIGIOUS ASSOCIATION (FRA) in 1867 and helped organize the RADICAL CLUB, a society for proponents of free thought. Membership in these organizations was heavily dominated by other Transcendentalists, and Bartol's later writings moved closer than ever to promoting the philosophy. In essays such as "Transcendentalism," which appeared in his 1872 book, *Radical Problems,* Bartol defended the subjective and intuitive aspects of Transcendentalism as a spiritual and philosophical defense against the increasingly dominant scientific models of late 19th-century intellectual culture. Like other Transcendentalists, Bartol did not reject scientific inquiry and advances but instead sought to make empirical methods compatible with personal spiritual motivations. Through gatherings such as the Free Religious Association, Bartol and his colleagues in free thought looked to other cultures and religious traditions for ideas and inspiration on meeting this goal. He published regularly on such themes in newspapers, including the FRA's own *Index.*

Cyrus Bartol's last book, *Principles and Portraits* (1880), was a collection of essays on his favorite literary and religious personalities, including William Ellery CHANNING, Ralph Waldo Emerson, and William SHAKESPEARE. Bartol again joined with Transcendentalist colleagues, such as Ednah Dow CHENEY, Elizabeth Palmer PEABODY, and David WASSON, as a lecturer and attendee at Bronson Alcott's CONCORD SCHOOL OF PHILOSOPHY AND LITERATURE in the 1870s and '80s. There he lectured on literary themes in the works of Dante, Ralph Waldo Emerson, Johann Wolfgang von GOETHE, and William Shakespeare.

Bibliography

Heath, William G. "Cyrus Bartol's Transcendentalism," *Studies in the American Renaissance* (1979): 399–408.

"The Bird and the Bell"
Christopher Pearse Cranch
(1874)

The title poem in Transcendentalist artist Christopher Pearse CRANCH's 1874 collection of poems, *The Bird and the Bell*, recalls the Cranch family's three-year stay in Italy coinciding with the European revolutions of the 1840s. The sounds of the church bells set against the songs of birds was a common image in Italian literature criticizing the Roman Catholic Church. Transcendentalist Cranch employs the birdsongs as a symbol of the freedom of the natural world, a "fresh message from the Beauty Infinite," only to be interrupted and taken over by the "weird tones" of the decidedly unnatural "brazen bell" of the nearby church. Cranch represents the Catholic Church not only through the sound of the bell but through gothic images of "chanting priests" and a "great ghost-organ." In his Transcendentalist interpretation of the reasons for revolution, it is nature rather than the church that offers an understanding of "the Beauty Infinite," or the Divine. The church offers "an empty feast"—in other words, nothing—justifying not only political but spiritual revolution. The future of Italy lies, according to Cranch, in the bird's song, in the images of nature as a representation of the living soul. Cranch's poem, and thus the revolution, ends triumphantly, when at the end of the poem an entire flock of birds returns, singing "Truth and Beauty," but now he as-

sures us that "No clang of hierarchal bells shall ring, / To drown your carol, in the airs that move / And stir the dawning age of Liberty and Love!"

Bibliography

The Life and Letters of Christopher Pearse Cranch, by his Daughter Leonora Scott Cranch. Reprint. Brooklyn, N.Y.: AMS Press, 1969.

Blake, Harrison Gray Otis
(1816–1898)

Harrison Gray Otis "H. G. O." Blake was a HARVARD DIVINITY SCHOOL student who sat on the committee that chose Ralph Waldo EMERSON as the 1838 commencement speaker. Emerson presented on that occasion his controversial "DIVINITY SCHOOL ADDRESS," which Blake promoted for post-commencement publication. Blake was trained for the Unitarian clergy but his views on organized religion and on the clergy in particular were so radically altered by his acquaintance with Transcendentalist Emerson and English writer Thomas CARLYLE that he early abandoned the ministry and instead pursued teaching as a vocation.

H. G. O. Blake was at the center of intellectual life in his hometown of Worcester, Massachusetts, and regularly arranged for Emerson and later Henry David THOREAU to lecture there in public halls and occasionally at meetings in his own home. Blake became a devoted disciple of Thoreau beginning in the 1840s, and the two men occasionally went on nature hikes together in and around CONCORD, MASSACHUSETTS. Blake and Thoreau maintained a voluminous correspondence until Thoreau's death in 1862. When Thoreau's sister, Sophia THOREAU, died in 1876 she willed all of her brother's manuscripts to the care of Blake, who edited his friend and mentor's nature journal notebooks and organized the writings into four seasonal volumes: *Early Spring in Massachusetts* (1881), *Summer* (1884), *Winter* (1888), and *Autumn* (1892). Throughout this period of editorial work in the 1880s, H. G. O. Blake continued his connections with the other Transcendentalists through his regular attendance at Amos Bronson

ALCOTT's CONCORD SCHOOL OF PHILOSOPHY AND LITERATURE.

Bibliography
Harding, Walter. *The Days of Henry Thoreau.* New York: Dover, 1982.

Blake, William
(1757–1827)

English poet and artist William Blake was one of the primary figures of English ROMANTICISM and therefore a major influence on the American Transcendentalist movement, which drew much of its literary and artistic aesthetic from romanticism. The Transcendentalists, in particular, were influenced by the romantic emphasis on imagination and on childhood, two of the main characteristics or themes of William Blake's own work. Blake's romantic sensibility, in both his poetry and the detailed illustrated engravings that accompanied his text, paid attention to and evoked sympathy for the realities of human existence.

In addition to providing engravings for his own poems, Blake also illustrated important works by other poets, such as John Milton, as well as scenes from the Bible, and was even commissioned to engrave a children's book by English feminist Mary Wollstonecraft. *Poetical Sketches* (1783) was his first book, but his most influential work began in 1789 with *Songs of Innocence,* a poetic tribute to childhood, a favorite theme of the romantics, including the Transcendentalists several decades later. The innocence of childhood represented to romantic poets, following Blake's lead, the beginnings of all humanity, the freedom and potential of humanity before the fall of Adam and Eve. The book was presented as a volume for children— "happy songs / Every child may joy to hear"—but it was also a reflection on the childlike in every person. In 1794 he tempered the optimism of *Songs of Innocence* by publishing an enlarged volume of poems intending to show "the two Contrary States of the Human Soul." The now expanded *Songs of Innocence and of Experience* includes the affirmations of the happy souls of children, countered with the *Songs of Experience,* which deal with human faults and evil. In this combined volume are some of Blake's most well-known poems, including "The Lamb," "The Tyger," and "Little Boy Lost," among others. All of the poems, of "innocence" and of "experience," are written from the point of view of children, who were believed to gauge more perceptively and accurately both the beauty and the injustices of the world.

Blake's influence on the American Transcendentalists included a rejection of the rational thought of the Enlightenment era in favor of an emphasis on human imagination, love, and subjectivity as the foundations of moral and social-political life. These themes were most prevalent in Blake's series of "Prophetic Books" of poetry, which included, most famously, *The Marriage of Heaven and Hell* (c. 1790) and *Milton* (1804–08). In these works Blake drew on the ideas of contemporary mystics, such as Emanuel Swedenborg, who also greatly influenced the Transcendentalists. William Blake never achieved great prominence or respect during his own lifetime, but today his poems and his drawings are appreciated as innovative and foundational aspects of the European romantic tradition.

Bibliography
Ackroyd, Peter. *Blake: A Biography.* New York: Knopf, 1996.

"Blight"
Ralph Waldo Emerson
(1844)

Ralph Waldo EMERSON's poem "Blight" was first printed in the Transcendentalist literary journal, the DIAL, in January 1844 under the title "The Times—A Fragment" and appeared in Emerson's 1846 collection of POEMS. "Blight" is an angry critique of humanity's contemporary relationship to nature, which is one of external scientific observation rather than mystical interdependence. Emerson begins the poem with a description of the "truths" of nature that were well known to previous generations, whose livelihoods depended upon an understanding of and interaction with the natural world as "a part of the round day, related to the sun." In that earlier state of being, "The old men studied magic in the flowers, / And human fortunes in astronomy, / . . . Preferring things to names." Emerson then laments that now he sees around him only "these young scholars, who invade our hills," who as "strangers to the stars" and, in their quest for scientific knowledge, "Love not the flower they pluck, and know it not, / And all their botany is Latin names." Beyond scientific pursuits, the general reaction of modern humans to nature is only to complain about its inconveniences: "The stunted trees look sick, the summer short, / Clouds shade the sun, which will not tan our hay." Emerson accuses his contemporaries of having only a superficial and therefore destructive relationship to the earth, acting as "thieves" and "pirates of the universe" who, in pursuing their own selfish human goals, have assured that "nothing thrives to reach its natural term; / And life, shorn of its venerable length, / Even at its greatest space is a defeat."

The Blithedale Romance
Nathaniel Hawthorne
(1852)

The novel *The Blithedale Romance* by Nathaniel HAWTHORNE was a fictional characterization of the Transcendentalist utopian community at BROOK FARM. The community of Brook Farm was founded by George RIPLEY at West Roxbury, Massachusetts, in 1841 as an attempt to create an ideal community as an alternative to capitalism, urbanization, slavery, and even the constraints of gender roles which so negatively affected 19th-century American society and economy. Many of Hawthorne's friends and colleagues, referred to in the novel as "visionary transcendentalists, who were still seeking for the better life," resided at the community between its founding in 1841 and its collapse in 1847. Brook Farm was based on a system whereby individual members would contribute manual labor just a few hours a day and have the rest of the time free for intellectual and spiritual pursuits, and Hawthorne hoped participation in the experiment would provide him with a place and time to write. Instead of finding time to pursue the life of the mind, however, Hawthorne found himself engaged in unending (and often unpleasant) tasks necessary just to keep the community afloat. He worked long days in agricultural labor and wrote to his fiancée, Sophia Peabody (HAWTHORNE), that, contrary to his expectations, residing at Brook Farm actually produced "an antipathy to pen and ink." He left the community briefly, returning once more to give it another try but again finding life at the farm too busy, he left for good after another few months. Ten years later, several years after Brook Farm had dissolved entirely, he revisited the experiment as the subject of a novel.

Hawthorne's fictional community of Blithedale reveals many of the problems and inconsistencies of the utopian socialist ideal, in particular the problem of committed individualists coming together in an effort to create community. The novel exposes the frailties of human beings rather than idealistic possibilities and comes to the conclusion that the problems that plague the larger society are ultimately reproduced within the smaller communal experiment, such as class divisions, the sexual division of labor, and personal relationships and character flaws. The community is doomed because it depends upon faulty individuals, many of whom are caricatures of Hawthorne's own friends among the Transcendentalists of Boston. Although contemporary and modern readers have sought to identify the basis of individual characters, it is more useful to read the characters as either composites of various actual figures or merely general types that Hawthorne either observed in his society or created out of his imagination.

Although a host of characters are introduced, the novel revolves around the relationships between four main characters. The novel opens with the poet Miles Coverdale's arrival at Blithedale. Coverdale, as the narrator and as the skeptical outsider, lends to easy identification as the voice of Hawthorne himself, and his experiences bear a close resemblance to Hawthorne's own time spent at Brook Farm. Upon arriving, Coverdale meets the feminist journalist and intellectual Zenobia, regarded by most readers to be closely based on Margaret FULLER, down to the fact that Zenobia, like Fuller, dies by drowning—Zenobia in the river, Fuller in the sea. While Fuller regularly visited and lectured at Brook Farm, unlike Zenobia, she never lived there full time. Coverdale then meets the fanatical reformer, Hollingsworth, who has brought along another resident, Priscilla, the younger, more beautiful, and more traditional model of womanhood than her half sister, Zenobia. The character of Hollingsworth is the most idealistic, but also most egotistical, of the reformers, and various scholars have linked this character with either the actual founder of Brook Farm, George Ripley, or a composite of some other Transcendentalist reformers.

The setting of the Blithedale community ultimately serves as merely an idyllic backdrop to the human drama unfolding among its residents. As the story progresses, both past and hoped-for romantic relationships between the various characters are revealed—relationships that undermine the work of the ideal community and lead to the characters' individual ruin, both economically and physically. Zenobia commits suicide because Hollingsworth loves her sister and not her, and Hollingsworth gives up his philanthropic and reform commitments due to guilt over Zenobia's death. Coverdale himself leaves the community for good due to, as he reveals to the reader much later, unrequited feelings for Priscilla.

The novel is not, however, entirely or even primarily a veiled (auto)biographical account of actual historical figures and events, nor a blatant condemnation of Transcendentalist efforts at social reform. Hawthorne insisted that he was presenting a "fictitious handling" of the Brook Farm experiment, not a factual history.

Bibliography
Mitchell, Thomas. *Hawthorne's Fuller Mystery.* Amherst: University of Massachusetts Press, 1999.

Boston Athenaeum

Chartered in 1807, the Boston Athenaeum was a literary and cultural center throughout the time of the Transcendentalists. The Athenaeum was founded as an extension of the members' library of the Anthology Society, a private club that collectively edited THE MONTHLY ANTHOLOGY and *Boston Review.* Ralph Waldo EMERSON's father, William Emerson, was a founding member of the Anthology Society and, thus, of the Boston Athenaeum. Members or subscribers to the Athenaeum had access to an extensive reference and periodical library—which included the best of both American and foreign works—as well as natural history and art exhibits and a lecture room. Ralph Waldo Emerson was a lifelong member.

"Boston Hymn"
Ralph Waldo Emerson
(1863)

Transcendentalist Ralph Waldo EMERSON wrote the poem "The Boston Hymn" in the midst of the Civil War as an antislavery celebration of President Abraham Lincoln's "Emancipation Proclamation." Emerson read the poem aloud at a public meeting on January 1, 1863, the date the Proclamation went into effect by freeing slaves in rebel states. It was first published four years later in Emerson's 1867 collection, MAY-DAY AND OTHER PIECES. The poem is written in the voice of God calling for freedom by reminding the United States of its higher, nobler, more democratic purpose. Emerson explicitly engages the language of "manifest destiny," or the belief that God had ordained this special purpose for America by providing access to the vast land reaching all the way to the Pacific Ocean. Emerson writes: "Lo! I uncover the land / Which I had hid of old time in the West, / As the sculptor uncovers the statue / When he has wrought his best." Side by side with the land is the democratic political system as a special feature of this divine purpose. He glorifies the fact that both "The young men and the sires, / The digger in the harvest field, / Hireling, and him that hires" are called together "in a pine statehouse" (the choice of pine wood as the building material emphasizes both the native and the humble status of American political institutions) to collectively "choose men to rule." In giving America this democracy in the first place God himself points out that "I break your bonds and masterships, / And I unchain the slave," so that America risks losing this special status by keeping some of its citizens enslaved: "To-day unbind the captive, / So only are ye unbound." Ultimately, then, the poem is a call to end slavery, but it also reminds listeners or readers of the divine meaning of the Civil War itself in preserving the Union.

The Bostonians
Henry James, Jr.
(1886)

The Bostonians was an 1886 novel by Henry JAMES, Jr., that provided a satire on upper-class Boston life during the time of the Transcendentalists and is presumed to caricature some of the Transcendentalists directly. One of the main characters is a strong-minded reformer, Olive Chancellor, whose primary cause is the emancipation of women. Another character, Miss Birdseye, was perceived by many at the time of the novel's publication to be representative of Transcendentalist reformer Elizabeth Palmer PEABODY, in whose parlor many reform meetings and CONVERSATIONS, about WOMEN'S RIGHTS as well as other issues, were held. In the novel, Miss Birdseye has orchestrated a meeting of women reformers to welcome one of the most celebrated feminists of their cause, Mrs. Farrinder. Olive Chancellor and Mrs. Farrinder are representatives of the new generation of feminists during the time such as Margaret FULLER, Elizabeth Cady Stanton, and others. One of the primary struggles in the novel is the relationship between Olive Chancellor and the younger Verena Tarrant, who is converted to the women's cause and trained by Olive to become a lecturer but then must choose between her career and the pull of marriage and family in her courtship with the southern lawyer, Basil Ransom.

Although many actual Bostonians thought that James's novel was an unfair and unflattering portrait of their society, the novel is an insider's view into, and criticism of, the social and political world of New England's reformer class, who possessed money and social standing and expected to use those assets to change the world in the mid-19th century.

Boston Quarterly Review
(1838–1842)

Orestes BROWNSON published the *Boston Quarterly Review* between January 1838 and October 1842 as a journal of critical thought within UNITARIANISM in general, and a space for Transcendentalism in particular. The paper was not merely a forum for intellectuals to talk to one another, however, as Brownson envisioned the *Boston Quarterly Review* as democratic forum bridging the gap between philosophers and ordinary people. He first articulated this concern in his 1836 *NEW VIEWS OF CHRISTIANITY, SOCIETY, AND THE CHURCH*—itself one of the markers of the beginning of the Transcendentalist movement—in which he wrote "The time is not far distant when our whole population will be philosophers, and all our philosophers will be practical men." Despite his affiliation with the movement, Brownson did not intend for the role of "philosophers" to be dominated by the voice of the Transcendentalists, as he opened up its pages to "the Transcendentalists, the Mystics, the Theosophists, the Idealists, (who) may make this journal at all times, if they choose, their medium of communication with the public."

Although Brownson had been a regular attendee of the TRANSCENDENTAL CLUB, his own views were more conservative than most of his colleagues in that group and, in his paper, he neither defended nor uncritically promoted the Transcendentalist viewpoint. Still, the periodical was central to the development of an early Transcendentalist literary community in that it predated the founding of the movement's own specific journal, the *DIAL*, in 1840. One essay in particular, "Thoughts on Unity, Progress, and Government" by S. D. Robbins in the April 1838 issue, articulated many of the central themes that would be developed by Ralph Waldo EMERSON a few months later in his "DIVINITY SCHOOL ADDRESS." A partial list of other writers published in the paper includes, from among the Transcendentalists, Amos Bronson ALCOTT, William Henry CHANNING, John Sullivan DWIGHT, Margaret FULLER, Theodore PARKER, Elizabeth Palmer PEABODY, and George RIPLEY.

As the editor for the *Boston Quarterly Review*, Brownson himself wrote most of the essays, and every issue included several reviews of recent American or European books. Besides his essays on religious or theological issues, Brownson also used the forum to publish several pieces related to his interest in democratic social reform. His July 1840 essay on "THE LABORING CLASSES" remains one of the most important critiques of capitalism of this era.

By the time he founded the *Boston Quarterly Review* Orestes Brownson had established his prominence as a writer in many other intellectual journals, such as the CHRISTIAN EXAMINER, and as an editor on papers such as *The Free Enquirer* and *The Philanthropist.* After ceasing publication of *Boston Quarterly Review,* Brownson spent two years writing for *The Democratic Review* before beginning another journal, BROWNSON'S QUARTERLY REVIEW.

Bibliography

Gohdes, Clarence L. F. *The Periodicals of American Transcendentalism.* Durham, N.C.: Duke University Press, 1931.

Bowen, Francis
(1811–1890)

As a conservative Unitarian, essayist, and editor of the NORTH AMERICAN REVIEW, Francis Bowen was one of the most vocal critics of Transcendentalism during the 1830s and 1840s. In the *North American Review* and, even earlier, in the CHRISTIAN EXAMINER, Bowen criticized Ralph Waldo EMERSON and George RIPLEY (both of whom published their first major Transcendentalist treatises in 1836) and others for their emphasis on intuition and an "inspirational" philosophy of unintelligible abstracts. He criticized the Transcendentalist approach to theology, in particular, which favored personal mystical experience over rational study of texts and dismissed their project as, if nothing else, arrogant: "From the heights of mystical speculation, they look down with a ludicrous self-complacency and pity on the mass of mankind." Bowen's own philosophical bent was toward the more rational Scottish COMMON SENSE PHILOSOPHY, which he understood as attacked by the tenets of Transcendentalism. He saw the Transcendentalist emphasis on the individual as the source of knowledge and power as dangerous in that it did away with the need for God and revelation. He warned that

"There are mysteries in nature which human power cannot penetrate."

Furthermore, Bowen's criticisms focused on the German influence in Transcendentalist thought, as evidenced by their enthusiasm for the writings and ideas of Johann Wolfgang von GOETHE, Immanuel KANT, Johann SCHILLER, and others. For Bowen, these "foreign" influences would serve only to "contaminate," not enrich, American intellectual life. Finally, and worse, considering its growth out of Unitarian Christianity, he saw how Transcendentalist tendencies could lead to atheism. The early public criticisms of conservatives like Bowen and Andrews NORTON ironically helped fuel the group and philosophical identity of Transcendentalism.

Bowen would eventually embrace some aspects of transcendentalist philosophic ideals and, like many of the Transcendentalists later in the century, became interested in HEGELIANISM; he even published a book on "foreign" philosophers, the 1877 *Modern Philosophy from Descartes to Schopenhauer and Hartmann.* Bowen was an important philosopher in his own right and spent his career from 1853 onward as a Harvard professor of religion and philosophy.

Bibliography

Howe, Daniel Walker. *The Unitarian Conscience: Harvard Moral Philosophy, 1805–1861.* Cambridge, Mass.: Harvard University Press, 1970.

Bradford, George Partridge
(1807–1890)

Teacher and member of BROOK FARM George Bradford befriended many of the Transcendentalists in CONCORD, MASSACHUSETTS, and was considered by most to be a fellow scholar, even though he published little original work. Bradford was a graduate of Harvard and occasionally gave lyceum lectures on literary themes. Most of his professional life was as a teacher, although he did publish one book of translations and a handful of articles. As a resident of Concord, Bradford had attended meetings of the TRANSCENDENTAL CLUB and was characterized by Ralph Waldo EMERSON as one of his few intellectual companions, and Amos Bronson ALCOTT credited Bradford with first introducing him to Emerson. Bradford was a close friend of Nathaniel HAWTHORNE as well. He had resided at George RIPLEY's utopian experiment at Brook Farm, but Bradford's "Reminiscences of Brook Farm by a Member of the Community" was not published until 1892, two years after his death.

Bibliography

Mathews, James W. "George Partridge Bradford: Friend of Transcendentalists," *Studies in the American Renaissance* (1981): 133–156.

"Brahma"
Ralph Waldo Emerson
(1857)

Along with the essay "Persian Poetry" (1858), the poem "Brahma" represents Ralph Waldo EMERSON's interest during this period of his career in Eastern religion, culture, and literature. Many of the Transcendentalists were interested in exploring non-Christian religions and were intrigued by what Hindu culture and religion could reveal about human ethics and universal themes. The short 16-line "Brahma" appeared in the first issue of the ATLANTIC MONTHLY (November 1857) and was published again 10 years later as part of Emerson's 1867 collection, MAY-DAY AND OTHER PIECES.

In Hinduism Brahma represents the eternal and infinite nature of the universal spirit, similar to Emerson's own conception of "THE OVERSOUL," the unifying power that encompasses God as well as humans and nature. As in the Bhagavad Gita, the central Hindu spiritual text, Brahma speaks in Emerson's poem to these themes of eternal life and of the universe as ruled by the force of life, not death. The opening lines of the poem are a rewriting of a key passage from the Bhagavad Gita on this theme. Emerson writes, in the voice of Brahma: "If the red slayer think he slays, / Or if the slain think he is slain, / They know not well the subtle ways / I keep, and pass, and turn again." For comparison, the original passage in the Bhagavad Gita reads: "He who thinks this self a killer / and he who thinks it killed, / both fail to understand; / it does not kill nor is it killed."

Emerson goes on to emphasize in the next stanza that, to Brahma, there are no opposing forces in the universe but, instead, all is interconnected: "Far or forgot to me is near; / Shadow and sunlight are the same." As in the Transcendentalist concept of the oversoul, this overarching force that is Brahma includes and encompasses all things within the universe: "And I the hymn the Brahmin sings." This line emphasizes that the teacher, the poet, and the song are all the same. Perhaps unintentionally, referring to himself as the Brahmin's poem might also be seen as a play on words since the term "BRAHMIN" was just coming into use in New England in the 1860s to refer to Boston's cultural elite as well. Lastly, Emerson emphasizes again that the individual is universal and, unlike the goal of heaven in his native Christianity, the universal truths are open to all. The last line of the poem—"But thou, meek lover of the good! / Find me, and turn thy back on heaven."—is Emerson's urging to seek out other spiritual belief systems besides Christianity as alternative sources for finding personal meaning.

Brahmin

Brahmin, or Boston Brahmins, refers to New England families who claim to be descendants of the original Puritan settlers and founders of Boston and the Massachusetts Bay Colony. In addition, and perhaps more important than being direct hereditary descendants, they claimed to be the cultural descendants of the American historical legacy of white Anglo-Saxon Protestants and, in the 19th century, made up not only the wealthiest class of Bostonians but the most highly educated and politically progressive as well. Ralph Waldo EMERSON's family traced its genealogy back to the founding generation of Puritan ministers and landowners.

The term *Brahmin* comes from India and refers to the highest caste in the social system. It is believed that the first American usage of the phrase to refer to a New England Brahmin class appeared in an 1860 ATLANTIC MONTHLY article by Oliver Wendell HOLMES, thus coming into use during the era of the Transcendentalists to refer specifically to upper-class Bostonians, many of whom were engaged in the literary and reform activities of the time. Culturally, the Boston Brahmin class was identified with Harvard College, through which intellectual as well as moral and religious values were disseminated to each new generation. It was at HARVARD DIVINITY SCHOOL in the early 19th century that Ralph Waldo Emerson and other young men of his generation were steeped in Unitarian thought and trained as ministers, lecturers, and writers. Critics, such as English reformer Harriet MARTINEAU and Henry JAMES, JR., in his novel THE BOSTONIANS, criticized members of New England's upper class, and the Boston Brahmins in particular, as exclusive and full of pretensions and hypocrisies, pointing out the limitations of their progressive reform politics in light of their investment in their social and economic standing.

Brisbane, Albert
(1809–1890)

Albert Brisbane was the primary person responsible for promoting the ideas of 19th-century French utopian socialist Charles Fourier among the Transcendentalists and throughout the United States in general. Through Brisbane, the Transcendentalists, and George RIPLEY in particular, brought Fourier's idea of the PHALANX as the model society to their community at BROOK FARM. Born in New York, Brisbane traveled and studied in Europe where he was introduced to utopian socialism through the writings of Fourier. Fourier himself died in 1837, after which time Brisbane returned to America and subsequently published his *Social Destiny of Man* in 1840. The book consisted of original writings by Brisbane as well as translations of many of Fourier's main texts. Its publication gained national attention for Brisbane who went on to write several essays on "associationism" and Fourier for the *NEW YORK TRIBUNE* and other periodicals, as well as another book, *Concise Exposition of the Doctrines of Association*, in 1843.

Brisbane's work was read by many of the Transcendentalists including George Ripley, who joined with Brisbane and Horace GREELEY in 1843 to establish a written constitution for the North American Phalanx community at Albany, New York. By January 1844 Ripley's community at Brook Farm revised its own constitution to reflect this new interest in FOURIERISM. The Fourier plan was ultimately too strict—and involved participation in too many undesirable tasks—to be attractive to the free spirits at Brook Farm, thus hastening the community's demise by 1847. Albert Brisbane never lived at Brook Farm in Massachusetts but instead concentrated his efforts in publishing out of New York. He established a Fourierist journal, *The Phalanx*, which existed between 1843 and 1845 and was succeeded by *THE HARBINGER*, the official journal of the Brook Farm community.

Bibliography
Francis, Richard. *Transcendental Utopias: Individual and Community at Brook Farm, Fruitlands, and Walden.* Ithaca, N.Y.: Cornell University Press, 1997.
Guarneri, Carl. *The Utopian Alternative: Fourierism in Nineteenth Century America.* Ithaca, N.Y.: Cornell University Press, 1991.

Brook Farm
(1841–1847)

The communal living experiment at Brook Farm was the largest scale and most successful attempt to translate the IDEALISM of Transcendentalist into practical living. Brook Farm was founded in April 1841 on a nearly 200-acre site in West Roxbury, Massachusetts, by former Unitarian minister George RIPLEY and his wife Sophia RIPLEY. The community grew slowly but steadily, attracting families as well as many single persons, although never more than 100 people lived there at any given time. Although many early members were drawn from among Boston's Transcendentalist community—joining the Ripleys were George William CURTIS, Charles DANA, John Sullivan DWIGHT, and Nathaniel HAWTHORNE— major figures such as Amos Bronson ALCOTT, Ralph Waldo EMERSON, or Margaret FULLER visited often but never joined the community.

For some, the experiment did not seem to be clearly enough linked to a Transcendentalist purpose. Fellow reformer Charles LANE—soon to be the founder with Bronson Alcott of another community at FRUITLANDS—critiqued Brook Farm in the January 1844 issue of the Transcendentalist journal, the DIAL, by arguing that there was no clear organizing principle or philosophy behind the creation of the community: "The motives which bring individuals there may be as various as their numbers." For his part, Ralph Waldo Emerson avoided organized reform efforts in general, articulating instead a belief in self-reform before the larger reforms of society could be undertaken. Additionally, he felt that communal living would stifle individual self-development. This was the case for Nathaniel Hawthorne, an original shareholder-member who soon discovered he could not both live there and write productively. Hawthorne ultimately caricatured the community's goals and members in his 1852 novel, THE BLITHEDALE ROMANCE.

George Ripley's stated objective for Brook Farm was to "insure a more natural union between intellectual and manual labor than now exists," and he believed that communal living and shared labor would be the way to best promote both social and individual development; as Ripley proposed the plan to Emerson in a fall 1840 letter, the goal would be to "combine the thinker and the worker as far as possible in the same individual" and thus eliminate distinctions and privileges of class. In the early or "Transcendental" years the community, then called the Brook Farm Institute of Agriculture and Education, worked toward this goal through a philosophy of shared work in distinct and focused areas of the farm—people might concentrate their efforts in farming, school-teaching, manufacturing, domestic work (such as cooking and housekeeping), or maintenance, depending on their interests and natural abilities. Although the community remained small, Ripley embraced grand social reform goals as he intended not only to reform the personal and work lives of the residents but for their community to provide a model for American society at large. The plan for the community, as well as its philosophical basis, was laid out by Ripley in the 1841 "Articles of the Association of the Subscribers to the Brook Farm Institute of Agriculture and Education." While much attention was paid to member's work lives, as much work had to be done, another important focus for Ripley in guiding the Brook Farm experiment was EDUCATION. For many, the highlight of the community was the school for children,

which drew students both from among the offspring of permanent residents and from the surrounding community. The school became the focus of much press about the experiment, and most accounts praised academics as well as the ideals of the Brook Farm school.

After 1844 the community reorganized as a PHALANX—and renamed itself the Brook Farm Association for Industry and Education—modeled on the ideas of French utopian socialist Charles Fourier, a philosophy known as FOURIERISM. Practically, this meant a reorganization of community members' work lives from a model which encouraged each individual to pursue the labor which most suited him or her to a model of strict regulation that required individuals to move in shifts from one task to another throughout the day. During this time Ripley promoted both the experiment and Fourier's ideas and began publication began of THE HARBINGER as the official newspaper of Brook Farm. Under the Fourierist plan construction began on the main building, the Phalanstery, but by then many members had already left and others had become disillusioned. In March 1846 the Phalanstery burned down before it was completed, a financial and emotional loss from which the community never recovered, and the experiment disbanded for good in September 1847.

Bibliography

Delano, Sterling. *Brook Farm: The Dark Side of Utopia.* Cambridge, Mass.: Harvard University Press, 2004.

Francis, Richard. *Transcendental Utopias: Individual and Community at Brook Farm, Fruitlands, and Walden.* Ithaca, N.Y.: Cornell University Press, 1997.

Guarneri, Carl. *The Utopian Alternative: Fourierism in Nineteenth-Century America.* Ithaca, N.Y.: Cornell University Press, 1991.

Brooks, Charles Timothy
(1813–1883)

Unitarian minister Charles Timothy Brooks introduced many German ideas and writers to the American Transcendentalists through his translations of authors such as Johann Wolfgang von GOETHE and Johann SCHILLER. At Harvard Brooks studied under Charles FOLLEN, the premiere German scholar of the time. Brooks's 1842 translations of German poetry, entitled *Songs and Ballads*, were published as part of the SPECIMENS OF FOREIGN STANDARD LITERATURE, a series edited by Transcendentalist reformer George RIPLEY. Brooks contributed two other Schiller translations—"The Emigrants" and "The Moorish Prince"—to the April 1844 issue of the Transcendentalist literary journal, the DIAL. The most important literary work of his career was his 1856 translation of Goethe's *Faust*, the first English version of the German tragedy published in the United States.

Charles Brooks also created a large body of written work out of his theological career and published several volumes of sermons, lectures, and religious-themed poetry, most of which has received little or no attention from literary scholars in favor of emphasis on his importance as a translator. His choice of German writers and poets for his translations as well as his own original work in the intricacies of Unitarian theology are evidence of his knowledge of and influence from the Transcendentalist movement. Many of his poems emphasize the spiritual and moral lessons to be drawn from nature. His 1882 translation of German poet Friedrich Ruckert's *The Wisdom of the Brahmin* was consistent with Unitarian-Transcendentalist interests in Eastern religion and philosophy, and Brooks dedicated the volume to fellow Transcendentalists Frederic Henry HEDGE and William Henry FURNESS.

Brooks was the first Unitarian minister in Newport, Rhode Island, where he lived for most of his professional life. This geographical distance from Boston limited his direct engagement with the Transcendentalist circle, but at Harvard he had established friendships with Christopher Pearse CRANCH, John Sullivan DWIGHT, and Theodore PARKER, and he corresponded regularly with these and others among Boston's literary and cultural elite. He also entertained visitors in Providence, including Ralph Waldo EMERSON, who met with Brooks there in early 1840. When the *Dial* magazine was started the next year, Emerson recommended Brooks to then-editor Margaret FULLER, but Brooks's translations did not appear in that forum until 1844. Charles Brooks's other primary literary contribution to the Transcendentalist movement was his biography of the revered Unitarian leader *William Ellery Channing: A Centennial Memory* (1880).

Bibliography

Myerson, Joel. *The New England Transcendentalists and the Dial: A History of the Magazine and Its Contributors*. London and Toronto: Associated University Presses, 1980.

Brown, John
(1800–1859)

John Brown was a radical antislavery activist from Kansas whose efforts were funded in part by several Boston Transcendentalists who were part of the SECRET SIX. On October 16, 1859, Brown and 20 other men, including his three sons, unsuccessfully raided the federal weapons arsenal at Harpers Ferry, Virginia, as part of a plan to arm southern slaves and create a rebellion. Authorities thwarted the plan, and Brown was captured almost immediately, tried, and swiftly executed.

Most of the Transcendentalists admired John Brown as an idealist committed to his cause. Both Ralph Waldo EMERSON and Henry David THOREAU had met him before the Harpers Ferry raid and pledged small amounts of money to his cause during the battles over free soil in Kansas and, later, to support Brown's family after his capture and execution. During Brown's trial in fall 1859, Emerson signed his name as part of a committee to "obtain contributions to aid in the defense of Capt. Brown and his companions on trial for their lives in Virginia." Both he and Thoreau were among those who spoke out publicly in Brown's defense, and Emerson even wrote a letter to Massachusetts Governor Alexander Wise describing Brown as "the rarest of heroes, a pure idealist with no by-ends of his own." In November 1859 Emerson delivered the first of his public lectures in defense of Brown in a speech entitled "Courage," in which he identified Brown as "the new saint awaiting his martyrdom." Thoreau also, despite his later emphasis on the strategy of nonviolent civil disobedience, argued for Brown's cause and was among those who established Brown's role as a martyr for ABOLITIONISM. On the day of

Brown's execution, December 2, 1859, Thoreau eulogized in his "PLEA FOR CAPTAIN JOHN BROWN" that "Some eighteen hundred years ago Christ was crucified. This morning, perchance, Captain Brown was hung. These are the two ends of a chain which is not without its links. He is not Old Brown any longer; he is an angel of light." In the coming months both Thoreau and Emerson delivered several lectures and wrote essays about Brown and the meaning of his actions and of his cause for American society.

As part of the Secret Six, other Transcendentalists Thomas Wentworth HIGGINSON, Theodore PARKER, and Franklin SANBORN put their money if not their names behind Brown. Members of the group went into hiding after Brown was captured, tried, and then executed. Higginson, in particular, regretted that they could not publicly support Brown at the time and had left him alone to be martyred for the cause. Immediately after Brown's death James REDPATH published a collection of essays, *Echoes of Harper's Ferry* (1860) to which several writers and reformers contributed, including Transcendentalists Emerson, Thoreau, and Parker, and poetry by Louisa May ALCOTT and Lydia Maria CHILD.

Bibliography

Gougeon, Len. *Virtue's Hero: Emerson, Antislavery, and Reform.* Athens: University of Georgia Press, 1990.

Renehan, Edward J., Jr. *The Secret Six: The True Tale of the Men Who Conspired with John Brown.* New York: Crown, 1995.

Brown, Theophilus
(1811–1879)

Theophilus (Theo) Brown was a Worcester, Massachusetts, resident who, as a member of the executive committee of the local lyceum in the early 1850s, worked to bring the Boston and CONCORD Transcendentalists to speak in his town. He was also part of a literary salon that invited figures such as Amos Bronson ALCOTT, Ralph Waldo EMERSON, and Henry David THOREAU to Worcester, where he occasionally allowed Alcott to use his home as a meeting place for his CONVERSATIONS. Although

he published some poetry in *Harper's*, Brown did not pursue a literary career but, rather, established himself as the center of Worcester community and intellectual life—friend Thomas Wentworth HIGGINSON referred to Brown as "the wit of the city."

Theo Brown also befriended other Transcendentalists and, along with Harrison Gray Otis BLAKE and David WASSON, followed the career of Henry David Thoreau in particular. He often visited H. G. O. Blake's home in Worcester for readings of Thoreau's letters, and both Blake and Brown visited Thoreau in Concord several times. The two friends accompanied Thoreau and Elizabeth HOAR on an 1858 trip to the White Mountains. Theo Brown was one of only 75 people to receive an advance copy from the publisher of Thoreau's first book, *A WEEK ON THE CONCORD AND MERRIMACK RIVERS* (1849).

Bibliography

Harding, Walter. *The Days of Henry Thoreau.* New York: Dover, 1982.

Brownson, Orestes Augustus
(1803–1876)

As an essayist and editor Orestes Brownson was at the center of the Transcendentalist controversy of 1830s Boston even though he experimented with a variety of philosophical and religious beliefs throughout his life and eventually became a Catholic. His most central role in the Transcendentalist debates was as editor of the *BOSTON QUARTERLY REVIEW* between 1838 and 1842. After a brief stint as a schoolteacher, Brownson turned his attention to issues of theology and reform. He wrote essays for reform newspapers and went on to serve in various editorial and ministerial positions with the Universalist and then Unitarian church. His primary income, however, was derived from his lecturing on the lyceum circuit, which he continued to pursue even after establishing himself with his own Unitarian pulpit in New Hampshire in 1832. A move to Massachusetts in 1834, along with his lectures and his writings in Unitarian papers, brought him into conversation with the Transcendentalist movement emerging at that time. In particular, Brownson met Henry David THOREAU, who had come to Brownson's town of Canton, Massachusetts, to work as a schoolteacher and who subsequently lived with the Brownsons for several weeks as a tutor for their young sons.

Brownson became increasingly interested in the plight of the working classes and in the ideas of French socialists. He brought these theories to bear on his own criticisms of organized religion and his spiritual eclecticism in formulating his 1836 book, NEW VIEWS OF CHRISTIANITY, SOCIETY, AND THE CHURCH, which was intended as the foundation of a new church. That same year, Brownson created his own Christian socialist church based on his views—the Society for Christian Union and Progress—while also serving as editor for the Boston Reformer. In 1838 he finally founded his own paper, the Boston Quarterly Review, through which his stated philosophical and reform goals were "to christianize democracy and democratize the church." Brownson wrote the majority of essays for the paper, but eventually many Transcendentalists contributed as well, such as Margaret FULLER, Theodore PARKER, Elizabeth Palmer PEABODY, and George RIPLEY among others.

Brownson was already immersed in this circle of fellow Unitarians and intellectuals from which he drew writers for his paper as he had attended TRANSCENDENTAL CLUB meetings and even held one meeting at his house in the Club's early months. Although at the center of this first phase of the movement and often associated with the radical Unitarianism of Ralph Waldo EMERSON and Theodore Parker that defined early Transcendentalism, Brownson almost immediately dissociated himself from the controversy and the more liberal aspects of Transcendentalist thought. He was critical of Emerson's NATURE, which appeared the same year as Brownson's New Views of Christianity, Society, and the Church. Brownson criticized what he perceived as irreligious and egotistical aspects of Emerson's thought in both Nature and the controversial "DIVINITY SCHOOL ADDRESS" (1838), although he still publicly defended the Transcendentalists as original and democratic thinkers.

Brownson's concerns turned more toward the political than the theological and his best-known essay was a piece entitled "THE LABORING CLASSES," published in the July 1840 issue of the Boston Quar-

terly Review. In this controversial essay Brownson blamed Christian leaders for supporting and benefiting from a social and economic system that oppressed working people and, accepting as fact the idea of benevolent slaveholding in the South, argued that wage laborers in northern factories were more exploited even than southern slaves, who had least had adequate food and shelter. Brownson predated Karl Marx by several years in calling for an uprising of working people, a class war, to bring about true social justice and equality.

Brownson had supported some Transcendentalist-inspired reform efforts, such as George Ripley's founding of the utopian socialist community at BROOK FARM, where Brownson's son resided for a period. Orestes Brownson made his final philosophical break with Transcendentalism with his 1844 conversion to Catholicism. In Catholicism Brownson found a more highly organized theology that restored the strong sense of historical tradition and the spiritual aspects he felt lacking in both Emerson's Transcendentalism and mainstream Protestantism. Having ceased publication of the Boston Quarterly Review in 1842, he created a new forum for his views with BROWNSON'S QUARTERLY REVIEW, the first major Catholic intellectual magazine in the United States. The magazine was published in two different phases, for a long period between 1844 and 1864 and resuming again after the Civil War briefly from 1873 to 1875. Although Brownson continued to engage many of the same philosophical and reform issues as his Transcendentalist friends, his perspective now came through the lens of Catholicism and his criticism of Transcendentalism thus became more outright. In 1845 he wrote an essay on "Transcendentalism, or the Latest Form of Infidelity," echoing criticisms of the philosophy and movement that harkened back to the 1830s when Brownson himself was considered part of the "new thought." During the gap in his own paper during the Civil War, Orestes Brownson continued to write for other Catholic papers, emerging as one of America's most influential Catholic apologists before his death in 1876.

Bibliography

Lapati, Americo D. Orestes A. Brownson. New York: Twayne Publishers, 1965.

Power, Edward J. *Religion and the Public Schools in Nineteenth-Century America: The Contribution of Orestes A. Brownson.* New York: Paulist Press, 1996.

Brownson's Quarterly Review
(1844–1865 and 1873–1875)

Brownson's Quarterly Review was founded by Orestes BROWNSON in 1844 as one of the earliest forums for Catholic philosophy and thought. Orestes Brownson was a Unitarian minister considered one of the founders of the early Transcendentalist movement. His 1836 NEW VIEWS OF CHRISTIANITY, SOCIETY, AND THE CHURCH was one of the defining texts of the new philosophy, along with Ralph Waldo EMERSON's NATURE, published the same year. Brownson was a member of the TRANSCENDENTAL CLUB, where he joined colleagues Emerson, Convers FRANCIS, Frederic Henry HEDGE, George RIPLEY, and others in discussing the new philosophy as it impacted liberal theology. Between 1838 and 1842 Orestes Brownson published the BOSTON QUARTERLY REVIEW, a paper whose main purpose was to spread the ideas of Transcendentalism. Brownson also wrote a column for the *Democratic Review,* but his views soon proved too controversial for that paper. Around 1844 Brownson distanced himself from Transcendentalism entirely by converting to Catholicism, and in January 1844 he began a new periodical, *Brownson's Quarterly Review.*

As he did for the *Boston Quarterly Review,* Brownson himself wrote most of the material that appeared in *Brownson's Quarterly Review.* Several articles dealt with his own personal spiritual journey that led him to the Catholic faith as well as his critique of Transcendentalism. Some of Brownson's views even caused trouble within the Catholic church to which he devoted his paper. He expressed controversial opinions on everything from theological debates within Catholicism to the role of parochial schools to anti-Irish sentiments aimed at the American Catholic community. Although Brownson's paper dealt primarily with theological issues related to Catholicism, he also devoted space to his social and political viewpoints on a range of issues. *Brownson's Quarterly Review* included articles on WOMEN'S RIGHTS and slavery. He used his paper as a forum for his political views, including defending South Carolinian John C. Calhoun's position on states' rights, a position that further alienated him from his New England contemporaries.

Brownson's Quarterly Review folded after subscriptions fell during the Civil War, but Brownson was able to resume publication in 1873 and continue for another two years. He continued his social and political as well as theological commentaries and, despite his controversial relationship to the church, in *Brownson's Quarterly Review* as well as in his other writings, Orestes Brownson became one of the most visible Catholic apologists of the mid-19th century.

Bibliography

Power, Edward J. *Religion and the Public Schools in Nineteenth-Century America: The Contribution of Orestes A. Brownson.* New York: Paulist Press, 1996.

Burns, Anthony
(1834–1862)

Anthony Burns was an alleged fugitive slave whose 1854 Boston trial rallied northerners, including many Transcendentalists, to the cause of radical ABOLITIONISM. Support for Burns was galvanized, in particular, through an anti–FUGITIVE SLAVE LAW group called the Vigilance Committee, led by radical Unitarian minister Theodore PARKER and whose members also included Samuel Gridley Howe, Samuel MAY, and Thomas Wentworth HIGGINSON. Parker would serve as Burns's lawyer for the trial, in which Burns, an African American who had been engaged in various industrial occupations in Boston, was now claimed as the property of a merchant from Alexandria, Virginia. The Vigilance Committee distributed flyers throughout Boston declaring a "Mock Trial" at the "Kidnapper's 'Court'" and urging Bostonians to "See to it that no Free Citizen of Massachusetts is dragged into Slavery, Without Trial by Jury! '76!" the final note an appeal to the revolutionary struggle that the "Men of Boston!" had initiated and won against British tyranny in 1776. These references were to the Fugitive Slave Law of 1850, under which Burns was arrested and against which the Vigilance Committee was organized. In addition to outrage over the Fugitive Slave Law, which not only implicated northern citizens and courts in the arrest and return of alleged fugitives, Burns's trial took place in the context of several other events that led the United States toward Civil War. In fact, Burns's arrest occurred on the very same day that Congress passed the controversial Kansas-Nebraska Act, which allowed that the western territories would decide the issue of slavery through popular sovereignty; that is, the decision would be made based on the vote of the territorial citizens. The Kansas-Nebraska Act was perceived by northerners as a major step toward opening the western territories to slavery and as evidence that southern Democrats controlled the will of Congress. Burns's return to slavery prompted Ralph Waldo EMERSON's 1855 speech on "AMERICAN SLAVERY."

Bibliography

Von Frank, Albert J. *The Trials of Anthony Burns: Freedom and Slavery in Emerson's Boston.* Cambridge, Mass.: Harvard University Press, 1998.

Cabot, James Elliot
(1821–1903)

As Ralph Waldo EMERSON's literary executor, James Elliot Cabot oversaw publication of Emerson's *Complete Works* (1883–93) and wrote *A Memoir of Ralph Waldo Emerson* in 1887, the first biography to incorporate previously unpublished personal letters and journals. Cabot graduated from Harvard College and spent several years in Germany reading idealist philosophy, essays by Emerson, and issues of the main American Transcendentalist journal, the Boston-based DIAL. Cabot returned to America where he entered Harvard Law School and, in early 1844, published an essay on Immanuel KANT in the *Dial*. Cabot followed up on the *Dial* essay by writing to Emerson, whom he had not yet met, with writing samples to be considered for future issues. The *Dial* ceased publication before any of Cabot's other pieces might have been considered, but Emerson was impressed with one essay, in particular, on the philosopher Spinoza and the correspondence between Cabot and Emerson began an important lifelong friendship.

Cabot went on to publish more than 50 essays, mostly on philosophical subjects, in various other journals, including the MASSACHUSETTS QUARTERLY REVIEW, which he coedited with Transcendentalist Theodore PARKER. His *Memoir of Ralph Waldo Emerson*, as well as the *Complete Works*, helped to establish the historical importance of both Emerson and the Transcendentalist movement in general for early 20th-century readers. James Elliot Cabot was perhaps the first historian of the movement to argue for the larger cultural and historical significance of Transcendentalism beyond Emersonian Boston when he characterized the intellectual genealogy of the movement from PURITANISM through European ROMANTICISM to ultimately a broad-ranging philosophical perspective that he defined as "a deeper way of feeling and enlarged way of thinking about all subjects."

Bibliography

Myerson, Joel. *The New England Transcendentalists and the Dial: A History of the Magazine and Its Contributors.* London and Toronto: Associated University Presses, 1980.

Simmons, Nancy Craig. "Arranging the Sibylline Leaves: James Elliot Cabot's Work as Emerson's Literary Executor." *Studies in the American Renaissance* (1983): 335–389.

Calvinism   *See* PURITANISM.

Cape Cod
Henry David Thoreau
(1865)

Cape Cod was a posthumously published travel narrative based on an October 1849 outing that Henry David THOREAU took with friend William Ellery CHANNING II. The account traces the two men's initial journey to and very brief stay in Cape Cod in 1849, but it also incorporates material from Thoreau's return alone the following June and two more trips (once more with Channing) spread out over several years in efforts to gather enough information about the region for a book-length account.

Thoreau initially presented some of his account as lectures in CONCORD, MASSACHUSETTS, and installments of the manuscript were published in three issues of PUTNAM'S MONTHLY MAGAZINE under editor George William CURTIS between June and August 1855. Ellery Channing assisted Thoreau's sister, Sophia THOREAU, in preparing the complete manuscript for publication after the author's death in 1862. *Cape Cod* was a popular travel narrative and was the first of Thoreau's works to be published abroad, appearing in England almost immediately after its initial release.

The core of the book, as with the earlier, more fully developed WALDEN, is Thoreau's engagement with the natural world. In the case of *Cape Cod*, the site of that engagement was not the forest or the pond, but the seashore and the ocean. Unfortunately he and Ellery Channing arrived upon the seashore immediately after a shipwreck had occurred and thus had drawn all of the townspeople out to see it. His first observations, therefore, provide a somewhat different perspective on humankind's relationship with nature: "The carcasses of men and beasts together lie stately up upon its shelf, rotting and bleaching in the sun and waves, and each tide turns them in their beds, and tucks fresh sand under them. There is naked Nature,—inhumanly sincere, wasting no thought on man, nibbling at the cliffy shore where gulls wheel amid the spray."

Although *Cape Cod* also provides details about local customs and industry, natural history, and the animal and plant life of the region, the sea dominates his experience there: "the dash and roar of the waves were incessant." The immensity, the violence, and the power of the Atlantic Ocean become the central point of understanding for Thoreau, one perceived in awe and fear: "This gentle Ocean will toss and tear the rag of a man's body like the father of mad bulls." As scholar Philip Gura points out, the sea held unknowable secrets for Thoreau but was "not simply a larger and deeper WALDEN POND." Thoreau himself

warned his readers that the ocean may at first appear to have a "pond-like look," but whereas Thoreau could and did measure the depth of Walden Pond, he was overcome by, in his words, "the immensity of the ocean" and declared that it was of no use to attempt to understand the true depths of the ocean since "it is two or three miles from the surface, and you are to be drowned so long before you get to it."

Bibliography

Gura, Philip F. "A wild, rank place": Thoreau's *Cape Cod*. In *The Cambridge Companion to Henry David Thoreau*, ed. Joel Myerson. Cambridge University Press, 1995, 142–151.

Thoreau, Henry David. *Cape Cod*. Edited by Joseph J. Moldenhauer. Princeton, N.J.: Princeton University Press, 2004.

Carlyle, Thomas
(1795–1881)

Scottish writer and scholar of German philosophy and literature Thomas Carlyle was one of the most significant contemporary influences on the American Transcendentalists. His most important essays included "State of German Literature" (1827) and "Signs of the Times" (1829). Through these and other writings he introduced American readers to the work of authors such as Johann Wolfgang von GOETHE, Immanuel KANT, Johann SCHILLER, and Madame Germaine de STAËL, among others. Among the Transcendentalists, James Freeman CLARKE and Margaret FULLER, in particular, were directly inspired by Carlyle to study German language and philosophy on their own. Clarke, and presumably other Transcendentalists, found in Carlyle "new and profound views of familiar truths, which seemed to open a vista for endless reflection."

Ralph Waldo EMERSON as well was influenced by the anonymously published essays in the *Edinburgh Review* that were authored by Carlyle. After he met with Carlyle personally on a European visit in 1833, Emerson became the chief promoter of Carlyle's work in the United States, arranging for Carlyle's book, *Sartor Resartus*, to be published in 1836, a text for which Emerson also wrote the introduction. Thomas Carlyle was in many ways Emerson's most important guide to German literature, in particular first introducing him to the ideas of Goethe and SCHILLER, the subject of an 1825 biography by Carlyle. Carlyle influenced Emerson's own literary work as well. Carlyle's *On Heroes, Hero-Worship and the Heroic in History* (1841) prompted Emerson's idea for a study of genius that resulted in *REPRESENTATIVE MEN*, published nearly 10 years later in 1850. As Carlyle wrote in *On Heroes*, "all things that we see standing accomplished in the world are properly the outer material result, the practical realization and embodiment, of thoughts that dwelt in the Great Men sent into the world." Emerson and Carlyle were regular correspondents throughout the period, although in *ENGLISH TRAITS* (1856) Emerson directly addressed the differences between his own and Carlyle's philosophy through a discussion of the differences between the United States and England. Emerson used Carlyle to highlight differences between English aristocratic culture and American democracy, and the two men had a personally strained relationship as Carlyle attacked ideas about racial equality and Emerson became increasingly involved in social reform through the 1850s, particularly ABOLITIONISM.

The central role of Carlyle in the development of Transcendentalism in the 1830s and 1840s was recognized beyond Emerson, however. In his important *TRANSCENDENTALISM IN NEW ENGLAND: A HISTORY* (1876), contemporary Octavius Brooks FROTHINGHAM acknowledged Thomas Carlyle's influence on the movement by boldly proclaiming, "Carlyle was the high priest of the new philosophy."

Bibliography

Harris, Kenneth Marc. *Carlyle and Emerson: Their Long Debate.* Cambridge, Mass.: Harvard University Press, 1978.

Weisbuch, Robert. *Atlantic Double-Cross: American Literature and British Influence in the Age of Emerson.* Chicago: University of Chicago Press, 1986.

Channing, Edward Tyrrel
(1790–1856)

Edward Tyrrel Channing was the brother of the revered Unitarian minister William Ellery CHAN-NING and a Harvard professor of rhetoric who had a direct influence on the emerging generation of Transcendentalists who made up his students, such as James Freeman CLARKE, Ralph Waldo EMERSON, Thomas Wentworth HIGGINSON, Henry David THOREAU, and Jones VERY, among others. Through his lecture topics, the example of his speaking style, and his commentary on their written work, Edward Channing shaped the development of his students as speakers and writers. In particular, it may have been from Channing that Emerson first heard the term "American Scholar," an idea which Emerson later used to articulate the role for thinking and speaking men as representative of their times. Additionally, Thoreau gave direct credit to Professor Channing for teaching him how to write. For these reasons Edward Channing deserves credit not for inspiring Transcendentalist ideas directly but for contributing to the development of a distinctly American literature during this time period.

Bibliography

Howe, Daniel Walker. *The Unitarian Conscience: Harvard Moral Philosophy, 1805–1861.* Cambridge, Mass.: Harvard University Press, 1970.

Channing, William Ellery
(1780–1842)

The most admired and influential theologian of UNITARIANISM of the early 19th century was the Reverend William Ellery Channing. He came from a prominent and successful family that included his brothers, Walter, who became the dean of Harvard Medical College, and Edward Tyrrel CHANNING, a Harvard professor of rhetoric. As a minister, cultural critic, and reformer, William Ellery Channing had a signal impact on the spiritual and intellectual development of Ralph Waldo EMERSON and the emergence of the New England Transcendentalist movement. Channing was a liberal Congregationalist minister whose 1819 sermon "UNITARIAN CHRISTIANITY" marked the beginning of the Unitarian movement in the United States with Channing as its primary spokesperson. Unitarians critiqued the orthodox Calvinist system of New England PURITANISM, which emphasized innate depravity and predestination, and promoted instead a humanistic emphasis on the individual soul, free will, and the subjective experience of religion. Channing's preaching gave coherence to other Boston liberals who then joined together as a new denomination, the Unitarians. Throughout all of his orations and writings Channing sought to moderate the split off into a new denomination by focusing on the positive approach to a spiritual life offered through Unitarianism, rather than defining the split solely in negative terms of a critique of Calvinism. More than a specific doctrine to adhere to, his sermons emphasized spiritual and moral ideals upon which individuals could build.

The young Ralph Waldo Emerson looked to the Reverend Channing as the model for his own career as a preacher. In his 1821 "Evidences of Revealed Religion" Channing upheld the early Unitarian position of the believers that the miracles of the Bible were caused by supernatural means but could also be comprehended through rational and human means. This is a theme he had begun in "Unitarian Christianity," in which he put forth a model for approaching the scriptures, arguing that the Bible's "meaning is to be sought in the same manner as that of other books." Many of the Transcendentalists would retain this Christian basis of belief in the miracles, but more radical thinkers like Emerson would eventually reject this and other aspects of Unitarian Christianity in favor of a more completely nonbiblical and humanistic stance. Channing's attempt to rationalize belief and to harmonize the natural and the divine or supernatural aspects of historical religion found voice in Emerson's early works, in particular his 1838 "DIVINITY SCHOOL ADDRESS."

Channing's most influential sermons for Emerson and the other young Unitarians also included his 1828 "LIKENESS TO GOD," which laid out a religion based on personal spiritual growth, and the 1838 "SELF-CULTURE," which identified self-improvement as both a spiritual and a social goal. Channing's philosophy of self-culture was his single most important contribution to 19th-century New England intellectual and theological history. Channing himself was never a member of the "new school" of Transcendentalist thought, but his ideas were central to the movement as they were developed more fully not only by Emerson but in the

writings of Transcendentalist thinkers both orthodox and radical, such as Orestes BROWNSON, Margaret FULLER, Frederic Henry HEDGE, Theodore PARKER, and Elizabeth Palmer PEABODY.

Channing's influence went beyond the pulpit, however, as he served as an important role model of literary and social life as well. He wrote numerous essays and literary reviews in the 1820s and 1830s, most notably calling for "The Importance and Means of a National Literature," the title of an 1830 essay. Through the example of his own career, Channing set a high standard for the cultural interests of the intellectual class to expand beyond merely the theological. The themes of this essay, in particular, were taken up by Ralph Waldo Emerson in his subsequent calls, most famously in the 1837 address "THE AMERICAN SCHOLAR," for example, for the development of a unique American literature and intellectual life beyond the influence of European custom and tradition.

Channing ultimately served as a perceptive critic and inspiration for those who aspired to literary careers, such as Emerson, Fuller, and others among the Transcendentalists, but he did not pursue a literary career himself. He was a minister for most of his career, although the latter part of his life was dominated by an increasing interest in social reform projects, such as the plight of the working classes, EDUCATION reform, and ABOLITIONISM. From his earliest days as a minister Channing had paid particular attention to the intellectual and spiritual needs of children and was a forerunner in the Sunday School movement for children's religious education. His first publication was an 1807 reprint of a sermon entitled "The Duties of Children," and he went on to work with other innovative educational reformers such as Transcendentalists Amos Bronson ALCOTT and Elizabeth Palmer Peabody, founder of the first kindergarten in America.

Like Emerson's "American Scholar" address, Channing's 1838 lecture on "Self-Culture" was a democratic call to workingmen to develop their own talents and potential through not only education but also the appreciation of literature and art. While Channing and Emerson thus emphasized the role and development of the individual in raising the status of the working classes, other reformers critiqued the narrow Transcendentalist focus on self-culture. Most notably, Orestes Brownson critiqued the limitations of self-culture as social reform when he wrote in his 1840 treatise, "THE LABORING CLASSES," that self-culture "cannot abolish inequality, nor restore men to their rights. As a means it is well, as an end it is nothing."

Channing would take a broader political view of societal problems in his most passionate cause: antislavery. As a young man Channing worked briefly as a tutor in Richmond, Virginia, where he was affected by viewing slavery firsthand, and he spoke out on the issue as early as the 1820s. In the 1830s he read and was inspired by Lydia Maria CHILD's antislavery treatise, *An Appeal in Favor of That Class of Americans Called Africans* (1833). He wrote his own text on the subject, *Slavery* (1835), in which he emphasized the moral and spiritual crisis of the institution of slavery in limiting the development of human beings, the individual slaves. His reform vision was thus grounded in his theological imperatives of "self-culture" and the belief that humans were made in the "likeness of God." Colleagues such as William Lloyd GARRISON criticized Channing for not taking a stronger political stance, and later, in the 1842 *The Duty of the Free States,* Channing took on the immoral laws that "the artificial organization called society" had created and under which all Americans were enslaved. Channing did not live to see the end of slavery in the United States, but he continued speaking out on the subject until his last months. His final public address was on the subject, a commemoration on the anniversary of the emancipation of slaves in the British West Indies, an event that he hoped would serve as an example for America to follow.

William Ellery Channing was one of the most prominent New Englanders of his time and a central figure in the religious and cultural history of that region. The scope of his influence is evident in the fact that the most radical Transcendentalists as well as their more conservative Unitarian colleagues and critics could claim him as a spiritual and intellectual forefather.

Bibliography

Delbanco, Andrew. *William Ellery Channing: An Essay on the Liberal Spirit in America.* Cambridge, Mass.: Harvard University Press, 1981.

Howe, Daniel Walker. *The Unitarian Conscience: Harvard Moral Philosophy, 1805–1861.* Cambridge, Mass.: Harvard University Press, 1970.

Channing, William Ellery, II
(1817–1901)

William Ellery Channing II was a minor Transcendentalist poet and the first biographer of Henry David THOREAU. His father, Walter Channing, was the dean of Harvard Medical School, and his famous uncles included the landscape artist Washington ALLSTON, Harvard professor Edward Tyrrel CHANNING, and the leader of early 19th-century UNITARIANISM, the Reverend William Ellery CHANNING, the senior. Friends and family referred to the younger Channing as "Ellery" to distinguish between the two men. Ellery Channing married the sister of Margaret FULLER, Ellen, and, after spending a brief period in Cincinnati where Channing served as a newspaper editor, the couple settled permanently in CONCORD, MASSACHUSETTS, where he befriended Ralph Waldo EMERSON, Elizabeth HOAR, and Henry David Thoreau.

Despite his strong familial and social connections with many of New England's cultural elites of the period, Ellery Channing was estranged from many in his prominent family and lacked a clear vocational purpose for his own life. He left Harvard College after only a few months, determined to become a poet but experimented with a variety of occupations over the years. He ultimately made his most significant literary contributions to the Transcendentalist movement in his writings about Henry David Thoreau. Ellery Channing in some ways replaced John THOREAU, the brother whom Thoreau had lost prematurely in 1842, and the two became especially close friends, confidantes, and walking partners. When Henry David Thoreau died in 1862 Channing immediately began publication of his "Reminiscences of Thoreau" in installments in the Boston *Commonwealth* magazine and expanded the work into the 1873 biography, *Thoreau: The Poet-Naturalist.*

Channing was in a particularly privileged position to set the terms of how his famous friend, and the movement of which he was a part, would be remembered. Scholars agree, however, that while Channing's biography of Thoreau provides important anecdotal insight by someone particularly close to Thoreau, and a more positive portrait of the man than provided publicly by Ralph Waldo Emerson, the text is unreliable for its use of unattributed journal entries by other figures mixed in with Thoreau's own writing and long quotes by Thoreau without reference to their original source. During the time he was preparing the manuscript for the biography he also assisted Thoreau's sister, Sophia THOREAU, in editing Thoreau's papers and manuscripts for publication, producing CAPE COD in 1865 and A YANKEE IN CANADA in 1866. Ellery Channing had, in fact, accompanied Henry David Thoreau on both of the excursions that formed the basis of these books drawn from Thoreau's travel notes. He later put together another article drawn from Thoreau's unpublished papers, "Days and Nights in Concord," published in *Scribner's Monthly* in 1878.

The *Thoreau* biography included a selection of touching "Memorial Verses" by Channing in honor of his friend. In fact, Ellery Channing was one of the most prolific poets of the early Transcendentalist movement. A mutual friend, Samuel Gray WARD, had sent a collection of Channing's poems to Ralph Waldo Emerson, and both Emerson and Margaret Fuller happily published Channing's verses in the DIAL magazine between 1841 and 1844. In fact, he became the third most regular contributor, after only editors Emerson and Fuller. One of the few prose pieces written by Channing was a semiautobiographical account of his interactions with the other Transcendentalists entitled "The Youth of the Poet and Painter," published serially in the last four issues of the *Dial*. He went on to publish seven book-length volumes of poem, between 1843 and 1886.

Despite the sheer numbers of poems that Ellery Channing wrote, his work received little critical notice or praise, and scholars do not regard him as a significant Transcendentalist poet. After early enthusiasm for his work, Emerson decided that Channing lacked the dedication or focus to be a true poet, as Channing often refused to edit or revise poems based on Emerson's suggestions before publication in the *Dial*. Thoreau had recognized Channing in the pages of WALDEN as "The

Poet," and the book includes quotes from some of his verses. Other friends such as Franklin Benjamin SANBORN (with whom Channing lived in the last years of his life) attempted to secure his colleague's literary legacy with such compilations as *Poems of Sixty-five Years* (1902), but in the end Channing produced no original literary work of lasting or critical measure. Even friend and early supporter Emerson wrote in the preface to one of Channing's own 1871 collections of poems, *The Wanderer,* that "He will write,—as he has ever written,—whether he has readers or not." W. Ellery Channing II is best remembered as an insider to the movement and most significantly for his friendship to and writings about Thoreau. He was, in the end, dedicated to promoting Thoreau's genius and importance more than his own.

Bibliography

Harding, Walter, ed. *The Collected Poems of William Ellery Channing the Younger.* Gainesville, Fla.: Scholar's Facsimiles and Reprints, 1967.

Hudspeth, Robert N. *Ellery Channing.* New York: Twayne, 1973.

Channing, William Henry
(1810–1884)

William Henry Channing (often called "Henry" to distinguish him from his other relatives of the same name) was one of the most reform-minded of the Transcendentalists. He was the nephew of the renowned Unitarian thinker Reverend William Ellery CHANNING on his father's side and Transcendentalist reformer Thomas Wentworth HIGGINSON on his mother's side. Henry Channing was a graduate of HARVARD DIVINITY SCHOOL where he befriended several of the Transcendentalists before he left Boston in 1839 to accept a position as pastor of a Unitarian church in Cincinnati. While in Ohio he began working with James Freeman CLARKE on the WESTERN MESSENGER, the earliest journal of Transcendentalist thought in the western region. Clarke had headquartered the paper in Louisville, Kentucky, but the magazine was eventually moved to Cincinnati where Channing took on a more direct role as coeditor. Channing's passion was for practical reform more than philosophy, and he moved on to other projects after the paper folded in 1841 and returned to the east coast.

Henry Channing was particularly involved in socialist-utopian experiments and philosophy. He was active in ABOLITIONISM and signed the petition for the CHARDON STREET CONVENTION in Boston before moving to New York where he edited the Fourierist journal THE PRESENT in 1843 and 1844. He helped found the AMERICAN UNION OF ASSOCIATIONISTS in 1846 as well as another utopian social reform journal, the short-lived SPIRIT OF THE AGE. He was friends with Margaret FULLER, who sought him out when she came to New York in 1844 to write for their mutual friend Horace GREELEY at the NEW YORK TRIBUNE. In 1840 and 1841 he contributed a series of short pieces to the Boston DIAL.

The influence of Transcendentalism informed all of his reform and literary work, including the publication of two biographies of important Transcendentalists: a three-volume biographical study of his prominent uncle, *Memoir of William Ellery Channing* (1848) and his coeditorship with Emerson and Clarke of the two-volume *Memoirs of Margaret Fuller Ossoli* (1852). Henry Channing was in turn remembered by his colleagues with Octavius Brooks FROTHINGHAM's 1886 publication of *Memoir of William Henry Channing*, which remains the only full-length biography of Channing.

Bibliography

Habich, Robert. *Transcendentalism and the Western Messenger: A History of the Magazine and Its Contributors, 1835–1841.* London and Cranbury, N.J.: Associated University Presses, 1985.

Myerson, Joel. *The New England Transcendentalists and the Dial: A History of the Magazine and Its Contributors.* London and Toronto: Associated University Presses, 1980.

"Character"
Ralph Waldo Emerson
(1844)

Published in ESSAYS: SECOND SERIES in 1844, Ralph Waldo EMERSON's essay on "Character" ex-

amines the creation of character through the relationship of the self to society, a theme followed throughout the collection in other essays such as "EXPERIENCE," "Manners," "Gifts," and "POLITICS." Emerson defines "character" as "a certain undemonstrable force, a Familiar or a Genius, by whose impulses the man is guided, but whose counsels he cannot impart," and, more broadly, as "nature in the highest form." Those of character are self-reliant individuals who serve as models and moral guides for the rest of society, regardless of whether they were acknowledged or appreciated in their own time. As in REPRESENTATIVE MEN (1850), Emerson's purpose in identifying character in "men of great figure, and of few deeds," is not to promote hero-worship but to emphasize the democratic belief that character exists as a "universal law," affecting every individual but in varying degrees: "Character is the moral order seen through the medium of an individual nature." Character then is not an action to be admired, and Emerson warns against the illusion that fame itself is representative of character. The action which is praised as a result of character is "nonconformity," for the "natural measure of this power is the resistance of circumstances." Since independence of thought is related to "purity" and self-sufficiency for Emerson, he moves within the essay from discussion of "men of great figure" in history to the simple example of children as possessing the highest character: "This masterpiece is best where no hands but nature's have been laid on it." He gives an account of an "occasion for thought" upon two "very young children," who followed only their own thought and seemed in their nonconformity to say, "I never listened to your people's law, or to what they call their gospel, and wasted my time. I was content with the simple rural poverty of my own: hence this sweetness."

Chardon Street and Bible Conventions

The Chardon Street and Bible Conventions were a series of three separate reform meetings held at the Chardon Street Chapel in Boston in November 1840, March 1841, and November 1841, and a site for early Transcendentalist movement in

ABOLITIONISM. A final meeting focused on the subject of the Bible was held at the Masonic Temple in March 1842, and therefore is sometimes not included as part of the Chardon Street conventions, but it is related in theme and in participants. By virtue of its location in Boston, the first meetings gathered together several Transcendentalists who joined with radical abolitionists and other "Friends of Universal Reform" to discuss, as William Lloyd GARRISON's newspaper *The Liberator* advertised, whether organized churches were of "Divine ordination" or were merely "inventions and traditions of men" which stood in the way of social reform efforts. More than location connected the Transcendentalists and the radical abolitionists of the 1830s and 1840s, as both movements were made up of individuals who had undergone spiritual crises that resulted in an anticlerical and anti-institutional stance. The Transcendentalists had split from the already liberal Unitarian church, and Garrisonian abolitionists condemned organized religion as well as the United States government for allowing slavery.

Attendees at the Chardon Street and Bible Conventions included such prominent abolitionists as William Lloyd Garrison and Maria Weston Chapman, and Transcendentalists Amos Bronson ALCOTT, Ralph Waldo EMERSON, Margaret FULLER, George RIPLEY, and Henry David THOREAU, among others. No official records exist from the meetings, only personal reflections and assessments from attendees, such as Emerson's review in "Chardon Street and Bible Conventions," published the following summer in the July 1842 issue of the Transcendentalist periodical, the DIAL. In this brief account Emerson reported more on the spectacle of the "disorderly" meeting of reformers than on any specifics of what was discussed: "Madmen, madwomen, men with beards, Dunkers, Muggletonians, Come-Outers, Groaners, Agrarians, Seventh-day-Baptists, Quakers, Abolitionists, Calvinists, Unitarians, and Philosophers,—all came successively to the top, and seized their moment, if not their *hour,* wherein to chide, or pray, or preach, or protest." According to this report, at least, the goal of the meeting was "simply the elucidation of truth" and, in the end, "no decision was had, and no action taken." Emerson later referred to the meetings indirectly in the 1844 lecture "NEW EN-

GLAND REFORMERS" in which he argued against the whole idea of organized reform movements, which stifled individualism and focused on one specific issue rather than seeing the interrelatedness of social problems.

Another Transcendentalist viewpoint came from Margaret Fuller, who attended the Convention with a specifically feminist, more than abolitionist, frame of mind. Within this combined community of abolitionist-activists and Transcendentalist-intellectuals, the question of WOMEN'S RIGHTS was already of rising interest. Just the year before the Chardon Street Conventions, in fall 1839, Fuller had begun her CONVERSATIONS FOR WOMEN to address the questions of woman's social subordination and right to personhood. She had hoped to hear about "religious institutions and the social position of women" at the convention, presumably because the attendees at Chardon Street were among some of the most radical women in the antislavery movement at that time. However, in December 1840 Fuller wrote to secretary Chapman that she was disappointed in the lack of attention to women's rights at the meetings as "not only I heard nothing that pleased me, but no clear statement from any one. . . . As far as I know you seem to me quite wrong as to what is to be done for woman!"

Despite these individual criticisms by leading figures, the Transcendentalists as a group were present and interested in the ideas of abolitionism and social reform as discussed at the Chardon Street Conventions, and several of them pursued further ties to the radical abolitionist cause in the following years.

Bibliography
Cole, Phyllis. "Woman Questions: Emerson, Fuller, and New England Reform." In *Transient and Permanent: The Transcendentalist Movement and Its Contexts,* eds. Charles Capper and Conrad Edick Wright. Boston: Massachusetts Historical Society, 1999, 408–446.

Cheney, Ednah Dow Littlehale
(1824–1904)

Ednah Dow Cheney was a reformer, writer, lecturer, and editor who, while still a teenager, attended Unitarian sermons and public lectures within the early Transcendentalist community. In her autobiography she recalled first attending a lecture by Ralph Waldo EMERSON with her parents at "the society for the diffusion of knowledge" so that by 1842, when she first heard Theodore PARKER preach, she "was not wholly unprepared to accept his ideas." She had also been introduced at a young age to reform ideas such as ABOLITIONISM and WOMEN'S RIGHTS. Cheney was already interested in questions of women's roles and status in society when she attended Margaret FULLER's CONVERSATIONS FOR WOMEN, an event she considered "among the greatest felicities of my life." Cheney was married briefly to artist Seth Cheney but was widowed early. The mother of a young daughter, she never remarried but instead launched a career as an activist, writer, and philanthropist.

While most of Cheney's published writings appeared in the later decades of the century, she was a prolific and highly visible feminist activist, lecturer, and educator from the 1840s onward. Her connections with Transcendentalism and feminism, including her childhood friendship with reformer Caroline DALL, led to her involvement with THE UNA, the first women's rights periodical, for which Cheney offered occasional book reviews and reports on the New England School of Design for Women, which she founded in 1851. Among her other social reform activities she cofounded and financially supported the New England Woman's Club (established in 1868), served as secretary in the New England Freedman's Aid Society (1867–75), became president of the New England Hospital for Women and Children after previously serving as its secretary (1887–1902), and worked as an organizer and officer in numerous local, state, and regional woman's suffrage organizations. She also lectured regularly on topics related to philosophy, art, and EDUCATION and published children's stories, fiction, biography, memoirs of other prominent women, and eventually her own *Reminiscences* (1902).

Despite her prolific career and writings, Ednah Dow Cheney has been recognized by scholars of Transcendentalism primarily in relation to her connection with Amos Bronson ALCOTT and his fam-

ily. She was a lifelong friend with the Alcotts, attended Bronson Alcott's CONVERSATIONS in the late 1840s and even helped him organize a series of talks just for women, and edited Louisa May ALCOTT's journals and letters for publication. She also wrote several books of her own and is regarded as the first American woman to publish on the aesthetics of art. Her definition of art as "thought in material form" is an example of the Transcendentalist understanding of a direct link between philosophical values and the expression of those values in one's work. In addition to her autobiography, which included a chapter on "Art," she published several articles and memoirs of other artists and collected together many of her later essays in a book entitled GLEANINGS IN THE FIELDS OF ART (1881). Cheney's Transcendentalism also shaped her involvement in the early women's rights movement. Whether in her remembrances of Margaret Fuller, who she named as one of the most significant intellectuals of the century, or in her analysis of Johann Wolfgang von GOETHE's view of womanhood, Ednah Dow Cheney consistently identified Transcendentalist ideals such as self-education, harmonious social relations, and the valuing of intuition as those which inherently supported the cause of woman in the 19th century.

After the Civil War, Cheney was invited by Bronson Alcott to be a lecturer at his CONCORD SCHOOL OF PHILOSOPHY AND LITERATURE. As a founding member, and as a lecturer every summer of the School's existence between 1879 and 1888, Cheney was one of the most prolific and significant figures in later-century Transcendentalism. Her lectures appear in all three of the official publications of the Concord School of Philosophy: CONCORD LECTURES ON PHILOSOPHY (1883), THE LIFE AND GENIUS OF GOETHE (1886), and THE GENIUS AND CHARACTER OF EMERSON (1898). In her writings and lectures, Ednah Dow Cheney continued through the end of the century to emphasize the themes that had engaged her as a Transcendentalist and a feminist since the 1840s.

Bibliography

Dykeman, Therese B. "Ednah Dow Cheney's American Aesthetics." In *Presenting Women Philosophers*, eds.

Cecile T. Tougas and Sara Ebenreck. Philadelphia: Temple, 2000, 41–50.

Wayne, Tiffany K. *Woman Thinking: Feminism and Transcendentalism in Nineteenth-Century America.* Lanham, Md.: Lexington Books, 2005.

"Chesuncook"   See THE MAINE WOODS.

Child, Lydia Maria Francis
(1802–1880)

Writer and reformer Lydia Maria Child participated in Transcendentalist activities in Boston of the 1830s and '40s and regularly engaged Transcendentalist themes in her literary works. Along with her brother, Convers FRANCIS, a Unitarian minister and one of the founding members and hosts of the TRANSCENDENTAL CLUB, she was drawn to the philosophy and formed lasting friendships with several Transcendentalists, including John Sullivan DWIGHT, Margaret FULLER, Theodore PARKER, and BROOK FARM residents Charles Anderson DANA and Sophia RIPLEY. Child's novel *PHILOTHEA*, published in 1836 just months before Ralph Waldo EMERSON's *NATURE*, is often acknowledged as the first Transcendentalist novel for its themes of neo-Platonic IDEALISM and ROMANTICISM. The novel received high praise in Transcendentalist circles, both informally and in published critical reviews, as did her published newspaper columns in *LETTERS FROM NEW YORK* (1843). Child attended Margaret Fuller's CONVERSATIONS FOR WOMEN in the 1840s and, under the editorship of Emerson, published an essay entitled "What is Beauty?" in the April 1843 issue of the Transcendentalist journal, the *DIAL*. In her 1845 review of Margaret Fuller's *WOMAN IN THE NINETEENTH CENTURY*, Child declared her colleague "a woman of more powerful intellect, comprehensive thought, and thorough education, than any other American authoress, with whose productions I am acquainted."

The Transcendentalist impulse led Child to eventually question New England's Calvinist heritage and the role of Christianity in general as a moral guide. These themes were explored in *THE PROGRESS OF RELIGIOUS IDEAS, THROUGH SUCCESSIVE AGES* (1855), a controversial work for the widely read and popular novelist Child. In this book she offered one of the first Transcendentalist forays into comparative religion studies and the serious analysis of non-Christian religions. Like many other Unitarian-Transcendentalists, her religious studies led her to join the FREE RELIGIOUS ASSOCIATION in 1876, an organization which she herself recognized as the outgrowth of ideas she had first explored and articulated many years earlier in *The Progress of Religious Ideas.*

Like other female Transcendentalist writers and thinkers (such as writer and reformer Caroline DALL), Child was interested in the question of WOMEN'S RIGHTS. As an author she focused on women's historical subordination and progress through such works as *The Biographies of Madame de Staël and Madame Roland* (1832) and *History of the Condition of Women, in Various Ages and Nations* (1835). These biographical and chronologically broad historical studies were offered as more substantial reading material for women readers and provided role models through highlighting women's historical contributions to their societies.

Child's interests were varied, however, and she did not identify explicitly or exclusively as a Transcendentalist writer. She was most well known in her own time, as she is today, for her domestic handbooks, juvenile literature and reform writings, especially related to ABOLITIONISM. The publication of *The Frugal Housewife* (1829) made her a household name and a national authority on domestic matters and, although never a mother herself, Child founded the first magazine directed specifically to children, *The Juvenile Miscellany* (1826–34). Late 20th-century scholars and students have been most interested in Child's reform novels, which dealt with racial and political themes, such as *Hobomok* (1824), a novel set in colonial times and dealing with the subject of miscegenation between an Indian man and a white woman, and her antislavery writings, especially the controversial political treatise *An Appeal in Favor of That Class of Americans Called Africans* (1833) and her editorship of the *National Anti-Slavery Standard* (1841–43). Lydia Maria Child's personal and professional connections with the Transcendentalists continued during this period of her most activist reform work, and she even reprinted Emerson's essay "MAN THE REFORMER" in the *Standard*.

Bibliography

Karcher, Carolyn L. *The First Woman in the Republic: A Cultural Biography of Lydia Maria Child.* Durham, N.C.: Duke University Press, 1994.

Cholmondeley, Thomas
(1823–1863)

Thomas Cholmondeley was an English aristocrat and friend of Henry David THOREAU. The two men met in Massachusetts at least three times, corresponded regularly, and exchanged books on several occasions. Cholmondeley first visited CONCORD in 1854, staying first with the Emersons and then with the Thoreau family. He also accompanied Thoreau and Harrison Gray Otis BLAKE on hikes in the mountains. Cholmondeley invited Thoreau to travel with him elsewhere, particularly to the West Indies and to visit him in England, but, although intrigued by his friend's travels, Thoreau preferred to explore his local surroundings, leading Cholmondeley to warn him of his solitary nature. The two men held quite different opinions on political and social issues, with Cholmondeley being much wealthier and more conservative than Thoreau, but they corresponded regularly about literary topics. On one occasion in 1855, Cholmondeley sent a large collection of books on Indian history and literature to his friend Thoreau, including translations of the Vishnu Purana and the Bhagavad Gita. Thoreau returned the favor by later sending Cholmondeley copies of some of the best in American literature, including his own *WALDEN* (1854), as well as Ralph Waldo EMERSON's *POEMS* (1847) and Walt WHITMAN's *LEAVES OF GRASS* (1855).

Bibliography

Harding, Walter. *The Days of Henry Thoreau.* New York: Dover, 1982.

Christian Disciple   *See* CHRISTIAN EXAMINER.

Christian Examiner
(1813–1869)

The *Christian Examiner* was the most important journal of UNITARIANISM during the first half of the 19th century and a forum for many of the earliest defining essays of the Transcendentalist movement in the 1830s. It was founded in 1813 by, among others, the Reverend William Ellery CHANNING as the *Christian Disciple* and continued publication until 1869. The paper was originally intended as a forum for bringing together geographically dispersed ministers of what was a loosely organized denomination until Unitarians formalized themselves into the AMERICAN UNITARIAN ASSOCIATION after 1825.

Frederic Henry HEDGE's essay on "Coleridge's Literary Character" was one of the first articulations of the "new thought" of Transcendentalism and first appeared in the *Christian Examiner* in 1833. Other Unitarian-Transcendentalists who published in its pages early on included Francis BOWEN, Orestes BROWNSON, and George RIPLEY. Within a context of experimentation within liberal Unitarianism, the controversy sparked by Transcendentalism was concentrated to a large degree in the pages of the *Christian Examiner*. Andrews NORTON, one of the most prominent Unitarian leaders of the time, was a member of the paper's editorial board. Norton threatened to break his ties with the magazine over the publication of a series of articles by George Ripley that sparked a debate over the divinity of Christ and, therefore, the nature of the miracles performed by Christ in the New Testament Gospels. Now referred to as the MIRACLES CONTROVERSY, this conversation in the pages of the *Christian Examiner* signaled the break of Transcendentalist thought from orthodox Unitarian Christianity and, in the case of Emerson and Ripley, the break of specific individuals from the ministry.

The paper went through several distinct editorial phases in the wake of the Transcendentalist controversy and the resulting split within Unitarianism. During the 1840s the paper maintained a conservative stance by limiting publication or even discussion of Transcendentalists in its pages, except perhaps condemnation of newer radical figures, such as Theodore PARKER. Commentary on Emerson, however, is conspicuously absent from the paper throughout most of the 1850s. In 1858 Frederic Henry Hedge took over as editor of the *Christian Examiner* and reestablished it as a forum for liberal ideas, including the exploration of the Unitarian connection to Transcendentalism. During his tenure as editor (1858–61), Hedge published essays praising Transcendentalists such as Emerson, Parker, and Henry David THOREAU, and his writers included a younger generation of Transcendentalist thinkers such as Octavius Brooks FROTHINGHAM, David WASSON, and John WEISS.

Christian Register
(1821–1961)

The *Christian Register* was the major periodical of UNITARIANISM throughout the heyday of 19th-century Transcendentalism, and several Transcendentalists contributed to the paper at one time or another, including Orestes BROWNSON, Elizabeth Palmer PEABODY, John WEISS, and George RIPLEY, who also served as a coeditor in the early years of publication. The *Christian Register* was founded in April 1821 and edited and owned by minister David Reed who described the general goal of the paper as to "inculcate the principles of a rational faith, and to promote the practice of genuine piety." The weekly paper was founded several years before Unitarians organized into the AMERICAN UNITARIAN ASSOCIATION (AUA) and remained independent of the AUA, which was primarily a loosely based organization of diverse Unitarian groups rather than a governing body. The *Christian Register* focused more on general liberal religious views than on news related to a specific church and included news and editorials on larger political and social reform issues as well.

Although not specifically a Transcendentalist periodical, in addition to publishing and following the writings of figures affiliated with Transcendentalism, which emerged out of debates within Unitarianism beginning in the 1830s, the editors of the *Christian Register* sometimes came to the defense of controversial Transcendentalist activities. The paper was one of the few publications that did not try to distance itself from Amos Bronson ALCOTT following a controversy over his 1836 CONVERSATIONS WITH CHILDREN ON THE GOSPELS. Alcott was publicly attacked in other papers for revealing his experimental teaching methods at the TEMPLE SCHOOL, which included engaging children on controversial topics related to sexuality and the perceived blasphemy of teaching a subjective approach to the Bible. The *Christian Register*, at that time under the editorship of a different minister named Chandler Robbins, sought to soften criticisms not necessarily by endorsing his methods but by defending Alcott, in general terms, as a "pure-minded, industrious, and well-meaning man." Furthermore, Alcott's assistant and transcriber for the volume, Elizabeth Palmer Peabody, defended him in the pages of the *Christian Register* in an anonymously published essay in which she urged, "Will this generation be so unwise as not to avail itself of the peculiar genius of this singular enthusiast; who is also a pure-hearted and devout man;—because he has some errors in detail?" Just two years later, editor Robbins would also defend Ralph Waldo EMERSON's controversial "DIVINITY SCHOOL ADDRESS" (1838) in the pages of the *Christian Register*.

In 1957 the name of the periodical was changed to the *Unitarian Register*, and just a few years later, in 1961, the paper was merged with the *Universalist Leader* and continued publication as the *Register-Leader*.

"Circles"
Ralph Waldo Emerson
(1841)

"Circles" appeared in Ralph Waldo EMERSON's collection of ESSAYS: FIRST SERIES (1841). The image of "Circles," a rhetorical device used in both the essay and the collection as a whole, is one of openness, without boundaries, and of constant renewal and movement and represents Emerson's idea that nothing is permanent: "Our life is an apprenticeship to the truth that around every circle another can be drawn: that there is no end in nature, that every end is a beginning, that there is always another dawn risen on mid-noon, and under every deep a lower deep opens." The essay is considered to be one of Emerson's best expressions of a core Transcendentalist IDEALISM—the belief that everything evolves and is related, moving outward from the individual, as expressed in the imagery of the first lines of the essay: "The eye is the first circle; the horizon which it forms is the second; and throughout nature this primary figure is repeated without end. It is the highest emblem in the cipher of the world."

As in his other writings, Emerson explores the relationship between the "Me" and the "Not Me"—between individual subjective reality and the material world of reality—in order to establish the predominance and importance of the individual, the "Me." He then moves on to describe, at the center of the circle of existence, the all-encompassing nature of the universe: "a circle whose center was everywhere, and its circumference nowhere." This universal force, the circle itself, defines and explains "every human action," but despite the seemingly fixed nature of this "first of forms," this "still and silent center of the universe," that defines all else, Emerson in fact emphasizes the hope and action of the individual in his or her current existence through "the creation of new thought," and the constantly changing and expanding of the universe within this primary circle of life: "The life of man is a self-evolving circle . . . without end." The image of the circle may also be interpreted as a life confined on all sides, but, on the contrary, the circle is the symbol of humanity itself and, in Emerson's more optimistic view, "there is no outside, no enclosing wall, no circumference to us." No one individual need feel confined by any limitations, for if "the soul is quick and strong, it bursts over that boundary on all sides, and expands another orbit," continuously creating new circles or spheres of experience within which each individual can work to construct a new and evolving self.

Emerson moves from discussing humanity and individuals in the abstract to applying the concept of "circles" to interactions in social life. The most vivid example is that of "conversation" which is, in fact, merely "a game of circles." CONVERSATION was understood by many of the Transcendentalists, not just Emerson, as an ideal mode of communication—one in which both participants could engage equally and take away from the interaction that which aided the development of their own self. Both Amos Bronson ALCOTT and Margaret FULLER held meetings in which they experimented with "conversation" as the primary teaching tool. In conversation, Emerson explained in his essay on "Circles," "we move outward, onward, beyond the thoughts of successive speakers, and are ultimately left with the splendor of silence." Conversation itself is a "system of concentric circles," in which we are introduced to the ideas of others for the purpose of establishing and evolving our own ideas about the topics. Through conversation one learns about the world, about others, and therefore about oneself, as one is always free to take what they want from the interaction: "I am only an experimenter. . . . No facts to me are sacred; none profane; I simply experiment, an endless seeker, with no Past at my back." Emerson's language from this section of the essay defining the relationship of the self to knowledge and history and experience would echo later in Walt WHITMAN's Transcendentalist-influenced poetry of the self, particularly "SONG OF MYSELF" in *Leaves of Grass* (1855).

"Civil Disobedience"
Henry David Thoreau
(1849)

Henry David THOREAU's "Civil Disobedience" is perhaps the best known piece of writing by an American Transcendentalist and is often cited as the best example of the movement's philosophical ideals translated into practical and political action. The essay was Thoreau's literary and political response to his arrest for refusal to pay a poll tax to fund a government that he opposed, primarily in its support of slavery and its expansion through the Mexican War. Thoreau's essay is an account of one man's acting in accord with his conscience, a critique of the majority rule mindset of the democratic state, and, finally, a model of nonviolent resistance as a viable and desirable form of political protest. It is in this last regard that Thoreau's writing has had its most lasting effect, inspiring political reformers, dissenters, and NONRESISTANCE leaders of the 20th century, such as Mohandas K. GANDHI, Martin Luther King, Jr., and others who have explicitly credited Thoreau as a role model.

Thoreau's protest began in 1846 during his stay at WALDEN POND in a one-room cabin he had built as an experiment in self-sufficiency and economy. Thoreau was charged and arrested for nonpayment of local poll taxes and spent one night in jail before a family member arrived and paid the tax for him. Thoreau had declared his nonpayment as a protest against the government but he was not the first Transcendentalist to do so. Fellow Transcendentalist and reformer Amos Bronson ALCOTT had refused to pay a tax three years earlier for the same antislavery reasons, but Alcott had not been arrested or jailed. Thoreau's own personal experience of civil disobedience gave an added political meaning to his stay at Walden and to the idea of self-reliance, for his wilderness retreat was now important to him as a place where "the State was nowhere to be seen." His account was presented first as an 1848 lyceum lecture in CONCORD, MASSACHUSETTS, on "The Relation of the Individual to the State" and appeared in print in May 1849 as "Resistance to Civil Government" in Elizabeth Palmer PEABODY's journal, AESTHETIC PAPERS. The title "Civil Disobedience" was given to the essay not by Thoreau but by his editors who printed it posthumously in the 1866 collection A YANKEE IN CANADA, with Anti-Slavery and Reform Papers.

The account of his arrest is inserted in the middle of the essay where he presents his night spent in jail as a metaphor for the state's only recourse in locking up physical bodies, or, in the case of war, etc., bringing bodies into its service, but the state's inability to change or control an individual's conscience. The majority of the piece shows how Thoreau's personal experience was translated into a larger critique of the mindless acceptance and even adoration most Americans seemed to be paying to their democratic government. Thoreau reminded his fellow Americans that people, not the government which people created, must be held responsible for the good and bad in America: "the government itself never furthered any enterprise. . . . It does not keep the country free. It

does not settle the West. It does not educate. The character inherent in the American people has done all that has been accomplished; and it would have done somewhat more, if the government had not sometimes got in its way." Likewise, the American people should not just be hapless bystanders while the government they created perpetuated, in Thoreau's eyes, multiple sins and injustices: "I cannot for an instant recognize that political organization as *my* government which is the *slave's* government also." For Thoreau the first step to change was resistance: "Let every man make known what kind of government would command his respect, and that will be one step toward obtaining it." Thoreau harked to the founding of the country to remind his readers that democracy was not the sole ideal Americans had fought for and held dear, for the country had been founded on "the right of revolution; that is, the right to refuse allegiance to and to resist the government." "Honest men," he went on, must sometimes "rebel and revolutionize." "I say, break the law. Let your life be a counter friction to stop the machine."

Increasingly influenced throughout the 1830s and 1840s by the leading voices of radical ABOLITIONISM, such as Wendell PHILLIPS and William Lloyd GARRISON, Henry David Thoreau did not just write abstractly about the need for individual conscience over law but provided a direct example of how people can take individual action against slavery by resisting the government. In "Civil Disobedience" Thoreau did not argue for a retreat from society; on the contrary, as Ralph Waldo EMERSON had done in "SELF-RELIANCE" (1841), Thoreau made a call to action as citizens of the country and the world. Thoreau was confident in criticizing his nation's government because of his Transcendentalist ideal of self-reliance. He brought his political resistance to bear on his philosophical ideals in pointing out that individuals who were not dependent on the government were free to criticize and thus change it: "You must live within yourself, and depend upon yourself . . . and not have many affairs." Both of these Transcendentalist writers argued, in different ways, for moral engagement with the problems of society, for looking inward to find solutions to the problems that plagued their times.

Bibliography

Chernus, Ira. *American Nonviolence: The History of an Idea.* Maryknoll, N.Y.: Orbis Books, 2004.

Glick, Wendell, ed. *The Higher Law: Thoreau on Civil Disobedience and Reform.* Princeton, N.J.: Princeton University Press, 2004.

Clapp, Eliza Thayer
(1811–1888)

Poet and Sunday school teacher Eliza Thayer Clapp was in sympathy with the Transcendentalist religious critique and befriended such figures as William Henry CHANNING, Frederic Henry HEDGE, Theodore PARKER, and Elizabeth Palmer PEABODY. When a friend sent some of her poems to Ralph Waldo EMERSON in 1840 he praised them for the poet's ability to see beyond the personal to the universal. Encouraged, she sent some of her writings to Margaret FULLER as editor of the new Transcendentalist literary journal, the *DIAL*. Fuller ultimately included four of Clapp's poems in the July 1841 issue of the paper and two more poems appeared a year later in the July 1842 issue. Her poems received the highest praise from readers and reviewers. A piece entitled "The Future is better than the Past" was even attributed to Emerson and erroneously printed multiple times under his name. Clapp continued to correspond with Emerson about her writing, but no further work was published in the *Dial*.

Bibliography

Myerson, Joel. *The New England Transcendentalists and the Dial: A History of the Magazine and Its Contributors.* London and Toronto: Associated University Presses, 1980.

Clarke, James Freeman
(1810–1888)

James Freeman Clarke was a Unitarian minister, writer, and editor of the *WESTERN MESSENGER*, which he helped found in 1836 as the first explicitly Transcendentalist periodical and a key forum for spreading Transcendentalist ideas in the western states. He attended Harvard with Oliver Wendell HOLMES and lifelong friend William Henry CHANNING and declared in his *Autobiography* that he "discovered that I was born a transcendentalist" when he began reading the works of Samuel Taylor COLERIDGE and Immanuel KANT. He also read Thomas CARLYLE and was thus brought in line intellectually and philosophically with the emerging Transcendentalist movement. In 1836 Clarke was one of the original members of the TRANSCENDENTAL CLUB. After graduating from HARVARD DIVINITY SCHOOL Clarke spent a brief period in Louisville, Kentucky, where he preached and worked on the *Western Messenger*. The magazine was originally a forum for liberal UNITARIANISM but Clarke used the paper to discuss social reform issues, especially antislavery, and to spread Transcendentalist ideas to the western United States. Clarke published many of the earliest poems of Ralph Waldo EMERSON and defended Emerson when the controversy over the "DIVINITY SCHOOL ADDRESS" broke out, just as he later defended Theodore PARKER from excommunication in the belief that the church must support the freedom of opinion.

Clarke himself never espoused the most radical and unorthodox aspects of Transcendentalism. He embraced the philosophical IDEALISM but remained a moderately conservative and thus popular church minister. He retained the belief that acceptance of Jesus Christ was a necessary component of faith and thus was, like his colleague Frederic Henry HEDGE, one of the thoroughly Christian Transcendentalists. After returning to Boston in 1841 Clarke founded a liberal congregation, the Church of the Disciples, and served as a minister there for most of the remainder of his life. He was also a liberal, but moderate, social reformer, speaking out for ABOLITIONISM and supporting EDUCATION reform and WOMEN'S RIGHTS, among other causes. In Boston he renewed his connections with the New England Transcendentalists, and both he and his sister Sarah Freeman CLARKE were close friends with Margaret FULLER, who was in fact a distant cousin. Under Fuller's editorship he published several poems in the Transcendentalist literary journal, the *DIAL*. He and Fuller corresponded almost daily and studied German literature together, especially the writings of Johann Wolfgang von GOETHE, and, along with Fuller and Hedge, Clarke is considered one of the key figures responsible for bringing German ROMANTICISM to its prominent place of influence in American Transcendentalism. In 1842 Clarke published a translation of another German work, *Theodore or the Skeptic's Conversion,* a novel by theologian Wilhelm de Wette, as part of George RIPLEY's multivolume series, SPECIMENS OF FOREIGN STANDARD LITERATURE.

In addition to his ministerial duties Clarke was a prolific writer who published innumerable books and pamphlets on religious as well as social themes. After Fuller's death Clarke collaborated with colleagues Ralph Waldo Emerson and William Henry Channing in the publication of MEMOIRS OF MARGARET FULLER OSSOLI (1852). Beginning in 1873 his sermons were regularly published in the *Saturday Evening Gazette.* Like other post–Civil War Transcendentalists he was increasingly interested in comparative religious studies and is most well known for one of the first historical surveys in the field, *Ten Great Religions: An Essay in Comparative Theology,* published in 1871 as the first of a two-volume study, followed in 1881 by a collection of sermons, *Events and Epochs in Religious History,* and in 1883 by volume two of *Ten Great Religions.* Clarke spent more than 25 years putting together these studies of all the world's major religious systems in an effort to understand religion historically and formulate an understanding of a "universal religion" which united all of mankind. Although he was himself a Christian and thus viewed the world's other religions through the lens of Christianity as itself a unifying religion, Clarke sought to truly understand and respect other religious traditions. His project was part of an interest in comparative religious study promoted by other Transcendentalists and Unitarians in the last half of the 19th century. His volumes constituted one of the first and most significant American contributions to the study of religion comparatively and historically. In 1876 Clarke offered the first courses in comparative religious studies at Harvard Divinity School. His Transcendentalism influenced not only his religious views but his literary and educational as well, as put forth in his 1880 essay collection, *Self-Culture: Physical, Intellectual, Moral, and Spiritual.*

James Freeman Clarke's prolific career as a writer on various religious themes highlighted the moderate and reform rather than literary aspects of his work, but, his contemporaries also regarded him as an inspired poet and a talented translator and literary critic. It was in this capacity that he edited the *Poems and Essays* (1886) of fellow Transcendentalist poet Jones VERY.

Bibliography

Habich, Robert. *Transcendentalism and the Western Messenger: A History of the Magazine and Its Contributors, 1835–1841.* London and Cranbury, N.J.: Associated University Presses, 1985.

Clarke, Sarah Freeman
(1808–unknown)

Sarah Freeman Clarke was one of only a few women to attend any meetings of the TRANSCENDENTAL CLUB and was a regular attendee at Margaret FULLER's CONVERSATIONS FOR WOMEN beginning in 1839. Clarke had close family ties and friendships with most of the major Transcendentalists. She was the sister of Unitarian minister and Transcendentalist James Freeman CLARKE and friends with Sophia Peabody HAWTHORNE. As a young woman she consulted with the romantic landscape artist Washington ALLSTON, who encouraged her to pursue a career in painting. She became a drawing teacher at Amos Bronson ALCOTT's TEMPLE SCHOOL, where her younger brother also attended, and stood by Alcott when his controversial teaching methods, as revealed in the 1836 publication of his CONVERSATIONS WITH CHILDREN ON THE GOSPELS, opened him up to public ridicule. She was also friends with Lydia Jackson, who, when she married Ralph Waldo EMERSON, became known as Lidian EMERSON. Ralph Waldo Emerson became one of Clarke's closest friends, offering her advice on her art and other matters. She regularly attended his lectures and supported him in the wake of criticism and controversy surrounding his 1838 "DIVINITY SCHOOL ADDRESS." Her journals and correspondence contain rare and important accounts of many of Emerson's lectures. She contributed a poem on "Dante" for the first issue of the Transcendentalist literary journal, the DIAL, in July 1840 and was later invited by her brother, James Freeman Clarke, to contribute to his paper, the WESTERN MESSENGER, but she never did.

Bibliography

Myerson, Joel. " 'A True & High Minded Person': Transcendentalist Sarah Clarke," *Southwest Review* (spring 1974): 163–172.

———. *The New England Transcendentalists and the Dial: A History of the Magazine and Its Contributors.* London and Toronto: Associated University Presses, 1980.

Clough, Arthur Hugh
(1819–1861)

Upon reading Ralph Waldo EMERSON, English poet and intellectual Arthur Clough identified with Emerson's IDEALISM and invited the Transcendentalist to Oxford in 1847. The two men met the following year and initiated a regular correspondence. Due in part to Emerson's example in resigning from the Unitarian ministry to pursue his calling and beliefs, Clough resigned from teaching at Oxford in 1848 when he could no longer in good conscience swear to his faith in the Anglican church. Emerson respected Clough's decision and encouraged him to come to the United States in search of work. Clough was unsuccessful and soon returned to England, but his sojourn in America was not entirely without benefit as Emerson had introduced him to many prominent New England intellectuals and writers such as Nathaniel HAWTHORNE, Henry Wadsworth LONGFELLOW, and Theodore PARKER. After Clough's death Emerson praised his friend by declaring that "I had found in London, the best American."

Bibliography

Biswas, Robindra. *Arthur Hugh Clough.* Oxford: Clarendon Press, 1972.

Lowry, Howard F., and Ralph Rusk, eds. *Emerson-Clough Letters.* Hamdon, Conn.: Archon Books, 1968.

Coleridge, Samuel Taylor
(1772–1834)

British poet and philosopher Samuel Taylor Coleridge was perhaps the most important contemporary literary influence on the American Transcendentalists. Through reading Coleridge, Transcendentalists such as Amos Bronson ALCOTT, William Ellery CHANNING, Ralph Waldo EMERSON, and Margaret FULLER were introduced to European ROMANTICISM and, in particular, to the most important German philosophers, most notably Friedrich SCHELLING, then unavailable in English translations. Coleridge's most important work for the New England Transcendentalists was his 1825 *Aids to Reflection.* James MARSH edited and wrote a useful introduction to the work in an 1829 American edition. It was this book that excited the thinkers associated with the emerging Transcendentalist movement and encouraged their criticism of the empirical method of Enlightenment thinker John LOCKE. Coleridge provided support for the Transcendentalist critique and articulated an alternative philosophy that valued the spiritual and the mental faculty of Understanding equal to or even more than Locke's emphasis on Reason.

While many liberal intellectuals were then engaged in reading Marsh's edition of *Aids to Reflection,* Frederic Henry HEDGE published a path-breaking review article on Coleridge in the CHRISTIAN EXAMINER in March 1833. Many credited Hedge's essay, "Coleridge's Literary Character," as the identifiable start of a "new school" of philosophy in the United States, the Transcendentalist movement. The *Christian Examiner* was the leading paper of UNITARIANISM at the time, and Hedge actually published a series of articles in 1833 and 1834 promoting the work not only of Coleridge but of the German philosophers he in turn relied upon, such as Immanuel KANT, Johann Fichte, and Friedrich Schelling, and Swedish mystic Emanuel Swedenborg. Ralph Waldo Emerson read Hedge's articles and praised them as "the best pieces that have appeared in the *Examiner,*" noting presciently that "he may help me."

Perhaps more than any other author, Samuel Taylor Coleridge influenced the early thought of Ralph Waldo Emerson and shaped his views on genius, on nature, and on spiritual truths as revealed through human intuition and understanding. The direct influence of Coleridge is most evident in Emerson's seminal work of 1836, NATURE, as well as his 1837 address on "THE AMERICAN SCHOLAR." The most important concept for Emerson, drawn from his readings of *Aids to Reflection* as well as *The Friend* (first published in 1812), was Coleridge's explanation of the distinction between Reason and Understanding. Emerson took from Coleridge a two-part explanation of the mind that informed Emerson's Transcendentalist philosophy. The first part was a belief in ideas as universal, as fixed and available to all humans. The second part was a belief in intuition as the source of arriving at these ideas or truths. Coleridge used the word *understanding* or *reflection* to speak of intuition. The idea that human intuition was the key to spiritual understanding was a radical challenge to orthodox religion in that the individual rather than theological doctrine became the source of spiritual truths. Emerson took Coleridge's explanation even further in asserting complete individual self-reliance on all matters.

The Transcendentalists relied upon other concepts from Coleridge's works, especially his literary and poetical theories as set forth in *Biographia Literaria* (1817). In the first full history of the movement, the 1876 TRANSCENDENTALISM IN NEW ENGLAND: A HISTORY, Octavius Brooks FROTHINGHAM confidently declared that "The prophet of the new philosophy in England was Samuel Taylor Coleridge; in the early part of the present century, perhaps the most conspicuous figure in our literary world."

Bibliography

Ashton, Rosemary. *The Life of Samuel Taylor Coleridge.* Cambridge, Mass.: Blackwell Publishing, 1996.

The College, the Market, and the Court
Caroline Dall
(1867)

Transcendentalist feminist Caroline DALL published her most thorough analysis of the social, economic, and legal condition of 19th-century women in her 1867 *The College, the Market, and the Court; or, Woman's Relation to Education, Labor, and Law.* Caroline Dall was a student of Margaret FULLER and a coeditor of the WOMEN'S RIGHTS newspaper THE UNA, published in the early 1850s. In her later career she worked to memorialize Fuller and the history of Transcendentalism. The 1860s, however, marked Dall's most prolific decade of publishing. She completed several full-length works during the Civil War decade, and *The College, the Market, and the Court* was perhaps her most widely read.

The book received positive reviews from the press, who acknowledged Dall as "widely known as one of the ablest and most earnest advocates of a radical change in the social position of woman." *The College, the Market, and the Court* brought together several of Dall's lectures and even previously published material—three lectures first published in *Woman's Right to Labor*, three lectures from *Woman's Rights under the Law*, three earlier unpublished lectures on the subject of women's EDUCATION, and additional information bringing the material in these lectures up to date with new statistics and analysis based on recent research. As the title indicates, Dall systematically analyzed woman's status by assessing their access to higher education (*The College*), to economic opportunities (*the Market*), and their treatment under the law (*the Court*).

Not surprisingly, Dall's conclusions were not encouraging. She documented and opposed women's exclusion from colleges and professional schools such as Harvard Medical School as well as unequal pay and lack of opportunities for women who did enter the paid labor force. Dall's strident critiques and sympathetic portrayal of the economic and moral plight of working women, even including prostitutes, made her work controversial but also set it apart from analyses of other middle-class reformers of her time. Lastly, her analysis of the American legal system criticized reliance on English common law, which kept women subordinate to men in all matters related to marriage, divorce, and property rights. The culminating issue in Dall's argument for women's equality in all of these other realms was woman's right to the franchise, or the vote.

In the end, Dall's thesis was influenced by her own Transcendentalist concern with woman's self-realization or self-culture. Dall was an educational reformer, but her definition of education included what she termed "unrestricted mental culture." She summed her argument up thus: "The right to education—that is, the right to the education or drawing-out of all the faculties God has given—*involves* the right to a choice of vocation; that is, the right to a choice of the end to which those faculties shall be trained." She argued that the vote was necessary in order to facilitate self-culture; without education or without full access to all fields of employment, women would not be able to pursue a VOCATION, their true calling, and therefore their potential would be limited. Once women were employed and participating in economic society, Dall argued that they would be entitled to be represented through the vote.

Bibliography

Wayne, Tiffany K. *Woman Thinking: Feminism and Transcendentalism in Nineteenth-Century America*. Lanham, Md.: Lexington Books, 2005.

Combe, George   *See* PHRENOLOGY.

Common Sense Philosophy

The American Transcendentalists were influenced by Scottish Common Sense Philosophy of the late 18th and early 19th centuries, primarily in their rejection of it as the primary philosophical system taught at Harvard College and within UNITARIANISM. The Scottish Common Sense school of thought was founded by Thomas Reid, as a reaction against the Enlightenment skepticism of David Hume that, according to Reid, did not take full account of the role of morality and religion in understanding the mind. "Common sense" as discussed by Reid and others encompassed not only our current understanding of practical sense or understanding but a recognition of human feeling and judgment in moral matters.

Placing a higher value on human intuition or judgment was attractive to the Transcendentalists,

many of whom had been trained in the Scottish philosophers while at HARVARD DIVINITY SCHOOL. Nineteenth-century Americans drew from the Common Sense school of thought the importance of self-consciousness and of observation in order to assess the meaning of an experience, rather than merely expecting an inherent or universal meaning. Furthermore, intuition brought forth truths and ideas that could not be gained from experience alone and therefore were not subject to the empirical tests or proofs demanded by previous philosophies, primarily that of John LOCKE. Although these aspects of Common Sense philosophy were important to Unitarianism, and the Transcendentalists eventually broke from the conservatism of Unitarianism as they learned it at Harvard, the Transcendentalists retained the Common Sense emphasis on valuing the intuition, a theme especially central to the writings of Ralph Waldo EMERSON and Henry David THOREAU, both of whom were well-grounded in the writings of Scottish Common Sense philosophers. Common Sense also reached the Transcendentalists through its influence on German and French writers who took up and reworked these earlier ideas.

Bibliography

Howe, Daniel Walker. *The Unitarian Conscience: Harvard Moral Philosophy, 1805–1861*. Cambridge, Mass.: Harvard University Press, 1970.

"Compensation"
Ralph Waldo Emerson
(1841)

Ralph Waldo EMERSON had written a poem entitled "Compensation" in 1841, and his philosophical essay of the same title appeared that same year in *ESSAYS: FIRST SERIES*. In the essay, Emerson explains how the Transcendentalist idea of "compensation" was different from the traditional definition of the term promoted by organized religion. In theological terms, "compensation" was similar to the idea of retribution, the belief that human actions on earth, whether good or evil, would be either rewarded or punished in the afterlife based on the decision of a nonhuman god. Emerson's philosophy rejected such theological connotations and instead argued that compensation or retribution comes from nature itself: "Every act rewards itself . . . integrates itself, in a twofold manner." At work here, as in Emerson's other writings, was the idea of "THE OVER-SOUL," or a universal soul or spirit governing and responding to human actions rather than a supernatural being such as the Christian God. The other key Transcendentalist reworking of this concept is the belief that actions are not compensated in the future, in the afterlife, but in the here and now; that immediately, and continually, "every act rewards itself."

In numerous examples throughout "Compensation," Emerson points out the "inevitable dualism" of the corresponding natural and human worlds: "Each thing is a half, and suggests another thing to make it whole; as spirit, matter; man, woman; odd, even." The human world is included in such dualities and therefore subject to the law of compensation because humans are part of nature: "Whilst the world is thus dual, so is every one of its parts." Emerson's formulation extends to an explanation or acknowledgement of evil and an argument for the system of morality of justice inherent in the natural universe. In the religious sense, evil is the opposite of God, of goodness, and something that must be avoided. But Emerson acknowledges evil as a necessary part of this dualistic universe, and therefore a characteristic of the Deity itself. Since the universe is entirely connected, nothing can be done in part that does not affect the whole; nothing can be done outside of oneself that does not, in turn, affect the inward self as well. Emerson links human social and spiritual life by choosing a relevant current social theme to make his spiritual analogy: "If you put a chain around the neck of a slave, the other end fastens itself around your own." As one recent biographer has noted, the essay might better have been termed "On Justice," since it does in fact present Emerson's theory on the nature of evil and justice, but "compensation" comes from "right action" as well, not only from evil; it includes reward, not only punishment. As Emerson simply states, "Love, and you shall be loved." Emerson explores the idea of justice and morality not only through social and economic relations but through personal relations as well.

Emerson's emphasis on duality and on justice and compensation would seem in some ways to limit his claims, in other writings, for the complete independence of the individual will. Indeed, perhaps his most famous defining statement on individualism, "SELF-RELIANCE," appears immediately before "Compensation" in this collection of essays. In "Compensation" he states "Our action is overmastered and characterized above our will by the law of nature." In some ways, then, the theory of "compensation" adds to and places a system of checks on unregulated individualism, for it places humankind within a moral universe, accountable not only to the self but to other humans and to nature as well. For Emerson the best life is one of "simplicity" and harmony with nature and society through self-respect. The essay thus turns from the seeming trap of natural law to one in which the individual will again rises as the decision-making source within nature. The remainder of the essay is somewhat more optimistic in emphasizing the moral virtue and "progress" of a life well lived. The individual is always changing, moving forward, in response to the changing movement of the universe around him or her. As an example of the hope and virtue that can arise out of despair, Emerson speaks of how his own life has been "compensated" by referring back to the loss of several loved ones—"The death of a dear friend, wife, brother, lover, which seemed nothing but privation"—and concluding that, although such pain could not be understood at the time, the loss "later assumes the aspect of a guide or genius." In other words, everything in the universe happens for a reason; even loss and death and evil are part of the plan of nature and add to the development of the individual soul. As in much of his other work, Emerson takes what seem to be basic tenets of Christian teachings and reworks them into humanistic, rather than God-mandated, guides for moral life.

Compromise of 1850 *See* FUGITIVE SLAVE LAW.

Concord, Massachusetts

Concord, Massachusetts, was the family home of Ralph Waldo EMERSON and a center of Transcendentalist social and literary culture throughout the 19th century. Located 20 miles northwest of Boston, Concord was established in 1635 as the first inland town in the Massachusetts Bay Colony. Its historical significance was further secured when it became the site of the first battle of the Revolutionary War in April 1775, a battle that Emerson memorialized in his poem, "CONCORD HYMN," in which he penned the now-famous lines, "Here once the embattled farmers stood / And fired the shot heard round the world." Although Concord thus had an important place in American colonial and revolutionary-era history, its reputation to this day owes most to its famous 19th-century residents.

Ralph Waldo Emerson was a descendant of one of the town founders, Peter Bulkeley. After Emerson settled there permanently in 1834 the town became associated with the Transcendentalist literary circle. In an effort to get closer to Emerson and his circle, the town drew many famous visitors and residents, including Amos Bronson ALCOTT, who moved his own family to ORCHARD HOUSE in Concord in 1840. As the home of writers such as Nathaniel HAWTHORNE, the town not surprisingly became the subject of various literary works. Nathaniel and Sophia Peabody HAWTHORNE lived for a brief time in the Emerson family home, THE OLD MANSE, the subject of a short story included in the collection MOSSES FROM AN OLD MANSE. Besides Emerson, perhaps Concord's most famous resident was Henry David THOREAU, whose association with the town in the popular imagination is one less literary and more environmental. Thoreau's famous experiment in self-reliance took place at WALDEN POND, located less than two miles outside of the village of Concord, a place that has become a symbol of humanity's right relationship with nature.

Many of the most prominent Transcendentalists are buried in Concord at the Sleepy Hollow Cemetery: Bronson Alcott, Ralph Waldo Emerson, Henry David Thoreau, and Elizabeth Palmer PEABODY, among others. Emerson was instrumental in the planning of the cemetery and delivered an address for its dedication. Because of its famous residents, Concord remains a popular destination for students, scholars, and enthusiasts seeking to be inspired by the surroundings that inspired the Transcendentalists.

Although the heyday of Transcendentalist activity in Concord was in the 1830s and 1840s, Emerson, especially, continued to attract students and followers to the town until his death in 1882. Bronson Alcott had long dreamed of making Concord an educational mecca and of founding a "Concord academy," a plan that led to the creation of his CONCORD SCHOOL OF PHILOSOPHY AND LITERATURE, which met during the 1870s and early 1880s and drew lecturers and visitors from all over New England and from as far west as St. Louis. Many friends, associates, and members of the literary community at Concord wrote memoirs based on their Concord connections, for example, Bronson Alcott's extremely popular CONCORD DAYS (1872) and Franklin Benjamin SANBORN's 1909 memoirs of New England life and, specifically, of Concord literary society, *Recollections of Seventy Years.*

Bibliography

Brooks, Paul. *The People of Concord: One Year in the Flowering of New England.* Chester, Conn.: Globe Pequot Press, 1990.

Concord Days
Amos Bronson Alcott
(1872)

Amos Bronson ALCOTT published his two most successful books in 1872, TABLETS and *Concord Days. Concord Days* was drawn from Alcott's day-to-day experiences as recorded in his personal journal and was presented as a straightforward but amusing account of a year of life in CONCORD, MASSACHUSETTS, surrounded by his famous friends and neighbors in the Transcendentalist community. Alcott realized the interest in New England authors and provided a portrait of the community life and personalities that produced the era's most well-known works of fiction and philosophy, by friends such as the reclusive Ralph Waldo EMERSON, the romantic Nathaniel HAWTHORNE, and the man of principle, Henry David THOREAU. Alcott presented these colleagues to his readers not merely to satisfy curiosity about the personal lives of such figures but as a way to introduce many of these writers and thinkers to a wider audience beyond New England. The publication of the book coincided with another of Alcott's tours through the western states, where he also lectured regularly on the contributions of these and other colleagues, such as Margaret FULLER, Henry Wadsworth LONGFELLOW, and Walt WHITMAN.

While *Concord Days* included many anecdotes as well as personal reflections on books and ideas, and was not meant to be a systematic presentation of Transcendentalist philosophy, it did reveal much about Alcott's own philosophy. He criticized thinkers and reformers who were "incapable of IDEALISM" and reiterated his own Transcendentalist belief in the possibility of human perfection: "Man becomes godlike as he strives for divinity." *Concord Days* was Bronson Alcott's most popular book as, by the 1870s, a wider American public was most interested in the famous literary figures of 19th-century Concord.

Bibliography

Dahlstrand, Frederick. *Amos Bronson Alcott: An Intellectual Biography.* East Brunswick, N.J.: Associated University Presses, 1982.

"Concord Hymn"
Ralph Waldo Emerson
(1837)

The "Concord Hymn: Sung at the Completion of the Battle Monument, April 19, 1837," is one of Ralph Waldo EMERSON's most well-known poems and also one of his earliest. Before this time, Emerson was primarily known as a lecturer and essayist and had yet to publish any poetry. Also known as the "Concord Ode," the poem, as indicated by its subtitle, was inspired by the public unveiling of a statue in CONCORD, MASSACHUSETTS, to celebrate the site and date of the first battle between the American and British forces that sparked the Revolutionary War. In this poem Emerson created one of the most memorable lines

in American poetry and history when he described the beginning of the American Revolution in Concord as "the shot heard round the world."

The short 16-line poem takes time and nature as its themes in assessing the historical and spiritual significance of the events in Concord of April 1775. The first stanza of the poem marks the passage of time by referring to the historical events and participants at the site of the bridge in Concord where the troops met: "By the rude bridge that arched the flood, / Their flag to April's breeze unfurled, / Here once the embattled farmers stood, / And fired the shot heard round the world." The second stanza again invokes time and nature—both represented as flowing water throughout the poem—as forces that would not be stopped in an assessment of the larger world significance of the age of revolution: "The foe long since in silence slept; / Alike the conqueror silent sleeps; / And Time the ruined bridge has swept / Down the dark stream which seaward creeps." The third stanza shifts the listener's or reader's focus from history back to those who presently stand at the same site, by the same river, to raise this monument, this "votive stone," and remember: "On this green bank, by this soft stream, / We set to-day a votive stone; / That memory may their deed redeem, / When, like our sires, our sons are gone." The reference to "our sons" indicates that the assembly gathered and the Concord monument are not just there to preserve the past but the future as well.

In the final stanza Emerson calls upon "Time and Nature" one more time in his hope that the monument, and the "Spirit" that it symbolizes, will last longer than the men who fought in the war: "Spirit, that made those heroes dare / To die, or leave their children free, / Bid Time and Nature gently spare / The shaft we raise to them and thee." Although much of Emerson's other, later, poetry was experimental in form and imagery, in the "Concord Hymn" he followed a more traditional poetic structure.

Concord Lectures on Philosophy
(1883)

An account of the 1882 summer session, *Concord Lectures on Philosophy* was one of only three full-length published accounts of the presentations given at the CONCORD SCHOOL OF PHILOSOPHY AND LITERATURE, which met each year between 1879 and 1888. Two other collections were edited by Franklin Benjamin SANBORN, *THE LIFE AND GENIUS OF GOETHE* (1886) and *THE GENIUS AND CHARACTER OF EMERSON* (1898). *Concord Lectures on Philosophy* was edited by Raymond Bridgman and included lectures or abstracts of lectures by the school's founder, Amos Bronson ALCOTT, and a range of other philosophers, reformers, writers, poets, and thinkers of the period.

A special day in the summer 1882 session was reserved for a commemoration of Ralph Waldo EMERSON, who had died earlier that year, and the collection includes Alcott's poetic eulogy of Emerson, "Ion: A Monody," also published in Alcott's *SONNETS AND CANZONETS*. Among others, reformers Ednah Dow CHENEY and Julia Ward HOWE each shared their own "Reminiscences of Emerson" and William Torrey HARRIS, Alcott friend and philosopher of HEGELIANISM from St. Louis, addressed "Dialectic Unity in Emerson's Prose." Harris spoke regularly throughout the summer, and the collection reprints his other lectures on diverse philosophical topics such as "Gnosticism and Neo-Platonism," "Socrates and Pre-Socratic Philosophy," "Philosophy of the Bhagavad Ghita," and "Historical Epochs of Art." Transcendentalist EDUCATION reformer and founder of the kindergarten movement, Elizabeth Palmer PEABODY, presented reflections on "Childhood." Transcendentalist biographer-historian Franklin Benjamin SANBORN, who served as Secretary of the Concord School, addressed "Oracles of New England" and presented "Readings from Thoreau's Manuscripts." Other lecturers included in the published collection were John Albee, Cyrus BARTOL, Joel Benton, C. E. Garman, R. G. Hazard, R. A. Holland, George Howison, Hiram Jones, George Lathrop, Martha P. Lowe, James McCosh, John Watson, and Alexander Wilder. Besides providing a representative history of the philosophical subjects covered at the school, the impetus for putting together the collection was, in part, a reaction to negative accounts of the school appearing in the press and an attempt to show the wide-ranging in-

terest and applicability of the various subjects touched upon by the lecturers.

Concord Lyceum

In 1829 Ezra RIPLEY was one of the founders of the Concord Lyceum, which was an important public forum for many of the Transcendentalists. The first American lyceum was founded in Massachusetts in 1826, modeled and named after Aristotle's school for adult education in ancient Greece. Over the next few decades the lyceum was one of the most popular forms of entertainment and most accessible forms of information on educational as well as social reform and political issues. Lyceum organizations were established throughout the country to present lectures, concerts, dramatic performances, and public debates. Abolitionist reformer and writer James REDPATH was the founder of the Boston Lyceum Bureau and was responsible for booking popular speakers such as Ralph Waldo EMERSON and Henry David THOREAU, whose public careers owed much to the rise of the lyceum movement in the mid-19th century.

In its first 50 years, the Concord Lyceum presented not only nearly 800 lectures but was as well a forum for public debates and concerts. Initially lyceum lectures were presented free to the public, but in 1856 tickets began to be sold. Lectures were given by distinguished visitors, as well as by Concord residents such as Thoreau, who also served as the Lyceum secretary, and Emerson, who gave nearly 100 public lectures at the Concord Lyceum. Other speakers from among the Transcendentalists included Orestes BROWNSON, James Freeman CLARKE, Frederic Henry HEDGE, Theodore PARKER, and Jones VERY. In addition, other prominent intellectuals, writers, and reformers were invited to give addresses at Concord, including Harvard Professor Louis AGASSIZ, *NEW YORK TRIBUNE* editor Horace GREELEY, and controversial abolitionist Wendell PHILLIPS.

Access to the lyceum was central as a testing ground for much of the Transcendentalists' written work. Many of Emerson's published essays were originally presented as lectures, as was Thoreau's *WALDEN*. Emerson, in his lyceum appearances not only at Concord but across the country, ultimately created a new profession in America, that of professional paid lecturer. The trademark written styles of both men reflected the rhetorical tools and tradition they perfected in oral presentation. For example, considering the essay first as an interactive public address helps explain the forcefulness and urgency of some of the Transcendentalists' most politically minded pieces, such as Thoreau's "A PLEA FOR CAPTAIN JOHN BROWN."

Bibliography

Field, Peter S. *Ralph Waldo Emerson: The Making of a Democratic Intellectual.* Lanham, Md.: Rowman & Littlefield, 2002.

Ray, Angela. *The Lyceum and Public Culture in the 19th-Century U.S.* East Lansing: Michigan State University Press, 2005.

"Concord Ode"   *See* "CONCORD HYMN."

Concord School of Philosophy and Literature

Between 1879 and 1888 the Concord School of Philosophy and Literature lecture series was held each summer in CONCORD, MASSACHUSETTS, the first year at the home of Amos Bronson ALCOTT and in subsequent years at a chapel built specifically for the school. Alcott's plans for the Concord School had been years in the making but were finally put into place following a series of "CONVERSATIONS" he held in the winter of 1878. That year Alcott convinced one of his western colleagues, Dr. Hiram Jones of the Plato Club in Jacksonville, Illinois, to visit Concord. In his travels westward in the early 1870s, Alcott had cultivated friendships in the literary-intellectual circles surrounding Jones in Illinois and William Torrey HARRIS, a Hegelian scholar and founder in 1867 of the JOURNAL OF SPECULATIVE PHILOSOPHY, in St. Louis, Missouri. Alcott's dream was to bring together in Concord the best thinkers from both eastern and western states to discuss philosophy, art, and literature in a conversational model of education.

The first session opened in July 1879 for a five-week course at the cost of 50 cents per lec-

ture, or approximately three dollars for each week's series. The school was more successful than even Bronson Alcott could have hoped; more than 400 people attended throughout that first summer with an average of 50 people in attendance at each individual lecture. The lecturers recruited by Alcott for the first session were Jones, Harris, poet David WASSON, and reformer Ednah Dow CHENEY. Cheney and Harris, along with Unitarian minister Cyrus BARTOL and the school's secretary Franklin SANBORN, would remain the most consistent of the regular faculty members, these four being the only ones to lecture every year of the school's existence. Throughout the years they were joined by a host of other Transcendentalists as lecturers and participants: among them were Ralph Waldo EMERSON, Frederic Henry HEDGE, Thomas Wentworth HIGGINSON, and Elizabeth Palmer PEABODY.

The 1870s and 1880s were a period of vibrant intellectual activity among the Transcendentalists. They gave lectures, published essays, and founded and joined organizations such as the FREE RELIGIOUS ASSOCIATION, the RADICAL CLUB, the AMERICAN SOCIAL SCIENCE ASSOCIATION, and the Concord School of Philosophy. The Concord School was the most explicitly Transcendentalist of the postwar organizations and the last major forum to have the regular participation of the older Transcendentalists who had been active since the 1840s. The very purpose of the Concord School—which was, according to Bronson Alcott biographer Frederick Dahlstrand, an interest "in maintaining the existence of a personal, self-conscious, spiritual cause above the material universe"—highlighted the tension between an earlier generation's Transcendentalist romanticism and the new intellectual culture of science and materialism. In fact, concern about this tension, and the desire to retain various aspects of the earlier tradition, was the subject of many lectures at the school; it was also the focus of contemporary criticisms and assessments of the school's philosophical purpose.

The Concord School of Philosophy arose within a personal intellectual crisis for Bronson Alcott that was, in fact, symptomatic of a larger intellectual shift within American culture toward the professionalization of knowledge. An emphasis on intuition, subjective knowledge, and self-culture as legitimate and alternative ways of knowing still had widespread relevance within and beyond the self-identified Transcendentalist community. Alcott himself was concerned about what he perceived as a decline of personal spiritual values as a guide for ethics and morality, and reliance instead upon religious dogmatism on the one hand and materialism and science (most notably the popularity of the ideas of Charles DARWIN) on the other. These concerns and contexts were the subjects of discussion at the Concord School of Philosophy each summer between 1879 and 1888.

The belief in the self-development of the individual remained an important concept beyond the 1840s, and in fact throughout the century, among Transcendentalists who emphasized personal fulfillment, rather than prestige or monetary gain, as the primary goal in pursuing a particular VOCATION. In 1885, just as in the 1840s, Transcendentalists invoked the figure of Johann Wolfgang von GOETHE as a model of individual intellectual development. In his Concord School lecture on Goethe John Albee stated, "Self-culture as now to be considered must be held up to the Goethean plan." It was within a Transcendentalist tradition of Goethean influence, and within a later century culture that dismissed Goethe's intuitive ways of knowing, that the Concord School of Philosophy devoted its 1885 summer session to lectures on *THE LIFE AND GENIUS OF GOETHE*. The Concord School lecturers on Goethe presented and reemphasized a model of self-education and vocational pursuit that was by then a 50-year tradition of Transcendentalist philosophic ideals on the subject. Besides the Goethe lectures, only two other sessions were recorded for publication: *CONCORD LECTURES ON PHILOSOPHY* reprinted the 1882 lectures, and *THE GENIUS AND CHARACTER OF EMERSON* was the result of the 1884 series on the Transcendentalist's most important and most thoroughly American philosopher.

HEGELIANISM, NEOPLATONISM, and Transcendentalism were the acknowledged philosophical influences behind the Concord School, although the public most explicitly identified it with the Transcendentalist movement due to the prominent role played by Bronson Alcott, Ralph Waldo Emer-

son, and others. As one contemporary account noted, "Transcendentalism was in a sense behind our Concord School, and if there had been no such movement, there would have been no School." Most historians have understood the closing of the School before the turn of the century as inevitable given that the Transcendentalist philosophy of subjective and universal knowledge was seen as outdated in the face of objective science and specialization.

Still, according to Bronson Alcott's most recent biographer, the Concord School of Philosophy and Literature was "the culmination of his career and his ultimate achievement." After the death of Ralph Waldo Emerson in 1882, Alcott, by then quite elderly himself and having suffered from a stroke, ceased direct participation in the school. The others continued on through 1887; in March 1888 Bronson Alcott died, and the only meeting held during the school's final summer was a one-day memorial service honoring their founder and mentor.

Bibliography

Dahlstrand, Frederick. *Amos Bronson Alcott: An Intellectual Biography.* East Brunswick, N.J.: Associated University Presses, 1982.

Wayne, Tiffany K. *Woman Thinking: Feminism and Transcendentalism in Nineteenth-Century America.* Lanham, Md.: Lexington Books, 2005.

The Conduct of Life
Ralph Waldo Emerson
(1860)

In 1860 Ralph Waldo EMERSON published his third collection of essays, *The Conduct of Life*. The book includes nine essays: "FATE," "Power," "Wealth," "Culture," "Behavior," "Worship," "Considerations by the Way," "Beauty," and "Illusions." These essays had originated as a series of lectures, and several had been previously published in the *ATLANTIC MONTHLY*. *The Conduct of Life* is unified through themes that Emerson had been exploring since the 1840s about power and self-identity, as he himself summed up the centralizing idea in the opening paragraph of the essay on "Power": "Life is a search after power."

The first and last essays, "Fate" and "Illusions," frame the collection with Emerson's deterministic statement that individual human beings have a notable lack of power in the world, are beset by constant limitations, and, finally, that free will, for the most part, is in fact an "illusion." While such a viewpoint may seem a less than satisfying unifying theme, the majority of the essays take a more positive Transcendentalist approach in urging readers to live a life of continual striving for power and influence, based on the development of individual talents and strengths. The essays examine in-depth various themes drawn from 19th-century American society and culture as Emerson observed it around him. As he states in the opening essay, however, the solution to problems of society is not to change society—"We are incompetent to solve the times"—but to change oneself—"the question of the times resolved itself into a practical question of the conduct of life. How shall I live?" In *The Conduct of Life* he attempts to give readers an answer to that question.

In "Wealth," which Emerson understands as one of the primary ways in which individuals currently attempt to derive "Power" in American society, Emerson offers an alternative understanding of the term to indicate not material abundance but "meaning" or "knowledge." He writes that "Wealth is mental; wealth is moral." True wealth comes, for Emerson, from balance and from investment, both economically and spiritually, in the right things: "The value of a dollar is, to buy just things: a dollar goes on increasing in value with all the genius, and all the virtue of the world. A dollar in a university, is worth more than a dollar in a jail; in a temperate, schooled, law-abiding community, than in some sink of crime, where dice, knives, and arsenic, are in constant play." Emerson's insistence on the morality of wealth, and the wealth of morality, can be read as a statement on the economic justification for slavery and the financial wealth of southern slaveholders—that they lack true wealth since financial gain does not make their system virtuous.

Like "Wealth," the other essays on "Culture," "Worship," and "Behavior" all address value judgments made in American society based on outward appearances. True "Culture" or "Worship," just like true wealth, cannot be perceived by the external senses; these social values have meaning only in relation to one's own personal power. The independent or self-reliant person knows the true or authentic meaning of these words. In "Worship," especially, Emerson sought to present previous themes in a new way. He takes a firm stand in arguing that there is no place for institutional religion in the development of individual souls: "God builds his temple in the heart on the ruins of churches and religions." People misunderstand worship as an outward behavior, when it should be perceived as a source of inward personal power. It was a controversial position to take that worship happens within "the heart," rather than in the "churches and religions," but it was, in fact, only an extension of the very idea upon which Emerson had begun his career more than two decades earlier. In his 1838 DIVINITY SCHOOL ADDRESS he had stirred controversy within UNITARIANISM by urging his listeners to look within themselves for salvation rather than to outside doctrines and creeds. Even in the Divinity School Address he retained some optimism in the role of the organized church and of ministers in their ability to aid parishioners in their spiritual quests. The negative response to the Divinity School Address, however, had resulted in Emerson's complete personal break from the church.

In addition, by 1860, when he published *The Conduct of Life*, Emerson was aligned philosophically with the radical ABOLITIONISM of reformers such as William Lloyd GARRISON and Frederick Douglass, who also criticized institutions, especially the United States government and American Christian churches, as immoral in their support of slavery. Ralph Waldo Emerson's overall tone in *The Conduct of Life*, then, may at first seem less affirmative and enthusiastic than his earlier writings in NATURE (1836) or REPRESENTATIVE MEN (1850), but it makes sense that Emerson had become more cynical by 1860, as the efforts of social reformers seemed increasingly ineffective and the violence of Civil War loomed as the inevitable route to ending the moral wrong of slavery. Emerson had come to realize that institutional reform was necessary, but that individuals must continue to develop and follow their own internal moral guides outside of those institutions. In that sense,

The Conduct of Life displays a more politically and reform-minded Emerson than some of his earlier works.

Bibliography

Lopez, Michael. "*The Conduct of Life:* Emerson's Anatomy of Power." In *The Cambridge Companion to Ralph Waldo Emerson*, eds. Joel Porte and Saundra Morris. New York: Cambridge University Press, 1999, 243–366.

Robinson, David. *Emerson and the Conduct of Life: Pragmatism and Ethical Purpose in the Later Work*. New York: Cambridge University Press, 1993.

conversation

Conversation was a mode of EDUCATION and of self-culture particularly favored by the Transcendentalists and a form experimented most notably by cultural and educational reformers such as Amos Bronson ALCOTT, Margaret FULLER, and Elizabeth Palmer PEABODY. The Transcendentalists were philosophically attracted to the spontaneity of conversation, which prompted utterances of thought unprocessed and unedited. In his essay "CIRCLES," Ralph Waldo EMERSON spoke of conversation as way of learning about oneself through others, as a necessary path to the perfection of "perfect understanding," of silence: "Conversation is a game of circles. . . . Good as is discourse, silence is better, and shames it. The length of the discourse indicates the distance of thought betwixt the speaker and the hearer. If they were at a perfect understanding in any part, no words would be necessary thereon."

Conversation was also considered to be the most democratic form of social interaction, a leveling between teacher and student, a rejection of high literary culture as the only route to knowledge (thus the appeal of this method for women and children), and, most important, a mode that depended upon the participation of all those present in order to be successful. For Transcendentalists this model could be traced back to the discussions held between Socrates and his students, referred to as the Socratic method of question and answer sessions that aided the questioner in arriving at his (or her) own answers. This mode

was actively pursued by the Transcendentalists both informally and formally in organized gatherings such as the TRANSCENDENTAL CLUB and, later, the CONCORD SCHOOL OF PHILOSOPHY AND LITERATURE.

Margaret Fuller is thought to have perfected the conversational model in her CONVERSATIONS FOR WOMEN held between 1839 and 1844. Fuller's talks were intended to provide "a point of union for thinking women" interested in discussing Transcendentalist philosophical and literary themes. For Fuller, as facilitator, the conversations were an effort at educational reform, a chance to draw on her talents and preparation as a teacher, but in a mode that drew together adult women to discuss complex themes. As conversations, rather than lectures or published essays, most of what was said at these meetings went unrecorded except for a few first-person accounts that survive. Fuller modeled her meetings on an earlier experiment by Elizabeth Peabody who had offered courses in history for adult women in the early 1830s.

Before sponsoring Fuller's talks in her own bookstore, Peabody was involved in another conversational project as an assistant at Bronson Alcott's experimental school for children, TEMPLE SCHOOL. Thanks to Peabody's detailed notes, Alcott's use of the conversational model was published as the 1836–37 CONVERSATIONS WITH CHILDREN ON THE GOSPELS. After creating some controversy about using this method with children, and about the subjects covered in his conversations, Bronson Alcott returned to teaching adults in his own series of CONVERSATIONS held in the 1848 at Elizabeth Peabody's bookstore in the tradition of Margaret Fuller's meetings. Alcott moved on, however, to explore the fully democratic and widespread appeal of conversations when he traveled throughout the western states offering conversations on a variety of topics.

It was within this context of a philosophical and pedagogical agenda that Fuller, Peabody, and Alcott were attracted to the educational model of drawing out their students, whether children or adults, through conversation. Unlike lectures or traditional teaching, conversation was valued as participatory and as a route to fostering the self-development of those in actual attendance. And unlike essays or other writings, the benefit was in being there, inspired by the other participants in a more spontaneous and interactive way than merely reading or listening to a lecture. Even in their written work, however, many Transcendentalists aspired to a conversational style of writing, and they identified specific examples of this art form in Samuel Taylor COLERIDGE's *Table Talk* (1835) (a title also used by Bronson Alcott for one of his later books) and *Conversations with Goethe*, an 1839 volume of translations by Margaret Fuller.

conversations
Amos Bronson Alcott

Amos Bronson ALCOTT held regular series of conversations first for children at his TEMPLE SCHOOL, then for adults in Boston, and, after the 1850s, in various locations on his western speaking tours. Perhaps more than any other Transcendentalist, Alcott was most committed to the idea of CONVERSATION as a teaching method, as a route to self-development, and as his preferred method of communication for the purpose of spreading his message of individual, cultural, and EDUCATION reform. Conversation, unlike lecturing, allowed smaller groups of individuals to interact with each other more directly. Alcott not only wanted to preach his own message but wanted to allow for the spontaneous development of new ideas that would aid in the growth of the individual souls present. Thus, conversation itself—the process— was Alcott's message of reform or renewal of the human spirit and society.

Alcott first experimented with conversation with young children, both in the regular classroom at Temple School and in a special Saturday series of *CONVERSATIONS WITH CHILDREN ON THE GOSPELS* (Elizabeth Palmer PEABODY's notes from the meetings were published in 1836) that he instituted. Alcott looked to the Gospel not only for discussion topics but at the model of Jesus whose teaching method, like Socrates as well, greatly relied on an informal conversational style. Alcott believed that the universal truths of the Gospels lay within the uncorrupted souls of children and needed only to be drawn out by a skilled teacher such as himself.

Alcott believed that he projected no ideas of his own in these meetings and was only facilitating the "spiritual direction" of the children's conversation. As he stated in *Conversations with Children on the Gospels*, "Education, when rightly understood, will be found to lie in the art of asking apt and fit questions, and in thus leading the mind by its own light to the perception of the truth."

The revelation of his pedagogy as well as his subject matter in teaching children created a controversy that resulted in the closure of the Temple School, but Alcott's interest in conversation as the ideal method of teaching others and of promoting self-development continued. He would find better success in conversing with adults, and in 1838 he embarked on what he termed a "ministry of talking" when he organized his first series of conversations for adults. For this project he looked to his Transcendentalist colleagues for assistance and as conversation participants. The first conversation was arranged by John Sullivan DWIGHT, and Ralph Waldo EMERSON was among those who attended the early series. Revealing the democratic intentions of conversation as a method, Alcott declared that "my talking is to reach all classes and ages," and he perceived such meetings as an alternative to the lyceum lecture circuit that increasingly defined the public careers of many of his colleagues. Alcott was never a regular or successful lecturer, and he embraced his unique contribution in comparison to his contemporaries, stating that "Garrison made the convention. Greeley made the newspaper. Emerson made the lecture. And Alcott is making the Conversation. These are all purely American organs and institutions, which no country nor people besides ours can claim as we can." Friends increasingly accepted this role for and view of Alcott as, in Emerson's words, a "majestic converser." The height of popularity for Alcott's conversations was between 1848 and 1853, during which time he regularly conversed with crowds of 50 or more people, and nearly every major reformer and Transcendentalist in the Boston area attended at least one time: Cyrus BARTOL, James Freeman CLARKE, Sarah Freeman CLARKE, William Henry CHANNING, Ednah Dow CHENEY (who helped arrange a special series just for women), Caroline DALL, John Sullivan Dwight, Ralph

Waldo Emerson, Nathaniel HAWTHORNE and Sophia Peabody HAWTHORNE, Thomas Wentworth HIGGINSON, Theodore PARKER, Elizabeth Palmer Peabody, and Edwin WHIPPLE.

Topics at Alcott's conversations covered many of the same issues engaging reformers, lecturers, and Transcendentalist writers at that time, from discussions of the soul, the nature of genius, humanity's relationship to the natural world, and reforming the church and social relations, to general topics related to philosophy and history. Like Margaret FULLER, who held her CONVERSATIONS FOR WOMEN between 1839 and 1844, Alcott would prompt discussion through a selected reading on a particular theme, and rely upon the attendees to pull the conversation out and direct it to their own needs and perspectives. As at Fuller's meetings, some attendees attempted to record the conversations and, in Alcott's case, several accounts were published in newspapers, including transcripts by both Ednah Dow Cheney and Caroline Dall, both of whom had also attended Fuller's conversations during the previous decade. Regardless of these efforts, conversation was a forum that did not lend itself well to publication, and such accounts were not only limited in their coverage but did not adequately reflect the spontaneous and interactive atmosphere that Alcott sought to cultivate.

Although it was increasingly difficult to earn a sufficient income through the conversations, throughout this period of the late 1840s and early 1850s Bronson Alcott focused on little else. He was convinced that his calling was in conversation, not in lecturing or publishing, and he broadened his vision beyond his New England friends and embarked on a conversational tour in the fall of 1853, first to upstate New York and then out to Ohio. In the late 1850s he traveled further west, through connections in Midwest cities such as St. Louis, where he achieved some fame and press coverage. As Alcott avoided controversial reform issues in favor of grand philosophical inquiries, his conversations also failed to attract those individuals whose energies were turned to reform and the politics of the Civil War, so that by the 1860s he began to have to look elsewhere for regular income and took a job with the CONCORD, MASSACHUSETTS, school district. After the Civil War Bronson Alcott

also began to pursue writing in earnest and published several books of personal reflections and philosophy, including the very popular CONCORD DAYS (1872), and TABLE-TALK (1877), itself an attempt to parlay the informal conversational style into print, among others.

Distinguished from his Transcendentalist colleagues such as Emerson, Fuller, and Henry David THOREAU, however, Bronson Alcott would leave no lasting literary legacy and would be remembered by friends and colleagues as a converser, not a great writer. The view of Alcott that would prevail was captured by James Russell LOWELL in his caricatures of New England literary figures, A FABLE FOR CRITICS. Lowell wrote of Alcott: "While he talks he is great, but goes out like a taper, if you shut him up closely with pen, ink, and paper." Throughout his life, Alcott retained his commitment to the development of ideas and of individual minds through the intimate atmosphere of conversation on spiritual and philosophical themes, culminating in the format of his CONCORD SCHOOL OF PHILOSOPHY AND LITERATURE in the 1870s and 1880s.

Bibliography

Dahlstrand, Frederick. *Amos Bronson Alcott: An Intellectual Biography.* East Brunswick, N.J.: Associated University Presses, 1982.

Conversations for women
Margaret Fuller
(1839–1844)

The Conversations were a series of Boston meetings for women organized and led by Transcendentalist Margaret FULLER between 1839 and 1844. As an attendee at the earlier primarily male TRANSCENDENTAL CLUB meetings, Fuller saw the need for a forum for "thinking women" to discuss issues such as EDUCATION, VOCATION, and reform through the Transcendentalist's preferred method of communication: CONVERSATION. She sought a way to combine her own intellectual interests with her talent for teaching and envisioned a role for herself in encouraging women to use their minds and talents beyond the expectations of a traditional female education. In first proposing the meetings in a letter to friend Sophia RIPLEY, Fuller presented the overarching theme of the Conversations as engaging women in questions that no one had asked of them before: "What were we born to do? How shall we do it?"

The first Conversation was held at noontime on November 6, 1839, at the Boston home and bookstore of Elizabeth Palmer PEABODY, the site of almost all subsequent meetings. The date and time were chosen to coincide with Ralph Waldo EMERSON's evening lecture series so that visitors from out-of-town would be able to attend both events. This gathering opened a 13-week series, a schedule that would be repeated each winter and spring for the next five years, with approximately 15 to 20 women attending on any given date. The meetings were exclusively for women except for a single mixed-sex season in 1841 which Emerson, George RIPLEY, and other male Transcendentalists attended. Fuller always charged a fee for attendance and thus the Conversations provided her with what she hoped other women could achieve: a vocation that utilized her talents and education, and an independent income.

Fuller chose the weekly themes, presented a lecture, and presided over the gathering by asking questions as well as suggesting topics for participants to write about on their own time between meetings. On one occasion she asked members to write about the intellectual differences between men and women. From this assignment Sophia Ripley wrote an essay that was then published in the *DIAL*, the movement's periodical edited at that time by Fuller. In "WOMAN," Ripley presented a Transcendentalist view on the conflict between the idea of "woman's sphere" and women's development as individuals. By publishing the essay in the *Dial*, Fuller highlighted the role that her Conversations had in sponsoring women as writers and thinkers within the Transcendentalist movement.

The Conversations brought women together to discuss literary and philosophical ideas as well as social reform and were, in fact, one of many associations that reform-minded Bostonians attended. Participants ranged from prominent activists and writers such as abolitionist Lydia Maria CHILD and educational reformer Elizabeth Palmer Peabody, to younger attendees, such as Ednah Dow CHENEY

and Caroline DALL, who would emerge as leaders of the WOMEN'S RIGHTS movement. By opening up a space for women to discuss issues of particular concern to their sex, Fuller brought feminism into "conversation" with the Transcendentalist movement and provided an intellectual starting point for the next generation of female thinkers.

Bibliography

Capper, Charles. "Margaret Fuller as Cultural Reformer: The Conversations in Boston," *American Quarterly* 39:4 (winter 1987): 509–528.

Conversations with Children on the Gospels
Amos Bronson Alcott
(1836)

Several of the Transcendentalists' most important early works were published in the signal year, 1836, including Amos Bronson ALCOTT's *Conversations with Children on the Gospels*. The book actually was the published notes of his assistant and colleague, Elizabeth Palmer PEABODY, from their work at Alcott's TEMPLE SCHOOL in Boston. *Conversations* included an introduction by Alcott entitled "The Doctrine and Discipline of Human Culture," a brief pamphlet he had published separately several months later and the clearest statement of his Transcendentalism and his perspective on teaching young children. Alcott's introduction, and the exposure of his methods of working with children in the classroom, subjected him to intense criticism and ultimately forced him to close down his school.

The controversy over Alcott's teaching methods revolved around his religious beliefs and his contribution to the Transcendentalist criticism of UNITARIANISM. Unlike his colleagues Ralph Waldo EMERSON, Convers FRANCIS, or George RIPLEY, all of whom also published foundational and controversial works in 1836, Bronson Alcott had no formal religious training or ties and was therefore more forthright in his criticisms of the established church and the promotion of his own ideas. His ideas fit within the emerging Transcendentalist focus on the divinity within individual human beings, and the ability to discern universal and spiritual truths outside of religious organizations or texts. Alcott's concerns were not theological or literary, as were those of his Transcendentalist friends at this time, but were primarily pedagogical in nature. His studies of human nature led him to focus on the innocence and untapped power of childhood as the closest route to uncovering divine truths. The interest in childhood for these reasons was a characteristic of the early 19th-century philosophy of ROMANTICISM he shared with many poets and writers of the era, such as William BLAKE. Alcott argued that it was the role of the teacher (and of parents) not to fill children with random and unrelated information, but, through CONVERSATION, to draw out the innate wonder and truths within children and aid them in their self-development, in reaching their full potential; or, as Alcott phrased it, the "glorious unfolding of the Godlike in man."

This was the goal of Transcendentalism in general, but for Alcott it would become the goal of early childhood education. Following Alcott's theoretical basis in his introduction, "The Doctrine and Discipline of Human Culture," Peabody provided transcripts of his theory in practice in a school of actual children. Public controversy surrounded not so much Alcott's methods but the nature of the subjects he encouraged his pupils to discuss. In pursuing self-development Alcott encouraged children to question rather than accept standard teaching about biblical subjects such as the Creation and the life of Jesus, applying them to their own lives rather than accepting them as God's final word. Alcott was accused in the press of blasphemy and of encouraging such among young children. Besides the spiritual problems, Alcott also engaged the students in what Elizabeth Peabody referred to as potentially scandalous "unveiled physiological references" having to do with topics such as birth and circumcision. Such references were, in fact, veiled and subtle, but Peabody was correct in assuming that the public, not to mention parents of Alcott's students, would not approve of such subject matter as suitable for discussion with children. Although several of his Transcendentalist colleagues publicly supported Alcott's efforts—among them James Freeman CLARKE, Ralph Waldo Emerson, and George Ripley—too

many parents pulled their children from his Temple School until he was finally forced to close it in 1838.

Although most critics focused on the subjects of Alcott's conversations with children, others may have resented Alcott's attempt to explicate scriptures and revise theology when he himself was not a member of the clergy. The idea that theological education was not necessary in order to have a personal spiritual relationship to God was one that Emerson, for one, also promoted, and that would soon be explored further by others among the Transcendentalists and ultimately set them apart philosophically and socially from the Unitarian ministerial elite. At the time, however, Alcott was more interested in being an innovative educational reformer and was disappointed and upset at the inability of his fellow humans to recognize the benefits of his services for their children. Bronson Alcott's future ventures into education and reform would continue to provoke controversy and criticism.

Bibliography

Dahlstrand, Frederick. *Amos Bronson Alcott: An Intellectual Biography.* East Brunswick, N.J.: Associated University Presses, 1982.

Conway, Moncure Daniel
(1832–1907)

Moncure Conway was a Unitarian minister, abolitionist, biographer and historian of the early Transcendentalist movement, and editor of the later Cincinnati-based Transcendentalist-inspired journal, THE DIAL (1860). Born in Virginia, Conway's spiritual and social journey took him from Methodism to QUAKERISM to UNITARIANISM and from a slaveholding family to radical ABOLITIONISM. In 1853 he entered HARVARD DIVINITY SCHOOL and subsequently befriended many of the Boston and Concord, Massachusetts, Transcendentalists including Ralph Waldo EMERSON, whose writings had influenced the young Conway toward an interest in Unitarianism (Conway even named his second child Emerson), and Theodore PARKER, who became an important mentor for Conway in both Transcendentalism and abolitionism. Conway spent time in Concord with

Emerson and Henry David THOREAU, solidifying his own philosophical and political beliefs.

After graduation Conway served as minister of a Washington, D.C., area Unitarian church and, in 1856, after being dismissed from his pulpit because of his antislavery views, moved to Cincinnati as pastor of the First Congregational Church. Conway was one of the western promoters of HEGELIANISM in the mid-19th century, and in 1860 he founded and edited *The Dial*, a monthly magazine inspired by the earlier 1840s Boston DIAL, edited by Margaret FULLER and, later, Emerson. Conway's Cincinnati *Dial* was an important tool in the spread of Transcendentalist ideas and writers to the western states. He invited his New England friends to speak at his church and both Emerson and Parker had lecture dates in Cincinnati. Another Transcendentalist friend and fellow radical Unitarian minister, William Henry FURNESS, performed Conway's wedding to Ellen Dana in 1858. His religious views ultimately became too radical even for his liberal Cincinnati audience, and his preaching against Christ's miracles as well as the Resurrection forced the congregation to split. Conway eventually left the Unitarian church and Cincinnati.

In addition to his philosophical and religious writings in *The Dial*, Conway worked effortlessly as an abolitionist and published several books and essays demanding the end of American slavery. At various times he served as a coeditor and columnist for the newspaper *The Commonwealth*, where he published writings by Amos Bronson ALCOTT, Louisa May ALCOTT, and Lydia Maria CHILD, among others. During the Civil War he traveled to England to promote his abolitionist views, and he ultimately accepted a position at a radical London church, South Place Chapel, where he remained for several decades. After the Civil War he continued to promote radical views on race relations, including support of interracial marriage and black suffrage. As a reformer he also publicly urged for WOMEN'S RIGHTS, sex education, and birth control. He also continued his pursuit of liberal theology with the publication of works on Eastern religious traditions and free religion, an idea that attracted many of the Transcendentalists in the later decades of the 19th century.

Moncure Conway retained his own philosophical and historical connection to Transcendentalism by promoting Emerson and other authors in England. He assisted Charles Eliot NORTON in collecting letters for the 1883 *Correspondence of Thomas Carlyle and Ralph Waldo Emerson*. His own contributions to memorializing the Transcendentalists were his biographies *Thomas Carlyle* (1881), *Emerson at Home and Abroad* (1882), *Life of Nathaniel Hawthorne* (1890), and his anecdotal accounts of his friendships in his 1904 autobiography.

Bibliography

d'Entremont, John. *Southern Emancipator: Moncure Conway, The American Years, 1832–1865*. New York: Oxford University Press, 1987.

Gohdes, Clarence L. F. *The Periodicals of American Transcendentalism*. Durham, N.C.: Duke University Press, 1931.

Cooke, George Willis
(1848–1923)

Unitarian minister George Willis Cooke was a younger or next-generation Transcendentalist whose writings provided important documentation and biographical work on the earlier movement. Cooke moved to CONCORD, MASSACHUSETTS, in 1880 where he met an elderly Ralph Waldo EMERSON and participated as an occasional lecturer at Amos Bronson ALCOTT's CONCORD SCHOOL OF PHILOSOPHY AND LITERATURE. As a self-described "disciple" of Emerson, Cooke wrote several works on the Concord philosopher including an early biography, *Ralph Waldo Emerson: His Life, Writings, and Philosophy* (1881), and a reference work, the *Bibliography of Ralph Waldo Emerson* (1908). At the suggestion of social reformer and Transcendentalist Ednah Dow CHENEY he also published an important biography of Transcendentalist music critic John Sullivan DWIGHT. Research for this book led to a later edition of Dwight's collected letters.

Cooke's other work included *The Poets of Transcendentalism* (1903), an anthology that was crucial in gathering together pieces published in scattered literary journals since the 1830s. In this book Cooke provided one of the first systematic definitions of Transcendentalist poetry as a genre. Its defining features, according to Cooke, stemmed from its emphasis on the individual poet's personal inspiration and relationship to art and to the universe or the "OVER-SOUL." Additionally, Cooke saw Transcendentalist poetry as inherently positive in tone due to beliefs in immortality through the Over-Soul and the natural moral goodness in humankind. In 1902 Cooke published a history of the Boston-based DIAL to accompany a 1902 reprint of the magazine for 20th-century readers—a history which is still useful to scholars and students today.

Cooke's other area of interest for study and writing was UNITARIANISM, which related to the historical themes and ideals of Transcendentalism he so admired, and liberal religion more broadly. As in his work on Transcendentalism, he emphasized the importance of Unitarianism on American thought and culture. In his seminal work, *Unitarianism in America: A History of Its Origin and Development* (1902), he even identified such famous non-Unitarians as Benjamin Franklin and Abraham Lincoln as important indicators of the Unitarian tradition because they shared and "accepted its principles of individual freedom, the rational interpretation of religion, and the necessity of bringing religious beliefs into harmony with modern science and philosophy." Despite his prolific literary production, Cooke's primary profession was as an ordained Unitarian minister who, throughout the period of his writings on literary subjects, held pastoral positions in both the Midwest and, later, in Massachusetts. In 1878 he helped found and edit a Chicago-based liberal religious journal, *Unity.* In 1891 Cooke became the pastor of a church in Lexington, Massachusetts, where Emerson himself had preached during his days as a Unitarian minister in the 1830s.

In all of his work George Cooke characterized Transcendentalism as a distinctly American phenomenon that had its historical roots less in European thought and philosophy and more in the intellectual heritage of New England PURITANISM, an argument that would form the basis of later 20th-century assessments of the movement. Cooke took an interest in other religious and literary themes and figures as well, but by preserving the record of historical Transcendentalism of the 19th century, he was instrumental in making it accessible and influential for 20th-century scholars. Cooke never called himself a Transcendentalist, consider-

ing himself a member of a more rational-scientific generation, although in all of his work he valued and promoted the same core ideals of humanism, social reform, and individual moral accountability that characterized the Transcendentalist thought of his subjects, in particular his hero, Emerson.

In April 1923 Cooke married fellow Unitarian minister Mary Lydia Leggett, who was, in fact, the first female graduate of HARVARD DIVINITY SCHOOL; unfortunately, George Cooke died unexpectedly just one week after their wedding.

Cousin, Victor
(1782–1867)

The Transcendentalists were interested in contemporary French philosopher Victor Cousin for his IDEALISM and his eclecticism of thought. It was through Cousin that many American readers were first introduced to the ideas of German philosophers such as Immanuel KANT and Georg Hegel (*see* HEGELIANISM). Among the Transcendentalists, George RIPLEY was most interested in Cousin's ideas. Ripley provided an 1838 English translation of Cousin in his *Philosopical Miscellanies from the French of Cousin, Jouffroy, and Benjamin Constant,* the first volume in his edited series, SPECIMENS OF FOREIGN STANDARD LITERATURE. While many of the subsequent volumes in *Specimens* were dedicated to the German idealists, Ripley opened the series with attention to French philosophy. Ripley's entire project was grounded in the idea of eclecticism, of gathering ideas and inspiration from a variety of sources, a method that Victor Cousin represented and promoted. Ripley praised Cousin for easily putting "the general reader in possession of the most valuable results of a profound philosophy," which was, in many ways, Ripley's own goal with his series of translations. Ralph Waldo EMERSON was introduced to NEOPLATONISM via Cousin, but eventually dismissed even Cousin's eclectism as too "mechanical" a method to yield any higher truths.

Bibliography
Leighton, Walter L. *French Philosophers and New England Transcendentalism.* New York: Greenwood Press, 1968.

Cranch, Christopher Pearse
(1813–1892)

Unitarian minister, poet, writer, musician, and artist Christopher Pearse Cranch experimented with a variety of VOCATIONS in an effort to pursue artistic work in line with his Transcendentalist philosophical and religious beliefs. His most important legacy is as one of the few significant Transcendentalist poets, along with Ralph Waldo EMERSON and Jones VERY. Cranch attended HARVARD DIVINITY SCHOOL with John Sullivan DWIGHT and Theodore PARKER and, after graduation, briefly served as a Unitarian minister before pursuing other literary and artistic interests. He traveled to several western cities working as a substitute guest preacher and settled briefly in Louisville, Kentucky. Between 1837 and 1839 he occasionally edited the Transcendentalist-inspired journal, the WESTERN MESSENGER, with colleague James Freeman CLARKE.

In the *Western Messenger*, Christopher Cranch published not only his own poetry but presented the ideas of New England Transcendentalists, particularly the writings and lectures of Ralph Waldo Emerson, to readers in western states. He praised Emerson's emphasis on independent thought and optimism in lectures such as "THE AMERICAN SCHOLAR" (1837) and the DIVINITY SCHOOL ADDRESS (1838) and defended Emerson against critics even though he did not necessarily share the radical conclusions drawn in those controversial speeches.

In the 1830s Cranch began to caricature his Transcendentalist colleagues with drawings representing lines or excerpts from their writings. For example, Cranch is responsible for the now famous "transparent eyeball" cartoon representing Emerson as a giant eyeball on thin legs, walking about seeing all around him; Cranch's original drawing was accompanied by text he transcribed from Emerson's NATURE (1836): "Standing on the bare ground,—my head bathed by the blithe air, & uplifted into infinite space,—all mean egotism vanishes. I become a transparent Eyeball." His many other drawings and caricatures not only of Emerson but of Theodore Parker and of the radical-versus-conservative debates of Unitarians George RIPLEY and Andrews NORTON, were private and uncollected until the mid-20th century and evidence from Cranch's own correspondence with friends indicates that they were meant as lighthearted engagements with their subjects, not criticisms.

Returning from the west to Boston Cranch continued to preach and became more closely involved with the Transcendentalist community, attending meetings of the TRANSCENDENTAL CLUB and publishing several poems in the movement's literary journal, the DIAL. He also published in THE HARBINGER, the paper for the BROOK FARM utopian community. Cranch never joined Brook Farm as a member, but he regularly visited and entertained the residents with musician friend John Sullivan Dwight. In 1844 he collected together many of his poems previously published in various periodicals as the volume, *Poems*, which he dedicated to Emerson. By this time, however, Cranch had married and was attempting to make a living as a landscape artist in New York. To this end, he traveled to Europe to study art. The Cranches traveled with friend George William CURTIS and met Margaret FULLER in Italy, where their first two children were born. Cranch had difficulty making a living as a painter and, during a second trip to Europe in the 1850s and '60s, he met and befriended James Russell LOWELL, who helped him edit and publish more of his poetry and translations. During this time Cranch also put his talents toward illustrating and writing his own children's stories, and he found modest success with his fantastical stories, *The Last of the Huggermuggers* (1856) and a sequel, *Kobboltzo* (1857), but it was as a poet that he was most consistent and prolific.

After the Civil War, Cranch returned to Massachusetts and rekindled friendships with many of his Transcendentalist colleagues. He joined the RADICAL CLUB and continued to publish, most significantly a translation of Virgil's *Aeneid* (1872) and further collections of poetry, including his largest work, THE BIRD AND THE BELL (1875), which included poems dedicated to friends such as George Curtis and Octavius Brooks FROTHINGHAM. He also continued to publish poems in periodicals such as the ATLANTIC MONTHLY and DWIGHT'S JOURNAL OF MUSIC, edited by his longtime friend, John Sullivan Dwight.

Contemporaries and historians have often characterized Cranch as an amateur who lacked the focus to pursue one strong vocational path, or, worse, a Transcendentalist of "wasted talents." However, his body of written work as well as his efforts in pursuing an artistic career in the face of dilemmas of art versus action, of inspiration versus duty, place him alongside many of his Transcendentalist colleagues who struggled with these same issues in their own lives.

Bibliography

Miller, DeWolfe F. *Christopher Pearse Cranch and His Caricatures of New England Transcendentalism.* Cambridge, Mass.: Harvard University Press, 1951.

Norko, Julie. "Christopher Cranch's Struggle with the Muses," *Studies in the American Renaissance* (1992): 209–227.

Curtis, George William
(1824–1892)

As a young man, writer, reformer, and lecturer George William Curtis sought out an education among Boston's literary and reform circles first by briefly residing at George RIPLEY's Transcendentalist-inspired utopian community BROOK FARM and, thereafter, moving to CONCORD, MASSACHUSETTS, to be under the intellectual influence of Ralph Waldo EMERSON. Curtis did not identify as a Transcendentalist himself, but he admired the philosophies and morals of leading figures, especially Emerson and Henry David THOREAU. He eventually even helped Thoreau build his cabin at WALDEN POND. Within this circle he formed other lasting friendships as well with men such as Christopher Pearse CRANCH and Theodore PARKER. Curtis submitted a poem, "A Song of Death," to the primary Transcendentalist literary journal, the *DIAL.* He was honored to earn his hero's praise and acceptance when Emerson selected the poem for publication in the July 1843 issue.

Curtis's association with Boston Transcendentalists was short-lived, however. He contributed no other pieces to the *Dial,* although his connections to the Transcendentalists and to Brook Farm led to the publication of more of his work in THE HARBINGER and THE PRESENT. After 18 months he finally left Brook Farm out of frustration with their utopian socialist reform philosophy. He wrote to his friend John Sullivan DWIGHT that, unlike the Brook Farmers, he believed "our evils are entirely individual, not social." This belief did not limit his desire for social reform, however, as George Curtis went on to become an ardent proponent of ABOLITIONISM and one of the most popular reform lecturers of his day. His Transcendentalist friendships had inspired his approach to social reform, as is evident in his 1856 speech entitled, "The Duty of the American Scholar to Politics and the Times." In this address he explicitly invoked Emerson's idea of "THE AMERICAN SCHOLAR" (the title of Emerson's 1837 address) by arguing for a more direct connection between individual conscience and social action.

Curtis ultimately had a long career as a journalist and newspaper editor. After serving as editor at PUTNAM'S MONTHLY MAGAZINE in the 1850s, he moved into a long career as a columnist and editor for *Harper's Monthly* and, later, *Harper's Weekly.* During this period he published a novel as well as essays on leading American authors such as Emerson and Nathaniel HAWTHORNE. His full-length biographies of *Emerson* and *Hawthorne* were both published posthumously, in 1896. During his lifetime, George William Curtis was one of the best-known and most highly regarded American journalists and authors.

Bibliography

Milne, Gordon. *George William Curtis and the Genteel Tradition.* Bloomington: Indiana University Press, 1956.

Myerson, Joel. *The New England Transcendentalists and the Dial: A History of the Magazine and Its Contributors.* London and Toronto: Associated University Presses, 1980.

D

Dall, Caroline Wells Healey
(1822–1912)

Caroline Dall was a lecturer, reformer, editor, preacher, and writer who, inspired early in life by Margaret FULLER, wrote widely on feminist issues from a Transcendentalist perspective. Dall's early introduction to the Transcendentalist community included attending a lecture by Ralph Waldo EMERSON at the Society for the Diffusion of Useful Knowledge in 1835 and a Theodore PARKER sermon in 1841. These activities coincided with her attendance in March 1841 at Margaret Fuller's CONVERSATIONS FOR WOMEN. Dall had been invited to this spring session by another key figure in the Transcendentalist community, and regular host of the Conversations, Elizabeth Palmer PEABODY. Dall believed that Peabody "would dearly love to make a transcendentalist of me—if she could," and, although she initially felt she had too much "common sense" to join the Transcendentalist ranks, her attraction to and immersion in this community of ideas set her life in that direction. Dall was attracted to the "new thought" and understood Transcendentalist philosophy to encourage intellectual freedom and expression of one's own opinions. She dedicated much of her writing career to accounts and analyses of Margaret Fuller's influence as a feminist and to issues related to the ideas and participants of the wider Transcendentalist movement. She described herself as "a Transcendentalist of the old New England sort" and became one of its first historians.

Caroline Dall began writing essays in the late 1840s on topics such as religion and reform and published consistently through the end of the century. Her essays and short fiction were regularly published in the popular and religious press, including periodicals such as ATLANTIC MONTHLY and the CHRISTIAN EXAMINER. In addition to her essays and book-length works, she also printed collections of her lectures on WOMEN'S RIGHTS issues—suffrage, prostitution, women's health, labor—was a prolific journal-keeper and corresponded with a wide range of 19th-century reformers, authors, and intellectuals.

In 1853 Caroline Dall began contributing to and coediting THE UNA, the women's rights newspaper founded by fellow activist Paulina Wright DAVIS. In 1855 Dall took over as the paper's primary editor for the last months of its existence. Her essays in *The Una* reflected Dall's belief that, while political gains such as the vote were an important goal for the women's movement, the everyday aspects of women's social subordination must first be challenged and changed. As a Transcendentalist, she called upon women to educate themselves for the VOCATION or calling that best suited their characters and interests, and then to work together to dismantle any obstacles to the pursuit of that calling—reform of self followed by reform of society.

Throughout the 1850s and 1860s, Dall contributed to the women's rights cause whether through biographies of great women in HISTORICAL PICTURES RETOUCHED (1860) or tackling controversial issues such as wage equality and the relationship between women's EDUCATION and the right to vote as discussed in THE COLLEGE, THE MARKET, AND THE COURT (1867). In this text Dall again applied the Transcendentalist philosophy of self-culture to the issue of women's rights by arguing that women cannot pursue self-culture and self-knowledge without access to education; that the goal of education is to prepare oneself for a vocation; that all employments should therefore be open to women so that they have the full freedom to follow their true calling; and, finally, that if women are employed and participating in economic society, they are entitled to be represented through the vote.

Caroline Dall was one of the most prolific later-century Transcendentalists, and after the Civil War she began to memorialize the movement by writing its history—first with MARGARET AND HER FRIENDS (1895), her first-person account of the 1841 season of Margaret Fuller's conversations for women, and then with her overview of the entire movement, TRANSCENDENTALISM IN NEW ENGLAND (1897). In her history she covered a range of topics and figures related to the movement, but her text differed significantly from the other major 19th-century history of the movement, Octavius Brooks FROTHINGHAM's TRANSCENDENTALISM IN NEW ENGLAND: A HISTORY (1876), in that Dall emphasized the central role of women. In Dall's words, the Transcendentalist movement began "with a woman's life and work" (referring to colonial religious dissenter Anne HUTCHINSON) and ended "with a woman's work and death" (a reference to Margaret Fuller). Dall believed that Transcendentalism was compatible with, in fact inspired, the women's rights movement. She explicitly argued that "the characteristics of the Transcendental movement were shown in the temper of its agitation for the rights of woman and the enlargement of her duties."

Caroline Dall had longed to be a Unitarian minister, the vocation of many of her male Transcendentalist colleagues, but the Unitarians did not ordain women during her career. Still, she considered herself to be a theologian and did serve as a guest preacher in the pulpits of various friends. In theological matters, she looked to her own minister Cyrus BARTOL and friend Theodore Parker as her mentors and, after the Civil War, published

several works dealing with religious themes. One of her pieces, *Nazareth,* was included, much to Dall's delight, along with writings by William Ellery CHANNING, Ralph Waldo Emerson, and Theodore Parker in a collection of "Memorable Sermons" published by the AMERICAN UNITARIAN ASSOCIATION.

Bibliography

Deese, Helen. "Transcendentalism from the Margins: The Experience of Caroline Healey Dall." In *Transient and Permanent: The Transcendentalist Movement and Its Contexts,* eds. Charles Capper and Conrad Edick Wright. Boston: Massachusetts Historical Society, 1999, 527–547.

Wayne, Tiffany K. *Woman Thinking: Feminism and Transcendentalism in Nineteenth-Century America.* Lanham, Md.: Lexington Books, 2005.

Dana, Charles Anderson
(1819–1897)

Teacher and journalist Charles Anderson Dana was Sophia RIPLEY's cousin and a founding member of and shareholder in George RIPLEY's utopian community at BROOK FARM. He had been introduced to Ripley's ideas, as well as those of Ralph Waldo EMERSON, while a student at Harvard. He was unable to graduate due to financial hardship and his failing eyesight, so when Ripley organized Brook Farm in the fall of 1841, Dana took the opportunity to leave school and join the community. Dana was one of the few people to remain at Brook Farm for the entire six years of its existence (1841–47), teaching languages and serving in various executive positions throughout the period, as well as meeting his wife there. He was an active American proponent of the philosophy of FOURIERISM and published essays on the subject, as well as his own poetry, in the Transcendentalist journal, the DIAL, and in Brook Farm's periodical, THE HARBINGER.

After the demise of Brook Farm Charles Dana did some German translation work, including translating part of *The Autobiography of Goethe* (1847) and a collection of children's stories. He ultimately pursued journalism in both Boston and New York, working with Horace GREELEY at the *NEW YORK TRIBUNE* as a foreign correspondent and later literary editor. Between 1858 and 1863 he collaborated again with George Ripley, this time in a literary effort with the publication of a comprehensive multivolume project which proved to be a great commercial and financial success for the two men: the *NEW AMERICAN CYCLOPEDIA: A Popular Dictionary of General Knowledge.* After a professional break with Horace Greeley and a political stint during the Civil War, Charles Dana returned to journalism and an opportunity to purchase the New York *Sun* newspaper, which he ran as his own independent forum from 1868 until 1897.

Bibliography

Steele, Janet E. *The Sun Shines for All: Journalism and Ideology in the Life of Charles A. Dana.* New York: Syracuse University Press, 1993.

Darwin, Charles
(1809–1882)

As philosophers and intellectuals, the Transcendentalists were interested in and grappled with British naturalist and scientist Charles Darwin's theories of natural selection and evolution. Because of the widespread influence of Darwinism on all aspects of 19th-century intellectual and cultural life, contemporaries were particularly interested in comparing the relationship between Transcendentalist philosophy and Darwinism. For example, Thomas Wentworth HIGGINSON addressed similarities between Darwin and Ralph Waldo EMERSON at an 1883 meeting of the FREE RELIGIOUS ASSOCIATION. Likewise, connections between and the compatibility of IDEALISM and the scientific materialism of Darwin (among others) was at the center of debates at Amos Bronson ALCOTT's CONCORD SCHOOL OF PHILOSOPHY AND LITERATURE. Alcott, for one, remained skeptical that the two could be reconciled, but Octavius Brooks FROTHINGHAM later concluded that, for him, the speculation of Transcendentalism had been superseded by science, in particular Darwinism, and he rejected the idea that social Darwinism did away with traditional (that is, religious) guidelines for morality, as critics feared.

Of all the Transcendentalists, fellow naturalist Henry David THOREAU, in particular, thoroughly read and commented upon Darwin's scientific work in his own journals. Darwin provided Thoreau with a model of the scientist-naturalist as observer and, in particular, an observer of plant life. In his "Voyage of a Naturalist Around the World," Darwin noted that "a traveler should be a botanist," and, indeed, Thoreau became the preeminent 19th-century traveler-botanist. Thoreau did not travel the world, like Darwin, but sought to travel in-depth into his local surroundings. He noted after reading of Darwin's method, "There would be this advantage in traveling in your own country even your own neighborhood, that you would be so thoroughly prepared to understand what you saw."

Henry David Thoreau eagerly read Darwin's *On the Origin of Species* as soon as it became available in early 1860. Darwin's theory of natural selection, or survival of the fittest, caused great moral controversy in Victorian society, although Darwin's examples of the benevolence along with the cruelties of nature fit with Thoreau's own observations and perspective. Thoreau also found Darwin's theories of adaptability compatible with his own work as he had discovered and shared his findings in his 1860 lecture, "THE SUCCESSION OF FOREST TREES." Thoreau found Darwinism appealing not so much because it introduced him to entirely new ideas, but because it supported Thoreau's own research and ideas about the interrelatedness of plant species that he had been developing independently at the same time that Darwin was writing.

Most of the Transcendentalists, including Ralph Waldo Emerson, accepted the science of Darwin's work, although another prominent naturalist within their circle, Harvard professor Louis AGASSIZ openly opposed Darwinism. It is not entirely surprising that Emerson and Thoreau, in particular, were open to accepting Darwin's ideas since Transcendentalism had already cast aside fixed doctrinal explanations for understanding the natural world and, more specifically, were invested in the idea of nature as a living, constantly changing force within the universe. Still, even Thoreau's relationship with Darwinism was limited by Transcendentalism's emphasis on humans and nature as evolving not only physically but, more important, spiritually toward perfection. The Transcendentalists ultimately were not committed to advancing scientific knowledge, specifically, but in understanding the spiritual or symbolic relationship between nature and humanity.

Bibliography

Walls, Laura Dassow. *Seeing New Worlds: Henry David Thoreau and Nineteenth-Century Natural Science.* Madison: University of Wisconsin Press, 1995.

White, Michael, and John Gribbin. *Darwin: A Life in Science.* New York: Dutton, 1995.

Davis, Paulina Kellogg Wright
(1813–1876)

Feminist writer and activist Paulina Wright Davis was the founder in 1852 of the first WOMEN'S RIGHTS periodical, THE UNA, which she coedited with Transcendentalist Caroline DALL. Davis was born in New York and spent most of her adult life in Providence, Rhode Island, where her work as a lecturer, writer, and editor brought her into contact with the extended reform communities of Boston and New York City. She was active in the health and women's rights movements as well as in ABOLITIONISM. Her published work consisted mainly of articles for *The Una,* for the post–Civil War woman's rights journal *Revolution,* and lectures and articles on health reform, which appeared in the *Water-Cure Journal.* In her essays in *The Una*—such as "Woman as Physically Considered" (February 1853) and "The Intellect of Woman" (March and April 1853)—Davis, inspired by Margaret FULLER, combined her feminist goal of "harmony between the sexes" with her particular interest in explaining the physical and intellectual differences between men and women. She was also responsible for promoting the ideas of FOURIERISM in the pages of *The Una* with editorials and letters on various utopian communities.

Davis was extremely active in the organized women's movement, serving in various positions from president of the first National Woman's Rights convention held in Worcester, Massachusetts, in 1850, to cofounding the New England Woman Suf-

frage Association in 1868, to serving as president of a local Rhode Island suffrage association. Her prominent role at conventions led to the publication of her 20-year anniversary *History of the National Woman's Rights Movement* (1870). Davis was one of the originators who put out a "Call" for a national woman's rights meeting in 1850 to be held in Worcester, Massachusetts. Davis's "Call" received more signatures of support from Massachusetts than from any other state, including the signatures of several people affiliated with Transcendentalism: Amos Bronson ALCOTT, William Henry CHANNING, Ralph Waldo EMERSON, and Thomas Wentworth HIGGINSON. Henry Channing, in fact, served as one of the vice presidents of the Convention.

The influence of Transcendentalism on her own thought—in particular through her friendship with Caroline Dall—as well as the predominance of Massachusetts reformers and the coinciding of the convention with Margaret Fuller's untimely death just three months prior, led Davis, as president of the convention, to speculate on Fuller's inspiration to those in attendance and on what her role might have been in the movement: "One great disappointment fell upon us. Margaret Fuller, toward whom many eyes were turned as the future leader in this movement, was not with us. The 'hungry, ravening sea,' had swallowed her up, and we were left to mourn her guiding hand—her royal presence. To her, I, at least, had hoped to confide the leadership of this movement. It can never be known if she would have accepted this leadership: the desire had been expressed to her by letter; but be that as it may, she was, and still is, a leader of thought—a position far more desirable than of numbers."

Bibliography

Wayne, Tiffany K. *Woman Thinking: Feminism and Transcendentalism in Nineteenth-Century America.* Lanham, Md.: Lexington Books, 2005.

"Days"
Ralph Waldo Emerson
(1857)

Conceived and composed in his journals years earlier, Ralph Waldo EMERSON's poem, "Days," was published in the first issue of the ATLANTIC MONTHLY in November 1857 and appeared 10 years later in his 1867 collection MAY-DAY AND OTHER PIECES. "Days" remains one of Emerson's most cited poems, and some critics say his best by far, in part due to the memorable phrases within the first lines: "Daughters of Time, the hypocritic Days, / Muffled and dumb like barefoot dervishes, / And marching single in an endless file." Here Emerson launches a melancholy visualization on the passing of days and seasons and eventually years. Emerson emphasized that each day was a gift to humankind and with each day came a challenge to make the most of it: "To each they offer gifts after his will, / Bread, kingdoms, stars, and sky that holds them all," but long before he published this poem Emerson regularly lamented his own feeling of inadequacy in fulfilling the promise of each new day.

As early as 1826 he had recorded a verse in his journal full of similar regrets ("My days roll by me like a train of dreams / A host of joyless undistinguished forms"); and again, in 1827 ("My days run onward like the weaver's beam"); sentiments he would more fully contemplate in this published poem several decades later. In "Days" Emerson moved this thought beyond just general melancholy about the human condition into a reflection on the wider role of the poet-philosopher in capturing the meaning of those days. Many of Emerson's writings, both prose and verse, addressed the role of the poet, and here he again related the question of VOCATION and of his own personal calling and experience as the poet. In this case, even the poet is unable to transcend the passage of time and can only sit idly by and watch his best laid plans, his "morning wishes," be taken over by the Day: "I, in my pleached garden, watched the pomp, / Forgot my morning wishes, hastily / Took a few herbs and apples, and the Day / Turned and departed silent. I, too late, / Under her solemn fillet saw the scorn." The day is over again, and here the poet can offer no resolution or advice, but the reader can only identify with this very human dilemma.

The poem takes as its theme the familiar perspective of the Transcendentalist Self, but this time Emerson focuses on the limitations of the individual self in the face of the forward march of time. "Days" thus stands out from other more optimistic Transcendentalist writings. Emerson would explore the boundaries of human will and power in other writings, such as in the essay "FATE."

"The Dead"
Jones Very
(1839)

Transcendentalist poet Jones VERY composed the poem "The Dead" sometime between September and December 1838 during a period in which he experienced an intense mystical experience that resulted in Very spending one month in an asylum. Although Very wrote some poetry both before and after what scholars refer to as his "ecstatic period" of late 1838 and 1840, poems such as "The Dead" and "THE NEW BIRTH" were among his most original and spiritually urgent writings and brought him to the attention of Ralph Waldo EMERSON and other Transcendentalists as one of their era's most significant poets. The 14-line poem, "The Dead," was published in Very's hometown paper, the *Salem Observer,* on January 5, 1839, and was subsequently included in the 1839 collection of *Essays and Poems: By Jones Very,* edited by Emerson.

Jones Very's intense experience in the fall of 1838 was not just a religious conversion but a period during which he was completely and temporarily overcome both emotionally and physically by an intense feeling of despair and renewal. Very's intensity shocked and concerned many of his friends and colleagues and is viewed by scholars as a possible manifestation of some level of mental illness. Very turned his energies during this period to writing, and while the poem "The New Birth" marked the beginning of Very's new spiritual outlook, "The Dead" moves to condemning humanity's general lack of spiritual reverence and meaning. "The Dead" moves in the poem actually refers to the living dead of humanity, going about their daily lives, in a state of spiritual emptiness: "I see them crowd on crowd they walk the earth / Dry, leafless trees no Autumn wind laid bare." Very warns that a life without God is not worth living, and he contrasts "the living God" with the dead-like state of humanity: "Their hearts the living God have ceased to know." He points out the hypocrisy of the spiritually dead mourning the physically dead: "And in their show of life more dead they live / Than those that to the earth with many tears they give."

Bibliography

Deese, Helen, ed. *Jones Very: The Complete Poems.* Athens: University of Georgia Press, 1993.

Dial
(Boston, 1840–1844)

The Boston-based *Dial* was the only journal published by the New England Transcendentalists as a group and thus stands as one of the most significant records of the movement's early development as a distinct literary voice. The first number was issued in July 1840, and the journal appeared quarterly for nearly the next four years with a peak of about 300 subscribers. The idea for the journal arose out of the TRANSCENDENTAL CLUB of the late 1830s as members realized the need for a forum for disseminating their ideas into the larger public. A brief discussion at the September meeting of the Transcendental Club led to the creation of the *Dial*. The first issue had an introductory notice that described the venture as "one cheerful rational voice amidst the din of mourners and polemics."

The prospect of a new journal was also appealing to the Transcendentalists involved as an alternative to the popular periodical literature of the day, the object of much criticism among the group of Boston intellectuals. The *Dial* was modeled instead on periodicals such as the English *Monthly Magazine*, which many New England Transcendentalists subscribed to and read, and the Cincinnati-based *WESTERN MESSENGER*, begun in 1835 and edited at various times by Transcendentalists James Freeman CLARKE and Christopher Pearse CRANCH, among others. In fact, the *Western Messenger* had already published many of the Unitarian and Transcendentalist writers who would later appear in the *Dial*.

George RIPLEY was to be the editor of the new journal. He solicited the first contributors and

agreed to be the business manager but determined he was too busy with other projects, in particular the editing of his series, SPECIMENS OF FOREIGN STANDARD LITERATURE, and the founding in 1841 of the utopian community at BROOK FARM, to continue to take on the work of a regular journal. Margaret FULLER agreed to serve as general editor and combined her work for the journal with her CONVERSATIONS FOR WOMEN that had just begun in the fall of 1839. She postponed the planned first issue from April to July 1840 and ultimately served as editor for the first two years of its publication. Ralph Waldo EMERSON took over as editor for the final two years, although Henry David THOREAU also stepped in to oversee one issue in April 1843.

Some of the most important Transcendentalist philosophical essays first appeared in print in the *Dial*, such as Fuller's "THE GREAT LAWSUIT. Man versus Men. Woman versus Women" (July 1843), which was later revised and expanded into book form as WOMAN IN THE NINETEENTH CENTURY (1845), and poems and essay fragments by Thoreau that were also eventually incorporated into other published works. The *Dial* also proved to be perhaps the only forum for early Transcendentalist poets such as Fuller, Ellen Sturgis HOOPER, Caroline Sturgis TAPPAN, and Jones VERY. Its pages were not limited solely to literary pieces, however, and included reports and insights on various Transcendentalist reform projects such as Elizabeth Palmer PEABODY's essay "Plan of the West Roxbury Community" (January 1842), an overview of the proposed utopian experiment at BROOK FARM, as well as some of Emerson's most important pieces, such as "MAN THE REFORMER" (April 1841) and "THE TRANSCENDENTALIST" (January 1842). Amos Bronson ALCOTT's primary contribution to the *Dial* was in his series of "ORPHIC SAYINGS" in the early issues. These collections of random mystical thoughts were caricatured in the regular press as absurdly unintelligible and became, unfortunately, the critic's representation of the movement as a whole.

In assessing the audience for the *Dial*, Emerson determined that its "writers were its chief readers." While this perspective does highlight the importance of the journal as a central site of literary gathering for those involved in the movement, readers and contributors to the *Dial* were drawn from a broader cross section of 19th-century literary and cultural life beyond just the self-identified Transcendentalists. Due to a dwindling subscriber list and the exhaustion and exasperation of Emerson in his editorial and writing duties, the *Dial* ended its publication with the April 1844 issue. By then the "new thought" that was Transcendentalism, as well as the Transcendentalists themselves, had spread into and influenced a broader geographical and literary realm, thanks in part to the brief existence of the *Dial.*

Bibliography

Myerson, Joel. *The New England Transcendentalists and the Dial: A History of the Magazine and Its Contributors.* London and Toronto: Associated University Presses, 1980.

The Dial
(Cincinnati, 1860)

The Dial of Cincinnati was one of the last published journals of the Transcendentalist movement. The paper was founded by HARVARD DIVINITY SCHOOL graduate Moncure CONWAY in 1860 and lasted through just 12 monthly issues. *The Dial* was founded as "a monthly magazine for literature, philosophy and religion" and took its name and inspiration directly from the earlier DIAL Transcendentalist journal of 1840s Boston. Along with the WESTERN MESSENGER, the St. Louis Philosophical Society, and significant western lecture tours of figures such as Amos Bronson ALCOTT and Ralph Waldo EMERSON, the Cincinnati *Dial* had an important role in the spread of Transcendentalism beyond New England and into midwestern states such as Ohio, Missouri, and Kentucky. An early review of *The Dial* noted the geographical importance and timeliness of the Cincinnati journal since, the reviewer felt, "Until now Boston has been the only place in the land where the inalienable right to think what you please has been practiced and upheld." The Ohio cities of Cincinnati and Columbus, in particular, had significant populations of German immigrants and thus were centers of intellectual interest in many of the

German philosophers central to American Transcendentalist thought, such as August and Friedrich SCHLEGEL, Johann Wolfgang von GOETHE, Johann SCHILLER, and, later, Georg Hegel (*see* HEGELIANISM).

Before founding the paper, Moncure Conway was already at the center of religious and philosophical conversations in Ohio, as a pastor and as a writer for numerous periodicals. The establishment of *The Dial* allowed him to put his thoughts and ideas promoting Transcendentalism together in one public forum. Conway alone authored 30 articles during the year of the paper's existence. Second to editor Conway, the most regular contributor was scientific writer Marx Lazarus, an associationist who had lived at BROOK FARM and a reformer who shared Conway's passion for ABOLITIONISM.

The Dial featured many book reviews as well as articles on UNITARIANISM and a tribute series to Theodore PARKER, who died that same year, 1860. Ralph Waldo Emerson was asked to contribute an essay on Parker but declined, but *The Dial* regularly reprinted poetry by Emerson as well as his essay on "Domestic Life" (October 1860) and a lecture, "The Story of West-Indian Emancipation" published in the November and December 1860 issues. Other reprints or original articles by Boston Transcendentalists were published, such as excerpts from Bronson Alcott's "ORPHIC SAYINGS," Caroline DALL on Margaret FULLER and WOMEN'S RIGHTS, Octavius Brooks FROTHINGHAM on Christianity, William FURNESS on Schiller, and the poetry of Franklin Benjamin SANBORN. With entries by and about names such as these, the Cincinnati *Dial* also serves as an important first history of the movement at this particular time, illustrating the important legacy of these writers to a younger generation that included Conway.

Conway blamed the short-lived nature of his journal on the intrusion of Civil War, although he planned to switch to a quarterly rather than monthly publication to keep the journal alive after the war. This never happened, however, and in 1862 Conway moved from Cincinnati back to CONCORD, MASSACHUSETTS, where he focused on his social reform interests and instead took over editorship of an abolitionist paper promoting immediate emancipation, *The Commonwealth.*

Bibliography

Gohdes, Clarence L. F. *The Periodicals of American Transcendentalism.* Durham, N.C.: Duke University Press, 1931.

Dickinson, Emily
(1830–1886)

Poet Emily Dickinson was a generation younger than most Transcendentalists, but the ideas of Ralph Waldo EMERSON, in particular, were among her strongest literary influences, and she had professional connections with the movement through her editor Thomas Wentworth HIGGINSON. Dickinson read many of Emerson's works from 1850 onward, and his model, perhaps more than any other, served to define poetry and the role of the poet during her formative years. She made explicit references to his writings in her letters, and Emerson traveled to her hometown of Amherst to lecture, but there is no evidence that she ever heard him speak or that the two met. Researchers have noted, however, that in addition to several books by Emerson, her personal library also included works by Margaret FULLER, Henry David THOREAU and Theodore PARKER.

That she absorbed Transcendentalist ideas directly into her poetic style and themes is most evident in the imagery of circles, orbs, and "circumference" that bears striking similarity to Emerson's "CIRCLES." An 1878 poem by Dickinson that appeared anonymously in print was misattributed to Emerson, evidence of how much their styles appeared similar to 19th-century readers. Her emphasis on looking inward, to one's own soul and consciousness, also echoed Transcendentalist themes, as did her ROMANTICISM, her appreciation of nature, and her self-reliant individualism. As a 19th-century New England poet Dickinson was immersed in the same literary and cultural milieu as the Transcendentalists—in her own words, she was "seeing New Englandly." Even though she did not explicitly identify with the movement, her writing emerged from the same contexts as that of her contemporaries Nathaniel HAWTHORNE, Walt WHITMAN, and Emerson himself, and her unique talents place her among these figures as one of the century's major authors.

Bibliography

Tufariello, Catherine. "'The Remembering Wine': Emerson's Influence on Whitman and Dickinson." In *The Cambridge Companion to Ralph Waldo Emerson,* eds. Joel Porte and Saundra Morris. New York: Cambridge University Press, 1999, 162–191.

A Discourse of Matters Pertaining to Religion
Theodore Parker
(1842)

In the wake of controversy over his South Boston Sermon, published as A DISCOURSE ON THE TRANSIENT AND PERMANENT IN CHRISTIANITY, Unitarian minister Theodore PARKER embarked on a lecture series in the fall of 1841 and quickly gathered his lectures together as A *Discourse of Matters Pertaining to Religion.* In 1841 Parker's South Boston Sermon had led many of his fellow Unitarian ministers to distance themselves from him, to ban him from speaking to the congregations, and to some even suggesting Parker be removed from the ministry. Parker maintained a loyal following, however, and was able to establish an alternative congregation. He took the lecture podium as a way to widen his audience and expand his influence beyond the church, however. His five courses on "Religion" drew large crowds and prompted Parker to collect and expand his talks into the nearly 500-page volume, A *Discourse of Matters Pertaining to Religion,* published in the spring of 1842.

A *Discourse of Matters Pertaining to Religion* is perhaps Parker's clearest statement of his Transcendentalist views and earned him even further controversy within the Unitarian church. Parker's book was the first in English to examine the ideas of August Comte, and he provided explication of other European thinkers, including the works of German biblical criticism then engaging the Transcendentalists in their critique of orthodox Christianity. Parker expected to have a career as a minister, however, and he remained, even after his ostracism from mainstream UNITARIANISM, one of the few Christian Transcendentalists to work within organized religion. Parker's critique sprung, like the other Transcendentalists, from the church's tendency to emphasize the rituals of what they termed "historical Christianity" rather than the spiritual depths of a prophetic religion. Rather than rejecting Christianity in favor of a reliance on divine revelation within the individual, Parker maintained that Christians should nurture their innate "religious sentiment" and are right in looking to God as the source of divine truths. One of the controversies of his work surrounded his treatment of the historical figure of Jesus. Parker, again like other Transcendentalists, held up Jesus as a moral model, but as a human model, subject to faults just as anyone else. Parker preached that Jesus taught about the true meaning of religion, but that he had no divine authority or miraculous powers, an argument made by other Transcendentalists, in what had come to be termed the "MIRACLES CONTROVERSY" of the 1830s.

Critics and readers expected controversy from Parker again, after the South Boston sermon the year before, and in *A Discourse of Matters* Parker again rejected the authority of the scriptures and reiterated the belief, shared by Ralph Waldo EMERSON, that the rituals of historical Christianity lacked spiritual meaning for most participants, and he now more emphatically questioned evidence for the miracles of the New Testament. As for organized religion, Parker rejected the idea of one true church and emphasized that no one church, not even Unitarianism, offered the only true route to salvation. Salvation and knowledge came from the individual soul, not solely from the Bible, and not from any church. The difference between Parker and his colleagues such as Ralph Waldo Emerson was that Emerson had left the church and organized religion behind entirely, whereas Parker continued to speak from his position as a minister and continued to pursue his career as a preacher. This was the source of the controversy for many of his Unitarian colleagues. As one fellow minister told Parker upon the publication of *A Discourse of Matters Pertaining to Religion*, "it augurs ill for a man, *within* the Church, to break its windows; we should more naturally expect, that they should be broken from *without*."

Bibliography

Grodzins, Dean. *American Heretic: Theodore Parker and Transcendentalism.* Chapel Hill: University of North Carolina Press, 2002.

A Discourse on the Latest Form of Infidelity
Andrews Norton
(1839)

Prominent Unitarian Andrews NORTON was perhaps Ralph Waldo EMERSON's most vocal and public critic in the 1830s, and Norton's *A Discourse on the Latest Form of Infidelity* was his book-length response to the controversy surrounding Emerson's 1838 DIVINITY SCHOOL ADDRESS. In August 1838, just one month after Emerson's address, Norton published his critique of "The New School in Literature and Religion" in the Boston *Daily Advertiser,* labeling Emerson the leader of an "insurrection of folly" poised to undo Christianity itself. Norton continued to speak against what he termed the "depraving literature and noxious speculations" of Transcendentalism, and in the following summer he published the fullest development of his critique as *A Discourse on the Latest Form of Infidelity.*

As a professor at Harvard and leading Unitarian theologian, Norton was in a position to decide what future ministers should be taught as well as the public position of UNITARIANISM, and Transcendentalism potentially threatened both. Norton was, in some ways, most outraged that Emerson had been given the floor at all at HARVARD DIVINITY SCHOOL, with the newest graduating class of ministers as his audience for what turned out to be an attack on organized religion and on Christianity itself. Emerson's address signaled his own personal final break from organized religion in that he denounced the very foundations of Christianity as a revealed religion. This, to Norton, was the final straw in a controversy within Unitarianism over the divinity of Christ and the role of the scriptures that had begun a few years earlier with the debate carried out between Norton and George RIPLEY over the MIRACLES CONTROVERSY. Now Emerson called upon the new class of ministers to proceed in their careers by following their hearts rather than the scriptures and to find the divine in man, in themselves. For Norton, it was blasphemous for Emerson to make such statements that amounted to nothing less than bold atheism, but it was especially outrageous that he had been asked to speak and had now spoken against religion at the very heart of Unitarianism's training ground at Harvard.

Norton, like other conservative Unitarians, was concerned with the Transcendentalist dismissal of the nature of Jesus' miracles. Transcendentalists like Emerson and Ripley proposed that the miracles could be explained as natural phenomena and were not supernatural proof of the divinity of Christ. For Norton, however, this view was unacceptable and certainly incompatible with any version of Christianity—in other words, it was blasphemy. Norton wrote that "Nothing is left that can be called Christianity, if its miraculous character be denied." Norton argued not only against the findings the Transcendentalism but against its methods as well. He rejected the idea of the intuition or of a "controlling power of intellect" as the determinant of human spirituality and favored instead a solid basis of theological and other truths that could be empirically known. For Norton, Christianity could not be subjectively known because of its basis in historical facts and in revealed scripture: "There can be no intuition, no direct perception of the truths of Christianity."

Norton not only attacked the Transcendentalists but also addressed the dangerous foreign or European influence of Transcendentalism on American letters. Aware of the influence of German philosophy and biblical criticism on the emergence of Transcendentalism in the 1830s, Norton attributed the Transcendentalist's "ill-understood notions" to their reading of "some of the worst German speculatists." For example, Norton singled out Friedrich SCHLEIERMACHER, whose theological studies influenced George Ripley's ideas in particular, as a "German pantheist."

Norton's *Discourse on the Latest Form of Infidelity* only forced adherents of Transcendentalism to respond further, and the public debate on the miracles and on historical Christianity continued. In October 1839 George Ripley published a response in the form of an article entitled "The Latest Form of Infidelity Examined," and Norton responded once again in turn with his "Remarks" on Ripley's review. With Emerson refusing to engage Norton directly and publicly, Ripley responded again as the strongest voice of the Transcendentalist side, until Theodore PARKER also took up the question and Norton's challenges in print before Norton finally

ended the cycle in 1840. After 1840 Norton focused his career on his own biblical scholarship, and he gave up sparring with the Transcendentalists after his final work on the subject, *The Evidences of the Genuineness of the Gospels,* was published in 1844.

Bibliography

Habich, Robert D. "Emerson's Reluctant Foe: Andrews Norton and the Transcendentalist Controversy," *NEQ* 65 (June 1992): 208–237.

Packer, Barbara. "The Transcendentalists." In *The Cambridge History of American Literature,* vol. 2: *1820–1865,* ed. Sacvan Bercovitch. New York: Cambridge University Press, 1995, 329–607.

A Discourse on the Transient and Permanent in Christianity
Theodore Parker
(1842)

Also referred to as the "South Boston Sermon" or the "South Boston ordination," Theodore PARKER's May 1841 address, published the following year as *A Discourse on the Transient and Permanent in Christianity,* was one of the most controversial moments in the early Transcendentalist movement and a turning point in Parker's career as a Unitarian minister. The sermon was prepared for the ordination of another minister and delivered on May 19, 1841, at Hawes Place Church in South Boston. Parker graduated from HARVARD DIVINITY SCHOOL in 1836 and was involved in various Transcendentalist clubs and activities. He had attended Ralph Waldo EMERSON's controversial DIVINITY SCHOOL ADDRESS in 1838 and was moved by Emerson's speech to write privately in his journal that "so beautiful, so just, so true, & terribly sublime was his picture of the fault of the church in its present position" that he resolved himself to "this week" begin writing his own "sermons, on the state of the church & the duties of these times." Still, Parker had some disagreements with Emerson over what he called some "philosophical untruths" in the address. He was uncomfortable with what he understood as Emerson's assertion that Man is not simply *like* God, but *is* God. Parker thus did not entirely affiliate himself with the most radical defenders of Emerson in the wake of the Divinity School Address controversy. Parker remained a committed Christian interested in religious reform. He would be shocked, therefore, to have his own position and credibility as a Christian challenged just a few years later.

Emerging from the Unitarian-Transcendentalist debates of the 1830s, Parker sought to sift through the points made by both sides on the questions of historical Christianity, the divinity of Christ, and the MIRACLES CONTROVERSY. In the South Boston Sermon or "Discourse," he spoke on the changes Christianity has undergone over time (the "transient"), balanced with attention to what constants might be identified (the "permanent"). He praised the life and example and words of the historical Jesus as the "permanent" or unchanging aspect of Christianity. However, like Emerson, who had left the ministry over the issue of whether to continue offering communion or THE LORD'S SUPPER, Parker argued that doctrines and rituals do change, and that external forms do not represent what it means to be a true Christian. On this point Parker presented the Transcendentalist view that there is not evidence that New Testament accounts, including the miracles of Christ, were divinely inspired or actually happened: "It has been assumed at the outset, with no shadow of a sufficient reason, that all of its authors were infallibly inspired, so that they could commit no error of doctrine or fact." Here he urged his listeners to consider that denial of the miracles did not deny Christianity, but in fact that Christianity was more than, and did not depend on, the miracles. He proposed that even if it were proved "that the gospels were a sheer fabrication, that Jesus had never lived," he challenged his listeners to comprehend that "Christianity would still stand firm," an assertion that conservative orthodox Christians found inconceivable.

In his sermon Theodore Parker sought to encourage the radicals to retain the historical Jesus as a moral and spiritual teacher of the eternal truths they were seeking, while he assured the conservatives that Christianity would in fact be strengthened by embracing the "permanent" truths but acknowledging and letting go of the "transient" beliefs and rituals. Although the sermon was delivered without incident, Parker biographer Dean Grodzins notes "within hours of the service, rumor spread that Parker had preached a strange, possibly infidel, perhaps even blasphemous sermon." Indeed, the South Boston Sermon set off a heated controversy to rival Emerson's Divinity School Address given three years earlier. Articles in the religious press condemned Parker, and the situation was made worse by the fact that his critics often misrepresented and distorted his statements in their own "summaries." This prompted Parker to publish *A Discourse on the Transient and Permanent in Christianity,* a 48-page version of the sermon, so that people could read it and decide for themselves. The criticisms forced Parker to publicly defend his religious views and, in the process, he became a sought-after lecturer beyond the pulpit. Still, he suffered professional persecution as a minister. He was no longer invited to exchange pulpits with other Unitarian ministers and serve as a guest preacher, his writings were rejected by the religious press (as were those of his defenders), he was no longer invited to speak at Harvard, and many of his friendships with more orthodox Christians suffered.

Theodore Parker did not, however, retreat from Unitarianism as colleagues such as Emerson or George Ripley had done but instead became the leading Transcendentalist spokesperson within the ministry. Shut out of many Unitarian circles and churches, his Boston friends and supporters embraced him by founding a pulpit especially for him at the Twenty-Eighth Congregational Society of Boston, where he preached for the next 15 years. *A Discourse on the Transient and Permanent in Christianity* is considered one of the most important defining sermons in the history of Unitarianism.

Bibliography

Grodzins, Dean. *American Heretic: Theodore Parker and Transcendentalism.* Chapel Hill: University of North Carolina Press, 2002.

Discourses on the Philosophy of Religion
George Ripley
(1836)

With the 1836 publication of his first book, *Discourses on the Philosophy of Religion Addressed to*

Doubters Who Wish to Believe, Unitarian minister George RIPLEY entered into a fierce public debate with prominent minister and Harvard professor Andrews NORTON that would ultimately characterize the split between UNITARIANISM and the "new school" of Transcendentalism. Ripley and his former HARVARD DIVINITY SCHOOL professor Norton had been exchanging a series of responses to each other in the form of articles in the religious press. Their debate centered upon the question of Christ's divinity and whether the miracles performed by Christ as described in the gospels were natural or supernatural phenomena, a discussion that became known as the MIRACLES CONTROVERSY within Unitarianism. Their responses and opinions on the issue grew from articles and reviews of each other's works to book-length explications of their positions, as in Ripley's *Discourses,* a collection of six essays and sermons on the topic.

The Unitarians were in the midst of a theological crisis, attempting to retain the name of Christian while increasingly questioning the ability to reconcile the supernatural aspects of Christianity with rational thought. Ripley took issue with attempts by some Unitarians to "prove" the miracles and to understand them as natural phenomena, manipulated by God, but scientifically knowable by humans if only we had the right methods and tools. Ripley did not argue that the miracles were supernatural or that they were proof of anything, including Christ's divinity. What he did put forth was the suggestion that even some natural phenomena are not "knowable" by scientific means alone. He rejected the idea of attempting to understand the significance of a religious text in scientific terms and argued instead that "true Believers" (as opposed to the "Doubters" of his title) relied not on their senses alone but were open to the intangible and subjective nature of spiritual truths and experiences as revealed through individual intuition. In fact, the external world of experience and nature was not objective at all but was always understood through individual subjective means: "It is from the cast and disposition of our souls that external nature derives its hues and conformations . . . the perception of beauty is in the soul." Like Ralph Waldo EMERSON, Ripley rejected the "cold, logical" approach to reli-

gion: "We would have these relations not only recognized, but felt. . . . We do not wish them to be treated as subjects of cold, logical discussion . . . but to be held up in living colors, as everlasting realities, in which every human being has a deep and vital interest."

Ripley's ideas were influenced by works of German theology, biblical criticism, and ROMANTICISM that many of the Transcendentalists were reading at this time. In particular, Ripley was an enthusiastic student of Friedrich SCHLEIERMACHER, and his arguments were grounded in, but expand upon, Schleiermacher's more mystical and inward-focused version of Christianity. Ripley's *Discourse* was in fact a full-length exploration of his Transcendentalist ideas and his contribution to the explosion of philosophical and religious works produced by the movement in 1836, a year that also saw the publication of Ralph Waldo Emerson's more secular NATURE, Orestes BROWNSON's *NEW VIEWS OF CHRISTIANITY, SOCIETY, AND THE CHURCH,* and Convers FRANCIS's *Christianity as a Purely Internal Principle,* all of which advanced a similar perspective on the intuitive and personal, rather than external or scriptural, experience of religion. Andrews Norton responded once again not only to George Ripley's ideas but to the personal charge that he was one of the "Doubters" within Christianity.

Bibliography
Crowe, Charles. *George Ripley: Transcendentalist and Utopian Socialist.* Athens: University of Georgia Press, 1967.

The Dispersion of Seeds   *See* "THE SUCCESSION OF FOREST TREES."

Divinity School Address
Ralph Waldo Emerson
(1838)

Transcendentalism arose in the United States in the 1830s as a crisis of faith, a reaction against orthodox Christianity, and nothing signals that break more clearly than Ralph Waldo EMERSON's address to the graduating class of HARVARD DIVINITY SCHOOL on July 15, 1838. The six young men who made up the senior class that year chose alumnus Emerson as their speaker and, by so doing, spurred a major controversy within Boston UNITARIANISM. In the wake of the controversy, the speech that most scholars still refer to as the Divinity School Address was quickly published as *An Address Delivered Before the Senior Class in Divinity College, Cambridge* (1838).

In his address Emerson questioned many of the foundations of traditional Christianity, arguing that rituals such as THE LORD'S SUPPER, or communion, were stripped of meaning in the way they were blindly followed in most churches, including Unitarian churches. Emerson argued that rituals and traditions remove people from the true source of spiritual strength rather than drawing them closer, as intended. He reminded his listeners that religion was best experienced by attention to the everyday, the appreciation of nature and of humanity. Emerson thus shifted the focus of religion, of Christianity in particular, from man's subordinate position under a benevolent God and a divine Christ, to the "sovereignty" of man's "inward nature" in urging the students, who were all future ministers, "to go alone . . . to be a divine *man.*" Emerson invited his listeners to perceive religion not as an institution or set of texts to be studied but as a living, subjectively experienced, "indwelling Supreme Spirit." He urged them to "Dare to love God without mediator or veil," thus calling into question their very training and purpose as ministers. The "Supreme Spirit" was articulated as Emerson's idea of the "OVER-SOUL," the primary force of the universe—a further secularization of the Unitarian's unified God—that is, the idea of a universal soul made up of God, humans, and nature together. Jesus Christ, in this formulation, exists primarily as a historical figure, a moral teacher rather than the ultimate presence of the divine on Earth.

The controversy within Boston's Unitarian community between more conservative ministers and those who had begun to espouse radical views such as Emerson's had already begun in the years leading up to his Divinity School Address. Emerson had resigned from a regular pastor position six years earlier, in 1832 over the issue of the Lord's Supper, although he continued to appear periodically as a guest preacher in friends' congregations. Additionally, 1836 had been a significant year of public criticism of followers of the "new thought" of Transcendentalism by their more conservative Unitarian colleagues; first, in the debates known as the MIRACLES CONTROVERSY between George RIPLEY and Andrews NORTON and, second, in the critical response by Norton and others to the publication of Emerson's NATURE. Thus the Transcendentalist controversy was well under way and the young men at Harvard specifically invited Emerson as their speaker knowing his views were radical and controversial.

Given the very public discussion of his ideas in these earlier debates, Emerson more than anyone else was surprised at the degree of controversy sparked by his address, but the Divinity School Address differed from his earlier writings, for Emerson presented not just his views on nature or on the state of American letters (as in his "AMERICAN SCHOLAR" speech at Harvard the year before), but this time he struck at what he termed "historical Christianity." Worse, in speaking at Harvard he brought his ideas to the very source of Unitarianism orthodoxy, its training ground for the ministry, directly challenging not only abstract theological tenets but many of his former faculty and colleagues in attendance that day. Emerson was accused of blasphemy, heresy, and atheism in scathing essays and editorials in the religious press, but he refused to respond publicly. He wrote in his private journals about his shock at the number and nature of the attacks. The critics only helped him sharpen his beliefs, however, and his 1841 collection of *Essays*, which included his most famous, "SELF-RELIANCE," was in some ways his public response and reassertion of the need to think for oneself outside of social, historical, and religious institutions. As strong as his critics were, however, his defenders were equally strong. The public support of colleagues such as James Freeman CLARKE, George Ripley, and Theodore PARKER helped to define the Transcendentalists as a group outside of and beyond liberal Unitarianism.

The Divinity School Address was thus a very public controversy, but it was also a personal statement and turning point for Emerson as an individual. Although he had already left the ministry, the Divinity School Address signaled the final step in his own mind away from the influence of his teachers and mentors at Harvard and toward finalizing his own career shift from minister to public intellectual. Not only was it several decades before he spoke at Harvard again, but Emerson never again spoke or wrote as a Christian—instead freeing himself from organized religion of any kind and signaling the beginning of a Transcendentalist literary, philosophical, and spiritual movement with Emerson as its most enduring spokesperson.

"Double Triangle, Serpent and Rays"
Margaret Fuller
(1844)

Margaret FULLER is not often regarded as a significant Transcendentalist poet, but "Double Triangle, Serpent and Rays" is perhaps Fuller's most well-known poem and the most anthologized. The short 10-line poem, however, was not published during her lifetime and was written only in her private journal. The poem was composed during one of Fuller's most prolific periods as a writer, during the summer and fall of 1844. During these months between her work as editor of the Transcendentalist journal, the DIAL, and moving to New York to write for the *Tribune*, Fuller wrote more than 30 poems and completed the manuscript for her seminal work, WOMAN IN THE NINETEENTH CENTURY.

In this poem, as well as many others, Fuller addressed the theme of finding spiritual or personal, as well as social, harmony. In "Double Triangle, Serpent and Rays" she returned to the theme of androgyny, the harmonizing of the male and the female, which had emerged in her earlier *Dial* essay, "THE GREAT LAWSUIT. Man *versus* Men. Woman *versus* Women." (July 1843), in which she mused that "male and female represent the two sides of the great radical dualism. . . . Fluid hardens to solid, solid rushes to fluid. There is no wholly masculine man, no purely feminine woman." As part of this effort to imagine harmony between the sexes, the poem "Double Triangle, Serpent and Rays" provides an image of wholeness to be achieved through the bringing together of the masculine and feminine within any particular individual: "When the perfect two embrace, / Male & female, black & white, / Soul is justified in space, / Dark made fruitful by light, / And, centred in the diamond Sun, / Time & Eternity are one."

An image representing to this poem was printed as the frontispiece to Fuller's 1845 *Woman in the Nineteenth Century*, linking the vision of her poetry to the reform work she performed through her theoretical writings. The image is one of interlocking triangles ("double triangle") surrounded by an image of wholeness in the form of a serpent holding its tail ("patient serpent, circle round, / Till in death thy life is found"), with rays of light emanating from the central image ("serpent and rays"). The central image of harmonizing dual forces served not only as a reform vision of a harmonious society, however. The metaphor also had a psychological dimension as an effort for the individual, Fuller herself no doubt, to harmonize dual interests and feelings, to come to a completeness or wholeness within oneself.

As a prominent female intellectual, Fuller was at odds with her society—if people did not denigrate her as a woman, they characterized her as "masculine." She was highly and classically educated, with no clear VOCATION to correspond to her knowledge and talents. She was unmarried yet had few options as an independent female in 19th-century society. The duality or "double"-ness of male and female was embedded not only in every aspect of social life but in individual bodies and minds as well. This theme or insight would be addressed by Fuller again in another unpublished poem, "To the Face Seen in the Moon," in which she acknowledged in less mystical terms that "through the woman's smile looks the male eye."

Bibliography
Steele, Jeffrey. *Transfiguring America: Myth, Ideology, and Mourning in Margaret Fuller's Writing.* Columbia: University of Missouri Press, 2001.

Duyckinck, Evert
(1816–1878)

Though not a Transcendentalist himself, Evert Duyckinck was part of a New York literary scene of the same time period. As an editor, journalist, and critic, Duyckinck actively promoted the work of American authors and, in particular, many of the Transcendentalists during the 1840s. He was most directly connected, both personally and professionally, to Herman MELVILLE, but as an editor at Wiley and Putnam he helped create a 19th-century literary canon and chose several New England writers as part of the Library of American Books series: Nathaniel HAWTHORNE's MOSSES FROM AN OLD MANSE and Margaret FULLER's PAPERS ON LITERATURE AND ART (1846) appeared under the imprint. With his brother, George Duyckinck, he put together an important early anthology of American writers, the 1855 *Cyclopaedia of American Literature*, which recognized the place of Ralph Waldo EMERSON, Margaret Fuller, Henry David THOREAU, and others as important figures in this most prolific period of American literary history, dubbed by Duyckinck biographer Samuel OSGOOD as the "American Renaissance." Duyckinck also worked to promote American authors as professionals by fighting for international copyright laws so that writers could profit more from their work.

Bibliography
Greenspan, Ezra. "Evert Duyckinck and the History of Wiley and Putnam's Library of American Books, 1845–1847," *American Literature* 64 (December 1992): 677–693.

Dwight, John Sullivan
(1813–1893)

Transcendentalist writer, reformer, and critic John Sullivan Dwight was a graduate of HARVARD DIVINITY SCHOOL who served briefly as a Unitarian minister before giving up the pulpit to pursue literature and music criticism. Class poet Dwight had attended Harvard with Charles Timothy BROOKS and Samuel OSGOOD and, later as a Divinity student, befriended Transcendentalists Christopher

Pearse CRANCH, a fellow musician, and Theodore PARKER. He thus became immersed in the center of Transcendentalist activity in the late 1830s and early 1840s, participating in Bronson ALCOTT's CONVERSATIONS and attending meetings of the TRANSCENDENTAL CLUB and later the SATURDAY CLUB. As part of this literary circle, he edited a translated volume on the *Select Minor Poems, Translated from the German of Goethe and Schiller* (1839) for George RIPLEY's series, SPECIMENS OF FOREIGN STANDARD LITERATURE. For this volume Dwight collaborated with several other Transcendentalist translators such as Brooks, Cranch, Margaret FULLER, Frederic Henry HEDGE, and others.

Dwight became an ordained Unitarian minister in 1840 but served as a regular pastor for only a year. While he thus had little success as a preacher, he fared better as a writer and had three pieces, including a revision of one of his sermons entitled "The Religion of Beauty," published in the first issue (July 1840) of the Transcendentalist literary journal, the DIAL. He submitted another one of his sermons to the journal in 1841, "Ideals of Every-Day Life," which was published in two parts in the January and April 1841 issues. He did not contribute to any future *Dial* issues, partly because his work was being submitted to music magazines and because he had joined his friend George Ripley as a member of the utopian community at BROOK FARM. Dwight lived at Brook Farm for three years where he played music for the residents' social events and contributed regular essays on music criticism to the experiment's official paper, THE HARBINGER. He was also the EDUCATION director at the community and published his own treatise on the utopian social theory of FOURIERISM, which was then the guiding philosophy at BROOK FARM, entitled *A Lecture on Association, in its Connection with Education* (1844). Dwight had faith in the idea of association as the key to social and moral regeneration, and he was one of Brook Farm's and Charles Fourier's most active and vocal supporters.

In 1852 he founded his own DWIGHT'S JOURNAL OF MUSIC, which had a long-lived success until 1881 and remains the most complete source on the history of music and music appreciation in 19th-century New England. Dwight was not only editor but primary contributor for the journal, in which he reported on concerts and musical events, provided biographies of composers, reprinted or translated European music and art news pieces, wrote critical reviews of major European and American works and composers, and promoted music education, since formal music study was not a part of the regular college curriculum at this time. As a pianist he was most fond of Beethoven and studied and promoted the composer at a time when his work was little known in American circles. In his writings he argued for an understanding and reading of music as literature and emphasized that composers were just as important and equal to poets and writers in the Transcendentalist belief that, just like art or poetry, "genuine classic music" could reveal universal moral truths to aid the social progress of humanity. To this end Dwight advocated the incorporation of musical study into the educational system as well as efforts to make music more accessible through programs such as public concerts. His emphasis on "genuine classical music," however, as well as his support of institutions for education about music reveal the limitations of Dwight's perspective as a radical supporter of innovation in the arts. He had a specific idea or model against which contemporary music was judged, and that was the symphonies of Ludwig van Beethoven.

He served as librarian and president of the Harvard Musical Association, but living until the end of the century, Dwight saw music become more professionalized in ways that made his own Transcendentalist perspective and amateur contribution obsolete. On the positive side, however, he had contributed to the incorporation of music and music appreciation into literary culture in general. Recognizing both of these developments, Dwight thus ceased publication of his journal in 1881. John Sullivan Dwight died in 1893, having lived long enough to see some of his own goals for music achieved, such as the establishment of a music professorship at Harvard and the founding of organizations such as the Boston Symphony Orchestra.

Bibliography

Myerson, Joel. *The New England Transcendentalists and the Dial: A History of the Magazine and Its Contributors.* London and Toronto: Associated University Presses, 1980.

Saloman, Ora Frishberg. *Beethoven's Symphonies and J. S. Dwight: The Birth of American Music Criticism.* Boston: Northeastern University Press, 1995.

Dwight's Journal of Music
(1852–1881)

The field of music criticism did not exist in the United States before John Sullivan DWIGHT founded *Dwight's Journal of Music* in 1852. It was in the pages of another Transcendentalist journal, THE HARBINGER, the official paper of the BROOK FARM utopian experiment, that Dwight provided the most significant essays on music criticism before he launched his own journal with support from the Harvard Musical Association. The timing of his project coincided with the emergence of a more institutionalized presence of music in Boston. The Music Hall was built in 1852, the same year his journal appeared, and in 1867 both the Boston Conservatory of Music and the New England Conservatory of Music were founded. Throughout this time period, for nearly three decades, *Dwight's Journal of Music* was the authoritative print source for information and analysis of the music world.

The central feature of the journal was reviews of concerts, operas, and other musical events in major U.S. cities from Boston, Philadelphia, and New York to Chicago, St. Louis, and even San Francisco. Dwight covered individual shows as well as tours of orchestras and individual instrumentalists and singers, both American and European performers. The journal thus carefully documents the rise and spread of American musical performance during this era. He reported on new musical societies and institutions such as the New York Philharmonic, the Boston Symphony Orchestra, and the Handel and Haydn Society. There was also a weekly insert of sheet music so that subscribers could play on their own. Although Dwight was the editor and primary contributor to *Dwight's Journal of Music*, book reviews and essays were published by other writers as well, including several younger figures who went on to become prominent music historians and critics in their own right.

Bibliography

Sablosky, Irving. *What They Heard: Music in America, 1852–1881, from the Pages of "Dwight's Journal of Music."* London and Baton Rouge: Louisiana State University Press, 1986.

Saloman, Ora Frishberg. *Beethoven's Symphonies and J. S. Dwight: The Birth of American Music Criticism.* Boston: Northeastern University Press, 1995.

"Each and All"
Ralph Waldo Emerson
(1846)

The poem "Each and All" was first published in 1839 in the Transcendentalist magazine, the WEST-ERN MESSENGER, as "Each in All," and was included in Ralph Waldo EMERSON's first collection of POEMS, published in late 1846. "Each and All" is Emerson's clearest expression of his idea of the wholeness of the universe, the interconnectedness of all parts in interdependence with one another: "All are needed each by one; / Nothing is fair or good alone." Although this would emerge as a major theme in Transcendentalist thought, and especially in nature writing, the inspiration for the poem can be traced to Emerson's earlier journals, in which he recorded observations made while walking along the seashore: "I remember when I was a boy going upon the beach and being charmed with the colors and forms of the shells. I picked many up and put them in my pocket. When I got home I could find nothing that I gathered, nothing but some dry ugly mussel and snail shells." Here the child learns a lesson in the interrelatedness of all parts of nature, in appreciating the shells as part of a larger environment and realizing that the beauty of even one part is lost when it is not seen as part of the whole.

In the poem, "Each and All," the adult Emerson reflects on the sense of loss that came from imposing his will upon nature but the sense of wholeness in recognizing the lesson: "Beauty though my senses stole; / I yielded myself to the perfect whole." The mature Emerson now considers that appreciating "beauty" alone should not be the foundation of humanity's relationship to nature. His first response is to dismiss his childhood "games" in favor of the pursuit of "truth": "Then I said, 'I covet truth; / Beauty is unripe childhood's cheat; / I leave it behind with the games of youth.'" He then considers that beauty is the route to truth—that, again to return to his original revelation, to perceive beauty one must understand the whole of the natural phenomena, not just a part. The understanding of the whole, through the use of all the human senses, leads one to universal truths. The poem abounds with references not only to seeing nature but smelling it, hearing it, feeling it. And in this extrasensory experience of appreciating the natural world, the poet, too, becomes one with nature—becomes a part of the perfect whole. The seashore episode is thus transformed into a Transcendentalist epiphany in which a single, seemingly insignificant, individual experience of nature is transformed into a more universal revelation about the natural world and humanity's place within it.

Eckermann, Johann Peter
(1792–1854)

Johann Peter Eckermann introduced the American Transcendentalists to the writings of Johann Wolfgang von GOETHE, one of the most influential thinkers in the development of Transcendentalist thought. Ralph Waldo EMERSON had read Eckermann's memoir of Goethe in the original German and determined that it "helps one much in the study of Goethe," but it was Margaret FULLER who helped spread the interest in Goethe, and therefore in German philosophy in general, among the Transcendentalists through her translation of Eckermann's 1836 *Conversations with Goethe.* The translation, published in 1839, was Fuller's first book, and it established her as one of the premiere Goethe readers and scholars in the United States.

Many of the Transcendentalists had reservations about Goethe's moral character that they drew from information about his personal life as well as that of his literary characters, that interfered with their understanding and appreciating of his philosophy. It was through Johann Eckermann's treatment that Goethe was made more acceptable to American readers and through Margaret Fuller's translation, in particular, that she herself was able to work through the connections between Goethe's interest to her both philosophically and psychologically.

Bibliography

Zwarg, Christina. *Feminist Conversations: Fuller, Emerson, and the Play of Reading.* Ithaca, N.Y.: Cornell University Press, 1995.

education

As reformers and as philosophers, the Transcendentalists were particularly concerned with education, and the careers of many Transcendentalists revolved around publishing pedagogical works, establishing and teaching at experimental or alternative schools for children and adults, and involvement in the same broader educational reform projects that engaged their 19th-century antebellum contemporaries. Among the major figures associated with Transcendentalism, Amos Bronson ALCOTT, Margaret FULLER, and Elizabeth Palmer PEABODY were especially interested in the role of education, specifically self-education, which was the key to the development of the individual and, ultimately, the reform of social relations.

The first half of the 19th century was the era of widespread public education, vocational colleges, and colleges for women, as well the rise of educational reformers and theorists who debated both the content and purpose of formal education. Transcendentalists were concerned about all types of education but were especially focused on education that took place outside of formal institutions and curriculum, particularly the education of children and of adult women. Self-education or self-culture, the lifelong project of learning about oneself, was at the heart of the Transcendentalist project, and CONVERSATION was a particularly favored teaching method among Transcendentalists wishing to formally facilitate self-culture. Even before his introduction to Transcendentalist ideas and colleagues, Bronson Alcott was well read in the educational philosophy of European thinkers, such as Johann PESTALOZZI, and began his career as a teacher. In 1834 Alcott founded his TEMPLE SCHOOL for children in Boston where he employed a unique (and ultimately controversial) method of encouraging children to inner study and reflection by drawing them out through conversation or discussions. Alcott, like Peabody and other Transcendentalists influenced by European ROMANTICISM, believed that children need not be taught but in fact inherently possessed spiritual knowledge and truth. Alcott eventually gave up teaching as a career, but he remained interested in adult education and self-education throughout the century. He lectured widely and held conversations for adults on various topics and, in the post–Civil War period, established the CONCORD SCHOOL OF PHILOSOPHY AND LITERATURE.

The view of education as the drawing out of the individual was the goal of Margaret Fuller as well in offering her CONVERSATIONS FOR WOMEN in Boston between 1839 and 1844. Fuller was particularly interested in the development not of children but of adult female selfhood in a society that limited women's educational and vocational options. Although she had worked previously as a schoolteacher, Fuller's long-term "dreams and hopes as to the education of women" were the inspiration for the Conversations and she felt this project would help her, in turn, realize her own "true VOCATION." Transcendentalists were always concerned about education as a dual project—the education of their students or participants, but also teaching as a calling on their own path to self-culture. Fuller's Conversations were the best example of the implementation of a personal project of self-education through her efforts to educate and guide other women in pursuit of their own self-knowledge.

Fuller's Conversations were held in the bookstore of Elizabeth Palmer Peabody, who at that time already had a record as an educational reformer, had been a teacher herself of both adults and children, and had collaborated with Transcendentalist colleague Bronson Alcott in his experimental schools in the 1830s. Her interest in and support of the utopian experiment at BROOK FARM was based on her belief that it was through the community's school for children, the education of the next generation, that true social change would be made possible. While involved in various experimental and controversial projects as a Transcendentalist, after the Civil War Peabody did become more interested in the role of institutions and she became famous as the founder of the American kindergarten movement and, along with William Torrey HARRIS, then superintendent of schools in St. Louis, helped to establish the first public kindergarten schools in the United States.

Peabody was a follower of the pedagogical writings of German educator Friedrich Froebel and focused her attention and her hopes for social reform on the very youngest students. Peabody was intrigued by Froebel's system of activities for young children, the goal of which were to draw out and uncover spiritual and moral truths within the individual child. Froebel's idea for a "child garden" emphasized the importance of play for moral development and was organized around participation in games, songs, and finger plays. In introducing these methods into early childhood education, Peabody explicitly challenged the emphasis on early reading then governing early instruction. Furthermore, she promoted an alternative purpose for education that focused on individual development rather than on filling students with a set course of common knowledge or information. In 1873 Peabody cofounded a journal, *The Kindergarten Messenger*, with her sister, Mary Mann, wife of education reformer and first secretary of the Massachusetts State Board of Education, Horace MANN. Peabody differed from re-

formers like Mann and was more closely aligned with her Transcendentalist colleagues in the belief in self-culture and the idea that the role of any educational program was to draw out the inner moral sense, not merely teach morality, and to develop the individual to his or her fullest potential, not merely teach a proscribed set of facts.

Bibliography

Dahlstrand, Frederick. *Amos Bronson Alcott: An Intellectual Biography.* East Brunswick, N.J.: Associated University Presses, 1982.

Ronda, Bruce. *Elizabeth Palmer Peabody: A Reformer on Her Own Terms.* Cambridge, Mass.: Harvard University Press, 1999.

Ellis, Charles Mayo
(1811–1878)

Charles Mayo Ellis is considered by many to have been the author of the anonymously published *An Essay on Transcendentalism,* an 1842 pamphlet which provided a basic overview of contemporary Transcendentalist beliefs on a range of topics such as "Art," "Religion," and "Criticism." The essay was favorably reviewed in the January 1843 issue of the movement journal, the DIAL, which lends credence to its acceptance among the Transcendentalists as representative of their views.

Ellis grew up in West Roxbury on the site that would become home to the BROOK FARM utopian community begun by Transcendentalist George RIPLEY in 1841. Soon after the dissolution of Brook Farm, Ellis published *The History of Roxbury Town* (1847). Ellis was a Harvard graduate who worked as a lawyer and was active as a social reformer, particularly for ABOLITIONISM. He defended his minister and lifelong friend Theodore PARKER in the Anthony BURNS fugitive slave case when Parker was brought up on contempt of court charges.

"Emancipation in the British West Indies"
Ralph Waldo Emerson
(1844)

"An Address in Concord on 1st August, 1844, on the Anniversary of the Emancipation of the Negroes in the British West Indies" was Ralph Waldo EMER-SON's most well-known speech in support of ABOLI-TIONISM and the only one on the topic published during his lifetime. CONCORD, MASSACHUSETTS, had its share of antislavery activists by the mid-1840s, and local abolitionists invited Emerson to give a public address reflecting on the British cause, a speech that was subsequently published as a pamphlet in both the United States and Britain. The year 1844 and the delivery of this address were turning points in Emerson's perception of the deeper harm of slavery and in his public role in the antislavery movement.

Emerson was particularly focused now, especially, on the effect of slavery on the slaves themselves: "I am heart-sick when I read how they came there, and how they are kept there. Their case was left out of the mind and out of the heart of their brothers. The prizes of society, the trumpet of fame, the privileges of learning, of culture, or religion, the decencies and joys of marriage, honor, obedience, personal authority . . . these were for all, but not for them." He provides an overview of the horrific details of the slave's journey, including being kidnapped from Africa, the cruelties of "the slave-ship . . . in whose filthy hold he sat in irons, unable to lie down," and the lack of basic human rights accorded a slave, including the inability to marry, to own property, or to even have rights to their own children.

Emerson's purpose was not merely to detail the horrors of slavery, however, as his main focus was on the fact that emancipation had been achieved in the British case. He now looked to the West Indies example to warn of the problems of emancipation and freedom that threatened to occur in America as well, and he pointed out that while emancipation is a cause for celebration, "the habit of oppression was not destroyed by a law and a day of jubilee." Emerson acknowledged that legal changes alone would not change hearts and customs, and "it soon appeared in all the islands that the planters were disposed to use their old privileges, and overwork the apprentices . . . and to exert the same licentious despotism as before." Emerson determined that "the love of power" was a "bitter element" within human nature that could not be ignored or outlawed and he pointed out

that emancipation was not enough, as "Parliament was compelled to pass additional laws for the defense and security of the negro." This is a foreshadowing of exactly what would happen in the United States after the Civil War as the federal government would need to have a continued role in implementing and overseeing civil rights legislation for the protection of former slaves.

Beyond the social and moral question of providing protections for one class of people against another's "love of power," Emerson also considers the achievement of emancipation from the perspective of the extreme economic advantage of slavery. He finds emancipation not just a moral victory but a remarkable "transaction" within a country so dedicated to "commerce." Here, again, the purpose is to reflect on the similarities between the British and U.S. situations and to counter the argument that emancipation would economically ruin the South and the nation as a whole. He only hoped that American abolitionists, also dwelling in a nation of commercial interests, could pull off such a moral victory of right over wrong.

Emerson makes clear the political purpose of examining the British situation: "Whilst I have read of England, I have thought of New England." In considering New England, it is significant that Emerson turns to directly address the government, specifically quoting the Constitution, to express his outrage that the United States does not work as a unified whole, as slaves can be held in one state but would be declared free in another. With this address, Emerson moved from contemplation of slavery as a philosophical problem to a more direct expression of moral outrage and a call for political action, directly engaging the question of law and policy and the responsibility of the government. Emerson now praises the role of the abolitionist movement in bringing people together to resist and attempt to change the law and politics: "I will say farther that we are indebted mainly to this movement . . . for the popular discussion of every point of practical ethics." Emerson, known for his politics of individual conscience, now emphasizes the need for collectivity and declares that "what great masses of men wish done, will be done."

Having addressed the various legal, economic, and political issues surrounding slavery and emancipation, Emerson now turns his attention to the question of the rights of the individuals who find themselves the victims of this system and makes his strongest statement for recognizing the equality and human rights of this long despised race: "The First of August marks the entrance of a new element into modern politics, namely, the civilization of the negro. A man is added to the human family . . . he will survive and play his part." Emerson sees the rise of "the negro" to play a larger more positive part on the world stage as the inevitable progressive movement of human civilization: "Seen in masses, it cannot be disputed, there is progress in human society. There is a blessed necessity by which the interest of men is always driving them to the right; and, again, making all crime mean and ugly." Emerson ends his address optimistically assuring that "the sentiment of Right . . . because it is the voice of the universe, pronounces Freedom."

Emerson's speech was reported and praised in the abolitionist papers by some of his most radical antislavery colleagues, such as Nathaniel Peabody ROGERS in the *Herald of Freedom* and William Lloyd GARRISON in *The Liberator*. The abolitionist movement rejoiced that Emerson not only allied himself with their cause but praised their work, as it was declared in *The Liberator* that "Before we saw notice of this celebration, we were not aware that Mr. Emerson had sufficiently identified himself with the abolitionists, as a party, to receive such a distinguished token of our confidence." After the speech, Emerson received letters of praise, even a medal of service from the American Anti-Slavery Society, and numerous invitations to speak at other abolitionist meetings from prominent figures in the cause such as Maria Chapman, Ellis Gray LORING, and John Greenleaf WHITTIER. Emerson would give subsequent addresses on the anniversary of emancipation in the British West Indies in August 1846 and 1849, and events of the late 1840s and throughout the 1850s would bring Emerson even more into the public realm of abolitionist activity. He became one of the most outspoken critics of the U.S. government with his "FUGITIVE SLAVE LAW ADDRESS" in 1851, and he was a supporter of John BROWN's antislavery raid in 1859.

Bibliography

Gougeon, Len. *Virtue's Hero: Emerson, Antislavery, and Reform.* Athens: University of Georgia Press, 1990.

Emerson, Charles Chauncy
(1808–1836)

Charles Chauncy Emerson was Ralph Waldo EMERSON's youngest brother—five years his junior—but the one with whom he had the closest relationship. Charles was the fourth Emerson brother to attend Harvard and was a prizewinning undergraduate even more academically successful than Ralph Waldo. After graduating from Harvard Charles studied the law, and in 1833 he became engaged to Elizabeth HOAR and planned to take over her father's law office in CONCORD, MASSACHUSETTS. Charles had been battling tuberculosis for some years, however, and died in 1836 at the age of 28 before the marriage took place. Out of duty to his brother, Ralph Waldo Emerson looked after Elizabeth Hoar as he would a sister, and Hoar became one of Ralph Waldo Emerson's closest friends; she never married and is reported to have worn black for 20 years in mourning for Charles.

Brothers Ralph Waldo and Charles had shared interests and conversations on many topics related to Transcendentalism in the 1830s, and Charles had been an important listener and critic in the development of Ralph Waldo's own ideas. Ralph Waldo Emerson declared that he and Charles "made but one man together." He posthumously published some of Charles's writings under the title "Notes from the Journal of a Scholar" in the first issue of the DIAL magazine in July 1840 and again in two editions of 1843.

Bibliography

Myerson, Joel. *The New England Transcendentalists and the Dial: A History of the Magazine and Its Contributors.* London and Toronto: Associated University Presses, 1980.

Emerson, Edward Waldo
(1844–1930)

The only son of Ralph Waldo EMERSON and Lidian Jackson EMERSON to survive into adulthood—first son Waldo died at age five—Edward Waldo Emerson became a chronicler of not only his father's life but also of Transcendentalism in general. He wrote a personal memoir of his father, eventually published in book form as *Emerson in Concord* (1889), and edited and annotated the Centenary Edition of his father's writings (1903–04) and the *Journals of Ralph Waldo Emerson* (1909–14). Edward also published memoirs and biographies of other important Transcendentalist figures such as his *Life and Letters of Charles Russell Lowell* (1907) and *Henry David Thoreau as Remembered by a Young Friend* (1917). Edward Emerson's writings provide important accounts of key figures within the movement from someone who knew them personally.

Edward did not himself pursue a literary career but was a graduate of Harvard College and medical school and worked as a physician in CONCORD, MASSACHUSETTS. He was also a member of the Massachusetts Historical Society and a supporter of the arts who spent time as a teacher at the Boston Museum of Fine Arts.

Emerson, Ellen Tucker
(1839–1909)

Ellen Tucker Emerson was the daughter of Ralph Waldo EMERSON and Lidian Jackson EMERSON, but was named after Emerson's first wife, Ellen Louisa Tucker Emerson, who had died of tuberculosis in 1831 after only 16 months of marriage. Daughter Ellen never married but instead retained the role of doting daughter, sister, and aunt throughout her adult life. As her father aged his sphere of popularity increased and Ellen traveled with him, aided him in preparing and presenting lectures, and assisted him in writing correspondences and greeting guests. She collaborated with James Elliot CABOT in editing Ralph Waldo Emerson's papers after his death, and she authored her own biography of her mother, *The Life of Lidian Jackson Emerson*, which was not actually published until 1980. Ellen's detailed journals, along with her own voluminous correspondences with friends and family members, illuminate many personal details about the Emerson household and the bustling CONCORD, MASSACHUSETTS, social life of which they were a part.

Emerson, Lidian Jackson
(1802–1892)

When Lydia Jackson married Ralph Waldo EMERSON in September 1835 she became known as Lidian, in reference to the mystical nickname he had given her: "my Lydian Queen." Lidian Emerson was a reluctant Unitarian and never considered herself a Transcendentalist like her husband. Like Ralph Waldo Emerson, however, she was particularly interested in the philosophy of Emanuel Swedenborg (*see* SWEDENBORGIANISM), about whom she corresponded with Elizabeth Palmer PEABODY. She rejected her Congregationalist upbringing, but throughout her spiritual searching she retained a belief in a personal God and a divine Christ, beliefs that gave her the strength to withstand what she termed the "Transcendental Times" of her husband's philosophical leadership. For his part, Ralph Waldo Emerson appreciated his wife's beliefs as a moral check on his own estrangement from Christianity.

The spiritual differences between the couple were occasionally the cause of tension and regret for Lidian, but she also at times playfully disagreed with her husband's philosophical tendencies. At one point she went so far as to pen in her private journals a satire on the moral excesses and social disgraces that one was in danger of committing if Transcendental "egoism" or reliance on "the Infallible Self" was taken to the extreme. This tirade was termed by daughter Ellen the "TRANSCENDENTAL BIBLE," and according to his journals Ralph Waldo Emerson found the essay amusing and witty. Regardless of their theological or philosophical differences, the Emersons enjoyed a nearly 50-year marriage, and Lidian was closely involved in her husband's career and was well known as an engaging hostess at their CONCORD, MASSACHUSETTS, home.

Lidian Emerson was already an involved reformer before her marriage, and she continued to devote her time and resources to a variety of causes including ABOLITIONISM, WOMEN'S RIGHTS, animal rights, the EDUCATION of children, and Indian rights. She was a regular member of the Anti-Slavery Society and even forbade her son, Edward, from fighting for the Union cause until emancipation was declared as the goal. She openly debated guests and correspondents on reform subjects and hosted club meetings at her home on occasion. Although she suffered from health problems for most of her life, she outlived Ralph Waldo Emerson by 10 years and died at age 90.

Bibliography

Carpenter, Delores Bird. *The Selected Letters of Lidian Jackson Emerson.* Columbia: University of Missouri Press, 1987.

Emerson, Ellen Tucker. *The Life of Lidian Jackson Emerson,* ed. Delores Bird Carpenter. Boston: Twayne Publishers, 1980.

Emerson, Mary Moody
(1774–1863)

Mary Moody Emerson was one of the primary intellectual influences on the premier Transcendentalist thinker, her nephew, Ralph Waldo EMERSON. "Aunt Mary," as Emerson referred to his never-married paternal aunt, was a model of female genius from whom he received not only many lessons as a boy, but regular correspondences and advice as an adult. Mary Moody Emerson advised her nephew, "Waldo," on personal and professional matters, and also discussed with him a variety of theological and philosophical texts. It was she who introduced him to many of the ideas and perspectives that would form the basis of his Transcendentalist break from UNITARIANISM in the 1830s and his formative views on nature, spirituality, and the soul.

Mary Moody Emerson was influenced by and in many ways embodied the intellectual currents of her time. Raised in the tradition of New England Puritan orthodoxy, her wide readings in Enlightenment thought led her to incorporate intuition and personal experience into her understanding of the divine. After her brother, William Emerson, died in 1811 when Ralph Waldo was only eight years old, Mary Moody Emerson took over as mentor and intellectual guide for all of her nephews and nurtured them toward their careers. By 1820 she had converted to Unitarianism, but she retained a belief in historical Christianity and in a God-centered religion and did not adopt the skepticism or the ratio-

nalism of the most liberal Unitarians. She led daily prayers for all the children and encouraged Ralph Waldo Emerson to read heavily in works of religious mysticism as well as John Milton's *Paradise Lost,* theological texts of American PURITANISM, and the Bible itself. Thus, although his father had been a liberal Unitarian, Ralph Waldo Emerson received a thorough education in the orthodox Calvinist tradition, or what he termed "that old religion," and, in his own words as he remembered his aunt's influence, the "prophetic and apocalyptic" aspects of religious experience.

In particular, Mary Moody Emerson primed Ralph Waldo Emerson to enter the ministry. Throughout the 1820s the two exchanged hundreds of letters through which his spiritual development is documented. Aunt Mary, whom he sometimes referred to in his own journals by the mystical anagram "Tnamurya," suggested readings for her nephew and directed him to a range of literary and spiritual writings, both contemporary and ancient. Ralph Waldo Emerson did become a Unitarian minister, but his aunt was disappointed when he resigned that post in 1832 in the face of a personal, philosophical, and career crisis that led him to eventually break with organized religion completely and promote his own individualist philosophy. He embarked on what would become his true VOCATION as a poet-philosopher and lecturer and, although Mary Moody Emerson retained her connection to the church, she did, ultimately, admire her nephew's courage to break free from institutions and rely on his own heart.

Mary Moody Emerson lived most of her adult life in Maine, but she had spent time in CONCORD, MASSACHUSETTS, to help care for and educate her nephews and was well connected to Boston-Concord literary and intellectual life throughout the height of the Transcendentalist movement. She participated in CONVERSATIONS and corresponded not only with her nephew Emerson but also with figures such as Elizabeth Palmer PEABODY and Henry David THOREAU. She read widely in the works of many of the Transcendentalists but did not contribute to the movement's literary output herself. She had published an early 1804 piece on her religious ideas in *THE MONTHLY ANTHOLOGY,* a literary paper founded in part by her brother,

William Emerson, Ralph Waldo's father, but there were few opportunities for publication for a woman of her generation, and a literary or ministerial career were out of the question. As such, the main outlet for her philosophical writings was in letters to her nephews and in her own personal diary or "almanack."

One of the main themes she engaged was that of humanity's relationship to *nature*. She provided her nephew with an understanding of the symbolic meaning of nature as a "wilderness," a corollary to the wilderness of the inner soul. While Ralph Waldo Emerson would reject his aunt's Calvinist beliefs in the inherent evil of the soul and the need for salvation, he did retain the more mystical idea of looking to nature for spiritual renewal. While much attention has been paid to the influence of Puritan theology on later Transcendentalism, that influence has only recently been traced to the important role that Mary Moody Emerson played in the development of Ralph Waldo Emerson's overall philosophy. Her voluminous personal writings and her correspondences with her nephew attest to what Mary Moody Emerson's biographer, Phyllis Cole, identifies as a "proto-Transcendentalist" belief system that illuminates much not only about early 19th-century literary culture, but, most intriguingly, about the depth of the Puritan-Calvinist source for key Transcendentalist ideas and the emergence of Transcendentalism in general.

Bibliography

Cole, Phyllis. *Mary Moody Emerson and the Origins of Transcendentalism: A Family History.* New York: Oxford University Press, 1998.

Emerson, Ralph Waldo
(1803–1882)

Lecturer and writer Ralph Waldo Emerson was the intellectual center of American Transcendentalism and one of the most important writers and thinkers in American literary history. Although many Americans had begun reading the works in English ROMANTICISM and German IDEALISM that inspired the new philosophy, the timing of a separate Transcendentalist movement began in the

1830s in the midst of a theological as well as personal career crisis for Ralph Waldo Emerson. As a Unitarian minister who left his post, as a prolific writer and thinker on all matters religious, literary, and social, Emerson embodied the movement of self-reliance and originality and gave it a voice. He also represented a uniquely American response to the philosophical and theological themes and critiques that characterized European literature of the era.

Ralph Waldo Emerson came from a long line of New England ministers and was the middle son of William Emerson, a liberal clergyman who had already rejected the PURITANISM of their ancestors, but who died when Waldo, as he was called, was only eight years old. Waldo Emerson and his four brothers were raised by their mother, Ruth Haskins Emerson, and educated in part by their eccentric but well-read paternal aunt, Mary Moody EMERSON, probably the most significant early influence on Emerson's intellectual and philosophical development. After graduating from Harvard, Waldo Emerson worked as a schoolteacher and assisted in putting his younger brothers through college as well. His family expected him to enter the ministry like his father, however, and he eventually returned to pursue this path as a student at HARVARD DIVINITY SCHOOL. He began preaching as a Unitarian minister before he received his degree and was a much-desired young speaker. At the age of only 25 he took over as pastor of Boston's Second Church, at about the same time that he began reading new thinkers such as Samuel Taylor COLERIDGE and Thomas CARLYLE. These European writers even further challenged his unease about religious tradition and the historical foundations of Christianity, beyond even his liberal UNITARIANISM.

While he thrived with the intellectual work of writing sermons and preaching, his wide readings in philosophy, literature, and theology led him to question the blind obedience displayed in church rituals such as the LORD'S SUPPER. In 1832 he resigned from the ministry in the aftermath of a controversy within his congregation over serving the Lord's Supper, a ritual Emerson felt was done out of tradition only without any personal spiritual meaning or not as an authentic expression of faith for those participating. Although he would appear as a visiting preacher in friends' congregations over the next few years, his break with the church had begun, and he had taken the first steps toward Transcendentalism in establishing the primacy of individual experience and personal conviction over church tradition.

His crisis over finding his true VOCATION corresponded with the personal crisis of the 1831 death from tuberculosis of his young wife, Ellen Tucker EMERSON, after less than two years of marriage. Emerson immersed himself in study and reading and, after resigning from his pulpit, traveled to Europe before deciding on the next direction to take for his life. He traveled through France, Italy, Scotland, and England, visiting many of the places and people he had only read about, including meeting with contemporary writers William WORDSWORTH, Coleridge, and Carlyle. Emerson began to cultivate his ideas about nature while in Europe and to piece together scientific and natural history essays and lectures that would lead to his seminal work, NATURE, published in 1836.

Upon his return, however, he lost his beloved brother, Charles Chauncy EMERSON, to tuberculosis as well. Emerson remarried, this time to a woman he called Lidian Jackson EMERSON, and embarked upon not only a new family life but a new career as an essayist and speaker. As one of the first professional speakers on the lyceum circuit, he lectured widely on topics such as history, natural history, literature, and self-culture. In 1836 his first book, *Nature,* appeared anonymously. It was in *Nature* that Emerson articulated the foundations of his Transcendentalist philosophy, a way to connect the material nonhuman world of nature (what Emerson termed the "Not-Me") with the spiritual world of the human self (in Emerson's terms, the "Me"). Through nature would be found the meaning of the larger world, the universe even, and thus the meaning or truth of human existence.

Nature was published the same year that the TRANSCENDENTAL CLUB was formed. The Club emerged out of a meeting between Emerson, Frederic Henry HEDGE, and George RIPLEY, and eventually brought together a diverse group of individuals interested in the emerging theological critique within liberal Unitarianism as informed by literary and philosophical movements of English romanti-

cism and German idealism. Through the Transcendental Club and the other activities it inspired, Emerson became friends with other important thinkers and writers, such as Amos Bronson ALCOTT, James Freeman CLARKE, Margaret FULLER, Theodore PARKER, Elizabeth Palmer PEABODY, and Henry David THOREAU. Soon there revolved around Emerson a group of people interested in reading works by Samuel Taylor Coleridge and Thomas Carlyle, whom Emerson had befriended in Europe and whose writings he was now editing for publication in the United States, as well as German thinkers such as Johann Wolfgang von GOETHE and Immanuel KANT. From the Transcendental Club emerged plans for a dedicated journal for the movement. The DIAL was formed in 1841, and Emerson served as coeditor with Margaret Fuller and eventually as primary editor. Through his work on the *Dial,* Emerson came into contact with an even greater range of writers and thinkers interested in new philosophical and religious ideas. From his position in CONCORD, MASSACHUSETTS, Ralph Waldo Emerson emerged as the social and intellectual center of the movement throughout the better part of the 19th century.

Soon following the publication of *Nature,* Emerson delivered two of his most important early addresses, both delivered at his alma mater, Harvard. In 1837 he presented his call for self-education in his "AMERICAN SCHOLAR" address. In 1838, however, his vision of independent thinking extended to a critique of the ministry in his speech to the graduating class at Harvard Divinity School. Known as the DIVINITY SCHOOL ADDRESS, Emerson's speech sparked a controversy even he was unprepared for as conservative Unitarians such as Andrews NORTON, in particular, attacked Emerson in the press and accused him of heresy and even atheism. Emerson did not respond to such critics publicly and only expanded his ideas more fully in his 1841 collection of *ESSAYS: FIRST SERIES.* The foundation of his philosophy, in his writings as well as his lectures, was not theological doctrine but a belief in personal experience and intuition. Over and over he emphasized the supremacy of the individual human soul, rather than doctrine, tradition, or social custom, in determining truth and the meaning of our existence. The one essay most characteristic of his philosophy and most widely quoted is "SELF-RELIANCE." His great work of biography, *REPRESENTATIVE MEN,* was published in 1850 and included essays on Plato (*see* PLATONISM), Goethe, Montaigne, William SHAKESPEARE, Napoleon, and Emanuel Swedenborg (*see* SWEDENBORGIANISM), all of whom had influenced Emerson's own development and who he now held up as "representative" of the potential for greatness and genius that resides in all individuals.

Ralph Waldo EMERSON primarily saw himself as a poet, although he is often less recognized as such, but for him "poet" was defined in the broadest sense and included his prose writing and lecturing. A poet for Emerson was closer in definition to a philosopher, someone who observed and interpreted the world around him for his contemporaries. While Emerson pursued his own career and self-development, he also sought out original and talented writers for the *Dial,* enthusiastically promoting the work of poets such as Christopher Pearse CRANCH, Caroline Sturgis TAPPAN, Henry David Thoreau, and Jones VERY, and a host of young writers and thinkers who impressed him. Besides his more famous prose writings, essays drawn primarily from lectures and from his voluminous and detailed journals, he himself published more than two dozen poems in the *Dial* and was encouraged enough to publish his first collection of *POEMS,* released on Christmas of 1846. He later gathered together his own collection of favorite poems and verses by other people in *PARNASSUS* (1874).

Although Emerson was often accused of abstract and inaccessible writing, he was not only a popular author and speaker but also a concerned social activist. In the 1850s he spoke on WOMEN'S RIGHTS and was increasingly drawn into the cause of ABOLITIONISM, speaking publicly against slavery and the government, in particular against the FUGITIVE SLAVE LAW.

Bibliography

Buell, Lawrence. *Emerson.* Cambridge, Mass.: Harvard University Press, 2003.

Richardson, Robert D., Jr. *Emerson: The Mind on Fire.* Berkeley: University of California Press, 1995.

Emerson, William
(1801–1868)

William Emerson influenced his younger brother, Ralph Waldo EMERSON, through reports of his theological studies at the University of Göttingen in Germany in preparation for the Unitarian ministry. After studying German philosophers and Bible critics, however, William decided he could not promote organized Christian religion, even UNITARIANISM (a decision Ralph Waldo would also later make for many of the same reasons), and became a lawyer instead. Biographers of Ralph Waldo Emerson point out that the older William directly influenced his brother through his letters home with discussions of German criticism and biblical scholarship. William ultimately anticipated Ralph Waldo's emphasis on the sovereignty of the individual's perception of and relationship to God and on a historical rather than miraculous or divine Christianity as put forth in Ralph Waldo's 1838 DIVINITY SCHOOL ADDRESS which signaled a Transcendentalist break from orthodox Unitarianism—for example, in 1824 William wrote to another brother, Edward, that "I do not find it needful to seek for proofs of the being and omnipresence of God in my metaphysical subtleties, for I find them in my own thoughts, in my own moral history."

William Emerson lived in New York for most of his professional life, and Henry David THOREAU served at one time as a tutor for Emerson's three sons. He retired to CONCORD, MASSACHUSETTS, however, and is buried there in Sleepy Hollow Cemetery among many of the Transcendentalists of his famous younger brother's circle.

English Traits
Ralph Waldo Emerson
(1856)

English Traits was Ralph Waldo EMERSON's least Transcendentalist or broadly philosophical work and, therefore, in many ways his most accessible. Still, it does not stand out from his other writing and, in fact, encompasses the same core of his philosophy about self-identity and cultural identity as detailed in his other major works of the 1850s, REPRESENTATIVE MEN (1850) and THE CONDUCT OF LIFE (1860). *English Traits* began as an 1848 series of lectures Emerson had given on his impressions of English life and culture drawn from two early trips to Europe. He first traveled to England in 1833 immediately after resigning from his position as a Unitarian minister. He returned to England in 1847–48 on a lecture tour at the height of his popularity as a speaker.

At the time *English Traits* was finally published in book form in the 1850s, the genre of travel narrative was immensely popular, accounting in part for the success of the book, but *English Traits* was less an account of his travels and more his impressions and critiques of America's English heritage, another topic of concern in 1850s literary culture. Emerson was fascinated with English culture and, especially, with America's emergence from and debt to that culture. In defining what was undeniably English about England, Emerson was helping to articulate what was distinctly American about American culture. An analysis of England was also a clue to America's future, as America was coming into its own economic and political maturity, the time was right to look to England, and Emerson, for one, saw warnings about what America should do or not do. Emerson believed in the cultural and even racial superiority of English culture, but he now saw problems with England's economic and political organization.

The book details Emerson's visits with prominent English writers and thinkers such as Thomas CARLYLE, Samuel Taylor COLERIDGE, and William WORDSWORTH. Emerson celebrated the genius of these writers while also presenting them as merely men of their time, as "representative" men who have faults and shortcomings, but who possess the same abilities as any of us to draw out our own personal genius. Other aspects of English culture were treated thematically in sections on "Race," "Ability," "Character," "Aristocracy," "Wealth," and "Religion," among other topics. Throughout, Emerson balances praise with straightforward critique about what he perceived to be the excesses of English culture. While England had achieved the material and economic success of a world power, Emerson's criticisms were meant to warn the United States of the spiritual and intellectual harm that could befall a nation driven by unlimited material gain and expansion. Emerson read widely not only in the literature and philosophy of ROMANTICISM but in English history as well, and in his view, 19th-century England was no longer capable of the sharp intellect and literary genius of previous generations. Publishing his book in the 1850s, Emerson had much to be concerned about as he perceived the state of American politics and culture at that time. The effects of expansionism and material greed were seen not only in the crass nature of the national consciousness but in the spread and brutality of slavery, an issue that would increasingly draw his attention throughout the decade.

Bibliography

Emerson, Ralph Waldo. *English Traits*. Edited by Robert E. Burkholder, Philip Nicoloff, Douglas Emory Wilson. Cambridge, Mass.: Harvard University Press, 1994.

Enlightenment   *See* LOCKE, JOHN.

Essays: First Series
Ralph Waldo Emerson
(1841)

Essays: First Series, a collection of revised lectures gathered together and published in January 1841, was Ralph Waldo EMERSON's primary public response to the controversy and criticisms surrounding his 1838 DIVINITY SCHOOL ADDRESS. The volume includes some of his most popular essays on topics to which Emerson applied his own philosophy of subjective experience and individual faith. *Essays: First Series* includes "HISTORY," "SELF-RELIANCE," "COMPENSATION," "SPIRITUAL LAWS," "LOVE," "FRIENDSHIP," "Prudence," "HEROISM," "THE OVER-SOUL," "CIRCLES," "INTELLECT," and "ART." Behind the simply stated titles are complex examinations of each topic intended to alter the reader's assumptions and previous knowledge about these individual themes. Contrary to contemporary criticisms that Emerson as a philosopher was not systematic enough, *Essays: First Series*, as with ESSAYS: SECOND SERIES, published three years later, is consistent with the key themes first addressed by Emerson in NATURE in 1836. These later essay collections only provide more in-depth analysis and explanation of the topics as he had more fully developed them in his writings and lectures in the intervening years. While the individual essays in the *First Series* deserve their own attention and the topics addressed stand alone as Transcendentalist themes, the collection should also be recognized as a whole.

Emerson opened *Essays: First Series* with "History," and the first line introduced an idea traced through all of his other work as a Transcendentalist philosopher: "There is one mind common to all individual men." Here Emerson introduces the idea of "the Over-Soul," developed more fully in a later essay by that name, an idea that he returns to again and again throughout the rest of the volume. It is the core of Emersonian philosophy, as introduced earlier in *Nature,* to assert the primacy of "individual men" as they are related to the whole, the "one mind." In "History" Emerson traces the relationship of the modern individual to human society in the past, bringing the past to bear directly on the present. All human actions, past and present, are connected in Emerson's formulation, because across time humans are connected by a universal morality, a universal mind. A focus on the present and the emergence of the individual at the center of universal existence is the theme developed to its fullest in the next essay, perhaps his most well-known and defining work, "Self-Reliance." Even though the individual reigns supreme in Emerson's thought, the interconnectedness of all humanity, past, present, and future, the "one mind," is carried throughout his exploration of the other topics as well.

With *Essays: First Series*, Ralph Waldo Emerson established himself as one of America's premier thinkers and as the main spokesperson for the Transcendentalist movement. As he was not yet widely known as a lecturer and essayist the book had only limited success in the United States. Critics focused on the lack of a theological, specifically Christian, framework for Emerson's humanist morality. Emerson's friend, Thomas CARLYLE, wrote the preface for an English edition of the book, drawing attention to the inspirational quality of the essays as "the soliloquy of a true soul, alone under the stars, in these days." The book introduced Emerson to a wider British audience and helped to pave the way for his warm reception as a lecturer when he toured England in 1848. Taken together, his two essay collections of the 1840s cover the foundations of Emersonian Transcendentalism, introducing his trademark rhetorical style, his penchant for memorable and quotable phrases, and the philosophical themes he would follow throughout his other writings as well: individualism, self-reliance, humanity's relationship with nature, and the quest for universal truths.

Bibliography

Von Frank, Albert J. *"Essays: First Series (1841)."* In *The Cambridge Companion to Ralph Waldo Emerson*, eds. Joel Porte and Saundra Morris. New York: Cambridge University Press, 1999, 106–120.

Essays: Second Series
Ralph Waldo Emerson
(1844)

Ralph Waldo EMERSON's *Essays: Second Series* was published in 1844, just three years after his ESSAYS: FIRST SERIES. These two collections of his most important early writings and lectures introduced various practical topics as seen through the lens of Transcendentalism. These volumes were published during a period of prolific thinking, writing and lecturing, as Emerson emerged as one of America's foremost American intellectuals. As editor of the Transcendentalist literary journal the DIAL during the 1840s, Emerson was also at the forefront of nurturing new American writers and thinkers. The *Essays: Second Series* includes eight essays—"THE POET," "EXPERIENCE," "CHARACTER," "Manners," "Gifts," "Nature," "POLITICS," "Nominalist and Realist"—and a reprint of his lecture from that year on "NEW ENGLAND REFORMERS." While the *First Series* took as its theme the power of the individual self, the *Second Series* essays are unified in their concern with the limitations to that self as it moved in the broader social and political world.

In opening the collection with the essay on "The Poet," Emerson introduces himself to the reader and positions himself as the interpreter of the ideas presented in the rest of the volume. Emerson summed up the more general question of how to locate the individual self in relation to other forces with the opening lines of the next essay, on "Experience": "Where do we find ourselves? In a series of which we do not know the extremes, and believe that it has none." The essays on "Politics" and "New England Reformers," the latter one of his most well-known pieces, explicitly addressed the question of the relation between the individual and the state. Emerson's individualism is democratic as he states in "Politics": "Of persons, all have equal rights, in virtue of being identical in nature." Furthermore, he articulated what, a few years later, would become the seminal idea of Henry David THOREAU's manifesto on "CIVIL DISOBEDIENCE." In "Politics," Emerson declared that, in matters of the individual's relationship to the law, "Every actual State is corrupt," even a democracy, and that "Good men must not obey the laws too well."

The lecture-turned-essay on "New England Reformers" was included in the volume as Emerson's response to the increased participation of many of his closest Transcendentalist colleagues in social and political reform movements, including ABOLITIONISM and the establishment of the local utopian communities at BROOK FARM and FRUIT-LANDS. Emerson maintained his own idea of reform coming from within the individual when he identified the best movements as those that showed "a tendency toward the adoption of simpler methods and an assertion of the sufficiency of the private man." He himself, however, would move from an observer and critic of organized reform to a more outspoken participant in the antislavery cause in the following decade of the 1850s.

Essays: Second Series was a more successful book for Emerson than the *First Series*. Although some similar criticisms were made of both volumes as lacking religious sentiment, by 1844 Emerson was well-regarded as a lecturer and writer, the intense controversy over Transcendentalism had mostly subsided, and the *Second Series* was overall favorably reviewed. For example, Frederic Henry HEDGE, a conservative Unitarian affiliated with the early Transcendentalists, but eventually a critic of their radical move away from Christianity, reviewed Emerson's essays in the CHRISTIAN EXAM-INER, declaring that "So long as there are lovers of fine discourse and generous sentiment in the world, they will find their own."

Everett, Alexander Hill
(1790–1847)

Alexander Hill Everett presented European literature and philosophy to American readers through his role as editor of the NORTH AMERICAN REVIEW from 1830 to 1835. In this forum he wrote essays on many of the European writers and thinkers that inspired the Transcendentalists during this same time, such as Thomas CARLYLE, Friedrich SCHILLER, and Madame de STAËL. Like Ralph Waldo EMERSON—and like Everett's older brother, the influential Harvard professor Edward EVERETT—Alexander Everett promoted participation in a transatlantic intellectual community at the same time that he encouraged the development of a distinctively American literary culture. This idea was fully developed as one of Emerson's own major intellectual legacies in his 1837 lecture, "THE AMERICAN SCHOLAR." Alexander Hill Everett's main work predated the Transcendentalist controversy by a few years, and he remained more philosophically conservative, determining the IDEALISM they espoused to be "an unsubstantial dream."

Everett, Edward
(1794–1865)

Harvard professor Edward Everett predated the Transcendentalists by a generation but was central in promoting the need for a distinctly American literature that would help spark the movement. In 1817 Everett graduated from the University of Göttingen in Germany and thus received the first Doctor of Philosophy (PhD) awarded to an American. That same year, he published in the NORTH AMERI-CAN REVIEW the first significant American commentary on Johann Wolfgang von GOETHE, who would quickly become one of the primary European influences for Transcendentalist thought. He went on to serve as editor of the *North American Review* in the early 1820s, and there he promoted American intellectual culture within the context of international literary criticism and reviews, as did his brother, Alexander Hill EVERETT, who edited the same journal in the 1830s.

Ralph Waldo EMERSON had been among Edward Everett's students at Harvard, where the professor first articulated many of the themes that Emerson would explore in his later "AMERICAN SCHOLAR" address of 1837, such as Everett's argument that Americans must break their intellectual ties from the European past and work to produce their own more vibrant native democratic culture. Everett had little to do with the radicalism of Transcendentalism, however, once the movement began. By the late 1820s he had switched careers from academics to a successful rise in politics, elected first as a Massachusetts Congress member, and then governor (1835–39), and eventually U.S. senator (1853–54). During that time he had returned to Harvard, briefly, as president in the late 1840s, and he was responsible for hiring naturalist Louis AGASSIZ as a professor and establishing the Lawrence Scientific School.

Bibliography

Varg, Paul A. *Edward Everett: The Intellectual in the Turmoil of Politics.* Selinsgrove, Pa.: Susquehanna University Press, 1992.

"Experience"
Ralph Waldo Emerson
(1844)

Published in *Essays: Second Series* in 1844 and probably Ralph Waldo EMERSON's most important essay in the volume, "Experience" takes as its theme the effect of life experience on Transcendentalist faith in the power of the individual. Recent biographer Robert Richardson suggests that nearly every one of Emerson's books contains an essay on "doubt" and, in *Second Series,* "Experience" is that essay. Here Emerson the philosopher confronts the realities of daily life and determines that "So much of our time is preparation, so much is routine, and so much retrospect, that the pith of each man's genius contracts itself to a few hours."

Here Emerson appears less optimistic than in some of his other writings, such as "SELF-RELIANCE," in which he celebrated the unlimited power of the individual self. Now, having more worldly "experience" himself, he determines that much of life is "illusion" and the individual in fact has only limited vision of the real world: "Life is a train of moods like a string of beads, and as we pass through them, they prove to be many-colored lenses which paint the world their own hue, and each shows only what lies in its focus." That "illusion" turns out to be but one fact controlling and limiting personal experience: "Illusion, Temperament, Succession, Surface, Surprise, Reality, Subjectiveness,—these are threads on the loom of time, these are the lords of life. . . . I know better than to claim any completeness for my picture. I am a fragment, and this is a fragment of me."

Unlike the earlier optimism of "HISTORY" (from *ESSAYS: FIRST SERIES*), in "Experience" Emerson presents a humanity with no connection to either past or future: "Where do we find ourselves? . . . We wake and find ourselves on a stair; there are stairs below us, which we seem to have ascended; there are stairs above us, many a one, which go upward and out of sight." Humankind is now barely able to navigate even the present and immediate world around us as "Sleep lingers all our lifetime about our eyes. . . . Ghostlike we glide through nature, and should not know our place again." The reader soon discovers that Emerson's melancholy observations emerge from his own attempt to deal with the loss and grief over the death of his five-year-old son, Waldo, in 1842. Emerson is disappointed to find that death, this most profoundly human "experience," has not inspired him to higher planes or provided him with deeper wisdom about the human condition. On the contrary, "I grieve that grief can teach me nothing, nor carry me one step into real nature."

Although Emerson has sunk to the depths of despair in this essay, he returns to the immediate world and ends the essay with a more positive assertion of the purpose of living and thinking and the possibility of "practical power." He determines that "Experience" itself is the point of life: "To finish the moment, to find the journey's end in every step of the road, to live the greatest number of good hours, is wisdom." He warns against only philosophizing or "thinking" about the world and urges his readers to live in the present moment. The essay ends with one of Emerson's most often cited lines: "The true romance, which the world exists to realize, will be the transformation of genius into practical power."

A Fable for Critics
James Russell Lowell
(1848)

Editor and literary critic James Russell LOWELL's 1848 satirical poem, *A Fable for Critics: A Glance at Some of our Literary Progenies,* included warnings of the potential excesses of Transcendentalist individualism and egoism. The book-length poem was published anonymously in 1848, although Lowell was soon detected as its author. It caricatures many of the leading writers and thinkers of the time, most of them contemporaries of Lowell's literary intellectual circle in Boston. The Transcendentalists were particularly favorite targets, and Lowell attacked them with sharp personal criticisms of their individual personalities and insider bickering. Among those subject to Lowell's humorous although at times harsh pen were Amos Bronson AL-COTT, Lydia Maria CHILD, Ralph Waldo EMERSON, Margaret FULLER, Nathaniel HAWTHORNE, and Theodore PARKER. He even turned his satire on himself: "There is Lowell, who's striving Parnassus to climb, / With a whole bale of *isms* tied together with rhyme."

Although some of the characterizations in *A Fable for Critics* may seem harsh and even unjust, scholars have noted Lowell's perceptive insights into the private personalities as well as public philosophies of many of the 19th century's most prominent literary voices. Lowell's criticism of Bronson Alcott as a successful orator but incomprehensible writer was one shared by many of Al-

cott's contemporaries, even among the other Transcendentalists: "While he talks he is great, but goes out like a taper, / If you shut him up closely with pen, ink, and paper." "Yonder, calm as a cloud, Alcott stalks in a dream, / And fancies himself in thy groves, Academe." Regarding Margaret Fuller, Lowell was the most venomous. Most scholars attribute his portrayal of the feminist author and conversationalist as a response to her disparagement of Lowell's writing abilities two years earlier in her "American Literature" essay which appeared in PAPERS ON LITERATURE AND ART (1846). Lowell's "verse," Fuller had written, "is stereotyped; his thought sounds no depth, and posterity will not remember him." For his part, in *A Fable for Critics* Lowell characterized Fuller (identified in the poem as "Miranda," an autobiographical character from Fuller's own 1845 text, WOMAN IN THE NINETEENTH CENTURY) as a self-promoting author who thought most highly of herself: "Miranda came up, and said, 'Phoebus! you know / That the Infinite Soul has its infinite woe, / As I ought to know, having lived cheek by jowl, / Since the day I was born, with the Infinite Soul.'" Of her actual literary production, Lowell quipped of "Miranda's own writings / (Which, as she in her own happy manner has said, / Sound a depth, for 'tis one of the functions of lead)" and that her life's work consisted of "unfolding a tale (of herself, I surmise, / For 'tis dotted as thick as a peacock's with I's)." The direct response to Fuller is clear since here he notably used the same metaphor Fuller used in her critique of his writing which "sounds no depth." Of Henry David THOREAU Lowell had even more contempt, especially of the younger man's attempts to follow in the footsteps of mentor Ralph Waldo Emerson rather than find his own way. He characterized Thoreau as one who walked "in Emerson's tracks with legs painfully short."

Although most of James Russell Lowell's verses seem to be unfair attacks on the vulnerabilities of many of the era's major writers, in particular those among the Transcendentalists, his genius was not as a poet but as a literary critic in identifying and bringing together these writers and acknowledging their cultural contribution—being subjected to Lowell's criticism in *A Fable for Critics* was a sign of their individual as well as group significance to 19th-century American literary culture.

"Fate"
Ralph Waldo Emerson
(1860)

Ralph Waldo EMERSON's lecture on "Fate" was published in 1860 as the opening essay of the collection, *THE CONDUCT OF LIFE*. In "Fate," Emerson posed the central theme of the volume—"The question of the times resolved itself into a practical question of the conduct of life. How shall I live?"—a question followed in subsequent related essays on "Power," "Wealth," "Culture," "Behavior," and others. Originally presented as a lecture in 1851, "Fate" is often considered his most significant piece from *The Conduct of Life* in that it attracted the most attention from contemporaries and is seen by scholars as an important turning point in Emerson's own thought and life. In the very idea of "Fate" can be traced Emerson's movement from an earlier enthusiastic celebration of self-culture to a more cynical midlife recognition of the limitations of personal power. In the context of the questions of slavery and civil war then engulfing mid-19th-century society, Emerson here engages the dilemma of hope, human will, and the possibility of reform. Emerson himself, between the two decades of 1840 and the essay's publication in 1860, had become increasingly involved in ABOLITIONISM, culminating in the disappointment he

shared with other northerners over John BROWN's failed raid on Harpers Ferry in late 1859. Here, in the essay on "Fate," Emerson takes a more sobering world-weary view of the "laws of the world," whether natural (such as race, sex, or parentage) or man-made (war or slavery, for example), which pose obstacles to any one individual's effort to change himself or herself and the larger world: "In our first steps to gain our wishes, we come upon immovable limitations."

Emerson did not mean to present these "laws of the world," his definition of "fate," as an entirely negative conception of humankind's place in the world. Fate alone is not at play, and in discussing fate "We have to consider two things: power and circumstance." In fact, "circumstance" relates most closely to what readers might understand as "fate" in that "the Circumstance is Nature. Nature is, what you may do. There is much you may not," but he does not approve of people using fate as an excuse to explain their entire circumstances in life: " 'Tis a weak and vicious people who cast the blame on Fate." "Power" must also be considered and if circumstance is "negative power," people are still capable of positive power through resistance, in exerting human will against fate. Personal power is, in Emerson's terms, "a stupendous antagonism" to fate.

Power, and the freedom which comes from it, is not just a question of exercising will, of changing one's circumstances in a physical sense. It is also a question of mental power, for Emerson argued that humankind is made up not just of nature but of mind: "Freedom is linked to the human power of thought, which allows us to foresee events, and sometimes control them." The human mind, then, is ultimately stronger than fate: "Intellect annuls Fate." Intellect is thus the power that humans should strive to accumulate in order to turn fate to beneficial uses: "Just as much intellect as you would add, so much organic power." For Emerson knowledge is power is the freedom to self-direct: "Of two men, each obeying his own thought, he whose thought is deepest will be the strongest character."

Emerson goes on to give specific examples of how the intelligence of humankind has overcome fate: "But every jet of chaos which threatens to exterminate us, is convertible by intellect into wholesome force." For example, humans have fought diseases, such as typhus or smallpox, with treatments and vaccines; ice freezes some people to death, but others have discovered the beauty of ice-skating; dangerous forces of nature have been harnessed to benefit humans in the form of wind power, steam, or electricity. Emerson takes some comfort in looking around and seeing that "when there is something to be done, the world knows how to get it done." For Emerson, again, the intellectual, the powers of the mind, must be balanced with the physical powers that make these amendments to fate: "Physical force has no value, where there is nothing else." The wonder of humankind's discovery of fire or electricity, he gives as an example, is that we need so little of it—too much of human force is as dangerous as the natural force: "The luxury of fire is, to have a little on our hearth."

Having posed the question of determining the right conduct of life, Emerson tackles the "immovable limitations" of "fate" and provides a new conception of human power and freedom that accepts the challenge of fate as a way to strengthen individual character: "The right use of Fate is to bring up our conduct to the loftiest of nature."

Felton, Cornelius Conway
(1807–1862)

Cornelius Conway Felton was a writer, classical scholar, and Unitarian who criticized the most radical aspects of Transcendentalism but shared an enthusiasm for German literature and philosophy that allied him with the early movement in some aspects. Specifically, Felton contributed a two-volume work of translation, *German Literature, Translated from the German of Wolfgang Menzel* (Vol. VII and Vol. IX, 1840) to George RIPLEY's SPECIMENS OF FOREIGN STANDARD LITERATURE, a series to which several of the major Transcendentalists also contributed. Felton had been involved in bringing Ralph Waldo EMERSON to Harvard in 1837 to deliver the "AMERICAN SCHOLAR" address, but his 1841 CHRISTIAN EXAMINER review of Emerson's ESSAYS: FIRST SERIES revealed his clearest criticisms of both Emerson and Transcendentalism in general. On the one hand he admitted that "some of the best writing of late years has proceeded from the pens of . . . Transcenden-

talists," but at the same time he saw Emerson as capable of "propounding the most amazing nonsense" and "contradictions." As a learned classical scholar himself, Felton questioned Emerson's originality: "To a very great extent, the new opinions, if such they may be called, are ancient errors and sophistries, mistaken for new truths." He later joined Emerson as a fellow member of the SATURDAY CLUB and lectured regularly at the CONCORD LYCEUM.

Cornelius Conway Felton published numerous translations and book reviews on a range of writers and thinkers of the day, but his most direct interaction with and influence on the Transcendentalists was in his role as a Harvard professor. His students included, at various times, James Russell LOWELL, Henry David THOREAU, and Jones VERY. In 1860 Felton became president of Harvard but had only a brief tenure as he died in 1862.

feminism *See* WOMEN'S RIGHTS.

"Fog"
Henry David Thoreau

Transcendentalist naturalist and poet Henry David THOREAU drafted at least four versions of the poem "Fog," including one which appeared within the text of his first book, the 1849 *A WEEK ON THE CONCORD AND MERRIMACK RIVERS*. Thoreau included the poem as part of his description of the mist surrounding the Merrimack River. Descriptions or reflections on mist or fogginess are, in fact, a regular theme in other writings by Thoreau, for example, in "SMOKE." The fog represents the unseen or, rather, the not fully seen, and thus is a metaphor for the truths of nature yet to be fully revealed to humanity. Most striking about the poem "Fog" is Thoreau's appeal to the senses in experiencing the fog: the readers sees the fog coming as a "Descended cloud fast anchored to the earth"; smells the fog as the "Incense of earth, perfumed with flowers—"; and can almost touch the fog as he describes its resemblance to tangible objects such as "earth-dream drapery / Dew cloth and fairy napkin."

Follen, Charles
(1796–1840)

Charles Follen only emigrated to America in 1824, but in the last two decades of his life he became an outspoken antislavery activist, was ordained as a Unitarian minister, secured a position as professor of German at Harvard, and befriended many within the Transcendentalist circle. Follen, in fact, offered the first German language courses at Harvard since, before that time, German was taught only by private tutors. As enthusiasm for German literature and philosophy was a central feature of early Transcendentalism, Follen found himself in the regular company of those who shared his interests in writers such as Johann Wolfgang von GOETHE and Friedrich SCHILLER, in particular Amos Bronson ALCOTT, Ralph Waldo EMERSON, Margaret FULLER, and Theodore PARKER. Within this circle he first met the Reverend William Ellery CHANNING, who influenced his own decision to become a Unitarian minister. He never held more than a brief position in his own congregation, however, partly due to his radical ABOLITIONISM, which had earlier threatened his Harvard career as well. In 1828 he married Eliza Lee Cabot (Follen) with whom he had a son, but his career and life in America were cut short when he died at age 44 in a shipwreck returning from Europe.

Bibliography
Spevack, Edmund. *Charles Follen's Search for Nationality and Freedom: Germany and America, 1796–1840.* Cambridge, Mass.: Harvard University Press, 1997.

Fourier, François-Marie-Charles   *See* FOURIERISM.

Fourierism

Charles Fourier (1772–1837) was a French utopian socialist thinker who directly influenced the reform efforts of major Transcendentalists, most notably George RIPLEY in his founding of the community at BROOK FARM. Fourier's ROMANTI-CISM and his mystical imagination led him to envision a complete redesign for society based on the rejection of capitalism and its underlying values. Fourier saw "morality" itself as a false system set up by current society to meet material and economic goals. In contrast, he not only rejected organized religion and the whole idea of sin but promoted unlimited desire and "Passions" as the motivating social force. He sincerely believed, with much controversy of course, that society would live without conflict if everyone were allowed to follow their own passions, their own inner desires, as a basis of personal, rather than social, morality. When Fourier spoke of the "Passions" he included everything from sexuality, love, wealth, and art, to good food and drink. He argued that most social problems and discord revolved around fighting over and preventing human desires. Fourier's system applied to economics because he believed that people should and would follow their passions into the types of work that they did and that the diversity of human interests and talents would assure that every type of work in society gets done. Fourier's theory of "Attractive Labor" was his main contribution to French utopian socialist thought and the economic system that attracted American reformers in particular.

In Fourier's system, society would be organized into "Associations" of people who lived together in small communities of "Phalanxes." Each PHALANX would be limited in size, in fact, in Fourier's formulation exactly 1,620 people were needed (no more, no less) to ensure an even representation among the various economic passions or interests, but society could not be organized solely around labor, so a variety of cultural events were promoted as well. When American reformers attempted to translate his ideas in their socialist opposition to American capitalism and industrialization, they emphasized his economic plan, while ignoring, or never fully understanding, his complex and controversial insistence on full sexual and physical desire as detailed in his original writings, including his rejection of conventional marriage and his condoning of even homosexuality and group sex.

Fourierism was brought to the United States in the early 1830s by Albert BRISBANE, an American disciple who had met Fourier in Paris. Brisbane wrote a column in Horace GREELEY's NEW YORK TRIBUNE in which he expounded his excitement about Fourier's plans for social reorganization. Brisbane translated several of Fourier's works into English, again emphasizing his ideas on labor and economy and omitting not only the sexually explicit material but much of Fourier's critique of Christianity as well. The first Fourierist community was founded in 1844 at the North American Phalanx in New Jersey and was amazingly long-lasting, existing until 1855. During that time period more than 30 more communities, or "phalansteries," were established in America, but overall Fourierism died out in the United States by the time of the Civil War.

Another of the most important Fourierist communities in America, and the one that engaged many of the Transcendentalists, was Brook Farm in West Roxbury, Massachusetts. George Ripley had founded Brook Farm as an alternative communitarian experiment based on the Transcendentalist ideals of self-culture and self-reliance, but after reading Fourier and meeting Brisbane, he and other leaders reorganized Brook Farm around Fourierist principles beginning in 1844–45. The community adopted Fourier's plan of "Attractive Labor" and was committed to a "cooperative" labor system whereby everyone participated in both the physical and intellectual labor needed to sustain an ideal society. The community was building a large phalanstery or dormitory when the building was lost in a fire, a financial disaster from which the experiment never recovered, and Brook Farm closed in 1846. Since Brook Farm had not originally been founded as a Fourierist community, and since its demise was linked to the burning of the phalanstery, many believed that the community ended because it had converted to Fourierism, although there is no indication that they would not have been successful under such a plan based on their large number of supportive members and the committed leadership of Ripley and others. In regards to the Transcendentalists, however, it was increasingly hard to justify a commitment to individual sovereignty with the highly organized and disciplined work schedules promoted by Fourier.

Only one major community was established in France during Fourier's lifetime. There remained, however, considerable interest in his ideas throughout the 19th century after his death, with phalanxes founded around the globe in Eastern Europe, South America, and France and North America. For the Transcendentalists and other reformers in the United States, the Civil War disrupted and changed the nature and focus of social and economic reform, and the experiment at Brook Farm became important primarily for its literary rather than utopian interest as a true alternative to the American economic system.

Bibliography

Beecher, Jonathan. *Charles Fourier: The Visionary and His World*. Berkeley: University of California Press, 1986.

Guarneri, Carl. *The Utopian Alternative: Fourierism in Nineteenth-Century America*. Ithaca, N.Y.: Cornell University Press, 1991.

"Fourierism"
Elizabeth Palmer Peabody
(1844)

"Fourierism" was one of three essays that Elizabeth Palmer PEABODY contributed to the Transcendentalist literary journal the DIAL on the subject of utopian social reform. Her essays were inspired by the utopian community at BROOK FARM, established by George RIPLEY and supported by many other reformers affiliated with Transcendentalism. Although first established in 1841 as an experiment in Transcendentalist self-reliance, Brook Farm reorganized in 1844 around the principles of Charles Fourier's theory of utopian socialism. "Fourierism" was the last essay in a trilogy by Peabody that, collectively, attempted to make the theory of FOURIERISM compatible with Peabody's own brand of Christian Transcendentalism.

The first essay in her series, "A GLIMPSE OF CHRIST'S IDEA OF SOCIETY" (*Dial*, October 1841), established Peabody's vision of Christian PERFECTIONISM as social reform that looked to Christ as the model of a perfect human being who successfully balanced social equality with individual rights and spiritual development. Peabody's second essay, "Plan of the West Roxbury Community" (*Dial*,

January 1842), turned attention specifically to the community at Brook Farm (located in West Roxbury, Massachusetts), as an example of the implementation of "Christ's Idea of Society." Peabody never lived at the community but visited regularly and used the *Dial* as a forum for promoting the experiment. In the last essay of the trilogy, "Fourierism" (*Dial*, April 1844), Peabody summarized the ideas of Charles Fourier as they were implemented at Brook Farm and as she herself was introduced to the philosophy at a recent Boston convention.

Peabody published "Fourierism" to coincide with Brook Farm's shift from a Transcendentalist emphasis on spiritual and intellectual culture to a Fourierist community and, as much as she was moving with the times in explaining what that shift meant, she also was reporting on some of the problems raised by critics of Fourier as they related to the community. Her efforts were complicated by the unfamiliarity with Fourier on the part of American critics as well as proponents: "The works of Fourier do not seem to have reached us." Peabody referred here to the fact that few Americans were reading Fourier directly for, at this time, even those enthusiastic about implementing Fourier's ideas knew the French philosopher primarily through the writings of his main American promoter, Albert BRISBANE, but Peabody's essay revealed as much about her own philosophy as it explained Fourier's. Peabody acknowledged that critics had focused on Fourier's unconventional sexual ideas and rejection of marriage and monogamy, and she even sympathized with some early concerns about Fourier: "For ourselves we confess to some remembrance of vague horror, connected with this name."

While others, such as Margaret FULLER, who discussed Fourier in her WOMAN IN THE NINETEENTH CENTURY published the following year in 1845, were attracted to Fourier's vision of radical social and sexual equality, for Peabody, Fourierism was compatible with Christian morality and, in particular, with her Christian ideal of marriage. In applying that ideal to practical social experiments, Elizabeth Peabody's main concern or criticism of Fourier, and, by extension, of the Fourierist community at Brook Farm, was that the system did not incorporate a strong enough role for the practice of religion. At the very least, even if Fourierism was not dependent upon Christian spirituality, she suggested that the Fourierist community not exclude a place for religious worship: "Let the Fourierists see to it, that there be freedom in their Phalanx for churches, unsupported by its material organization, and lending it no support on its material side. Independently existing within them, but not of them . . . and pressing on to the stature of the perfect man, they will finally spread themselves in spirit over the whole body." In Peabody's philosophy, there was no possibility of the full development of the individual, the attainment of "the perfect man," outside of a Christian context, and she wanted to make sure this aspect was included in reformist plans for the perfect society.

Bibliography

Ronda, Bruce. *Elizabeth Palmer Peabody: A Reformer on Her Own Terms.* Cambridge, Mass.: Harvard University Press, 1999.

Francis, Convers
(1795–1863)

Unitarian minister, historian, and Harvard professor Convers Francis was one of the more moderate thinkers and writers within Transcendentalist circles. He was an original member of the TRANSCENDENTAL CLUB and through his Harvard and Unitarian connections befriended many notables within the movement, including radicals such as Ralph Waldo EMERSON, Theodore PARKER, whom Francis had tutored, and Francis's own sister, Lydia Maria (Francis) CHILD, author of the Transcendentalist novel, PHILOTHEA, and a friend of Margaret FULLER's. Convers Francis was proficient in several languages and was particularly well regarded as a scholar of German language and theology, an interest shared by many of his Transcendentalist friends in the early years of the movement. Francis was known for moderation in his views and, while he supported many political and social reforms, such as ABOLITIONISM, he was never an outspoken social or theological critic like Child or Parker. In spiritual matters Francis emphasized the internal experience of religion and the influence of nature, but he maintained adherence to the external forms of tradition and ritual unlike his radical anti-institution colleague Emerson.

As a writer Convers Francis published several early essays in the *Christian Disciple* and CHRISTIAN EXAMINER, wrote translations of German stories and contributed regularly to the children's periodical, the *Juvenile Miscellany*, published by his sister, Lydia Maria Child. Although most of his early writings were on religious themes, including publication of some of his own sermons, he eventually became best known as a historian of colonial New England. Following the publication of a history of his hometown of Waterford, Massachusetts, in 1836 he published his most well regarded work, a biography, entitled *Life of John Eliot, the Apostle to the Indians*, a scholarly work that earned him membership in the Massachusetts Historical Society. That same year also saw his most important theological work in light of his involvement with the Transcendentalists, a Unitarian pamphlet entitled *Christianity as a Purely Internal Principle*, which emphasized the intuitive and personal aspects of religion. Francis was completely aware of the debates within UNITARIANISM during that important year of 1836, and he perceived the wedge between liberal and conservative sides brought on by the publications of his various radical friends such as Amos Bronson ALCOTT, Orestes BROWNSON, Ralph Waldo Emerson, and George RIPLEY. Francis characterized the split as one between the "English" (meaning the orthodox and empiricist) and the "Germans" (meaning those, namely the Transcendentalists, inspired by German biblical studies in their unorthodox spiritual IDEALISM).

Despite such acute perceptions so early in the movement, and his personal and ideological affiliations with Transcendentalism during these years, Francis remained above the controversy and sought to balance the traditions of the church and the intellectual openness of theological debate, both of which he valued greatly. As moderator and oldest member of the Transcendental Club, other members appreciated Francis's ability to serve, as Alcott phrased it in a letter to Emerson, as a "balance wheel to keep all movements in fit order." When Emerson's DIVINITY SCHOOL ADDRESS wedged the final division between conservative and radical,

Francis defended him on grounds of freedom of interpretation, although he did not necessarily accept Emerson's views. He equally defended friend and protégé Theodore Parker against ridicule and censure during the early 1840s in the wake of Parker's controversial A DISCOURSE ON THE TRANSIENT AND PERMANENT IN CHRISTIANITY.

Despite such alliances with radical Unitarians and sympathies with what he sarcastically referred to in his journal as "the horrible crime of transcendentalism," Convers Francis was appointed a professor at HARVARD DIVINITY SCHOOL in 1842, a position he held for the remainder of his life. Most of his Transcendentalist colleagues believed that Francis was of great benefit to the conservative Divinity School in that he encouraged students to think for themselves and "liberalized" the atmosphere at Harvard. As a respected liberal Unitarian, Convers Francis thus served as an important influence and mentor for several younger Transcendentalists as well, including not only Parker but also Caroline DALL and Octavius Brooks FROTHINGHAM.

Free Religious Association (FRA)

Founded in 1867, the Free Religious Association (or FRA) was one of the most important sites of activity for the post–Civil War Transcendentalist movement. Its members included such prominent figures as Cyrus BARTOL, Lydia Maria CHILD, Octavius Brooks FROTHINGHAM (who served as the first president of the FRA in 1867–78), Thomas Wentworth HIGGINSON (who also served a term as president of the association), David WASSON, and John WEISS. Many of the younger members were continuing the radical tradition of theological critique within UNITARIANISM which began with founding Transcendentalists such as Ralph Waldo EMERSON and Theodore PARKER. Emerson supported and attended meetings of the group as well as serving as a vice president under Frothingham, and Amos Bronson ALCOTT was a major force in its organization, although he eventually left the group over philosophical disagreements. The FRA was not strictly a Transcendentalist meeting, however, and included many other Unitarians and a range of prominent liberal reformers among its ranks.

The establishment of the Free Religious Association was a response to attempts by American Unitarian leadership to regulate and maintain orthodoxy within the churches. The broader free religious movement was critical of orthodoxy and of organized religion and its institutions, including even those within Unitarianism. Proponents of free religion instead emphasized an individualized approach to spirituality and even to theology and thus the appeal among those associated with Transcendentalism. The continued presence of such an anti-creed and anti-institutional strain of radical Unitarianism was central to the eventual movement in the 20th century of the Unitarian church as a whole toward religious liberalism and free thought.

The FRA was founded in 1867 by Unitarian radicals who began to consider forming a new, more open, and inclusive organization that would represent the interests of a variety of independent churches, not just Unitarian churches. Ralph Waldo Emerson spoke at the first organizational meeting in 1867, and the association declared as its purpose to "promote the interests of pure religion, to encourage the scientific study of theology, and to increase fellowship in the spirit." As in the earlier Unitarian-Transcendentalist debates of the 1830s, the radicals of the FRA envisioned religion as based on the principles of spirituality, not on a specific doctrine or text, but, in line with post-Civil War intellectual developments, they framed their new debates and purposes in the context of a more systematic study of comparative religion, the "scientific study of theology." The FRA bridged the concerns of two different generations of intellectuals, and there were thus two different agendas or strains of thought within the Free Religious Association—the Transcendentalist emphasis on intuition and subjective belief side-by-side with the younger members who were increasingly influenced by more scientific and evolutionary thought.

Although the FRA grew out of Unitarianism, the organization was open to members of any church or believers of any religion. Free Religion itself was not a separate religion, and many members had ties to specific churches that limited their participation in critiques within the FRA. Like Transcendentalism itself, the FRA lacked a unifying doctrine, and the idea of universal acceptance and individual experience of religion meant that the association had no official position on the debates it hoped to engage. Because of its nonsectarian identification, the FRA was criticized as non-Christian, which also caused problems for its Christian members.

In addition to regular meetings, the FRA sponsored lecture series, held annual conventions, and published tracts on various topics related to the spiritual principles shared by all religious traditions. The movement had two periodicals, *The Radical*, founded in 1865, and *The Index* (also known as the *Free Religious Index*), a weekly journal founded in 1870, both of which served as forums for the essays and articles of many of the Transcendentalists during this time. In addition, both radicals and conservatives met to further discuss and debate at the RADICAL CLUB, a social group also founded by Cyrus Bartol in 1867 and which included many FRA members. The height of activity for the FRA was the final decades of the 19th century, but as Unitarianism itself became a more open and universal faith, there was less need for a separate radical organization.

Like Transcendentalism, the FRA was formed out of IDEALISM, the belief in universal principles, and out of a humanist commitment to the development and education of the individual as the true purpose of religion. As Octavius Brooks Frothingham explained, "The Dignity of Human Nature must be our watchword. . . . This doctrine does not belong to a sect or a church, but to all mankind. It assumes an entirely new conception of the basis of religious faith . . . it exactly reverses the ancient order of thought, and builds up from a completely original foundation." Frothingham established a church in New York where he preached these ideas, originally a Unitarian church but one that attracted an audience made of people of different religious backgrounds, or of no religious affiliation at all.

In addition to the periodicals, the *Index* and *The Radical*, several influential books on free thought and on comparative religious studies were produced out of the movement as well. Lydia

Maria Child's THE PROGRESS OF RELIGIOUS IDEAS, THROUGH SUCCESSIVE AGES was published in 1855 and thus predated the organization of the FRA, and post–Civil War works by free religion advocates included Bartol's *Radical Problems* (1872), Frothingham's *The Religion of Humanity* (1873), and James Freeman CLARKE's *Ten Great Religions: An Essay in Comparative Theology* (1871 and 1883), and *Events and Epochs in Religious History* (1881).

Bibliography

Dahlstrand, Frederick. *Amos Bronson Alcott: An Intellectual Biography.* East Brunswick, N.J.: Associated University Presses, 1982.

Gabriel, Ralph Henry. *The Course of American Democratic Thought.* Westport, Conn.: Greenwood Press, 1986.

French, Daniel Chester
(1850–1931)

Daniel Chester French was a CONCORD, MASSACHUSETTS, sculptor who created busts of many prominent 19th-century figures, including friends Ralph Waldo EMERSON and Amos Bronson ALCOTT, with whose daughter, May Alcott, French had studied art. Emerson highly praised the lifelike quality of French's work, and French prided himself on having captured Emerson's own "glorifying expression" in the statue that today sits at the Concord Public Library. By the time Emerson sat for him in 1879, however, French had already established a reputation for his bronze statue of *The Minute Man* memorializing the start of the American Revolution 100 years earlier at the battle of Concord. The town of Concord held an extravagant dedication ceremony of the statue at the Concord Bridge on April 17, 1875, an event attended by President Ulysses S. Grant among other dignitaries. The monument includes Emerson's poem the "CONCORD HYMN" engraved on its base, and Emerson spoke at the dedication ceremony, a speech that, according to literary executor James Elliot CABOT, may have been the last original address that Emerson wrote. Daniel Chester French later gained national recognition as the sculptor who created the monument of a seated

Abraham Lincoln that marks the Lincoln Memorial in Washington, D.C.

Bibliography

Richman, Michael. *Daniel Chester French: An American Sculptor.* Washington, D.C.: Preservation Press, 1983.

"Friendship"
Ralph Waldo Emerson
(1841)

Ralph Waldo EMERSON's essay on "Friendship" appeared in his 1841 ESSAYS: FIRST SERIES. Several of the essays in the volume deal with the theme of human social relations, and "Friendship" does so most directly. The essay is a reflection of the theme in Emerson's own personal life, a working out of the idea of friendship for a man who in most other forums emphasized the solitary nature of human existence. The theme was probably prompted by the challenges Emerson faced in understanding the nature of specific relationships with friends such as Amos Bronson ALCOTT and Henry David THOREAU, but also particularly with women: his first wife, Ellen Tucker EMERSON, his second wife, Lidian Jackson EMERSON, and the friendships he negotiated with Transcendentalist colleagues Margaret FULLER and Caroline Sturgis TAPPAN. Emerson idealized the relationships he had had with many of his closest friends and family members who were taken from him by early deaths, such as his brothers, his first wife, his firstborn child, Waldo, and, of course, Margaret Fuller, who died in a shipwreck in 1850, at the height of their personal and professional engagements. Death emerges as a theme in "Friendship" as the ultimate loss, pure loneliness, the one thing that cannot be either fully understood or "transcended." Because of the transitory nature of human relationships, Emerson regularly resisted seeing his friendships as permanent, therefore limiting the commitment or intimacy that his friends could expect, and often demanded, from him.

For Emerson, any relations that interfered with the life of the mind, with writing, could not be sustained or fully pursued. In the essay "Friendship" he acknowledged the benefits and rewards of friendship, such as love and caring, the intellectual excitement of CONVERSATION, and the resulting self-growth that comes from interaction with others. This aspect of his analysis in the essay was drawn directly from conversations he was then having with friends, primarily with Caroline Sturgis (later Tappan), over the nature of friendship. Emerson and the much-younger Sturgis self-consciously enacted a model of friendship learned from their readings of Johann Wolfgang von GOETHE and his younger female protégée, Bettina von Arnim. Just as they felt they had found an acceptable model of friendship (and of male-female friendship in particular), Emerson's reservations prevented him from continuing the relationship in that mode. He pulled back, much to Tappan's confusion and dismay. During the writing of "Friendship" in 1840–41 Emerson was also engaged in extended private conversation and correspondence with Margaret Fuller over the meaning of friendship in general, and theirs in particular, which was thoroughly grounded in intellectual compatibility. Like Caroline Sturgis, Fuller demanded more of Emerson—more openness, more intimacy—and he struggled to understand what that "more" would mean, both practically and philosophically.

The interactions with these women brought up not only issues of propriety in a relationship between a married man and his younger unmarried female friends but his friendships also posed a larger philosophical problem for Emerson as a Transcendentalist. In considering "Friendship" Emerson attempted to reconcile intellectual and emotional dependency on friends with his theory of individualism and "SELF-RELIANCE," which is included in this same 1841 volume of *Essays*. In "Friendship" he asserted that "We walk alone in the world. Friends, such as we desire, are dreams and fables." He concludes that on some level friendship and self-reliance were not at odds with one another, in fact they depended upon one another in an ironic way since the main function of friends was as a route to understanding the self: "The soul environs itself with friends that it may enter into a grander self-acquaintance or solitude." Emerson himself had to ultimately admit that friends are "a sort of paradox in nature." For

in contributing to the development of the individual self, friends become secondary to that self, and one thus eventually outgrows those particular friendships: "That which is so beautiful and attractive as these relations, must be succeeded and supplanted only by what is more beautiful, and so on for ever." In this sense, friends are only the outward or public representation of the inner self. At the end of the essay, therefore, Emerson returns to his earlier pessimism in determining that as something only transitory, of this world, "Friendship, like the immortality of the soul, is too good to be believed."

Bibliography

Sebouhian, George. "A Dialogue with Death: An Examination of Emerson's "Friendship," *Studies in the American Renaissance* (1989): 219–239.

Smith, Harmon L. *My Friend, My Friend: The Story of Thoreau's Relationship with Emerson.* Amherst: University of Massachusetts Press, 1999.

Steele, Jeffrey. "Transcendental Friendship: Emerson, Fuller, and Thoreau." In *The Cambridge Companion to Ralph Waldo Emerson*, eds. Joel Porte and Saundra Morris. New York: Cambridge University Press, 1999, 121–139.

Frothingham, Nathaniel Langdon
(1793–1870)

Nathaniel Langdon Frothingham succeeded William Emerson, the father of Ralph Waldo EMERSON, as minister of the First Unitarian Church of Boston, where he served for 35 years. Before his ordination in 1815, Frothingham held a position as Harvard's first professor of oratory and rhetoric. Frothingham was a close friend of the Emerson family, and he corresponded with Ralph Waldo Emerson regularly throughout the period of Emerson's break from UNITARIANISM. Emerson thought that Frothingham was sympathetic enough to his own ideas to invite him to an early meeting of the TRANSCENDENTAL CLUB, which Frothingham declined, and to send him a copy of NATURE when it was published in 1836. Frothingham ultimately represented the older more conservative generation of Unitarians who opposed Transcendentalism. He, in fact, was the chair of the committee that sought to remove radical Theodore PARKER from the ministry in 1843 in the wake of Parker's unorthodox South Boston sermon, revised and published as A DISCOURSE ON THE TRANSIENT AND PERMANENT IN CHRISTIANITY.

In the Parker case, as well in other matters, Frothingham's views differed from the younger generation, including those of his son, Octavius Brooks FROTHINGHAM, an advocate of free religion (and first president of the post–Civil War–era FREE RELIGIOUS ASSOCIATION) and one of the earliest historians and biographers of the Transcendentalists. In 1890 Octavius Brooks Frothingham memorialized his father's role in the religious debates of his generation when he published his history of Boston Unitarianism 1820–1850: A Study of the Life and Works of Nathaniel Langdon Frothingham. Another child, daughter Ellen, published several volumes of translated German literature, including at least one title by Johann Wolfgang von GOETHE. Nathaniel Frothingham published regularly in the religious press, in particular the conservative Unitarian journal, the CHRISTIAN EXAMINER. In addition to a treatise on Deism or Christianity published in 1845, several of Frothingham's sermons were published as well as occasional poetry, which he collected together for the 1855 Metrical Pieces, Translated and Original.

Bibliography

Caruthers, J. Wade. Octavius Brooks Frothingham: Gentle Radical. Tuscaloosa: University of Alabama Press, 1977.

Frothingham, Octavius Brooks
(1822–1895)

Octavius Brooks Frothingham was a younger generation Transcendentalist who is most well-known as a biographer of several major figures, the first historian of the movement with the publication of his 1876 TRANSCENDENTALISM IN NEW ENGLAND: A HISTORY, and first president of the FREE RELIGIOUS ASSOCIATION, founded in 1867. Frothingham was a graduate of Harvard, where he befriended Samuel JOHNSON and Thomas Wentworth HIGGIN-SON and where his uncle, Edward EVERETT, had been one of Ralph Waldo EMERSON's professors. He was one of the youngest members of the TRANSCENDENTAL CLUB in the early years of the movement, and he went on to train for the Unitarian ministry at HARVARD DIVINITY SCHOOL where, by that time, as Frothingham later wrote, " 'Transcendentalist,' [was] a term of immeasurable reproach."

Frothingham published several articles in the conservative Unitarian paper, the CHRISTIAN EXAMINER, but he had already formed some more radical ideas due to the influence of Transcendentalism. Radical preacher Theodore PARKER was a mentor to Frothingham and introduced him to German biblical criticism, although his own father, Nathaniel FROTHINGHAM, was a conservative Unitarian who had participated in the attempt to oust Parker from the ministry in 1843 in the wake of controversy over Parker's A DISCOURSE ON THE TRANSIENT AND PERMANENT IN CHRISTIANITY. Octavius Frothingham had his own difficulties establishing himself in a permanent post as minister due to his radical theology as well as his antislavery views. Frothingham shared many of Emerson's beliefs about organized religion and dogma as hindrances to the development of the individual soul—for example, like Emerson, Frothingham objected to the ritual of THE LORD'S SUPPER and refused to serve communion to his congregation. In 1854 he preached a sermon in response to the Anthony BURNS fugitive slave case in Boston and chastised Christians for not speaking out against the treatment of Burns as well as not actively working against slavery in the United States: "The Christian Church universal of this country . . . is blind and indifferent to the most hideous Institution now existing under the sun; an institution which, on an enormous scale, outrages human rights and crushes human nature." Frothingham's ABOLITIONISM extended to the publication of a tract on Colonization (1855) and a speech before the American Anti-Slavery Society.

The year after his sermon on the Burns case, Frothingham moved from his congregation in Salem, Massachusetts, to a Unitarian church in New Jersey, and finally to New York where he eventually broke from Unitarianism and established his own Independent Liberal Church. Frothingham welcomed to his church "Unitarians, Universalists, 'come-outers,' spiritualists, unbelievers of all kinds, anti-slavery people, reformers generally . . . materialists, atheists, secularists, positivists—always thinking people." Frothingham's independent congregation was ultimately one of the largest gatherings in New York, where he regularly preached to audiences of 600 or more. Buoyed by his success with his Independent church, Frothingham was moved to help found the Free Religious Association in 1867, an organization that attracted many former Unitarians. Frothingham served as first president of the FRA from 1867 to 1878 and on at least two occasions secured Ralph Waldo Emerson as a speaker. For Frothingham, as for Emerson, free religion meant "absolute freedom of thought in the study of religious literature" and "the superiority of practical morality to dogma." Throughout the 1870s, Frothingham published regular articles in the FRA's main paper, the *Index*. In addition to essays and lectures for the FRA, Frothingham published several hundred of his sermons as well as a book on *The Religion of Humanity* (1872). In this book Frothingham explained what had become for him a more scientific approach to the study of theology, incorporating his various philosophical influences, from Transcendentalism to HEGELIANISM to DARWINISM.

The emphasis on "practical morality" and on reform is what Frothingham ultimately praised most in his history of the Transcendentalist movement. In *Transcendentalism in New England* Frothingham identified his own list of the most important figures within the movement, devoting one chapter each to Amos Bronson ALCOTT, Ralph Waldo Emerson, Margaret FULLER, Theodore Parker, and George RIPLEY. Other thinkers and writers are discussed in a section on "Minor Prophets" which included Cyrus BARTOL, William Henry CHANNING, James Freeman CLARKE, and Thomas Wentworth Higginson. This section allowed Frothingham to give attention to many of his colleagues in the post–Civil War generation, although he did not detail his own contribution. Among the earlier original Transcendentalists, Frothingham made a glaring omission in excluding Henry David THOREAU from his history, perhaps showing his commitment to the Emersonian strain of the movement, but still somewhat surprising

given his particular interest in the "practicality" or reform aspect of Transcendentalism.

As an insider and contemporary, as well as self-appointed historian of the movement, Octavius Brooks Frothingham also published biographies of his Transcendentalist colleagues such as his mentor *Theodore Parker* (1874), founder of the utopian community at BROOK FARM *George Ripley* (1883), and a *Memoir of William Henry Channing* (1886), as well as one of the earliest comprehensive histories of New England Unitarianism during his father's time, *Boston Unitarianism 1820–1850: A Study of the Life and Work of Nathaniel Langdon Frothingham* (1890). Taken together, his published works present the full scope of the Transcendentalist movement, from its earliest beginnings in Unitarianism to the implications of its theological and intellectual legacy through the post–Civil War period.

Bibliography

Caruthers, J. Wade. *Octavius Brooks Frothingham, Gentle Radical*. Tuscaloosa: University of Alabama Press, 1977.

Fruitlands
(1843–1844)

Fruitlands was a utopian community established in Massachusetts by Transcendentalist Amos Bronson ALCOTT and English reformers Charles LANE and Henry Wright. The experiment lasted only eight months, from June 1843 to January 1844, and drew minor interest from among the local Transcendentalist and reform communities. The two men published their proposal for the community in the Transcendentalist journal the DIAL (July 1843) and advertised in various other publications, but they ultimately attracted few members. The list of permanent settlers was made up primarily of the Alcott and Lane families and a few early supporters. They envisioned Fruitlands as an experiment in communitarian living, a "true harmonic association," backed by a reform idealism of self-sufficiency and opposition to mainstream American values such as personal property ownership, commercialism, and slavery. Although Alcott had conceived of the idea after talking to reformers in England, a number of such communities had already arisen in the United States in the 1820s and 1830s to serve as models. Some of these early communitarian experiments were religion-based (such as the Shakers and Mormons), and others had secular purposes and goals (such as Robert Dale Owen's utopian community at New Harmony, Indiana). Of course, Alcott and Lane also had the example of the more significant and more successful Transcendentalist utopian experiment at BROOK FARM, established just two years earlier in 1841.

Alcott had a more mystical and ascetic plan for Fruitlands than the intellectual-socialist community of Brook Farm, which was eventually modeled on the theories of French utopian socialist Charles Fourier (see FOURIERISM). The members of Fruitlands were to live off of the land and provide themselves with food, shelter, and clothing, but for the individual rather than purely social rewards of separating themselves from a capitalist-slave economy while also fostering a spiritual belief in minimalism and cultivation of the soul. In the name of animal rights the community would follow a strict vegetarian diet and forego not only the use of leather and wool products but also the use of animals as farm labor or even manure as fertilizer, thus further limiting the types of crops they could harvest. In the name of ABOLITIONISM and human rights they would also resist the wearing of cotton and the use of other slave products such as sugar.

With these limitations as to diet and clothing and agricultural methods, the philosophic ideals of Alcott and Lane quickly met with practical problems after they moved their families onto the farm. The physical rigors as well as the financial strain of self-sufficiency wreaked havoc on relations between the founding members. The people, problems, and conflicts at Fruitlands formed the basis for Louisa May ALCOTT's later fictionalized account, "TRANSCENDENTAL WILD OATS." First published in 1873, this short story is a satire on her childhood experience in the community and on the incompatibility of philosophical IDEALISM with true social reform. It is also a poignant account of the abusive nature of such experiments toward women as laborers, even in the "ideal" society. Abigail May ALCOTT, Louisa's mother, had often been the only adult woman at Fruitlands and as

such had shouldered an unequal burden of the cooking, cleaning, and child-rearing as well as caring for the male members and guests. For all of the reform causes and ideals that Fruitlands was meant to reflect, the subordinate role of women was apparently not challenged nor even discussed.

Within just a few months of moving to the community Abigail Alcott became physically ill from the diet and hard work. Charles Lane's espousal of celibacy and the dissolution of the conjugal family caused further conflicts between the married Alcotts, and after Lane eventually left to join the Shakers, Bronson Alcott was forced to abandon the experiment at Fruitlands. For a while he still pursued the idea of community-based living but never found a utopian experiment he could commit to and never attracted enough potential members to start another one of his own.

Bibliography

Dahlstrand, Frederick. *Amos Bronson Alcott: An Intellectual Biography*. East Brunswick, N.J.: Associated University Presses, 1982.

Francis, Richard. *Transcendental Utopias: Individual and Community at Brook Farm, Fruitlands, and Walden*. Ithaca, N.Y.: Cornell University Press, 1997.

Fugitive Slave Law
(1850)

The federal Fugitive Slave Law of 1850 (also referred to as the Fugitive Slave Act) enraged many northerners, including many Transcendentalists, and promoted a broader public outcry against slavery for the first time, in particular in response to the celebrated Boston case of Anthony BURNS. The Fugitive Slave Law stated: "No person held to service or labor in one State, under the laws thereof, escaping into another, shall, in consequence of any law or regulation therein, be discharged from such service or labor; but shall be delivered up on claim of the party, to whom such service or labor may be due." Additionally, the law made it mandatory for northern law enforcement and even common citizens to assist in the recovery, detention, and return of fugitive slaves. The law would also deny accused runaways any legal protections and thus favor the southern slaveholder by denying the accused a jury trial and declaring that they would not be able to testify on their own behalf. The justice system was further stacked against any defendants brought to trial as the judges would receive 10 dollars for every fugitive returned to white hands, but only five dollars if they determined the accused should go free. This system was not only a harsh crackdown on actual runaways but endangered the lives of free blacks as well since, on the sole basis of a white southerner's claim of ownership, any black could be removed to the south in the hands of a slaveholder. The atmosphere of fear engendered by the Fugitive Slave Law led to the development of an elaborate Underground Railroad system to assist former slaves to escape even further north, into Canada.

Although many northern states attempted to circumvent or ameliorate the law, the Supreme Court upheld the constitutionality of the federal mandate. The Fugitive Slave Law was a turning point on the road to Civil War for the United States in that it forced a wider spectrum of northerners, even those not previously associated with ABOLITIONISM, to take a stand on slavery as the northern population were now implicated in supporting southern slavery directly. The Fugitive Slave Law was part of the overall Compromise of 1850 between northern and southern congressmen, a concession to the South in exchange for banning the slave trade in Washington, D.C., and bringing California into the union as a free state.

"Fugitive Slave Law Address"
Ralph Waldo Emerson
(1851)

Ralph Waldo EMERSON delivered an antislavery address in May 1851 as part of his public response to the 1850 passage of the federal FUGITIVE SLAVE LAW, which had been supported by Massachusetts Senator Daniel WEBSTER. More specifically, Emerson was moved to action when the law was challenged in a Boston case in April 1851 and upheld as constitutional. Both Emerson and Theodore PARKER were among the Transcendentalists who spoke out to protest the decision on the local case,

and Emerson immediately responded by urging readers of the abolitionist newspaper, *The Liberator,* to "protest for humanity against the detestable statute of the last congress." CONCORD, MASSACHUSETTS, citizens responded to Emerson's call and to his leadership by delivering a petition signed by 36 people asking him to give a public "opinion upon the Fugitive Slave Law, & upon the aspects of the times." Emerson agreed and on May 3, 1851, spoke in Concord, acknowledging that "the last year has forced us all into politics."

Beginning with his earlier 1844 address on "EMANCIPATION IN THE BRITISH WEST INDIES," Emerson had become an increasingly public voice in the antislavery debates and now clearly aligned himself even more clearly with ABOLITIONISM. By 1851, in the aftermath of the Fugitive Slave Law decision, his language was unapologetic and his message one of political action. In addressing the effects of the federal Fugitive Slave Law as it was being applied locally, his anger was directed not just to the South but to northerners as well, who would support and assist in such efforts. With Webster's actions in Congress and the outcome of the Boston case, the slavery issue had come close to home and Emerson physically felt it: "I wake in the morning with a painful sensation, which I carry about all day, and which, when traced home, is the odious remembrance of that ignominy which has fallen on Massachusetts, which robs the landscape of its beauty, and takes the sunshine out of every hour."

In "Emancipation in the British West Indies" Emerson made a strong moral appeal to the effect of slavery on the slaves themselves, detailing their conditions and victimization within the system. Now, in the "Fugitive Slave Law Address," Emerson grieved for the fugitive slave, those who managed to escape their circumstances, and who, thinking that the northern states represented not only safety but enlightenment, would find instead that "the learning of the universities, the culture of elegant society, the acumen of lawyers, the majesty of the bench, the eloquence of the Christian pulpit, the stoutness of Democracy, the respectability of the Whig party are all combined to kidnap him." Thus, in addition to the dangers awaiting the fugitive, Emerson also grieved the loss of the ideal he held of his own home, of what Massachusetts, even Boston, represented to him.

Emerson then turned his attention to the Fugitive Slave Law itself and, finding that the higher law of the Constitution had failed them all, made an appeal to a higher spiritual law, the moral law of justice and of right over wrong. Tracing the Western legal tradition from classical to Enlightenment-era English and American political philosophers, all the way to Thomas Jefferson, he counters and singles out Daniel Webster by arguing that "the great jurists" were part of a tradition in which "all affirm that it is a principle in law that 'immoral laws are void,'" and they would have found the Fugitive Slave Law an "immoral law." Emerson attacks Webster directly as outside of this tradition of "great jurists" and instead as merely one who "obeys his powerful animal nature," and who has situated himself as "the head of the slavery party in this country." In other words, Webster's motivation arose from politics rather than ideals and so Emerson must address him and the law in political terms. He next addressed the political argument of the Fugitive Slave Law as a compromise in the interest of preserving the Union by noting that the law itself was divisive, for "as soon as the constitution ordains an immoral law, it ordains disunion."

The situation forced Emerson the philosopher not only into taking a political position, but, in a departure from his other writings, into offering specific political solutions, forcing him to contemplate "the only practicable course." Emerson asked what his listeners would have asked of him: "What shall we do?" And he answers, "abrogate this law; then, proceed to confine slavery to the slave states, and help them effectually to make an end to it." While reversing the Fugitive Slave Law and then abolishing slavery itself were the primary goals, Emerson went a step further and directly advocated civil disobedience, in the tradition of Henry David THOREAU. Emerson is clear: "This law must be made inoperative. It must be abrogated and wiped out of the statute-book; but whilst it stands there, it must be disobeyed."

Emerson's appeal thus combined a strategy of refusing to abide by immoral laws as motivated by individual conscience with a direct call for collective social action in ending the law, both strategies

of the abolitionist movement throughout the heated decade of the 1850s. Abolitionists acknowledged and praised Emerson's leadership, his call to action, and the importance of someone of his reputation and position addressing this issue. Senator Charles SUMNER wrote to Emerson that he "rejoiced in reading this morning that you had spoken on the great enormity," and assured him that "your judgment of the Fugitive Slave Bill posterity will adopt, even if the men of our day do not. But you have access to many who, other Anti Slavery speakers cannot reach. Your testimony, therefore, is of peculiar importance." Emerson delivered versions of the Fugitive Slave Law Address on more than one occasion and, although it was never published in his lifetime, it appeared in later collections of his works.

Bibliography

Gougeon, Len. *Virtue's Hero: Emerson, Antislavery, and Reform.* Athens: University of Georgia Press, 1990.

Fuller, Sarah Margaret
(1810–1850)

Writer and reformer Margaret Fuller was one of the major New England Transcendentalists and the most prominent female thinker within the circle during the 1830s and 1840s. In particular she brought a feminist perspective and interpretation to the main tenets of Transcendental philosophy as recorded in accounts of her CONVERSATIONS FOR WOMEN and her most substantial written work, WOMAN IN THE NINETEENTH CENTURY, published in 1845. She was one of the first female journalists to hold a position as a regular correspondent at Horace GREELEY's NEW YORK TRIBUNE. Ralph Waldo EMERSON was one of her closest friends, and the two influenced each other's thought on everything from friendship to art to the nature of genius. She also had an intimate and sometimes intense relationship with Nathaniel HAWTHORNE, for whom Fuller served as literary inspiration for many female characters in his short stories and novels.

Fuller received a rigorous classical education at home from her father and was fluent in several languages, including Latin, Greek, French, Italian, and German. She became a schoolteacher, first at

Amos Bronson ALCOTT's alternative TEMPLE SCHOOL, then offering night classes for women in languages and poetry, and for two years teaching at a school in Providence, Rhode Island. Fuller missed Boston, however, and was becoming restless with school teaching, seeking a different outlet for her intellectual and creative impulses. Upon returning to Boston, she reunited with friends such as William Henry CHANNING, James Freeman CLARKE, and Frederic Henry HEDGE and became a part of the circle of emerging Transcendentalists. She was one of the few women to attend the first meetings of the TRANSCENDENTAL CLUB, and she emerged as a serious student of German philosophers, in particular of Johann Wolfgang von GOETHE. Fuller became the preeminent Goethean scholar in America with the publication not only of the first English translation of Johann ECKERMANN's *Conversations with Goethe* (published in 1839 as part of George RIPLEY's *SPECIMENS OF FOREIGN STANDARD LITERATURE* series) but also with her original translation of one of Goethe's plays, *Torquato Tasso* (which she completed as early as 1834 but which was not published until after her death), and her unfinished and never-published full-length biography of the thinker.

Her background as a teacher and her experience as one of the few women among the core of Transcendentalist men inspired her decision to reach out to and engage other women during the theological and cultural controversies of the 1830s and 1840s. She began her Conversations for women in the fall of 1839 with the plan to provide, as she wrote to friend Sophia RIPLEY, "a point of union to well-educated and thinking women in a city which, with great pretensions to mental refinement, boasts at present nothing of the kind." Fully aware of the limited opportunities for women to pursue either an EDUCATION or a VOCATION, Fuller challenged her participants with questions that guided her own life as a woman, "What were we born to do? How shall we do it?" In the Conversations she came closer to what she felt was her true purpose as a teacher: drawing out the ideas of others to stimulate her own thinking on various topics.

During this same time period the Transcendentalists decided to establish their own literary journal and the *DIAL* was founded in 1840 with Fuller as its first editor and one of its primary writers for the first two years of the journal. As editor of the *Dial* Fuller contributed her own poetry and literary reviews and introduced new writers such as Henry David THOREAU. It was in the *Dial* of July 1843 that Fuller published her essay, "THE GREAT LAWSUIT. Man versus Men. Woman versus Women." She spent the next year revising and expanding the essay into her most fully developed political-philosophical statement, *Woman in the Nineteenth Century*, the first book-length feminist work by an American author. The book (and the woman) became an inspiration to the emerging WOMEN'S RIGHTS movement of the same time, and feminist reformers and thinkers throughout the 19th century drew on Fuller's rhetoric to make claims to women's economic, social, political, and, most important, intellectual equality.

By the time *Woman in the Nineteenth Century* appeared in print Margaret Fuller had gone in another vocational direction in moving to New York to write for the *Tribune*. Editor Horace Greeley had been impressed with Fuller as a writer and thinker and provided her a regular column as a forum for her literary criticism and reviews on every important American and European work during this time period. Her essays for the *Tribune* also include some of her most political and reform-minded writing on issues ranging from slavery to prison reform to women's rights. She again seized an opportunity for professional and personal advancement in 1846 when she made her first trip to Europe and secured an agreement with Greeley to serve as a foreign correspondent for the paper. She primarily reported back to New York in a series of dispatches on "THINGS AND THOUGHTS IN EUROPE," covering events surrounding the Italian Revolution of 1848. Most of Fuller's biographers agree that her time in Italy, more than any other period, allowed Fuller to fulfill her goal of using her intellectual gifts in the service of meaningful political work; or, in Fuller's own words, "building the life of action upon the life of thought." This is what she had encouraged in her Boston protégées and what she sought in her own life. It is what other Transcendentalists hoped for as well, as Emerson put it in his essay "EXPERIENCE," to cultivate "the transformation of genius into practical power."

While in Italy, Fuller established herself as a mature politically engaged intellectual, but she also crossed major personal milestones in her relationship with Italian revolutionary Marchese Giovanni Ossoli and the September 1848 birth of a son, Angelo. Fuller had left the United States as an independent unmarried career woman, a leading female genius, but she faced an uncertain reception and future in her home country as she left Italy in the spring of 1850. Fuller never made it home, however, as she and her young family were all drowned when their ship wrecked off the coast of Fire Island, New York, on July 18, 1850. Upon hearing the news Ralph Waldo Emerson immediately sent Henry David Thoreau to the site to gather any news or remnants of Fuller's belongings. Emerson specifically hoped to recover Fuller's manuscript history that she had been writing on the Italian revolution, but Thoreau returned empty handed.

Fuller's life and work were thus cut short—she was only 40 years old at the time of her death—and her controversial legacy began. She became the symbol of American feminism to her followers in the women's rights movement. She remained an idealized woman of genius for her Transcendentalist friends such as Emerson. For some of her contemporaries she was a role model for women who pursued careers. For others she was an example of a true woman succumbing to the martyrdom of love and motherhood, but for most Margaret Fuller remained a paradox, an exceptional intellect who both challenged and was confined by her culture's expectations of womanhood.

Bibliography

Capper, Charles. *Margaret Fuller: An American Romantic Life.* Vol. 1. *The Private Years.* New York: Oxford University Press, 1992.

Von Mehren, Joan. *Minerva and the Muse: A Life of Margaret Fuller.* Amherst: University of Massachusetts Press, 1994.

Furness, William Henry
(1802–1896)

Reformer, writer, and Unitarian minister William Henry Furness established himself as a Transcen-

dentalist during the 1830s "MIRACLES CONTROVERSY" in which he supported the humanity rather than divinity of Jesus and the idea that Jesus' miracles could be explained by natural laws, even though humans did not yet have the moral perfection to understand those laws. Furness moved from Boston to Philadelphia after graduating from HARVARD DIVINITY SCHOOL and thus was geographically removed from the center of Transcendentalist activity. He was invited to, but could not attend the TRANSCENDENTAL CLUB upon its founding in 1836, but that same year he joined with the Transcendentalists in publishing his contribution to the "new thought" with his *Remarks on the Four Gospels,* the book which established his view on the miracles and placed him in the camp of radical UNITARIANISM.

Furness's book appeared at the exact moment as a wave of Transcendentalist works such as Ralph Waldo EMERSON's *NATURE* and Orestes BROWNSON's *NEW VIEWS OF CHRISTIANITY, SOCIETY AND THE CHURCH.* When Furness was writing his book he consulted with his former Harvard professor, conservative Unitarian Andrews NORTON, who disapproved of Furness's thesis that humans must look into their own hearts and minds—their intuition—rather than to Christianity to discover truth about themselves and the natural world. In this regard, Jesus Christ was seen as a moral teacher but not a supernatural being. Other Transcendentalists such as James Freeman CLARKE praised the book, but Norton saw this belief as atheism, as negating the need for Christianity, and he became one of the most vocal critics of the Transcendentalism of Emerson, Furness, Theodore PARKER, and George RIPLEY in the ensuing controversy that entangled the Unitarian church in light of such writings. Furness stuck with his views on the matter but attempted to clarify them in 1838 when he revised and reprinted *Jesus and His Biographers.*

As a child, Furness had attended school with Emerson, and the two boys even collaborated on a project together. The letters of the two men were edited by Furness's son, Horace Howard Furness, and published as *Records of a Lifelong Friendship 1807–1882* (1910). Furness was also a lifelong friend of Amos Bronson ALCOTT and corresponded throughout the century with several of his fellow Transcendentalist-Unitarian colleagues from the early days, such as James Freeman Clarke, Christopher Pearse CRANCH, Convers FRANCIS, Frederic Henry HEDGE, and Theodore Parker. In fact, Furness was a prolific translator of German works, another trait he shared with several of his Transcendentalist friends, and he collaborated with Hedge in translating *Prose Writers of Germany* (1848). Furness was also a reformer who used his pulpit to speak on ABOLITIONISM. He urged his congregation to oppose the FUGITIVE SLAVE LAW that angered so many of his fellow northerners, and he even participated in the Underground Railroad to aid fugitive slaves in escaping to Canada. Like many of his Boston colleagues, Furness praised John BROWN and even wrote a hymn, "Song of Old John Brown," to memorialize his antislavery raid.

Bibliography

Hoffman, R. Joseph. "William Henry Furness: The Transcendentalist Defense of the Gospels," *NEQ* 56 (1983): 238–260.

Gandhi, Mohandas K.
(1869–1948)

Mohandas K. Gandhi was a 20th-century Indian leader and peace activist who was influenced by the writings of Transcendentalist naturalist-poet Henry David THOREAU. Sources differ on how and when Gandhi was introduced to Thoreau's writings, but sometime around 1900, either while he was serving his own jail sentence for refusal to pay a tax or through his connections with Thoreau biographer Henry SALT, Gandhi read Thoreau's seminal essay on NONRESISTANCE, or nonviolent resistance, "CIVIL DISOBEDIENCE." Gandhi most likely read WALDEN as well, but it was in "Civil Disobedience" that he found a kindred spirit. Both Gandhi and Thoreau served jail time for refusal to pay taxes and, although they lived and practiced their "civil disobedience" within very different political contexts, Gandhi later wrote about his experience in terms very similar to Thoreau's 1849 account. Gandhi, like Thoreau, found that only the body could be imprisoned while "the prisoner's soul is free" and, in his own account, Gandhi quoted Thoreau directly in saying that "I did not for a moment feel confined, and the walls seemed a great waste of stone and mortar." Gandhi referred to Thoreau's work as a "masterly treatise" and acknowledged that "it left a deep impression on me." Gandhi later translated and published "Civil Disobedience" in the South African newspaper *Indian Opinion*.

Gandhi was obviously heavily influenced by Thoreau's methods and writings, but he did interpret their actions somewhat differently. He at first rejected the idea of civil disobedience, preferring instead to think of his actions as "resistance" rather than "disobedience." Gandhi coined the Sanskrit term *satyagraha*, which translates as "force of truth" or "force of love." Gandhi explained "satyagraha" himself as "the vindication of truth not by infliction of suffering on the opponent but on one's self." While Thoreau called upon more people, "ay, if one honest man, in this state of Massachusetts," to be willing to "be locked up in the county jail" on behalf of ABOLITIONISM Gandhi called for "patience and sympathy" in expecting one's opponent to change his or her ways and the cultivation of inner strength as one's most powerful tool. In this sense, ironically, Gandhi's method was more in line with the Transcendentalism of Thoreau's day in the emphasis on the strength and control of one's self rather than attempting to influence and control others. As an activist, however, Gandhi moved beyond the individualist aspect of satyagraha, and his message became the basis of a mass movement for social change, something that the Transcendentalists in general, not just Thoreau, were unable to do in the political context of the 19th century. Satyagraha included a range of methods of nonviolent resistance, from noncompliance, such as Thoreau and Gandhi practiced in their stance against unjust or immoral taxes, to fasting, prayer, and other nonviolent actions. This is the legacy—from Henry David Thoreau through Mahatma Gandhi—that influenced the strategies of other 20th-century activists as well, including the Reverend Martin Luther King, Jr., in the American civil rights movement of the 1950s and 1960s.

Bibliography

Chernus, Ira. *American Nonviolence: The History of an Idea.* Maryknol, N.Y.: Orbis Books, 2004.

Kaur, Harpinder. *Gandhi's Concept of Civil Disobedience: A Study with Special Reference to Thoreau's Influence on Gandhi.* New Delhi: Intellectual, 1986.

Garrison, William Lloyd
(1805–1879)

William Lloyd Garrison was, for many, the public face of radical ABOLITIONISM in the American 19th century and was admired by many of the Transcendentalists for his strategy of moral suasion and calling attention to individual conscience rather than directly engaging what he perceived as a corrupted political system. In his lectures and in the reform newspaper he founded in 1831, *The Liberator*, Garrison called for the "immediate emancipation" of African-American slaves. As one of the founders of the New England Anti-Slavery Society, Garrison had personal and professional connections with many Massachusetts reformers, including Transcendentalists such as Amos Bronson ALCOTT, William Henry CHANNING, Henry David THOREAU, and Theodore PARKER. Garrison personally brought many of this community into the abolitionist cause and in the 1840s Ralph Waldo EMERSON described Garrison as one of "the five or six personalities that make up . . . our American existence." Most of the Transcendentalists held antislavery beliefs and several were active, like Garrison, as speakers and writers for the abolitionist cause. Garrison joined them at the CHARDON STREET AND BIBLE CONVENTIONS, an early location for organizing antislavery commitments among Boston's literary and reform community. It was William Lloyd Garrison who called a July 4, 1854, meeting to protest the capture and return of fugitive slave Anthony BURNS, a case that outraged and galvanized the Boston reform community. It was at that meeting that Thoreau gave one of his most politically charged speeches, "SLAVERY IN MASSACHUSETTS," and the same meeting at which

Garrison escalated tensions over the issue by publicly burning a copy of the U.S. Constitution.

Bibliography

Gougeon, Len. *Virtue's Hero: Emerson, Antislavery, and Reform.* Athens: University of Georgia Press, 1990.

The Genius and Character of Emerson
Franklin Benjamin Sanborn
(1898)

The Genius and Character of Emerson is a collection of lectures from a special 1884 session of the CONCORD SCHOOL OF PHILOSOPHY AND LITERATURE commemorating Transcendentalist thinker Ralph Waldo EMERSON. The Concord School of Philosophy met every summer between 1879 and 1888 and Franklin Benjamin SANBORN served as the school secretary. The 1884 lecturers covered all aspects of Emerson's career and influence: Amos Bronson ALCOTT presented "Ion: A Monody," Ednah Dow CHENEY on "Emerson and Boston," Julian HAWTHORNE on "Emerson as an American," M. Rene de Poyen Belleisle on "A French View of Emerson," Cyrus BARTOL on "Emerson's Religion," Elizabeth Palmer PEABODY on "Emerson as Preacher," Franklin Benjamin SANBORN on "Emerson Among the Poets," "Poems in Honor of Emerson" presented by Emma Lazarus, Ellery CHANNING, Sanborn, and Mrs. E. C. Kinsey, Edwin D. Mead on "Emerson's Ethics," Julia Ward HOWE on "Emerson's Relation to Society," George Willis COOKE on "Emerson's View of Nationality," William Torrey HARRIS on "Emerson's Philosophy of Nature," Protap Chunder Mozoomdar on "Emerson as Seen from India," and William Torrey Harris again on "Emerson's Orientalism" and "Emerson's Relation to Goethe and Carlyle." *The Genius and Character of Emerson* was one of only three published volumes of lectures from the school, the others being CONCORD LECTURES ON PHILOSOPHY (1883) and THE LIFE AND GENIUS OF GOETHE. (1886).

Gerando, Joseph Marie, Baron de
(1772–1842)

Baron de Gerando was a French educational theorist and philosopher who greatly influenced the ideas and work of American Transcendentalist reformers of EDUCATION, Amos Bronson ALCOTT and Elizabeth Palmer PEABODY. In the 1830s Peabody translated Gerando's works into English editions that were reprinted as late as 1860. His most influential text, *Self-Education: or, The Means and Art of Moral Progress,* formed the foundation of Bronson Alcott's educational philosophy as implemented in his TEMPLE SCHOOL. George RIPLEY also read and reviewed *Self-Education* in the CHRISTIAN EXAMINER, and drew upon Gerando's ideas for the school set up at the utopian experiment at BROOK FARM. While Alcott, Peabody, and Ripley were most interested in applying ideas to their educational reform projects, other Transcendentalists read Gerando's work on the history of philosophy. Ralph Waldo EMERSON, Margaret FULLER, and Henry David THOREAU all made references to reading Gerando's philosophy of eclecticism, a significant influence on the development of Transcendentalist thought as well.

"Give All to Love"
Ralph Waldo Emerson
(1847)

Ralph Waldo EMERSON's poem "Give All to Love" was published in his first collection of POEMS (1847) and, like much of his other poetry, grapples with the struggle between the individual and social demands on the self. The dilemma between giving of oneself to others while still retaining integrity of the self was, in this case, explored through the theme and imagery of love. Emerson opens the poem with recognizing the competing demands to the self and advises to not hold back on giving attention to wherever you are needed: "Give all to love; / Obey thy heart; / Friends, kindred, days, / Estate, good-fame, / Plans, credit, and the Muse— / Nothing refuse." The primary symbol of love in the poem is the sun, which both rises and sets, but, "Though thou loved her as thyself," that should not discourage one from experiencing the day. This image of nature is personified by the end of the poem as a "she": "Cling with life to the maid." "She" or a woman is also symbolic of the earth, another force or element of nature. To give to both

the sun and earth, to love oneself, an ideal, and to love another person, highlights Emerson's belief that the sun, earth, and humanity are not separate, but their symbolic meanings are, in fact, unified into a whole, the universe. Since humans are part of the universe, even when humans die or love is unrequited, the love that was generated goes on, enriching the universe: "Though her parting dims the day, / Stealing grace from all alive; / Heartily know, / When half-gods go, / The gods arrive." Emerson may have been referring here to the memory and death of his first wife, Ellen Tucker EMERSON, and other poems in the collection also make reference to love, "Eros," and to remembrances of a loved one gone, "Thine Eyes Still Shined."

Gleanings in the Fields of Art
Ednah Dow Cheney
(1881)

Gleanings in the Fields of Art is a collection of lectures and essays by feminist reformer and art theorist Ednah Dow CHENEY. Cheney was heavily influenced in her theory of art by Transcendentalist Margaret FULLER, and Cheney's writings illuminate, as one scholar has noted, perhaps the most important "Transcendentalist aesthetic" of art beyond Fuller's own. Aesthetics dealt with the concept of beauty and defining the source, characteristics, and purpose of beauty in art. For classical thinkers, beauty was revealed through imitation, a concept rejected by ROMANTICISM of the late 18th and early 19th centuries. For romantic philosophers and artists, art was judged by its inspiration and reflection of nature, and the beauty of nature was conveyed not through pure imitation but through the artist's own interpretation or representation which was meant to draw out the perhaps not obvious beauty of nature. As Ralph Waldo EMERSON stated in his essay on "ART," "the painter should give the suggestion of a fairer creation than we know."

In addition to the influence of Transcendentalism on her work, Ednah Dow Cheney was a lifelong student of aesthetic theories and of many prominent artists of her day, including her husband

Seth Cheney and Boston's most regarded local artist of the time, Washington ALLSTON, who was admired greatly by the Transcendentalists. Unlike other Transcendentalists who translated their sense of aesthetics into their writing, poetry, or music, Cheney developed the most thorough and systematic aesthetic theory as related to painting and the practical arts. For her, art informed all other aspects of expression and, in her *Reminiscences,* she declared that "Transcendentalism is the philosophy of Ideal Art."

Like Emerson, Cheney understood art as a representation of higher ideals "though in a material form." Unlike Emerson, however, Cheney did not feel that art must serve as a purely unifying force. For Cheney, striving for "absorption in unity" of distinct elements risked losing insight into the separate distinct parts, and her aesthetic of art as outlined in *Gleanings in the Fields of Art* emphasized the coming together of opposites. She outlined a series of dichotomies as the subject of art, which was not only "thought," as Emerson had stated, but "feeling" as well, the "material" alongside, not superior to, the "spiritual," celebrating nature as well as humanity. Cheney also spoke of art as an ideal marriage, combining the masculine and the feminine in an aesthetic that appreciated and celebrated both. Cheney's aesthetic, then, is an androgynous emphasis on "duality" as the ideal, rather than just "unity," and in this sense her theories were aligned with those of her mentor, Margaret Fuller, especially as Fuller discussed in her 1845 feminist text, WOMAN IN THE NINETEENTH CENTURY. Cheney did share with Emerson the idea that "Human life itself is the greatest of all forms of art," but she was also inspired by Fuller's feminist-Transcendentalism and applied it to her own specific focus on art.

Ednah Dow Cheney's essays on art were the first fully formulated aesthetic theories from an American artist and writer and were uniquely inspired by her association with Transcendentalism. Some of the essays featured in *Gleanings in the Fields of Art* were reprinted from lectures given at the CONCORD SCHOOL OF PHILOSOPHY AND LITERATURE, at which Cheney was a regular speaker during the school's existence between 1879 and 1888.

Bibliography

Dykeman, Therese B. "Ednah Dow Cheney's American Aesthetics." In *Presenting Women Philosophers*, eds. Cecile T. Tougas and Sara Ebenreck. Philadelphia: Temple, 2000, 41–50.

"A Glimpse of Christ's Idea of Society"
Elizabeth Palmer Peabody
(1841)

Transcendentalist reformer and publisher Elizabeth Palmer PEABODY contributed the essay "A Glimpse of Christ's Idea of Society" as part of a trilogy on the theoretical underpinnings of the utopian communal experiment at BROOK FARM, established by George RIPLEY at West Roxbury, Massachusetts, in 1841. The essay was printed in the October 1841 issue of the Transcendentalist literary journal, the DIAL, and was followed by "Plan of West Roxbury Community" in the January 1842 issue, and "FOURIERISM" in April 1844. The idea for Brook Farm had been formulated out of discussions held in Peabody's own Boston bookstore and, although she never lived at the community, she lent her voice of support through her writings in the *Dial.*

In "A Glimpse of Christ's Idea of Society," Peabody translates the ideals of the community through her own particular lens of Christian PERFECTIONISM in social reform. Peabody retained a strong faith in Christianity and balanced her Transcendentalist individualism with a strong social vision based on the moral example of Jesus Christ. In the essay Peabody presented "Christ's idea of society" as an attempt toward perfection of the individual soul as well as "the social principle" which, ideally, should "cherish and assist" the soul in its quest. Peabody the Transcendentalist articulated the theme of self-culture as the philosophical ideal, in language similar to her colleagues Ralph Waldo EMERSON and Margaret FULLER, when she argued "the final cause of human society is the unfolding of the individual man into every form of perfection . . . according to the inward nature of each." Peabody's vision promoted development of the individual at the same time that it checked excessive individualism by linking personal or spiritual goals with ideals for social organization.

Elizabeth Peabody had dedicated much of her professional life to this point as a teacher and educational reformer and theorist. Thus it is not surprising that Peabody emphasized EDUCATION as the key to social and individual reform: "In the true society, then, Education is the ground Idea." The idea of "Christ"—which Peabody likened to the same principle called by other names such as "Law" or "Freedom"—was, she posited, "the only university of Education worthy the name." Although she would more explicitly address the Brook Farm experiment in her later essays, in "A Glimpse of Christ's Idea of Society" Peabody was working toward an examination of utopian socialism, and of the social theories of Charles Fourier in particular, as a model of the harmony of the individual with social interests.

Godwin, Parke
(1816–1904)

Writer and reformer Parke Godwin was associated with the Transcendentalists through his involvement at BROOK FARM, the utopian community established by George RIPLEY in 1841. Godwin lived in New York, but through his reform work and newspaper editing he had made contacts with Ripley and other Transcendentalists such as Orestes BROWNSON, William Henry CHANNING, and Ralph Waldo EMERSON. Godwin never joined the community at Brook Farm, but he took an active interest in the experiment as one of the premiere American disciples of French utopian socialist Charles Fourier (see FOURIERISM). He wrote articles for Fourierist journals, including The Phalanx and Brook Farm's THE HARBINGER, and published two books on socialism and FOURIERISM. In 1846 he was one of the founders and a secretary of the New York-based AMERICAN UNION OF ASSOCIATIONISTS, an organization created to bring together geographically diverse communities and individuals interested in promoting Fourier's ideas in the United States. When the Associationists took over publication of The Harbinger after the 1847 demise of Brook Farm, Godwin became the editor. He took on this role not only because he had an interest in Fourierism but because he had an interest in Fourierism but

because he had experience in newspaper editing, having founded his own paper, the Pathfinder, in 1843. Fellow reformer Elizabeth Palmer PEABODY solicited an essay from Godwin for her 1849 AESTHETIC PAPERS and, in the 1850s, he went on to work as an editor at PUTNAM'S MONTHLY MAGAZINE and other New York magazines.

Bibliography
Guarner, Carl. The Utopian Alternative: Fourierism in Nineteenth Century America. Ithaca, N.Y.: Cornell University Press, 1991.

Goethe, Johann Wolfgang von
(1749–1832)

The German idealist philosopher Johann Wolfgang von Goethe was one of the major intellectual influences on American Transcendentalism. As recent historian Gustaaf Van Cromphout has noted, "Almost every Transcendentalist had something negative or positive to say about G[oethe]." Reflecting later in his journals on the ideas that developed among his Transcendentalist colleagues in the 1830s and 1840s, Ralph Waldo EMERSON wrote, "Goethe was the cow from which all their milk was drawn." As a near contemporary the Transcendentalists held up Goethe as an example of genius; as a philosopher the main idea that the Transcendentalists drew from Goethe was that of self-culture, the development of the individual soul as the main purpose of life.

Goethe exerted perhaps his most powerful influence on the thinking of Ralph Waldo Emerson and Margaret FULLER, who sought more than any other to make Goethe's ideas applicable to their own lives and philosophy. The American Transcendentalists first came to Goethe through the translations of English writer Thomas CARLYLE in the 1820s. Although several of them could read and study Goethe in the original German language, such as Margaret Fuller and James Freeman CLARKE who were particularly interested in German writers, and both of whom wrote articles or essays on Goethe, Fuller was responsible for making Goethe more widely available to American readers when, in 1839, she provided the first English translation of Johann Peter ECKERMANN's *Conversations with Goethe in the Last Years of His Life*; she also published book-length translations of Goethe's *Torquato Tasso* and the novel *Die Gunderode* by Goethe's literary colleague and correspondent Bettine von Arnim. Considered together with her unfinished and never-published biography of the German philosopher, Fuller's writings constitute the first and most substantial body of critical work on Goethe by a single American author.

Goethe inspired Margaret Fuller's feminist Transcendentalism as she identified him as one of three "prophets of the coming age" (along with Charles Fourier [*see* FOURIERISM] and Emanuel Swedenborg [*see* SWEDENBORGIANISM] whose ideas had specific relevance for the social and cultural position of women. According to Fuller in *WOMAN IN THE NINETEENTH CENTURY* (1845), Goethe in his "continued efforts at self-culture, takes as good care of women as of men" primarily due to the "suggestions to his mind" provided by prominent women in his life. Looking at the influence of women such as Goethe's mother and sister, but especially at female characters and heroines in Goethe's literary creations, Fuller found that "In all these expressions of Woman, . . . (Goethe) aims at pure self-subsistence, and a free development of any powers with which they may be gifted by nature as much for them as for men. They are units, addressed as souls." In Fuller's interpretation of Goethe, then, were the foundations and aims of her own philosophy: a belief that the main human goal was to grow and develop as individuals to our highest potential.

For his part, Ralph Waldo Emerson was most attracted to Goethe's theories of literature and history. It was in Goethe's writing on history that Emerson was introduced to the idea of "representative" figures, of important or select individuals who symbolically stood in for an age or an ideal. This philosophy and framework of history directly informed Emerson's own approach in *REPRESENTATIVE MEN* (1850), in which he named Johann Wolfgang Von Goethe as Western intellectual history's representative "Writer" (Chapter VII). In this essay Emerson chose Goethe as representative because Goethe himself sought to *be* representative, to encompass "universal nature, universal truth." Emerson praised the man whose

purpose in life was the pursuit of truth for the purpose of self-development, as revealed for Emerson in the title of Goethe's autobiography, "Poetry and Truth out of my Life."

Bibliography

Cromphout, Gustaaf Van. *Emerson's Modernity and the Example of Goethe.* Columbia: University of Missouri, 1990.

Zwarg, Christina. *Feminist Conversations: Fuller, Emerson, and the Play of Reading.* Ithaca, N.Y.: Cornell University Press, 1995.

"Goethe; or, the Writer"   *See* REPRESENTATIVE MEN.

"The Great Lawsuit"
Margaret Fuller
(1843)

"The Great Lawsuit. Man *versus* Men. Woman *versus* Women" was an essay by Margaret FULLER published in the July 1843 issue of the *DIAL*, the Transcendentalist literary journal previously edited by Fuller but in 1843 edited by Ralph Waldo EMERSON. "The Great Lawsuit" expanded upon themes Fuller addressed in her series of CONVERSATIONS FOR WOMEN held between 1839 and 1844. The essay provided Fuller's fully developed feminist Transcendentalist ethos in that she addressed the idea of female self-culture, the need for women's EDUCATION and independence and social and cultural reform to raise woman's status.

The "Great Lawsuit" that Fuller referred to was the worldwide and historical battle not only between the sexes but, as her subtitle clearly indicated, between the idea and customs of manhood or womanhood and between actual men and women. One of the most striking aspects of Fuller's feminist writing is her challenge to cultural expectations of women *and* men, and her goal not only of advancing the position of woman but of harmonizing relations between the sexes and thus among humanity as a whole. Still, she argued that this project must begin with raising the status of women since, as she put forth, "the idea of man, however imperfectly brought out, has been far more so than that of woman, and that an improvement in the daughters will best aid the reformation of the sons of this age."

In "The Great Lawsuit" Fuller addressed the same goals and issues that had motivated her Conversations for women, which were still ongoing at the time of the essay's publication. Fuller used the same language of encouraging women by bringing them together to discuss their status. In "The Great Lawsuit," as in her letters to friends about the Conversations, she lamented that "The difficulty is to get them to the point where they shall naturally develop self respect, the question how it is to be done." While Fuller thus hoped to reform women's own images of themselves, she also emphasized that even if women did "naturally develop self respect," they would still need opportunities for pursuing self development and thus simultaneous reform of institutions and social customs was necessary as well.

Although the essay was widely reviewed in various periodicals in Boston and New York, Fuller's ideas would reach a broader audience beyond those interested in Transcendentalism when she revised and considerably expanded the essay into the 1845 book WOMAN IN THE NINETEENTH CENTURY. The book proved to be Margaret Fuller's most important and influential work as it provided theoretical and rhetorical power to the emerging WOMEN'S RIGHTS movement of the same time and influenced the next generation of feminist activists and writers.

Bibliography
Reynolds, Larry J. "From *Dial* Essay to New York Book: The Making of *Woman in the Nineteenth Century.*" In *Periodical Literature in Nineteenth-Century America,* eds. Susan Belasco Smith and Kenneth M. Price. Charlottesville: University of Virginia, 1995, 17–34.

Greaves, James Pierrepont
(1777–1842)

English reformer James Pierrepont Greaves was heavily influenced by the educational philosophy of Transcendentalist Amos Bronson ALCOTT. It was through Greaves's own work that Alcott was introduced to and understood the ideas of Johann PESTALOZZI. For his part, when Greaves read reports of Alcott's work at the TEMPLE SCHOOL, as recorded in Elizabeth Palmer PEABODY's RECORD OF A SCHOOL, the two men began a correspondence. Soon after, in 1838, Greaves founded the ALCOTT HOUSE in England, a boarding school inspired by the methods Bronson Alcott used at the Temple School as well as the health and political reform ideas then occupying Greaves's mind. In 1842 Alcott traveled to England and visited the school founded upon his model. Although Greaves died before Alcott arrived and, therefore, the two men never met, the transatlantic ties between reformers were further strengthened when Alcott met with Greaves's colleague Charles LANE who accompanied Alcott back to the United States and became the cofounder of the utopian community at FRUITLANDS.

Bibliography
Francis, Richard. *Transcendental Utopias: Individual and Community at Brook Farm, Fruitlands, and Walden.* Ithaca, N.Y.: Cornell University Press, 1997.

Greeley, Horace
(1811–1872)

Prominent 19th-century reformer, politician, and journalist Horace Greeley supported Transcendentalist literary efforts in the pages of the NEW YORK TRIBUNE, the paper Greeley founded in 1841 and edited for 30 years. New Yorker Greeley did not identify as a Transcendentalist himself, although he claimed to "like its spirit and its enobling tendencies." He positively reviewed and reprinted excerpts from the movement's Boston literary journal, the DIAL, as well as works by Ralph Waldo EMERSON and Henry David THOREAU. Greeley came into contact with other Transcendentalists, such as William Henry CHANNING and George RIPLEY, through their mutual reform interests. Greeley was particularly attracted to the utopian socialist ideas of Charles Fourier (*see* FOURIERISM) and contributed financially to Ripley's experimental community at BROOK FARM as well as writing articles for the American Fourierist paper, THE HARBINGER. Ripley served as a literary critic for Greeley's *Tribune,* and, after the demise of Brook Farm, reformer Charles DANA served as Greeley's chief editorial assistant. Greeley's most famous Transcendentalist writer for the *Tribune* was Margaret FULLER, feminist author and founding editor of the *Dial,* who worked for Greeley first as a literary critic beginning in 1844 and then as a foreign correspondent from Europe, sending dispatches for her column "THINGS AND THOUGHTS FROM EUROPE" from 1846 until her death in 1850. In reform and literary endeavours Greeley was attracted to and supported the work of the Transcendentalists and, undoubtedly, the philosophy had an influence on his own approach to a wide range of social issues, from ABOLITIONISM to labor reform to WOMEN'S RIGHTS.

Bibliography

Fahrney, Ralph Ray. *Horace Greeley and the Tribune in the Civil War.* New York: Da Capo Press, 1970.

Lunde, Erik S. *Horace Greeley.* Boston: Twayne, 1981.

Greene, William Batchelder
(1819–1878)

Reformer and writer William Batchelder Greene had more radical and even more eclectic interests than many of his Transcendentalist peers and was known as man who courted debate and controversy. He served briefly as an Army lieutenant before resigning and joining George RIPLEY's utopian community at BROOK FARM. Through his contacts at Brook Farm he met several of the Transcendentalists including Orestes BROWNSON and Elizabeth Palmer PEABODY. Through Peabody's introductions he eventually traveled to CONCORD, MASSACHUSETTS, to meet Ralph Waldo EMERSON. Throughout the 1840s Greene participated in many Transcendentalist activities such as attending meetings of the TOWN AND COUNTRY CLUB and participating in Amos Bronson ALCOTT's public series of CONVERSATIONS. Greene's first published piece of writing was an essay on "First Principles" published in the January 1842 issue of the Transcendentalist literary journal, the *DIAL,* then under Ralph Waldo Emerson's

editorship. His respect for and interest in Emerson and in Transcendentalism led Greene to enter HARVARD DIVINITY SCHOOL, and he briefly served as a Unitarian minister. He also published a short treatise on *Transcendentalism* (1849) around the same time that he contributed an article on Emerson's "Human Pantheism" for the periodical of American FOURIERISM, SPIRIT OF THE AGE. The rest of Greene's writing career was dedicated to radical stances on labor and political reforms.

Bibliography

Myerson, Joel. *The New England Transcendentalists and the Dial: A History of the Magazine and Its Contributors.* London and Toronto: Associated University Presses, 1980.

Greenough, Horatio
(1805–1852)

Horatio Greenough is considered the first professional American sculptor. Although born in Boston and a graduate of Harvard, Greenough first met Ralph Waldo EMERSON while studying art in Florence, Italy. Greenough completed most of his well-known works while in Italy, but he corresponded regularly with Emerson. The two men met again in Washington, D.C., in 1843 when Greenough's sculpture of George Washington was placed on display in the Capitol rotunda. Harvard professor Edward EVERETT wrote: "I regard Greenough's 'Washington' as one of the greatest works of sculpture of modern times. I do not know the work which can justly be preferred to it, whether we consider the purity of the taste, the loftiness of the conception, the truth of the character, or the accuracy of an anatomical study and mechanical skill." Still, the classical style sculpture created some controversy among an American public with more modern tastes, and the statue was moved several times before finding a permanent home at the Smithsonian Institute in Washington, D.C., where it can be seen today. After graduating from Harvard, Greenough was mentored by another Boston artist and favorite among the Transcendentalists, Washington ALLSTON. In addition to portrait busts and statues, Greenough completed sculptures of idealized virtues and religious symbolism as well, such as "The Guardian Angel," "Venus contending for the Golden Apple," and "Lucifer." Horatio Greenough and Ralph Waldo Emerson shared similar ideas about art and aesthetics, and Emerson praised Greenough as an original American artist. Besides that of George Washington, Greenough completed busts of an impressive list of other famous American political and even literary subjects, including Presidents John Adams and John Quincy Adams, novelist James Fenimore Cooper, and Supreme Court Chief Justice John Marshall. Greenough spent the last several years of his life working on a four-statue commission by Congress when he died prematurely in 1852.

Bibliography

Metzger, Charles R. *Emerson and Greenough: Transcendental Pioneers of an American Esthetic.* Berkeley: University of California Press, 1954.

Grimm, Herman
(1828–1901)

Independent scholar and historian Herman Grimm was a friend and correspondent of Ralph Waldo EMERSON and the biggest promoter of Emerson's Transcendentalist philosophy in 19th-century Germany. After writing biographies of Michelangelo and Raphael, Grimm was appointed professor of art history at the University of Berlin. The American Transcendentalists knew of and were interested in Grimm as well because his wife, Gisella von Arnim Grimm, was the daughter of Bettina Brentano von Arnim, who was in turn a literary confidante of Johann Wolfgang von GOETHE, one of the major influences on the Transcendentalists and one of Emerson's *REPRESENTATIVE MEN* (1850) of history. After reading Emerson's *ESSAYS: FIRST SERIES* (1841), Grimm recalled that "I followed his thoughts, word for word. . . . Everything seemed to be old and well known, . . . and everything was new as if I was learning it for the first time." Grimm promoted Emerson in Germany by translating his essays on "Shakespeare" and on "Goethe" from *Representative Men* and writing German essays on Emerson. The two men began corresponding in 1856, and they met one time in Italy in 1873. Emerson may also have been the inspiration for a character in an 1867 novel by Grimm.

H

Hale, Edward Everett
(1822–1909)

Unitarian minister, writer, and editor Edward Everett Hale was brought into contact with the Transcendentalists through his family connections to both the newspaper business and Harvard College. His father, Nathan Hale, was one of the owners of the *Boston Daily Advertiser,* and his uncle Edward EVERETT was a Harvard professor whose students included Ralph Waldo EMERSON among others. Hale himself graduated from Harvard in 1839 as the class poet but went on to study theology independently. In addition to his long career as a reform-minded minister, Hale was an extremely prolific writer who published literally hundreds of books, novels, sermons, essays, and short stories. His literary interests included early reporting for the Boston *Daily Advertiser* and serving as coeditor of the CHRISTIAN EXAMINER along with Frederic Henry HEDGE between 1857 and 1861. He collaborated with Hedge again in founding the Examiner Club in 1863, of which Hale eventually served as president.

Hale often preached on reform themes, especially ABOLITIONISM, and his first major book, *Kanzas and Nebraska* in 1854, urged Americans to keep the territory free from slavery. (The spelling of Kanzas with a "z" was thought to more accurately reflect the native American pronunciation of the word and was used by other reformers, such as Thomas Wentworth HIGGINSON in his 1856 book, *A Ride Through Kanzas.*) Perhaps Hale's most well-known story is "The Man Without a Country" (1863), a story of patriotism and loyalty, which condemned unchecked individualism and has been adapted numerous times in the 20th century for the stage, screen, and opera.

Beyond his professional relationships with figures such as Frederic Henry Hedge or James Freeman CLARKE, also a member of the Examiner Club, Edward Everett Hale was interested in the Transcendentalists primarily as 19th-century literary figures. In 1891 he edited the *Autobiography, Diary and Correspondence* of fellow Unitarian minister James Freeman Clarke. He lectured on Ralph Waldo Emerson and published a collection of Emerson's essays. Finally, Hale's own autobiography, the immensely popular *A New England Boyhood,* was published in 1893. In 1903 Hale became the chaplain for the U.S. Senate. At the time of his death in 1909, Edward Everett Hale was a prominent and much beloved American figure.

Bibliography
Adams, John R. *Edward Everett Hale.* Boston: Twayne, 1977.

"Hamatreya"
Ralph Waldo Emerson
(1846)

Ralph Waldo EMERSON's poem "Hamatreya" was published in his 1847 volume of POEMS. He composed the verse during a period in which he was heavily influenced by readings in Hindu and Islamic literature and poetry, reflected in another of his more well known poems as well, "BRAHMA," published in 1867 in a separate collection, MAY-DAY AND OTHER PIECES. Also during the mid-1840s Emerson made his largest land purchases, acquiring the 14 acres at WALDEN POND, which he visited daily. The Eastern influences as well as his reflections on land ownership are both present as themes in the poem. "Hamatreya" was Emerson's interpretation or translation of a passage from the Hindu spiritual text, the Vishnu Purana. He had copied into his 1845 journal the lines "I will repeat to you, Maitreya, the stanzas that were chanted by the Earth." Emerson appropriated the earlier name of "Maitreya" into the westernized "Hamatreya" (the Greek prefix "hama" meaning "all together") and "the stanzas chanted by the Earth" into the second part of his poem, "the Earth-Song."

The poem opens by further mixing western and eastern in describing the human relationship to the land of the earliest settlers of CONCORD, MASSACHUSETTS: "Bulkeley, Hunt, Willard, Hosmer, Meriam, Flint" were the first European owners of the land that Emerson now partly owned and through whom he therefore attempted to work out the dilemma of his "possession" of the land. The first settlers, many of them Emerson's own ancestors, owned the land but were also dependent upon it for "Hay, corn, roots, hemp, flax, apples, wool, and wood." Their farming efforts were symbolic of the reciprocal relationship between humans and nature, and in the next part of the poem Emerson pointed out that these men did not see that they, too, were part of and subject to nature; that their ownership of the land was temporary and that they themselves would become a part of that land when they died. "Where are these men?" he asks, and finds them "Asleep beneath their grounds; / And strangers, fond as they, their furrows plough." The men did not have a spiritual or Transcendental relationship to nature, but in fact a very real physical relationship through their own mortality and burial: "Earth laughs in flowers, to see her boastful boys / Earth-proud, proud of the earth which is not theirs; / Who steer the plough, but cannot steer their feet / Clear of the grave." These lines were again drawn from the original

Hindu text, which Emerson copied in his journal as "Earth laughs, as if smiling with autumnal flowers to behold her kings unable to effect the subjugation of themselves." Here Nature, or Hamatreya, not only repossesses humans but mocks them, for it is Nature that is immortal and transcendent.

The second section, "Earth-Song," turns from the reflections of the landlords and their descendants to the perspective of the earth itself and the poet asks us to "Hear what the Earth says. / Mine and yours; Mine, not yours, / Earth endures." The Earth has "old sea" and "old shores" but has to wonder, again mockingly, "where are the old men?" The question or dilemma of ownership is resolved by nature who, obviously, owns the men, not the other way around. Although Emerson drew his inspiration and some of his lines from the Vishnu Purana, the views on nature in the poem were ultimately more consistent with Emerson's Transcendentalism than with traditional Hindu beliefs.

The Harbinger
(1845–1849)

The Harbinger was the official journal of the Transcendentalist utopian experiment at BROOK FARM. The first issue appeared in June 1845 at the time that the community had reinvented itself as a PHALANX modeled on the utopian socialist philosophy of French socialist Charles Fourier. Brook Farm had been established in 1841 as an experiment in self-reliant living, but in May 1845 George RIPLEY and the other members adopted a new constitution that reorganized work and life at the community according to FOURIERISM and began their newspaper, *The Harbinger*, to promote and explain the new philosophy.

The editors of *The Harbinger* did not intend for the paper to be limited to their small community but instead envisioned it as more generally "devoted to the cause of a radical, organic social reform" and "the principles of universal unity as taught by Charles Fourier." In fact, the paper already had a history of its own as it had been the successor of an earlier Fourierist paper, *The Phalanx*. The paper ultimately provided very little information about Brook Farm itself, and as the community came to an end in 1847 the paper moved again, this time to New York City where it continued as a publication of the AMERICAN UNION OF ASSOCIATIONISTS until 1849. The scope of *The Harbinger,* under the Associationists and editorship of Parke GODWIN, was broadened in hopes of attracting more subscribers. The new prospectus of 1847 read: "In conducting *The Harbinger* for the future the editors intend to relieve it of the abstract character which, to a certain degree, it has hitherto borne, and to give much larger space to General Topics, to the News of the Day, and to comments on Passing Events." The paper did ultimately address a broad range of reform issues including EDUCATION, WOMEN'S RIGHTS, and ABOLITIONISM—all from the perspective of utopian socialism.

Many Transcendentalists who were not directly affiliated with Brook Farm, but who had written earlier for the DIAL, contributed pieces to *The Harbinger.* These included not only *The Harbinger* editors George Ripley, John Sullivan DWIGHT, and Charles Anderson DANA, but also James Freeman CLARKE, Christopher Pearse CRANCH, Frederic Henry HEDGE, and others. The majority of the content of *The Harbinger,* specifically the emphasis on communitarian and social reform, however, was more closely related to its immediate predecessors, *The Phalanx,* and *The Present,* than to the Transcendentalist literary emphasis of the *Dial.* In addition to providing details of Fourierist philosophy, including translations of French writings by Fourier and other socialists, however, *The Harbinger* did publish occasional poetry and literary and music reviews. The unique attention to music criticism can be attributed to the fact that one of the coeditors was John Sullivan Dwight, a music critic and theorist who went on to found the very successful *DWIGHT'S JOURNAL OF MUSIC* between 1852 and 1881.

Bibliography

Delano, Sterling. *The Harbinger and New England Transcendentalism: A Portrait of Associationism in America.* London: Associated University Presses, 1983.

Gohdes, Clarence L. F. *The Periodicals of American Transcendentalism.* Durham, N.C.: Duke University Press, 1931.

Harris, William Torrey
(1835–1909)

William Torrey Harris was a prominent philosopher of HEGELIANISM and a lecturer involved in a variety of post–Civil War Transcendentalist activities, most significantly as a friend of Amos Bronson ALCOTT and participant at the CONCORD SCHOOL OF PHILOSOPHY AND LITERATURE. Harris was a self-taught scholar of German literature and thought and a central figure in the St. Louis philosophical school. Through the writings of Thomas CARLYLE, Ralph Waldo EMERSON, and Theodore PARKER, he became interested in the ideas of Johann Wolfgang von GOETHE and Immanuel KANT, and ultimately the ideas of German philosopher Georg Hegel. Harris became perhaps the most prominent voice of Hegelian IDEALISM in 19th-century America.

While still a student at Yale University, Harris attended lectures of radical Transcendentalist thinkers such as Amos Bronson Alcott, also an educational reformer, and Theodore Parker. After leaving Yale Harris moved to St. Louis where he eventually worked as a grammar school teacher. He joined a radical group of thinkers and reformers at the St. Louis Philosophical and Literary Society, where he was first introduced to the ideas of Hegel. As a teacher and reformer, Harris sought to apply the philosophy to educational reform. Harris became the superintendent of St. Louis schools where he instituted the kindergarten as part of the public school system and worked to standardize curricula at each grade level. The theory of kindergarten education had been drawn from the work of another German theorist, Friedrich Froebel, whose ideas were promoted in the United States by educational reformers such as Transcendentalist Elizabeth Palmer PEABODY, who established the first kindergarten in the United States in 1860.

During this same period Harris helped found the St. Louis Philosophical Society in 1866 with many of his school system colleagues as well as members of the earlier similarly named Philosophical and Literary Society. It was Harris who proposed that the group begin its own publication and the *JOURNAL OF SPECULATIVE PHILOSOPHY* was founded the following year. The *Journal* was immensely successful and became one of the most important forums for American philosophical thought. It featured writing by the most prominent thinkers and writers of the age, including educator John Dewey, Transcendentalist Frederic Henry HEDGE, author William JAMES, and, of course, Harris.

In 1878 Harris brought his ideas to his friend Bronson Alcott in CONCORD, MASSACHUSETTS. The two had met when Alcott traveled to the western states with his "CONVERSATIONS" and lectures, and Harris soon planned a summer seminar in Concord. The session was a success, and Harris and Alcott joined with Franklin Benjamin SANBORN to organize another session the following summer. Out of these plans came the Concord School of Philosophy and Literature, which met every summer between 1879 and 1888. The school brought together Harris and the St. Louis Hegelians with many of Alcott's Transcendentalist colleagues in a series of public lectures and seminars. Many of Harris's lectures from the school were reprinted in in the 1883 volume of CONCORD LECTURES ON PHILOSOPHY. During this period, however, both Transcendentalism and Hegelian philosophy were being replaced by the new scientific models of social Darwinism (see DARWIN, CHARLES) and PRAGMATISM. In addition, many of the individual adherents to these ideas who had built careers working outside of professional academic circles, including both Alcott and Harris, no longer held cultural authority as philosophers.

William Torrey Harris introduced many Americans to the ideas of Hegel, which ultimately merged well with Transcendentalist idealism and, in particular, with the desire to apply philosophical ideals to practical life. Harris eventually published much of his intellectual work dating back from this period in his book *Hegel's Logic: A Book on the Genesis of the Categories of the Mind,* not published until many years later in 1890. Harris left his position as superintendent of schools in Missouri in 1880 and continued his career as a writer, primarily on issues of educational philosophy. Although many of his reforms, such as kindergarten and the separation of children into grade levels, had been incorporated into the public schools, by the time of his death in 1909 the field of pedagogy was moving away from the philosophic idealism of an earlier

age toward more empirical and technical methods of observing and assessing students.

Bibliography

Leidecker, Kurt F. *Yankee Teacher: The Life of William Torrey Harris.* New York: Kraus, 1971.

Pochmann, Henry A. *New England Transcendentalism and St. Louis Hegelianism.* New York: Haskell House, 1970.

Harvard College　　*See* HARVARD DIVINITY SCHOOL.

Harvard Divinity School

Most of the major Transcendentalists were trained as Unitarian ministers at Harvard Divinity School: James Freeman CLARKE, Ralph Waldo EMERSON, Theodore PARKER, George RIPLEY, Thomas Wentworth HIGGINSON, and many others. Founded by Puritans (*see* PURITANISM) in 1636 as a school for training ministers for the new colonies, Harvard College remained the educational and cultural center of Boston's BRAHMIN intellectual and social life through the 19th century. In 1805 Henry Ware, Sr., became a professor and served as the main intellectual force at the Divinity School for the next several decades. Beginning in the 19th century under Ware, the faculty broke with the school's Calvinist heritage and became increasingly drawn to the ideas of liberal UNITARIANISM, leading some more orthodox Christians to found alternative theological schools. By the 19th century, Harvard was well established as a general undergraduate liberal arts college and, in 1819, the ministerial training was separated to form the Divinity School.

Almost all of the major male Transcendentalists were educated at Harvard, and many returned to the school as professors and speakers throughout the century. The ministry was one of only a few professional vocational options for young men in the first half of the 19th century and, among religiously liberal New Englanders, the Unitarian pulpit held particular intellectual appeal. Unitarianism in general and the school in particular were at the center of controversy in the 1830s with the new ideas of Transcendentalism. In his 1838 DI-VINITY SCHOOL ADDRESS, Ralph Waldo Emerson criticized the rituals and traditions, including Harvard and its Unitarian faculty, that emphasized dogma and study over true spirituality. Although the 1838 address and resulting public controversy signaled Emerson's own final break from Unitarianism (and from Harvard, where he did not speak again until after the Civil War), the Divinity School was still central to the spread of early Transcendentalism. In 1842 Convers FRANCIS, founding member of the TRANSCENDENTAL CLUB, became a faculty member at the Divinity School, thus solidifying the next generation's direct link between Transcendentalism and the training of Unitarian ministers. Beginning in the 1840s the school became what historian Gary Collison characterizes as "an almost continuous Transcendentalist breeding ground." Other Transcendentalists also served as periodic instructors at the school, including James Freeman Clarke and Frederic Henry HEDGE in the 1850s.

By the late 19th century, Harvard Divinity School was no longer exclusively associated with Unitarianism. As many Unitarians themselves became more interested in comparative and universal religion (such as the Transcendentalist-Unitarians who founded the FREE RELIGIOUS ASSOCIATION), the Harvard seminary began to offer, and still does today, a wider nondenominational theological curriculum.

Bibliography

Collison, Gary. " 'A True Toleration': Harvard Divinity School Students and Unitarianism, 1830–1859." In *American Unitarianism, 1805–1865,* ed. Conrad Edick Wright. Boston: Massachusetts Historical Society and Northeastern University Press, 1989, 209–237.

Howe, Daniel Walker. *The Unitarian Conscience: Harvard Moral Philosophy, 1805–1861.* Cambridge: Harvard University Press, 1970.

Hawthorne, Julian
(1846–1934)

Julian Hawthorne was the son of Nathaniel HAWTHORNE, one of the most important novelists of the mid-19th century, and Sophia (Peabody) HAWTHORNE, an artist and the sister of Transcendentalist Elizabeth Palmer PEABODY. As a writer Julian Hawthorne lived under the daunting example of his father's achievements. The younger Hawthorne eventually produced his most critically acclaimed work not in fiction, but in biographical and historical studies, including studies of his father's life and works and published editions of family papers.

Julian Hawthorne attended Harvard and initially worked as an engineer in New York City before pursuing a literary career. Recognized because of his father's name, he sold his first short stories to various periodicals beginning in the 1870s. His first novel, *Bressant,* was published in 1873. The novel was reviewed in relation, again, to Julian's famous father, with various critics seeing this connection as either an asset or a liability to the younger writer, and scholars continue to find influences of theme and style passed from father to son. Although dismayed by such comparisons with his father, Hawthorne continued to publish several novels as well as historical works and was most productive as a journalist and writer of essays and short stories.

His two-volume biography, NATHANIEL HAWTHORNE AND HIS WIFE, created some controversy among surviving members of the Transcendentalist literary community when it was published in 1884 and 1885. In this edited collection of his parent's notebooks and correspondence, son Julian included private entries in which Nathaniel Hawthorne had denounced Margaret FULLER both personally and professionally. Julian used this material from his parents to denounce Fuller and her major feminist work, WOMAN IN THE NINETEENTH CENTURY (1845).

Julian Hawthorne's work was a major factor in establishing Nathaniel Hawthorne's place within the male American Renaissance tradition of the 1840s alongside Ralph Waldo EMERSON, Herman MELVILLE, Henry David THOREAU, and Walt WHITMAN, but his criticisms of Margaret Fuller led many of her still-surviving friends to rise to her defense with a flurry of editorials denouncing Julian's work and attempting to salvage Fuller's reputation. Still, Julian Hawthorne went on to write another well-regarded biographical study of his father's era in *Nathaniel Hawthorne and His Circle* (1903).

Bibliography

Bassan, Maurice. *Hawthorne's Son: The Life and Literary Career of Julian Hawthorne*. Columbus: Ohio State University Press, 1970.

Mitchell, Thomas. *Hawthorne's Fuller Mystery*. Amherst: University of Massachusetts Press, 1999.

Hawthorne, Nathaniel
(1804–1864)

Although author Nathaniel Hawthorne was critical of many aspects of the philosophy, his personal associations with the Transcendentalists meant that he was both closely influenced by and himself influenced the mid-19th century movement. Hawthorne was first introduced to Transcendentalist philosophy through his friend, bookstore owner and reformer, Elizabeth Palmer PEABODY, whose sister, Sophia Peabody (HAWTHORNE), he eventually married. Before their marriage, Nathaniel spent some time at the BROOK FARM utopian community in West Roxbury, Massachusetts, where he hoped to find the time to write. Instead, he found himself immersed in long hours of agricultural labor that prevented his creative production, and he eventually left the community after only a few months. He drew upon the experiences at Brook Farm a decade later as the setting for his 1852 novel, THE BLITHEDALE ROMANCE. Between 1842 (the year of their marriage) and 1845 the Hawthornes lived in CONCORD, MASSACHUSETTS, at THE OLD MANSE, the family home of Ralph Waldo EMERSON, where Nathaniel was finally able to devote time to his writing.

Although his wife, Sophia, and his sister-in-law, Elizabeth Peabody, were actively involved in Transcendentalist activities, Nathaniel Hawthorne remained aloof from many of the social and cultural interactions that defined the Transcendentalist community throughout the 1840s. Ralph Waldo Emerson characterized his neighbor as living in a "painful solitude" throughout this period, although Hawthorne did form strong friendships with William Ellery CHANNING II and Henry David THOREAU. Hawthorne spent many hours with Thoreau in nature, perhaps appreciating the latter's search for "solitude" as well, and he promoted Thoreau's literary efforts. Hawthorne's relationship

with one other Transcendentalist, Margaret FULLER, was especially complex. Fuller was a close friend of both of the Hawthornes, and she spent many hours at their home and in conversation with Nathaniel. Fuller presented a paradox of female genius and friendship to Hawthorne and to have informed many of his female characters. Through characters such as Zenobia in *The Blithedale Romance* and Hester Prynne in THE SCARLET LETTER, Hawthorne worked out his own ideas about women's roles, feminism, and relations between the sexes.

Overall, his Transcendentalist friends and neighbors exerted a strong influence on Nathaniel Hawthorne's literary life. His novels and short stories engage a range of Transcendentalist philosophical and social themes, and many of his characters were drawn from his Transcendentalist acquaintances. In the 1843 story "The Celestial Railroad" he explicitly presented the satirical image of the "Giant Transcendentalist" who "shouted after us, but in so strange a phraseology that we knew not what he meant, or whether to be encouraged or affrighted." Most of his characterizations of the movement and its ideas, however, were presented more subtly in the form of cautionary tales about the extremes of individualism and reliance on human beings. For example, the pitfalls of philosophic IDEALISM and PERFECTIONISM are addressed in short stories such as "RAPPACCINI'S DAUGHTER" and "The Birth-Mark," and satires of individual Transcendentalists, such as Ralph Waldo Emerson or Margaret Fuller, may be found in the short story "THE OLD MANSE" and in the novel *The Blithedale Romance*.

On the other hand, scholars have pointed out how thoroughly Transcendentalist themes of self-reliance, social reform, the hypocrisy of religion, the problem of evil, and the influence of the natural world on human thoughts and actions do in fact permeate Hawthorne's writings. For example, his 1850 novel *The Scarlet Letter* is one of the most scathing 19th-century critiques of historical PURITANISM, the intellectual and theological legacy of the New England Transcendentalists. The novel also provides two of the strongest, most independent female characters in literature of this time period in the mother-daughter pair of Hester and

Pearl. Even *The Blithedale Romance,* which is rightly seen as a critique of the blind idealism of the movement, still shows a perceptive understanding of the experiment and the philosophy guiding it and a grappling with what he perceived to be the limitations of that philosophy. In the end, Hawthorne was most like the Transcendentalists in looking to the interior life for clues about the outward life, and in taking the mystery of human nature and the development of the individual soul as his main themes in most of his romances.

Despite their differences and their inability to form a close personal relationship, Nathaniel Hawthorne emerged along with Ralph Waldo Emerson as one of the most important writers of the American Renaissance, part of the rise of a distinctly American literature during the mid-19th century.

Bibliography

McFarland, Philip. *Hawthorne in Concord.* New York: Grove Press, 2004.

Wineapple, Brenda. *Hawthorne: A Life.* New York: Knopf, 2003.

Hawthorne, Sophia Peabody
(1809–1871)

Artist and writer Sophia Peabody was the sister of Transcendentalist reformer and publisher Elizabeth Palmer PEABODY and, in 1842, became the wife of author Nathaniel HAWTHORNE. As a young woman in Boston Sophia studied visual arts and was encouraged by Ralph Waldo EMERSON and artist Washington ALLSTON to pursue an artistic career. After painting for several years and producing several works, Peabody traveled to Cuba with another sister, Mary, who worked as a governess on a plantation. Sophia's voluminous correspondences from the year and a half spent in Cuba were bound and published as the *Cuba Journal,* a multivolume collection read by many of her Boston friends and acquaintances. Sophia Peabody resumed her art upon returning to the United States but married Nathaniel Hawthorne in 1842 and completed her last painting just before the birth of their first child in 1844. The Hawthornes subsequently had two more children.

Their son Julian HAWTHORNE was a prominent later century writer and editor who published the earliest biographical information on Sophia in an edited collection of his parents' notebooks entitled *NATHANIEL HAWTHORNE AND HIS WIFE* (1884).

The early influence of Transcendentalism on Sophia, especially in relation to her views on nature, is most apparent in the *Cuba Journal,* as well as later references in her personal journals and notebooks. Probably due to her sister Elizabeth Peabody's influence, but also her own earlier artistic apprenticeship, Sophia was arguably more enthusiastic about Transcendentalism than her literary husband, who is best known for his critiques of many of the ideas and figures associated with the movement in novels such as *THE BLITHEDALE ROMANCE* (1852).

Nathaniel Hawthorne died in 1864 leaving Sophia with still young children and few financial resources. She maintained the family's solvency by publishing portions of his notebooks and, later, her own *Notes on Italy and England,* a record of the family's time spent in Europe while Nathaniel Hawthorne served as consul to Liverpool. She eventually returned to Europe, first to Dresden and then to London with her daughters, where she died in 1871.

Bibliography

Marshall, Megan. *The Peabody Sisters: Three Women Who Ignited American Romanticism.* Boston: Hougton Mifflin, 2005.

Valenti, Patricia Dunlavy. *Sophia Peabody Hawthorne. A Life, Volume 1, 1809–1847.* Columbia: University of Missouri Press, 2004.

Hedge, Frederic Henry
(1805–1890)

Unitarian minister, writer, and editor Frederic Henry Hedge was a preeminent German scholar and a major figure in the early years of the Transcendentalist movement. Hedge, in many ways, helped to found the movement with a series of early articles in the *CHRISTIAN EXAMINER* in 1833 and 1834 that were responsible for introducing the ideas of Samuel Taylor COLERIDGE to the American Transcendentalists who incorporated Coleridge's ideas about intuitive knowledge as one of the core aspects of their own philosophy. Ralph Waldo EMERSON, in particular, was influenced by Hedge's reviews of both Coleridge and Emanuel Swedenborg (see SWEDENBORGIANISM) in these early publications. At the age of only 13 Hedge had studied in Germany where he was introduced to the literary and philosophical IDEALISM of Immanuel KANT, Friedrich von SCHILLER and Johann Wolfgang von GOETHE. He returned from Germany to attend HARVARD DIVINITY SCHOOL and, although he moved to Maine in 1835 to serve as a Unitarian minister in Bangor, he regularly visited Boston and Cambridge and retained close ties with many Unitarian-Transcendentalists.

Hedge had befriended Ralph Waldo Emerson at Harvard and was drawn into the circle of friends that also included Convers FRANCIS, Margaret FULLER, Elizabeth Palmer PEABODY, and George RIPLEY. His *Christian Examiner* articles on Coleridge and others introduced this circle to the philosophy of intuition then prominent in German thought and which the American Transcendentalists soon adopted as part of their way of thinking. It was Hedge who proposed to Emerson the idea of a "symposium" to bring together those interested in discussing "theological and moral subjects," and he regularly attended the resulting TRANSCENDENTAL CLUB, which was founded in 1836. Contemporaries often referred to the gatherings as "Hedge's Club," acknowledging both his intellectual influence on the discussions taking place and the fact that the club mostly met when he was in town. Hedge had been among those members of the Transcendental Club who supported the idea of a new journal for the emerging movement, but his relocation to Maine prohibited his direct involvement.

When the DIAL was founded by George Ripley and others in 1840 Hedge declined editor Margaret Fuller's request for contributions, first citing other responsibilities, but then finally admitting to Fuller that he did not wish to be associated with Transcendentalism at all for fear of being labeled "an atheist in disguise." After his initial reticence, however, Hedge did finally contribute several pieces to the *Dial* including a poem and two translated pieces—playing it safe by engaging with literary, rather than theological themes. As he

lamented in a letter to colleague Convers Francis, even this small hint of association with Transcendentalism "frightened" his "ultra conservative" congregation in Maine and he narrowly escaped having to resign his post.

By 1840 even greater controversy had descended upon the movement and Hedge was withdrawing from association with many of the most radical figures such as Amos Bronson ALCOTT, Ralph Waldo Emerson and Theodore PARKER. Hedge retained a foundational belief in the divinity of Jesus Christ and condemned the critiques of orthodox Christianity put forth by Emerson and Parker, refusing to allow either man to speak in his pulpit. Although Hedge was theologically conservative, his philosophical and reform interests still kept him tied to Boston intellectual circles. He preached what he himself characterized in an 1841 lecture as an "enlightened conservatism."

It was Hedge's literary interests that allied him more closely with the Transcendentalists. His 1848 *Prose Writers of Germany* was the first American anthology of German fiction and criticism and established him as an important scholar of German literature. He also translated German poetry and wrote critical reviews for a variety of New England periodicals. In 1858 Hedge took over editorship of the *Christian Examiner,* a position he held for only three years. He was most influential as president of the AMERICAN UNITARIAN ASSOCIATION between 1859 and 1863. During this time Hedge had a central role in holding the Unitarian denomination together through defining its theological basis. Transcendentalism was one of the early threats to Unitarian unity, and in his 1861 book, *Recent Enquiries in Theology,* Hedge addressed the challenge posed by Transcendentalism, followed up by his 1865 *Reason in Religion* which examined the possibility of a Transcendental Christianity that rejected Lockean empiricism in favor of intuition but still had a basis in historical Christianity.

Having left Maine and returned to Boston in the 1850s, Frederic Henry Hedge embarked on a career as Harvard professor of church history and German and continued to move within Transcendentalist circles. He retained many of his earlier friendships for the rest of his life, despite his theological differences with many of his colleagues. He was in attendance at most of the social and intellectual gatherings dominated by Transcendentalists in the second half of the 19th century, such as the SATURDAY CLUB, the RADICAL CLUB, and, finally, Bronson Alcott's CONCORD SCHOOL OF PHILOSOPHY AND LITERATURE, where Hedge occasionally lectured.

Bibliography

LeBeau, Bryan F. *Frederic Henry Hedge: Nineteenth Century American Transcendentalist.* Allison Park, Pa.: Pickwick Publications, 1985.

Wells, Ronald Vale. *Three Christian Transcendentalists: James Marsh, Caleb Sprague Henry, and Frederic Henry Hedge.* New York: Octagon Books, 1972.

Hedge's Club   *See* TRANSCENDENTAL CLUB.

Hegel, Georg Wilhelm Friedrich   *See* HEGELIANISM.

Hegelianism

The early Transcendentalists were influenced by Hegelianism, the philosophy of German thinker Georg Wilhelm Friedrich Hegel (1770–1831), primarily through secondary readings in other German writers, such as Johann Wolfgang von GOETHE. Hegel preceded the Transcendentalists by a generation, but many were introduced to his ideas through the writings of Goethe, who greatly influenced the major Transcendentalists in the 1830s, especially Ralph Waldo EMERSON and Margaret FULLER. Hegelianism's clearest influence on earlier Transcendentalist thought was the belief in an "Absolute Mind," an idea similar to Emerson's "OVER-SOUL," and the understanding of history as a process with the goal of bringing together the human mind and the natural world.

Hegel's ideas were taken up more directly and systematically by American philosophers in the late 19th century. After the Civil War, Transcendentalist reformers reflected Hegelian ideas in their EDUCATION reform and other social science projects and were particularly attracted to Hegel's method and his ideas on the dialectic of the human mind and on history. Emerson was usually critical of such overarching and systematic methods as offered by Hegelianism, but his readings of Hegel through other proponents of German IDEALISM distilled the philosophy into a usable more Transcendentalist form.

The most prominent American Hegelian of the 19th century was William Torrey HARRIS of the St. Louis school of philosophy. Harris was a close friend and associate of Amos Bronson ALCOTT, and the two shared an interest in educational reform. Alcott, like Emerson, resisted formal structural arguments and never embraced Hegelianism directly. Harris eventually wrote the first biography of Alcott, with coauthor Franklin Benjamin SANBORN, and was also the editor of the influential *JOURNAL OF SPECULATIVE PHILOSOPHY*, through which he promoted Hegel's ideas. Many of the Transcendentalists, including Alcott and Emerson, published in Harris's journal in the 1860s and 1870s. Harris himself published an essay in the *Journal of Speculative Philosophy* on "The Dialectic Unity in Emerson's Prose," in which he tried to reconcile Emerson's Transcendentalism with Hegelianism through a study of Emerson's rhetorical style of constructing an essay.

Bibliography

Goetzmann, William, ed. *The American Hegelians: An Intellectual Episode in the History of Western America.* New York: Knopf, 1973.

Pochmann, Henry A. *New England Transcendentalism and St. Louis Hegelianism.* New York: Haskell House, 1970.

Hennell, Charles Christian
(1809–1850)

Charles Hennell was a British writer and critic whose 1838 *An Inquiry into the Origin of Christianity* and 1839 *Christian Theism* confirmed the Transcendentalist belief in nature as the source of religious truth and the rejection of the miracles of Christ. Hennell was not trained in biblical criticism but through his own studies reached many of the same conclusions as the prominent German scholars read by so many of the Transcendentalists. Ralph Waldo EMERSON first asked William Henry CHANNING to review Hennell is work for the Transcendentalist literary journal, the DIAL, but Channing declined and Theodore PARKER wrote the review instead for the October 1843 issue. Parker's praise of Hennell's "natural" Christianity, that is, his lack of formal theological training, sparked a controversy and a letter to Emerson as editor for the *Dial* from a Unitarian minister reproving the "infidelity" of both Parker and Hennell. Emerson refused to publish the letter in the *Dial,* however, and the denouncement was published separately as a pamphlet.

Bibliography

Myerson, Joel. *The New England Transcendentalists and the Dial: A History of the Magazine and Its Contributors.* London and Toronto: Associated University Presses, 1980.

Henry, Caleb Sprague
(1804–1884)

Caleb Sprague Henry introduced Americans, and the Transcendentalists in particular, to the ideas of French philosopher Victor COUSIN with an 1834 translation of Cousin's influential "Critical Examination of Locke's Essay on the Human Understanding," published under Henry's title *Elements of Psychology.* The Transcendentalists were most interested in Cousin's eclectic philosophy, and the challenge that such a method posed to Enlightenment thinker John LOCKE's empiricism was attractive to Transcendentalists such as George RIPLEY and Orestes BROWNSON but brought criticism to Caleb Henry from the religious press. Henry himself was religiously conservative and was not a Transcendentalist. Criticisms from conservatives were strong, however. Professors at Princeton Theological Seminary condemned Henry for promoting Cousin, whose philosophy they argued "makes sad havoc with Christianity." Henry felt his opponents misunderstood Cousin's ideas, but he also refused any responsibility for how the Transcendentalists used Cousin and resisted any links to what he termed

that "quality of transcendental cloud and moonshine out of Ralph Waldo Emerson." Victor Cousin's claim that Lockean sensationalism could not completely account for the human acquisition of knowledge may have attracted even a Christian like Caleb Henry to the philosophy, but Henry's readings of Cousin did not suggest the same secular applications as made by Emersonian philosophy. Henry was undeterred, however, and continued to publish several more editions of Cousin's work, introducing Cousin not only to the Transcendentalists but to a wider English-speaking audience as well.

Bibliography

Wells, Ronald Vale. *Three Christian Transcendentalists: James Marsh, Caleb Sprague Henry, and Frederic Henry Hedge.* New York: Octagon Books, 1972.

Herald of Freedom   *See* ROGERS, NATHANIEL PEABODY.

"Heroism"
Ralph Waldo Emerson
(1841)

Ralph Waldo EMERSON presented "Heroism" as part of a new series of nine lectures in Boston, which began in December 1837, and included with few revisions in his collection of ESSAYS: FIRST SERIES published in 1841. Emerson was becoming increasingly popular as a lyceum speaker, and "Heroism" was one of his most well-received lectures of this series. In "Heroism" Emerson made one of his earliest published comments on slavery and ABOLITIONISM with a controversial reference to the recent mob killing of the Reverend Elijah Lovejoy for attempting to publish an antislavery newspaper in Illinois. Although social reform and political statements were not Emerson's main purpose in 1837, or even in 1841 when the lecture was published, Emerson was moved to speak on Lovejoy's case and honor the man who died for principles: "It is but the other day, that the brave Lovejoy gave his breast to the bullets of the mob, for the rights of free speech and opinion, and died when it was better not to live."

"Champions and martyrs" were not the only kinds of heroes that Emerson celebrated, and the essay addresses heroism in much broader terms. "Heroism" is "wild courage," but, specifically, the courage of the individual soul to resist conventional wisdom, thus Emerson's appreciation of Lovejoy not only for the specific cause for which he died but for his courage in standing against popular opinion: "The hero is a mind of such balance that no disturbances can shake his will, but pleasantly and as it were merrily he advances to his own music." Heroism was thus not outward show, although in the case of "champions and martyrs" it did manifest as an outward deed. More importantly, heroism was an individual characteristic, an internal quality that governed one's own soul and set one apart, an idea he would develop further in later essays such as "CHARACTER" (1844) and in the individual examples given in REPRESENTATIVE MEN (1850). Heroism is similar to character in that it "is a obedience to a secret impulse of an individual's character."

It is typical of Emerson to take the listener or reader from the grand extremes of an ideal to its relevance in the everyday and in every person. Heroism was at the core of Emersonian self-reliance: "Self-trust is the essence of heroism." In this sense, Emerson's heroism was defined as a courage that relates not only to extreme situations, such as standing up publicly for ideas or facing martyrdom for a cause. Heroism, "self-trust," was necessary and put to the test in every aspect of daily life. Emerson gives examples of the difficulties of human life, from disease and mortality to the inconveniences of domestic life, all of which require a certain level of heroism to face down: "Time is slit and peddled into trifles and tatters. A door is to be painted; a lock to be repaired; a cord of wood is wanted; the house smokes; or I have a headache; . . . these eat up the hours." It takes courage, or heroism, to make an "extraordinary" life out of such circumstances, for "the characteristic of heroism is its persistency. All men have wandering impulses, fits, and starts of generosity. But when you have chosen your part, abide by it, and do not weakly try to reconcile yourself with the world. The heroic cannot be common, nor the common the heroic."

Higginson, Thomas Wentworth
(1823–1911)

Reformer, editor, literary critic, and author Thomas Wentworth Higginson is best known for his role in promoting the literary career of Emily DICKINSON and editing her poems, but he was a friend and chronicler of many within the Transcendentalist movement as well. He entered Harvard College at the age of only 13, where he was promptly introduced to Transcendentalism. He was heavily influenced by individual figures such as James Freeman CLARKE, Theodore PARKER, and Ralph Waldo EMERSON and once remarked that his daily reading always included "a dose of Emerson." Like Clarke and William Henry CHANNING, Higginson was unorthodox in his religious beliefs and became increasingly interested in comparative religious studies. He had graduated from HARVARD DIVINITY SCHOOL but soon left the Unitarian ministry to pursue reform work and lecturing. In the 1850s he briefly found a home preaching at the Worcester Free Church, a group who appreciated Higginson's radical reform positions. He eventually resigned that position as well in the name of radical politics.

Like others among his Transcendentalist colleagues, Higginson's theology included a strong sense of social responsibility and a commitment to almost every social reform of the century, but ABOLITIONISM in particular. While at Harvard he had also been introduced to abolitionism through hearing William Lloyd GARRISON speak, through the example of Theodore Parker, and through the writings of Lydia Maria CHILD. Higginson became an outspoken abolitionist and as one of the Boston SECRET SIX—along with Samuel Gridley Howe (husband of reformer Julia Ward HOWE), Theodore Parker, Franklin Benjamin SANBORN, Gerrit Smith, and George Stearns—he helped raise money for John BROWN's radical antislavery activities which culminated in Brown's arrest after the failed attack on the Harpers Ferry arsenal in the fall of 1859. Higginson joined the Union army during the Civil War and eventually became the colonel of one of the first black regiments in South Carolina. He wrote about his experiences in the 1870 *Army Life in a Black Regiment.*

Higginson was also an advocate of WOMEN'S RIGHTS and wrote several essays and delivered speeches supporting the women's cause. He once protested against a temperance convention for its failure to allow women to speak on its platform, and for over a decade he coedited and contributed regular essays for the women's rights periodical, *Woman's Journal.* He wrote several controversial and influential writings on the subject of women's rights including *Woman and Her Wishes* in 1854 and an 1869 treatise entitled *Ought Women to Learn the Alphabet?*—a rhetorical question that Higginson posed to address the problem of women's education.

In 1884 Higginson published a full-length biography of Margaret FULLER called *Margaret Fuller Ossoli.* His was one of the most balanced views of Fuller from a contemporary, mostly due to the fact that, unlike earlier biographers, he drew heavily upon previously unpublished materials such as personal letters, travel diaries, and recently translated correspondence between Fuller and her Italian husband. Ultimately, Higginson focused in-depth on Fuller's importance within the Transcendentalist movement—her CONVERSATIONS FOR WOMEN, her editorship of the DIAL, and her writings on Johann Wolfgang von GOETHE—and argued that she should be seen as the equal, at least, of figures such as Emerson and one of the most important writers of the century. (He honored both Fuller and Emerson by naming his only child Margaret Waldo Higginson.) His interests in women's EDUCATION and in Margaret Fuller's place in history may explain the fact that, at the time of his death, he was writing a full-length study on "The Intellectual History of Woman," which he never finished.

Thomas Wentworth Higginson's prolific writing career included many other political essays, literary reviews, short stories, and novels. He produced a significant amount of historical work, although he never considered himself a historian by profession. He was once considered for a position on the history faculty at Harvard, which he did not receive, and he was offered a position at the University of Nebraska, which he did not accept. Instead, he wrote popular history books, and his most successful of these were written for children. Books in his *Young Folks' History* series were translated into several languages and sold hundreds of thousands of copies for use in schools.

Higginson's 1898 reminiscences, *Cheerful Yesterdays,* contain the most information about his connection with other Transcendentalists, although he also published numerous essays and encyclopedia entries about individual thinkers and writers involved in the movement.

Bibliography

Meyer, Howard N. *The Magnificent Activist: The Writings of Thomas Wentworth Higginson.* Cambridge, Mass.: Da Capo Press, 2000.

Tuttleton, James W. *Thomas Wentworth Higginson.* Boston: Twayne, 1978.

Historical Pictures Retouched
Caroline Dall
(1861)

One of three books that Transcendentalist feminist Caroline DALL published in one year, *Historical Pictures Retouched: A Volume of Miscellanies* was a compilation of articles Dall had previously published in THE UNA, the WOMEN'S RIGHTS periodical coedited by Dall and reformer Paulina Wright DAVIS. As the book's title suggests and as the Preface made explicit, History, for Dall, was a feminist project and more women were needed as historians due to the fact that "many an historical judgment waits to be reversed." Dall acknowledged the many women who worked as historians and biographers, emphasizing such pursuits as particularly desirable VOCATIONs for thinking women. She presented two types of historians, "the Seekers and the Observers," and noted that women heretofore had practiced primarily as "Seekers," those who "collect, collate, test, and simplify material; to decide what is worth saving." However, History would not do justice to women's lives until more women did the work of "Observers," those who "make use of this material, and permit philosophic thought, general knowledge, and rare culture, to do their work with the accumulations so brought together." In his 1837 address on "THE AMERICAN SCHOLAR," Ralph Waldo EMERSON had proposed a similar conception in his idea of the scholar as a "Watcher" who was "to observe and report" on the world around him. Emerson expected that only a very few in society would be inclined to "adopt it as their vocation." Caroline Dall was one of those few as it was as an "Observer" that she defined her own work as an intellectual and as a cultural critic.

Dall's "reversal" of "historical judgment" was focused on illuminating the contributions of exceptional women, either women already well-known historically but who had been misrepresented, or unknown women who had done significant work in traditionally male fields such as philosophy, politics, or medicine. Caroline Dall took *vocation* as the primary theme of much of her written work on women in both historical and contemporary times. In *Historical Pictures Retouched* she was most interested in great female intellects at work. This text marked the beginning of Dall's lifelong role as a historian, specifically her interest in women's history, as central to her own Transcendentalist vision of self-development and of reform. For the series of biographical essays in *Historical Pictures Retouched,* Dall chose prominent female figures in various historical periods, from the Greeks to the Italian Renaissance to the English Enlightenment, specifically intellectual or professional women whose reputations and contributions had been misrepresented or denigrated in some way perhaps like Dall herself. Two figures that garnered considerable space in Dall's writings were the Greeks Aspasia (fifth century B.C.E.) and Hypatia (fifth century C.E.). The subtitles of these chapters reveal Dall's approach to the history of women: "Aspasia: What may truly be said for her, rather than what has been said against her" and "Hypatia, a sketch and a review: The Historic Fact, and a Protest against the Fictitious Aspersion."

Bibliography

Wayne, Tiffany K. *Woman Thinking: Feminism and Transcendentalism in Nineteenth-Century America.* Lanham, Md.: Lexington Books, 2005.

"History"
Ralph Waldo Emerson
(1841)

"History" is the opening essay in Ralph Waldo EMERSON's 1841 collection of *ESSAYS: FIRST SERIES.*

The essay takes as its theme the centrality of the individual examined through the relationship of contemporary humankind with the historical past. In the opening lines of "History," Emerson articulated his core Transcendentalist concept that "There is one mind common to all individual men. Every man is an inlet to the same and to all of the same . . . Of the works of this mind, history is the record." The universal mind was an idea he would explore further in the same volume in his essay on "THE OVER-SOUL." By placing "History" as the first essay in this volume, Emerson uses humanity's relationship to "History" as the foundation for a discussion throughout the rest of the book of the nature of the human mind and soul in current times. Ultimately, he concludes that while humans owe a debt to their heritage and past, the soul is ever progressing forward and the current human condition is that which is most important: "All inquiry into antiquity . . . is the desire to do away this wild, savage and preposterous There or Then, and introduce in its place the Here and the Now." History, in this formulation, is not a fixed set of knowledge about the past but the foundation for a subjective and individual relationship to it since "there is a relationship between the hours of our life and the centuries of time."

As "all history becomes subjective," Emerson argues then that "there is properly no History; only Biography." By this he means that the proper study of the past is the study of individuals who stand out from their times as those who have pursued genius in some way, a belief that would inspire his 1850 collection of essays on REPRESENTATIVE MEN. Furthermore, as put forth in *Representative Men,* to study and understand great individuals in the past is to understand oneself. Emerson goes on to detail that every aspect of "public" and "private" life has a history, whether nature, literature, civil life, or art, "all public facts are to be individualized, all private facts are to be generalized." At the center of the discussion remains the individual self and, in his personalization of history, Emerson argues that history is the story of the successive stages not just of civilization but of the individual as well. Each person experiences and develops through each historical age; that is, each person has within him (or her) self characteristics of the ancients, the Middle Ages, the modern world, and every time/stage in between. He argued that each person passes "through the whole cycle of experience" and "should see that he can live all history in his own person." History, therefore, is not a collection of unrelated or impersonal facts, "a dull book," but a study of one's very self, as each individual "shall walk incarnate in every just and wise man," a theme, again, guiding his choices for the six *Representative Men* (Plato, Swedenborg, Montaigne, SHAKESPEARE, Napoleon, and GOETHE) of his later collective biography.

In "History" Emerson provided then not only a model for studying history but a model for writing it as well. He urges in the conclusion of the essay that "broader and deeper we must write our annals . . . if we would trulier express our central and wide-related nature." The Transcendentalist mode of approaching history was not through an allegedly objective "path of science and of letters," an amassing of facts, but as a personal exercise in "stand[ing] nearer to the light by which nature is to be read." And, as in nature, so in history, and therefore so in individuals, in that "there is at the surface infinite variety of things; at the centre there is simplicity of cause."

The essay "History" then repeats many of the familiar Transcendentalist themes found in NATURE (1836) and throughout the remaining essays in this 1841 volume: the relationship of humanity to nature and to the past, a progressive view of civilization, an emphasis on the present (the "Here and Now") as the most significant moment in any individual life, and, most definitively, the primacy of the individual perspective and meaning over institutional or textual authorities such as colleges and history books.

Hoar, Edward Sherman
(1823–1893)

Edward Sherman Hoar was a member of a leading CONCORD, MASSACHUSETTS, family that included his father Judge Samuel Hoar and his sister, Elizabeth HOAR, an intimate friend of the Emerson family who had once been engaged to Ralph Waldo EMERSON's brother, Charles EMERSON. Edward Hoar was a graduate of Harvard and became a lawyer and district attorney in California, where he had traveled during the Gold Rush. Although trained as a lawyer, he had a passionate interest in botany and natural history and was one of Henry David THOREAU's closest friends. The two regularly explored together in and around Concord, and Hoar accompanied Thoreau on several momentous wilderness expeditions. He is the unnamed companion in the section of THE MAINE WOODS that recounts an 1857 trip the two men took together. Hoar befriended other noted scientists of his time including Harvard professor Louis AGASSIZ. Edward Hoar collected plant specimens throughout his life, and his collection, which included specimens gathered by Thoreau as well, was eventually donated to the New England Botanical Club.

Bibliography
Harding, Walter. *The Days of Henry Thoreau.* New York: Dover, 1982.

Robbins, Paula I. *The Royal Family of Concord: Samuel, Elizabeth, and Rockwood Hoar and Their Friendship with Ralph Waldo Emerson.* Philadelphia: Xlibris, 2003.

Hoar, Elizabeth
(1814–1878)

Elizabeth Hoar was engaged to Charles EMERSON, Ralph Waldo EMERSON's brother, who died in 1836 four months before their scheduled wedding. Both she and Ralph Waldo Emerson grieved over Charles's death for many years—reportedly, she wore black for 20 years in mourning for Charles. Elizabeth never married, and Ralph Waldo Emerson treated her as a sister throughout her life and she became one of his closest confidantes. He nicknamed her "Elizabeth the Wise" and, in a poem he wrote about her, declared that "My sister is a Greek in mind & face" and "that no judge or scribe / Could vie with her unerring estimate." She was a close friend not only of the Emerson family but of many of the leading Transcendentalists living in and around CONCORD, MASSACHUSETTS, such as

Amos Bronson and Abigail May ALCOTT, Margaret FULLER, and Henry David THOREAU, a schoolmate of both her and her brothers. She was herself a member of a prominent Concord family. The daughter of the infamous Judge Samuel Hoar, who later became a Massachusetts state senator and then U.S. Congressman, she had the full advantage of a private education alongside her brothers, attending and graduating from the Concord Academy, a school cofounded by her father in 1822. She was trained in several languages and had at one time tutored Richard Fuller, the younger brother of Transcendentalist Margaret Fuller, in Greek. Hoar spent most of her adult life independently pursuing her love of learning and reading.

Elizabeth Hoar was one of only three women—along with Margaret Fuller and Sophia RIPLEY—in attendance at the first meetings of the TRANSCENDENTAL CLUB. She was especially good friends with poet Caroline Sturgis (TAPPAN), with whom she regularly attended Margaret Fuller's CONVERSATIONS FOR WOMEN beginning in 1839 as well as Bronson Alcott's later CONVERSATIONS. In 1843 Hoar contributed a translated piece called "Discoveries in the Nubian Pyramids" to the Transcendentalist literary journal, the DIAL, According to Emerson's own notebooks, Elizabeth Hoar also supported the magazine in many unofficial roles assisting him with preparation of manuscripts during his tenure as editor. After the death of Margaret Fuller in 1850, Hoar translated from Italian to English the private correspondence of Fuller and her Italian husband, Giovanni Ossoli, in preparation for publication. One of her few other literary contributions was a rare account of the life of Sarah Alden Bradford RIPLEY written for an 1876 book of historical portraits of *Women of Our First Century.*

Bibliography
Maxfield-Miller, Elizabeth. "Elizabeth of Concord: Selected Letters of Elizabeth Sherman Hoar to the Emerson Family and the Emerson Circle." *Studies in the American Renaissance.* (1984, 1985, 1986).

Myerson, Joel. *The New England Transcendentalists and the Dial: A History of the Magazine and Its Contributors.* London and Toronto: Associated University Presses, 1980.

Holmes, Oliver Wendell
(1809–1894)

Writer and first biographer of Ralph Waldo EMERSON, Oliver Wendell Holmes shared the BRAHMIN cultural and social milieu of the Boston Transcendentalists but was too scientifically rather than spiritually minded to accept the philosophy. In his early career, Holmes balanced poetry writing with medical study as he was a Harvard professor of anatomy and served for six years as dean of Harvard Medical School, and he was in attendance when Ralph Waldo Emerson gave his 1837 address at Harvard on "THE AMERICAN SCHOLAR." Holmes was also popular as a lecturer and Unitarian reformer and held a place at the center of Boston intellectual and social life. By the 1850s Holmes was primarily a man of letters, attending meetings of the SATURDAY CLUB and publishing regularly as a poet and essayist. He contributed to the ATLANTIC MONTHLY (even suggesting the name for the paper founded in 1847) and eventually published three novels. Many of his writings took up Transcendentalist themes and figures, mostly in satire, although he was influenced by the philosophy enough that some of its main tenets made their way into his own thought. His 1885 biography of *Ralph Waldo Emerson* was an important early work by a contemporary, but it has been criticized by modern scholars for its emphasis on Emerson as a genteel philosopher, while ignoring the Transcendentalist's commitment to social reform, especially ABOLITIONISM.

Bibliography
Gougeon, Len. *Virtue's Hero: Emerson, Antislavery, and Reform.* Athens: University of Georgia Press, 1990.

Hooper, Ellen Sturgis
(1812–1848)

Poet Ellen Sturgis Hooper regularly contributed to the Transcendentalist movement's literary journal, the DIAL, and her poetry was privately circulated and read by many of her Boston friends who were then themselves forming the core of the Transcendentalist movement, including Ralph Waldo EMERSON, Margaret FULLER, and Elizabeth Palmer PEABODY. Both Emerson and Fuller sought out Hooper's poems, as well as those of her sister, Caroline Sturgis (TAPPAN), for the *Dial*, for they regarded both women's verses as among the best the movement had to offer. Ellen Sturgis ultimately contributed 11 anonymous poems to the magazine, several of which were incorrectly attributed to other Transcendentalists. Her poems were well received, and one of the *Dial* pieces, entitled "I slept and dreamed that life was Beauty," was even translated into Italian and subsequently misattributed to Immanuel KANT. Henry David THOREAU reported positively to Emerson on her poetry and even quoted from her poem "The Wood Fire" in a chapter of his 1854 *WALDEN*.

It was Hooper who urged Elizabeth Palmer Peabody to host "reading parties" for their female friends, and Peabody's weekly meetings predated by several years Margaret Fuller's similar concept for the CONVERSATIONS FOR WOMEN which began in 1839. Sturgis was a participant at Fuller's meetings as well and was further involved in Transcendentalist activities as a regular attendee of Emerson's lectures and a member of Unitarian minister James Freeman CLARKE's Boston congregation.

Ellen Sturgis Hooper died from tuberculosis at the age of only 36, the mother of three children. Her daughter, Clover, eventually married Henry Adams. Upon Ellen's death in 1848 Margaret Fuller planned a private printing of her collection of poems, but this did not happen until Hooper's son published a limited edition in the 1870s. Emerson chose three of her poems for representation in his 1874 collection, *PARNASSUS*.

Bibliography

Myerson, Joel. *The New England Transcendentalists and the Dial: A History of the Magazine and Its Contributors.* London and Toronto: Associated University Presses, 1980.

Howe, Julia Ward
(1819–1910)

Writer, poet, and composer Julia Ward Howe was a colleague and sometime host of the Boston intellec-

tual circle that included Transcendentalists such as Ralph Waldo EMERSON, Margaret FULLER, and Theodore PARKER, among others. Julia Ward Howe was married to Samuel Gridley Howe, an advocate of the blind and deaf and a social reformer with whom she founded an antislavery paper, the Boston *Commonwealth*. Although not generally regarded as a Transcendentalist herself, Julia Ward Howe's writing and reform commitments reflected the influence of the philosophy, especially her 1854 book of poetry, *Passion-Flowers*. She was committed to ABOLITIONISM and peace activist and prominent figure in the WOMEN'S RIGHTS cause and she aligned with other Boston Transcendentalists, such as feminists Ednah Dow CHENEY and Caroline DALL, to promote Margaret Fuller's legacy at the end of the 19th century. Howe published two books about Fuller—a biography, *Margaret Fuller*, and an edited collection of *Love-Letters of Margaret Fuller*. These works emphasized Fuller not only as an intellectual but as a woman and they provided alternative readings of Fuller's literary and social significance. Howe remained aligned with Transcendentalist philosophical efforts through her participation in Amos Bronson Alcott's CONCORD SCHOOL OF PHILOSOPHY AND LITERATURE, where she lectured on Margaret Fuller and on the influence of German thinker Johann Wolfgang von GOETHE, one of the most important influences on Transcendentalism and on Fuller in the 1830s. Julia Ward Howe is best known today as the composer of "The Battle Hymn of the Republic," the 1861 Civil War anthem which begins with the line, "Mine eyes have seen the glory."

Bibliography

Williams, Gary. *Hungry Heart: The Literary Emergence of Julia Ward Howe.* Amherst: University of Massachusetts Press, 1999.

"The Humble-Bee"
Ralph Waldo Emerson
(1846)

Ralph Waldo EMERSON wrote "The Humble-Bee" in the spring of 1837, and the poem was first published in 1839 in the Transcendentalist magazine, the *WESTERN MESSENGER*, and finally appeared in

Emerson's first collection of POEMS, published in late 1846. Emerson wrote in his journal of 1837 that "The humblebee and the pine warbler seem to me the proper objects of attention in these disastrous times," referring to the financial panic of that year that left many, Emerson included, at risk for losing their investments. The poet thus turned away from the worries and concerns of the material world which are mocked by "the yellow-breeched philosopher . . . sipping only what is sweet." Nature is unaffected by the complications and crises of the human world of economics and politics and instead continues on as always before: "Aught unsavory or unclean / Hath my insect never seen." Emerson did not mean to ignore the issues that affected human life or to attempt to provide a simple solution to human problems but only shifted the perspective to show that any individual has within him (or her) the power to decide what is most important and enriching in this world; that depending on where you look, you can find beauty or you can find chaos, but you yourself decide how to respond to either.

Humboldt, Alexander von
(1769–1859)

German naturalist and explorer Alexander von Humboldt was a prominent scientist of the first half of the 19th century and highly regarded among the Transcendentalists, in particular Ralph Waldo EMERSON and Henry David THOREAU, as a "universal man." Humboldt was widely known in intellectual circles for his travels into the interior of South America between 1799 and 1804, the first European to explore the region in depth. Humboldt wrote about his explorations and observations related to the geography, weather, and ecological systems of the region in his *Personal Narrative*, a widely read and popular work. Emerson read Humboldt while still a student at Harvard in the 1810s or 1820s but was still interested in his ideas as late as the 1860s. Emerson was attracted to Humboldt's broad-ranging scientific interests and referred to him in his journals as "one of those wonders of the world . . . who appear from time to time, as if to show us the possibilities of the human mind." Naturalist-

philosopher Henry David Thoreau was even more directly influenced by Humboldt's example, singling him out as the model scientist in his 1842 "A Walk to Wachusett." Thoreau read Humboldt's *Cosmos and Aspects of Nature* (five volumes, published between 1845 and 1862), a monumental work that established Humboldt as the premiere man of science of his time. Along with Charles DARWIN, it was Humboldt who most directly influenced Thoreau in his methods of collecting, measuring, and interpreting information gathered from his own natural expeditions. These scientists also provided Thoreau with a model for interpreting the specifics of his observations into a larger theory of humanity's relationship to the whole of nature.

Harvard professor of natural history Louis AGASSIZ was a student and follower of Alexander von Humboldt who organized a celebration of the centennial of Alexander von Humboldt's birth, at which many of those associated with Transcendentalism honored the scientist. Ralph Waldo Emerson, Frederic Henry HEDGE, Julia Ward HOWE, and Thomas Wentworth HIGGINSON were among those who gave addresses in Humboldt's honor. Despite their acknowledgment of his influence, Humboldt actually differed significantly from the other German writers read by the Transcendentalists, in that he emphasized an empirical approach to scientific study, but Humboldt's appreciation of the power of the natural world and his belief in the interconnectedness of all natural phenomena and processes appealed to Transcendentalist beliefs about the role of the scientist-naturalist.

Bibliography
Walls, Laura Dassow. " 'The Napoleon of Science': Humboldt in Antebellum America," *19th-Century Contexts* 14:1 (1990): 71–98.
———. *Seeing New Worlds: Henry David Thoreau and Nineteenth-Century Natural Science*. Madison: University of Wisconsin Press, 1995.

Hunt, Benjamin Peter
(1808–unknown)

Benjamin Peter Hunt was a student and friend of Ralph Waldo EMERSON who, after moving to

Jamaica in 1840, remained in contact with Emerson and submitted a series of articles on the West Indies to the Transcendentalist literary journal, the DIAL. Although encouraged by Emerson to pursue literary interests, Hunt was more of a conversationalist than a writer and established a career as a merchant in Jamaica. He did continue to work on book-length writings of life in the West Indies, but none of these longer narratives were ever published.

Bibliography

Myerson, Joel. *The New England Transcendentalists and the Dial: A History of the Magazine and Its Contributors*. London and Toronto: Associated University Presses, 1980.

Hutchinson, Anne
(1591–1643)

Anne Hutchinson was a colonial woman who immigrated to Massachusetts from England and quickly emerged at the center of the religious and social controversy of ANTINOMIANISM within early PURITANISM. Hutchinson was a highly educated daughter of an English clergyman and a follower of the preacher John Cotton, whom she and her merchant husband would follow to New England. She promoted Cotton's ministry by holding meetings in her home to discuss his sermons, but the conversations soon turned to criticism of the other ministers in the colony, whom Hutchinson accused of preaching that salvation could be attained through good works or deeds, rather than through God's grace alone as the Puritans believed. She was put on trial by the political and religious leaders of the Massachusetts Bay Colony in 1637–38 and, although the trial records make it difficult to discern the specific charges against her, it is apparent that her meetings and her message were viewed as disruptive to the theological as well as social and gender hierarchies necessary for peaceful government in the Puritan colony. The governor, John Winthrop, banished Hutchinson, her family, and her followers from the colony, and just a few years later she and most of her family were killed by Native Americans in New York.

Nineteenth-century writers and thinkers, including those among the Transcendentalists, were particularly interested in Anne Hutchinson as part of a distinctly American legacy of religious and intellectual dissent. WOMEN'S RIGHTS advocate Caroline DALL looked to Hutchinson as a feminist as well as a model of Transcendentalist-style radicalism and mysticism. Nathaniel HAWTHORNE was, in several of his works of fiction, concerned with New England's Puritan legacy and its elements of sin, heresy, and punishment, and echoes of Hutchinson's 17th-century trial can be read in the trial and social persecution of the character of Hester Prynne in THE SCARLET LETTER (1850). Nineteenth-century UNITARIANISM itself was based on a rejection of the Calvinist theological heritage of New England Puritanism, explaining why many of the Transcendentalists continued to be interested in the theological, literary, and genealogical legacy of Puritanism.

Bibliography

Lang, Amy Schrager. *Prophetic Woman: Anne Hutchinson and the Problem of Dissent in the Literature of New England*. Berkeley: University of California Press, 1987.

"I am a parcel of vain strivings tied" *See* "SIC VITA."

idealism

Idealism was the primary philosophical outlook of the American Transcendentalists and was drawn primarily from their readings in European thinkers such as Samuel Taylor COLERIDGE, Immanuel KANT, and Emanuel Swedenborg (*see* SWEDENBORGIANISM). Transcendentalist idealism, however, was not a direct reiteration of these sources but an eclectic mix that included influences from PLATONISM and NEOPLATONISM and a philosophy formed in large part in opposition to other intellectual traditions, such as the Enlightenment rationalism or "empiricism" of John LOCKE and of the Scottish COMMON SENSE school. Transcendentalists rejected the reliance on external or sensual experience, or "materialism," as the only source of knowledge and emphasized instead the value of human intuition and extrasensory perception as a route to moral and spiritual truths. Although idealism offered an alternative meta-philosophy for integrating all aspects of human experience, Ralph Waldo EMERSON, in defining Transcendentalism itself, recognized the specific historical contexts and philosophical traditions out of which his philosophy grew and defined it in the most basic terms as "Idealism, as it appeared in 1842." In the 19th century, popular usage of the term *idealism* referred to the optimistic belief in the perpetual progress of civilization and in the perfectability of the social world. Idealism was offered as an alternative to the materialistic values of commercialism and expansion that characterized 19th-century American culture and jeopardized morality. In this sense, then, idealistic philosophy propelled the social reform efforts of many in the Transcendentalist community, including their commitment to ABOLITIONISM.

Idealism looked beyond the material world, then, to a level of existence informed by the mind, by ideas. As Emerson once wrote, "The sensual man conforms thoughts to things; the poet conforms things to his thoughts." For the Transcendentalists, equally important to the emphasis on ideas was the primacy of the human mind, the belief that individual intuition perceives the truth of all things. Idealism, then, emphasized the power of the individual and elevated the individual human mind and consciousness to the level of the divine.

"Intellect"
Ralph Waldo Emerson
(1841)

Ralph Waldo EMERSON's essay on "Intellect" appeared in the 1841 *ESSAYS: FIRST SERIES* and continues the main themes of that collection of individual development and intellectual self-reliance as traced in the other essays such as, "HISTORY," "SELF-RELIANCE," "THE OVER-SOUL," "CIRCLES," and "ART." The essay also echoes many of the themes of his earlier 1837 address at Harvard on "THE AMERICAN SCHOLAR." In both instances Emerson emphasized that the intellect was not something to be developed through specialized study of other writers and thinkers but must be cultivated from within or else we risk becoming "prisoners of ideas." The intellect is cultivated by pursuit of truth, not merely of knowledge, one of the foundational themes of Emersonian Transcendentalism.

Emerson stated in the opening of the essay his intention and desire, as well as his doubts, in addressing the subject: "Gladly would I unfold in calm degrees a natural history of the intellect, but what man has yet been able to mark the steps and boundaries of that transparent essence?" Even after the publication of the essay in 1841, Emerson remained interested in the idea of the history of the mind, a subject that formed the basis of many subsequent lectures, some of which were collected together after his death in *Natural History of Intellect*. Emerson's interest in the "Intellect" as a topic was broadly defined and wide-ranging, encompassing inquiries into knowledge, truth, memory, intuitiveness, and the process and sources of inspiration. Emerson was extremely ahead of his time in considering the workings of the mind without the benefit of scientific findings in fields such as psychology, which emerged in the early 20th century. What Emerson did in "Intellect" was to consider the act of thinking and the development of the individual mind within a Transcendentalist's metaphysical or spiritual framework. His inquiry led him to an understanding of the process and progress of thought in terms of the individual's openness to the phenomena of epiphany: "What is the hardest task in the world? To think. I would put myself in the attitude to look in the eye an abstract truth, and I cannot. . . . We say, I will walk abroad, and the truth will take form and clearness to me. We go forth, but cannot find it. It seems as if we needed only the stillness and composed attitude of the library, to seize the thought. But we come in, and are as far from it as at first. Then, in a moment, and unannounced, the truth appears. A certain,

wandering light appears, and is the distinction, the principle we wanted. But the oracle comes, because we had previously laid siege to the shrine."

This explanation of the growth of the intellect fit within Emerson's perspective of Transcendentalist individualism, for while the epiphany is an outside experience of truth acted upon the mind, he stressed the individual's role in nurturing or preparing for the experience. Epiphany or inspiration does not affect each person in the same way, for "each mind has its own method." Indeed, he concluded, "We are all wise. The difference between persons is not in wisdom but in art." By way of example, he calls upon the figure of the great poet, William SHAKESPEARE, who would reappear later in Emerson's 1850 study of REPRESENTATIVE MEN. To make the point that "genius" or "intellect" a matter of "art," of conscious development, and not of innate ability, he considered that "perhaps if we should meet Shakspeare, we should not be conscious of any steep inferiority, no: but of a great equality,—only that he possessed a strange skill of using, of classifying, his facts, which we lacked." This is what separates intellect from knowledge, for the scholar studies great minds of the past, but the thinker recognizes that "the Bacon, the Spinoza, the Hume, Schelling, Kant, or whosoever propounds to you a philosophy of mind, is only a more or less awkward translator of things in your consciousness, which you have also your way of seeing." He challenged that "God offers to every mind its choice between truth and repose" and urged his readers to choose to actively seek the truth. According to Emerson, the individual would be rewarded for such by growth in self-knowledge.

Bibliography
Buell, Lawrence. *Emerson*. Cambridge, Mass.: Harvard University Press, 2003.

"Ion: A Monody"   *See* SONNETS AND CANZONETS.

J

James, Henry, Jr.
(1843–1916)

Author Henry James, Jr., was a generation younger than most of the Transcendentalists and, while recognizing the philosophy's importance in New England literary and intellectual history, he also criticized and caricatured what he termed the "Concord-haunting figures" associated with 19th-century Transcendentalism and with the community surrounding Ralph Waldo EMERSON in particular. James, one of the most significant and prolific American writers of his time, was the son of writer and reformer Henry JAMES, SR., and the brother of psychologist and philosopher William JAMES. In novels such as *Daisy Miller* (1879), *The Portrait of a Lady* (1881), and, most notably, THE BOSTONIANS (1886), Henry James, Jr., commented upon the lifestyle, sensibilities, and excesses of upper-class Americans, both at home and abroad. *The Bostonians* was a satirical commentary upon New England's reformer class and the Transcendentalists in particular. Although he denied a direct link between his characters in *The Bostonians* and specific individuals associated with Transcendentalism, contemporaries and scholars alike have seen similarities between the novel's characters and the activities of Boston's thinkers and reformers in the mid-19th century.

In both his fiction and nonfiction, James effectually dismissed Transcendentalist literary and reform experiments as abstract IDEALISM without much relevance or interest beyond the closed community of CONCORD, MASSACHUSETTS. While James did admire Ralph Waldo Emerson personally, he criticized the attention lavished on those who flocked around Emerson and who, in James's view, were "not so much interesting themselves as interesting because for a season Emerson thought them so." Writing in the very different intellectual and political context of the post–Civil War period, James ultimately viewed Emerson's ideas as the quaint domain of an earlier bygone era: "Transcendentalism has come and gone . . . and the novelty of the Unitarian creed, and the revelation of Goethe, and the doctrine of a vegetable diet, and a great many other reforms then deemed urgent."

Bibliography
Menard, Louis. *The Metaphysical Club: A Story of Ideas in America.* New York: Farrar, Straus, and Giroux, 2001.

James, Henry, Sr.
(1811–1884)

Henry James, Sr., was the father of novelist Henry JAMES, JR., writer and philosopher William JAMES, and writer and lecturer Alice James. After studying theology and subsequently rejecting plans to become a Calvinist minister, James, Sr., was influenced by the mystical philosophy of SWEDENBORGIANISM and the utopian ideals of FOURIERISM that so intrigued many of the Transcendentalists as well during the same time period of the 1840s. Henry

James, Sr., was friends with Ralph Waldo EMERSON as well as with Thomas CARLYLE, and he was close colleagues with American promoters of Fourierism in New York, such as Albert BRISBANE, Parke GODWIN, and George RIPLEY. Although he never identified as a Transcendentalist, James took up many similar themes as the Transcendentalists in his lectures and writings on American culture, society, and the individual self. Although James, too, rejected religious institutions, he ultimately disagreed too much with Transcendentalist IDEALISM and accused the major thinkers, especially Emerson, of not dealing sufficiently with the problem of evil and for rejecting all theological models as possible sources of knowledge. Intrigued by Emerson, James was still led to conclude that his friend was "philosophically infirm" who "lived by perception" alone, at the expense of social experience. His criticisms of other figures were even more harsh and less grounded in specific philosophical differences; for example, he referred to Amos Bronson ALCOTT as simply "an egg half hatched." As a social reformer with a communitarian sensibility (thus his attraction to Fourierism), James felt that Transcendentalist "self-reliance" placed dangerously too much emphasis on the individual and bordered on egotism.

Henry James, Sr., published several books explaining his religious and social reform beliefs about "the immanence of God in the unity of mankind." In 1844 he had either a religious conversion or a mild nervous breakdown brought on by his study of Swedenborgianism. Later, in 1869, he published a study on *The Secret of Swedenborg*. James did not become a disciple of Emanuel Swedenborg, but the experience and the model of a more mystical humanistic religion influenced James's literary and social commitments for the rest of his life. His reform philosophy combined individual and social change and was articulated most fully in his books *The Nature of Evil* (1855) and *The Social Significance of Our Institutions* (1861).

Bibliography

Menard, Louis. *The Metaphysical Club: A Story of Ideas in America*. New York: Farrar, Straus, and Giroux, 2001.

James, William
(1842–1910)

William James was the son of writer and reformer Henry JAMES, SR., and the older brother of novelist Henry JAMES, JR. William James studied science and medicine at Harvard before accompanying professor Louis AGASSIZ on a zoological expedition to Brazil in 1865–66. James returned to complete his education and became a teacher and lecturer on physiology and psychology at Harvard. He published regularly in periodicals, and in 1890 he completed a classic textbook on *The Principles of Psychology*. Perhaps James's most important psychological work remains his 1902 *The Varieties of Religious Experience*, but William James is most well known as the founder of the philosophical concept of PRAGMATISM. His 1907 book on *Pragmatism* explained the belief that ideas only have meaning if they can be felt or experienced. James argued that for any belief, whether scientific or personal or religious, to be true and meaningful to a particular individual, it had to have benefit in the practical world of human happiness and lived experience.

Pragmatism was in many ways influenced by and served as an extension of the Transcendentalism of the previous generation. William James had family and social connections to the Boston Transcendentalists, as his father, Henry James, Sr., was friends and colleagues with Ralph Waldo EMERSON, George RIPLEY, and others. Henry James, Sr., had reservations about Transcendentalism as a philosophy that influenced his son's approach as well. Still, William James's philosophy of pragmatism included an emphasis on the individual mind and subjective experiences as the source of spiritual or philosophical truths. Like the Transcendentalists, William James rejected the need for religious institutions to convey spiritual knowledge and promoted instead human intuition as a psychological guide. James's philosophy of pragmatism was ultimately more systematic and more applicable to a range of situations, both personal and institutional. James was involved in a variety of reform efforts, including ABOLITIONISM, WOMEN'S RIGHTS, and EDUCATION reform, as were many of the Transcendentalists, but he criticized Transcendentalism as too broad and too abstract, as not focused enough on contemporary social issues: "An entire world is the smallest unit with which the Absolute can work, whereas to our finite minds work for the better ought to be done within this world."

Bibliography

Gale, Richard. *The Philosophy of William James.* New York: Cambridge University Press, 2005.

Menand, Louis. *The Metaphysical Club: A Story of Ideas in America.* New York: Farrar, Straus, and Giroux, 2001.

Johnson, Samuel
(1822–1882)

Samuel Johnson was a younger generation Transcendentalist who published widely on the topic of eastern and comparative religious traditions, a topic that engaged many of the Transcendentalists during the post–Civil War decades. As the title of his series, *Oriental Religions and Their Relation to Universal Religion,* indicates, Johnson sought to merge eastern spirituality with Christianity in pursuit of a universal human religion. His work was the most comprehensive explanation of an idea explored by both Ralph Waldo EMERSON and Henry David THOREAU in their earlier interest in eastern spirituality but was particularly reflective of the projects of other Transcendentalists in the later period also interested in comparative and universal religion, such as Lydia Maria CHILD, James Freeman CLARKE, and Octavius Brooks FROTHINGHAM.

At Harvard Johnson had befriended Samuel Longfellow, with whom he traveled to Europe and collaborated on a *Book of Hymns* (1864). After graduating from HARVARD DIVINITY SCHOOL Johnson had difficulty securing a regular position with a Unitarian church in part due to his radical politics. Johnson supported ABOLITIONISM and had himself written for William Lloyd GARRISON's paper *The Liberator* and for the *Anti-Slavery Standard.* Johnson also resisted the idea of individual congregations affiliating with the AMERICAN UNITARIAN ASSOCIATION, and he finally established his own

Independent Church in Lynn, Massachusetts, where he served as minister for 17 years.

Although Johnson had a scholarly interest in universal religion, he resisted joining the FREE RELIGIOUS ASSOCIATION that attracted the attention of so many of his colleagues precisely because he was against such institutions on principle. Johnson published three volumes in his *Oriental Religions* series on *India* (1872), *China* (1877), and *Persia* (1885), the last volume published after his death under the editorship of his colleague Octavius Frothingham, founder and president of the Free Religious Association.

Bibliography

Jackson, Carl T. *The Oriental Religions and American Thought: (19th-century Explorations.* Westport, Conn.: Greenwood Press, 1981.

Jouffroy, Theodore Simon
(1796–1842)

Theodore Jouffroy was a French philosopher who influenced the Transcendentalists through his own reworking of the ideas of Charles Fourier (*see* FOURIERISM) and Victor COUSIN, which, in turn, were taken up by American reformers who founded the utopian community at BROOK FARM. Jouffroy promoted the ideas of the Scottish COMMON SENSE school of philosophy and the use of reason over faith and, although the Transcendentalists rejected many aspects of the Common Sense philosophy, they too were interested in the system of human faculties explained by writers such as Jouffroy. Jouffroy presented a system of six different human faculties or senses that, taken together, defined the individual and from which the "truth," or common sense, would emerge: pleasure, pain, intelligence, expression, movement, and volition. For the Transcendentalists, Jouffroy's formulation valued the development of these faculties within the individual and thus provided individual rather than institutional means to arriving at philosophical truths.

Jouffroy was included with other French and German writers in George RIPLEY's *Philosophical Miscellanies* (1839), which made up the first two volumes of Ripley's multivolume series, SPECIMENS OF

FOREIGN STANDARD LITERATURE. In 1840–41 the Reverend William Ellery CHANNING translated Jouffroy's *Introduction to Ethics* as two more volumes in Ripley's *Specimens*. George Ripley himself was particularly interested in Jouffroy and drew upon his ideas in planning the utopian community at Brook Farm.

Bibliography

Leighton, Walter L. *French Philosophers and New England Transcendentalism*. New York: Greenwood Press, 1968.

Journal of Speculative Philosophy
(1867–1893)

The *Journal of Speculative Philosophy* was the first English-language journal devoted specifically to philosophy as a separate field, although it also addressed cultural themes such as art, literature, science, and religion, as part of moral philosophy. The *Journal* was begun in 1867 by William Torrey HARRIS as an outgrowth of the St. Louis Philosophical Society. The society had been meeting regularly for nearly a year when Harris suggested they needed their own journal. The St. Louis group, influenced primarily by the ideas of German philosopher Georg Hegel (known as HEGELIANISM), was concerned primarily with tempering the extremes of American individualism by applying philosophical ideals to the problems of practical life and social problems.

The Civil War had a profound effect on American philosophers, and the St. Louis Society, through the *Journal of Speculative Philosophy*, offered alternative ways to think through national moral and political problems. In this sense, then, the *Journal* was their contribution to social reform efforts of their time. Harris's motto for the *Journal* was that philosophy "can procure for us God, Freedom, and Immortality," exemplifying his high expectations for moral philosophy and the engagement of 19th-century intellectuals with social and political issues. The *Journal* ultimately had great intellectual influence beyond the St. Louis circle and reflected various philosophical views beyond the primarily Hegelian outlook of its founders, most notably in addressing the IDEALISM and hu-

manism of other German thinkers such as Johann Wolfgang von GOETHE and Johann SCHILLER. The *Journal* included writings by contemporary European philosophers and was widely read in Europe as well. More important, it provided a forum for American philosophers and thus the beginnings of a formal philosophical tradition in this country. In the decades after the *Journal of Speculative Philosophy* ceased publication, philosophy would become increasingly professionalized within the universities and organized through the American Philosophical Association, founded in 1901.

Bibliography

Goetzmann, William, ed. *The American Hegelians: An Intellectual Episode in the History of Western America*. New York: Knopf, 1973.

Judd, Sylvester
(1813–1853)

Sylvester Judd was the author of one of the few novels, *Margaret* (1845), associated with the Transcendentalist movement. While Lydia Maria CHILD's 1836 PHILOTHEA was the first specifically Transcendentalist novel, Judd's work was distinctive for its New England setting. Judd was a graduate of HARVARD DIVINITY SCHOOL and an ordained Unitarian minister and, although he never identified as a Transcendentalist (in fact, he denied the association), some contemporaries perceived him as such due to his connection with many of the main figures of the movement as well as the themes of his novel. Ralph Waldo EMERSON, Margaret FULLER, and Theodore PARKER all read and praised his novel. Fuller reviewed the book as evidence of "a distinctive American literature," and James Russell LOWELL went even further in declaring Judd's *Margaret* as "the most emphatically American book ever written." In his history of the movement, Octavius Brooks FROTHINGHAM credited the novel with presenting "the whole gospel of Transcendentalism in religion, politics, reform, social ethics, personal character, professional and private life." These comments were high praise indeed from the New England Transcendentalists who sought to promote American thought and literature as distinctive from the European tradition.

Margaret abounds with Transcendentalist themes of childlike innocence, communion with nature, and utopian IDEALISM expressed through the main character, whose name in fact must have been seen as a reference to Margaret Fuller. In the novel, Margaret is an independent orphan who lives in and is nurtured by nature. Significantly, Margaret finds in nature the acceptance and beauty she cannot find in the church. Margaret ultimately finds human companionship and culture in her marriage to the Unitarian, Mr. Evelyn. Her conversations with him seem to echo specific passages from Ralph Waldo Emerson's work, NATURE (1836), and, early in their relationship, she declares her Transcendentalism to him in revealing that "In myself seems sometimes to reside an infant Universe."

Sylvester Judd had befriended poet Jones VERY in college and was present when Ralph Waldo Emerson delivered his "AMERICAN SCHOLAR" address of Harvard in 1837. He was undoubtedly inspired by Emerson's ideas and by the general Transcendentalist reverence for nature as well as its critique of traditional Christianity but, more like William Ellery CHANNING or Theodore Parker, Judd retained the idea of the importance of Jesus Christ. Unlike those Transcendentalists who broke with organized religion completely, Judd retained his connection with UNITARIANISM in his role as a minister in Augusta, Maine. Ultimately, his novel, *Margaret,* included a strong religious element influenced by the New England Calvinist tradition as much as by Transcendentalism. Sylvester Judd published other novels and poems, but any further connection to the Transcendentalist movement was cut short by Judd's early death in 1853.

Bibliography

Hathaway, Richard D. *Sylvester Judd's New England.* University Park: Pennsylvania State University Press, 1981.

K

Kant, Immanuel
(1724–1804)

German philosopher Immanuel Kant greatly influenced the Transcendentalists through his intuitive or "transcendental" philosophy, although much of their reading of Kant was a reinterpretation rather than a clear understanding of his original ideas. What they read in Kant beginning in the 1830s already fit in with their own developing philosophy of mystical self-reliance and their critique of the empirical or rational thought of John LOCKE. For Kant, from whom they borrowed the term *transcendental*, the term applied to any aspect of the spiritual or nonmaterial world of experience. In their appropriation of Kantian IDEALISM and of this term, the American Transcendentalists focused more specifically on elevating the idea of human "intuition" above other spiritual or philosophical concepts in Kant's transcendental sphere. As set forth in Ralph Waldo EMERSON's essay "THE TRANSCENDENTALIST," the debt to Kant was acknowledged, but the explanation was American: "that whatever belongs to the class of intuitive thought, is popularly called at the present day Transcendental."

Most of the Transcendentalists read Immanuel Kant, specifically his *Critique of Pure Reason*, through English-language translators and interpreters, which also influenced their understanding of his ideas. Most learned of Kant through analyses and appropriations by influential writers such as Thomas CARLYLE and Samuel Taylor COLERIDGE, while a few, such as Frederic Henry HEDGE and Theodore PARKER, read Kant in the original German.

kindergarten   *See* EDUCATION.

Kneeland, Abner
(1774–1844)

Abner Kneeland was a Universalist minister who was defended by the Transcendentalists, in particular Ralph Waldo EMERSON, when he was convicted and imprisoned in 1838 on charges of blasphemy and atheism. Kneeland was the editor of the *Olive Branch*, a free-thought newspaper, and he founded an association of "free enquirers" after leaving his position with the Universalist church. In 1833 he published a series of three articles in the *Boston Investigator*, where he served as editor, and was brought up on charges of blasphemy against the Christian religion.

The Transcendentalists, many of them still connected to the Unitarian church and thus invested in their Boston social status, did not necessarily share Kneeland's most radical political and social views, such as his association with free love and birth-control advocates, his support for worker's rights, or his political backing of Democratic President Andrew Jackson, but Kneeland's trial for blasphemy concerned radical Unitarians who were concerned about their own right to free speech surrounding critiques of conservative Christianity. When Kneeland was imprisoned in 1838, the Reverend William Ellery CHANNING initiated a petition to the governor of Massachusetts on Kneeland's behalf, a petition signed by Ralph Waldo Emerson and other Transcendentalists. The controversy over Kneeland's case had an effect on Emerson's own controversial DIVINITY SCHOOL ADDRESS a few months later, when those within the conservative Unitarian community turned against Emerson with similar charges. Reciprocating the support he had received, Kneeland defended Emerson's rights to express his views, allying himself with Emerson's cause and stating that the beliefs expressed by Emerson were "our own faith and our doctrine."

Bibliography

Burkholder, Robert E. "Emerson, Kneeland, and the Divinity School Address." *American Literature* 58 (March 1986): 1–14.

Kraitsir, Charles
(1804–1860)

Charles Kraitsir was a Hungarian professor of languages and linguistics who influenced the American Transcendentalist's views on these subjects through their readings of his 1846 book, *The Significance of the Alphabet,* and his 1852 book, *Glossology: Being a Treatise on the Nature of Language and the Language of Nature.* Kraitsir had helped a group of Polish exiles escape from their country in the 1830s and eventually migrated himself from England to the United States. He found a position as professor of languages at the University of Virginia but left the South over opposition to slavery. Kraitsir settled in Boston where he established a language school and met Transcendentalist reformer and bookstore owner Elizabeth Palmer PEABODY, who was enthusiastic about his work and worked as his assistant. Peabody recorded his 1845 lecture series in Boston and published her notes as the influential pamphlet, *The Significance of the Alphabet.* Henry David THOREAU in particular was influenced by Kraitsir's philosophy of language and incorporated aspects into his own written style. The Transcendentalists were particularly interested in Kraitsir's theory of language as symbolic, as a vehicle for conveying meaning about the world, but without inherent or universal meaning itself. For the Transcendentalists, the whole of nature as well as religion itself was a symbolic language, and thus Kraitsir's views supported their broader philosophical tendencies. Kraitsir argued that although there was no universal language, all languages had common origins and thus common meaning to a unified humanity. Elizabeth Peabody was the Transcendentalist most consistently intrigued with the theory and history of language. In addition to her studies and writings on the Hebrew language and poetry, she promoted Kraitsir's ideas specifically in her 1849 AESTHETIC PAPERS. Charles Kraitsir relocated to New York and, after the publication of *Glossology,* he contributed to the NEW AMERICAN CYCLOPEDIA edited by Charles Anderson DANA and George RIPLEY.

Bibliography

Gura, Philip. *The Wisdom of Words: Language, Theology, and Literature in the New England Renaissance.* Middletown, Conn.: Wesleyan University Press, 1981.

"Ktaadn"   *See* THE MAINE WOODS.

L

"The Laboring Classes"
Orestes Brownson
(1840)

Trancendentalist Orestes BROWNSON published his most well known and most controversial article, "The Laboring Classes," in the July and October 1840 issues of the paper he then edited, the *BOSTON QUARTERLY REVIEW.* "The Laboring Classes" was ostensibly an overview of the conditions of England's industrial working class, but Brownson ultimately compared the English labor system with that of slave labor in the southern United States. Through these examples Brownson developed a substantial general critique of American capitalism and determined that, in all cases, the interests of labor and of the business class could never be reconciled and in essence predicted that America would see bloodshed between these two sides before change would happen. Most controversially, although condemning the system of slavery, Brownson ultimately determined that it was still yet preferable to the industrial wage labor characteristic of the working class in the northern states in the mid-19th century. Furthermore, Brownson's criticism reached beyond the business class who controlled labor and looked to the role of the church in ameliorating the condition of the poor. Brownson's essay thus ended as an attack on American Christianity and organized religion that he felt ignored the moral teachings of Christ in favor of sanctioning the exploitation of labor and protecting the interests of the business class. His solution proposed involved the abolishment of private property as well, for only when property ownership was related to production, that is, owned by the workers themselves, would the promises of a democratic state extend to all citizens. In calling for the reform and even abolishment of the church as well as of both wage and slave labor, Orestes Brownson's exposé earned him critics from all sides.

Lane, Charles
(1800–1870)

Charles Lane was an English social and political reformer who came to America in 1842 to establish the utopian community at FRUITLANDS with Transcendentalist Amos Bronson ALCOTT. Lane had worked with James Pierrepont GREAVES at the AL-COTT HOUSE in England, a school for children modeled on Alcott's work at the experimental TEMPLE SCHOOL in Boston. Lane had corresponded with Alcott about EDUCATION reform, and the two men shared an interest in health reform and vegetarianism as well. Bronson Alcott traveled to England in spring 1842 where he met with Lane and the two began plans for a "true harmonic association," a utopian community committed to self-sufficiency and the development of the individual as the key to social change. Along with the Alcott family and his young son, William, Charles Lane lived at Fruitlands between June 1843 and January 1844.

During that time Lane came into contact with the broader literary and reform culture of the

Transcendentalist movement, and he corresponded with figures such as Ralph Waldo EMERSON and Henry David THOREAU. Under Emerson's editorship, Lane contributed regularly to the movement's main literary journal, the DIAL, the only foreign-born essayist included in its pages. Lane had read the first issues of the *Dial* while still in England and, after meeting Alcott, wrote a review of the *Dial* and an essay on "Transatlantic Transcendentalism" for the English *Union.* Among his writings for the Boston *Dial* was a two-part article on his English colleague "James Pierrepont Greaves" (October 1842 and January 1843), an announcement of "Fruitlands" (July 1843), and comments upon other American social experiments such as in "A Day with the Shakers" (October 1843) and "Brook Farm" (January 1844). Lane and his son, in fact, joined a group of Massachusetts Shakers after Fruitlands dissolved and lived within this religious-utopian community before returning again to England. Lane resumed his previous career as a journalist and planned to, but apparently never did, write a history of his time at Fruitlands. It was Bronson Alcott's daughter, Louisa May ALCOTT, who memorialized the community in her 1876 short story, "TRANSCENDENTAL WILD OATS," a satirical account of the failed experiment that portrayed Lane's role through the unsympathetic character of Timon Lion.

Bibliography

Francis, Richard. *Transcendental Utopias: Individual and Community at Brook Farm, Fruitlands, and Walden.* Ithaca, N.Y.: Cornell University Press, 1997.

Leaves of Grass   See "SONG OF MYSELF."

Letters and Social Aims
Ralph Waldo Emerson
(1876)

In 1876 Ralph Waldo EMERSON, with the assistance of editor and literary executor James Elliot CABOT, put together a collection of previously unpublished essays, *Letters and Social Aims.* The volume included one of Emerson's most important pieces, and the longest essay in the collection, "Poetry and Imagination." This essay alone is longer than his earlier seminal book, NATURE (1836). In "Poetry and Imagination" Emerson fully developed his theory of the symbolic use of language first discussed in *Nature,* and the nature of the literary process: "A good symbol is the best argument . . . indeed Nature itself is a vast trope, and all particular natures are tropes." "The poet accounts all productions and changes of Nature as the nouns of language, uses them representatively." For Emerson, "Poetry is the only verity. . . . As a power, it is the perception of the symbolic character of things, and the treating them as representative."

Letters and Social Aims also includes Emerson's only theoretical essay on "Persian Poetry." Emerson had read and been inspired by eastern literature and poetry since the early 1840s when he composed poems such as "BRAHMA" and "HAMATREYA." His essay in *Letters and Social Aims* helps explain his thinking behind the writing of these earlier poems. Emerson admired the poet Hafiz, for example, because he "praises wine, roses, maidens, boys, birds, mornings and music, to give vent to his immense hilarity and sympathy with every form of beauty and joy."

Letters from New York
Lydia Maria Child
(1843–1845)

Transcendentalist feminist, author, and reformer Lydia Maria CHILD published two volumes of her newspaper columns, *Letters from New York,* in 1843 and 1845. The "letters" originally appeared as regular columns in the *National Anti-Slavery Standard,* edited by Child in 1841–43, and later in the *Boston Courier.* By the 1840s, Lydia Maria Child was well known as the author of the first Transcendentalist novel, PHILOTHEA (1836), editor of a children's journal, and an antislavery writer and activist. Child left her position as editor of the *National Anti-Slavery Standard* in 1843 but continued to support herself by writing regular columns for the paper. Her *Letters from New York* were extremely popular with readers and combined a high literary style and philosophical grounding in Transcendentalism with her commitment to political reform and social justice, through a focus on the problems of urban life. While writing from an antislavery perspective, Child skillfully connected the moral impulse that drove ABOLITIONISM to a wider array of social problems affecting not only southern slaves but also the urban poor, immigrants, and women. She wrote on themes such as poverty, prostitution, alcoholism, prison reform, religious tolerance, and race relations. Child's overall vision was one of applying the American ideals of social equality and diversity to areas of practical concern and making her readers aware of their own assumptions and prejudices which prevented these ideals from being achieved.

The influence of Transcendentalism was evident not only in Child's general reform commitments but in her writing style as well. Colleague Thomas Wentworth HIGGINSON reviewed the first series of *Letters from New York* in the reform paper, THE PRESENT, calling Child's work "a perfect encyclopedia of anecdotes and interesting realities, in endless variety. . . . There is a quickness, a brilliancy in her comparisons and analogies." Child herself acknowledged the particular "quickness" of her writing style as an aesthetic choice of allowing an unfettered flow of thoughts, musing that "My pen . . . paces or whirls, bounds or waltzes, steps in the slow minuet, or capers in the fantastic fandango, according to the tune within." Indeed, this free-flowing style undefined by any other genre was one consciously adapted by other Transcendentalists, such as Ralph Waldo EMERSON, Margaret FULLER, and Henry David THOREAU, and the trademark characteristic of the most successful Transcendentalist poet, Walt WHITMAN. Emerson appreciated Child's writing style as well and emphasized the work's literary quality over its success as a call to reform, declaring *Letters from New York* "a most salutary infusion of love into American literature." Child also shared with Walt Whitman and with Margaret Fuller a focus on urban and social problems and, in his review of *Letters,* Thomas Wentworth Higginson acknowledged that Child brought the same Transcendentalist IDEALISM to bear on a different realm of human experience in appreciating that "the Beautiful does not exist for her only in the moonlight trembling on

the quiet water . . . ; she finds it equally in the dark gray city, where beats the sorrowing, striving heart of man."

Child sought for her *Letters from New York* to have broader appeal beyond the readership of the *Anti-Slavery Standard* newspaper and in collecting the columns together in book form she made editorial changes to that effect. Ironically, given Child's reputation and since the columns were originally published in an antislavery paper, Child downplayed the politicized issue of slavery in the book, omitting some of the more radical comments and criticisms of the U.S. government, for example. The commercial success of the first collection in 1843 prompted the printing and equal success of a second volume in 1845.

Bibliography
Karcher, Carolyn L., ed. *A Lydia Maria Child Reader.* Durham, N.C.: Duke University Press, 1997.

The Liberator See GARRISON, WILLIAM LLOYD.

The Life and Genius of Goethe
Franklin Benjamin Sanborn
(1886)

The Life and Genius of Goethe was a collection of lectures from a special 1885 session of the CONCORD SCHOOL OF PHILOSOPHY AND LITERATURE devoted to the influence and ideas of German thinker Johann Wolfgang von GOETHE. The Concord School of Philosophy met every summer between 1879 and 1888 and Franklin Benjamin SANBORN served as the school's secretary. The 1885 lectures on Goethe included H. S. White on "Goethe's Youth," John Albee on "Goethe's Self-Culture," Thomas Davidson on "Goethe's Titanism," Cyrus BARTOL on "Goethe and Schiller," Frederic Henry HEDGE on "Goethe's Marchen," Franklin Benjamin SANBORN on "Goethe's Relation to English Literature," William Ordway Partridge on "Goethe as a Playwright," Ednah Dow CHENEY on "Das Ewig-Weibliche" (the "ever-womanly" or eternal feminine concept in Goethe), S. H. Emery, Jr., on "The Elective

Affinities," Caroline K. Sherman on "Child Life as Portrayed by Goethe," Denton J. Snider on the "History of the Faust Poem," Julia Ward HOWE on "Goethe's Women," and William Torrey HARRIS on "Goethe's Faust." Only two other volumes of lectures from the school were published: CONCORD LECTURES ON PHILOSOPHY (1883) and THE GENIUS AND CHARACTER OF EMERSON (1898).

"Life Without Principle"
Henry David Thoreau
(1863)

Henry David Thoreau worked to revise the essay "Life Without Principle" during the last months of his life, but it was not published until October 1863, a year after his death, in the ATLANTIC MONTHLY. Thoreau had originally presented the material as a lecture in the mid-1850s under various other titles. Although shorter than many of his other influential works, "Life Without Principle" contains the basic foundations of his larger philosophy that he had developed more fully in other writings: self-reliance and attention to the principles of a simple life. As in WALDEN and "CIVIL DISOBEDIENCE," Thoreau warned readers to avoid being influenced by institutions, such as the church and state, as well as by public opinion and even your closest neighbors. For Thoreau, the only law or principle that governs is that within oneself.

"Likeness to God"
William Ellery Channing
(1828)

The Unitarian Reverend William Ellery CHANNING's "Likeness to God" was a sermon presented in 1828 and one of the most significant impacts on the development of early Transcendentalist thought within UNITARIANISM. In the sermon, the liberal minister and reformer Channing explored humankind as a reflection of God and humanity's relationship to God, practiced through religion, which should include "high aspirations, hopes, and efforts," spiritual characteristics motivated by our sense of being "like" God. The human relationship

to God, in Channing's view, was one that involved not solely, or even primarily, obedience, but emulation: "To honor him, is not to tremble before him as an unapproachable sovereign, not to utter barren praise which leaves us as it found us. It is to become what we praise. It is to approach God as an inexhaustible Fountain of light, power, and purity. It is to feel the quickening and transforming energy of his perfections." This is an early utterance of the 19th-century religious idea of PERFECTIONISM that permeated many other spiritual and reform movements of the era. The idea that the purpose of religious belief and practice was to strive toward perfection as modeled by Jesus Christ came to dominate evangelical religion and was the impetus for humanitarian reforms such as ABOLITIONISM. The abstract idea that to reach one's full human potential was the closest route to God, or the divine in general, became a foundation of Transcendentalist philosophy as well. The Reverend William Ellery Channing made explicit the connection between spiritual belief and social reform, or moral action. The perfectionism of aspiring to be God-like meant aspiring to create a world in which God could thrive: "Whenever we think, speak, or act, with moral energy, and resolute devotion to duty . . . then the divinity is growing within us, and we are ascending towards our Author." This idea had a profound influence and was echoed throughout the coming decades in the writings of Ralph Waldo EMERSON, although, for Emerson, unlike Channing, the spiritual work of thinking, speaking, and acting with moral energy could be best done on individual terms, outside of the framework of the organized church.

Little Women
Louisa May Alcott
(1868–1869)

Originally published in two volumes (September 1868 and April 1869), Little Women: Meg, Jo, Beth, and Amy was a semiautobiographical account of four sisters and established Louisa May ALCOTT as the best-loved children's writer of the 19th century. Alcott wrote the novel at the suggestion of her publisher that she capitalize on the success of stories for and about the adventures of young boys by writing a book for girls. The book was hugely successful and was followed by two sequels: *Little Men* and *Jo's Boys.* Louisa May Alcott was the daughter of Transcendentalist reformer Amos Bronson ALCOTT and Abigail May ALCOTT. She had only to look to her own life for inspiration, as she was the second sister in a family of four girls: Anna (the model for the character "Meg" in the novel), Louisa ("Jo"), Elizabeth ("Beth"), and Abby May ("Amy"). The story traces the journeys of these four girls into young womanhood, emphasizing not only their happy home and family life together but their different personalities, virtues, talents, and interests. In volume two, the girl's individual stories are traced into full adulthood as they make choices about college, marriage, and travel to Europe.

Readers are taken along with Jo (the alter ego of Alcott herself) as she pursues a writing career and with the heartbreaking tragedy of angelic and quiet Beth succumbing to a long bout with scarlet fever (as Alcott's own sister, Elizabeth, died from a prolonged illness brought on by scarlet fever in 1858 at the age of only 23). In all instances, from childhood to adulthood, Alcott presents not only the story of a family but of each sister as an individual in her own right and therefore makes available to her young readers, mostly girls, a range of character types and therefore the possibility of a variety of options for women, rather than one narrowly defined role of domesticity and motherhood as presented in other moralistic literature of the time. Especially in the memorable character of Jo, Louisa May Alcott seemed to work out her own identity as a young woman dedicated to her family, but with her own individual talents and goals to nurture, providing a model of how to be both a woman and a writer at a time when the two roles still seemed contradictory.

Locke, John
(1632–1704)

American Transcendentalism, and 19th-century ROMANTICISM in general, emerged as part of a cul-

tural rejection of the empirical rationalism of British philosopher John Locke. Locke was perhaps the most significant influence on the Enlightenment era, and his works fueled major intellectual shifts in Europe as well as the United States in the 18th century in the realms of politics, with *Two Treatises of Government* (1690), and religion, with *Essay Concerning Human Understanding* (1690). His *Two Treatises* formed the foundation of 18th-century political culture with its emphasis on life, liberty, and property as the basis of natural human rights, ideas that were later appropriated in the American context by Thomas Jefferson in the Declaration of Independence, in which "property" was replaced with the more general "pursuit of happiness."

Aside from the political implications of Locke's work, his writings had further cultural impact in transforming people's understanding of religious experience and belief. Locke not only advocated religious toleration, which was a radical idea, but in the *Essay Concerning Human Understanding,* he emphasized that all knowledge and ideas are gained from lived experience, from observation of the physical world around us. This idea, and a more general rational approach to knowledge exemplified by the Enlightenment, directly resulted in the formation of liberal Christian denominations, most notably UNITARIANISM, in the late 18th and early 19th centuries. The Unitarians saw in Locke a common sense approach to religion that valued education, reflection, and rational, even scientific, thought over the emotionalism and faith as promoted in the religious revivalism of the masses during this same time period. Enlightenment thought had a firm place in the curriculum at HARVARD DIVINITY SCHOOL, where Unitarian ministers, and most of the Transcendentalists, were educated.

Beginning in the early 19th century, however, even as Unitarianism was establishing itself as a rational religion, thinkers and writers, both literary and theological, influenced by European romanticism began to reject the rigid empiricism of Locke, however, in favor of the value of human perception, or intuition, in revealing spiritual truths. In 1829 James MARSH wrote an introduction to and published an American version of English writer

Samuel Taylor COLERIDGE's *Aids to Reflection* that had a significant impact on the Unitarian-Transcendentalist understanding of Coleridge and rejection of Locke. Marsh argued that Locke's ideas were not only limited but were in fact incompatible with liberal Christianity itself in that Locke presented "a system of philosophy which excludes the very idea of all spiritual power and agency." That is, Locke left no room for the idea of the soul and its development or growth separate from the physical world. Greatly influenced by Marsh's argument, although Marsh himself did not identify as a Transcendentalist, this anti-Lockean sentiment which privileged individual "power and agency" in all things spiritual as well as philosophical, became the foundation of Transcendentalism as it developed in the 1830s. Transcendentalism argued that Enlightenment thought, and Unitarianism in particular, went too far away from acknowledging a place for faith and spirituality in individual development. Transcendentalism was by definition, then, a break from what many proponents perceived as the rigid empiricism of Unitarianism as a result of this outgrowth from Enlightenment thought—what Ralph Waldo EMERSON referred to as the "corpse-cold" feeling of Unitarianism.

The Transcendentalists critiqued the lack of mysticism and spiritualism of Unitarianism, and they did so by reaching back to directly engage and critique the Enlightenment thinkers they read at Harvard, and John Locke specifically. Transcendentalism valued the senses, the physical observation of nature as one route to spiritual meaning, but not at the cost of ignoring the inner senses, such as intuition. Eventually, the intuition—meaning a subjective inner interpretation of events, natural processes, and of religion itself—replaced the need for reliance on any outside sources, such as church or Bible. Ironically, then, Transcendentalism was influenced directly by Locke and Enlightenment thought in rationalizing religion to the point of finding it unnecessary and promoting instead the restoration of faith and belief in individuals, in one's self.

Unitarians engaged in a rational study of the Bible, analyzing it through scientific methods to understand the supernatural events included within it, such as the accounts of the miracles performed by

Jesus. John Locke, and the Unitarians who read and were influenced by him, such as the Reverend William Ellery CHANNING, were not complete skeptics, however, and left room for "revelation" in their analysis, accepting as a starting point, for example, that the Bible itself was the revealed word of God and therefore must be *true*, needing analysis only to be truly *understood*. Channing accepted the eyewitness accounts contained in the Bible as proof for the miracles. Following Locke's theories, the Unitarians believed that the Bible would not contain acts against the laws of nature and science—it was only that humans had not accurately defined methods of understanding some laws and therefore fully understanding or explaining the so-called supernatural events of the Bible. In demanding proof and asserting a foundational belief in the reliability of the biblical record, Locke, and later the Unitarians, only presented a method more grounded in Enlightenment rationalism than the religious "enthusiasm" of those who accepted on faith alone, without empirical evidence. Locke rejected the idea of "illumination without search, of certainty without proof." He warned against "the extravagancy of enthusiasm, and the error of wrong principles," both of which the Unitarians of the late 18th and early 19th centuries saw in the religious revivalism and "awakenings" taking place in America at that time. Grounded in Locke, Unitarians offered instead a scholarly rational approach to religion, to belief itself, and promoted their methods through the Harvard curriculum with an emphasis on the reading of Enlightenment texts, including John Locke.

By the first decade of the 19th century, however, other philosophical schools had emerged whose purpose was to critique Locke and the Enlightenment thinkers. Young Harvard students were excited by extracurricular readings in Scottish COMMON SENSE PHILOSOPHY and in the literary and biblical criticism of European romanticism. These alternative readings mounted a powerful critique against the rational and empirical methods of Locke as applied to the realms of philosophy, religion, and literature and instead emphasized the role of individual human judgment and intuition as reliable tools for determining moral and spiritual truths. The Transcendentalists emerged, then, from among the young Harvard students who simultaneously began to rebel against John Locke, against the rigidity of Unitarianism, and against the educational methods of Harvard itself.

Bibliography

Packer, Barbara. "The Transcendentalists." In *The Cambridge History of American Literature,* vol. 2: 1820–1865, ed. Sacvan Bercovitch. New York: Cambridge University Press, 1995, 329–607.

Longfellow, Henry Wadsworth
(1807–1882)

Poet and Harvard professor of languages, Henry Wadsworth Longfellow was perhaps the most well-known American poet of the 19th century through such popular verses as "The Psalm of Life," "Paul Revere's Ride," and the narrative poem, *The Song of Hiawatha.* Longfellow is acknowledged as the most important poet of American ROMANTICISM and, although he did not identify as a Transcendentalist himself, he worked under the same New England literary and social influences and read widely in many of the same European thinkers who influenced American Transcendentalist philosophy. Before settling into his position as a Harvard professor, Longfellow traveled throughout Europe studying languages and literature. He met Thomas CARLYLE, who introduced him to the German romantic writers Johann Wolfgang von GOETHE and Friedrich SCHILLER, whose ideas influenced his own style of poetry. In the United States Longfellow published not only poetry but also book reviews and scholarly essays on language theory in the NORTH AMERICAN REVIEW. His 1842 *Poems on Slavery* was dedicated to the Unitarian Reverend William Ellery CHANNING, who typified the early elite liberal Christian antislavery position. Like the Transcendentalists, particularly Ralph Waldo EMERSON and Margaret FULLER, Longfellow was particularly interested in promoting American authors and the emergence of an independent American literature and wrote a famous 1837 review of Nathaniel HAWTHORNE's *Twice-Told Tales* that helped to establish Hawthorne's literary reputation and career.

Henry Wadsworth Longfellow left Harvard in 1854 to focus on his own writing, specifically his poetry. He organized a group of New England intellectuals into the "Dante Club" to assist and inspire him in producing a translation of *The Divine Comedy,* which was published in three volumes between 1865 and 1867 and is generally considered one of his most significant works. Longfellow was promoted by his publisher, Ticknor and Fields, as one of the most significant American writers of his time, along with other clients of the publisher, such as Ralph Waldo Emerson, James Russell LOWELL, and John Greenleaf WHITTIER, and was included in literary anthologies and textbooks circulated among a wide general audience.

Longfellow was connected to the Transcendentalists also through his brother, Samuel Longfellow (1819–92), a Unitarian minister active in Transcendentalist activities. In addition to collaborating with Thomas Wentworth HIGGINSON on a book, Samuel Longfellow also wrote a two-volume 1886 biography of his famous brother.

Bibliography

Calhoun, Charles C. *Longfellow: A Rediscovered Life.* Boston: Beacon Press, 2004.

"The Lord's Supper"
Ralph Waldo Emerson
(1832)

"The Lord's Supper" is the name given to Ralph Waldo EMERSON's most famous sermon, delivered at his Second Church congregation in Boston on September 9, 1832, as an explanation for his resignation from the ministry. Emerson had attempted to resign by writing a letter to the congregation, but they refused his request, forcing him to provide a more complete explanation in the form of this sermon. The church finally accepted his resignation in late October 1832. In "The Lord's Supper" Emerson explained that his opposition to the tradition of serving communion to his congregation prevented him from fulfilling his duties as their pastor: "It is my desire, in the office of a Christian minister, to do nothing which I cannot do with my whole heart." He opened the address by acknowledging the contentiousness of the issue: "In the history of the Church no subject has been more fruitful of controversy than the Lord's Supper."

Communion, or the Lord's Supper, consists of a ritual in which church members remember the suffering of Jesus Christ on the cross by consuming some type of unleavened bread or cracker (a symbolic representation of the body of Christ) along with red wine or grape drink (representing his blood). While acknowledging that Jesus brought his disciples to participate in this ritual with him in the New Testament, Emerson insisted this was only a symbolic lesson for his immediate followers before he died, not a mandate for churches to continue the practice on a regular basis: "Jesus did not intend to establish an institution for perpetual observance." The Lord's Supper was not only irrelevant for contemporary religion but even harmful, for it had become, Emerson feared, a rote practice, devoid of any deeper spiritual meaning for participants. Emerson had come, by this time in his career, to articulate a full-fledged critique of the spiritually vacant adherence to the rituals of what he termed "historical Christianity," including but not limited to the Lord's Supper. He was dismayed that liberal Unitarians especially continued to unquestioningly follow such formal aspects of orthodox Christianity.

Emerson had several reasons—personal, vocational, and philosophical—for removing himself from the ministry in 1832. In emphasizing his problem with the Lord's Supper, Emerson was drawing on his extensive readings that paved the way for the emergence of his Transcendentalist philosophy. He was influenced in particular by the Swedish mystic Emanuel Swedenborg (see SWEDENBORGIANISM), who warned against tradition and outward practices of religion in favor of "genuine" spiritual experience. The Lord's Supper had no genuine meaning for Emerson, and he could not in good conscience lead the ceremony for his congregants. His separation from the church, based on his belief in the value of conscience over religious tradition, was the first step toward formulating his own philosophy of Transcendentalism.

Loring, Ellis Gray
(1803–1858)

Ellis Gray Loring was a prominent Boston abolitionist and lawyer who was connected with the Transcendentalists both socially and in reform activities. Loring counted Ralph Waldo EMERSON among his classmates in grammar school as well as later at Harvard. Loring shared Emerson's interest in Scottish writer Thomas CARLYLE and aided Emerson in editing an important four-volume collection of Carlyle's *Critical and Miscellaneous Essays* in 1838. While the two thus shared philosophical interests, Loring also influenced Emerson politically through ABOLITIONISM. He inspired and advised Emerson on at least one of the Transcendentalist's public addresses on the slavery issue. Many other prominent reformers and abolitionists gathered around Loring, who had participated with William Lloyd GARRISON in the founding of the New England Anti-Slavery Society in 1832, and who was closely associated with Lydia Maria CHILD and Wendell PHILLIPS. In 1836 Loring contributed to the abolitionist cause in his capacity as a lawyer by successfully arguing an important case before the Massachusetts Supreme Court that resulted in the decision that the legal status of "slave" did not exist in Massachusetts, and therefore any slave brought into state was considered free. Loring was also among the signers, along with Emerson and William Ellery CHANNING, of an 1838 petition supporting the right to free speech of radical Abner KNEELAND, tried and convicted of blasphemy.

Bibliography
Gougeon, Len. *Virtue's Hero: Emerson, Antislavery, and Reform.* Athens: University of Georgia Press, 1990.

"Love"
Ralph Waldo Emerson
(1841)

Ralph Waldo EMERSON's "Love" was part of a series of lectures on human life and culture delivered in Boston beginning in December 1838 (winter 1838–39) and published in ESSAYS: FIRST SERIES in 1841. Although Emerson focused on other types of love, such as "FRIENDSHIP," in the essay of that name, the essay on "Love" is primarily a discussion of romantic love, or Eros. In the opening paragraph Emerson forcefully and eloquently defines love as "a private and tender relation of one to one, which is the enchantment of human life, which, like a certain divine rage and enthusiasm, seizes on man at one period, and works a revolution in his mind and body." Emerson himself acknowledged that this flow of emotion or sentiment from him might seem uncharacteristic: "I have been told, that in some public discourses of mine my reverence for the intellect has made me unjustly cold to the personal relations." Emerson regretted that others had judged him in this "disparaging" way, for, as a philosopher, he was thoroughly interested in the question of "the enchantment of human life." In fact, he concluded, "The power of Love is indeed the great poem of nature."

"Passion," which Emerson used as synonymous with the type of "love" he was exploring, "rebuilds the world for the youth. It makes all things alive and significant." In fact, it is in the experience of loving another that, ultimately, the self becomes more whole, thus bringing love into the Transcendentalist focus on self-development. The person who finds love finds that "he is somewhat; he is a person; he is a soul." Love also aids in the soul's appreciation of and relationship to nature: "Nature grows conscious." Awareness heightened by love, the individual finds that "Every bird on the bough of the tree sings now to his heart and soul. The notes are almost articulate. The clouds have faces as he looks on them . . . the peeping flowers have grown intelligent . . . nature soothes and sympathizes."

Love was not only a personal experience of "revolution" or heightened consciousness, however, as the relationships that arise from it had social implications as well, as love "unites him to his race, pledges him to the domestic and civic relations . . . establishes marriage, and gives permanence to human society." Emerson's biographer notes that this essay was published at a difficult time in his marriage to Lidian Jackson EMERSON, and Ralph Waldo Emerson may have drawn as much of his recollections of the power of desire and emotions from his earlier love for and marriage to Ellen Tucker EMERSON, his first wife, who died quite young. In fact, throughout the essay, Emerson celebrated the early stages of love, of Eros, but acknowledged this as a temporary state as "even Love which is the deification of the per-

sons must become more impersonal every day." The essay was thus not a celebration of marriage, as a social institution, and, in fact, Emerson wrote no essay on marriage, per se. In his journals he often recorded his disillusionment with marriage and its hindrance to the experience of the ideal ever-perfecting love relationship. In the conclusion of the essay on "Love," in fact, he somewhat shockingly admitted that "slowly and with pain, the objects of the affections change, as the objects of thought do," recognizing that there can be no growth without change. The essay was primarily a celebration of the ecstasy of an idealized love relationship, which is not intended to be permanent but "must be succeeded and supplanted only by what is more beautiful, and so on for ever."

Marriage, love, and the nature of friendship were all increasingly topics of debate among Emerson's Transcendentalist colleagues, both male and female. At the time he wrote this essay, Ralph Waldo Emerson had intense personal relationships with and was engaged in conversations about love and friendship with women friends, such as Margaret FULLER and Caroline Sturgis (TAPPAN), and most likely considered the nature of love and desire within such friendships. The essay on "Love" could be seen, then, as part of that larger conversation which was carried on in person, in journals and letters, and in the publication of essays and poems. Marriage and ideal relations between the sexes were also topics at the center of Margaret Fuller's WOMAN IN THE NINETEENTH CENTURY, published in 1845, as well as in many of her poems. Emerson also wrote a poem on "Initial, Daemonic, and Celestial Love," celebrating love as ultimately transcending the earthly limitations on relationships between two people.

Lowell, James Russell
(1819–1891)

James Russell Lowell was one of the most important literary critics of the 19th century and influential to New England intellectual culture in general, and the Transcendentalists in particular, as editor of periodicals such as the ATLANTIC MONTHLY and the NORTH AMERICAN REVIEW. He attended Harvard College where he was designated class poet the year of his graduation in 1838. His *Class Poem* was a poorly written satire of many of the intellectual and reform tendencies of the era, including WOMEN'S RIGHTS, temperance, and Transcendentalism. During his final term at Harvard he had traveled to CONCORD, MASSACHUSETTS, where he met Ralph Waldo EMERSON and others within the movement. His opinions and criticisms of Transcendentalism did not change, but his writing and humor were more skillfully put to use when he tried again at satirical verse in the 1848 A *FABLE FOR CRITICS*.

After Harvard Lowell obtained a law degree, but he was not interested in being a lawyer and quickly gave up the law in pursuit of a literary career. He lectured at the CONCORD LYCEUM on "Modern Poetry" and submitted his own poetry for publication to several magazines. His sonnet "To a Voice Heard in Mount Auburn" was published in the January 1841 issue of the Transcendentalist journal, the DIAL, and he also contributed to THE HARBINGER, the paper of the BROOK FARM experiment. When his *A Year's Life* was published the same year, however, the book received a less than favorable review by Margaret FULLER in the *Dial*. Still, another set of his poems appeared in the January 1842 issue of the journal. Ultimately Lowell's wife, Maria White, who had been an attendee at Fuller's CONVERSATIONS FOR WOMEN, was more interested in Transcendentalism than her husband. In 1843 he founded his own magazine, *The Pioneer,* which printed only three issues but published such important writers as Nathaniel HAWTHORNE and Edgar Allan POE and, from among the Transcendentalists, John Sullivan DWIGHT, Elizabeth Palmer PEABODY, and Jones VERY.

While as an editor and critic he would eventually become personally involved with the careers of many of the Transcendentalists, James Russell Lowell never aligned himself philosophically with the movement. He felt that many of their ideas were too extreme and individualistic. He did, however, become an especially close friend of Ralph Waldo Emerson whom he published regularly in his periodicals and helped establish as one of the major writers of the period. Lowell dedicated his own most significant collection of literary essays,

Among My Books: Second Series (1876), to Emerson. His relationship with Henry David THOREAU, however, was less genial, as the two had disagreements over Lowell's censorship of lines from one of Thoreau's essays submitted to the *Atlantic Monthly*. He was personal friends with minor figures such as George William CURTIS and John Sullivan Dwight, but Amos Bronson ALCOTT, Margaret Fuller, Theodore PARKER, and others were harshly caricatured as egotistical and even incomprehensible pseudo intellectuals in *A Fable for Critics*. Alcott and Fuller were singled out for further discussion in his "Studies for Two Heads," published the same year in Lowell's collection of *Poems*.

Other than these satirical rhymes about Transcendentalist personalities and his contrasting celebration of Emerson, Lowell curiously wrote very little about the actual movement and its literary or philosophical impact. Many years later he wrote retrospective essays on Emerson and on Thoreau that dealt more with their personal and historical interest than philosophical ideas. Most scholars agree that Lowell was too practical and commonsensical a thinker and reformer to have much use for abstract Transcendentalist musings or for the celebrity worship that many, even Emerson, seemed to attract. Of Emerson's followers he had the most disdain, for, in his opinion, they completely failed to think for themselves. He wrote to a friend of his impressions upon meeting Thoreau for the first time: "It is exquisitely amusing to see how he imitates Emerson's tone & manner. With my eyes shut I shouldn't kn[ow] them apart." This was the opinion he put forth more publicly in his caricature of Thoreau in *A Fable for Critics*.

James Russell Lowell's concerns were ultimately more political than philosophical. He became increasingly involved in ABOLITIONISM, publishing numerous essays on the subject and becoming an editor during the 1840s for the *National Anti-Slavery Standard,* where he wrote poems under the name of Yankee Hosea Biglow. This persona and popularly successful experiment in writing led to the 1862 publication of *The Biglow Papers*.

In 1857 the *Atlantic Monthly* was founded with Lowell as editor. He published many of his own poems and other writings in the paper, but by this time he had moved beyond his criticisms of the Transcendentalists. At the same time, his role in American letters was acknowledged in his appointment as professor of belles lettres at Harvard, a position he held for the next two decades. James Russell Lowell never gained critical acclaim for his own writing, although scholars now view his verses and, in particular, his humorous style in the tradition of popular or democratic as well as political poetry. His most influential role in the 19th-century literary market was as an editor and critic of his contemporaries.

Bibliography

Duberman, Martin. *James Russell Lowell*. Boston: Houghton Mifflin, 1966.

lyceum   *See* CONCORD LYCEUM.

Lyell, Charles
(1797–1875)

The Transcendentalists read the works of British geologist Charles Lyell and heard him lecture in Boston. Lyell was perhaps the most well-known geologist of his era and helped spread the science to a broader and more popular audience. Lyell linked current geologic evidence to the past in showing how the Earth changed over time, slowly and in cycles, not progressively as other theories assumed. While Ralph Waldo EMERSON initially found Lyell's three-volume *Principles of Geology* "only a catalogue of facts," the influence of Lyell's scientific, rather than religious, theories of the Earth's history were evident in Emerson's 1844 essay on "Nature" in which he noted that "Geology has introduced us to the secularity of nature."

It was Henry David THOREAU, who in his own work as a naturalist-scientist was most directly influenced by Charles Lyell's geologic studies. Thoreau knew that the Earth and nature are constantly changing, but he specifically addressed the idea of geological layers in A WEEK ON THE CONCORD AND MERRIMACK RIVERS: "I thrust this stick many aeons deep into its surface. . . . The newest is but the oldest made visible to our senses." The earth's history, for Thoreau, had correlations with human history and actions. In the broadest terms, Lyell's science of the significance of small changes over time fit with the Transcendentalist social project as well, which focused on the actions of the individual as important to the whole of human history and progress.

Bibliography

Rossi, William. "Poetry and Progress: Thoreau, Lyell, and the Geological Principles of *A Week*," *American Literature* 66 (June 1994): 275–300.

M

The Maine Woods
Henry David Thoreau
(1864)

Published two years after his death, *The Maine Woods* is a collection of three separate essays by Henry David THOREAU, recounting three different wilderness excursions: "Ktaadn," "Chesuncook," and "Allegash and East Branch." Much of his material from these trips was originally presented as lyceum lectures, and two of the three essays were previously published as magazine articles before their appearance in *The Maine Woods*. The essay "Ktaadn, and the Maine Woods" was serialized in five issues of the *Union Magazine of Literature and Art* between July and November 1848; "Chesuncook" originally appeared in three issues of the ATLANTIC MONTHLY between June and August 1858; but "Allegash and East Branch" had never been published before appearing in the final text of *The Maine Woods*. The essays were collected and edited by friend William Ellery CHANNING II and sister Sophia THOREAU following Henry David Thoreau's death in 1862. Written over a period of 16 years, then, the sections of *The Maine Woods* vary in theme and style; taken together, the essays highlight Thoreau's development as a writer and a naturalist.

During his stay at WALDEN POND in 1846 Henry David Thoreau made a sojourn into "the woods of Maine." During this trip Thoreau made his climb of Mount Ktaadn (or Katahdin), the highest peak in Maine, and the subject of the first part of *The Maine Woods*, "Ktaadn." Just the year

before the mountaintop had been reached by two Boston acquaintances of Thoreau's, Edward Everett HALE and William Francis Channing, cousin of Transcendentalist friend William Ellery Channing II. In addition, Thoreau's interest in Maine and in the mountains in particular was spurred by personal connections to the region, such as distant relatives of his father who lived in Bangor and with whom the family regularly visited, and the fact that state geologist Charles T. Jackson was the brother of Lidian Jackson EMERSON, wife of Ralph Waldo EMERSON. Thoreau's written account of his own ascent up "Ktaadn" resembled in some ways his approach to the wilderness as detailed in his book-length A WEEK ON THE CONCORD AND MERRIMACK RIVERS (1849)—which he was writing at the same time he made the Ktaadn trip—with its literary and mythological allusions and its relation of the physical journey of the climb with the spiritual journey of the individual.

The essay on "Chesuncook" was inspired by an 1853 trip which took Thoreau down from the mystical mountaintop into an examination of the life of the Indian hunters who inhabited the region. In presenting the essay to *Atlantic Monthly* editor James Russell LOWELL, Thoreau declared that "the Moose, the Pine Tree & the Indian" were its main subjects. Indeed, Thoreau recounted an incidence of the useless slaughter of a moose by one of his white companions and equated such an act with the destruction of the forests as well. Although at first Thoreau idealized the world of the Indian natives, he ultimately found that they, too, were interested in exploiting animals for profit with the sale of furs and skins, and, in one instance at least, had adopted other negative habits due to contact with Europeans. "Chesuncook" therefore shows Thoreau struggling with the concept of "the wild" versus "civilization" and placing the paradox of native peoples living in the 19th century at the center of that struggle. Thoreau studied and made journal notes on volumes and volumes of anthropological works on primitive cultures during this period of his Maine trips and, according to some scholars, his writings in "Chesuncook" and "Allegash" (the last section of The Maine Woods) were his most thorough analyses of native Americans.

A native American, his friend and guide Joseph Polis, emerges as the central figure in his final Maine experience, "Allegash and East Branch." Accompanied by CONCORD, MASSACHUSETTS, friend Edward Sherman HOAR, and Polis, a representative of the Penobscot Indians, Thoreau traveled the greatest distance in this 1857 trip. Thoreau sought to learn all he could about native culture and survival from Polis, even though Polis was also a Christian and wealthy landowner. As scholar Joseph Moldenhauer points out, Joe Polis ultimately represented for Thoreau the Indian peoples who were caught between "primitive" and "civilized" societies, "between woods and village," but this situation also accurately describes Thoreau himself, in these essays, as well as in the more fully developed WALDEN (1854).

The "Allegash" essay shows Thoreau's scientific tendencies more than the other pieces in his detailed and knowledgeable interest in Maine flora and fauna. The Maine Woods includes an Appendix of Thoreau's listings of plants and trees to be found in Maine, but in the essay he characterized science as insufficient for interpreting his encounter with the natural world, preferring spiritual explanations for certain phenomena. Ultimately, in all of the essays in The Maine Woods, science and mysticism are combined for Thoreau in an overall appreciation of nature.

Bibliography
Moldenhauer, Joseph J. "The Maine Woods." In The Cambridge Companion to Henry David Thoreau, ed.

Joel Myerson. New York: Cambridge University Press, 1995, 124–141.
Sayre, Robert F. Thoreau and the American Indians. Princeton, N.J.: Princeton University Press, 1977.

Mann, Horace
(1796–1859)

Educational reformer Horace Mann had both professional and personal connections to the Transcendentalists. He shared reform interests with many of them who were teachers at various types of experimental schools and who were involved in issues related to public EDUCATION. Ultimately, however, in his position as the head of the first Massachusetts Board of Education, Mann differed from the Transcendentalists in that he sought reform through institutions rather than emphasizing belief in the autonomy of the individual. He was particularly criticized by Orestes BROWNSON, who disagreed with and thought impossible and irreligious Mann's proposal of a nonsectarian curriculum in the public schools. Mann was especially close friends with Nathaniel HAWTHORNE and Sophia (Peabody) HAWTHORNE and with Elizabeth Palmer PEABODY. Despite his intense intellectual friendship with Elizabeth Peabody, in 1843 Mann married the third Peabody sister, Mary.

Bibliography
Messerli, Jonathan. Horace Mann: A Biography. New York: Knopf, 1972.

"Man the Reformer"
Ralph Waldo Emerson
(1841)

Ralph Waldo EMERSON first delivered his lecture on "Man the Reformer" in January 1841, and it was published in the April 1841 issue of the Transcendentalist literary journal, the DIAL. "Man the Reformer" was primarily a response to the communitarian experiment at BROOK FARM, which engaged the energies of many of the Transcendentalists beginning in 1841. Brook Farm was founded by George RIPLEY as a utopian community. Although

Emerson provided financial support for the community, he promoted instead a vision of individual reform as the basis of social change. In "Man the Reformer" Emerson makes clear his stance that the plan for social reorganization instituted at Brook Farm, based on the division of labor according to specialized tasks and individual talents, was not as desirable or efficient as an "economy" based on self reliance: "How can the man who has learned but one art, procure all the conveniences of life honestly? . . . Can anything be so elegant as to have few wants and to serve them oneself?" Emerson used this occasion of reflecting on self-reliance and on the value of labor to comment as well on the issue of slavery. In "Man the Reformer," he reminds readers that the productivity of the South depended not upon industrious planters but upon slave labor and that, in the North, "the abolitionist has shown us our dreadful debt to the Southern negro. In the island of Cuba . . . one dies in ten every year, of these miserable bachelors, to yield us sugar."

Margaret and Her Friends
Caroline Dall
(1895)

Besides scattered references in letters and autobiographies, there are only two extant accounts of Margaret FULLER's famous series of Boston CONVERSATIONS FOR WOMEN: notes on the 1839 season recorded by Elizabeth Palmer PEABODY and the 1841 season recorded by Caroline DALL, which she published in 1895 as *Margaret and Her Friends; or, Ten Conversations with Margaret Fuller upon the Mythology of the Greeks and Its Expression in Art.* The spring season held between March 1 and May 6, 1841, at the home of George RIPLEY was the only session of Conversations to include both women and men. Fuller had begun the Conversations for women in the fall of 1839 but decided to open up the meetings to men since, according to Dall, Fuller "had great need of money" and so hoped that inviting men would increase paid attendance. She also hoped to stimulate conversation between the sexes by including many of her closest male friends—in Dall's words, "the gentle-

men who were accustomed to talk with her"—in her experiment.

Margaret and Her Friends is thus one of the few historical accounts of Fuller's work in this genre as the Conversations, by definition, were not intended to produce written texts to be analyzed and studied, and thus little is known about what went on at such events. Dall's account provides information on the format and topics discussed, and on Fuller's role as facilitator. The theme for the 1841 season was Greek mythology, and participants at one or more of the weekly gatherings (besides Dall who apparently attended all 10 meetings) included Amos Bronson ALCOTT, James Freeman CLARKE, Ralph Waldo EMERSON, Frederic Henry HEDGE, Elizabeth HOAR, Elizabeth Palmer Peabody, George and Sophia RIPLEY, Caroline Sturgis TAPPAN, and Jones VERY. Dall recreated the conversational style by keeping track of each speaker and her or his comments and then annotating with her own observations and biographical notes on those in attendance. Dall ultimately concluded that Fuller was at her best when in the company of women and that the mixed-sex experiment was not a success. Dall made notes about the men interrupting—in Emerson's case he ignored Fuller's direction and instead "pursued his own train of thought"—and in general disrupting Fuller's efforts to guide the conversation along the chosen theme. According to Dall, "Margaret" herself "never enjoyed this mixed class, and considered it a failure so far as her own power was concerned." This summation may be accurate as the Conversations returned the next season as a forum for women only.

The fact that Dall did not publish her transcribed notes of the 1841 meeting until more than 50 years later perhaps limits their reliability as a firsthand account, but the account reveals much about Margaret Fuller's legacy at the end of the century. By the 1890s Dall herself was one of the last of the living Transcendentalists, and many former colleagues were beginning to memorialize the movement by writing personal memoirs or biographies of key figures. Dall had been influenced by Fuller and had written consistently on her since their meeting in the 1840s. As a writer and editor of *THE UNA* WOMEN'S RIGHTS paper Dall reviewed Fuller's works and referenced the ideas of *WOMAN*

IN THE NINETEENTH CENTURY, Fuller's 1845 feminist manifesto, in her own writings in the intervening years. The same year that she published *Margaret and Her Friends,* Dall also delivered a lecture on the history of the Transcendentalist movement as a whole. Published two years later as *TRANSCENDENTALISM IN NEW ENGLAND* (1897), Dall's history placed Fuller at the center of the meaning of the movement as an intellectual and as a feminist. When Dall decided to publish her firsthand account of Fuller's Conversations, she had her own voluminous notes and reflections on Fuller's importance, but she also sought out other surviving Transcendentalists to gather information to supplement her own record.

Bibliography

Myerson, Joel. "Mrs. Dall Edits Miss Fuller: The Story of *Margaret and Her Friends," Papers of the Bibliographical Society of America* 72:2 (1978): 187–200.

Marsh, James
(1794–1842)

James Marsh was a Congregationalist minister and president of the University of Vermont who in 1829 issued the first American edition of English romantic writer Samuel Taylor COLERIDGE's *Aids to Reflection,* one of the most important works explaining the emergence of Transcendentalism. Marsh provided an explication of Coleridge's ideas in a "Preliminary Essay" and in annotations of the text, aids for his American readers. Marsh further spread the influence of Coleridge and of German philosophers in the United States by editing two other Coleridge texts and translating several German works.

Although now identified for his importance to the early movement, James Marsh himself was not a Transcendentalist. As an orthodox Christian Marsh was drawn to Coleridge's ROMANTICISM and ideas for spiritual renewal, not the theological criticism that emerged within the Transcendentalist controversy. He turned down invitations both to attend meetings of the TRANSCENDENTAL CLUB and to write for the movement's literary journal, the *DIAL,* and once characterized Transcendentalism in general as "a rather superficial affair." Re-gardless, both Marsh and the Transcendentalists were attracted to Coleridge's rejection of the Enlightenment belief that Reason was acquired through empirical knowledge and believed, instead, that true Reason and knowledge could only be attained through reflection, or self-knowledge.

Like Caleb Sprague HENRY, whose translations of Victor COUSIN also influenced the emergence of Transcendentalism, Marsh attempted to distance himself from the ideas he inadvertently promoted. His interest in Coleridge was, again like Henry in relation to Cousin, centered on introducing a more self-conscious individual spirituality into Christianity, not in critiquing the need for Christianity. Marsh tried to reconcile Coleridge with religion, indeed saw Coleridge as adding needed depth to rational UNITARIANISM. James Marsh did, however, understand the logical extreme of Coleridge's principles in doing away with reliance on theology, a position that the many of the Transcendentalists would eventually advocate.

Bibliography

Carafiol, Peter. *Transcendent Reason: James Marsh and the Forms of Romantic Thought.* Tallahassee: University Presses of Florida, 1982.

Wells, Ronald Vale. *Three Christian Transcendentalists: James Marsh, Caleb Sprague Henry, and Frederic Henry Hedge.* New York: Octagon Books, 1972.

Martineau, Harriet
(1802–1876)

Harriet Martineau was a British journalist and abolitionist who embarked on a tour of the United States beginning in 1834, during which time she was introduced to many prominent American politicians, writers, and thinkers, including many among the Transcendentalists. Martineau came from a prominent Unitarian family and therefore had connections within the church during her travels. In Massachusetts she met and stayed with revered Unitarian leader William Ellery CHANNING, and met both Ralph Waldo EMERSON and Margaret FULLER. After returning to England, Martineau gathered together her firsthand observations about America into two books: *Society in*

America (1837) and *Retrospect of Western Travel* (1838). She also remembered some of her American experiences and colleagues in her later widely read *Autobiography* (1877).

In *Society in America*, Martineau, in a project similar to Alexis de Tocqueville's *Democracy in America*, also published in the 1830s, provided a European's perspective on the success of the American political and social system. For Martineau, the most obvious shortcoming to America's promise was the institution of slavery. Martineau was outspoken in regards to ABOLITIONISM, and in all of her writings she criticized the Southern slave power as well as the American government. She made many friends, of course, among Northern reformers involved in the abolitionist movement, but she also made enemies due to her criticism of the church. Given her own background and her firsthand knowledge of American UNITARIANISM, she was particularly critical of those among the Northern elite who did not do enough against slavery. In *Society in America* she declared, "I can come to no other conclusion than that the most guilty class of the community in regard to the slavery question at present is, not the slaveholding, nor even the mercantile, but the clerical: the most guilty, because . . . they profess to spend their lives in the study of moral relations, and have pledged themselves to declare the whole counsel of God." There were a few Unitarians who stood apart in Martineau's assessment, including several in Massachusetts affiliated with Transcendentalism. She was a close friend of William Ellery Channing, who did speak out against slavery, and her respect for Ralph Waldo Emerson's philosophical commitment to self-reliance and "moral independence" meant that she held back from criticizing his relative lack of involvement in abolitionism in the 1830s.

Harriet Martineau also met Amos Bronson ALCOTT, whose educational treatises she passed on to friends in England, and Margaret Fuller. Martineau was decidedly less tolerant of Fuller's lack of involvement with abolitionism compared to her commentary on Emerson. It was not until her 1877 *Autobiography*, however, more than 25 years after Fuller's death, that Martineau unleashed her harshest criticism of Fuller's priorities. Although Martineau was not in America at the time Fuller held her famous CONVERSATIONS FOR WOMEN, Martineau focused on Fuller's Transcendentalist activities at the expense of broader social commitments, a demand she never made of Emerson's work and life. Martineau described Fuller as "living and moving in an ideal world" consisting of "the most fanciful and shallow conceits which the transcendentalists of Boston took for philosophy." She made the accusation that while "Margaret Fuller and her adult pupils" at the Conversations were "talking about Mars and Venus, Plato and Goethe, and fancying themselves the elect of the earth in intellect and refinement, the liberties of the republic were running out as fast as they could go." In other words, these Bostonian women of means should have put their time and their energy to better use, such as fighting against slavery. This criticism was not entirely fair as many of Fuller's "adult pupils" were in fact drawn from Boston's reform community and themselves had strong ties to the abolitionist movement during the 1840s and 1850s—women such as Ednah Dow CHENEY, Caroline DALL, Lydia Maria CHILD, and Lidian EMERSON.

Bibliography

Hoecker-Drysdale, Susan E. *Harriet Martineau: First Woman Sociologist.* New York: St. Martin's Press, 1992.

Martineau, James
(1805–1900)

Unitarian minister and professor of philosophy James Martineau was the younger brother of English reformer Harriet MARTINEAU. James Martineau was perhaps the most well-known Unitarian theologian in England whose liberal writings were read by many Unitarians in New England. He was influenced by the same European philosophers of IDEALISM and ROMANTICISM as the American Transcendentalists and shared many of their criticisms of conservative UNITARIANISM. He regularly read the works of Ralph Waldo EMERSON as well as the American movement's literary journal coedited by Emerson, the *DIAL*. Martineau's most important book for the Transcendentalists was *The Rationale of Religious Inquiry*, published in 1836, the same year as many of the seminal Transcendentalist works, such as Emerson's NATURE. In this work, Martineau proposed a method of reforming English theology by looking outside of the scriptures and theological doctrine and toward human self-consciousness as a moral guide. Martineau's writing was reviewed favorably in the American Unitarian press, in particular in early reviews by George RIPLEY in the CHRISTIAN EXAMINER. Martineau was not as overtly politically active as his sister, Harriet Martineau, and apparently he never traveled to the United States as she did, but he was sought out by American travelers such as Ralph Waldo Emerson and Margaret FULLER on their separate European trips. Fuller heard Martineau speak and reported in one of her European dispatches for the NEW YORK TRIBUNE in 1846 that "his powers and views do find a true harmony." James Martineau's most sustained correspondence with an American contemporary was with fellow Unitarian minister William Ellery CHANNING.

Massachusetts Quarterly Review
(1847–1850)

The *Massachusetts Quarterly Review* was founded by radical Unitarian minister Theodore PARKER in 1847 as a forum for Transcendentalist reform interests. Parker explicitly intended his paper as not only a successor but as an evolved version of the earlier DIAL journal, which had represented the Boston movement during its tenure between 1840 and 1844. In Parker's own words, the *Massachusetts Quarterly Review* was envisioned as the "*Dial* with a Beard," that is, a mature version of the movement and its primary proponents. The demise of the *Dial* was necessary, according to Ralph Waldo EMERSON, as he wrote in a letter to William Henry FURNESS, so that the writers established there could move on, "write in their own names, and go to their proper readers." The *Massachusetts Quarterly Review* was intended as one such forum to reach those readers and many in the movement, including Emerson, Amos Bronson ALCOTT, James Freeman CLARKE, John Sullivan DWIGHT, and others, had joined Parker in planning for a new periodical.

Despite these explicit Transcendentalist connections, many of the earlier and prominent *Dial*

voices were absent from the *Massachusetts Quarterly Review*. Emerson wrote an introductory piece for the first issue and was initially listed as one of the editors, but he ultimately had little to do with the project, and neither Bronson Alcott, Margaret FULLER, or Henry David THOREAU ever wrote for Parker's paper. Emerson had hoped that the *Massachusetts Quarterly Review* would have a more literary emphasis, but under Parker's leadership it ultimately differed from the *Dial* in casting a wider net into the more explicitly political arena of antebellum reform. Specifically, articles on ABOLITIONISM made up a significant portion of the paper, and Parker published pieces by prominent antislavery activists such as Wendell PHILLIPS and Samuel Gridley Howe. Although reform was a regular theme that linked many of the *Massachusetts Quarterly Review* writers together, the magazine still covered a range of topics in its pages (religion, philosophy, science) and thus was not focused completely enough on abolitionism to retain an audience interested in that subject. Like the *Dial* before it, the *Massachusetts Quarterly Review* lasted barely three years, ceasing publication in 1850.

Bibliography
Gohdes, Clarence L. F. *The Periodicals of American Transcendentalism*. Durham, N.C.: Duke University Press, 1931.

Grodzïns, Dean. *American Heretic: Theodore Parker and Transcendentalism*. Chapel Hill: University of North Carolina Press, 2002.

May, Samuel Joseph
(1797–1871)

Unitarian minister and reformer Samuel Joseph May was a member of the TRANSCENDENTAL CLUB and an educational reformer intrigued by the theories and teaching of Transcendentalist Amos Bronson ALCOTT. Alcott introduced May to the ideas of Swiss educational theorist Johann PESTALOZZI and, in 1827, May introduced Alcott to his sister, Abigail May (ALCOTT), who subsequently married Bronson Alcott. Samuel May had an impact on American EDUCATION by working with Horace MANN in instituting Massachusetts's public school system and later establishing the first free public, and first desegregated, school system in Syracuse, New York, and in 1865 he was elected president of the Syracuse Board of Education. He studied at HARVARD DIVINITY SCHOOL and was ultimately a beloved minister whose New York congregation was renamed the May Memorial Church in his honor.

Samuel May was perhaps best known as a radical antislavery activist who lectured widely on the issue and promoted the education of black children as well. He helped found the American Anti-Slavery Society and was a colleague in the cause of ABOLITIONISM along with Lydia Maria CHILD, William Lloyd GARRISON, and Theodore PARKER. May sought to use the Unitarian pulpit as a forum for his antislavery addresses and, while some ministers resisted allowing the slavery controversy into their congregations, in 1831 Emerson allowed May to preach at his church in Boston. May's work pushed the Reverend William Ellery CHANNING to take a stand on the issue, resulting in Channing's book on *Slavery* (1835), which established Channing as one of the most reform-minded of the liberal Unitarians. May's own 1836 book, *Slavery and the Constitution,* was an even more radical analysis of the theoretical foundations that allowed slavery to continue. May spoke out against the FUGITIVE SLAVE LAW and continued his human and civil rights work beyond the issue of slavery in fighting for the rights of freedpeople during and after the Civil War. Social reformer Samuel Joseph May also argued for women's equal education, and he regularly attended WOMEN'S RIGHTS conventions during the last two decades of his life.

Bibliography

Yacovone, Donald. *Samuel Joseph May and the Dilemmas of the Liberal Persuasion.* Philadelphia: Temple University Press, 1991.

May-Day and Other Pieces
Ralph Waldo Emerson
(1867)

May-Day and Other Pieces was the second of Ralph Waldo EMERSON's two published poetry collections, the first being POEMS in 1847. The connecting theme of *May-Day* is that of the beauties of nature and the interrelatedness of all parts of nature to the universal whole, a verse counterpart to the philosophy defined in his seminal 1836 work, NATURE. *May-Day* contains some of Emerson's most well-known poems, such as "THE ADIRONDACS," "BRAHMA," and "DAYS." Emerson included a poem "In Memoriam" to his brother Edward EMERSON who had died; he also included a lengthy 45-page poem by Edward entitled "The Last Farewell." A section called "Quatrains" is reminiscent of the style of his Transcendentalist colleague Amos Bronson ALCOTT. Published at the end of the Civil War, the collection also includes several references to the issue of slavery and to the Civil War, such as in "BOSTON HYMN" and a poem entitled "VOLUNTARIES" on the deaths of members of the Massachusetts all-black regiment and their leader, Robert Gould Shaw.

Melville, Herman
(1819–1891)

Herman Melville, best known as the author of *Moby-Dick* (1851), was a contemporary of the New England Transcendentalists but had little personal contact with the major figures. He did hear Ralph Waldo EMERSON lecture, and he subsequently read the essays, poems, and other writings of major figures, such as Emerson, Nathaniel HAWTHORNE, and Henry David THOREAU. He also read widely in the European thinkers who influenced American Transcendentalism, such as Thomas CARLYLE, Samuel Taylor COLERIDGE, and Johann Wolfgang von GOETHE. Melville's direct response to Transcendentalist thought is best recorded in the comments or annotations he made in his own copies of Emerson's writings. In general, Melville was intrigued and in agreement with many of Emerson's ideas. In the end, however, he found aspects of Emersonian Transcendentalism too egotistical or cold. His knowledge of the movement, combined with his reserved hesitation to embrace the philosophy thoroughly or directly, places him in the same category as contemporaries Nathaniel Hawthorne and Edgar Allan POE.

Indirect responses to Transcendentalism are found in Melville's works of fiction, such as his phenomenal *Moby-Dick*, a novel that engages on several levels the theme of a correlation between nature and human existence. In addition, scholars have taken Melville's many references to PLATONISM as evidence of the influence of Emerson's writings, particularly of Plato as discussed in Emerson's REPRESENTATIVE MEN (1850). Less positively, Melville's 1857 novel, *The Confidence-Man*, includes what some scholars see as overt caricatures of Emerson, in the character of Mark Winsome, and of Transcendentalism in general. As a reader, then, but also as a member of the same mid-19th century literary and social circles, Herman Melville was influenced by the same themes of ROMANTICISM and individualism found in the writings of the Transcendentalists.

Bibliography

Hardwick, Elizabeth. *Herman Melville*. New York: Viking, 2000.

McLoughlin, Michael. *Dead Letters to the New World: Melville, Emerson, and American Transcendentalism*. New York: Routledge, 2003.

Memoirs of Margaret Fuller Ossoli
William Henry Channing, James Freeman Clarke, Ralph Waldo Emerson
(1852)

In July 1850 Transcendentalist feminist Margaret FULLER was returning home to the United States from Europe when her ship, the *Elizabeth*, was grounded and sank off the coast of Fire Island, New York. At the time of her death Fuller was working as a foreign correspondent for Horace GREELEY's NEW YORK TRIBUNE, writing a regular column, "THINGS AND THOUGHTS IN EUROPE," on events she witnessed during the Italian Revolution in particular. Upon her death Fuller's family had hoped that Greeley would gather and publish some of her writings as a memorial. Greeley did not do so, but Fuller's colleagues and friends among the Transcendentalists immediately planned to publish a group biography to include their reminiscences of Fuller along with selected correspondence and writings.

Ralph Waldo EMERSON was most certainly Margaret Fuller's closest friend among the Transcendentalists. The two shared an intense intellectual companionship and challenged each other on all themes philosophical and social, from the nature of genius and friendship, to marriage and WOMEN'S RIGHTS. James Freeman CLARKE knew Fuller before the emergence of a unified Transcendentalist movement, and the two had excitedly studied German together so that they could read writers such as Johann Wolfgang von GOETHE and Friedrich SCHELLING in the original language. William Henry CHANNING was a close confidante and correspondent of Fuller's, and the two shared many of the same social reform commitments, such as ABOLITIONISM and women's rights. Together these three men edited and published the two-volume *Memoirs of Margaret Fuller Ossoli*, published in 1852, a monumental work that defined Fuller's place in 19th-century American literary history. In addition to shaping Fuller's reputation as a conversationalist, writer, and thinker, the project of editing the *Memoirs* between 1850 and 1852 had a significant impact on Emerson's work and thought during this time. Fuller had been a constant presence in his life during the critical years of forming his own Transcendentalist philosophy and now he had to come to terms with the meaning of her short life and the ideas she so vigorously pursued. He described her, in short, as a "brave, eloquent, subtle, accomplished, devoted, constant soul."

Despite the close association of these three editors with their former colleague and their obvious grasp of and respect for her intellectual power, the completed *Memoirs* is neither a particularly useful account of Fuller's work nor an entirely fair portrayal of her life. Part of the problem was that her American friends were ultimately writing in response to rumors about Fuller's character as a woman. In particular, while in Italy she had at some point married a man named Giovanni Ossoli and given birth to a son, Angelo, both of whom died with her in the shipwreck. Fuller had chosen to keep these facts of her personal life secret, revealing the news by letter to only a few close friends and family members. After her death, there were speculations about the exact nature of her relationship with Ossoli, whether and when they had married, and about her ability to combine motherhood with her work as a journalist. Fuller's friends, Channing, Clarke, and Emerson, understood their project, the first memorial to Fuller after her death, as a way to salvage her reputation and ultimately presented her more as a tragic heroine than an intellectual. In addition to collecting together reminiscences by many friends and associates, the book is primarily drawn from Fuller's own writing in her letters and journals. These writings, however, were heavily edited and even partially censured by Channing, Clarke, and Emerson to fit their purpose for the project and to reveal a Fuller they felt fit for the public. Thus not only is the volume of limited usefulness, but many contemporary scholars are now appalled to find that in putting the *Memoirs* together, Channing, Clarke, and Emerson literally cut apart pages from Fuller's original journals and letters, thus ruining the originals. Fuller's family was not entirely pleased with the portrayal of Fuller's less likeable personality traits, but, overall, the book was warmly received by the public, a rousing commercial success that was reprinted in multiple editions through the end of the century.

Bibliography

Zwang, Christina. *Feminist Conversations: Fuller, Emerson, and the Play of Reading.* Ithaca, N.Y.: Cornell University Press, 1995.

"Merlin"
Ralph Waldo Emerson
(1846)

Ralph Waldo EMERSON's poem "Merlin" was first published in POEMS (1847) and includes two parts or even two separate poems usually referred to as "Merlin I" and "Merlin II." The main theme of the poem is the role of the poet and the true voice of poetry: "The kingly bard / Must smite the chords rudely and hard, / As with hammer or mace; / That they may render back / Artful thunder, which conveys / Secrets of the solar track." The poem's title most likely refers to a sixth-century poet or bard named Myrrdhin who, as "Merlin," is the ideal poet: "Merlin's blows are strokes of fate." The

poet's words should reflect on a variety of themes, presented by Emerson as a list which included "the forest tone" of nature, "manly hearts," "orators," "city arts," and "wars." As all topics are open to the poet, the poet should not be bound by any specific structure or rules of poetry writing: "Great is the art, / Great be the manners, of the bard. / He shall not his brain encumber / With the coil of rhythm and number; / . . . Nor count compartments of the floors, / But mount to paradise / By the stairway of surprise." Form and structure do not make the poem, says Emerson, but rather substance and message.

Emerson gives a hint in "Merlin I" of the final accomplishment of the poet: "Merlin's mighty line / Extremes of nature reconciled." It is in "Merlin II" that Emerson explains how the poet takes these "extremes" and through his verse shows how "Balance-loving Nature / Made all things in pairs." In other words, the poet reveals the larger meaning and order behind the seeming chaos of nature. The first part of "Merlin II" begins by cataloging this dualism and symmetry in nature: two feet, two hands, "Each color with its counter glowed; / To every tone beat answering tones." "Merlin II" differs in both rhyme and meter from the first part of the poem as Emerson experimented with different ways for the poet to get his message across, moving from the more conventional four-line stanzas of the first section to the irregular lengths and rhyming schemes of the second. "Merlin II" also emphasizes the effect of poetry on the poet, the price that he must pay for taking on this role. Despite encouragement to reach beyond the restrictions of "rhythm and number," Emerson's final poem is much more conventional in form than the original freer verse he drafted in the pages of his journal in 1845.

miracles controversy

The "miracles controversy" refers to the first major public debate between Unitarians and Transcendentalists in 1836 over whether belief in the miracles performed by Jesus Christ in the New Testament of the Bible was a necessary foundation of Christian belief and, additionally, whether the miracles themselves were in fact supernatural events or were symbolic of Christ's teachings. The controversy arose when Unitarian and Harvard professor Andrews NORTON responded to an article by George RIPLEY in the CHRISTIAN EXAMINER in which Ripley argued that the miracles were not necessary to prove the truth or importance of Christ's teachings. Norton responded to Ripley's article in a piece in the CHRISTIAN REGISTER, calling Ripley's views a dangerous precedent for Unitarians in questioning the divinity of Jesus himself and, therefore, the very basis of Christianity. In Norton's view, without the miracles as an example of Jesus' divinity, without his supernatural powers, there was no basis for Christianity as a religion of revelation from a personal God. For Ripley and other Transcendentalists, however, the "truth" of Christianity was in its moral teachings, not in its supernatural events. Norton was thus responding to Ripley directly but was also reacting to the proliferation of theological critique that characterized the emergence of the new Transcendentalist movement as a split within UNITARIANISM.

Norton was motivated to speak up and call attention to the dangers and excesses of Transcendentalism in relation to Christian beliefs because, that same year, in 1836, a proliferation of foundational Transcendentalist texts were published that challenged Christian spirituality and questioned institutional practices, including Ralph Waldo EMERSON's NATURE and Convers FRANCIS's *Christianity As a Purely Internal Principle*. The controversy continued in the press as Ripley, in turn, responded again to Norton, accusing Norton of questioning Ripley's own beliefs as a Christian. Another writer anonymously came to Norton's defense and agreed that the divinity of Christ had to be revealed to Jesus' listeners, to Christians, through some supernatural acts, or miracles, although this writer was less critical of Transcendentalism as a whole.

Two years later, Andrews Norton was the most vocal public critic of another Transcendentalist controversy, this time in response to Ralph Waldo Emerson's DIVINITY SCHOOL ADDRESS. Emerson again addressed the issue of Christ's miracles and concluded that the stories of the miracles were symbolic and that Christianity was

revealed to individuals through living a life of Christian principles, not through reading about outward signs and events in the Bible. By this time, 1838, many of the Transcendentalists, including former ministers such as Ripley and Emerson, had broken ties with organized Unitarianism, and Norton was responding to the broader principles of Transcendentalism itself, which he felt had gone beyond theological debate to utter atheism and, worse, to questioning the authority of the ministry. Norton pointed out that Emerson "professes to reject all belief in Christianity as a revelation," and therefore "he makes a general attack upon the Clergy." Unlike Ripley, Emerson chose not to respond publicly to Norton, but others came to Emerson's defense. Orestes BROWNSON praised the open spirit of Emerson's address in the WESTERN MESSENGER, and Theodore PARKER agreed that the proof of Christ's divinity should come from faith, not from belief in the outward signs of the miracles. George Ripley also again engaged Norton's criticisms and reconfirmed the position that the miracles were not necessary to Christian belief and that there were other ways to accept and believe the teachings of Christ.

"Montaigne; or, the Skeptic" *See* REPRESENTATIVE MEN.

The Monthly Anthology
(1803–1811)

One of the first editors of *The Monthly Anthology* was William Emerson, Ralph Waldo EMERSON's father, and Mary Moody EMERSON published an early piece in the paper. The magazine was founded in 1803 and helped to establish New England, and Boston in particular, as the center of 19th-century American literary culture. The magazine, which was published between 1803 and 1811, was among the first American journals to serve the dual interests of liberal religion and literary criticism and covered topics related to history, theology, science, and literature. While the editors drew upon their European educations and influences, the magazine's main goal was to cultivate American genius for its own sake but also in the hopes that America would someday influence European arts and letters. In 1805 William Emerson formed the Anthology Society as a committee of his Harvard graduate intellectual friends—including Unitarian Andrews NORTON, who would later be one of Ralph Waldo Emerson's most outspoken critics—to help write for and edit the magazine each month. This arrangement proved difficult to sustain in producing a monthly journal as the friends tended more toward socializing at their meetings than official magazine business. The Anthology Society had influence beyond just its publication efforts, however, as its informal member's library was officially chartered by the state legislature in 1807 as the BOSTON ATHENAEUM, a cultural institution that would be central in nurturing and advancing the next generation of New England intellectuals, including the Transcendentalists.

Moods
Louisa May Alcott
(1864)

Moods was the first novel published by Louisa May ALCOTT, author of the later best-selling LITTLE WOMEN (1868) and daughter of Transcendentalist thinker and reformer Amos Bronson ALCOTT. Louisa May Alcott attributed the title, *Moods*, to a quote taken from the essay "EXPERIENCE" by Transcendentalist philosopher and family friend, Ralph Waldo EMERSON: "Life is a train of moods like a string of beads; and as we pass through them they prove to be many colored lenses, which paint the world their own hue, and each shows us only what lies in its own focus."

Alcott's novel follows the lead female character, Sylvia Yule, from childhood through adolescence and into womanhood. Through Sylvia, Alcott explored the difficulties that women in 19th-century society encountered as they faced the limitations of female social roles surrounding EDUCATION, relationships with men, and marriage. Sylvia challenges the separation of boys' and girls' experiences into young adulthood by going on a weeklong river trip with her brother and two other young men, reminiscent of the wilderness expeditions under-

taken by Henry David THOREAU as a young man. In fact, the rest of the novel centers upon a romantic triangle that develops between Sylvia and the two men she meets on the trip, Geoffrey and Adam, characters based, in fact, upon real-life friends, Ralph Waldo Emerson and Henry David Thoreau. These characters embody not only prominent individual Transcendentalists personally known to Louisa May Alcott, but each man exemplifies a different type of relationship and different Transcendentalist definitions of love and friendship from which Sylvia could choose. Friend and WOMEN'S RIGHTS reformer, Caroline DALL, critiqued the manuscript and helped arrange for the novel to be published.

Bibliography
Deese, Helen R. "Louisa May Alcott's Moods: A New Archival Discovery," *NEQ* 76:3 (September 2003): 439–455.

Mosses from an Old Manse
Nathaniel Hawthorne
(1846)

Mosses from an Old Manse is a collection of short stories by Nathaniel HAWTHORNE. The volume opens with an introductory essay on "THE OLD MANSE" itself, a guide through the house and study that inspired his writing. The house had historic and literary significance in that it belonged to the Emerson family, and Ralph Waldo EMERSON had most recently resided there. Hawthorne explained that, in sharing Emerson's house and study, he hoped to benefit from the same inspiration in writing his own stories.

Some of Hawthorne's most well-known short tales appear in *Mosses from an Old Manse*. After "The Old Manse" are "The Birthmark" and "RAPPACCINI'S DAUGHTER," both cautionary tales about the human and emotional costs of the fanatical pursuit of science, and "Young Goodman Brown," the story of an unfortunate marriage. Also included in the collection are "Feathertop: A Moralized Legend," "Roger Malvin's Burial," "Earth's Holocaust," and "The Artist of the Beautiful," a story most clearly influenced by Emersonian ideas.

Muir, John
(1838–1914)

The Scottish-born John Muir immigrated to Wisconsin at the age of 11 and became, along with Transcendentalist Henry David THOREAU, one of the most important and well-known naturalists in American history. Muir was a mountaineer, ecologist, and conservationist who helped found and served as first president of the Sierra Club beginning in 1892. Muir was central to the late 19th-century movement for preserving national parks. Although he was headquartered in the West and therefore geographically removed from the Transcendentalist community in CONCORD, MASSACHUSETTS (as well as being a generation younger than most of them), he was directly influenced by the writings of both Thoreau and Ralph Waldo EMERSON, and most scholars of Muir associate him and his ideas with the same impulses that fueled the Transcendentalist movement.

Muir is best known for his writings on Yosemite and California's Sierra Mountains. His most "transcendental" work is his 1894 *The Mountains of California*, which expresses some of the same tendencies toward PANTHEISM apparent in nature writings by the New England Transcendentalists. Muir was most like Henry David Thoreau in his approach to the wilderness and his own role as a scientist-naturalist. Like Thoreau at WALDEN POND (and in his 1854 account of *WALDEN*), Muir's study of the western Sierras was a journey of scientific exploration of the wilderness as much as a journey and exploration of the self. Muir was a conscientious student of Thoreau, making regular notations in the margins of his copies of Thoreau's works, carrying on an ongoing conversation with Thoreau through his texts.

Muir's own beliefs about nature were less like Emerson's. Whereas Emerson the idealist saw the Self at the center of the universe, the individual as the primary route to the Divine, Muir (like Thoreau) put nature in that role. For Muir nature enfolded humankind, rather than humans shaping nature through their own thought as Emerson wrote. Their different views, as well as their differences in age, became apparent when Emerson traveled throughout the west in 1871 and visited Muir in Yosemite. Emerson saw in John Muir, as he had in Thoreau, someone whose talents were wasted in his solitary wilderness existence and proposed to Muir instead that he consider a career as an intellectual and teacher in the East. Muir would not leave the West, of course, and was disappointed in Emerson's ability to truly appreciate what Muir saw in the Sierras. Emerson was quite elderly by this time and not interested in the rough existence of an independent naturalist. Regardless, Muir read Emerson for inspiration and Emerson respected Muir, with Emerson writing about him in his journal alongside Thoreau and others as "My men," representative men of his own age.

Bibliography
Fleck, Richard. "John Muir's Homage to Henry David Thoreau," *Pacific Historian* 29 (summer–fall 1985): 55–64.

Turner, Frederick. *John Muir: Rediscovering America.* Cambridge, Mass.: Perseus, 2000.

N

"Napoleon; or, the Man of the World"

See REPRESENTATIVE MEN.

Nathaniel Hawthorne and His Wife
Julian Hawthorne
(1884)

Nathaniel Hawthorne and His Wife is an edited collection of novelist Nathaniel HAWTHORNE's notebooks and correspondence, in which son Julian HAWTHORNE included a controversial 1858 entry by his father which cruelly criticized Transcendentalist Margaret FULLER. Margaret Fuller died in an 1850 shipwreck returning to the United States from a tour of Europe and a lengthy stay in Italy, and she was supposed to have had a manuscript history of the Italian Revolution with her when she was lost at sea. In his notebook several years later, Nathaniel Hawthorne recorded an acquaintance's negative speculations about Fuller's final years in Italy and completed the entry with his own denunciation of her as a woman—"she had not the charm of womanhood"—and as an intellectual—"Margaret had quite lost all power of literary production, before she left Rome . . . and the History of the Roman Revolution, about which there was so much lamentation, in the belief that it had been lost with her, never had existence." Hawthorne concluded his entry with the observation that, despite Fuller's vain efforts "to make herself the greatest, wisest, best woman of the age," ultimately "she proved herself a very woman, after all, and fell as the weakest of her sisters might."

Julian Hawthorne's motives for wanting to disassociate his father from Fuller appear to have been both personal and political. As the title of his collection indicated, *Nathaniel Hawthorne and His Wife* was intended as a celebration of his parent's marriage. In this sense, son Julian wanted to present a picture of a wholesome union untainted by speculations about his father's friendship with the unmarried Fuller, who was in fact a significant source of literary inspiration for the novelist. Secondly, Julian Hawthorne's own criticisms of the 19th-century WOMEN'S RIGHTS movement are revealed in his treatment of the figure of Margaret Fuller. He went beyond publishing his father's notes and took great liberties in editing and even rewriting some of his mother, Sophia Peabody HAWTHORNE's, letters and journal entries on Fuller as well. In particular, Julian included an 1845 letter in which Sophia supposedly stated that if Fuller "were married truly, she would no longer be puzzled about the rights of woman."

Nor did Julian Hawthorne make any efforts to hide his own agenda. As editor, he wrote an introduction to his mother's letter that included his own analysis of Fuller's 1845 book WOMAN IN THE NINETEENTH CENTURY: "She produced a book in which the never-to-be-exhausted theme of Women's Rights was touched upon." Furthermore, he assured readers that Sophia Hawthorne would not have been allied with Fuller's feminism since "married women . . . whose domestic affairs sufficiently occupied them, were not likely to be cordial supporters of such doctrines as the book enunciated."

Julian Hawthorne's work was a major factor in establishing Nathaniel Hawthorne's place within the male American Renaissance tradition of the 1840s alongside Ralph Waldo EMERSON, Herman MELVILLE, Henry David THOREAU, and Walt WHITMAN. It also worked to exclude the only woman ever seriously considered for canonization, Margaret Fuller. At the time *Nathaniel Hawthorne and His Wife* was printed, many of Fuller's Transcendentalist colleagues and followers were still living— friends such as Christopher Pearse CRANCH, Caroline DALL, and Julia Ward HOWE—and they wrote reviews and editorials to salvage her reputation as an important writer and as a close friend of both Nathaniel and Sophia Hawthorne.

Bibliography

Mitchell, Thomas. *Hawthorne's Fuller Mystery*. Amherst: University of Massachusetts Press, 1999.

Nature
Ralph Waldo Emerson
(1836)

Ralph Waldo EMERSON's *Nature* is one of the most important works in 19th-century American literature and philosophy and certainly Emerson's best-known work. *Nature* was published anonymously in 1836, appearing in the same year as several other Transcendentalist treatises signaling the start of the new movement, such as Orestes BROWNSON's *NEW VIEWS OF CHRISTIANITY, SOCIETY, AND THE CHURCH*, Convers FRANCIS's *Christianity as a Purely Internal Principle*, and Lydia Maria CHILD's novel, *PHILOTHEA, A ROMANCE*. Although *Nature* is usually considered as one long essay, the book actually included an introduction and eight separate sections on "Nature," "Commodity," "Beauty," "Language," "Discipline," "Idealism," "Spirit," and "Prospects." The original anonymously published text of *Nature* was not widely read, but Emerson reprinted the text along with a collection of his key lectures of the 1830s and 1840s for the 1849 edition, *Nature; Addresses, and Lectures*. Ultimately,

Nature established Ralph Waldo Emerson as the primary intellectual force behind the Transcendentalist movement.

Nature clearly illuminates Emerson's translation of German IDEALISM and English ROMANTICISM into a distinctly American Transcendentalism. Emerson presented a philosophy of nature as understood through the direct experience of the individual soul, not through scientific methods or reason, and proposed that through such an understanding of nature one becomes closer to God or to divinity. In *Nature* Emerson thus provided the foundations of his Transcendentalist philosophy, which rejected the intellectual tradition of the Enlightenment (exemplified by the rationalist philosophy of John LOCKE) as well as the theological tradition of Christianity (specifically, for Emerson in 1836, the doctrines of New England UNITARIANISM). These were the ideas to which he would return again and again and expand upon in his later writings.

In the first section of *Nature* Emerson provides the core definition of nature as everything which is "not me," that is, everything outside of the "me" of the individual soul or mind, including even one's own body as it is part of the material rather than spiritual world. The individual must be an observer of the "not me" and must accept nature on its own terms, while also understanding that every thing that exists in nature has its correspondent in the spiritual world and is reflective of some higher, or "transcendental," truth about human existence and morality. The purpose of life is to observe, study, and decipher these meanings from the natural world by understanding one's personal relationship to nature. Study and observance of nature provides one with spiritual connection to the universe as a whole, if only one is willing to really see what surrounds us. Emerson relies upon the metaphor of seeing, and the image of the eyes, as the route to absorbing what nature has to offer. In an oft-quoted passage (famously caricatured by Christopher Pearse CRANCH) Emerson defines himself as "a transparent eyeball; I am nothing; I see all; the currents of Universal Being circulate through me." It is in moments of true observation and acceptance rather than of intellectual reason or empirical study that we are most open to receiving insight and revelation about the world around us and, thus, ourselves: "the whole of nature is a metaphor of the human mind."

Another section of the essay deals with nature as "Commodity." Nature fundamentally provides food or other raw materials to meet human needs, a "steady and prodigal provision." Beyond and even superior to its usefulness in this way to humans is nature's "Beauty." In its physical beauty nature fulfills the spiritual need of humans to witness perfection. It is especially important that humans, having been pulled into business so far removed from the natural world, return to nature for regeneration: "The tradesman, the attorney comes out of the din and craft of the street, and sees the sky and the woods, and is a man again." Throughout, Emerson defines nature's importance as a "Language," a metaphorical system of symbols that provides meaning for everyday life. While Emerson's book was a spiritual guidebook for any individual, he also established a special role for the poet in receiving and understanding the symbolic language of nature. Setting up another theme that can be traced throughout his writing career, Emerson argued that some people are more perceptive and open to nature and that the role of the poet is to interpret nature for others. Nature is still humanity's best teacher, however, and the laws and forces of nature provide models for understanding any aspect of human life: "Space, time, society, labor, climate, food, locomotion, the animals, the mechanical forces, give us sincerest lessons, day by day, whose meaning is unlimited."

Bibliography

De Groot, Jean, ed. *Nature in American Philosophy.* Washington, D.C.: Catholic University of America Press, 2004.

neoplatonism

Neoplatonism was a later and more mystical modification of the IDEALISM of ancient Greek philosopher Plato and formed the central basis of many of Ralph Waldo EMERSON's Transcendentalist ideas. It was through neoplatonist philosophers, particularly the third-century writer Plotinus and fifth-century Proclus, that the Transcendentalists understood Plato, whom they modified within their own specific cultural and literary contexts. Emerson was probably first introduced to neoplatonism through 18th-century English translations and editions as well as through summaries of Victor COUSIN's *Introduction to the History of Philosophy,* translated into English in 1832. Emerson acknowledged the influence of the neoplatonists directly when he cited Plotinus on the title page of NATURE in 1836: "Nature is but an image or imitation of wisdom, the last thing of the soul; nature being a thing which doth only do, but not know."

PLATONISM provided the Transcendentalists with a foundational understanding that all things are knowable and that all knowledge is related. Neoplatonism extended that idea with the belief that all unified knowledge emanates from an overarching universal force, what Emerson would term "THE OVER-SOUL," an idea presented and explored more fully in the essay which appeared in ESSAYS: FIRST SERIES, 1841. In Emerson's formulation, humanity achieves a state of perfection when, through the pursuit of self-knowledge, a unification with the over-soul is achieved; this was a core Transcendentalist concept pursued by other major writers, such as Henry David THOREAU.

Neoplatonism expanded on Plato's system of universal forms or ideals, such as Beauty, Truth, and Justice, by searching for the source of those forms. In Plotinus's terms, the source is defined as "the One," an idealized understanding of the universe existing as a direct moral influence or force in human life, an idea adapted by Emerson as the Over-Soul. Plotinus defined "the One" as the ideal that "emanates" throughout the known world. Emerson built on this idea of the universe as a positive force and on the uniting of the human with the divine as the goal for self-development. Individual human souls existed as part of the One, but humanity struggled between the material and the spiritual worlds. Humans aspired toward perfection by resisting the temptations of the physical world and reaching toward union with the spiritual force of the One; in neoplatonist terms, this was accomplished not through the Christian framework of religious practice and communion with God but in the humanist emphasis on self-development, on inward reflection and thought.

Neoplatonism was most evident in Emerson's early writings of the 1840s as he sought to develop his own idea of the relationship of the individual soul and mind to the universal or the Over-Soul. In several of the *Essays: First Series* from 1841, including "The Over-Soul," "CIRCLES," and "SPIRITUAL LAWS," Emerson praised human thought and consciousness itself as evidence of the divine and sought out ecstasy as an intellectual rather than religious experience. Union with the One was sought through an experience of mental clarity that Emerson found, for example, in the ecstatic experience necessary to write poetry. The poet was, by definition, one who was most open to communication with the universe, aware of his surroundings, and able to convey that experience in writing, a state of being to which all persons should aspire.

In his 1848 *A FABLE FOR CRITICS,* James Russell LOWELL characterized Emerson as "a Plotinus Montaigne," emphasizing Emerson's affinity for neoplatonist idealism as communicated through his preferred forum as an essayist. Besides Emerson, Amos Bronson ALCOTT was also significantly influenced by Plato and by the neoplatonism of Plotinus, in particular the ideas of the unity of man, nature, God, and universe, of individual souls "emanating" from the One, and Alcott's belief that "man is a soul informed by divine ideas." More than any other Transcendentalist, Alcott continued to pursue neoplatonist idealism after the Civil War in his CONVERSATIONS and at the CONCORD SCHOOL OF PHILOSOPHY AND LITERATURE.

Neoplatonism appealed to the Transcendentalists as a model of spirituality outside of a Christian framework, a worldview in which nature, humanity, and God were all part of the same universal force, the One, and an emphasis on the importance of human thought in propelling the universe in a positive direction. Although Transcendentalism drew from many sources, including Christianity itself as well as other world religions, neoplatonism was at once a more rational or scientific approach to some of the same questions addressed by Christianity and allowed for a more mystical spirituality than Unitarian Christianity.

Bibliography
Allen, Gay Wilson. *Waldo Emerson: A Biography.* New York: Viking, 1981.

New American Cyclopedia
George Ripley
(1863)

In most of his broad literary endeavors, Transcendentalist reformer George RIPLEY sought to bridge the gap between high and popular culture by presenting the best ideas to a wide audience—what he termed "the common mind"—and the *New American Cyclopedia: A Popular Dictionary of General Knowledge,* coedited with Charles Anderson DANA, came closest to that goal. Previous projects had included the multivolume edited collection of translations of the most important European philosophers and thinkers made available to American readers in the *SPECIMENS OF FOREIGN STANDARD LITERATURE.* Published between 1838 and 1842, *Specimens of Foreign Standard Literature* included volumes and contributions by Ripley as well as by James Freeman CLARKE, John Sullivan DWIGHT, Margaret FULLER, and others. Another project, the 1852 *A Handbook of Literature and the Fine Arts,* coedited with Bayard Taylor, was still even less specialized and reached for a general reading audience interested in literary and aesthetic themes. It was through the 16-volume *New American Cyclopedia* that Ripley finally reached beyond a readership among the intellectual elite and found the "common" audience he so desired to reach, and the work became the most popular encyclopedia of its time.

As with his *Specimens of Foreign Standard Literature,* Ripley sought to set the cultural "standard" of his time with a general reference work that included comprehensive coverage of topics related to American culture, science, arts, and literature. Ripley and Dana served as coeditors of the *New American Cyclopedia,* although it was primarily Ripley who assigned topics and organized and edited the work of hundreds of contributors not only in the original volumes but also in subsequent editions, supplements, and condensed versions of the work. Authors for *Cyclopedia* entries included

Transcendentalist colleagues such as Ralph Waldo EMERSON and Theodore PARKER, as well as some of the most important literary and intellectual figures of the time, such as historian George BANCROFT, *NEW YORK TRIBUNE* editor Horace GREELEY, critic James Russell LOWELL, and Karl Marx. Even with such established and prominent writers, Ripley himself conducted a significant amount of research to ensure accuracy and the orderly presentation of facts, often consulting with several experts on a specific topic. He sought to be comprehensive in coverage, even in the face of criticism, for example, of including articles on non-Christian religions and of publishing Jewish and Catholic authors.

The *New American Cyclopedia* was a career success for its editors, both critically and financially. Newspaper reviews declared the *Cyclopedia* the most important reference work to date. The multiple editions sold well over one million copies in George Ripley's lifetime alone, establishing him as a writer and intellectual and allowing him finally able to pay off his numerous debts remaining from the folded experiment at the utopian community of BROOK FARM.

Bibliography

Crowe, Charles. *George Ripley: Transcendentalist and Utopian Socialist.* Athens: University of Georgia Press, 1967.

The New Birth
Jones Very
(1838)

Sometimes referred to as "The New Life" after the first line—" 'Tis a new life—thoughts move not as they did"—Transcendentalist poet Jones VERY composed the poem, "The New Birth" in September 1838 in the midst of an intense mystical experience that resulted in Very's one-month stay in an asylum. Although Very wrote some poetry both before and after what scholars refer to as his "ecstatic period" of late 1838 to 1840, poems such as "The New Birth" and "THE DEAD" were among his most original and spiritually urgent writings and brought

him to the attention of Ralph Waldo EMERSON and other Transcendentalists as one of their era's most significant poets. The 14-line poem, "The New Birth," was published in Very's hometown paper, the *Salem Observer,* on October 27, 1838, and was subsequently included in the 1839 collection of *Essays and Poems: By Jones Very,* edited by Emerson.

Jones Very's intense experience in the fall of 1838 was not just a religious conversion but a period during which he was completely and temporarily overcome both emotionally and physically by an intense feeling of despair and renewal. Very's intensity shocked and concerned many of his friends and colleagues and is viewed by scholars as a possible manifestation of some level of mental illness. Very turned his energies during this period to writing, and this particular poem marks the moment of his spiritual transformation, which Very specifically tried to articulate: "thoughts move not as they did / With slow uncertain steps across my mind . . . Fast crowding on each thought claims utterance strong."

"The New Birth" was in fact an "utterance strong," using the almost apocalyptic language of a natural force: "The heavens and earth—Their walls are falling now—. . . / . . . Storm-lifted waves swift rushing to the shore." His purpose was to convey the power and intensity of his own mystical experience, but he subsequently moves from describing his own "Start from death's slumbers" in "The New Birth" to decrying the spiritual lifelessness of those around him in the poem "The Dead." With "The New Birth" Very entered into not only his most excitable but his most productive writing period, with most of his output published in the *Salem Observer* over the course of a few months.

Bibliography

Deese, Helen, ed. *Jones Very: The Complete Poems.* Athens: University of Georgia Press, 1993.

Newcomb, Charles King
(1820–1894)

Charles King Newcomb had a brief association with the Transcendentalists in the early 1840s as a resident of George RIPLEY's utopian community at

BROOK FARM and a contributor to the Boston-based Transcendentalist literary magazine, the DIAL. Ralph Waldo EMERSON published Newcomb's story, "The First Dolon," in the July 1842 issue of the *Dial*. Emerson had recognized Newcomb as a young man of genius, but critics referred to the story as an example of the incomprehensible mysticism of the Transcendentalist movement. There are references in Emerson's correspondence to another story by Newcomb, and in his own private journals Newcomb wrote more than 1,000 poems, but he had no other work published besides the early *Dial* submission.

Margaret FULLER was a personal friend of his mother's and became a mentor for Newcomb, 10 years her junior, when he moved from Rhode Island to Massachusetts. He had given up plans to pursue the ministry, and his mother had called on Fuller with concern about his rising interest in Catholicism, or what his mother termed "the Superstition of Romanism." Correspondence between and referring to him and Fuller indicate that he may have become romantically interested in Fuller, a fact that led to the mutual cessation of their correspondences after 1840, but in 1841 he found a home at Brook Farm, where he lived until 1845. At the Brook Farm community he was able to live as an eccentric among eccentrics. He continued an interest in Catholic mysticism and fellow Brook Farm residents later remembered the relics and pictures of saints which adorned his room. Newcomb befriended other Transcendentalists such as Elizabeth HOAR and Caroline Sturgis (TAPPAN), whom he also pursued romantically, but their involvement too died down and Newcomb never married.

In early 1842 Charles Newcomb finally met Ralph Waldo Emerson, a friendship that resulted in Newcomb's publication in the pages of the *Dial*. While other Transcendentalists were less enthusiastic about Newcomb's style and writing in "The First Dolon," historian Joel Myerson speculates that the piece may have had particular appeal to Emerson, who pushed for its publication and personally copy-edited the manuscript, because of veiled references to Emerson's young son, Waldo, who had died just months earlier in January 1842. Newcomb referred to "the assumption of the hero-boy," a "beautiful boy, with long auburn-brown hair," descriptions of

the character "Dolon" which match descriptions of Waldo in Emerson family correspondence that Newcomb had borrowed to read during the months he was drafting his story. Although Newcomb began work on a "Second Dolon," and was urged by Emerson to finish it for the *Dial*, Newcomb ultimately lacked the health and motivation to sustain regular literary production. Emerson sadly wrote, "Where are all the fine stories I was to have from your imaginative pen which so took my love, & excited so many hopes?" After leaving Brook Farm, Charles Newcomb left Massachusetts and faded from contact with his Transcendentalist friends, living out his life in Rhode Island, then Philadelphia and, finally, Europe, where he died.

Bibliography

Myerson, Joel. *The New England Transcendentalists and the Dial: A History of the Magazine and Its Contributors.* London and Toronto: Associated University Presses, 1980.

New Connecticut: An Autobiographical Poem
Amos Bronson Alcott
(1881)

In the midst of the success of his CONCORD SCHOOL OF PHILOSOPHY AND LITERATURE, and a hectic schedule of lecture tours in the western states, Transcendentalist Amos Bronson ALCOTT published *New Connecticut, An Autobiographical Poem* (1881). Alcott was at the height of his popularity and determined that there was enough public interest in an account of his early life. Most of the material for *New Connecticut* came from journals and writing produced several decades earlier. Alcott's most imaginative work and best writing success had come as a poet more than a prose writer, and so he presented his autobiography in the form of an epic poem with a section of notes even longer than the actual poem. *New Connecticut* is not the story of Bronson Alcott's entire life to that date, however, but in fact covers only his earliest years of childhood and struggle before he became involved in the Transcendentalist community of ideas in the early 1830s. In presenting a story of basic American values and in ending the story before his career as a teacher, theorist, poet, and reformer had begun, however, there was little to connect the simplistic morality tale of his early life with the enthusiastic experiments in EDUCATION, community living, and unorthodox spirituality that characterized his later career as a Transcendentalist.

"New England Reformers"
Ralph Waldo Emerson
(1844)

Originally presented as a lecture in March 1844, Ralph Waldo EMERSON's "New England Reformers" was published in his *ESSAYS: SECOND SERIES* (1844). The essay was Emerson's response to the explosion of organized reform efforts—"the great activity of thought and experimenting"—engaging many Americans in the antebellum North, including many of the Transcendentalists, who were prominent in EDUCATION reform, WOMEN'S RIGHTS, ABOLITIONISM, and Utopian reform efforts. As he discussed in other essays and lectures, Emerson's overall philosophy emphasized the reform of the individual self as the source of power for larger social change, and for this perspective Transcendentalism in general has been criticized for a lack of attention to the specific social and political questions of the age. "New England Reformers" does begin with a somewhat ridiculous accounting of the many organized reform efforts of the day. Emerson detailed the incredible number and variety of reform associations surrounding him in the 1830s and 1840s: "temperance and NONRESISTANCE societies . . . movements of abolitionists and of socialists . . . of homeopathy, of hydropathy, of mesmerism, of PHRENOLOGY . . . Others attacked the institution of marriage, as the fountain of social evils." Declaring "what a fertility of projects for the salvation of the world!" Emerson was dismayed at the continual splitting of reform causes into ever more specific and separate issues. More disturbing, in his perspective, is the blind devotion of individuals to reform organizations, each to their own cause with their own agendas, methods, and solutions. Emerson believes that the solution lies within the individuals themselves, if only they would see it.

Emerson did not deny the need for reform or the genuine social, political, and economic problems that concerned reformers. He also held out an optimistic belief that society was moving forward and that most of the goals of reformers would eventually be realized. He also believed, however, that reformers were emphasizing the differences and disagreements among individuals, rather than recognizing what unites us as human beings. He argued that "the disparities of power in men are superficial," and that, through "frank and searching CONVERSATION" would emerge "a perfect understanding, a like receiving, a like perceiving, abolished differences." In the end, Emerson urged those interested in reforming society to look within and to nurture their own moral selves as models of the change and goodness they wished to see in society. For such an individualistic philosophy Emerson was criticized in his own time as someone who stood apart from the momentous social issues that engrossed antebellum society, most notably slavery, of which little is said in the essay. "New England Reformers" is obviously reflective of Ralph Waldo Emerson's position on reform in the mid-1840s; but he himself would be drawn more directly into public reform activity, in particular into the antislavery cause, throughout the 1850s.

New Jerusalem Magazine
(1827–1893)

The *New Jerusalem Magazine* was an American journal of SWEDENBORGIANISM and was an important site for the Transcendentalists to gather information on the philosophy of Swedish mystic Emanuel Swedenborg. Founded in Boston in 1827 by the primary American proponent of Swedenborgianism, Sampson REED, the magazine greatly influenced the thought of Ralph Waldo EMERSON, in particular, who heavily referenced the magazine in his own reading journals and notebooks and eventually chose Swedenborg, the "Mystic," as one of his *REPRESENTATIVE MEN* of history. Swedenborgian philosophy provided Emerson with a mystical IDEALISM and the theory of correspondences between the physical and moral worlds that was articulated in speeches and writings such as *NATURE*, "THE

AMERICAN SCHOLAR," "The Uses of Natural History," and "THE POET." In fact, in the cases of *Nature* and "The American Scholar," these writings were mistaken by some readers as publications of the New Church, the primary organization of Swedenborgian followers. Such mistakes were corrected in the pages of the *New Jerusalem Magazine*, however, since, although Swedenborg heavily influenced Emerson's thought, Sampson Reed felt Transcendentalism to be more eclectic and less spiritual than Swedenborgianism. Specifically, Swedenborgians affiliated with the New Church were less committed to the social reform issues that engaged many American Transcendentalists interested in the mystic's ideas. The *New Jerusalem Magazine* engaged with the Transcendentalists directly by reviewing and critiquing in its pages the writings of not only Emerson, but of figures such as Amos Bronson ALCOTT, Reverend William Ellery CHANNING, and James Freeman CLARKE.

Bibliography

Brock, Erland, ed. *Swedenborg and His Influence.* Bryn Athyn, Pa.: Academy of the New Church, 1988.

"The New School in Literature and Religion"   *See A DISCOURSE ON THE LATEST FORM OF INFIDELITY.*

New Views of Christianity, Society, and the Church
Orestes Brownson
(1836)

New Views of Christianity, Society, and the Church was the first book published by Transcendentalist Orestes BROWNSON and appeared in 1836 alongside such works as Ralph Waldo EMERSON's *NATURE,* and Convers FRANCIS's *Christianity as a Purely Internal Principle,* as a marker of the beginning of the Transcendentalist movement. That same year Brownson founded the Society for Christian Union and Progress and, in the book intended as a guide or handbook for the Church, he presented his vision for a "Church of the Future," founded on a Christian-socialist philosophy that erased the distinctions between the Protestant and Catholic faiths. Brownson found fault with both traditions within Christianity, as well as with general practice and institutions of 19th-century American religion. Brownson's theological critique was coupled with his inspiration for social and institutional reform based on his readings of European thinkers such as Victor COUSIN and Friedrich SCHLEIERMACHER and the French utopian socialism of Saint-Simon. Drawing on these German and French critics and romantic reformers, which many of the Transcendentalists were then reading, Brownson sought to synthesize church reform with a vision of social progress and individual PERFECTIONISM, all in the form of a new church.

As a reform mission, the target audience for the new church and the book, *New Views of Christianity, Society, and the Church,* was Boston's working class. Brownson had been encouraged by fellow reformers Unitarian Reverend William Ellery CHANNING and George RIPLEY to establish a church particularly for the working-class community for the purpose of inspiring in them an everyday accessible religion, which, these reformers felt, current religions (especially elite UNITARIANISM) did not promote. Between 1836 and 1844, Brownson's Society for Christian Union and Progress met in Boston to regular audiences of hundreds. Brownson preached that Christianity was not a religion of abstract principles and study but was applicable to everyday life. Similar to what Ralph Waldo Emerson would say in his DIVINITY SCHOOL ADDRESS in 1838, Brownson wanted to de-emphasize the role of the institutional church and encourage believers to integrate the universal principles of Christian spirituality into an emphasis on individual and social progress.

Although articulated within a Transcendentalist framework, neither Orestes Brownson's *New Views of Christianity, Society and the Church* nor his church generated any public criticism and debate, as did the work of Emerson or of George Ripley. First of all, Brownson was not calling for a rejection of traditional religion altogether but only seeking to reform its institutions. Secondly, Emerson's audience and forum for the Divinity School Address was HARVARD DIVINITY SCHOOL's elite

Unitarian clergy, who felt personally attacked by Emerson and therefore compelled to respond, whereas Brownson addressed and had committed himself to the spiritual and social lives of the working class. To paraphrase Brownson himself in one of his articles in the BOSTON QUARTERLY REVIEW, his goal was in democratizing Christianity, and this was the idea he promoted in his most influential reform pieces, such as his 1840 "THE LABORING CLASSES." Lastly, although Brownson, like Emerson, also rejected Unitarianism, in the end he did not reject Christianity or organized religion and, in fact, converted to Catholicism, arguably the most conservative and most institutional religion at that time. Orestes Brownson maintained his focus on reform and theological concerns in his paper, BROWNSON'S QUARTERLY REVIEW, the first major Catholic intellectual magazine in the United States, and became well-known as a public Catholic figure in the 19th century.

Bibliography

Lapati, Americo D. *Orestes A. Brownson.* New York: Twayne Publishers, 1965.

New York Tribune
(1841–1872)

The *New York Tribune,* under the general editorship of founder Horace GREELEY, was one of the earliest and the most widely read "penny daily" papers of the 19th century, and many Transcendentalist thinkers and reformers wrote for its pages. Greeley launched the *New York Tribune* in April 1841 and edited the paper until his death more than 30 years later. His vision was to provide an inexpensive alternative to the sensationalistic news-oriented dailies by focusing instead on informative cultural and political issues. The paper throughout this time was synonymous with the name of Horace Greeley, as most newspapers directly reflected the views of their editors. Greeley's views were representative of many liberal Northerners of his time, and those views were spread to a wider audience, beyond just New York, with Greeley's launch of a weekly national edition of the *Tribune.*

Horace Greeley was a reform-minded northerner who championed the common man and supported the cause of labor, WOMEN'S RIGHTS, ABOLITIONISM, FOURIERISM, and a host of other radical reforms in the pages of his paper. Greeley championed the cause of the working classes in the pages of the *Tribune,* where even Karl Marx was employed as a correspondent. But Greeley also made a commitment to actual workers at the paper by supporting the organizing efforts of printers and instituting a *Tribune* profit-sharing plan for the paper's employees. His concern about labor equality was related to his interest in utopianism, and he supported the establishment of utopian communities in both the East and West, where the community of Greeley, Colorado, was named after him. The paper was further aligned with utopian movements by the presence of reformers Charles Anderson DANA and George RIPLEY, both of whom worked for the paper in prominent editorial positions for extended periods of time. Dana served as Ripley's editorial assistant for 15 years, and for 30 years Ripley edited the first and one of the longest running regular newspaper book review columns.

In 1844 Transcendentalist feminist reformer Margaret FULLER moved from editing the DIAL with Ralph Waldo EMERSON in Boston to become a literary critic for Greeley's *Tribune* in New York. In this role, Fuller provided book reviews and regular commentary on social and political reform as well as literary themes. At the *Tribune* Fuller defined the role of the critic and promoted new American writers to the widest audience possible. Many of Fuller's *Tribune* articles and reviews were collected together for the 1846 volume, PAPERS ON LITERATURE AND ART. A few years after joining the *Tribune,* Fuller took the opportunity to go to Europe with friends and, rather than see her leave the paper, Greeley redefined her position as the first foreign correspondent for the *Tribune.* In her column, "THINGS AND THOUGHTS IN EUROPE," Fuller provided regular dispatches on European radicalism, news of revolution, and cultural and literary matters, writing for the *Tribune* until her death in 1850 upon returning to the United States.

Under Greeley, the *New York Tribune* also addressed the important domestic political issues of the day, most notably the events leading up to and through the Civil War. The paper espoused anti-slavery and, by the 1850s, explicitly Republican Party views, whether in opposition to the Mexican War, in criticism of the 1854 Kansas-Nebraska Act, which ostensibly allowed for slavery in the western territories, or in the eventual support of Abraham Lincoln for president in 1860. Greeley himself was a member of the Republican Party, but when he supported the release of Confederate President Jefferson Davis after the war, he lost nearly half his subscriptions to the *Tribune*, which by 1860 had reached nearly 200,000.

Horace Greeley died in 1872 and soon after, under the control of Ogden Mills Reid, the *Tribune* was merged with the *New York Herald* and re-named the *New York Herald Tribune*, a paper which continued until 1947.

Bibliography

Bean, Judith Mattson, and Joel Myerson, eds. *Margaret Fuller, Critic: Writings from the New-York Tribune, 1844–1846.* New York: Columbia University Press, 2000.

Fahrney, Ralph Ray. *Horace Greeley and the Tribune in the Civil War.* New York: Da Capo Press, 1970.

Reynolds, Larry J., and Susan Belasco Smith, eds. *"These Sad But Glorious Days": Dispatches from Europe, 1846–1850, Margaret Fuller.* New Haven, Conn.: Yale University Press, 1991.

Nietzsche, Friedrich
(1844–1900)

German philosopher Friedrich Nietzsche made well known his regard for the ideas and life of American Transcendentalist Ralph Waldo EMERSON. Nietzsche's own philosophy in many ways represented the response to and extension of Transcendentalist ideas into the next generation. As a young man Nietzsche read Emerson and drew from Emerson's work directly in formulating some of his most important ideas. For example, he drew upon Emerson's essay "HISTORY" in writing his own "On the Use and Disadvantage of History for Life" (1873). In Emerson, Nietzsche found and agreed with the questioning of all historical forms and rit-

uals, including religion and morality, in favor of a personal relationship to the past. Nietzsche, how-ever, was ultimately a more systematic philosopher than Emerson the idealist and found that Emerson lacked a "strict discipline." Nietzsche was also more strictly humanist than Emerson, whose for-mulation of the "OVER-SOUL" took away, in Nietzsche's view, the idea of full reliance on the self and the primacy of the individual will. In that sense, Friedrich Nietzsche's engagement with Emersonian Transcendentalism was to take it a step further, away from its origins in ROMANTICISM, and make it applicable to the concerns and realities of the following generations.

Bibliography

Mikics, David. *The Romance of Individualism in Emerson and Nietzsche.* Athens: Ohio University Press, 2003.

Stack, George J. *Nietzsche and Emerson: An Elective Affinity.* Athens: Ohio University Press, 1992.

nonresistance

Nonresistance, also referred to as nonviolent resistance, is the term used to define a pacifist approach to political change in the 19th century as exemplified by many Transcendentalist reformers, most notably Henry David THOREAU. A strategy of nonresistance ultimately created a paradoxical situation for reformers, especially those involved in ABOLITIONISM, as more direct and even violent modes of political action became increasingly used and necessary in the fight against slavery. While the term originated among religious radicals in 17th-century England, in 1838 American reformers created the New England Non-Resistance Society, an offshoot of the American Peace Society. Proponents of nonresistance rejected war or any kind of violence as a valid strategy, and they went even further by refusing to support governments or other institutions which employed violence or force in any situation. Based on such beliefs, members of nonresistance groups—sometimes referred to by contemporaries as "no-government men"—did not participate in politics at any level, including declining to vote, hold office, sit on juries, and, in some cases, even pay taxes. They declared themselves to be living under and held to God's laws, not the laws of man.

Among the most prominent "no-government men" in mid-19th-century reform politics was radical abolitionist William Lloyd GARRISON, who declared in the September 1838 issue of his newspaper, *The Liberator*, that "We recognize but one King and Lawgiver, one Judge and Ruler of mankind." It was such radical and non-compromising sentiments that ultimately led to a split within Garrison's American Anti-Slavery Society between those who saw the need to work within the political system to end slavery and those, like Garrison, who rejected the American political system as the primary cause and supporter of slavery.

Among the Transcendentalists, nonresistance was taken up by those engaged in radical reforms, such as abolitionism and utopianism. Charles LANE, cofounder with Amos Bronson ALCOTT of the utopian community at FRUITLANDS, argued that the U.S. government's use of force interfered with individual rights, a position he argued in a series of essays on "Voluntary Political Government" published between 1842 and 1844. Both Lane and Alcott practiced not just nonresistance but refused to pay taxes as well, actions which resulted in Alcott's 1843 arrest and jailing. This was a stance later taken by Henry David Thoreau, who was familiar with both Alcott's actions and Lane's essays, which Thoreau reviewed for the Transcendentalist paper, the DIAL, in 1844. Thoreau protested against a government that supported slavery and was willing to enter into the Mexican War to encourage its spread. In refusing to pay his poll taxes, Thoreau was arrested and spent one night in jail in 1846, the incident that formed the basis of his 1848 address at the CONCORD LYCEUM that became his most famous essay, "Resistance to Civil Government," later and more widely known as "CIVIL DISOBEDIENCE."

Thoreau also praised other reformers who practiced nonresistance, such as in his account of "Wendell PHILLIPS Before Concord Lyceum," which was published in Garrison's *Liberator*. In this essay Thoreau noted that the purpose of Phillips's lecture was "to show what the state, and above all the church, had to do, and now, alas!

Have done, with Texas and slavery, and how much, on the other hand, the individual should have to do with the church and state." Like many other proponents of nonresistance, especially those influenced by William Lloyd Garrison, Thoreau included "the church," organized religion, as another institution which infringed upon individual rights and supported the agenda of the government, and thus must be avoided or "resisted" by individuals. Despite the similarities with Garrisonian approaches to non-resistance, and his involvement with abolitionist organizations, Thoreau went even further in "Resistance to Civil Government" by urging others to avoid paying taxes or otherwise supporting the government, arguing that "those who call themselves abolitionists should at once effectually withdraw their support, both in person and in property, from the government of Mass."

Not all Transcendentalists saw such positions as necessarily realistic in the current fight against slavery. In his essay on "NEW ENGLAND REFORMERS," Ralph Waldo EMERSON saw nonresistance as more of an ideal to be striven for, but questioned how effective were the "solitary nullifiers, who throw themselves on their reserved rights . . . who reply to the assessor, and to the clerk of the court, that they do not know the State." Of his friend Thoreau's act of resistance that landed him in jail, Emerson referred to him not as an example for others to follow but merely as "a poor good beast who means the best." Especially after 1850, when the FUGITIVE SLAVE LAW and the Boston trial of Anthony BURNS forced a response from reserved abolitionists such as Emerson, the cause seemed to call for more active engagement with politics rather than resistance or retreat. This did not mean that Emerson advocated war, as many abolitionists had begun to. Heavily influenced by QUAKERISM, Emerson advocated pacifism. In 1849 his essay on "War" was published along with Thoreau's on "Resistance to Civil Government" in Elizabeth Palmer PEABODY's anthology, *AESTHETIC PAPERS*. In this essay Emerson advocated and praised "the extreme peace doctrine" as evidence that humans could rise above violence as a solution. Later, in 1856, Emerson wrote in *ENGLISH TRAITS* that "the gun that does not need another gun, the law of love and justice alone, can effect a clean revolution."

The revolution against slavery, however, had turned increasingly to violence and, in 1859, when radical abolitionist John BROWN launched a millennial attack upon Harpers Ferry, Virginia, in the name of inspiring slave revolt, many Boston reformers, including among the Transcendentalists, supported Brown, either financially or in spirit. Even Henry David Thoreau, in public addresses such as "A PLEA FOR CAPTAIN JOHN BROWN," praised Brown's courage and contributed to Brown's immediate status as a martyr for the cause, holding him up as a Christ-like figure, a moral example. Less than two years after Brown's raid, Thoreau, Emerson, Alcott, and others who had practiced and preached nonresistance lent their voices and support to the Union cause, backing the federal government in the final quest to end American slavery.

Bibliography

Chernus, Ira. *American Nonviolence: The History of an Idea.* Maryknol, N.Y.: Orbis Books, 2004.

North American Review

The *North American Review* was a conservative Boston-based periodical that had begun publication in 1815 but by the 1840s was an important site of information on and criticism of literary Transcendentalism. The *North American Review* published on a range of topics from literature and history to science and politics. The works of both Ralph Waldo EMERSON and Henry David THOREAU, among others, were reviewed in its pages, with mixed results. James Russell LOWELL praised Emerson as an original American genius who "speaks for what is highest and least selfish in us," but another reviewer, Francis BOWEN (who served as editor of the paper from 1843 to 1853), characterized Emerson as a creator of "fantastic nonsense." Some Transcendentalists wrote for the paper, such as James Freeman CLARKE's historical essays in 1836 and 1837 and Frederic Henry HEDGE's 1856 review of Margaret FULLER's *At Home and Abroad.* Emerson also contributed seven essays to the *North*

American Review, most of them after the Civil War, though, rather than during the antebellum heyday of Transcendentalist writing and thinking.

Norton, Andrews
(1786–1853)

As the leading professor of theology at HARVARD DIVINITY SCHOOL and an outspoken critic of Transcendentalist tendencies, Andrews Norton had an important influence on the emerging younger generation who would become well known in the movement. Norton found himself at the center of the Transcendentalist controversy of the 1830s, when he criticized the writings of George RIPLEY and Orestes BROWNSON that had appeared in the *CHRISTIAN EXAMINER,* a conservative Unitarian paper with which Norton was affiliated. Norton's response to Ripley was published in another paper, the *Boston Advertiser,* setting off a debate within UNITARIANISM over whether the miracles performed by Christ according the Bible truly happened (i.e., supernatural occurrences) or were merely symbolic and could be explained by natural laws. Norton was upset that such discussions were taking place at all among Christians, and, worse, in a Christian newspaper, and his attack, along with counterresponses by Ripley and others, set off what became known as the "MIRACLES CONTROVERSY" that was a turning point in eventually separating the Transcendentalists from their Unitarian beginnings and affiliations.

Less than two years after the debate with Ripley had begun, Ralph Waldo EMERSON delivered his DIVINITY SCHOOL ADDRESS to Harvard's graduating class of future ministers. Andrews Norton was one of the few people in actual attendance at the lecture and again responded with criticism to the "new school in literature and religion" as represented by Emerson's speech. Norton publicized his own views in a newspaper editorial to the *Boston Advertiser,* calling Emerson a "false preacher" and "a sort of a mad dog," the likes of whom "could have a disastrous effect upon the religion and moral state of the community."

This time Norton went beyond individual attacks and followed up with a book-length direct response to Transcendentalism in general. He published A DISCOURSE ON THE LATEST FORM OF INFIDELITY in 1839, in which he took a stand against the debunking of Christ's miracles and the Transcendentalist acceptance of a "historical" but not "divine" Jesus, by reiterating the traditional Christian view of the miracles as evidence themselves of Christ's divinity. Norton's criticisms quickly faded, however, as Transcendentalism gained legitimacy and a wider following among New England intellectuals, and by 1840 he withdrew from direct public confrontation with the radicals.

Although Andrews Norton had thus established his place in history as a critic of Ralph Waldo Emerson and of Transcendentalism, he was also a prominent theologian and prolific writer in his own right. After retiring from Harvard, he continued his biblical studies and maintained his position regarding the divinity of the New Testament, culminating in the publication of his multivolume work *Evidences of the Genuineness of the Gospels* between 1837 and 1844.

Bibliography

Habich, Robert D. "Emerson's Reluctant Foe: Andrews Norton and the Transcendentalist Controversy," *NEQ* 65 (June 1992): 208–237.

Wright, Conrad Edick, ed. *American Unitarianism, 1805–1865*. Boston: Massachusetts Historical Society and Northeastern University Press, 1989.

Norton, Charles Eliot
(1827–1908)

Unlike his father, Unitarian minister and critic of Transcendentalism Andrews NORTON, writer and editor Charles Eliot Norton promoted the ideas of the Transcendentalists and worked to secure Ralph Waldo EMERSON's literary and cultural legacy. Specifically, Charles Norton was the editor of an 1884 collection of correspondence between Emerson and Thomas CARLYLE and lectured regularly on Emerson's importance to American intellectual culture. Norton was a personal associate of Emerson and of James Russell LOWELL, and he joined these and others of the Transcendentalists as a member of the SATURDAY CLUB. He also worked with Lowell in establishing the *ATLANTIC MONTHLY*, a periodical that was an important forum for Emerson and other New England intellectuals.

Charles Eliot Norton was a protégé of art critic and friend of the Transcendentalist John RUSKIN, through whom Norton developed his perspective on art as a moral guide and on Italian art, in particular, as a model of the highest standard. His interest in Italy, after traveling and studying there, extended to Italian writers and a special attraction to Dante, who was the subject of several of his essays and books. At Harvard beginning in the 1870s, Norton offered the first American university courses in art history, with the support of his cousin, Charles Eliot, who was then president of Harvard.

Although Emerson had once been the most important American intellectual for Charles Eliot Norton, after the Civil War his own philosophical tendencies shifted so that Emerson seemed more and more a product of an earlier and different generation. Norton began to criticize Transcendentalist ROMANTICISM and optimism as he was part of the postwar generation of intellectuals who promoted more objective scientific methods of knowledge. He ultimately characterized Ralph Waldo Emerson as "the most innocent, the most inexperienced of men who have lived in and reflected on the world."

Bibliography

Turner, James. *The Liberal Education of Charles Eliot Norton*. London and Baltimore: Johns Hopkins University Press, 1999.

"Ode, Inscribed to W. H. Channing"
Ralph Waldo Emerson
(1847)

Ralph Waldo EMERSON wrote the poem "Ode, Inscribed to W. H. Channing" in response to the annexation of Texas that brought on the Mexican War in 1845–46. Emerson was opposed to the war over Texas out of concern over the spread of slavery. While Emerson was criticized by contemporaries and early historians for maintaining a distance from the political work of ABOLITIONISM and of pro-union efforts, he often put his philosophical and spiritual beliefs to the test in public speeches and poetry on the issue. In the case of this poem, Emerson had been approached by his colleague, reformer William Henry CHANNING, nephew of the great Unitarian leader William Ellery CHANNING, to make a public statement on the issue of slavery, which Emerson refused to do at this time. Henry Channing was then promoting the idea of northern secession from slaveholding states, a political position with which Emerson could not agree. He did put his thoughts and his direct response to Channing into the form of poetry, however, and "Ode" was included in his first published collection of POEMS in 1847.

Far from being apathetic or apolitical in regards to the events bubbling up around him, Ralph Waldo Emerson believed strongly that it was the poet's role, more than the politician's or the preacher's, to emphasize the higher ideals of human life as the route to resolution over moral issues rather than get bogged down in the political specifics. In "Ode, Inscribed to W. H. Channing," Emerson presented his belief that the great reform work was reform of individual minds, and only then would reform of society take place. Furthermore, the individual most suited to changing minds and ideas was the poet, with his access to a language outside of and above that of either the politician or the minister. As Emerson's most radical colleagues, such as William Lloyd GARRISON and Henry David THOREAU, had pointed out, the state and the church had done more to entrench slavery, so how could these institutions be expected to stop it? Emerson, the poet, points out that just like North and South, church and state— or the spiritual and the material—were "two laws discrete, / Not reconciled."

Emerson agreed with Channing's position against slavery, he only differed in the means of effecting reform. For Emerson, self-reliance was supreme over allying oneself with leaders in the movement who are more concerned with the political strategy and compromise than the higher values of a just cause and the underlying evil that allowed slavery in the first place. Emerson's emphasis on truth and personal power, and his resistance to allying with organized reform efforts, led many to criticize him of professing support for the cause but remaining distanced by wasting time formulating philosophical solutions to an urgent political and social crisis. The poem was Emerson's stance on political and social reform in the 1840s. Throughout the 1850s, however, he became increasingly more politicized on the topic, as the issue of slavery made its way closer to home with the FUGITIVE SLAVE LAW of 1850, the trial of fugitive slave Anthony BURNS in 1854, and, finally, radical abolitionist John BROWN's raid in 1859. Emerson spoke out publicly in support of John Brown and undeniably against slavery in other poems such as "BOSTON HYMN" in 1863, in the midst of the Civil War.

The Old Manse

In 1770 Ralph Waldo EMERSON's grandfather, the Reverend William Emerson, built the family home, later called the Old Manse, on 22 acres in CONCORD, MASSACHUSETTS. Ralph Waldo Emerson lived there with his mother in 1834–35 immediately preceding his marriage to Lydia Jackson (Lidian EMERSON) and it was during this time that he composed NATURE (1836). The house, with its scenic and historic surroundings situated as it is on Monument Street just a few yards from the Old North Bridge, a site best-known as the location of the first battle of the Revolutionary War on April 19, 1775, also served as inspiration for Nathaniel HAWTHORNE's MOSSES FROM AN OLD MANSE (1854), a collection of short stories which includes "THE OLD MANSE" and which he wrote while living there with his wife, Sophia Peabody HAWTHORNE. The Hawthornes had moved into the Old Manse on their wedding day on July 9, 1842, and Henry David THOREAU planted a garden there for the newlyweds. Nathaniel Hawthorne was inspired by the natural and historic landscape in his writings about the house that appeared in his journals as well as in Mosses. It was Hawthorne who gave the home the name Old Manse, as "manse" means both a "mansion" and "a minister's home."

The Hawthornes lived at the Old Manse for three years—their first child, Una, was born there in 1844—until Emerson's half uncle, the Reverend Samuel RIPLEY and his wife Sarah Alden Bradford RIPLEY decided to move back to Samuel's childhood home. The Ripleys entertained many of Concord's literary figures during their residency at the Old Manse, including, among the Transcendentalists, Amos Bronson ALCOTT, and Franklin Benjamin SANBORN. Descendants of the Emerson and Ripley families continued to occupy the house until 1939. Today the house is a preserved historic site and can be toured by visitors who will see much of the original furniture, including pieces purchased by Emerson's grandfather as early as 1767, and the upstairs study where both Emerson and Hawthorne produced major literary works of the Transcendentalist era.

For more information
http://www.concord.org/town/manse/inhabitants.html

"The Old Manse"
Nathaniel Hawthorne
(1846)

"The Old Manse" is the title essay in Nathaniel HAWTHORNE's 1846 collection of short stories, MOSSES FROM AN OLD MANSE. The OLD MANSE refers to the home in which Hawthorne lived while writing these stories, a home belonging to ancestors of Ralph Waldo EMERSON and in which Emerson himself had recently lived and worked. The house was located in CONCORD, MASSACHUSETTS, and while residing there Hawthorne counted Emerson, Henry David THOREAU, and others among the Transcendentalists as his neighbors.

The house was not only previously occupied by Ralph Waldo Emerson but it was situated in a historically significant location as well. Visible from Hawthorne's study in the Old Manse was the site of the battle of Concord that commenced the fighting in the American Revolution. In the story collection Hawthorne invited his readers along as "guests" to tour both the outside and inside of the house so that they might understand how his residence in this historic house provided inspiration for the stories that follow. In addition to describing the outside scene, Hawthorne described the interior decoration of the house, the pictures and stories of the ancestors who dwelled there, and even the books shelved in the library. His tour also included the study once used by Emerson, and Hawthorne hoped that he himself would find within its walls his own inspiration, "an intellectual treasure in the Old Manse well worth those hoards of long-hidden gold which people seek for in moss-grown houses."

Although the stories that follow in *Mosses from an Old Manse* do not deal with themes related to the House itself, they were all written from the study he described to the reader in his introductory piece on "The Old Manse."

Orchard House

Between 1858 and 1877 Transcendentalist Amos Bronson ALCOTT lived with his family at Orchard House in CONCORD, MASSACHUSETTS. The house was originally built in the early 1700s and was situated on 12 acres of land and apple orchards. The Alcott family lived at Orchard House longer than any other residence, as they often moved due to financial difficulties or to participate in Bronson Alcott's reform experiments, such as the community at FRUITLANDS, where the family lived, unhappily according to Louisa May ALCOTT, for seven months during 1843 and 1844. Louisa's years at Orchard House, however, were the happiest of her life and were recorded in her best-selling novel, *LITTLE WOMEN*, which she wrote and published in 1868 while living there. Today the home is a historic site and can be toured by visitors who will see the structure unchanged since the 19th century, including much of the original furniture owned by the Alcott family.

For more information

http://www.louisamayalcott.org

"Orphic Sayings"
Amos Bronson Alcott
(1840–1841)

The "Orphic Sayings" were a series of short philosophical statements by Transcendentalist reformer and writer Amos Bronson ALCOTT published in the literary journal, the DIAL. Colleague Ralph Waldo EMERSON had once termed Alcott an "Orphic poet" and early on saw in Alcott the gifts of a prophet or seer. Emerson was unsure about publishing the sayings, for fear that Alcott would be misunderstood, but he and *Dial* coeditor Margaret FULLER wanted to give Alcott a place in the new journal. He offered a series of 50 "Orphic Sayings" for the magazine's first issue in July 1840, and another 50 appeared in the January 1841 issue. The name for the new journal, the *Dial*, had been suggested by Alcott himself, and the first saying invoked the image: "Thou art, my heart, a soul-flower, facing ever and following the motions of thy sun, opening thyself to her vivifying ray, and pleading thy affinity with celestial orbs. Thou dost 'the livelong day Dial on time thine own eternity.' "

Alcott gave his writings the name "Orphic Sayings" in reference to the prophecies of Orpheus that released Eurydice from Hades in the Greek myth. He believed that brief poetic statements more accurately reflected his thought than longer elaborative essays and, just as importantly, such a style required that the reader form his or her own relationship to the ideas expressed rather than have the author provide extended analysis. Not only the ideas but the actual structure of the writing was inconsistent and abstract. Alcott intended the statements as guides or inspirations to the soul on ways of being and, as such, he purposefully rejected conventional forms of narrative and genre, and thus the random thoughts lacked any coherent philosophical theme. To him they expressed the core of philosophical truths without wasting space on "insignificant detail."

Ralph Waldo Emerson's first instinct was correct, and the publication of the abstract and mystical phrasings brought immediate ridicule upon Bronson Alcott, the magazine, and the Transcendentalist community as a whole by those who wished to discredit them. One reviewer referred to the *Dial* as "the ravings of Alcott and his fellow zanies." Particularly harsh was the New York *Knickerbocker*'s parody of Alcott in a series of "Gastric Sayings." His friends at the *Dial* did not want to publish any more "Orphic Sayings," and Alcott himself eventually decided that even the *Dial* was too conventional and not open-minded enough to appreciate his style. Unfortunately, a reputation for inaccessible and even nonsensical writings plagued Bronson Alcott for the remainder of his career. Decades later, commentators on the CONCORD

SCHOOL OF PHILOSOPHY AND LITERATURE referred to the "Orphic utterances" of Alcott at the school.

Unfortunately, Alcott's entire reputation as a writer and as a Transcendentalist rested upon this collection of brief pronouncements on human culture and character, despite his numerous other writings and his reform work. It is true that, unlike his Transcendentalist colleagues such as Ralph Waldo Emerson or Henry David THOREAU, whose works have endured overtime in part because of the ability of readers to extract brief phrases with universal meaning, Alcott's sayings were so abstract and oddly written as to completely obscure any larger or timeless interpretation. As Alcott biographer Frederick Dahlstrand observed, the problem of the "Orphic Sayings" was that "As philosophy they were useless because there was no thread tying them together in a system. As prophecy they were powerless because of their lack of concrete, captivating, or inspiring imagery." Still, while lacking clarity as a unifying whole, many of the themes and ideas articulated by Alcott in the "Orphic Sayings," were typical of themes addressed by other Transcendentalists, such as his pronouncement that "Every soul feels at times her own possibility of becoming a God; she cannot rest in the human, she aspires after the Godlike."

Although public ridicule prevented him from presenting any more such material to the *Dial,* the mystical style of the "Orphic Sayings" was one that Bronson Alcott turned to again. Years later he published a series of brief prophetic poems he called "Philosophemes" in the JOURNAL OF SPECULATIVE PHILOSOPHY and, in 1877, he gathered together more than 100 short paragraphs on topics "Practical" and "Speculative" into a popular book, *TABLE-TALK.*

Bibliography

Dahlstrand, Frederick. *Amos Bronson Alcott: An Intellectual Biography.* London and Toronto: Associated University Presses, 1982.

Osgood, Samuel
(1812–1880)

Unitarian minister Samuel Osgood was involved with Transcendentalism as a regular attendee of the TRANSCENDENTAL CLUB and, after moving from New England to the Ohio Valley, as a substantial contributor and editor of the first Transcendentalist periodical, the WESTERN MESSENGER. During his tenure with the *Western Messenger,* Osgood authored as many as 65 articles, possibly more, in which he presented Transcendentalist ideas and philosophy to readers in the western states. He introduced Ralph Waldo EMERSON, specifically, in that magazine with an 1837 review of the recently published NATURE. Osgood was ultimately a more conservative Unitarian than many of the New England Transcendentalists, but he was open to new ideas and experimented in his own writing with the implications of the new philosophy. He defined his own approach of taking the best of both old and new, European and American, traditional and radical ideas as "eclecticism." In 1842 Osgood contributed a translated volume of the writings of German theologian Wilhelm De Wette on *Human Life: or Practical Ethics* for George RIPLEY's series of works important to the Transcendentalists, SPECIMENS OF FOREIGN STANDARD LITERATURE. In 1849 Samuel Osgood returned to the East coast to preach in New York where, between 1850 and 1854, he edited another periodical, the *Christian Inquirer.*

Bibliography

Green, Judith Kent. "A Tentative Transcendentalist in the Ohio Valley: Samuel Osgood and the *Western Messenger,*" *Studies in the American Renaissance* (1987): 79–92.

"The Over-Soul"
Ralph Waldo Emerson
(1841)

"The Over-Soul" was published in Ralph Waldo EMERSON's ESSAYS: FIRST SERIES (1841), but the central thought of a primal mind, a cosmic unity, is one found throughout Emerson's writings. He defines this unity in "The Over-Soul" as "the soul of the whole; the wise silence; the universal beauty to which every part and particle is equally related; the Eternal One." "The Over-Soul" is Emerson's most fully developed presentation of a universal human force that replaces a belief in God or the supernatural. The Over-Soul both guides and is changed by humankind. According to Emerson, the universe of thought and action is in constant movement, and human beings are caught up in that eternal flowing movement: "Man is a stream whose source is hidden. Our being is descending into us from we know not whence." The Over-Soul is a "flowing river, which . . . pours for a season its streams into me," the "Unity . . . within which every man's particular being is contained and made one with all other; that common heart . . . that overpowering reality."

This is one of the most recurrent paradoxes of Emerson's Transcendentalist philosophy, the belief in the primacy of the individual, but that individual as always a part of a larger whole of a universal life force, a theme explored in other essays as well, most notably in Emerson's theory of "COMPENSATION." It would seem difficult to justify a belief in such an overarching force or "flowing river" of which all humankind is a part and still maintain the imperative of individual conscience and will. For Emerson, however, the Over-Soul does not dictate or even guide human behavior but, rather, all humans contribute, for better or worse, to the nature of the Over-Soul. Individual human beings gain their strength and wisdom from the Over-Soul and therefore must give over to it. We are reflections or manifestations of the universal power, but it is human beings that give it that power in the first place.

Called by different names, the idea of unity, or of "the One," is a key point of Emerson's philosophy and is mentioned in most of his other major lectures and essays. This idea had been introduced but not fully explored in Emerson's earlier works, such as NATURE (1836), and become a regular presence in other essays and poems and one of the foundational points characteristic of Emersonian Transcendentalism. In "SELF-RELIANCE," ironically his manifesto of individualism, he writes that all are combined "into the ever-blessed ONE." Likewise, a "fountain of power" from which we draw, and an "original unit" of which we are all a part, are mentioned in "THE AMERICAN SCHOLAR." For Emerson, true individualism and originality of thought are accessed through "the influx of the Divine mind into our mind," which leads to a Transcendentalist version of spiritual "revelation" and growth: "Let man then learn the revelation of all nature, and all the thought to his heart; this, namely; that the Highest dwells with him; that the sources of nature are in his own mind." In his critique of orthodox Christian theology, Ralph Waldo Emerson had appropriated its language to detail a relationship not between God and the self but between the humanistic Over-Soul and the Self. Emerson's Over-Soul is a more mystical celebration of the subjective and individual within the universal.

P

Palfrey, John Gorham
(1796–1881)

John Palfrey was a Massachusetts abolitionist and one of the few politicians admired and publicly supported by Ralph Waldo EMERSON. Emerson participated in Palfrey's 1851 congressional campaign by delivering his "FUGITIVE SLAVE LAW ADDRESS" on numerous occasions in support of Palfrey's Free Soil ticket. Emerson had been politicized the previous year against the FUGITIVE SLAVE LAW and against Daniel WEBSTER's support of it and so came to the aid of Palfrey as a northern politician willing to speak out against the law. Palfrey's Free Soil party was not the party of ABOLITIONISM—that is, the ending of slavery was not their primary goal—but the party at least was against the implicit support and protection of slavery given by federal fugitive slave legislation. The Free Soil party had been founded in 1848 and, although it included some antislavery members, its primary platform was containing slavery in the southern states and preventing its spread into the western territories and states.

Emerson and Palfrey had both literary and political connections before they came together on the 1851 campaign. Palfrey served as editor of the *NORTH AMERICAN REVIEW* during the height of the Transcendentalist controversy between 1835 and 1843. He was also a friend of Lidian EMERSON and a Unitarian minister and dean at Harvard who had declared Ralph Waldo Emerson's 1838 DIVINITY SCHOOL ADDRESS "folly," if not "downright Atheism." Palfrey left the ministry for politics and whatever theological differences between the two, they eventually shared the same political focus, first in their objection to the annexation of Texas, and in 1851 with Emerson agreeing to assist Palfrey, whom he now referred to as "my friend," in his bid for Congress.

Throughout the late 1840s and by 1850, Emerson was increasingly recognized and sought out as a public voice against slavery. Despite the popularity of Emerson's address on the Fugitive Slave Law, John Palfrey lost the election, although he did receive the majority votes in Emerson's own district, which included CONCORD. Disappointed that his friend lost, but also that the Whig candidate had won the seat, Emerson warned in his journal that, after the betrayal of Daniel Webster, northern politicians "have shown their teeth unmistakeably" and the people "shall not be deceived again" into thinking that the North would be protected from compromise with the southern slave states.

Bibliography
Gougeon, Len. *Virtue's Hero: Emerson, Antislavery, and Reform.* Athens: University of Georgia Press, 1990.

Palmer, Joseph
(1791–1875)

Joseph Palmer was a Massachusetts farmer, reformer, and resident of the utopian community at FRUITLANDS during its entire brief existence. He was committed to the plan set forth for the community by founders Amos Bronson ALCOTT and Charles LANE, although Palmer did not affiliate with the Transcendentalists on other projects. After the demise of Fruitlands, Palmer bought the property, which had been held under the trusteeship of Ralph Waldo EMERSON, and attempted to establish another utopian community at the same location. Louisa May ALCOTT remembered Joseph Palmer through the character of "Moses White" in her fictional satirical account of her father's experiment, "TRANSCENDENTAL WILD OATS." Palmer's eccentricities earned him a local reputation when he was ostracized and eventually personally accosted for wearing a beard in his hometown. When Joseph Palmer tried to defend himself against harassers who attempted to shave him, he was arrested for assault and spent more than a year in jail. He is remembered on his gravestone as the man who was "Persecuted for Wearing the Beard."

Bibliography

Rose, Anne C. *Transcendentalism as a Social Movement, 1830–1850.* New Haven, Conn.: Yale University Press, 1981.

pantheism

Pantheism is the worldview that sees God and nature as the same and, since some Transcendentalists, in particular Ralph Waldo EMERSON and Henry David THOREAU, seemed to "worship" nature as a God or at least emphasized that nature was divine, Transcendentalism was characterized by some as a pantheistic spirituality. As Transcendentalist contemporary Samuel JOHNSON explained, pantheism "confounds God with the universe." Although the term *pantheism* did not come into use until the 18th century, pantheistic ideas can be traced in the classical tradition of PLATONISM and, later, NEOPLATONISM, as well as in a variety of religious traditions, including Buddhism, Hinduism, and Judeo-Christian mysticism. In addition to reading widely in such philosophical and mystical traditions, the American Transcendentalists also encountered pantheistic ideas and spirituality in the 19th-century German IDEALISM of Friedrich

SCHELLING and, most important, Johann Wolfgang von GOETHE, which philosophized a personal and immanent God rather than the distant God of history. Through the tenets of European ROMANTICISM as well, notably in the work of Samuel Taylor COLERIDGE and poet William BLAKE, the Transcendentalists were immersed in a literature of communion with and appreciation of nature. Finally, Emerson's poetry as well was heavily influenced by the pantheistic traditions and symbolism of Eastern philosophy and literature. From Hinduism and from the Eastern mystical poets Emerson drew inspiration for the imagery found in his poems, such as "BRAHMA," "HAMATREYA," and "WOODNOTES," in which he praises "the eternal Pan."

Pantheism differs from and is seen as antithetical to orthodox Christianity, in one sense then, because it challenges biblical morality, since in pantheism there is no moral obligation to God but only to oneself and to the abstract goal of seeking to perfect oneself. In addition, biblical Christianity teaches that God is not only separate from but creator of and therefore above nature. For Ralph Waldo Emerson, nature existed to inspire the divine in man, and all of humanity, nature, indeed all of the universe, was connected as one, therefore as equals. Transcendentalists did not engage the question of a single God as creator of the universe but instead emphasized the interconnectedness of all and looked to nature, like a god itself, for its symbolic relationship to the individual and to human society. Pantheism, then, fit within a Transcendentalist worldview that saw all of creation as interrelated and nature as the language of creation, an alternative to the separation between humans and nature, between the physical and spiritual worlds, that characterized western biblical-based religions.

Ralph Waldo Emerson's pantheism can be seen throughout his writings, from his foundational work in *NATURE* (1836), through his essays and poems. In fact, one reviewer of Emerson's *ESSAYS: FIRST SERIES* (1841) titled his review "Pantheism" and warned that Emerson's "transfusion of God into the universe destroys our very idea of God." Indeed, it was the pantheistic extremes of Emerson's language that were caricatured in the drawings by Transcendentalist artist Christopher Pearse CRANCH. Cranch focused in on Emerson's description in *Nature* of the "occult relationship between man and vegetable" and drew humorous sketches of half-man, half-vegetable figures to accompany Emersonian quotes such as "I expand and live in the warm day, like corn and melons."

While Cranch was an insider and sympathizer of Emerson's ideas, serious critics of Transcendentalism, such as conservative Unitarian Andrews NORTON, were alerted to the philosophy's pantheistic elements and equated it with atheism and heresy. In A DISCOURSE ON THE LATEST FORM OF INFIDELITY (1839), Norton's response to Ralph Waldo Emerson's DIVINITY SCHOOL ADDRESS, Norton identified pantheism behind the Transcendentalist insistence that God was not a personified being but a universal force, and that the miracles performed by Jesus in the Bible were only symbolic of moral lessons, not supernatural events that defied laws of nature. Continuing with the MIRACLES CONTROVERSY, which had embroiled Norton with other Transcendentalists, namely George RIPLEY, in previous years, Emerson stated in the Divinity School Address that "the very word Miracle . . . is Monster; it is not one with the blowing clover and falling rain." Emerson insisted that nature itself was an everyday miracle and that the focus on unprovable events of the past as described in the Bible was misguided. The Transcendentalists were not privileging the scientific method, per se, in demanding proof for the miracles, but instead were denying that any "miracles" were truly supernatural events since, as critics of pantheism recognized, for Transcendentalists God was synonymous with nature and nature (therefore God) was bound by physical laws or explanations.

Ralph Waldo Emerson was only the most vocal or prominent Transcendentalist to espouse pantheistic principles. Henry David THOREAU was also singled out, not surprisingly, given his work as a naturalist and his commitment to seeing the actual as well as symbolic relationship of humanity to nature in works such as WALDEN (1854) and various essays.

Bibliography

De Groot, Jean, ed. *Nature in American Philosophy.* Washington, D.C.: Catholic University of America Press, 2004.

Papers on Literature and Art
Margaret Fuller
(1846)

Editor Evert DUYCKINCK asked Transcendentalist Margaret FULLER to gather several essays and literary reviews together as part of a series on American authors for Wiley and Putnam's publishers, resulting in Fuller's *Papers on Literature and Art* (1846). Fuller was at the time the main literary critic for Horace GREELEY's *NEW YORK TRIBUNE* and had edited and written extensively for the Transcendentalist literary journal she helped found, the *DIAL*, between 1840 and 1844. The emphasis of Fuller's essays was British and American literature, and she planned a second volume on other European authors, which the publishers were not interested in producing. *Papers on Literature and Art* was thus made up primarily of Fuller's writings from these other forums, although one of the most important pieces, "American Literature, Its Position in the Present Time, and Its Prospects for the Future," was written exclusively for this volume. In this essay, Fuller drew on her vast literary knowledge to assess the state of American literature at the time. Transcendentalism itself arose as a cultural movement promoting independent American literary culture, in debt to but now separate from the looming history of European thought and literature. Like her colleague Ralph Waldo EMERSON, then, Fuller called for the full development of a uniquely American literature drawing on the strengths of American culture. She argued that America's history and identity, indeed the very physical landscape, were now so entirely different from its European, primarily English, heritage, that new thoughts and ideas must be established and encouraged: "What suits Great Britain, . . . does not suit a mixed race continually enriched with new blood from other stocks . . . with ample field and verge enough to range in and leave every impulse free, and abundant opportunity to develop a genius wide and full as our rivers, flowery, luxuriant, and impassioned as our great prairies, rooted in strength as the rocks on which the Puritan fathers landed."

Although America had yet to enter into the international intellectual scene with its own meaningful contribution, when Margaret Fuller looked around her she saw the beginnings of a distinctly American literary model, and she provided a survey of promising work in several genres. The writers she held out as examples included Washington Irving, James Fenimore Cooper for his "noble romance of the hunter-pioneer's life," and her own friend Nathaniel HAWTHORNE, who was yet to emerge, as Fuller predicted, as one of the era's most significant and well-known novelists. While she named these promising individual writers of fiction who managed to capture the distinct spirit and essence of American society and history in their works, Fuller found only "scanty" evidence of an American contribution in poetry. Of the premier poets of her time, she judged that "posterity will not remember" James Russell LOWELL (a comment that may explain, in part, the harshness with which he portrayed Fuller in his 1848 A FABLE FOR CRITICS), and that Henry Wadsworth LONGFELLOW's verse was "artificial and imitative."

The most important and original American writer in Fuller's assessment was her own close friend Ralph Waldo Emerson. Emerson was an essayist, poet, and philosopher who, she predicted, would be one of the few of the current age "likely to live and be blessed and honored in the later time." Fuller's opinions on almost all counts are thus incredibly prescient for someone writing in the 1840s, before most of the authors about whom she wrote were known beyond a small circle of New England elites. In fact, many critics chided Fuller for ignoring the most popular and commercially successful writers in America and praising only those authors who came from her own "clique" and, worse, interpreting their "unpopularity" itself as proof of their "original merit." When *Papers on Literature and Art* appeared in print Margaret Fuller had already sailed for Europe where she would turn from literary criticism and write for the *New York Tribune* as a foreign correspondent.

Bibliography

Bean, Judith Mattson, and Joel Myerson, eds. *Margaret Fuller, Critic: Writings from the* New-York Tribune, *1844–1846.* New York: Columbia University Press, 2000.

Parker, Theodore
(1810–1860)

Theodore Parker was a religious reformer, ardent abolitionist, WOMEN'S RIGHTS supporter, and the most important Transcendentalist Unitarian minister. He graduated from HARVARD DIVINITY SCHOOL in 1836 and was involved in early Transcendentalist activities as a member of the TRANSCENDENTAL CLUB and contributor to the movement's literary journal, the *DIAL*. As the remaining leader of radical UNITARIANISM after other Transcendentalists had left the ministry, Parker became an important mentor and colleague to other liberal Christian friends such as Elizabeth Palmer PEABODY, younger Transcendentalists such as Caroline DALL and Octavius Brooks FROTHINGHAM (who published an 1874 biography of Parker), and ministers Thomas Wentworth HIGGINSON and David WASSON.

Theodore Parker was born into a large family with no money for formal education. He was expected to work on the farm, but he loved books and was entirely self-taught before applying for admission to Harvard. He still could not afford to enroll officially so he embarked upon a period of independent study of the entire undergraduate curriculum. He was able to get a job as a schoolteacher but had to use much of his salary to hire a substitute for himself to help his father run the family farm. While working as a teacher he met Convers FRANCIS, a Unitarian minister who became Parker's mentor and sponsored him into Harvard Divinity School. Parker soon befriended other young men who would be associated with the emerging Transcendentalist movement, including Christopher Pearse CRANCH and John Sullivan DWIGHT. In 1837 he married Lydia Cabot, whose wealthy family helped support the couple. He took a position as a regular minister at West Roxbury, Massachusetts (the site chosen in 1841 for George RIPLEY's utopian community, BROOK FARM, which Parker regularly visited), but retained his connections with the Boston-Cambridge intellectual circles. During this time he was heavily influenced by readings in German biblical criticism, embracing ideas and methods that led him even more toward the radical ideas of the emerging Transcendentalist thought.

Parker was a regular attendee of the Transcendental Club during this time and came to admire Ralph Waldo EMERSON greatly. He attended many of Emerson's lectures and was present for Emerson's 1838 Harvard DIVINITY SCHOOL ADDRESS. Although Parker had some reservations about Emerson's humanistic conception of God, he was exhilarated by Emerson's ideas in general and inspired to begin work on his own statement on the state of the current Unitarian church and historical Christianity. Parker's 1841 "South Boston Sermon," published the following year as A DISCOURSE ON THE TRANSIENT AND PERMANENT IN CHRISTIANITY, was his own Transcendentalist manifesto and propelled him to the center of the Transcendentalist controversy. In the sermon Parker not only questioned the necessity of a divine conception of Jesus and the belief in the supernatural, including Christ's miracles, but like Emerson, he criticized other liberal Unitarians for preaching a version of Christianity which they themselves did not fully embrace.

Parker's sermon set off a controversy within the liberal religious community to rival that of Emerson's address three years earlier. Critics proposed that he be removed from the ministry. This did not happen formally, but informally he was barred from preaching in the congregations of many former friends, and the religious press now rejected his writings. Most painfully, his radicalism meant severed relationships from his more orthodox friends, including former mentors Convers Francis and Andrews NORTON, who had emerged as one of the most vocal critics of the Transcendentalism with which Parker was now most clearly associated. Unlike Emerson, however, Parker was a committed Christian who believed in God and who wished to remain in the ministry. He eventually gave up his West Roxbury position when his Boston friends and supporters gathered together as the Twenty-Eighth Congregational Society and created a pulpit especially for him. The Society rented halls to accommodate audiences of thousands who came to hear Parker preach as well as discuss the important political and social topics of the day. The controversy from his *Discourse on the Transient and Permanent* had propelled Parker beyond a preacher to become a popular lecturer on a variety of topics and finally garnered the wider audience that he had craved in his early days as a parish minister. He eventually traveled as far west as Illinois and Wisconsin on the lecture circuit.

In the immediate aftermath of the controversy, however, he gave a series of lectures in Boston on his Transcendentalist view of "Religion" which became the basis for another publication, the 500-page A DISCOURSE OF MATTERS PERTAINING TO RELIGION (1842), which was revised multiple times over the next decade. Shut out of the liberal religious press, he found a new forum for his opinions in the Transcendentalist journal, the *Dial*, and his writings appeared in all four volumes of the periodical, published between 1840 and 1844. The first issue of July 1840 featured an essay by Parker on "The Divine Presence in Nature and in the Soul," and other issues featured his literary review essays, reprinted sermons, and even poems. The *Dial* provided Parker with a platform for his controversial views, but as he had already made a name for himself, his notoriety also contributed to the relative success of the magazine.

The *Dial* ceased publication in 1844, and Parker's attention had increasingly turned more toward social reform issues such as urban reform, antipoverty, prison reform, EDUCATION reform, women's rights, and, especially, ABOLITIONISM. In 1847 he founded his own reform periodical, the MASSACHUSETTS QUARTERLY REVIEW, which he envisioned explicitly as a more politically minded Transcendentalist alternative to the literary *Dial*. His paper had strong ties to the abolitionist movement but also featured Parker's continued interest in theological and literary topics. The magazine ceased publication in 1850, but Parker's involvement in antislavery activities only increased after this time with the passage of the new fugitive slave laws. As part of the Compromise of 1850, the FUGITIVE SLAVE LAW was a concession to the southern states in the form of a promise of to return runaway slaves who managed to reach the North back to their owners. Parker was among those who urged northern citizens to actively disobey the laws. He became the chairman of the Boston Vigilance Committee, a citizen's group that not only vowed to help hide fugitive slaves if called upon but provided legal and financial assistance to them as well. When a fugitive slave, Anthony BURNS, was arrested in Boston in 1854, Parker became the spokesperson for Burns's cause and was himself arrested and jailed for inciting a public riot that led to the death of a policeman. Parker was released and never charged.

In 1859 Parker traveled with his wife to the Caribbean in an attempt to rest and recover his failing health. From there he went to Europe where he remained involved in political events in the United States, writing a defense of failed antislavery crusader John BROWN upon hearing of his arrest and impending execution in late 1859. Theodore Parker never returned to the United States, however, as he died in Italy in May 1860.

Bibliography

Grodzins, Dean. *American Heretic: Theodore Parker and Transcendentalism.* Chapel Hill: University of North Carolina Press, 2002.

Parnassus
Ralph Waldo Emerson
(1874)

In late 1874 Ralph Waldo EMERSON published *Parnassus,* an edited collection of his favorite poems. The title word *Parnassus* refers to the mountain in Greece of great importance in Greek mythology. Not only was the mountain Parnassus a sacred place of worship of certain gods, but it was believed that the presence of the Muses at Parnassus made it a site of inspiration for musicians and poets. Little attention has been paid to this volume produced late in Emerson's life when his failing health forced him to increasingly rely upon other people, namely his daughters, Edith and Ellen EMERSON, and his eventual literary executor, James Elliot CABOT, to prepare materials for publication, and therefore the role of editor of the volume may not have belonged to Emerson alone. Furthermore, *Parnassus* itself does not include original work by Emerson.

In fact, although the volume was not published until 1874, Emerson had been gathering poems and passages for such a project throughout the preceding decades of his most prolific activity. Emerson regularly transcribed his favorite poetry into his journals and notebooks, and several of the poems included in *Parnassus* had been entered into and commented upon in his journals as much 50 years earlier. By at least 1850 Emerson planned to collect these diverse notations together into a full-length volume of selected poems, and his daughter, Edith, began copying out his chosen passages. After the publication of the second collection of his own poems, MAY-DAY AND OTHER PIECES, in 1867 Emerson began serious work on the idea for *Parnassus.*

The very act of conceiving of such a volume and the work of selecting the poems to include in the anthology ultimately reveal much about Emerson's vision of the role of poetry and of poets in society. As literary scholar Ronald Bosco argues, *Parnassus* is more than a disjointed collection of favorites, "it is a master poem of Emerson's own making." The poems and excerpts he chose spoke to him personally and met different criteria within his theories of poetry and readership. They are presented to the readers of *Parnassus* as examples of "genius" and "originality," ideas he had developed in earlier lectures and essays, specifically his lectures on "Poetry and Imagination" and "Quotation and Originality" that were collected and published in the 1876 volume, LETTERS AND SOCIAL AIMS. The essay on "Poetry and Imagination" is, in fact, the source for most of the ideas presented in Emerson's brief "Preface" to *Parnassus.*

The more than 500-page *Parnassus* is dominated by English and American writers. In the preface, Emerson gives credit to William SHAKESPEARE as the creator of "a universal poetry." Other writers heavily cited include Geoffrey Chaucer, William WORDSWORTH, John Milton, Samuel Longfellow, John Greenleaf WHITTIER, and a select few of Emerson's 19th-century American contemporaries, whether known or unknown, such as William Ellery CHANNING II, Julia Ward HOWE, James Russell LOWELL, his own brother Edward EMERSON, and Transcendentalist poets Jones VERY, Ellen Sturgis HOOPER, and Caroline Sturgis TAP-

PAN. Emerson sought not to establish or confirm a canon of great poetry, but instead to present a range of talents and themes that reflected his theory of good poetry as that which fosters a meaningful relationship between poet and reader, and, specifically, a relationship analogous to the human connection with nature.

Reviewers criticized the volume for the exclusion of American poets before 1800 as well as the blatant omission of important contemporary poets such as Edgar Allan POE and, most notably, Walt WHITMAN, a writer many considered representative of American poetry and, in particular, reflective of the literary influence of Emersonian Transcendentalism. Emerson offered no explanation for his choices other than that they were his alone. Despite such criticisms, *Parnassus* was a success for Ralph Waldo Emerson, a success he modestly attributed to his established reputation more than the merits of the book alone. A second edition appeared just months after the first publication with successive editions printed until well after Emerson's death.

Bibliography

Bosco, Ronald A. " 'Poetry for the World of Readers' and 'Poetry for Bards Proper': Poetic Theory and Textual Integrity in Emerson's *Parnassus*." In *Studies in the American Renaissance*, (1989): 257–312.

Peabody, Elizabeth Palmer
(1804–1894)

As a reformer Elizabeth Palmer Peabody applied Transcendentalist ideas to practical issues and as a publisher and bookstore owner she facilitated the spread of those ideas during the crucial early days of the movement. Both of her parents were educators, and she received a rigorous education at home, including learning several languages. She took on responsibility for the EDUCATION of her siblings until establishing herself as a teacher in her own private school. At the age of 18 she moved to Boston where she operated a school, used her connections to attended lectures at Harvard, and studied Greek with Ralph Waldo EMERSON. While tutoring the young daughter of the influential Unitarian Reverend William Ellery CHANNING, Peabody began working as an unpaid assistant to Channing, who became an important mentor to her. Channing greatly influenced her liberal religious beliefs as well as her literary and reform spirit, as he did for other Unitarian-Transcendentalists, although in less direct and personal ways. As a woman Peabody could not be a minister, but she wrote essays on theological issues, including an early series on "The Spirit of the Hebrew Scriptures" published in successive issues of the *CHRISTIAN EXAMINER* during 1834. Her concerns about the authority of biblical scriptures were spiritual as well as historical, and she continued throughout her career to emphasize historical study as a source of tradition as well as a guide to the present. At the time of writing her biblical essay she was also engaged in writing a multivolume text on the study of history. In 1856 she published one of the earliest textbooks devoted to the history of the United States.

In the early 1830s Peabody supplemented her teaching with evening courses in history for adult women in a series of meetings similar to Margaret FULLER's famous CONVERSATIONS FOR WOMEN a decade later. Her teaching experience and her interest in new educational theories led her to join Amos Bronson ALCOTT at his TEMPLE SCHOOL in Boston. Peabody recruited students for the school and served as a teacher and assistant to Alcott, recording and presenting his methods in the 1835 *RECORD OF A SCHOOL*. Against her advice, Alcott published a second unedited version the following year as *CONVERSATIONS WITH CHILDREN ON THE GOSPELS*, a volume that incited public controversy over Alcott's presentation of improper subject matter to children and forced Peabody to leave the Temple School. She did attempt to clear her name from association with Alcott by publishing yet another edition of *Record of a School*, this time including an introduction that clarified the differences between Alcott's and her own theories.

Having been introduced to Transcendentalist ideas and circles in Boston, Elizabeth Palmer Peabody was friends with many in the early movement and was involved in a variety of their literary and social reform endeavors. She was one of the few women to attend meetings of the TRANSCENDENTAL CLUB and she had close contact with Ralph Waldo Emerson, Margaret Fuller, and her childhood neighbor from Salem, Nathaniel HAWTHORNE, whom she personally nurtured and encouraged to publish his fiction. She herself published several of his early stories for children in 1840 and 1841 after establishing her own press. Peabody never married but her family, social, and reform ties remained close as Nathaniel Hawthorne eventually married her sister Sophia Peabody (HAWTHORNE), and her sister Mary Peabody married educational reformer Horace MANN.

In 1840 Elizabeth Palmer Peabody, sponsored and supported by her Boston friends, embarked on a new career by opening a bookstore and library on West Street in Boston. Through Peabody the early Transcendentalists gained access to vast literary resources, including many European books and periodicals then available nowhere else in Boston. Peabody offered not only readings in literature, history, philosophy, and the natural sciences, but she provided art supplies and various other items as well. The bookstore soon became a literary and social center of Boston intellectuals in general and Transcendentalism in particular. While the bookstore opening was planned for early 1840, Peabody opened her parlor doors at this location in the fall of 1839 to host Margaret Fuller's first series of Conversations for women. The final meeting of the Transcendental Club was held there as well the following fall. By the time the members of that Club had decided to put together their own journal, Peabody was actively publishing books on literary and reform themes through her own press.

Beginning in January 1842 Peabody published six issues of the Transcendentalist literary journal, the *DIAL*, after which time the editors sought a publisher with a broader and more established market. Regardless, the magazine ceased publication in 1844. Peabody contributed several essays to the *Dial:* "A GLIMPSE OF CHRIST'S IDEA OF SOCIETY" (October 1841), "Plan of West Roxbury Community" (January 1842), and "FOURIERISM" (April 1844), all of which addressed Peabody's interest in and support of the utopian communal experiment at BROOK FARM recently established by friends George RIPLEY and Sophia RIPLEY. She also con

tributed a translated piece, "The Preaching of Buddha," to the January 1844 issue. In 1849 Peabody ventured into print with her own edited journal, *AESTHETIC PAPERS*, a single issue which included many seminal essays and represented the best thought of the early Transcendentalist movement, including the first appearance in print of Henry David THOREAU's essay, "Resistance to Civil Government" (*see* "CIVIL DISOBEDIENCE").

Her interests in educational philosophy and reform characterized Elizabeth Palmer Peabody's work beyond the Transcendentalist circle. With her mother and sisters she founded and contributed to a short-lived journal, *The Family School,* and she became particularly interested in the ideas of European thinkers such as language theorist Charles KRAITSIR and Friedrich Froebel. She became an assistant at Kraitsir's Boston school, and her notes from his lectures were published as his 1846 book, *Significance of the Alphabet.* Peabody worked effortlessly to promote both Kraitsir and Froebel in the United States. References to Kraitsir appear in her essays in *Aesthetic Papers,* but her most enduring legacy is as the founder of the first English-speaking kindergarten in America in 1860 based on Froebel's ideas. She traveled to Europe in 1867–68 to learn more firsthand about systems of early childhood education and returned with a renewed and clarified sense of reform purpose. She wrote several pamphlets on the kindergarten system and worked to have them adopted by the public schools. Between 1873 and 1877 she promoted her ideas through her writing and editing of the journal *The Kindergarten Messenger.*

Peabody remained active in Transcendentalist circles in the post–Civil War period as well. She attended and lectured at old friend Bronson Alcott's CONCORD SCHOOL OF PHILOSOPHY AND LITERATURE. Throughout this period she also maintained her commitment to education reform, as well as working on behalf of native American rights; in particular she assisted Paiute leader Sarah Winnemucca in arranging lecture dates and published several reports by Winnemucca on the conditions of Indian life. Even with old age Peabody's memory remained sharp, and she was considered by many to be a fount of information about her famous friends and colleagues of the early Transcendentalist movement. In 1880 she finally published a memoir of her mentor, *Reminiscences of Rev. Wm. Ellery Channing.* Like other Transcendentalists, Elizabeth Palmer Peabody's interests and writings were wide-ranging, encompassing a variety of literary, theological, and reform issues of her day, but her most significant contributions were in educational reform and in approaching all of her subjects through the lens of historical perspective.

Bibliography

Marshall, Megan. *The Peabody Sisters: Three Women Who Ignited American Romanticism.* Boston: Houghton, Mifflin, 2005.

Ronda, Bruce A. *Elizabeth Palmer Peabody, A Reformer on Her Own Terms.* Cambridge, Mass.: Harvard University Press, 1999.

perfectionism

Like many of their early 19th-century contemporaries, the Transcendentalists believed in the possibility of human perfection, or perfectionism, as a guiding theory behind religious and social reform movements in the United States. The Transcendentalist emphasis on the development of the individual's full potential, and their optimistic belief in the forward progress of human society, corresponded with the idea that human beings themselves could reach moral and spiritual perfection. The idea of perfectionism had its basis in New Testament of the Bible itself, when the apostle Paul designated the work of the church as "for the perfecting of the saints" until all had achieved "the measure of the stature of the fullness of Christ." In the United States perfectionism became widespread during the period of religious revivalism of the 1830s after evangelist Charles Grandison Finney presented an 1837 lecture series on "Christian Perfection." Finney explicitly tied the individual goal of perfectionism with a moral reform impulse to perfect society at large.

For perfectionist reformers, the ultimate human model of perfection was found in the figure of Jesus Christ. For Christians, although Jesus was the divine son of God and thus not subject to human laws and morality, the very purpose of Jesus' existence in the human world was an example of the perfect man.

The Transcendentalists rejected the divinity of Christ but retained Jesus the man as a historical example of the perfected human being, not as the incarnation of God into man, but in secular terms as a moral teacher and guide. The perfect human being was self-sufficient, self-controlled, and guided by a subjective personal morality that nonetheless was motivated out of concern for society at large. Christian Transcendentalists emphasized these aspects of Jesus' character in assessing their own social reform projects. For example, Elizabeth Palmer PEABODY articulated a "Christian socialism" in looking to Jesus' teachings and the example of his life to determine the viability of the communitarian experiment at BROOK FARM as a true path to social perfection. In her essay "A GLIMPSE OF CHRIST'S IDEA OF SOCIETY," Peabody determined that Brook Farm did meet these standards in that social harmony proceeded from the Transcendentalist attention to EDUCATION and individual development. Perfectionism was attained by individuals who strove to be like Jesus or like God, or, in Transcendentalist terms as explained by George RIPLEY, to become "partakers of the Divine nature." In his 1836 *DISCOURSES ON THE PHILOSOPHY OF RELIGION,* Ripley expressed optimism that "man has the power of conceiving of a perfection higher than he has ever reached."

Bibliography

Abzug, Robert H. *Cosmos Crumbling: American Reform and the Religious Imagination.* New York: Oxford University Press, 1994.

Pestalozzi, Johann Heinrich
(1746–1827)

Swiss educational reformer and theorist Johann Heinrich Pestalozzi had an important influence on the educational philosophy of American Transcendentalists such as Amos Bronson ALCOTT and Elizabeth Palmer PEABODY. The Transcendentalists first read of Pestalozzi in the writings of Madame de STAEL and, later, in the *American Journal of Education.* Pestalozzi's ideas spread through the American EDUCATION reform community. Alcott and Peabody were most attracted to his belief in children's innate moral goodness and access to spiritual truths.

Through Pestalozzi, teachers and reformers such as Alcott and Peabody (in their joint work at the TEMPLE SCHOOL in the 1830s, but also in their individual projects and writings), developed a theory of teaching that emphasized self-culture, or individual intellectual growth, as the goal of education, and established alternative methods toward that goal. It was primarily through Bronson Alcott that Pestalozzi's ideas traveled to England through the work of James Pierrepont GREAVES, who founded the ALCOTT HOUSE in 1838 modeled after the Temple School in Massachusetts.

phalanx

Based on the ideas of French utopian socialist Charles Fourier (*see* FOURIERISM), a phalanx was a new model for social organization. Fourierist Americans in the 1830s and 1840s established several phalanxes, or utopian communities, from New York and Ohio to Texas and Massachusetts. BROOK FARM in West Roxbury, Massachusetts, was created in 1841 by Transcendentalist George RIPLEY as an experiment in communal living based on the Transcendentalist ideal of self-sufficiency but converted to an explicitly Fourierist phalanx in 1844.

An ideal phalanx was made up of a specific and equal number of men and women of different ages, character types, and VOCATIONS or talents. The community would be productive and labor would be fair and harmonious by having members rotate among the different work duties according to their interests and individual abilities, or what Fourier called "passions." The idea was that as a group the community had a "unity of interests," which was best realized through promoting individual happiness. The plan was for a scientifically organized community and a rational work schedule that would meet all the labor and economic needs of the ideal society that would, in turn, provide a model for society at large to follow. The basic functioning of the phalanx would be agricultural, with supplemental attention to self-sufficient handcrafts such as textile production and furniture making and, most important for social and economic equality, all land, buildings, and equipment were to be cooperatively owned by all community members. The idea of the phalanx was promoted in various periodicals devoted to the ideas of Charles Fourier, such as THE PRESENT, *The Phalanx*, and Brook Farm's own THE HARBINGER. Although other phalanxes enjoyed moderate successes in the United States, the planned phalanx at Brook Farm was short-lived. After the community adopted plans to convert to a Fourierist phalanx in 1844, construction began on the main building, The Phalanstery, but the building burned down before it was completed, and the community disbanded permanently in 1847.

Bibliography

Guarneri, Carl. *The Utopian Alternative: Fourierism in Nineteenth Century America.* Ithaca, N.Y.: Cornell University Press, 1991.

Phillips, Wendell
(1811–1884)

Wendell Phillips was one of the most prominent radical abolitionists, supported and admired by both Ralph Waldo EMERSON and Henry David THOREAU. A graduate of Harvard, Phillips allied with William Lloyd GARRISON in the cause of ABOLITIONISM after 1835. As part of the most radical wing of the abolitionist cause, Phillips, like Garrison made as many enemies as friends even within their own movement. Even though Emerson avoided the tactics and organizations of the abolitionists throughout the 1840s, and found Phillips particularly harsh in his presentation, he defended Phillips's right to speak at the CONCORD LYCEUM when more conservative community members thought his appearance would be too controversial. Emerson heard Phillips speak on more than one occasion and eventually warmed to Phillips as he himself became more involved in the cause in the 1850s. He admired Phillips especially as a speaker and determined that he was perhaps "the best generator of eloquence I have met for many a day." Emerson's opinion may have been changed by his wife's interest in both Phillips, whom Lidian EMERSON deemed "the great man of this earth." Henry David Thoreau was more forthcoming in his approval of Phillips, commenting on one of his Concord addresses in *The Liberator* and praising him personally as a man of "freedom and steady wisdom, so rare in the reformer, with which he declared that he was not born to abolish slavery, but to do right." After the Civil War, Wendell Phillips continued to pursue his reform commitments in the WOMEN'S RIGHTS and labor causes.

Bibliography

Bartlett, Irving H. "The Philosopher and the Activist," *New England Quarterly* 62 (June 1989): 280–296.

Stewart, James Brewer. *Wendell Phillips: Liberty's Hero.* Baton Rouge: Louisiana State University Press, 1986.

Philothea, a Romance
Lydia Maria Child
(1836)

Set in Ancient Greece and regarded as the first, and some would say only, Transcendentalist novel, *Philothea* was, in author Lydia Maria CHILD'S own words, a "rise into the ideal," into "the beauty of other worlds," away from "the practical tendencies of the age." The book was in some ways a Transcendentalist response to the rationalist appreciation of ancient Greece represented in Frances Wright's widely popular novel, *A Few Days in Athens*, originally published in 1822 but with several reprinted editions, including one in Boston as late as 1850. For her portrayal of Athenian democracy Child drew instead on influences of English ROMANTICISM, SWEDENBORGIANISM, and NEOPLATONISM as well as the IDEALISM of Transcendentalism in its look backward to ancient Greece for inspiration and influence.

Child's novel also reflected her own dilemma as a female intellectual in the 19th century. In the novel's preface she explicitly stated that in her own dreams she struggled with reconciling the interests, concerns, and persona of "Philothea" with that of the "Frugal Housewife," the title of her domestic manual published in 1829. The text of the story itself played out the Transcendentalist conflict between philosophic idealism and material reality within another specifically feminized dilemma: private versus public roles. This tension was reflected in Child's use of the contrasting characters of the

self-sacrificing Philothea and the intellectual courtesan Aspasia. Despite internal conflicts about her own role as a woman writer, *Philothea* reestablished the literary fame of Lydia Maria Child. The novel was well received within reform circles and particularly among the Transcendentalists.

Bibliography

Cameron, Kenneth, ed. *Philothea, or Plato Against Epicurus: A Novel of the Transcendental Movement in New England, with an Analysis of Background and Meaning for the Community of Emerson and Thoreau.* Hartford, Conn.: Transcendental Books, 1975.

Karcher, Carolyn L. *The First Woman in the Republic: A Cultural Biography of Lydia Maria Child.* Durham, N.C.: Duke University Press, 1994.

phrenology

Phrenology, the science of the brain and human behavior as revealed in the physical structure of the skull, briefly engaged the interest of the American Transcendentalists in the mid-19th century. The science of phrenology was founded by German-born Franz Josef Gall and excitement over phrenology had already spread throughout western and northern Europe by the time Gall's associate, Johann Gaspar Spurzheim, arrived in the United States in the summer of 1832 for a lecture tour. Spurzheim concentrated his efforts in the Boston area where he found enthusiastic audiences but, unfortunately, he died in America only three months after arriving. He had paved the way, however, for the reception of another phrenologist, Scottish philosopher and reformer George Combe, a few years later and the subsequent popular spread of phrenological ideas in the 1830s and 1840s.

George Combe captured the attention of several among the Transcendentalists, most notably Amos Bronson ALCOTT, Ralph Waldo EMERSON, and Theodore PARKER. Combe's *The Constitution of Man*, published in 1829, and his 1837–38 lecture tour in the United States brought the ideas of European phrenologists to an even wider popular audience. Phrenology, as presented by Combe and Spurzheim, appealed to the Transcendentalists because it emphasized self-knowledge and active and systemized inquiry into the relationship between the body and the mind, between nature and oneself.

Both Alcott and Emerson, Combe's most sincere early admirers among the Transcendentalists, eventually lost interest in phrenology after it became increasingly mainstream and "vulgarized," in Emerson's words, through the efforts of American publisher-phrenologists Orson and Lorenzo Fowler. In the end the Transcendentalists rejected the rigid categories of the mind imposed by the phrenological maps of the skull and were unable to reconcile those categories with a belief in the transcendent soul that had primacy over the physical body. Emerson, however, remained intrigued and repeatedly returned to the topic in his published and private writings. One of his earliest responses was in the 1839 essay "Demonology," that discounted the skills of the phrenologists while still holding out the possibility that "a man's fortune may be read . . . in the outlines of the skull." In his later address on "NEW ENGLAND REFORMERS" (1844), Emerson cataloged a whole range of enthusiastic reformers he saw around him, "the adepts at homeopathy, of hydropathy, of mesmerism, of phrenology," most of which he saw as only current fads. Emerson later acknowledged, however, in his "Historic Notes of Life and Letters in New England," the cultural significance of popular enthusiasm for the science, declaring that it was part of a much needed rejection of "too formal science, religion and social life," and that it had contributed to the "sharpness of criticism, an eagerness for reform" that characterized the era.

For a time, at least, however, phrenology provided Bronson Alcott, especially, with an educational model for the scientific study and observation of the human mind. He carefully observed his own children at play and recorded notes on the various strengths and faculties they exercised, using language based on the phrenological model he first encountered through the work of George Combe. James Freeman CLARKE, as well, had attended Spurzheim's lectures while still a student at Harvard and later mentioned Spurzheim's influence in several essays in *Self-Culture* (1890). For those who had

not had the opportunity to hear Spurzheim speak, American editions of his works were readily available, as were critical reviews in early Unitarian and Transcendentalist press. Frederic Henry HEDGE did not see the relevance of phrenology to Transcendentalism in his 1834 review of Spurzheim in the CHRISTIAN EXAMINER, in which he dismissed phrenology as "a branch of the sensual school." Orestes BROWNSON as well wrote on the "Pretensions of Phrenology" as limiting human free will in his 1839 BOSTON QUARTERLY REVIEW.

Phrenology ultimately had a literary and cultural impact beyond the mixed response of Boston Transcendentalism. The language and imagery of phrenology, whether praised or criticized, appears in numerous novels and poetry of the era, in the writings of Nathaniel HAWTHORNE, Herman MELVILLE, Edgar Allan POE, and Walt WHITMAN, among others.

Bibliography

Stern, Madeleine B. *Heads and Headlines: The Phrenological Fowlers.* Norman: University of Oklahoma Press, 1971.

———. "Emerson and Phrenology," *Studies in the American Renaissance* (1984): 213–228.

Tomlinson, Stephen. *Head Masters: Phrenology, Secular Education, and 19th-Century Social Thought.* Tuscaloosa: University of Alabama Press, 2005.

Plato See PLATONISM.

"Plato; or, the Philosopher" See
REPRESENTATIVE MEN.

Platonism

The philosophical tenets of Platonism were among the most significant influences on American Transcendentalism. The Transcendentalists read the writings of the philosopher Plato (427–347 B.C.E.) through 19th-century translations and critical interpretations and were drawn to the comprehensiveness of Plato's worldview. Platonism provided a non-Christian framework for understanding the relationship between the material world and the spiritual world and emphasized the spiritual world as more important—a concept that appealed to Transcendentalists in their critique of the Enlightenment emphasis on empirical evidence gained through the senses. Platonism thus fit within 19th-century ROMANTICISM's rejection of Enlightenment rationalism and the romantic emphasis on the subjective truths of individualism. One of the main premises of Platonism was that evidence from the physical world is, in fact, not reliable or satisfactory as a way to measure and understand "reality."

Unlike later Christian philosophers, Plato lacked a belief in a supreme creator or god and instead focused on humanity, the individual, at the center of the material and spiritual worlds and on intuition as the superior source of knowledge about the self and the universe. The Transcendentalists were attracted to this secular framework for empowering individuals with the ability to find their own route to the universal ideals, or forms, of Goodness, Truth, and Beauty. Plato was one of the earliest philosophers to develop a universal and systematic theory of IDEALISM, which Emerson attempted as well in his own Transcendentalist worldview. The influence of Plato, however modified, is most evident in Emerson's earliest published work, including *NATURE* (1836), with its emphasis on the natural world as manifestations of the universal truths and beauty, and his *ESSAYS: FIRST SERIES* (1841) with its pieces on "THE OVER-SOUL" and the celebration of a spiritual "LOVE." Elsewhere, Emerson considered the Platonic or idealized conceptions of love and beauty in the person of his deceased first wife, Ellen Tucker EMERSON, whom he described as "an Ideal that, if I were a Platonist, I should believe to have been one of the Forms of Beauty in the Universal Mind." Margaret FULLER discussed Platonic love with Emerson and invoked the idea in her 1845 *WOMAN IN THE NINETEENTH CENTURY.* No one more systematically dealt with the impact of Platonism on philosophic thought than Ralph Waldo Emerson and Plato earned a spot as Emerson's representative "Philosopher" in his 1850 text *REPRESENTATIVE MEN.* Regardless of Transcendentalist

or other modifications, Emerson declared Platonism as foundational to all other philosophy, stating that "Out of Plato come all things that are still written and debated among men of thought."

Amos Bronson ALCOTT was probably the Transcendentalist who most consistently and for the longest time relied upon Platonism, as revealed in his journals and CONVERSATIONS. After the Civil War, Alcott visited Plato clubs in his travels to midwestern cities and Alcott espoused the Platonist idea of the material world as only representative or symbolic of higher ideals. Alcott, like other Transcendentalists, also looked to the classical philosophers, both Plato and Socrates, for their model of CONVERSATION as their ideal teaching method for fostering self-development through drawing out the ideas and souls of participant-students. Alcott eventually incorporated many aspects of NEOPLATONISM into his philosophy as well, as did all of the Transcendentalists with their seeking to understand not just the material world, but the spiritual and mental realms as well.

Other Transcendentalists ultimately used Plato's theory of the forms as the basis of a new post-Christian humanist religion. As George RIPLEY explained in a letter to Theodore PARKER, "The Good, the Beautiful, the True is the Holy Trinity which commands the conviction of my intellect and the admiration of my heart . . . The adoption of this faith seems to me to be the turning point of humanity." In expanding upon Plato's ideas to fit within the intellectual and theological contexts and debates of the 19th century, then, the Transcendentalists were ultimately influenced even more by neoplatonism than by Platonism itself. Platonism provided only insight into the ideals, and not into the interconnectedness of those ideals with human life, nature, and the universe, and so they modified Platonism through the more mystical vision offered by neoplatonism. Whereas Platonism focused on defining the ideal forms, neoplatonism looked beyond the forms, which originated in some outward source, to a more mystical realm of experience and gave signal importance to, as Alcott put it, the "Mind and Its Ideas."

Bibliography

Allen, Gay Wilson. *Waldo Emerson: A Biography*. New York: Viking, 1981.

Dahlstrand, Frederick. *Amos Bronson Alcott: An Intellectual Biography*. East Brunswick, N.J.: Associated University Presses, 1982.

"A Plea for Captain John Brown"
Henry David Thoreau
(1859)

Henry David THOREAU published three essays in defense of abolitionist John BROWN, who was tried and executed for raiding the federal arsenal at Harpers Ferry, Virginia. "A Plea for Captain John Brown" was the first of his addresses, followed by "Martyrdom of John Brown" (1859) and "The Last Days of John Brown" (1860). Brown had many supporters among Boston reformers, including the Transcendentalists. Franklin Benjamin SANBORN arranged for Brown to visit CONCORD, MASSACHUSETTS, where he met Thoreau on more than one occasion. Brown was at that time attempting to gather support and financial assistance, although it is unlikely that Thoreau knew ahead of time about the plan to attack Harpers Ferry. After Brown was arrested many Northern abolitionists distanced themselves from any knowledge of Brown and his violent strategy, but Henry David Thoreau continued to publicly support and even praise the fact that Brown at least acted on his convictions. It was Thoreau who called a Concord meeting in October 1859 to discuss Brown's trial. Many opposed the meeting for fear of appearing to ally with Brown, but Thoreau gave his address, "A Plea for Captain John Brown" to a full crowd. He presented the same speech a few nights later at a meeting at Theodore PARKER's Boston church, and one more time within the week in Worcester, Massachusetts, at the request of his friend Harrison Gray Otis BLAKE. The original plan was to print the lecture in pamphlet form and sell it to raise funds "for the benefit of Captain Browns's family." The pamphlet never appeared, but the address was published the following year as part of James REDPATH's collection, *Echoes of Harper's Ferry* (1860).

Henry David Thoreau's series of essays on John Brown were his most politically motivated contributions to ABOLITIONISM, and some scholars have even seen his defense of Brown as uncharacteristic support for explicitly political reform rather than for the individual spiritual reform advanced in his other works. Even the antislavery paper owned by William Lloyd GARRISON, *The Liberator*, was surprised that "the hermit of Concord" had been finally been roused "from his usual state of philosophic indifference, and he spoke with real enthusiasm," which was not an entirely fair assessment given Thoreau's association with and support of radical abolitionists such as Garrison and Wendell PHILLIPS.

While it is true that Thoreau was responding to a specific event and championing a man who resorted to violent martyrdom as a reform strategy, John Brown did act as an individual, outside of the government as well as organized reform. For Thoreau, then, Brown was an example of a man of personal conviction willing to stand up for moral wrongs and was most impressive in his willingness to defy tradition as well as law. In this regard, rather than vilifying and denouncing Brown, Thoreau argued that antislavery advocates should see him as the martyr for their cause, a martyr in the sense that Christ himself was a martyr. Thoreau explicitly made this comparison: "Some eighteen hundred years ago Christ was crucified; this morning, perchance, Captain Brown was hung." In the end, John Brown was, in Henry David Thoreau's words, "a transcendentalist above all, a man of ideas and principles"

Poe, Edgar Allan
(1809–1849)

Author Edgar Allan Poe was one of the most well-published and outspoken critics of Transcendentalism in the 19th century. At the same time, he was a contemporary whose writings reflect many of the Transcendentalists' literary influences. Poe was a scathing critic, and his reviews of the Transcendentalists were filled with his characteristically sharp wit. In a review of Nathaniel HAWTHORNE's *Twice-Told Tales*, Poe wrote that he thought Hawthorne might do better as a writer if he would "come out from the OLD MANSE" and "hang (if possible) the editor of 'The DIAL.'" Here Poe made reference to both the direct and indirect influence of Ralph Waldo EMERSON as the former editor and therefore overseer of Transcendentalist literary production through the movement's journal, the *Dial*, but also a reference to the Hawthorne's stay at the Emerson family home in CONCORD, MASSACHUSETTS, during the writing of *Twice-Told Tales*.

Poe targeted Ralph Waldo Emerson for his own writings as well, not just as the literary center of Transcendentalism in general. Poe critiqued Emersonian Transcendentalism as "obscurity for obscurity's sake" and, at various times, as "metaphor run mad" and a philosophy overly fond of "Carlylisms," a reference to Emerson's friendship and literary promotion of English writer Thomas CARLYLE. Although he decried the philosophical abstractions of such writers, Poe praised others as individuals. He thought Margaret FULLER a capable writer and even adopted similar mystical allusions and IDEALISM as the Transcendentalists in his own writings, such as in the novel *Eureka* and in the essay "The Poetic Principle" (1850).

Although a prolific writer himself, Edgar Allan Poe was based in New York and was thus not part of the New England literary and social scene that defined Transcendentalist Boston and Concord (a region termed by Poe as the "Frogpond") in the 1830s and 1840s. Much of his criticism of the Transcendentalists was lumped together with his anti-Boston sentiments and his different views on social reform and literary culture, views that had little to do with the Transcendentalist writers directly. Poe did not share a passion for reform or an interest in the causes of ABOLITIONISM, WOMEN'S RIGHTS, or other progressive movements that he associated with a New England morality.

Bibliography

Fisher, Benjamin Franklin, ed. *Poe and His Times: The Artist and His Milieu.* Baltimore: Edgar Allan Poe Society, 1990.

Meyers, Jeffrey. *Edgar Allan Poe: His Life and Legacy.* New York: Cooper Square Press, 2000.

Poems
Ralph Waldo Emerson
(1847)

Listed with a publication date of 1847, but actually released on Christmas 1846, *Poems* is the first of only two book-length collections of poetry published by Ralph Waldo EMERSON, the second being *MAY-DAY AND OTHER PIECES*, published in 1867. *Poems* includes 59 of Emerson's most well-known early poems on diverse themes of nature, mythology, love, and reform, including "BACCHUS," "BLIGHT," "CONCORD HYMN," "EACH AND ALL," "GIVE ALL TO LOVE," "HAMATREYA," "THE HUMBLE-BEE," "MERLIN," "ODE, INSCRIBED TO W. H. CHANNING," "THE RHODORA," "SAADI," "THE SNOW-STORM," "THE SPHINX," "THRENODY," and "URIEL." The collection was reviewed by *The Boston Courier* as "one of the most peculiar and original volumes of poetry ever published in the United States." Several of the poems had been published in the Transcendentalist press, either in the *WESTERN MESSENGER* (such as "Each and All" and "The Humble-Bee" in February 1839 and "The Rhodora" in July 1839) or the *DIAL* ("The Problem" in the July 1840 issue, "The Sphinx" and "The Snow-Storm" in January 1841, "Saadi" in October 1842, "Blight" in January 1844, and "The Visit" in April 1844).

Emerson's poetry was, in fact, original in that it differed greatly from the most popular American poets of his time, such as William Cullen Bryant, Henry Wadsworth LONGFELLOW, or Edgar Allan POE. Emerson's poems differed in structure and style from these other widely read poets, and critics of Emerson's poetry focused on these differences as well as differences of theme. While Emerson did, in fact, take up similar themes of the natural world and of reform issues as his contemporaries in the age of ROMANTICISM, critics pointed out that Emerson's poems lacked certain conventions of religious language and themes. Even his Transcendentalist colleagues commented upon the lack of religious sentiment in Emerson's poems. Unitarian minister Cyrus BARTOL reviewed *Poems* for the *CHRISTIAN EXAMINER* and noted the absence of Christian principles. Orestes BROWNSON went so far in the *MASSACHUSETTS QUARTERLY REVIEW* as to refer to the poems as "hymns to the devil." While Brownson had by this time dissociated himself from Transcendentalism and had, in fact, converted to Catholicism, such comments had more to do with 19th-century definitions of poetry and provide insight into how even liberal Christians expected religious, and not just spiritual, themes and conventions as the language of poetry. Certainly one could argue that all of Emerson's poetry did address spiritual themes, but from the perspective of the individual and of humanity's relationship to nature, not to God. Even fellow Transcendentalist and *Dial* coeditor Margaret FULLER had her own criticisms of the poetry; she did not specifically call for religious references in poetry, but she did note that Emerson's poems were "mostly philosophical, which is not the truest kind of poetry." Still, Fuller ranked Emerson as a poet, high "in melody, in subtle beauty of thought and expression."

"The Poet"
Ralph Waldo Emerson
(1844)

Ralph Waldo EMERSON's "The Poet" is the first selection in his 1844 collection of *ESSAYS: SECOND SERIES* and serves, in one sense, as an introduction to Emerson himself as a poet and writer. After establishing the purpose and role of "The Poet," Emerson went on to publish his own first book of *POEMS* in 1847. In the essay "The Poet," he had established the idea of the poet as an interpreter of ideas engaged in the process of thinking, not just rhyming, explaining that it is "not metres, but a metre-making argument that makes a poem." "The Poet" is arguably Emerson's most important contribution to American literary criticism and the seminal 19th-century statement on a new poetic aesthetic.

Emerson begins the essay with a call to free poetry from self-styled literary critics whose "knowledge of the fine arts is some study of rule and particulars, or some limited judgment of color or form, which is exercised for amusement or for show." Emerson declares, instead, that "there is no doctrine of forms in our philosophy," that is, in Transcendentalism. Poetry should emerge only

from "the instant dependence of form upon soul," not upon outward "rules and particulars." Emerson's is an organic aesthetic of poetry, that is, the belief that the form (the structure, the rhyme, etc.), as well as the language, of poetry emerges only from "a thought so passionate and alive that, like the spirit of a plant or an animal, it has an architecture of its own, and adorns nature with a new thing." Poetry not only emerges from nature but then also becomes a part of nature, contributing to the beauty of the world. The Poet is not just a writer, one who, in Emerson's terms, might be skilled at making metres. The Poet must be more, the interpreter of nature and of humanity, a creator of "arguments." The Poet exists then as a prophet almost, who therefore must be somewhat removed from the cares of the world, must "know the muse only" and must "lie close hid with nature" in order to be receptive to its message. Poetry exists not so much in the mind of the poet, since, coming from nature directly, "poetry was all written before time was," but it is the Poet's job to translate the language of nature into the language of humanity.

Despite this special role of the Poet, however, in the essay Emerson rejected the idea of "the fine arts," promoting instead a more democratic vision of access to poetry. "The poet is representative" and must speak to all people and thus must be a most humble and humane person himself. This idea of a "representative" American poet later inspired Walt WHITMAN to imagine that he was such a poet as Ralph Waldo Emerson described. Emerson may or may not have seen Whitman as the embodiment of this ideal, but Emerson did make a call for a distinctly American contribution to poetry, which Whitman certainly offered. Interestingly, however, when he looked for his ideal poet for the 1850 collection of essays, *REPRESENTATIVE MEN*, Emerson did not find his example from America's many emerging poets, but reached further back to hold up William SHAKESPEARE as representative of the poetic genius. Shakespeare was the model poet based on his universal genius, his ability to speak to each new generation through detailing experiences common to all humanity. In Emerson's view, Shakespeare was the example of a Poet who was able to transcend his own time and place and speak to the larger realm of human experience; a master not only of words, but also of thought and experience, was Emerson's ideal Poet.

"Politics"
Ralph Waldo Emerson
(1844)

Ralph Waldo EMERSON's "Politics" was included in the 1844 collection ESSAYS: SECOND SERIES. While the previous essays in the anthology, and in the earlier 1841 volume, ESSAYS: FIRST SERIES as well, dealt with the broad themes of Transcendentalism, the essay on "Politics" represented a shift to the more practical application of that philosophy. The primary theme of "Politics" is the relationship of the individual to the institutions that govern society, and the subsequent need to protect individuals from the unchecked power of such institutions. Emerson's challenge to institutional authority was espoused in other essays and lectures, such as the rejection of the theological authority of the church and of even the Bible in the DIVINITY SCHOOL ADDRESS, and the self-reliance outside the university as promoted in "THE AMERICAN SCHOLAR." "Politics" continued along this theme but, like the work of Henry David THOREAU and others, examined the more complex relation of humans to politics and the law, institutions that might restrain, but that also can be reformed.

Emerson urged his readers, first of all, to recognize that such institutions as "the law" are entirely human-created and specific to a time and place, merely "man's expedient to meet a particular case," and therefore can be changed or even dismantled by man since the system is only "a rope of sand which perishes in the twisting," but the "young and foolish" cannot rush into altering the law or the government. In one sense, Emerson is quite conservative in that he upholds the thinking of his time regarding the purpose and desirability of government—primarily, for the protection of private property. Regardless of what reformers might do, he shifted from emphasizing the law as "man's expedient" to identifying a "higher law" which dictated that "the property will, year after year, write every statute that respects property."

The "higher law" is one that develops naturally from the needs of any given society, and for Emerson the protection of property was the primary need of the United States in the mid-19th century. Emerson's views may seem somewhat conservative in light of more radical socialist options being articulated during his own time, such as the rejection of the idea of private property at the utopian communities of BROOK FARM or FRUITLANDS.

In criticizing those who might be "defensive of property," however, Emerson turned his critique to the larger political system and, in particular, to the system of political parties that defined American national politics. Emerson did not support either party but, instead, pointed out the threats that parties, in general, posed to democracy and to individuals. Parties themselves take on the worst characteristics of individuals, as they tend only to "degenerate into personalities." Both conservative and progressive parties were prone to these faults: "A party is perpetually corrupted by personality. . . . They reap the rewards of the docility and zeal of the masses which they direct. Ordinarily, our parties are parties of circumstance, and not of principle . . . parties which are identical in their moral character, and which can easily change ground with each other, in the support of many of their measures." Unfortunately, "From neither party, when in power, has the world any benefit to expect in science, art, or humanity, at all commensurate with the resources of the nation," since "The spirit of our American radicalism is destructive and aimless . . . not loving." Still, Emerson retained some hope for the United States and did not "despair of our republic," but, instead, he believed that there was a higher law that would shine through and that his readers should "trust infinitely to the beneficent necessity which shines through all laws."

In favor of the view that Ralph Waldo Emerson's essay on "Politics" was radical for its time are certain passages that would be echoed a few years later in the writings of his colleague, Henry David Thoreau. Thoreau became known for his resistance to the government and the arbitrary laws of humankind, specifically as articulated in his most famous essay, "CIVIL DISOBEDIENCE," first published in 1849. Writing in 1841, Emerson presaged Thoreau's indictment that "Every actual State is corrupt. Good men must not obey the laws too well." And, like Thoreau, Emerson held that through it all the individual "good men" must rise above a system which risked infringing on individual liberties and freedom: "Hence the less government we have the better,—the fewer laws, and the less confided power." The ultimate solution to the potential abuse and inherent shortcomings of the political system was the self-government of the individual within that system.

By the time Ralph Waldo Emerson published "Politics," he was becoming more interested in applying Transcendentalist philosophical frameworks to the pressing social and political issues of his day, most notably, ABOLITIONISM. In the 1840s he increasingly moved toward a more public stance against slavery in the United States. In this context, his analysis of the American political system is evidence of his interest in a more practical Transcendentalism that could make a contribution to the radical reform conversations. His primary goal was to retain a commitment to the idea that individual conscience should rise above the mundane context of party politics and majority rule. In this sense, Emerson offered not so much practical solutions to specific problems but a model for engagement within the political system.

Powers, Hiram
(1805–1873)

American sculptor Hiram Powers established a studio in Florence, Italy, that served as a base for American intellectuals and artists traveling abroad, including his friends among the Transcendentalists. He was especially close with Margaret FULLER, Nathaniel HAWTHORNE, and Sophia Peabody HAWTHORNE, and with English writers Robert and Elizabeth Barrett Browning and Charles Dickens. Powers was therefore an important figure for Transcendentalists in that he helped facilitate a transatlantic intellectual culture by introducing his American friends to European artists and thinkers.

Hiram Powers established his early reputation in Washington, D.C., in the 1830s, where he sculpted busts of such prominent political figures as John C. Calhoun, Andrew Jackson, and Daniel WEBSTER. His statues of Thomas Jefferson and Benjamin Franklin remain in the U.S. Capitol building today. In 1837 Powers left America for Italy to pursue a more serious independent art career. His 1843 marble sculpture, *Greek Slave*, was his greatest achievement and established him as the preeminent 19th-century classical sculptor.

Bibliography

Colbert, Charles. *A Measure of Perfection: Phrenology and the Fine Arts in America.* Chapel Hill: University of North Carolina Press, 1997.

Wunder, Richard P. *Hiram Powers: Vermont Sculptor, 1805–1873.* Cranbury, N.J.: Associated University Presses, 1991.

pragmatism

Pragmatism was a distinctly American philosophy that emerged in the 1870s as a direct response to but also a critique of the Transcendentalism of the previous generation. The primary American proponents of pragmatism in the late 19th and early 20th centuries were William JAMES and John Dewey. Like Transcendentalism, pragmatism insisted on the consideration of subjective experience in determining philosophical and moral truths, and therefore the belief that any such truths were influenced by a particular perspective, and thus subject to change. Pragmatists accepted that truth and knowledge were only temporary, compared to the Transcendentalist emphasis on truths as perpetually and universally applicable to humanity throughout time. Unlike Transcendentalism, pragmatism rejected the idea of any universal truth outside of but influencing human experience, such as the Transcendentalist idea of the OVER-SOUL. Thus influenced by and responding to the Transcendentalism of Ralph Waldo EMERSON and others, William James's philosophy of pragmatism was ultimately less speculative and insisted instead that any philosophical or moral theories be subjected to the methods of scientific investigation; that is, that truths themselves are determined as such by virtue of having some practical or "pragmatic" application. Although the philosophy was at its height between the 1890s and

1930s, pragmatism remains a relevant mode of philosophical inquiry to this day.

Bibliography

Robinson, David. *Emerson and the Conduct of Life: Pragmatism and Ethical Purpose in the Later Work.* New York: Cambridge University Press, 1993.

Pratt, Minot
(1805–1878)

Naturalist Minot Pratt was one of the original members and shareholders of the Transcendentalist-inspired utopian experiment at BROOK FARM. He lived there with his wife and three children who were born there between the founding of the community in 1841 and his departure in 1845. During that time Pratt was consulted by founder George RIPLEY on a range of matters related to running the farm and officially served, at various times, as a director of agriculture and as a trustee of the community. According to reports and memoirs by fellow members, Pratt was one of the most valued participants for his farming and management skills. He reluctantly left the community as his own family was growing and moved to CONCORD, MASSACHUSETTS, where he pursued his studies of local plant life, culminating in the publication of his "Flora of Concord."

The Present
(1843–1844)

Transcendentalist social reformer William Henry CHANNING established the short-lived literary journal, *The Present,* in 1843. Only seven issues were printed out of Channing's base in New York between September 1843 and April 1844. At the time of its publication Henry Channing was also a regular contributor to the primary journal of literary-philosophical Transcendentalism, the DIAL, but he sought an alternative forum for his more reform-minded emphasis. The *Dial* review of *The Present* in January 1844 declared it a "valiant and vivacious journal." In the inaugural issue of *The Present* Channing indicated that the paper would "reflects

the Signs of the Times" in its discussion of "the various questions of Reform which are now interesting our communities." Channing's commitment to reform is seen in the paper's connections, in particular, with the utopian experiments at BROOK FARM and FRUITLANDS and with Channing's promotion of *The Phalanx,* the official paper of American FOURIERISM. *The Present* also announced conventions of social reform organizations and reviewed books by and of interest to those involved in various associationist communities. Both Amos Bronson ALCOTT and Charles LANE, founders of Fruitlands, contributed pieces to *The Present.* *The Present* also emphasized writings by French socialists directly, not just American disciples—translations of writings by Pierre Leroux and Victor Considerant were among the most notable. Other Transcendentalists who published in *The Present* were Christopher Pearse CRANCH, Thomas Wentworth HIGGINSON, William Ellery CHANNING, and Margaret FULLER.

Bibliography

Gohdes, Clarence L. F. *The Periodicals of American Transcendentalism.* Durham, N.C.: Duke University Press, 1931.

The Progress of Religious Ideas, Through Successive Ages
Lydia Maria Child
(1855)

Lydia Maria CHILD's *The Progress of Religious Ideas, Through Successive Ages* was a product of Transcendentalist interest in comparative religious studies that eventually led to the creation of the FREE RELIGIOUS ASSOCIATION in 1867. *The Progress of Religious Ideas* was a three-volume study of all the major religions of the world since ancient times—Hinduism, Buddhism, Jainism, Confucianism, Taoism, and Zoroastrianism; Egyptian, Chaldaic, Greco-Roman, and Celtic myths and cults; Judaism, Christianity, and Islam. Child's stated purpose was, through "complete impartiality," to demonstrate "the beauties and blemishes" of each religion "as it appeared to those who sincerely believed it to be of divine origin." The free religious impulse was not merely a scholarly interest in comparative cultures, however, but an attempt to promote acceptance for religious diversity by understanding humanity's universal quest for meaning and spirituality. Child explicitly explained this project in the preface to her work: "I wished to show that theology is not religion; with the hope that I might break down partition walls."

Few of her fellow 19th-century Americans were ready for the idea of equal consideration of a diversity of religious views, and members of the clergy especially denounced her work. Child's *Progress of Religious Ideas* depended upon the work of biblical critics who, as the Transcendentalists had discovered, took the focus off of Christianity as the only possible source of spiritual revelation and inspiration, so that even liberal Reviewers criticized her work as having "too great prejudice against the sacred Books of Christians." Comparative religious study was a radical departure from traditional theological study, but Lydia Maria Child was still a product of her own time in that she tended to measure other religions and cultures up against the Protestant Christianity of 19th-century America, which, in her mind, was itself the symbol of "progress." Child's purpose was not only theology, however, and as an active reformer engaged in a variety of political issues, most notably ABOLITIONISM, she also made note of not just different spiritual beliefs but social issues of slavery and WOMEN'S RIGHTS as dealt with in other cultures and throughout history. Religious and social radicals, therefore, such as her Transcendentalist colleague and minister Theodore PARKER, praised her effort as "*the* book of the age; and written by a *woman!*"

Lydia Maria Child's *The Progress of Religious Ideas, Through Successive Ages* was the first systematic study of comparative religion in the United States. Throughout the decades following its publication, other Transcendentalists and members of the Free Religious Association researched and published on the topic. Cyrus BARTOL, James Freeman CLARKE, and Octavius Brooks FROTHINGHAM all published on comparative and universal theology, and Child responded to such works as an established authority. When Clarke published his book on *Ten Great Religions: An Essay in Comparative Theology* in 1871, Child criticized him for not

fully acknowledging the interrelatedness of those various religions, in particular what Christianity had borrowed from other religions, such as Buddhism and Hinduism. She followed up on such radical ideas she had first explored in *The Progress of Religious Ideas* with articles in the ATLANTIC MONTHLY.

Bibliography

Karcher, Carolyn L. *First Lady of the Republic: A Cultural Biography of Lydia Maria Child.* Durham, N.C.: Duke University Press, 1994.

———, ed. *A Lydia Maria Child Reader.* Durham, N.C.: Duke University Press, 1997.

Puritanism

Puritanism was the religion of the English settlers of the Massachusetts Bay Colony in the 17th century and the foundation of a New England cultural and intellectual tradition that was important in the development of 19th-century intellectual culture, in particular the emergence of Transcendentalism. Puritanism gets its name from its inception in the 16th century as a religious and political reform movement interested in "purifying" the Church of England of its Catholic influences. It emerged, therefore, as part of the Protestant Reformation theology of John Calvin and was based on Calvinist doctrines such as the belief in innate human depravity, the power of God's grace over human will, and predestination, or the belief that God had already determined who was saved and who was not. Calvinism remained the dominant American theology through the mid-18th century when these tenets met challenges from new religious sects and more emotional and less rationalistic modes of religious practice in the so-called Great Awakening period of religious revivalism. The Puritan legacy of American Calvinism was finally challenged directly in the early 19th century by UNITARIANISM, which emphasized the role of the individual, free will, and self-culture in spiritual growth and salvation.

As a response to and, in some cases, rejection of New England Unitarianism, Transcendentalism represented the last break with the Puritan theological legacy, although the cultural and historical connection to Puritanism remained central to the identity of Boston's BRAHMIN class. The Puritans placed a high value on EDUCATION and had established the first American college, HARVARD DIVINITY SCHOOL, in 1636, initially concerned with the education of ministers but quickly becoming a general college for any boys who wished for an education beyond grammar school. As colonists, the Puritans were concerned about the long-term survival of their community and their ideals, and they recognized the role that education played in carrying out their mission. The legacy of the Puritan education system continued to dominate a Harvard education through the early 19th century.

While Transcendentalist philosophy of the 19th century seemed to be an extreme move away from earlier Puritanism, it owed much to certain aspects of Puritan thought, in particular the emphasis on the development of the individual soul. The Puritan belief in predestination meant that one could not work to secure one's own salvation, so one's main purpose was to live a moral life and prepare oneself, mentally and emotionally, to receive God's grace, should you be chosen. This "preparation for grace" translated into the Unitarian emphasis on SELF-CULTURE, as preached by the Reverend William CHANNING in the early 19th century. Channing's self-culture, with its emphasis on formal education as well as self-knowledge, was then taken up by Ralph Waldo EMERSON in Transcendentalism's more explicit emphasis on the cultivation of the individual for the sake of individual growth and human progress, rather than for the theological purpose of pleasing God or securing salvation.

The Puritan problem of dissent was just as influential and interesting to 19th-century theologians and writers as core Puritan beliefs. In the 17th century, dissent within Puritanism took the form of ANTINOMIANISM, which meant "anti-law" and referred to the belief, articulated by dissenters such as Anne HUTCHINSON, that God's law was more important than human law. Antinomianism thus posed a threat to the authority of the church and to social order. In the 19th century, Transcendentalists, in their rejection of orthodox Christianity, were charged with and even sometimes embraced the tradition of antinomianism. The Transcendentalists explicitly rejected the laws of institutional and biblical authority in favor of a higher spiritual law of individual conscience and subjective experience. Ralph Waldo Emerson acknowledged in his 1841 lecture that "THE TRANSCENDENTALIST" "easily incurs the charge of antinomianism by his avowal that he, who has the Lawgiver, may with safety not only neglect, but even contravene every written commandment." In using a term that referenced Puritanism and its dissenters. Emerson and other Transcendentalists explicitly drew upon the Puritan tradition in coming to terms with not only their history, but their own philosophical leanings. In his 1836 NATURE, which serves as one of the defining texts of the beginning of the Transcendentalist movement, Emerson assessed his contemporary times by stating that "Our age is retrospective. It builds the sepulchers of the fathers."

While Transcendentalism was a rejection of the religion and rules of "the fathers," as Emerson noted, it also built upon and was influenced by history and tradition. Ironically, then, while the 19th-century heirs of New England religious life rejected so much of that tradition, even much of Christianity itself, they looked to the Puritans for inspiration, primarily as dissenters. In "The Transcendentalist," Emerson made the explicit historical connection between 17th-century Puritans and 19th-century Transcendentalists when he explained that "this way of thinking," that is the spirit of dissent and antinomianism, when "falling on popish times made protestants and ascetic monks . . . on prelatical times, made Puritans and Quakers; and falling on Unitarian and commercial times, makes the peculiar shades of IDEALISM which we know."

Although many of the Transcendentalists were Boston Brahmins, claiming genealogical or historical ties to the New England Puritan founders, Ralph Waldo Emerson, in particular, was the descendant of several generations of ministers and of Peter Bulkeley, one of the original founders of CONCORD, MASSACHUSETTS. This familial connection not only tied Emerson himself to Concord, a town with which he also became associated, but made a tie that he acknowledged and grappled with in literary terms in poems such as "HAMATREYA," which named Bulkeley specifically.

Beyond just the Transcendentalists, many of the most revered distinctly American writers and thinkers of the 19th century were New Englanders whose writings dealt with, in some way, coming to terms with the Puritan past. Writers such as James Fenimore Cooper, Nathaniel HAWTHORNE, and Catherine Maria Sedgwick, to name just a few, explored themes such as individualism, self-reliance, the frontier, and American exceptionalism and nationalism, by addressing the historical legacy of Calvinism and the usefulness of religious orthodoxy in general. Hawthorne as well grappled with the legacy of sin, heresy, and punishment in his own Puritan ancestry through the themes and characters in the novel *THE SCARLET LETTER* (1850).

Beyond their literary interests, 19th-century reformers drew on the Puritan legacy for ideas about an idealized community life that would serve as an example to the rest of society. The New England Puritans envisioned their own colonial experiment as a "city on a hill," serving as an example for the world below. In the 19th century, utopian reformers incorporated scientific methods and critiques of contemporary social and economic life and created a variety of utopian communities, both religious and secular, such as BROOK FARM, motivated directly by Transcendentalist ideals, Amos Bronson ALCOTT's FRUITLANDS, the Shakers, and the Mormons.

Bibliography

Lang, Amy Schrager. *Prophetic Woman: Anne Hutchinson and the Problem of Dissent in the Literature of New England.* Berkeley: University of California, 1987.

Miller, Perry. *Errand into the Wilderness.* Cambridge, Mass.: Harvard University Press, 1956.

Putnam's Monthly Magazine

Putnam's Monthly Magazine of American Literature, Science, Art was started and ended in three different time periods, the first series of 1853 through 1857 being the most relevant for the Transcendentalists. *Putnam's* was one of the most important literary magazines of the 1850s and its founding coeditors included George William CURTIS and Parke GODWIN. Although the magazine was based out of New York, it encompassed much of American literary culture of the time and included several New England Transcendentalists as contributors. Excerpts of both *An Excursion to Canada* and *CAPE COD* by Henry David THOREAU were anonymously serialized in 1853 and 1855, respectively. George William Curtis took issue with several passages in Thoreau's writings, however—what he termed Thoreau's "heresies"—and his editorial licenses caused a rift between him and Thoreau that resulted in suspension of the serialization plans and only portions of these works appearing in the magazine. Writing by James Russell LOWELL, Charles Eliot NORTON, George RIPLEY, and others appeared in its pages as well. While the paper was best known for its publication of original literary pieces as well as reviews and criticism, it also published political commentary, including a strong editorial stance toward ABOLITIONISM, and pieces on travel, nature, and even urban architecture. In fact a young Frederick Law Olmsted, later renowned as a landscape architect and designer of New York's Central Park, served at one time during this period as a managing editor at *Putnam's*. The original magazine financially folded in 1857, and George William Curtis attempted unsuccessfully to keep the magazine afloat by taking personal responsibility for many of its debts. Publisher George Putnam and his son later reestablished the magazine bearing their name for a stint between 1868 and 1870 and again between 1906 and 1910.

Q

Quakerism

Quakerism was a Protestant Christian sect founded in England in the mid-17th century by George Fox, and it had a direct effect on Ralph Waldo EMERSON's development of a Transcendentalist spiritual ethic. The foundation of Quaker belief is the idea of an "inner light" within each individual, which is an unmediated access to God or the divine, without outward intervention by the church, its clergy, or doctrines. Also known as the Society of Friends, a name drawn from originally calling themselves "Friends of Truth," the name *Quaker* seems to have arisen from both a spiritual and physical aspect of their religious practice—the physical shaking of some adherents as a response to the experience of having God or the Spirit move through them.

The Quaker's foundational belief in spiritual equality, that is, that the Spirit resided in and could speak through any person, translated into a vision of social equality. Quakers resisted human and social forms of inequality and institutional, political, or legal restrictions on individual conscience. In the 18th century, the Quakers became the first religious sect to officially ban slavery, and over the next century Quaker reformers were prominent public spokespeople in the 19th-century movements for ABOLITIONISM and, again due to the belief in spiritual equality, WOMEN'S RIGHTS. The emphasis on an individual relationship to God, the belief in an "inner light" guiding one to right action, meant that many Quaker women

were called as ministers and missionaries. The Quaker reform tradition also appealed to Transcendentalists, and many reformers from both groups worked as colleagues on various issues. Both Ralph Waldo Emerson and Amos Bronson ALCOTT, as well as their wives, Lidian EMERSON and Abigail May ALCOTT, were friends and fellow reformers with Quaker abolitionist and women's rights advocates such as Sarah and Angelina Grimke and Lucretia Mott. So closely linked were their ideas of individualism and social justice that Henry David THOREAU once described a speech of Lucretia Mott's as "Transcendentalism in its mildest form."

Ralph Waldo Emerson read many Quaker histories, admired George Fox, and was heavily influenced in his own early preaching by the idea of a personal "God within," which paralleled the Quaker idea of the "inner light." The inspiration and righteous dissent of Quakerism may have had a part in Emerson's decision to leave the ministry and make his final break with the UNITARIANISM. In 1835 Emerson presented a lecture on George Fox, whom he characterized as a "representative man," an idea he would return to in his 1850 book of that title. In the 1830s, however, Fox, for Emerson, was an example of the ideal form of "religious sentiment," and Emerson mentioned Fox in other contexts as well, such as in NATURE (1836) and in the essay on "THE OVER-SOUL." Transcendentalism ultimately went much further than Quakerism, however, and the similarities were more philosophical than theological. As Octavius Brooks FROTHINGHAM pointed out in his 1876 *TRANSCENDENTALISM IN NEW ENGLAND: A HISTORY,* the Quaker inner light was supernatural, while the Emersonian Transcendentalist idea was more humanist, a striving for the God within as part of human nature, not separate from it. While the Quakers believed that God spoke the truth through humans, if humans would only open themselves up to receiving God's message, Emerson's point was that "We are all discerners of spirits."

Still, if asked to choose, Emerson seems to have identified more with the Quakers than any other Christian group of his times, declaring that, spiritually speaking at least, "If I am anything, I am a Quaker."

Bibliography
Irie, Yukio. *Emerson and Quakerism.* Tokyo: Kenkyusha, 1967.

R

Radical Club

The Radical Club was a Boston social group founded by Unitarian minister Cyrus BARTOL in 1867 as an offshoot of the FREE RELIGIOUS ASSOCIATION (FRA). Both the FRA and the Radical Club attracted many of the Transcendentalists in the post-Civil War period, and attendees and speakers at Radical Club monthly meetings included a mix of both older and younger generation Transcendentalists, including Amos Bronson ALCOTT, James Freeman CLARKE, Christopher Pearse CRANCH, Ralph Waldo EMERSON, Frederic Henry HEDGE, Thomas Wentworth HIGGINSON, Julia Ward HOWE, Elizabeth Palmer PEABODY, and David WASSON, among others. While the FRA was made up of former Unitarians who had broken off from the denomination and embraced the search for a free or universal human religious experience, the Radical Club was open to both radicals and more mainstream Unitarians interested in open debate and discussion. Club proceedings were sometimes reported in the NEW YORK TRIBUNE. Peaceful debate was difficult to sustain, however, given public criticism of the club and the diverse denominational affiliations of members, and the club disbanded in 1880.

Bibliography

Gabriel, Ralph Henry. *The Course of American Democratic Thought.* Westport, Conn.: Greenwood Press, 1986.

"Rappaccini's Daughter"
Nathaniel Hawthorne
(1846)

First published in 1844 in the *Democratic Review*, Nathaniel HAWTHORNE's short story "Rappaccini's Daughter" appeared in 1846 as part of the collection MOSSES FROM AN OLD MANSE. As in the "The Birth-Mark," another story within the same collection, "Rappaccini's Daughter" addresses darker themes such as the excesses of science, the subversive power of sexuality, and the subordinate position of women within society, all examined through the lens of Transcendentalism which influenced Hawthorne at that time.

The story revolves around one Giovanni Guasconti who lives in an apartment overlooking a garden owned by Dr. Rappaccini. Rappaccini's daughter, Beatrice, tends the flowers and herbs there where Giovanni wonders if he has found an "Eden of the present world." The garden, like the Garden of Eden in the Bible, has one especially intriguing and beautiful but poisonous plant at its center. Only Beatrice can safely tend the plant because her father has exposed her to its poison since her birth, allowing her to form an immunity to its dangers, but her immunity also means that she herself is now poison to any who comes near her. Giovanni receives an antidote to Beatrice from Dr. Rappaccini's rival, Professor Baglioni. Before he can give it to Beatrice, however, so that they may fall in love, Giovanni discovers that he, too, has been poisoned.

Instead of embracing Beatrice now, he turns in rage against her and gives her Baglioni's potion which, in fact, kills her. Dr. Rappaccini supposedly had only wanted to give Beatrice powers beyond that of a "weak woman," but she declares that she would have rather been able to love than to have power. Through Rappaccini, as well as his rival Baglioni, Hawthorne critiques the human costs of the unchecked quest for scientific knowledge. Through the men's treatment of Beatrice—her father in sacrificing her and Giovanni in rejecting her— Hawthorne examines the subordination of women and the paradoxical fear of female power.

Transcendentalist scholars have observed that Hawthorne modeled the character of Beatrice on Margaret FULLER, whose power as an intellectual woman presented a "mystery" and paradox to him as well. Hawthorne had an especially close and ambivalent relationship with Fuller during his stay at the OLD MANSE in CONCORD, MASSACHUSETTS, the town itself an Eden of knowledge for Hawthorne. Through their conversations, both privately and in print in the form of reviews of each other's works, Fuller challenged Nathaniel Hawthorne to consider not only the powerlessness of women but also the self-centered excesses of male theories of individualism and knowledge—the two major themes of the story. In addition, the competing visions of female and male relationships to nature in the garden— Beatrice's as nurturing, Rappaccini's as intellectually exploitative—can be seen as representative of Hawthorne's complex and ambivalent relationships with the personalities and philosophies of Margaret Fuller and Ralph Waldo EMERSON, respectively.

Bibliography

Mitchell, Thomas. *Hawthorne's Fuller Mystery.* Amherst: University of Massachusetts Press, 1998.

Record of a School
Amos Bronson Alcott
(1835)

Transcendentalist reformer Amos Bronson ALCOTT published notes from his classes with children at his experimental TEMPLE SCHOOL as *Record of a School: Exemplifying the General Principles of Spiritual Culture* in 1835. Alcott opened the Temple School in the fall of 1834 with just 30 students enrolled. After creating controversy within the conventional school system, Alcott planned to use the Temple School as an experiment for his theories of EDUCATION. In particular, he sought to develop the children's souls as much as their minds and hoped, through his example and through children, to eventually reform the larger society. Elizabeth Palmer PEABODY signed on as Alcott's assistant and a fellow teacher at the school and, as part of her duties, she kept detailed notes of daily activities at the school. Her notes of the first year were published in July 1835 as *Record of a School,* an account that provided insight into Alcott's teaching methods, the subjects covered, and his interactions and discussions with the children.

Initial public reaction to Alcott's method was positive, but some critics began to express concern over issues ranging from putting too much pressure on the students to presenting them with potentially blasphemous beliefs about the nature of God and the soul. Alcott was not deterred by these early warnings, however, and remained enthusiastic about his experiment and confident in the support of his students and their parents, as well as his Transcendentalist friends. He began to hold additional Saturday discussion groups, or CONVERSATIONS, with the students specifically on the subject of the Gospels and the moral teachings of Jesus. Elizabeth Peabody also attended these Saturday meetings beginning in the fall of 1835 and again recorded the sessions. If *Record of a School* had raised some early concerns, the publication in 1836 of Peabody's *CONVERSATIONS WITH CHILDREN ON THE GOSPELS* brought enough ridicule and public outcry to bring the Temple School experiment to a close, as the book revealed Alcott speaking with children on such topics as human sexuality and reproduction, and parents quickly withdrew their children.

Bibliography

Dahlstrand, Frederick. *Amos Bronson Alcott: An Intellectual Biography.* East Brunswick, N.J.: Associated University Presses, 1982.

Redpath, James
(1833–1891)

Writer, reformer, and abolitionist James Redpath was connected with the Transcendentalists as a lyceum lecture organizer and participated in the public outcry of many Bostonians over the arrest of radical abolitionist John BROWN. Redpath worked as a writer for the NEW YORK TRIBUNE and had met Brown while reporting in Kansas. He also traveled throughout the South where he witnessed slavery firsthand, and published widely on the topic, including, at one time, promoting a plan for African Americans to be freed and moved to Haiti. Although Redpath was an outspoken advocate of ABOLITIONISM, and more forthrightly advocated violence as a necessary strategy to bring about the end of slavery, he found allies among the Transcendentalists when it came to honoring the martyrdom of John Brown. Redpath was in attendance at the CONCORD, MASSACHUSETTS, meeting called by Henry David THOREAU to show support for Brown on the eve of his execution. Redpath gathered together the addresses given on Brown's behalf, including Thoreau's "A PLEA FOR CAPTAIN JOHN BROWN" into the 1860 collection *Echoes of Harper's Ferry*. Other Transcendentalists who appeared in Redpath's volume were Ralph Waldo EMERSON ("John Brown"), James Freeman CLARKE ("Causes and Consequences of the Affair at Harper's Ferry"), and William Henry FURNESS ("Bunker Hill and Harper's Ferry were both Failures"). Redpath turned to Henry David Thoreau again for contribution to a biography, *The Public Life of Captain John Brown* (1860), a book he dedicated to his colleagues in remembering Brown's life and contribution: Emerson, Thoreau, and radical abolitionist Wendell PHILLIPS.

After the Civil War, James Redpath continued to commit his time and energy to helping the former slaves, through establishing social services such as schools and an orphan asylum. In Boston Redpath worked as the organizer of the Lyceum Bureau (the name of which was eventually changed to the Redpath Lyceum Bureau), where he arranged lectures by Ralph Waldo Emerson, Horace GREELEY, Julia Ward HOWE, and others. In 1886–87 Redpath edited the NORTH AMERICAN REVIEW, where many of his writer-colleagues were also published.

Bibliography

Horner, Charles F. *The Life of James Redpath and the Development of the Modern Lyceum.* New York: Barse and Hopkins, 1926.

Reed, Sampson
(1800–1880)

Sampson Reed was the foremost American promoter of the philosophy of Emanuel Swedenborg and, as the founder of NEW JERUSALEM MAGAZINE, was the chief communicator of Swedenborg's ideas to Transcendentalists such as Ralph Waldo EMERSON. Reed had been interested in Swedenborg early on as a teenager and had, in fact, been acquainted with Emerson while both young men were students at Harvard. Thus, before Reed even founded *New Jerusalem Magazine,* Emerson had been exposed to Reed's early writings on the subject, such as his 1821 "Oration on Genius" and the 1826 book *Observations on the Growth of the Mind.* In 1827 Reed was one of the founders of the *New Jerusalem Magazine* (1827–93), the forum for his own ideas for the rest of his life as the magazine outlived Reed by several years.

Reed's writing on SWEDENBORGIANISM, in his books and in the *New Jerusalem Magazine,* was the source for many Transcendentalist ideas and a particular influence on Emerson. Reed discussed themes such as nature's relationship to man through the idea of "correspondences" which detailed the connections between the natural and spiritual worlds. These ideas and others were rearticulated by Emerson in his earliest writings, including NATURE published in 1836. Sampson Reed himself, however, did not identify as a Transcendentalist, as he thought the philosophy of Emerson and others went too far in asserting the self-determination of genius and thought rather than an emphasis on the more Swedenborgian belief in genius as a result of man's opening up to or "reception" of a divine will rather than pure agency.

Bibliography

Brock, Erland, ed. *Swedenborg and His Influence.* Bryn Athyn, Pa.: Academy of the New Church, 1988.

Representative Men
Ralph Waldo Emerson
(1850)

Representative Men is a collection of six biographical sketches drawn from lectures presented by Ralph Waldo EMERSON in both the United States and England in the late 1840s. Emerson focused on six men as representative of different roles or geniuses throughout history in essays on "Plato; or, the Philosopher," "Swedenborg; or, the Mystic," "Montaigne; or, the Skeptic," "Shakspeare; or, the Poet," "Napoleon; or, the Man of the World," and "Goethe; or, the Writer." The book begins with an important additional essay "On the Uses of Great Men." *Representative Men* was in many ways inspired by English writer Thomas CARLYLE's 1841 book, *On Heroes, Hero Worship and the Heroic in History*, but Emerson had a more democratic vision than his friend and colleague in moving beyond admiring heroic figures for their superhuman roles in history, to seeing even the greatest men as only representative of the best of their ages and every person as capable of such greatness: "Engineer, broker, jurist, physician, moralist, theologian, and every man . . . is a definer and map-maker of the latitudes and longitudes of our condition." Emerson's main point in singling out these representative geniuses was to highlight how they possessed universal qualities common to all humans; that is that "great men" should be admired not for what they accomplished as individuals but for what they inspired in others. What makes men great is not some unique or special capabilities, but the fact that their common abilities, their genius, had been nurtured to their full potential.

Emerson's approach to history, in this and other works (such as he outlined in his 1841 essay on "HISTORY"), was thus biographical, but by biographical he means not just the study of individual biographies, but the study of humanity as a whole and thus of oneself. As he stated in the opening essay of *Representative Men* on "The Uses of Great Men," "The genius of humanity is the real subject whose biography is written in our annals." In the essay on "Goethe," Emerson emphasized that the best way to understand humanity was through in-depth understanding of individual, "representative," figures rather than reading a dry historical account of events: "There must be a man behind the book . . . It makes a great difference to the force of any sentence whether there be a man behind it or no." An interest in biographical details alone, however, was not sufficient, for what must be asked of each hero is insight into the essential question of "How shall we live?" To the extent that the thinkers and writers in each category helped address that question as it related to different aspects of individual "genius," they were chosen as representative.

PLATONISM, for Emerson, "represents the privilege of the intellect, the power, namely, of carrying up every fact to successive platforms," and thus represents the foundation for all other ideas. Perhaps Emerson chose Plato as his first representative man in the series, the first essay, since, according to Emerson, it is "impossible to think, on certain levels, except through him." Plato is representative of the Platonic ideal in each person and of philosophy in all things: "Out of Plato come all things that are still written and debated among men of thought." As he would do in each of the other essays, Emerson also pointed out the shortcomings or failures of Plato as a philosopher, a strategy that enforced Emerson's idea that the men are only representative of what other men are capable of, but were just as susceptible to the limitations of human nature. Emerson's main critique of Plato is that in only describing ideals, Plato did not devise a systematic philosophy, a criticism others, in turn, would make of Ralph Waldo Emerson.

While Plato was the man of ideas, the philosopher, 18th-century thinker Emanuel Swedenborg (*see* SWEDENBORGIANISM) represented for Emerson the relationship between humanity and nature, "The Mystic" who has "access to the secrets and structure of nature by some higher method than by experience." That method is what Emerson, in tradition of "the ancients," calls "ecstacy," or the act of "getting out of their bodies to think." According to Emerson, Swedenborg was able to see through and beyond his own times, to understand and "anticipate" the connection between spiritual and scientific knowledge. Unlike some of the other representative men, however, Swedenborg was so advanced that he was not appreciated in his own times, "uncomprehended by them, and requires a long focal distance to be seen." While Swedenborg's method is praised, his downfall, his "vice," was his reliance upon a Christian framework and "his theological bias thus fatally narrowed his interpretation of nature." In addition, Emerson concludes that his language lacked the beauty to make his ideas accessible and attractive: "In his profuse and accurate imagery is no pleasure, for there is no beauty. We wander forlorn in a lack-lustre landscape."

Of the six essays in *Representative Men*, the chapter on "Montaigne; or, the Skeptic" is perhaps the most well known. Sixteenth-century French essayist Michel Eyquem de Montaigne was one of Emerson's favorite authors, and he recalled in *Representative Men* that when he first read Montaigne's *Essays* (1580), "it seemed to me that I had myself written the book, in some former life, so sincerely it spoke to my thought and experience." Emerson chose no scientists as representative geniuses, and the essay on Montaigne perhaps reveals why: the representative skeptic reminds us "that there is no practical question on which any thing more than an approximate solution can be had." The lesson of Montaigne is to accept nothing at face value but instead test all theories and experiences as they relate to one's own self. Emerson felt that living life with this intelligently critical eye prevented one from being taken in by false ideas. At the same time, the skeptic takes ideas very seriously and therefore builds character and conviction in building up his own self and his own ideas against those around him. Emerson emphasized, however, that while the skeptic is always questioning and adopts a mode "of consideration," this does not mean that his ideas are grounded on "unbelief" or on "universal doubting." On the contrary, the skeptic looks beyond the material basis of belief "in accepting the affirmations of the soul."

Elizabethan poet William SHAKESPEARE was Emerson's representative "Poet." Shakespeare's greatness was "forced onward by the ideas and necessities of his contemporaries." As literary figures, Shakespeare and Goethe were the best examples of translating ideas about the relationship between humanity and nature into words, into poetry and prose that others can benefit from. Shakespeare's lasting influence and his greatness, and therefore the greatness of any poet, "consists in not being original at all," but "in being altogether receptive" of the world around him. Emerson's comments upon Shakespeare's originality as beside the point spoke to 19th-century debates about the authorship of many of Shakespeare's plays, debates that engaged some of his Transcendentalist colleagues during the 1850s (*see* BACON, DELIA). Emerson sought to rise above such questions and established his admiration for Shakespeare as a poet and as "a heart in unison with his time and country," and therefore as a model for his own call in the 19th century for an American poet.

Emerson's interest in the French leader Napoleon Bonaparte may have indeed sparked the idea for this collective biography. Emerson considered Napoleon perhaps the most important person in the 19th century and considered his qualities to be representative of the time: "The history of Bonaparte is the commanding romance of modern times because every reader studies in it his own history." In other words, Napoleon's greatness came not from his being exceptional but for his possessing "the qualities and powers of common men." In that sense, although Napoleon was great for a time, Emerson also used him to point out the frailties of human nature and the transience of earthly or political glory. Like Emerson's other representative men, Napoleon was a "creature of circumstances," born into and responding to a specific time in history. Again, as with the other men chosen for Emerson's collection, Napoleon's faults and limitations are just as important lessons as his greatness. In the end, he was "no hero, in the high sense," doomed by his own "sensual and selfish" nature.

Johann Wolfgang von GOETHE represents "the Writer" who, for Emerson, was representative of humankind's ability to translate the natural and the spiritual into words, making ideas accessible and universal. From Goethe we can learn, according to Emerson, that "We too must write Bibles, to unite again the heavens and the earthly world." Goethe teaches through his creative works and the subjects he has chosen, particularly his creation of *Faust,* that "The secret of genius is to suffer no fiction to exist for us; to realize all that we know; in the high refinement of modern life, in art, in sciences, in books, in men, to exact good faith, reality and a purpose; and first, last, middle and without end, to honor every truth by use."

In each essay, Emerson balanced praise with comments on the limitations of each hero, and thus the limitations within any individual. Each stands alone but all are needed for completeness. For example, Plato's IDEALISM is limited without acknowledgment of the prophetic and spiritual, while, conversely, Swedenborg's mysticism and symbolism are difficult to understand without practical application. It is up to the reader or student of these great men to draw upon the strengths of each, and, in order to be useful as heroes, each "must be related to us, and our life receive from him some promise of explanation." Interestingly, Emerson chose no Americans as representative writers and thinkers. This decision was in line with his feeling expressed elsewhere that America had not yet produced its great poets and writers. The only traditionally military or political "hero" is Napoleon, whom Emerson admires as an "incarnate Democrat" who will be remembered for his "directness of action." Besides Napoleon, however, Emerson's heroes are primarily literary figures drawn from a classic or contemporary European intellectual tradition, most of them with specific influence upon Ralph Waldo Emerson individually and on American Transcendentalism as it developed beginning in the 1830s. The six men chosen by Emerson represented ideas, not solely of their times but, specifically, various aspects of the human intellect or mind and ideals to which each individual could aspire.

"Resistance to Civil Government" *See* "CIVIL DISOBEDIENCE."

"The Rhodora"
Ralph Waldo Emerson
(1847)

Ralph Waldo EMERSON wrote the poem, "The Rhodora," in 1834, and it was first published in his 1847 collection, POEMS. "The Rhodora" is a good example of the influence of English ROMANTICISM on the American Transcendentalists in the poem's reverence for nature and belief in the ability of the individual soul to be touched by the natural world. In the poem, Emerson observes nature and details a Transcendentalist understanding of how, in this case, a vision of this New England native flower inspired his impulse to write a poem: "In May, when sea-winds pierced our solitudes, / I found the fresh Rhodora in the woods." Thus the artist's creativity itself springs from interaction with nature. The middle of the poem, its literal center, provides Emerson's aesthetics of art for the sake of beauty: "Tell them, dear, that if eyes were made for seeing, / Then Beauty is its own excuse for being." Emerson the Transcendentalist sees himself as an individual—as well as all of humankind—reflected in nature. In the last line of the poem nature is a metaphor for humanity's place in the universe. Addressing the flower directly he leaves the reader with the revelation that god created both nature and man out of the same impulse: "The self-same Power that brought me there brought you."

Emerson's relationship with the Rhodora, with nature in general, is contemplative but intellectual; the poem flows along a Transcendentalist philosophical guideline in which inspiration by nature leads to an understanding of nature, and understanding nature leads to a revelation of God's will in placing man in nature for this purpose of receiving wisdom. Henry David THOREAU is more often considered the Transcendentalist's representative nature writer, but in "The Rhodora" and other poems and writings, Ralph Waldo Emerson presents a somewhat different, more cerebral, record of the Transcendentalist interacting with the natural world.

Ripley, Ezra
(1751–1841)

The Reverend Ezra Ripley was the stepgrandfather of Ralph Waldo EMERSON and a conservative minister of the old style against which the Transcendentalists of Emerson's generation rebelled. Emerson never knew his natural grandfather, who died when Emerson's father, William Emerson, was a young child. Ezra Ripley married Ralph Waldo Emerson's grandmother and took over not only raising the family but the grandfather's properties and his ministerial position as well.

Ezra Ripley was, in fact, a member of a middle generation between the Congregationalist orthodoxy of 18th-century PURITANISM still remaining in New England and the split within the church that gave rise to UNITARIANISM in the first decades of the 19th century. Thus, opinions about his place within the history of Unitarianism, and therefore his influence on the Transcendentalists, differ. In Ralph Waldo Emerson's eulogy and reminiscences, published in the ATLANTIC MONTHLY in 1883 as "Ezra Ripley, D.D.," he presented his prominent relative as the last of a dying breed of Calvinists, a man "identified with the ideas and forms of the New England Church, which expired about the same time with him." Others, however, understood Ezra Ripley as an emerging liberal who had rejected Calvinist doctrines in his own church and, although not embracing the name of Unitarianism, opened the way for its challenges.

Regardless, Ezra Ripley was a well-known and highly regarded member of CONCORD, MASSACHUSETTS, religious and social circles, and his influence and legacy were widespread. He was the owner of the OLD MANSE, the house in Concord where Ralph Waldo Emerson had boarded with his grandparents before his marriage, a period during which he composed NATURE (1836) and several of his early Transcendentalist lectures. Author Nathaniel HAWTHORNE also briefly lived at the house where he wrote a collection of short stories, MOSSES FROM AN OLD MANSE. Hawthorne referred to Ripley in this text as a ghost and inspiration dwelling within the house and admired not his theological but his domestic legacy as one who had lovingly tended the grounds and orchard.

Ripley, George
(1802–1880)

George Ripley was one of the central figures of the early Transcendentalist movement as a Unitarian minister, editor, and social reformer and is best remembered as the founder of the utopian community at BROOK FARM in 1841. He was close friends with fellow liberal clergyman Theodore PARKER and had attended Harvard with Ralph Waldo EMERSON who was, in fact, his cousin. Ripley's career and interests, in many ways, followed the trajectory of the development and spread of the Transcendentalist philosophy. He helped spark its early theological debates, spread its literary message, and translate the philosophical ideals into practical reform projects.

Like Ralph Waldo Emerson and Frederic Henry HEDGE, Ripley read voraciously in German literature and philosophy, and he corresponded on the subject with Thomas CARLYLE. Along with Emerson and Hedge, Ripley helped found the TRANSCENDENTAL CLUB as a meeting place to discuss their new ideas. The first gathering of the club was held at Ripley's house, and he was a regular attendee during the four years of its existence. Realizing the need among the Transcendentalists and other English-speaking scholars for a source of information on European writers and thinkers, Ripley embarked on editing a multivolume series of translations of influential French and German works. His SPECIMENS OF FOREIGN STANDARD LITERATURE was published in 14 volumes between 1838 and 1842. Ripley contributed the first two volumes in the series, *Philosophical Miscellanies, Translated from the French of Cousin, Jouffroy, and Benjamin Constant* (Vols. I–II, 1838) and subsequent translations and editorial assistance were provided by other Transcendentalists, including William Henry CHANNING, James Freeman CLARKE, John Sullivan DWIGHT, and Margaret FULLER, among others.

Ripley graduated from HARVARD DIVINITY SCHOOL and was central to the development of a Transcendentalist philosophy in his early radical writings in papers such as the CHRISTIAN EXAMINER and the CHRISTIAN REGISTER, where he served as a co-editor. Two years before Ralph Waldo Emerson's DIVINITY SCHOOL ADDRESS, conservative Unitarian Andrews NORTON had reacted against George Ripley's radicalism by accusing him of liberalism and even atheism, critiques that Norton would soon extend to Transcendentalism in general. Ripley and Norton addressed each other in public debate, first in a series of articles in the pages of the religious press, and then through full-length published defenses of each position. Ripley, like other Transcendentalists trained in liberal UNITARIANISM, preached an intuitive and subjective approach to understanding "Divine Truths," rather than reliance on the Bible, which was only a historical, not divinely inspired, record of early Christianity. Ripley published an 1836 collection of sermons, DIS-COURSES ON THE PHILOSOPHY OF RELIGION. Addressed to Doubters Who Wish to Believe, and Andrews Norton responded directly with Evidences of Genuineness of the Gospels (1837). And although Andrews Norton's subsequent A DISCOURSE ON THE LATEST FORM OF INFIDELITY (1839) was a response to Emerson's Divinity School Address, Norton had formulated his anti-Transcendentalist position in the preceding years through his critique of George Ripley. Ripley, in fact, in his own defense of Emerson and in the tradition of sparring with Norton, responded once more in print with a series of pamphlets titled "The Latest Form of Infidelity" Examined. A Letter to Mr. Andrews Norton (1839).

During this heated period during which the Transcendentalist controversy engaged Boston's religious community, George Ripley and other members of the Transcendental Club were conceiving a plan for the movement's own journal. Ripley was initially intended as the DIAL's first editor, but deciding he was too busy with other projects—most notably editing the Specimens of Foreign Standard Literature series—Margaret Fuller stepped in as editor for the first two years of the journal's existence. Ripley remained involved as the business manager for the Dial and as occasional contributor of book reviews and articles. One of the essays he contributed, "Brownson's Writings," praised the commitment to social reform and progress of his friend Orestes BROWNSON. It was a commitment that Ripley would soon share as his career expanded to include that of utopian reformer.

Ripley's engagement with Transcendentalist ideas and controversy soon strained his relationship with and commitment to the church and he resigned from the ministry in early 1841. He immediately embarked on plans for the creation of a utopian social experiment on a 170-acre farm at West Roxbury, Massachusetts. Ripley envisioned Brook Farm as the practical application of Transcendental IDEALISM, a way to reform society by reforming individuals. At Brook Farm all members would be expected to contribute to both the manual and intellectual labor of the community, ensuring not only that all of the work of this model society would get done but that a balance within each individual would develop as well; as Ripley put it to Emerson in a fall 1840 letter outlining his plan, the goal would be to "combine the thinker and the worker as far as possible in the same individual," and thus create a socialist democracy. At its height, membership at Brook Farm was about 150 people, but Ripley's main goal was for this small community to provide a model that could be implemented within the broader American society.

In 1845 Ripley founded THE HARBINGER, which was ostensibly a journal for news and theoretical pieces related to the community and to American FOURIERISM, but which ultimately provided a forum for many of the Transcendentalists not directly affiliated with Brook Farm, such as Christopher Pearse CRANCH, Thomas Wentworth HIGGINSON, and James Russell LOWELL. The Dial had ceased publication the year before, and many of its writers and contributors turned to The Harbinger with their literary reviews, poetry, and criticism.

George Ripley and his wife, Sophia RIPLEY, founded, directed, and lived at the Brook Farm community until its collapse in 1847, after which time George Ripley had little contact with or interest in the activities of the Transcendentalists. After Brook Farm ended, The Harbinger was moved to New York City where Fourierist Parke GODWIN took over editorship and the Massachusetts-based Transcendentalists had little more to do with the magazine. Ripley remained affiliated with the paper until it folded in 1849. He was invited to join the NEW YORK TRIBUNE as book review editor and chief literary critic, filling the position left open by Margaret Fuller's untimely death in 1850. At the Tribune Ripley embarked on yet another phase of his Transcendentalist career as he became a prominent journalist, critic, and reviewer of nearly every major writer of his day.

George Ripley's contribution to the spread of American literary and cultural knowledge reached its peak with his coeditorship (along with Charles

Anderson DANA) of the immensely popular NEW AMERICAN CYCLOPEDIA: *A Popular Dictionary of General Knowledge,* 16 volumes published between 1858 and 1863. The series also earned Ripley more money than any other project he had undertaken as it was reprinted several times and sold more than one million copies. More importantly, the *Cyclopaedia* continued Ripley's legacy of spreading knowledge across (and thus blurring the lines between) social and economic classes by providing an accessible reference and translating high cultural ideals into practical information for the general reader or citizen.

Bibliography

Crowe, Charles. *George Ripley: Transcendentalist and Utopian Socialist.* Athens: University of Georgia Press, 1967.

Francis, Richard. *Transcendental Utopias: Individual and Community at Brook Farm, Fruitlands, and Walden.* Ithaca, N.Y.: Cornell University Press, 1997.

Ripley, Samuel
(1783–1847)

As Ralph Waldo EMERSON's half uncle Unitarian minister Samuel Ripley was a friend and supporter of many of the Transcendentalists during the height of the controversy of the late 1830s. He was the son of Emerson's paternal grandmother and her second husband, the Reverend Ezra RIPLEY. Samuel Ripley was a minister as well as a schoolteacher who, along with his wife, Sarah Alden Bradford RIPLEY, ran one of the most respected boy's schools in New England. Ralph Waldo Emerson worked as a tutor at the school while a student at Harvard, as did his brothers, and his first sermon was delivered in 1826 at his uncle's congregation in Waltham, Massachusetts.

Samuel Ripley was not a Transcendentalist himself but, due in no small part to his family connections, he retained an open mind about the challenges that Transcendentalism presented to orthodox UNITARIANISM during the 1830s and remained a friend and supporter of many major figures in the movement. After the 1838 controversy surrounding Emerson's DIVINITY SCHOOL ADDRESS many Unitarian ministers refused to allow Emer-

son to preach to their congregations, but Ripley, although he disagreed with and was alarmed by aspects of Emerson's speech, still kept his pulpit open to his nephew. He also allowed Theodore PARKER to continue visiting his congregation after Parker's preaching inspired controversy that led to his being shut out of other Unitarian churches. Similarly, when his cousin, George RIPLEY, was embroiled in the MIRACLES CONTROVERSY in the pages of the Unitarian press, Samuel Ripley came to his defense against fellow minister Andrews NORTON. In 1846 Ezra Ripley returned to his childhood home at the OLD MANSE in CONCORD, MASSACHUSETTS, where he and his wife Sarah regularly hosted and entertained many within the Transcendentalist circle.

Ripley, Sarah Alden Bradford
(1793–1867)

Sarah Alden Bradford Ripley was married to Ralph Waldo EMERSON's half uncle, Unitarian minister Samuel RIPLEY, and was a friend and hostess to many of the Transcendentalists at her homes in Waltham and later in CONCORD, MASSACHUSETTS. Sarah Bradford had been classically educated by her father and studied several languages including Latin, Greek, and German. She and her family were members of William Emerson's (father of Ralph Waldo) congregation in Boston, and Ralph Waldo's aunt, Mary Moody EMERSON was a mentor and guide to the young Sarah. She married into the family in 1818 as the wife of minister and teacher Samuel Ripley, and the two operated a boy's school to prepare young men for Harvard. Sarah not only taught at the school but supervised the education of her younger siblings as well as her own seven children.

Sarah Ripley attended meetings of the TRANSCENDENTAL CLUB when they were hosted at Ralph Waldo Emerson's house, and she was one of the few women to do so. She supported Emerson by attending his lectures and reading his works. She read the same works in English ROMANTICISM and German criticism that influenced the Transcendentalists and also became increasingly theologically skeptical, although she did not ultimately identify as a Transcendentalist herself, finding the philosophy still too mystical for her rational mind.

Bibliography

Goodwin, Joan W. *The Remarkable Mrs. Ripley: The Life of Sarah Alden Bradford Ripley.* Boston: Northeastern University Press, 1998.

Ripley, Sophia Willard Dana
(1803–1861)

With her husband George RIPLEY, Sophia Willard Dana Ripley cofounded and promoted the Transcendentalist-inspired utopian experiment at BROOK FARM (1841–47). Sophia Ripley was born in Boston and as a young woman became a teacher at a school she founded with her mother and sister. Their students included children, both sons and daughters, of many families affiliated with the emerging Transcendentalist movement: the Channings, the Higginsons, the Lowells. Sophia's sister married the famous landscape artist Washington ALLSTON, and in 1837 Sophia married Unitarian minister George Ripley. Sophia Ripley participated in a variety of Transcendentalist activities throughout the 1830s and '40s, including hosting the first meeting of the TRANSCENDENTAL CLUB, which her husband also cofounded, at their home in 1836, making her one of the few women to attend those meetings. It was to Ripley that Margaret FULLER first proposed the idea of her CONVERSATIONS FOR WOMEN, and Sophia became a regular attendee once the meetings commenced in 1839. Several of the meetings of the 1841 season were held at the Ripley home.

Sophia Ripley composed an essay on "WOMAN" as a prompt for one of the conversations, and Margaret Fuller, then editor, published the piece in the Boston-based Transcendentalist literary journal, the DIAL. In "Woman," Ripley argued against restrictions on women's social and intellectual lives, declaring "All adjusting of the whole sex to a sphere is in vain," but rather that "what is individual and peculiar to each" should determine one's sphere. Beyond this essay Sophia Ripley did not pursue a literary career nor participate in the emerging WOMEN'S RIGHTS movement, but the ideas that she was introduced to and developed at the Conversations would echo in the works of her friend Fuller as well as other feminist writers and thinkers. Ripley's essay on "Woman" appeared in the January 1841 issue of the *Dial,* and the July 1841 issue featured two more of her writings, an essay on "Painting and Sculpture" and a "Letter" reporting on what she and her husband had observed upon a visit to a socialist community in Ohio. According to Ralph Waldo EMERSON's journals, he also counted Sophia Ripley a close friend and supporter of the *Dial* who aided him with tasks associated with producing the paper during his turn as editor.

The Ripleys' dual interests in socialist reform and Transcendentalist self-reliance led them to found the Brook Farm Institute of Agriculture and Education in 1841, where Sophia Ripley served as a teacher of history and languages, domestic laborer and manager, and tireless promoter of the experiment. Contemporary accounts never fail to mention Sophia's efforts in keeping the community together, and ensuring its success until she disagreed with her husband's transformation of the community into a PHALANX, a planned community based on the ideas of French utopian socialist, Charles Fourier. The community disbanded in 1847 due to tensions surrounding the shift to FOURIERISM as well as financial difficulties and, finally, a fire that destroyed many of the main buildings. After the demise of Brook Farm the Ripleys dissociated themselves from Boston Transcendentalism by subsequently moving to New York where they struggled financially to recover from Brook Farm-related debts. Sophia worked as a teacher and, in 1847, converted to Catholicism, the religion she followed until her death in 1861.

Bibliography

Myerson, Joel. *The New England Transcendentalists and the Dial: A History of the Magazine and Its Contributors.* London and Toronto: Associated University Presses, 1980.

Raymond, Henrietta Dana. *Sophia Dana Willard Ripley.* Portsmouth, N.H.: Peter E. Randall, 1994.

Robbins, Samuel D.
(1812–1884)

Samuel Robbins was a colleague of many of the major Transcendentalists and published in several of the movement's periodicals, including THE HARBINGER, the WESTERN MESSENGER, and the BOSTON QUARTERLY REVIEW. Robbins attended meetings of the TRANSCENDENTAL CLUB and was friends with Amos Bronson ALCOTT and William Henry CHANNING, who arranged for Robbins to publish in the *Western Messenger*. Channing characterized Robbins as more of a "mystic" than a "philosopher," and Robbins mused in the direct style of Ralph Waldo EMERSON that "the Infinite is in us." The influence went both ways, however, as Robbins's anonymously published article in the April 1838 issue of the *Boston Quarterly Review*, "Thoughts on Unity, Progress, and Government," is believed to have been an influence on Emerson's DIVINITY SCHOOL ADDRESS, delivered later that same year. Like Emerson, Samuel Robbins declared that "Individual minds are the best interpreters of the Divinity" and came to the same radical conclusion that individuals are capable of seeking out knowledge without the intervention of institutions and authorities. He lamented that "truth has been shrouded by the initiated, theology by the priest, nature by the professor," and that this perceived monopoly on knowledge had "frightened young and credulous minds from researching the more profound religion of Humanity, the more glorious science of the soul." A few years later, the January 1841 issue of the DIAL included a review of Robbins's sermon on "The Worship of the Soul." Despite these seemingly obvious rhetorical and literary associations with Emerson's Transcendentalism, Samuel Robbins had little further connection with the movement.

Bibliography

Habich, Robert. *Transcendentalism and the Western Messenger: A History of the Magazine and Its Contributors, 1835–1841.* London and Cranbury, N.J.: Associated University Presses, 1985.

Rogers, Nathaniel Peabody
(1794–1846)

Both Ralph Waldo EMERSON and Henry David THOREAU admired and were influenced by the writings of reformer Nathaniel Peabody Rogers, who worked as a lawyer before becoming editor of the abolitionist paper, the *Herald of Freedom*, the journal of the New Hampshire Anti-Slavery Society. Henry David Thoreau contributed a review of the "Herald of Freedom" in the April 1844 issue of the Transcendentalist journal, the DIAL, and later sent Rogers a copy of Emerson's address on "EMANCIPATION IN THE BRITISH WEST INDIES." Rogers appreciated the attention from the Transcendentalists and saw Thoreau, in particular, as a kindred spirit in the cause of ABOLITIONISM. He was not entirely approving of Emerson's address, however, as Emerson proposed that the U.S. government purchase the freedom of slaves, whereas radical abolitionist Rogers was against any form of compensation to southern slaveholders or any acknowledgment by the government of the institution of slavery. Emerson accepted Rogers's criticism of his own lack of radicalism on the subject and wrote privately in his journal that Rogers "spoke more truly than he knew, perchance, when he recommended an Abolition-Campaign to me. I doubt not, a course of mobs would do me much good."

The *Herald* under the editorship of Nathaniel Peabody Rogers presented a moderate thoughtful view of the slavery issue and won the support and admiration of reformers such as Henry David Thoreau. In his *Dial* review, Thoreau praised the *Herald of Freedom* for "such timely, pure, and unpremeditated expressions of public sentiment, such publicity of genuine indignation and humanity . . . the most generous gifts which a man can make." Rogers eventually adopted a more Emersonian viewpoint that focused on the need for individual reform and turned against antislavery societies themselves, putting himself and his paper at odds with his own former allies and organizational affiliations. In December of 1844 Rogers was ousted from his role as editor of the *Herald*, a move that brought Emerson to Rogers's defense. Rogers died the following year, but Thoreau, for one, had taken

Rogers's message to heart and worked to revise his earlier article on the "Herald of Freedom." Writing after Rogers's death, Thoreau mused that "now there is no one in New England to express the indignation or contempt which may still be felt at any cant or inhumanity." Nathaniel Peabody Rogers's example of radical reform may have ultimately inspired Thoreau's 1849 "Resistance to Civil Government," later published as "CIVIL DISOBEDIENCE," in which he presented his own radical stance against a government that supported slavery.

Bibliography

Gougeon, Len. *Virtue's Hero: Emerson, Antislavery, and Reform.* Athens: University of Georgia Press, 1990.

romanticism

Romanticism is the name given to a literary and artistic impulse of the late 18th and early 19th centuries, emerging first within various European contexts, but becoming one of the major factors in the development of the American Transcendentalist movement beginning in the 1830s. The Transcendentalists drew upon romantic thought in the formulation of an "organic" aesthetic, the foundational Transcendentalist theory that language and art are expressions or translations of nature and that human and universal meaning is to be found in the forms of nature.

Romantic thought emerged in Europe in the aftermath of the French Revolution and incorporated the new political ideals of individualism and natural rights, but it was also a response to and critique of the rationalist methods of Enlightenment thought. Romanticism instead promoted subjective experience and emotional responses over reason and looked to nature for human inspiration and guides to moral life. At the center of the romantic aesthetic was the artist—painter or poet—whose works represented not just individual expression, which was highly valued, but translations of universal themes for all of humanity. The beginning of European romanticism is generally dated to the emergence of English poets such as William BLAKE, William WORDSWORTH, and Samuel Taylor COLERIDGE in the 1790s, poets of individualism,

nature, emotions, and the imagination who worked outside traditional literary forms and structures, and all favorites of the American Transcendentalists a generation later. In Germany romanticism took the form of idealist philosophy more than poetry and produced thinkers such as Immanuel KANT, Johann Wolfgang von GOETHE, August SCHLEGEL, and Friedrich SCHLEGEL, among others, all of whom were translated by and circulated among the American Transcendentalists in the 1820s and 1830s. These works were the source of inspiration for key Transcendentalist ideas about nature and self-culture in the works of Ralph Waldo EMERSON, Henry David THOREAU, and others identified with the American romantic-Transcendentalist aesthetic of the mid-19th century, such as Nathaniel HAWTHORNE and Walt WHITMAN.

Rowse, Samuel Worcester
(1822–1901)

Artist Samuel Worcester Rowse is best known for his portraits of Ralph Waldo EMERSON and Henry David THOREAU, created in the 1850s. Rowse had sketched Thoreau's likeness while boarding with the Thoreau family in CONCORD, MASSACHUSETTS, in the summer of 1854. Thoreau's friends and family admired the portrait, and Sophia THOREAU reported that "His friends all consider it an excellent likeness." The portrait hung in the Thoreau home until 1877, when the house was purchased by Amos Bronson ALCOTT, who donated the drawing to the Concord Free Public Library. Rowse began a portrait of Ralph Waldo Emerson in 1858, which today is displayed at the Emerson home in Concord. The finished portrait was actually Rowse's second attempt at drawing Emerson, the first sketch deemed unsuccessful by Rowse but liked well enough by Emerson's wife, Lidian EMERSON, to have been photographed and given out to other family members. Of the final portrait, Emerson's friend from the ADIRONDACK CLUB artist William Stillman declared Rowse's drawing "the most masterly" depiction of Emerson, accurately portraying Emerson's character, notably "the subtle intelligence mingling with the kindly humor in his face, thoughtful, cordial, philosophic." In 1864 Rowse joined the SATURDAY CLUB, whose members included Emerson and others among the Transcendentalists.

Samuel Rowse was a celebrated and successful artist in his time and was commissioned to do portraits of other literary figures such as Nathaniel HAWTHORNE, Henry Wadsworth LONGFELLOW, and James Russell LOWELL. Although he visited France and England, where he met artist John RUSKIN, Samuel Rowse determined that his best artistic work could be done in the United States: "The proper study of mankind is man, and I can study him and myself better in America than anywhere else."

Bibliography

Cameron, Kenneth Walter. "The Rowse Drawings of the Emersons," *ATQ* 13:2 (winter 1972): 49–52.

Ruskin, John
(1819–1900)

British writer, reformer, philosopher, and artist John Ruskin was perhaps the most important art critic of the 19th century, and his ideas on nature in art directly corresponded to the American Transcendentalist aesthetic of the same time period. Like the American Transcendentalists, Ruskin was immersed in the language of ROMANTICISM and looked to art and the artist's imagination for the revelation of nature's spiritual lessons for human existence. In his major works, *Modern Painters* (1843–46 and 1856–62) and *The Stones of Venice* (1851–53), Ruskin emphasized the role and presence of God in the artist's creations more than the secular Transcendentalists who were interested in the individual's direct relationship to nature. Ruskin's own paintings became popular for a time in the United States in the late 1840s and brought him to the attention of the Transcendentalists.

American artist and colleague of Ralph Waldo EMERSON, William Stillman, sought to directly apply Ruskin's ideas to an American aesthetic of landscape and nature painting, through the journal *The Crayon,* founded by Stillman in 1855.

Ruskin was important to the Transcendentalists' generation for his critical views and theory of the purpose of art and of the role of the artist, but his greatest influence would be on the next generation of American artists, who focused in on the importance of nature in art, as a counterbalance to increasing urbanization and industrialization, at the same time that they moved away from the broader Transcendentalist worldview of nature worship or appreciation. Ruskin, along with American artist William Morris, was instrumental in the emergence of the American Arts and Crafts movement at the end of the 19th century. The Arts and Crafts movement emphasized the use of natural materials, handmade objects, and simple designs in an aesthetic grounded in the idea of the human need for connection to the natural world. The influence of Transcendentalism and of Ruskin's own earlier romanticism remained an integral part of the Arts and Crafts movement, however, as artists continued, into the 20th century, to explicitly associate the aesthetic with the Transcendentalist values of Emerson, Henry David THOREAU, and Walt WHITMAN, in the previous generation. John Ruskin was a tutor and mentor to many artists of his time, teaching art and drawing at the Working Men's College in London for many years before accepting a position as art professor at Oxford, where a school is named after him.

Bibliography

Batchelor, John. *John Ruskin: A Life.* New York: Carroll and Graf, 2000.

Birch, Dinah, ed. *John Ruskin: Selected Writings.* New York: Oxford University Press, 2004.

S

"Saadi"
Ralph Waldo Emerson
(1842)

First published in the Transcendentalist literary magazine, the DIAL (October 1842), and later in POEMS (1847), "Saadi" is Ralph Waldo EMERSON's tribute to the Persian author in whose words he found his own Transcendentalist idea of the role of the poet. Sa'di (Emerson changed the spelling to Saadi) was a 12th-century poet whom Emerson read and commented upon in his journals, where he translated some of Sa'di's most famous poems. In "Saadi" he idealizes and identifies with the poet and his quest for solitude—God himself having "straitly charged him, Sit 'aloof,' "—with only the muse as his companion. Saadi sits outside of the everyday noisiness of human life, even though his role is to understand humanity and to find beauty and inspiration in the ordinary and in nature: "Though there come a million / Wise Saadi dwells alone. / Yet Saadi loved the race of men,—/ No churl immured in cave or den—." Finding solitude within society, then, is not always easy for the poet, however, who must remember to "mind thy rhyme" and "let the great world bustle on / With war and trade, with camp and town." The poet is to let others be concerned about daily cares and worries, while he looks "to the height of mighty Nature" for inspiration: "Yet before the listener's eye / Swims the world in ecstasy, / The forest waves, the morning breaks, / . . . And life pulsates in rock or tree. / . . . Suns rise and set in Saadi's

speech." "Saadi" is one of Emerson's clearest statements on the role and purpose of the poet, a recurring theme explored in other poems and essays as well. Emerson himself called it a "poem on poetical ethics."

"The Sacred Marriage"
Margaret Fuller
(1845)

Margaret FULLER included the poem, "The Sacred Marriage," at the very end of her first book, WOMAN IN THE NINETEENTH CENTURY, published in 1845. She had begun composing the poem in her private journals, where there were several more stanzas to the poem that she did not include in the final version. "The Sacred Marriage" refers to a marriage not between actual men and women, but between the masculine and the feminine within each individual. Fuller's is a vision of an androgynous self as the ideal realization of a complete individual personality and, by extension, a unified humanity. "Twin stars that mutual circle in the heaven, / Two parts for spiritual concord given." "With child-like intellect discerning love, / And mutual action energizing love, / In myriad forms affiliating love." This image of duality and unification represents a balance between the female and the male but also between the inward self and the outward world, a balance that Fuller, especially, struggled with as a woman of genius in a society that offered little acknowledgment and even fewer outlets for women's artistic or professional interests.

The themes of the struggle for unification and for an authentic expression of the female self appeared regularly in Fuller's other writings, such as in the poems, "DOUBLE TRIANGLE, SERPENT AND RAYS" and "To the Face Seen in the Moon," as well as in her full-length writings such as *Woman in the Nineteenth Century*, in which "The Sacred Marriage" appeared. The poem's inclusion at the end of her most significant full-length feminist work had the effect of leaving the reader with a clear understanding of Fuller's vision of the work the book was meant to do; that is, to promote the cultural reform project of recognizing woman as an individual complete self and to erase the artificial distinctions that proscribed masculine and feminine ways of being in a way that kept woman subordinate, both socially and intellectually.

Bibliography

Steele, Jeffrey. *Transfiguring America: Myth, Ideology, and Mourning in Margaret Fuller's Writing.* Columbia: University of Missouri Press, 2001.

St. Louis Philosophical Society   *See* William Torrey HARRIS.

Salt, Henry Stephens
(1851–1939)

English author Henry Salt is best known as the earliest serious biographer of Henry David THOREAU. Salt's *The Life of Henry David Thoreau* (1890) was the first biography to analyze Thoreau's major writings in the context of detailing the Transcendentalist poet–naturalist's life. Although Salt never met Thoreau, who died in 1862, Salt was able to draw upon firsthand correspondences and reminiscences from Thoreau contemporaries and colleagues such as Franklin Benjamin SANBORN and Harrison Gray Otis BLAKE. Salt sought to portray the significance of Thoreau's political philosophy as the foundation of personal practices such as his antiwar stance, his vegetarianism, and his lifestyle of voluntary simplicity and self-reliance. Attempting to counter some of the criticisms of

Thoreau during his own time, Salt argued that "We shall do wisely in taking him just as he is" and astutely looked to Thoreau's own friend, Ralph Waldo EMERSON, as the unfortunate source of many of the unjust portrayals of Thoreau, encouraging readers to "doubt whether Emerson had really gauged his friend's mind as fully as he imagined." Salt was not particularly impressed with Emerson's place in the canon or with the attention to the influence of Transcendentalism on Thoreau. He characterized Thoreau as "an Individualist of the most uncompromising type" but resisted associating Thoreau or his individualism with Emersonian Transcendentalism. Salt held up Thoreau's "sound practical frame of mind" in contrast to the "vague mysticism" of Transcendentalism and anticipated that, especially through WALDEN, "Thoreau's genius will eventually be at least as highly valued as Emerson's" or others among "the Concord group."

Henry Salt's attraction to Henry David Thoreau was in part due to his own socialism, which he saw as aligned with Thoreau's personal and political philosophy against government and capitalism. Before the publication of his biography, Salt published several articles about Thoreau, the first of which appeared in the November 1885 issue of *Justice*, a socialist paper of the Democratic Federation. In this essay Salt declared that, although his hero lived too soon for designation as a Socialist, "Thoreau did a real service to the cause of Socialism by practically demonstrating the truth of Socialist calculations and proving how little labour is sufficient to support mankind."

Henry Salt's biography of Henry David Thoreau never sold well, but it received favorable reviews and was read by Mahatma GANDHI, who was directly influenced by Thoreau's actions and ideas. It was not the only work on Thoreau completed by Salt, however, as he also published several articles and collected editions of Thoreau's works in *Anti-Slavery and Reform Papers* (1890), *Selections from Thoreau* (1895), and *Poems of Nature* (1895), which Salt coedited with Franklin Benjamin Sanborn.

Bibliography

Hendrick, George. *Henry Salt: Humanitarian Reformer and Man of Letters.* Urbana: University of Illinois Press, 1977.

———— et al., eds. *The Life of Henry David Thoreau, by Henry Salt.* Urbana: University of Illinois Press, 2000.

Sanborn, Franklin Benjamin
(1831–1917)

As an editor, journalist, and biographer Franklin Benjamin Sanborn did more than any other contemporary to promote Transcendentalism among the next generation. He was commissioned by Amos Bronson ALCOTT to write a biography, *Amos Bronson Alcott: His Life and Philosophy* (1893), which he coauthored with another Alcott friend, William Torrey HARRIS. He supplemented that work with a second book on Alcott's reform experiments, *Bronson Alcott at Alcott House, England, and Fruitlands, New England (1842–1844),* published in 1908. Sanborn edited the writings of several other Transcendentalists and wrote a biography of Nathaniel HAWTHORNE, two works on Ralph Waldo EMERSON, and three different biographies of Henry David THOREAU. These works were in addition to several editions of Thoreau's collected letters and writings, including a revised and expanded edition of *WALDEN* which reincorporated materials that Thoreau had edited out. Finally, in 1909, Sanborn published his own two-volume memoirs, *Recollections of Seventy Years,* which contain many more details on life and work within New England (especially CONCORD, MASSACHUSETTS) literary society.

As a teenager Sanborn read with interest the works of Ralph Waldo Emerson, whom he first met in 1853. After graduating from Harvard, where he had helped found *The Harvard Magazine,* Sanborn moved to Concord and became a teacher in the school attended by the children of Emerson and Hawthorne. In Concord he befriended many others among the Transcendentalists, such as Alcott, Theodore PARKER, and Thoreau. He was personally closest to Emerson but most interested in the life and writings of Thoreau, whom he often accompanied on nature walks.

Sanborn's acquaintance with Theodore Parker strengthened his own ABOLITIONISM, and he would join with Parker, Thomas Wentworth HIGGINSON,

and three other men as the SECRET SIX, who helped fund and support the antislavery crusade of John BROWN in 1859. Sanborn was an outspoken and active abolitionist and a member of the Massachusetts Free Soil Association whose purpose was to keep slavery out of the new western territories. In 1857 Sanborn first met Kansas free-soil radical John Brown. During Brown's trial and execution after his unsuccessful raid on Harpers Ferry, members of the Secret Six went into hiding. Sanborn initially fled to Canada, and after he returned to Concord, federal marshals attempted to arrest him but were thwarted by the efforts of Sanborn's friends, including Emerson. The Massachusetts Supreme Court ultimately declared that the attempted arrest of Sanborn and others was illegal, and none of the Secret Six were ever charged in the Brown conspiracy. In 1885 Sanborn published a biography and collection of John Brown's correspondence.

Franklin Sanborn also had an enduring career as a journalist. He published in various periodicals from the ATLANTIC MONTHLY to the Cincinnati-based THE DIAL. From 1856 until the end of his life he was a regular weekly correspondent and book reviewer for the *Springfield Republican,* and between 1863 and 1867 served as editor of the Boston antislavery paper, *The Commonwealth.* In 1865 he helped found—along with other Transcendentalist reformers such as Caroline DALL and Thomas Wentworth Higginson—the AMERICAN SOCIAL SCIENCE ASSOCIATION (or ASSA) and edited the Association's annual report, *The Journal of Social Science.* Sanborn was the leading force behind the ASSA throughout its existence. His interests in the social sciences and social reform led to offering the first college course in Social Science at Cornell University, where he was also a lecturer from 1884 to 1887.

During the post–Civil War period he continued his close association with the older generation of Transcendentalists in helping to organize, with Bronson Alcott and William Torrey Harris, the CONCORD SCHOOL OF PHILOSOPHY AND LITERATURE. Sanborn lectured at least once at the school, which met every summer between 1879 and 1888. More important, he collected and published editions of special sessions at the Concord School—*THE GENIUS AND CHARACTER OF EMERSON* (1898) and *THE LIFE AND GENIUS OF GOETHE* (1886)—

that serve as the only full-text records of many of the lectures presented and thus an important source for understanding the themes and figures of later century Transcendentalism.

As a contemporary, but a younger member of the circle, Franklin Sanborn was less interested in living and writing about Transcendentalist philosophical ideals and more dedicated to memorializing his well-known and prolific Concord neighbors. His ultimate goal was to tie Transcendentalism to a specific historical and social context and thus secure its place in literary history and in the history of social reform. Ultimately, his own literary contribution to the movement is in his meticulous recording of the events, writings, and lives of major Transcendentalists whom he either knew personally or followed as a devoted disciple. Modern scholars, however, have pointed out that although Sanborn's works were important in keeping Transcendentalism at the forefront of American literary culture, many of his memoirs and biographies suffer from inaccuracies and, in the case of his revision of Thoreau's *Walden*, gross editorial licenses. Still, his tireless reform work as well as his personal relationships with many of the Transcendentalists provide valuable insider details about the movement's history.

Bibliography

Haskell, Thomas L. *The Emergence of Professional Social Science: The American Social Science Association and the Nineteenth-Century Crisis of Authority*. Urbana: University of Illinois Press, 1977.

Sand, George
(1804–1876)

French novelist George Sand (a pseudonym of Amandine-Aurore-Lucile Dupin, baroness Dudevant) was a contemporary of the American Transcendentalists and attracted attention in literary communities on both sides of the Atlantic due to her controversial life as a divorced woman author who dressed and published as a man. She took her pseudonym, Sand, from a shortened version of her friend's name, Jules Sandeau, with whom she had a romantic and professional collaboration resulting in the publication of several journal articles as well as her first novel in 1831. George Sand went on to support herself and her two children by publishing nearly 80 popular novels and plays. Given her rebellion against marriage, her personal independence found through writing, and her arguments for social reform, Sand become a heroine of American feminists, including Margaret FULLER and others within the Transcendentalist circle. Like the Transcendentalist's writings, Sand's novels fit within a tradition of ROMANTICISM that emphasized the beauty and IDEALISM of nature. So closely was Sand's project seen to that of their own, in 1855 feminist Transcendentalist Caroline DALL translated and serialized segments of Sand's novel, *Spiridion*, in the pages of THE UNA WOMEN'S RIGHTS newspaper. Georges Sand's most important novels are considered to be *The Haunted Pool* (1846) and *The Master Bell-Ringers* (1853).

Saturday Club

The Saturday Club was established in 1854 as a literary society comprised of many prominent Boston intellectuals and writers, including several members of the earlier TRANSCENDENTAL CLUB and TOWN AND COUNTRY CLUB. The group met on the last Saturday of each month to discuss presentations by members on various subjects, including the politics of slavery and ABOLITIONISM as the recent Anthony BURNS case in Boston had, in part, prompted the club's organization at this particular time. Among the Saturday Club's members were Harvard naturalist Louis AGASSIZ, Ralph Waldo EMERSON, poet Henry Wadsworth LONGFELLOW, novelist Nathaniel HAWTHORNE, Oliver Wendell HOLMES, and many others. In 1858 attendee William Stillman organized several members of the Saturday Club into the ADIRONDACK CLUB for a wilderness adventure in the Adirondack Mountains.

The Scarlet Letter
Nathaniel Hawthorne
(1850)

Nathaniel HAWTHORNE's 1850 novel, *The Scarlet Letter*, deals with the themes of sin, heresy, and the legacy of New England PURITANISM, and the relationship between society and the individual, between Christian morality and personal truth, themes influenced by Hawthorne's association with Transcendentalist philosophy. There are only four main characters involved in the psychological drama that unfolds: Hester Prynne, put on trial for adultery; the Reverend Arthur Dimmesdale; Roger Chillingworth, a physician; and Hester's daughter born out of wedlock, Pearl. Hester lives alone, her husband presumed dead, but she has given birth to a child and refuses to name the father. Hester's punishment is public ridicule in being forced to wear a red letter "A" sewn to her dress and she and her daughter are subsequently shunned from regular society. The reader slowly learns that the father of the child is Dimmesdale, and the mysterious stranger physician, Chillingworth, is actually Hester's husband, who has returned to the village but is recognized by no one. Only Hester knows the truth about these men, but she chooses not to reveal the identity of either and takes her punishment alone.

On one hand, the novel is a commentary on actual historical events and a condemnation of Puritan society. Indeed, Hawthorne's own ancestors were involved in the Massachusetts witchcraft trials and so he has a personal stake in coming to terms with the New England past. In persecuting Hester Prynne, but not recognizing Chillingworth as a deserter, or Dimmesdale as the actual father of the child, the Puritan religious and political system failed because it relied upon external rather than internal motivations and guides to "truth," revealing Hawthorne's Transcendentalist perspective on their actions. And since the person punished was, like many of the accused witches, a woman, the novel can also be read even as a feminist condemnation of the unfair treatment of women. It is Hester who has to pay the price for the sexual relationship, socially in becoming an outcast, and financially and emotionally in being left alone to care for the child, while Dimmesdale is protected from suspicion by his status as a minister, a prominent male in the community. Many have seen similarities between the case of Hester Prynne and the colonial-era trial of Anne HUTCHINSON for religious and gender dissent, a trial which continued

to capture the imagination of Hawthorne and many of his contemporaries in the 19th century.

Finally, the novel is also a Transcendentalist story of the strength of individual character. Hester is a model of self-reliance, living, literally, in the wilderness, on the outskirts of society, but she is also independent in a psychological sense, rising above the social condemnation because she carries within her the truth about her husband and about Dimmesdale, who remains psychologically tortured with the knowledge of his sin, which ultimately makes him physically ill. Besides Hester, it is the child Pearl who is perhaps the most Transcendentalist-inspired character in the novel. Pearl, whose very name is taken from nature, has to grow up alone, and her only playmate is nature. While other colonists fear the harshness of the wilderness, as well as the native Americans who live there, Pearl finds peace and comfort in the woods. Other Puritans cannot appreciate nature because they place too much emphasis on social and religious dramas, According to Hawthorne's Transcendentalist-inspired critique of the role of the church in limiting the spiritual development of the individual. The beauty and spiritual renewal of nature is a theme introduced in the very opening scene of the novel, where the narrator describes a beautiful rose bush that blooms in full color outside the prison. Nature offers sustenance even in the midst of such sad and dreary social drama, but by the end of the novel it is Pearl, the innocent child, who flourishes and blooms outside of and above the society into which she was born.

Hawthorne leads the reader to neither judge nor pity Hester Prynne, or Pearl, as did their Puritan contemporaries. Shunned by others, Hester lives a life of virtue and charity, making her living as a seamstress sewing clothes for the poor. The novel insists that all humans are full of sin, but that we each must find our own internal strength and seek our own routes to personal salvation.

Schelling, Friedrich Wilhelm Joseph von
(1775–1854)

German philosopher Friedrich Schelling was one of the most influential contemporary European thinkers on the development of American Transcendentalist thought. Schelling published more than 15 books, including the 1800 *System of Transcendental Idealism* and his 1809 *Philosophical Inquiries into the Nature of Human Freedom*. Schelling was an idealist philosopher of German ROMANTICISM and shared with the American Transcendentalists a focus on the subjective experience of individuals and a critique of the empiricism of Enlightenment rationalism. Like other German philosophical trends, such as HEGELIANISM, Schelling was part of a school of post-Kantian thinkers who attempted to move beyond Immanuel KANT's framework of reason and understanding and sought instead to reintegrate the objective or tangible and the subjective or ideal by identifying both aspects as part of the "reality" of human experience. In NATURE (1836), Ralph Waldo EMERSON himself defined the purpose of philosophy as "for all that exists conditionally to find a ground unconditional and absolute," which is what Schelling attempted to solve in his philosophy. Despite the fact that Schelling offered the clearest Transcendentalist answer to this problem of philosophy, there were no English translations of his work available at the time that Emerson and other American Transcendentalists were writing. They accessed Schelling's ideas through his influence on other European thinkers such as Victor COUSIN and, especially, Samuel Taylor COLERIDGE in his book *Biographia Literaria*, which had an enormous role in the emergence of Transcendentalism in the United States. Coleridge drew explicitly upon Schelling's Transcendental philosophy of connecting the realm of "nature" with that of the "self or intelligence," which in turn influenced Emerson and others.

In particular, Frederic Henry HEDGE's 1833 review of Coleridge's work is often identified as the start of the Transcendentalist movement, and Hedge also acknowledged that it was Schelling who "endeavours to show that the outward world is of the same essence with the thinking mind, both being different manifestations of the same divine principle." Since few Americans read the German language, Hedge's work was critical in the early years, and it was not until the 1840s that more American thinkers gained access to Schelling

directly, either through his writings or through attending his lectures in Germany. While visiting Germany, young American Charles Stearns WHEELER attended Schelling's lectures and sent notes back to Ralph Waldo Emerson, who published them in the DIAL in 1843. Another European traveler, James Elliot CABOT, heard Schelling speak and provided Emerson with early English translations of some of Schelling's essays before publishing a Schelling lecture in Frederic Henry Hedge's 1848 collection, *The Prose Writers of Germany*. Beyond this early interest among the Transcendentalists, little of Frederich Schelling's work is available in English even to this day, and he never developed a place in American scholarship as did his contemporaries Coleridge, Kant, or Hegel.

Bibliography

Elfe, Wolfgang, James Hardin, and Gunther Holst, eds. *The Fortunes of German Writers in America: Studies in Literary Reception*. Columbia: University of South Carolina Press, 1992.

Vogel, Stanley M. *German Literary Influences on the American Transcendentalists*. New Haven, Conn.: Yale University Press, 1955.

Schiller, Johann Christoph Friedrich von (1759–1805)

German poet, historian, and playwright Johann Friedrich Schiller was, along with Johann Wolfgang von GOETHE, one of the most significant German thinkers of interest to the American Transcendentalists in the 1830s and 1840s. Thomas CARLYLE published an 1825 English language biography, *Life of Schiller*, which introduced many of the Transcendentalists to the German writer. By 1832 Ralph Waldo EMERSON set about to look into Schiller himself and recorded in his journal: "I propose to myself to read Schiller of whom I hear much. What shall I read?" Colleagues James Freeman CLARKE, John Sullivan DWIGHT, and Margaret FULLER all had particular interests in Schiller as well as other German writers of the time and in translating important works into English. Clarke had plans to translate Schiller's drama about Joan of Arc, and Dwight translated *Select Minor Poems* of Schiller and Goethe as part of George RIPLEY's 14-volume SPECIMENS OF FOREIGN STANDARD LITERATURE. In 1836 and 1837 Margaret Fuller was teaching German classes in Boston and in Rhode Island and used Schiller's plays as texts. Fuller focused most of her translation and critical study on Goethe, and in 1845 she had the opportunity, in her capacity as literary critic for the NEW YORK TRIBUNE, to review the recent publication of a book of *Correspondence Between Schiller and Goethe*. Schiller resonated for other Transcendentalists in their own writings, such as Frederic Henry HEDGE, who wrote on many German writers for the CHRISTIAN EXAMINER, and Charles Timothy BROOKS, who published two Schiller translations: *Wilhelm Tell* (1838) and *Homage of the Arts* (1847). Between those projects Brooks had also contributed translations of two Schiller poems—"The Emigrants" and "The Moorish Prince"—to the April 1844 issue of the Transcendentalist literary journal, the *DIAL*. Even after the Civil War, the Transcendentalists remained interested in Johann Schiller's writings and Unitarian minister Cyrus BARTOL gave a lecture on "Goethe and Schiller" at Amos Bronson ALCOTT's CONCORD SCHOOL OF PHILOSOPHY AND LITERATURE.

Bibliography

Elfe, Wolfgang, James Hardin, and Gunther Holst, eds. *The Fortunes of German Writers in America: Studies in Literary Reception*. Columbia: University of South Carolina Press, 1992.

Vogel, Stanley. *German Literary Influences on the American Transcendentalists*. New Haven, Conn.: Yale University Press, 1955.

Schlegel, August Wilhelm von
(1767–1845)

Along with his brother, Friedrich SCHLEGEL, writer and philosopher August Schlegel was one of the founders of German ROMANTICISM and therefore of particular interest to the American Transcendentalists of the same era. Together, August and Friedrich Schlegel founded and edited the main journal of the German movement, the *Athenaum*, between 1798 and 1800. A few of the early Transcendentalists read German in the original, and Margaret FULLER read Schlegel and other German writers throughout the 1830s. Ralph Waldo EMERSON read Schlegel in translation, including an 1833 edition of Schlegel's *Course of Lectures on Dramatic Art and Literature*.

August Schlegel influenced the Transcendentalists with his "organic" theory of growth and development of human society and culture. As related to art, this romantic ideal emphasized the artist or the author as rising out of, and representing, specific cultural circumstances, a rejection of the classical theory of art or literature that emphasized fixed forms and aesthetic ideals. For Schlegel, William SHAKESPEARE was a perfect example of the organic or "natural" artist, able to both reflect and transcend the values of historical and cultural context through individual characters who resonated with universal traits. Undoubtedly, Ralph Waldo Emerson's interest in Shakespeare, whom Emerson later identified as the representative or ideal Poet in REPRESENTATIVE MEN (1850), was influenced by Schlegel's romantic interpretation of the dramatist. Schlegel embarked upon an ambitious undertaking to translate the plays of William Shakespeare into German and ultimately completed about half of the project. August Schlegel associated with other prominent German thinkers also read by the Transcendentalists, such as Johann Friedrich SCHILLER, and Madame Germaine de STAEL, for whom Schlegel was a traveling companion throughout Europe and a literary adviser in the early 1800s. After de Stael's death, Schlegel became a professor of literature at Bonn University, where he became Germany's first specialist in Sanskrit language and literature.

Bibliography

Elfe, Wolfgang, James Hardin, and Gunther Holst, eds. *The Fortunes of German Writers in America: Studies in Literary Reception*. Columbia: University of South Carolina Press, 1992.

Vogel, Stanley. *German Literary Influences on the American Transcendentalists*. New Haven, Conn.: Yale University Press, 1955.

Schlegel, Friedrich
(1772–1829)

Along with his brother, August SCHLEGEL, writer and philosopher Friedrich Schlegel was one of the founders of German ROMANTICISM and therefore of particular interest to the American Transcendentalists of the same era. Together, August and Friedrich Schlegel founded and edited the main journal of the German movement, the *Athenaum*, between 1798 and 1800. Friedrich Schlegel wrote a series of experimental literary works in the late 18th and early 19th centuries and, like his brother, had a particular interest in the language and literature of India. Friedrich Schlegel lectured widely and served in various political positions as well as writing. As a romantic thinker, Schlegel recognized what he called the "romantic irony" that truth comes from experience, but that experience varies and is always changing. In 1808 Friedrich Schlegel converted to Catholicism and became much more conservative in his thinking and writing. The Transcendentalists would have read Schlegel in the mid-19th century, in the decades after his death, when his philosophies of history and literature were translated into English.

Bibliography

Elfe, Wolfgang, James Hardin, and Gunther Holst, eds. *The Fortunes of German Writers in America: Studies in Literary Reception.* Columbia: University of South Carolina Press, 1992.

Vogel, Stanley M. *German Literary Influences on the American Transcendentalists.* New Haven, Conn.: Yale University Press, 1955.

Schleiermacher, Friedrich
(1768–1834)

The American Transcendentalists read German theologian Friedrich Schleiermacher as part of their general interest in German ROMANTICISM and IDEALISM. Ralph Waldo EMERSON and George RIPLEY were the Transcendentalists most influenced by Schleiermacher in the development of their spiritual ideas and their criticism of the rational religious forms of UNITARIANISM. Ralph Waldo

Emerson first heard of Schleiermacher from his older brother, William EMERSON, who was studying in Germany and excitedly shared his readings of German biblical criticism with his brothers. By the 1830s, Ralph Waldo Emerson's friends in Boston, such as James Freeman CLARKE and Frederic Henry HEDGE, were also enthusiastically reading German writers and encouraging Emerson, who was making his own break from organized religion, to read Schleiermacher's mystical theology.

Drawing on the same readings in classical (such as PLATONISM) and contemporary idealism (such as Immanuel KANT) as the American Transcendentalists were studying, Schleiermacher promoted the idea of a unified spiritual force in the universe and, therefore, of God as an immanent force in individual lives. In works such as *Brief Outline of the Study of Theology* (1811), Schleiermacher provided a theology based on awareness of the individual soul and its place in the immediate world, including nature, rather than a disconnected religion based on the study of texts. These ideas appealed immensely to, and echoed the emerging ideas of, the Transcendentalists in their critique of Unitarianism and their search for a more meaningful, less rational, approach to spirituality and nature. The idea that religion, meaning a spiritual experience of God as well as a guide to truth and morality, resided within a person and not in some outside sources, was the foundation of Emerson's own Transcendentalism as articulated in his earliest works such as NATURE (1836), the DIVINITY SCHOOL ADDRESS (1838), and many of the ESSAYS: FIRST SERIES (1841). In Schleiermacher is found a more Christian-based theological justification for Transcendentalist individualism, spiritual connection with the natural world, and Emersonian "SELF-RELIANCE."

Despite the direct influence on Emerson's ideas, it was George Ripley who emerged as Friedrich Schleiermacher's greatest American proponent and translator. Ripley called Schleiermacher "the greatest thinker who ever undertook to fathom the philosophy of religion" and used Schleiermacher as the basis of his arguments against the Unitarian emphasis during the 1820s and 1830s on the scientific-historical study of the Bible. Transcendentalist critic Andrews NORTON

criticized Schleiermacher as "the German pantheist" and engaged with Ripley, most directly, on the
question of finding historical proof for the miracles
of the Bible. Ripley, of course, argued that the
question of seeking rational explanations for miracles and of rational study of the Bible was misguided since, as Schleiermacher explained, religious
truth and experience can only be found within,
from a personal experience of God, not from a text
written hundreds of years ago.

Schleiermacher gave Ripley and others an alternative way to discuss spirituality not as Christian
doctrine but as "a life in the infinite nature of the
universe, in one and all, in God." Transcendentalists
such as Emerson and Ripley, especially, were ultimately more humanist than mystical in their spirituality. Where these thinkers finally departed from, or
at least expanded upon, Schleiermacher was in
moving away from the idea of a personal God and
on the purpose of religion as exploring this relationship, and in focusing instead on the individual
human soul itself as the location of "the infinite"
and "the eternal"; on the individual as the center of
the universe itself. George Ripley's DISCOURSES ON
THE PHILOSOPHY OF RELIGION, Addressed to Doubters
Who Wish to Believe depended upon Schleiermacher
as a starting point, but Ripley went on to argue for
self-reliance, rather than reliance on or direction
from God, as the foundation of religion. He wrote
that it is an individual's "inward nature, which is
the source of more important and comprehensive
ideas . . . and he follows the decision of these ideas
as the inspiriting voice of God." There was a series
of Transcendentalist books published in 1836, along
with Emerson's *Nature* and Ripley's *Discourses,* that
put forth a new type of inward-focused spirituality
and owed a debt to Friedrich Schleiermacher's influence, either directly or indirectly, such as William
Henry FURNESS's *Remarks on the Four Gospels,* and
Orestes BROWNSON's *NEW VIEWS OF CHRISTIANITY,
SOCIETY, AND THE CHURCH.*

Bibliography

Crowe, Charles. *George Ripley: Transcendentalist and
Utopian Socialist.* Athens: University of Georgia
Press, 1967.
Elfe, Wolfgang, James Hardin, and Gunther Holst, eds.
*The Fortunes of German Writers in America: Studies
in Literary Reception.* Columbia: University of South
Carolina Press, 1992.
Vogel, Stanley M. *German Literary Influences on the
American Transcendentalists.* New Haven, Conn.:
Yale University Press, 1955.

School for Human Culture   *See* TEMPLE SCHOOL.

Scottish Common Sense School   *See* COMMON SENSE PHILOSOPHY.

Secret Six

One New Yorker and five Bostonians—several of
them affiliated with Transcendentalism—called
themselves the Secret Six and quietly financed
abolitionist John BROWN's raid on the arsenal at
Harpers Ferry, Virginia, in the fall of 1859: writer
and editor Franklin Benjamin SANBORN, editor
Thomas Wentworth HIGGINSON (who would later
become a colonel of Massachusett's first black regiment during the Civil War), Samuel Gridley
Howe, Unitarian minister Theodore PARKER,
George Luther Stearns, and New York abolitionist
Gerrit Smith. Most of the men—except for Higginson, who was the most optimistic—realized that
Brown's mission was doomed but supported his
cause and, although most had previously promoted
nonviolent political protest, supported Brown's
radical strategy of direct action in this case in the
hope that it would force the issue of slavery upon
the nation's conscience.

Smith had known Brown the longest, and the
others were spurred in their enthusiasm for his radical plans by events following passage of the 1850
FUGITIVE SLAVE LAW—legislation that Parker called
"the formal federal endorsement of kidnapping."
Even before the Fugitive Slave Law was enacted at
the federal level, both Parker and Howe were members of a Boston committee that aided fugitive
slaves in the area. Soon Higginson was a member of
the committee as well—bringing together half the
members of what would become the Secret Six—
and many meetings were held at Parker's home.

Stearns had also attended meetings, and after the Fugitive Slave Law was in effect he opened his own home as a stop on the Underground Railroad. These men all became involved in planning the hiding, escape, and trials of fugitive slaves in Boston in the years immediately leading up to Brown's raid, and in New York in 1852 Smith himself had taken up arms to rescue a fugitive slave.

Throughout 1858 and early 1859 John Brown unfolded details for his Virginia plan and received responses from members of the Secret Six. In early 1859 Sanborn had brought Brown to speak in CONCORD, MASSACHUSETTS, where Ralph Waldo EMERSON and Henry David THOREAU became interested in his cause as well. Brown indicated that he would need money to purchase arms and other supplies for the mission and called a meeting with the Massachusetts men in February 1859 to discuss his plan. The supporters worked clandestinely as fund-raisers and, after the failure of the mission and Brown's arrest in October 1859, and upon learning that seizure of Brown's personal belongings had revealed a large number of letters, possibly implicating the Secret Six and others, Sanborn and others consulted a lawyer and went into hiding. Indeed, the press exposed letters from Howe, Sanborn, and Smith that were found among Brown's papers. During Brown's trial and execution, the men denied any beforehand knowledge of the attack or any association with Brown; Parker was already away in Italy, where he died soon after in 1860; Smith was committed to an insane asylum after announcing that he wished his fate to be tied with Brown's; Howe, Sanborn, and Stearns fled to Canada, but none of the men were ever charged as coconspirators.

In 1909, at the time of the 50th anniversary of Brown's raid, a humbled and even angry Thomas Wentworth Higginson regretted that he had not "been the one to make my brave, mad, noble friend step back from martyrdom." He referred to himself and his wealthy socially protected colleagues in harsh terms as "six Peters, all who denied John Brown at least once through some word or act before the cock crowed."

Bibliography
Renehan, Edward J., Jr. *The Secret Six: The True Tale of the Men Who Conspired with John Brown*. New York: Crown, 1995.

"Self-Culture"
William Ellery Channing
(1838)

Unitarian leader William Ellery CHANNING's 1838 sermon on "Self-Culture" influenced the spiritual and social consciousness of the emerging Transcendentalists with its idea of the self-improvement of the individual soul as the primary goal of a religious and social life. The address was published under the full title, *Self-Culture. An Address Introductory to the Franklin Lectures, Delivered at Boston, September, 1838* and in it, Channing offered a plan for both personal and social reform in the continual striving toward self-improvement and growth. Through "self-culture" any individual could rise to their fullest potential. Channing was speaking directly to a working-class audience, and his speech specifically addressed self-culture not as a philosophy for the leisure class but as something within the reach of all, regardless of their level of education or their need to labor for wages. He emphasized that "A man, who follows his calling with industry and spirit, and uses his earnings economically, will always have some portion of the day at command; and it is astonishing, how fruitful of improvement a short season becomes, when eagerly seized and faithfully used." With frugality and commitment any individual could find the time and motivation to cultivate the soul.

"Self-Reliance"
Ralph Waldo Emerson
(1841)

The essay "Self-Reliance" is regarded as Ralph Waldo EMERSON's most fully developed statement on the philosophy of individualism that characterized the Transcendentalist movement. The essay was drawn from Emerson's journal notes and various lectures of the 1830s but was first published in 1841 as part of the collection, *ESSAYS: FIRST SERIES*. While many of the ideas and specific statements put forth by Emerson in this essay may seem like truisms for Americans today, the philosophical idea of self-possessed and intellectually self-reliant individuals, existing outside of religion or politics or even tradition, was radical for his time. Emerson's definition of genius as subjectively understood was not only radical but wildly democratic in that he declared that *every* person possessed genius: "To believe your own thought, to believe that what is true for you in your private heart is true for all men—that is genius." Emerson urged every person to rely on no one except him (or her) self. This required, on some level, a turning away from society and a focus instead on one's own nature and inner voice. Society, according to Emerson, means conformity, a forced "consistency" of manners and behaviors that is nothing less than "a conspiracy against the manhood of every one of its members." From Emerson's understanding of the word *consistency* comes one of the most well-known quotes from "Self-Reliance": "A foolish consistency is the hobgoblin of little minds, adored by little statesmen and philosophers and divines." It is more important to "trust thyself," than to listen to the mandates of the leaders of society, of "statesmen and philosophers and divines," or to worry what others think of you.

Emerson's goal was not merely to promote unchecked individualism without regard at all to society. He believed that the creation of more self-reliant individuals would eventually benefit society in specific ways. Most significantly, self-reliance called traditional religious practices and beliefs into question. Religious practices such as prayer, for example, forced people into dependent relationships vis-à-vis God as well as the church leadership. Emerson straightforwardly pronounced that "As men's prayers are a disease of the will, so are their creeds a disease of the intellect." Here was Emerson at his most radical in terms of rejecting the religious beliefs of his society, mainly Christianity, and urging his readers as well to formulate their own independent ideas and beliefs instead. If more people were truly self-reliant, vacuous religious beliefs and rituals would be replaced by "the contemplation of the facts of life from the highest point of view."

"Self-Reliance" returned to another regular theme within Emerson's writing: the need for distinctly American ways of being and thinking, the cultivation of an American culture. A nation of self-reliant individuals, he believed, would be a nation of people devoted to cultivating the best of American culture and thought rather than seeking inspiration from European sources. Finally, the creation of self-reliant citizens would benefit society necessarily as people came to understand and find true happiness within themselves rather than in the outward pursuit of wealth and material advancements, the gain of which too often brings negative consequences for society. In Emerson's words, "Nothing can bring you peace but yourself. Nothing can bring you peace but the triumph of principles." Lest they think a self-reliant life is unattainable, or cannot lead to great things both for the individual and for society, Emerson leaves the reader with specific examples of great men throughout history who exhibited the traits he discusses.

Shakespeare, William
(1564–1616)

The plays of Elizabethan writer William Shakespeare were immensely popular and regularly staged in the United States during the 19th century. The Transcendentalists were particularly interested in Shakespeare as a writer whose genius revealed universal messages. Ralph Waldo EMERSON gave two early lectures on Shakespeare in Boston in 1835 and discussed Shakespeare as the ideal poet in the 1841 essay "THE POET," an idea expanded upon in the essay devoted exclusively to "Shakspeare; or, the Poet" in the 1850 collection, REPRESENTATIVE MEN. Shakespeare was of interest to philosophers of ROMANTICISM in general, and August SCHLEGEL, for example, worked during this time period to translate all of Shakespeare's plays into German.

Although popular and of interest to a variety of thinkers and writers, William Shakespeare's plays were controversial in 19th-century America. Walt WHITMAN, for example, did not think that Shakespeare's aristocratic themes and characters were applicable or healthy in a democratic society such as the United States. Emerson was more interested in a Transcendentalist perspective on

Shakespeare the man as poet and writer and praised him for his ability to understand and translate the issues of his own time into universal themes that reached beyond time and country. Other Transcendentalists besides Emerson paid critical attention to the plays of Shakespeare as well. Margaret FULLER referred to Shakespeare in her 1843 essay, "THE GREAT LAWSUIT," in which she used the character of Cordelia as an example of certain female virtues represented by Shakespearean heroines. Poet Jones VERY wrote two essays on Shakespeare and was ultimately concerned with the lack of religion, specifically Christian morality, in Shakespeare's plays. Henry David THOREAU also had less praise for Shakespeare than Emerson, although Emerson's intention was always to emphasize the creative and universal aspects of writing literature that Shakespeare embodied, more than any specific plays or themes.

Still other Transcendentalists were drawn into discussion about William Shakespeare as a writer through an interesting and controversial debate over the authenticity of Shakespeare's authorship of certain plays. Historian and lecturer Delia BACON dedicated her final years to researching her theory that political collaborators had written several of Shakespeare's plays for political purposes, and she was, for a time, befriended, promoted, and supported by Transcendentalists such as Caroline DALL, Nathaniel HAWTHORNE, Elizabeth Palmer PEABODY, and even Ralph Waldo Emerson. Long after Delia Bacon's research and life ended, having never proven her theory and been discredited by mental illness, Caroline Dall addressed the debate again in a later essay entitled, "What We Really Know about Shakespeare."

Bibliography

Marovitz, Sanford E. "Emerson's Shakespeare: From Scorn to Apotheosis." In *Emerson Centenary Essays,* ed. Joel Myerson. Carbondale: Southern Illinois University Press, 1982.

Wynkoop, William M. *Three Children of the Universe: Emerson's View of Shakespeare, Bacon, and Milton.* The Hague: Mouton, 1966.

"Shakspeare; or, the Poet"   *See* REPRESENTATIVE MEN.

"Sic Vita"
Henry David Thoreau
(1841)

First published in the July 1841 issue of the Transcendentalist literary journal the DIAL, Henry David THOREAU's poem "Sic Vita" is also often referred to by the first line, "I am a parcel of vain strivings tied." Although Thoreau's contribution to American literature would ultimately rest more upon his prose writings, such as the 1854 account of his solitary existence in the cabin in the woods, WALDEN, Ralph Waldo EMERSON early on encouraged Thoreau as a poet and sent Thoreau's poems to *Dial* editor Margaret FULLER, who published several of them. In his journals and published texts Thoreau often mixed his poetry in with prose and "I am a parcel of vain strivings tied" was included in his 1849 A WEEK ON THE CONCORD AND MERRIMACK RIVERS.

According to Franklin Benjamin SANBORN in his 1917 biography of Thoreau, this particular poem was written as early as 1837 and may have been responsible for Emerson discovering the young Thoreau as a poet. Thoreau gave the poem, along with "a bunch of violets" (referenced in the poem), to Lucy Jackson Brown, the sister of Lidian EMERSON who was then staying with the Thoreau family. "Sic Vita," like "SYMPATHY" and others, is considered one of Thoreau's love poems, but Brown was more of a family friend and a woman whom the young Thoreau greatly admired. It was, in fact, Lucy Brown who showed Thoreau's poetry to her brother-in-law, Ralph Waldo Emerson, facilitating the two men's fateful meeting that same year.

"Sic Vita" is a reflection on the sources of inspiration and on humanity's connection with nature and with one another. The opening lines indicate a feeling of loss of such connection, of being separated from one's true nature and source of sustenance, as are cut flowers: "I am a parcel of vain strivings tied / By a chance bond together, / Dangling this way and that, their links / Were made so loose and wide . . . / A bunch of violets without their roots." Like cut flowers, human life is short and in "vain," time spent in "a bare cup": "And here I bloom for a short hour unseen, / Drinking my juices up, / With no root in the land." In the end, however, even one with such a fate might still hope for a meaningful connection: "But now I see I was not plucked for naught, / And after in life's vase / Of glass set while I might survive, / But by a kind hand brought / Alive / To a strange place." Thoreau's colleague, Amos Bronson ALCOTT, perhaps recognizing the poignancy of those lines for his friend whose own life was "a short hour," read the poem at Thoreau's funeral in May 1862.

slavery   *See* ABOLITIONISM.

"Slavery in Massachusetts"
Henry David Thoreau
(1854)

Henry David THOREAU delivered his address, "Slavery in Massachusetts," at a July 4, 1854, antislavery meeting called by William Lloyd GARRISON in protest of the arrest and return of fugitive slave Anthony BURNS. While Garrison outraged conservatives at this event by burning a copy of the U.S. Constitution, Thoreau's words were equally virulent when he declared in his address that "My thoughts are murder to the State." Thoreau's address was printed a few weeks later in an issue of Garrison's abolitionist newspaper, *The Liberator*. Thoreau and Garrison both directed their statements toward northern reformers, politicians, and sympathizers who would decry slavery in the South or in the western territories but not take a principled and public position against the workings of the FUGITIVE SLAVE LAW in their own region. As in "CIVIL DISOBEDIENCE," Thoreau called on his listeners or readers to follow their inner moral compass rather than the arbitrary laws of government: "They are the lovers of the law and order who observe the law when the government breaks it." Thoreau's own philosophy of reform included reform of the individual as the first priority, but also a commitment to dismantling immoral institutions, including the press and the church, both of which Thoreau and radical abolitionists accused of supporting or defending slavery. Again, as with "Civil Disobedience," "Slavery in Massachusetts"

was a response to a specific incident in Henry David Thoreau's experience, but it included a universal message as a model of political action and individual consciousness. He reminded his readers that "The law will never make men free; it is men who have got to make the law free."

Sleepy Hollow Cemetery   *See* CONCORD, MASSACHUSETTS.

Smith, Elizabeth Oakes
(1806–1893)

Elizabeth Oakes Prince Smith was a well-known poet, novelist, editor, and journalist who was influenced by the Transcendentalist feminism of Margaret FULLER. Smith was friends with many in Fuller's circle and contributed to the Transcendentalist-edited WOMEN'S RIGHTS periodical, *THE UNA*, under the editorship of Caroline DALL. Born and raised in Maine, Smith lived her adult life at the literary center of New York and is therefore representative of the wider parameters of the Transcendentalist community beyond New England. As a young woman she originally planned to become a teacher, but, at the urging of her mother, was married instead at the age of 16. She ultimately made a career for herself as a writer, editor, reformer, and lecturer on topics such as prison reform, children's rights, and women's rights. When she moved from Maine to New York she was immersed in the literary scene of that antebellum city. She traveled widely as one of the first women on the lecture circuit and shared lyceum dates with prominent figures such as Ralph Waldo EMERSON and abolitionist Wendell PHILLIPS. When in Massachusetts, she visited with Amos Bronson ALCOTT and Abigail May ALCOTT, the Emersons, and Henry David THOREAU. As coeditor (with her husband Seba Smith) of *Emerson's Magazine and Putnam's Monthly* in the 1850s, Smith was approached by Bronson Alcott to consider the short stories of his daughter Louisa May ALCOTT for publication.

Beyond personal and professional connections with Boston's reform and literary communities,

Elizabeth Oakes Smith's most clear association with Transcendentalist ideas and philosophy is evident through her book-length feminist treatise, WOMAN AND HER NEEDS (1851). This text is similar in rhetoric and philosophy to Margaret Fuller's WOMAN IN THE NINETEENTH CENTURY, published just a few years earlier, with its emphasis on cultivating woman's genius and its historical and contemporary examples of independent and intellectual women. Smith had met Fuller in New York and, interestingly, the two would have similar career trajectories. Fuller had served as a literary critic and later as a foreign correspondent for the NEW YORK TRIBUNE during the late 1840s. Just months after Fuller's untimely death in 1850, Smith became a regular contributor to the *Tribune,* beginning with a series of articles, "Woman and Her Needs," coinciding with the first national Woman's Rights Convention held in October 1850. Like Fuller, whose *Woman in the Nineteenth Century* had begun as a journal article in the DIAL, Smith's newspaper essays between November 1850 and June 1851 were gathered together and published in book form.

Smith's approach to social reform shared the Emersonian concern that organized single-issue reform hindered individual development and thought. Although a prominent and outspoken women's rights advocate, in *Woman and Her Needs* Smith declared herself independent of any particular organization and, even though she attended annual conventions, perceived herself as a "solitary lantern," taking into consideration "the many converging lights of many minds" in "arriving at truth to my own mind." In this way Smith articulated the Transcendentalist desire to pursue reform not only *of* individuals but *as* individuals, guided by their own sense of truth and right.

Bibliography

Bean, Judith Mattson. " 'A *Presence* Among Us': Fuller's Place in Nineteenth-Century Oral Culture," *ESQ: A Journal of the American Renaissance* 44 (1998): 79–123.

Wayne, Tiffany K. *Woman Thinking: Feminism and Transcendentalism in Nineteenth-Century America.* Lanham, Md.: Lexington Books, 2005.

"Smoke"
Henry David Thoreau
(1843)

Writer and naturalist Henry David THOREAU's poem "Smoke" appeared in the April 1843 issue of the Transcendentalist literary journal, the DIAL. Ralph Waldo EMERSON was then general editor of the Boston-based *Dial,* but Thoreau was actually serving as guest editor for the April 1843 issue while Emerson was out of town. Thoreau was a regular contributor to the *Dial* since its inception three years earlier, in 1840, and the April 1843 issue included several of his pieces, including "Smoke." The short, unrhymed 10-line poem is sometimes referred to as "Light-winged Smoke" or by the full first line, "Light-winged Smoke, Icarian bird." Although Thoreau's prose writings, especially the 1854 WALDEN, ultimately overshadowed his poetry, Emerson for one early on encouraged Thoreau as a poet. In his journals and published texts Thoreau often mixed his poetry in with prose and "Smoke" was included in the text of *Walden.*

As in several other poems, such as "FOG," "The Sluggish Smoke," and "Woof of the Sun, Ethereal Gauze," "Smoke" deals with a partially obscured or clouded aspect of the natural world. The smoke fills the sky and obscures humanity's view of the heavens, for it is "By night star-veiling, and by day / Darkening the light and blotting out the sun." The first line identifies the smoke as an "Icarian bird," a representative of nature but also a figure from classical Greek mythology who, flying too near the sun is burned or melted, thus producing the smoke. The bird then could be seen as a warning to humans in their quest for knowledge, characterized in the poem by the sun. While the dangers of the sun are then implied by the reference to the Icarian bird, in the last lines the poet produces his own alternative source of heat and light: fire. As an invention of mankind, fire represents humanity's cleverness and self-sufficiency. Additionally, it produces no smoke, but only a "clear flame," and Thoreau makes a plea to "Go thou my incense upward from this hearth, / And ask the gods to pardon this clear flame." Like much of Henry David Thoreau's writing, both prose and poetry, "Smoke" deals with the balance between humanity's desire for both worldly invention and harmony, or correspondence, with the natural and spiritual worlds. Indeed, this is the overarching theme of *Walden*, where the poem appeared.

"The Snow-Storm"
Ralph Waldo Emerson
(1841)

One of several of Ralph Waldo EMERSON's best poems written during the productive year 1834, "The Snow-Storm" relies upon the familiar Transcendentalist theme of looking to nature for meaning about human existence. The poem was first published in the January 1841 issue of the Transcendentalist literary journal, the *DIAL* and appeared in the 1847 collection of *POEMS*. "The Snow-Storm" is divided into two sections with the first emphasizing the outward focus on nature and the second illuminating an inward focus on the spiritual reflection inspired by nature. In the case of the winter storm and winds, Emerson portrays humans trying to imitate or capture the power and beauty of nature but who, in the end, can only "mimic in slow structures, stone by stone," nature's work, "the frolic architecture of the snow." There was in fact a great snow storm in New England in December 1834, but Emerson had conceived the idea for the poem at least two years earlier, according to his journal, when he proposed to write a lecture on "God's architecture," with a focus on "a sketch of a winters day." In the poem, it is nature, not humanity, that builds the most beautiful structures or "architecture": "Come see the north-wind's masonry. / Out of an unseen quarry evermore." A few years later in his 1841 essay on "HISTORY," Emerson interestingly returned to this same imagery of comparing nature's snow to the stonework of a mason: "I have seen a snow-drift along the sides of the stone wall which obviously gave the idea of the common architectural scroll to abut a tower."

Some critics consider Emerson's "The Snow-Storm" to be the best or clearest expression of the Transcendentalist organic theory that humanity takes cues and larger meaning from forms found in nature. And, in this sense, the poet himself, although only a "fierce artificer" of nature, like nature is free to complete work which is "So fanciful, so savage, nought cares he / For number or proportion." Emerson's poem influenced a similar theme in John Greenleaf WHITTIER's later poem, "Snow-Bound," which includes a long section of Emerson's "The Snow-Storm" as an epigraph.

Society and Solitude
Ralph Waldo Emerson
(1870)

Society and Solitude is a collection of essays by Ralph Waldo EMERSON, derived primarily from lectures delivered after 1858 and published in 1870. The collection includes 12 essays, the first of which is also titled "Society and Solitude," followed by essays on "Civilization," "Art," "Eloquence," "Domestic Life," "Farming," "Works and Days," "Books," "Clubs," "Courage," "Success," and "Old Age." The title piece deals with the conflicting needs of the individual to commune and interact with other people socially and the need for solitude in order to think and commune with oneself. According to Emerson, "men cannot afford to live together on their merits, and they adjust themselves by their demerits."

Overall, the essays in *Society and Solitude* are distinguished from earlier collections in that Emerson's writing style as well as his subject matter was intended to reach a broader audience. The essays deal less with philosophical abstractions and more with themes related to everyday life and experience. The essays are held together by the overarching issue of how to balance the solitude needed in order for self-development with commitments to society, a universal issue that Emerson himself struggled with. It was perhaps for these reasons that friend and correspondent Thomas CARLYLE characterized *Society and Solitude* as Emerson's best book to date: "Such brevity, simplicity, softness, homely grace; with such penetrating meaning, soft as silent electricity goes."

The book sold well, perhaps for the reasons Carlyle mentioned, but Emerson was more modest about the reasons for his success: "Old age is a good advertisement. Your name has been seen so often that your book must be worth buying."

Bibliography

Allen, Gay Wilson. *Waldo Emerson: A Biography.* New York: Viking Press, 1981.

"Song of Myself"
Walt Whitman
(1855)

"Song of Myself" was the opening poem in Walt WHITMAN's monumental 1855 collection, *Leaves of Grass.* Whitman envisioned all of *Leaves of Grass* as a long poem about and for the United States, "the greatest poem," and about its representative citizen, "the song of a great composite Democratic Individual, male or female." The poem, "Song of Myself," then is as much about the nation as about an individual, Whitman. The poem is a cataloging of the natural and human surroundings that the poet witnessed around him at the particular historical moment of mid-19th century America and a reflection on the destiny of the nation. As the opening poem, "Song of Myself" sets the tempo and the theme for the rest of the collection, but it is also among Whitman's most "transcendental" poems and shares with Transcendentalist philosophy the interest in human experience and in understanding the place of humans within nature and the universe. Walt Whitman's personal and professional relationships with the Transcendentalists were limited and subject to some tension, but in looking outward to nature and the cosmos for clues as to the inward state of humanity, Whitman's writing conveyed the particular influence of colleagues such as Ralph Waldo EMERSON and Henry David THOREAU. One of Emerson's most well known poems, "BRAHMA," was originally entitled "The Song of the Soul," reminiscent of the language of Whitman. Walt Whitman's free and rhythmic writing style in turn influenced other poets of his generation, such as Emerson and Emily DICKINSON.

Bibliography

Loving, Jerome. *Emerson, Whitman, and the American Muse.* Chapel Hill: University of North Carolina Press, 1982.

Sonnets and Canzonets
Amos Bronson Alcott
(1882)

Sonnets and Canzonets was Transcendentalist writer and reformer Amos Bronson ALCOTT's last published book and is considered by many scholars to be his best work of poetry. Franklin Benjamin SANBORN assisted Alcott in editing the collection of brief poetic reminiscences of his well-known friends and acquaintances within New England literary circles. The *Sonnets and Canzonets* were written in a similar style as Alcott's earlier work, *CONCORD DAYS,* and included tributes to his wife, Abigail May ALCOTT and his daughter Louisa May ALCOTT, as well as famous friends from among the Transcendentalists, such as Cyrus BARTOL, William Henry CHANNING, Ednah Dow CHENEY, Ralph Waldo EMERSON, Margaret FULLER, Nathaniel HAWTHORNE, Henry David THOREAU, Theodore PARKER, Elizabeth Palmer PEABODY, and Franklin Benjamin Sanborn. Alcott also paid tribute to his prominent and influential colleagues in the reform community, primarily proponents of ABOLITIONISM such as John BROWN (who he deemed "a prophet of God, Messiah of the slave"), William Lloyd GARRISON, and Wendell PHILLIPS. Alcott referred to novelist Hawthorne as a "Romancer, far more coy than that coy sex!," and, in a reference to Hawthorne's fictionalized account of PURITANISM, *THE SCARLET LETTER,* described him as a "Painter of sin in its deep scarlet dyes, . . . New England's guilt blazoning before all eyes." Alcott included two sonnets dedicated to his CONCORD, MASSACHUSETTS, neighbor, Henry David Thoreau, whom he described as the "Concord Pan," an idealist not fully understood or appreciated by his contemporaries, perhaps how Alcott also felt about himself. Of Thoreau he wrote: "Much do they wrong our Henry, wise and kind, . . . / Forsaking manners civil and refined / To build thyself in Walden woods a den,—/ Then flout society, flatter the rude hind. / We better knew thee, loyal citizen!"

Ralph Waldo Emerson, not surprisingly, received perhaps the most attention in *Sonnets and Canzonets*. Alcott included four sonnets on Emerson and reprinted "Ion: A Monody," a tribute to their friendship which spanned nearly a half century. Alcott's eulogizing poem was also presented as a memorial to Emerson at the July 1882 session of the CONCORD SCHOOL OF PHILOSOPHY AND LITERATURE. Of his friend Emerson, Alcott wrote: "And life-long hath it been high compliment / By that to have been known, and thy friend styled, / Given to rare thought and learning bent; . . . / Permit me then, thus honored, still to be / A scholar in thy university."

Like Emerson and other Transcendentalist-inspired poets, Bronson Alcott rejected traditional forms and structures in his writing, making both his poetry and his prose difficult for readers and reviewers to appreciate, both then and now. Regardless, *Sonnets and Canzonets* was considered among his best work, probably due to popular interest in its various literary personalities. *Sonnets and Canzonets* was published in February 1882, by which time many of the people whom Alcott remembered in the book were already dead. Alcott was able to present Ralph Waldo Emerson with a copy of the book in April just days before Emerson's death.

Bibliography

Dahlstrand, Frederick. *Amos Bronson Alcott: An Intellectual Biography.* East Brunswick, N.J.: Associated University Presses, 1982.

South Boston Sermon   *See* A DISCOURSE ON THE TRANSIENT AND PERMANENT IN CHRISTIANITY.

Specimens of Foreign Standard Literature
George Ripley
(1838–1842)

George RIPLEY, Transcendentalist reformer and founder of the BROOK FARM utopian community, edited the 14-volume book series *Specimens of Foreign Standard Literature* as one of the earliest unifying projects of the emerging Transcendentalist movement. Many of the contributors to Ripley's series were among the members of the TRANSCENDENTAL CLUB, established in 1836 and representing the emerging interest in European writers among American intellectuals. The *Specimens of Foreign Standard Literature* was a series of English translations of European philosophers, writers, and poets, and it became not only an important reference source for American scholars and intellectuals but encouraged the key voices of the early Transcendentalist movement to promote their own philosophy through selecting, translating, and annotating those noteworthy works which they found inspiring or important. Ripley's intention was to provide English-language access to foreign works and thus stimulate new directions in American thought and culture. As Ripley wrote to his friend Convers FRANCIS in an early proposal for the series, the collective work of this group of emerging scholars would create a "Library, which would do honor to our land and enlarge the cultivation of our people." Historian of Transcendentalism Perry Miller has pointed out that the intention was also to set a standard of cultural knowledge and, that by explicitly using the word *Standard* in his series title, Ripley was countering criticisms of Transcendentalism as "new thought" by pointing out that well-read Europeans were already familiar with such works.

Ripley himself contributed the first two volumes in 1838 under the title, *Philosophical Miscellanies, Translated from the French of Cousin, Jouffroy, and Benjamin Constant.* Other volumes published as part of the series included John Sullivan DWIGHT's *Select Minor Poems, Translated from the German of Goethe and Schiller;* Margaret FULLER's *Conversations with Goethe in the Last Years of His Life* (the first English translation of Johann ECKERMANN's biography of Johann Wolfgang von GOETHE); *German Literature, Translated from the German of Wolfgang Menzel,* contributed by Cornelius Conway FELTON; Theodore JOUFFROY's *Introduction to Ethics,* translated by William Henry CHANNING; Wilhelm De Wette's *Theodore; or, the Skeptic's Conversion,* translated by James Freeman CLARKE; De Wette's *Human Life; or, Practical Ethics,* translated by Samuel OSGOOD; and Charles Timothy BROOKS's *Songs and Ballads; Translated from Uhland, Korner,*

Burger, and Other German Lyric Poets. Still other Transcendentalists were involved in the series as some of the volumes were collaborations among multiple authors and translators.

Bibliography

Crowe, Charles. *George Ripley: Transcendentalist and Utopian Socialist.* Athens: University of Georgia Press, 1967.

"The Sphinx"
Ralph Waldo Emerson
(1841)

Ralph Waldo EMERSON's poem, "The Sphinx," was first published in the January 1841 issue of the Transcendentalist literary journal, the DIAL, and later included as the first poem in his 1846 collection, POEMS. By placing "The Sphinx" at the beginning of his book Emerson presents the riddle of the poem as an invitation to his collection, into his own mind and the riddle of all of his writing. "The Sphinx" details a conversation between a poet and the Sphinx, who challenges humankind to unravel the mysteries of nature and the universe, including the existence and fate of humanity itself: "Who'll tell me my secret, / The ages have kept?— / I awaited the seer, / While they slumbered and slept;— / "The fate of the man-child; / The meaning of man; / Known fruit of the unknown; / Daedalian plan."

In the middle of the poem the poet finally answers the challenge and replies that humans have been unable to answer such questions because they too often seek with the eyes and not the soul: "Whose soul seeks the perfect, / Which his eyes seek in vain." Here Emerson inserts his own Transcendentalist answer to the mysteries proposed by the Sphinx in promoting a more holistic and eternal view of nature and human existence rather than seeking answers in the objective scientific world of experience: "Profounder, profounder, / Man's spirit must dive;" Furthermore, Emerson as the poet chides humans for their impatience and shortsightedness in always looking for "new" explanations rather than appreciating the wisdom of "old": "The heavens that now drawn him / With sweetness untold, / Once found,—for new heavens / He spurneth the old."

Ultimately the poet solves the Sphinx's riddle by realizing that "Thou art the unanswered question" because "each answer is a lie"; that is, there is no right answer because there are multiple answers. This conclusion reveals another tenet of Emerson's Transcendentalism in that the answers are as varied and individual as the questions, that each person must solve his or her own riddle. In the poem, the poet so advises the Sphinx accordingly—"So take thy quest through nature, / It through thousand natures ply"—and in querying "a thousand voices" she indeed concludes, with Emerson, that if a person seeks out even one aspect of the mysteries of life, he or she will understand it all: "Who telleth one of my meanings, / Is master of all I am."

Since "The Sphinx" was one of Emerson's most popular poems and one of his personal favorites, he provided further clues to the riddle of the poem when he wrote, "I have often been asked the meaning of "The Sphinx." It is this,—The perception of identity unites all things and explains one by another, and the most rare and strange is equally facile as the most common. But if the mind live only in particulars, and see only differences . . . then the world addresses to this mind a question it cannot answer, and each new fact tears it to pieces, and it is vanquished by the distracting variety."

Spirit of the Age
(1849–1850)

William Henry CHANNING began publishing the reform-minded *Spirit of the Age* as the official paper of the AMERICAN UNION OF ASSOCIATIONISTS and an immediate successor to THE HARBINGER. The first issue of the *Spirit of the Age* appeared in July 1849, just five months after *The Harbinger* ceased publication. Channing sought to continue through this paper the work of American reformers and communities committed to FOURIERISM, such as those involved with BROOK FARM, where *The Harbinger* had been published. Several former members of Brook Farm, and writers for *The Harbinger,* continued on as writers for *Spirit of the Age* in what

Channing as editor identified as efforts to "introduce the era of Confederated Communities." The founder of Brook Farm, Transcendentalist George RIPLEY, aided in many of the editorial duties for *Spirit of the Age*. Charles LANE, cofounder with Amos Bronson ALCOTT of the utopian community at FRUITLANDS, supplied the paper with social reform news from England. The *Spirit of the Age* ceased publication in 1850 and was the last Fourierist periodical to garner support from Transcendentalist reformers involved in the movement.

Bibliography

Gohdes, Clarence L. F. *The Periodicals of American Transcendentalism.* Durham, N.C.: Duke University Press, 1931.

Guarneri, Carl. *The Utopian Alternative: Fourierism in Nineteenth-Century America.* Ithaca, N.Y.: Cornell University Press, 1991.

spiritualism

The term *spiritualism* had two meanings in the context of 19th-century American culture and Transcendentalism. The practical meaning of "spiritualism" described the practice and belief, widely popular in the mid-19th century, of communicating with the spirit world, including the dead. A more philosophical explanation of *spiritualism* was the belief that there was an experiential as well as symbolic connection between the natural world and the spiritual world. Both senses of the term had meaning and relevance for the American Transcendentalists.

The use of a medium to help the living communicate with the dead was a popular practice throughout 19th-century America and Europe. Communication could take place through dreams, prophecy, trances, hypnotism, or physical contact, such as messages from the dead through the movement of furniture, the appearance of apparitions or ghosts, speaking or singing through the medium, or, in one popular phenomena, spirits sending messages through rapping on tables. It was through a famous series of "table rappings" that the practice of spiritualism gained a following in the United States. In March 1848 the Fox sisters of New York reported that spirits were attempting to communicate to them through rapping and knocking on their house. The sisters positioned themselves as mediums for the spirits and took their message on a cross-country tour. They performed séances for eager audiences and inspired the creation of spiritualist clubs as well as magazines and papers devoted to the "science." The popularity of séances and spiritual gatherings spread across geographical and class lines, as intellectuals, writers, reformers, and even some scientists in both Europe and America became enthusiastic participants.

Among the Transcendentalists in New England, response and participation was mixed, but not absent. While in Europe in the 1850s, Sophia Peabody HAWTHORNE had been introduced to the craze through friends Elizabeth Barrett Browning and sculptor Hiram POWERS. For the culturally curious and open-minded, spiritualism went alongside interest in other new scientific inquiries about the mind-body connection, such as PHRENOLOGY and mesmerism. For his part, Nathaniel HAWTHORNE, with a literary reputation to protect, was more reserved, calling spirit-rapping "the strangest and most bewildering affair I have ever heard of." When asked to endorse or assist in the publication of a book on modern spiritualism, he tried to be polite in replying to the author: "My reputation (what little there is of it) has already too much fog and mist diffused through it; and if the public find me setting myself up as a sponsor of other people's books of dream craft and witchery, I shall get a very bad name." Still, and perhaps because of Sophia Hawthorne's involvement, spiritualism intrigued him. He addressed the practice in his 1852 novel, THE BLITHEDALE ROMANCE, in which he ultimately tested spiritualism against Transcendentalist commitments to free will and independence of thought, both of which were compromised when participants entered into hypnotic trances. Henry David THOREAU was less interested in considering all sides of spiritualism and more disapproving of those who practiced it in his own town. He wrote to his sister that "CONCORD is just as idiotic as ever in relation to the spirits and their knockings."

Ralph Waldo EMERSON also dismissed the fad but went even further in warning against its actual dangers. He referred to the practice as "pseudo-spiritualism" and criticized the mediums who sought profit through taking advantage of desperate family members. While his own philosophy was founded on the principle that "all nature is rich," spiritualists were engaged in "a series of conspiracies to win from nature some advantage without paying for it." Emerson expanded his criticism of the greed and immorality that fueled attempts to communicate with the spirit world in several writings, including the essay "Success," from the 1870 book *SOCIETY AND SOLITUDE,* an 1877 essay on "Demonology" that appeared in the *NORTH AMERICAN REVIEW,* and the 1860 book *THE CONDUCT OF LIFE.* In these writings he characterized spiritualism as a "black art," with no value for scientific knowledge or advances, which represented a regression of human moral and intellectual development. Through "the deliration of rappings . . . thumps in table-drawers," he warned that "we ape our ancestors . . . stagger backward to the mummeries of the Dark Ages."

Emerson was critical of the practice of spiritualism and of the fraud of the belief in communicating with the dead, but he did not reject the idea that a spiritual or nonmaterial world, an alternative reality, existed. In fact, the metaphysical belief in "spiritualism" was central to his Transcendentalist philosophy during this same time period. Spiritualism in this sense of the term could be traced back to the ideas of Plato (*see* PLATONISM), upon which Emerson and other "spiritualist" philosophers of the 19th century relied quite heavily. Transcendentalists believed that the physical world of nature was a symbolic language for larger spiritual themes and that, in fact, nature was but the physical manifestation of a universal force, Emerson's "OVER-SOUL," of which humanity was also a part. Emerson reworked various aspects of this theory in writings such as his seminal foundational work, *NATURE* (1836), as well as essays such as "CIRCLES," "SPIRITUAL LAWS," and "Swedenborg; or, the Mystic," but spiritualism had literary expression in other Transcendentalist writings such as the nature journals of Henry David Thoreau and the mystical prose and poetry of Amos Bronson ALCOTT. Indeed, given the contemporary cultural debates about the validity of spirit rappings and of the pseudosciences in general, the spiritualist tendencies of Transcendentalist philosophy were also the source of some criticism, as evidenced by the caricatures of Emerson's nature religion and his melding of the physical and spiritual worlds represented by the drawings of Christopher Pearse CRANCH.

Bibliography

Braude, Ann. *Radical Spirits: Spiritualism and Women's Rights in Nineteenth-Century America.* Bloomington: Indiana University Press, 2001.

"Spiritual Laws"
Ralph Waldo Emerson
(1841)

Sections of "Spiritual Laws" originated in lectures given by Ralph Waldo EMERSON in 1837, but it was first published as a coherent piece in his early significant collection of *ESSAYS: FIRST SERIES* (1841). In this collection of essays that, in addition to "Spiritual Laws," included such important pieces as "SELF-RELIANCE" and "THE OVER-SOUL," Emerson first systematically presented the foundations of his Transcendentalist philosophy as it had been developing throughout the previous decade. In "Spiritual Laws" Emerson defined the laws that governed human existence within the universe. Emerson attempted to bring such abstract and universal forces into focus through an emphasis on simplicity—"our life might be much easier and simpler than we make it"—and on nature as the place where the example of simplicity and "optimism" is revealed: "A little consideration of what takes place around us every day would show us, that a higher law than that of our will regulates events." Through nature, according to Emerson, humankind learns to value such "laws" as respect and self-reliance. The whole of nature, the universe, becomes a more important moral teacher, then, than any human-made institution or rules. In particular, spiritual lessons or laws of nature should replace the spiritually damaging laws of religious dogma: "Our young people are diseased with the theological problems of original sin, origin of evil, predestination, and the like. . . . A simple mind will not know these enemies." Emerson had no use for these particular theological questions. He was not advocating nonthinking, however, but instead reliance on self and nature for answers to life's problems.

In advocating that individuals strive for divinity "by contenting ourselves with obedience" to the lessons of the universe, Emerson introduced one of the main paradoxes of Transcendentalist philosophy as discussed in other essays as well; that is, how to balance the acceptance of laws already existing in the universe with the primacy of the individual and free will or free choice. Obeying nature is obeying our selves, our own inner laws, which are consistent with the universal laws, since humanity is one with the universe: "Place yourself in the middle of the stream of power and wisdom which animates all whom it floats, and you are without effort impelled to truth, to right, and a perfect contentment. . . . Then you are the world, the measure of right, of truth, of beauty." Emerson addressed the paradox of free choice by reframing the definition of "choice" itself. He argued that "what is commonly called *choice* among men . . . But that which I call right or goodness, is the choice of my constitution." In other words, individuals only do what is the right choice for them, the right "*calling* in his character," whether they are conscious of that choice or not: "What your heart thinks great, is great. The soul's emphasis is always right."

Looking to the natural world for "Spiritual Laws," or lessons, about human life was a foundational Transcendentalist theme that was subsequently and repeatedly explored not only by Emerson but by other Transcendentalists as well, most notably Henry David THOREAU. In this context of determining what was universally right or great, Emerson also addressed the theme of individual greatness that he would explore in his full-length book REPRESENTATIVE MEN a few years later. He pointed out that being universal, the soul is therefore democratic, and all people are "of an identical nature," only with different talents and circumstances.

Spurzheim, Johann Gaspar   *See* PHRENOLOGY.

Staël, Germaine de
(Anne-Louise-Germaine Necker, baroness of Staël-Holstein)
(1766–1817)

Madame de Staël, as she was known in print, was a French intellectual and romantic theorist who became one of the favorite authors of the American Transcendentalists. De Staël was regarded by many as an example of the ideal type of female genius. She was a theorist, novelist, and salonnière, or hostess of intellectual gatherings or discussions. Transcendentalists such as Margaret FULLER, Theodore PARKER, and George RIPLEY became interested in de Staël's most widely read work, the 1807 novel *Corrine,* for its representation of female genius. Ralph Waldo EMERSON read de Staël as early as the 1820s and was particularly influenced by her 1810 book, *De l'Allemagne,* an overview of German culture and thought that, in effect, provided a critique of the entire Enlightenment tradition, beginning with John LOCKE, all the way through Immanuel KANT, that Emerson and others had been taught at Harvard. De Staël inspired readers to look to German writers, in particular, for alternative sources of philosophical and theological insight and criticism and models of a philosophy of intuition and individualism, the core values of European ROMANTICISM. De Staël's work, like that of English writer Samuel Taylor COLERIDGE, introduced American readers, whose access to non-English language texts was extremely limited in the earliest decades of the 19th century, to the freshest ideas and massive changes taking place in European intellectual history up to that time.

Most of the Transcendentalists were enthralled by the figure of Madame de Staël, not only for her work in intellectual history but also for the fact that she was a prominent female thinker and author. Emerson eventually named de Staël as one of the few notable women of intellect that history had produced, a list that also included his own aunt, Mary Moody EMERSON. Lydia Maria CHILD chose two female French intellectuals as the subject of her 1832 work, *The Biographies of Madame de Staël and Madame Roland.* For many readers, the fictional character of *Corrine* and the author de Staël were sometimes confused as the same, as when William Henry CHANNING said of his colleague Margaret Fuller, who held her CONVERSATIONS FOR WOMEN in the tradition of de Staël's salons, that "Miss Fuller represents Mme. de Staël more than any woman I know" and referred to Fuller as "a Yankee Corinna."

Stetson, Caleb
(1793–1870)

Caleb Stetson was a graduate of HARVARD DIVINITY SCHOOL and a Unitarian minister whose classmates or contemporaries included James Freeman CLARKE, Ralph Waldo EMERSON, Margaret FULLER, Frederic Henry HEDGE, and George RIPLEY. Through various reform activities, such as attending ABOLITIONISM meetings, Stetson also befriended others among the Transcendentalists, including Henry David THOREAU. Stetson was a regular attendee of the TRANSCENDENTAL CLUB and hosted at least one meeting at his own house. Stetson was interested in the questions raised by Transcendentalism as they related to UNITARIANISM, as the topic at the Transcendental Club meeting at his house in May 1838 was "Is Mysticism an element of Christianity?," and two months later, in July 1838, he attended Emerson's controversial DIVINITY SCHOOL ADDRESS. Despite moving within these same circles, both socially and professionally, Stetson was not particularly involved in Transcendentalist activities in general. He wrote periodically in the Unitarian press, including the CHRISTIAN EXAMINER, in which Stetson wrote a mostly positive review of Margaret Fuller's 1844 SUMMER ON THE LAKES, although a hint of his disagreement with the Transcendentalists is evident in his criticisms of Fuller's observations on nature as being records of "what is passing in her own soul" more so than "the objective realities which present themselves to the senses."

Although Caleb Stetson never published in the Transcendentalist's own paper of this time, the DIAL, he was connected closely enough with the group to attend an 1847 meeting with Amos Bronson ALCOTT, William Henry CHANNING, Ralph Waldo Emerson, Theodore PARKER, and others to discuss a successor to the Dial; a conversation which resulted in the creation of the MASSACHUSETTS QUARTERLY REVIEW. He had little further involvement with Transcendentalist ventures beyond the 1840s, however.

Stone, Thomas Treadwell
(1801–1895)

Unitarian minister and lecturer Thomas Treadwell Stone had religious, literary, and reform connections to nearly all of the major Transcendentalists and contributed to the DIAL magazine in the early 1840s. A native resident of Maine, Thomas Stone was a close friend of Mary Moody EMERSON, through whom he learned of and eventually met her nephew, Ralph Waldo EMERSON. Stone began regular contact with the Boston Transcendentalists and attended meetings of the TRANSCENDENTAL CLUB, the first organized meeting of people interested in the new philosophy. When the Dial was established, both Emerson and Margaret FULLER mentioned Stone as a desired and possible contributor for the paper. The January 1841 issue included his essay "Man and the Ages" and a year later, in January 1842, his "Calvinist's Letter" was published. The latter was based on an earlier letter Stone had written to Mary Moody Emerson regarding issues of Transcendentalist faith.

Stone's engagement with Transcendentalism led him to convert to UNITARIANISM, and he finally moved from Maine to Massachusetts in 1846 to accept a post as minister in Salem. He willingly exchanged pulpits with even the most controversial Transcendentalist ministers, such as Theodore PARKER. In 1852 he was removed from his congregation, not because of his involvement in the religious controversy of Transcendentalism, but over his radical ABOLITIONISM and his acceptance of black parishioners. He found other ministerial positions over the coming decades and continued to lecture publicly on history and literature. In 1856 he presented a lecture on "The Preacher" to the HARVARD DIVINITY SCHOOL that drew explicitly upon Ralph Waldo Emerson's DIVINITY SCHOOL ADDRESS given in that same venue nearly 20 years before. Stone reiterated Emerson's call for preachers to be guided by the inward spirit rather than the outward forms of historical Christianity. By 1856, however, Stone's words were received as benign inspiration for young liberal Unitarians rather than as the serious theological challenge Emerson had presented in the 1830s.

In Massachusetts, Thomas Stone became increasingly involved in Transcendentalist social and literary activities, hosting Amos Bronson AL-COTT's CONVERSATIONS and entertaining colleagues such as Emerson, Nathaniel HAWTHORNE and Sophia Peabody HAWTHORNE, Elizabeth Palmer PEABODY, and George RIPLEY at his home. He ultimately published two books—*Sermons* (1854) and *The Rod and the Staff* (1856)—that upheld an Emersonian-Transcendentalist vision of a spirituality based on intuition and personal experience.

Bibliography

Myerson, Joel. *The New England Transcendentalists and the Dial: A History of the Magazine and Its Contributors.* London and Toronto: Associated University Presses, 1980.

"The Succession of Forest Trees"
Henry David Thoreau
(1860)

Henry David THOREAU's lecture, "The Succession of Forest Trees" was delivered in September 1860 at the Middlesex Agricultural Society at the CON-CORD, MASSACHUSETTS, Town Hall and was first printed in the *NEW YORK TRIBUNE* in October 1860. The lecture, drawn from his research and journal notes from the previous decade, is one of his least known literary works, but it was his most important contribution to 19th-century scientific knowledge. Thoreau worked to expand his ideas into a book, *The Dispersion of Seeds,* which was never published but was a 354-page draft manuscript left at the time of his death.

The lecture was directed to the general townspeople of Concord and, specifically, to those engaged in agriculture, as part of Thoreau's effort to educate the public about the use and loss of the forests. "The Succession of Forest Trees" provided the history of the forest, the information that the human community needed in order to cultivate and profit from but also respect and preserve the landscape. Later, in his unpublished manuscript for *Dispersion of Seeds,* Thoreau advocated appointing public guardians of the forest, a precursor to the 20th-century idea of forest rangers and overall government protection and regulation of the forests.

"Succession" was perhaps Henry David Thoreau's most widely read essay during his lifetime. Besides this essay, Thoreau was not generally known for campaigning publicly on specific issues related to wilderness or agriculture, nor for addressing a more general science-minded audience. This essay marked one of the few times he specifically sought to apply his knowledge as a naturalist to solving a problem related to the human impact on nature. Even among this audience at the Agricultural Society, Thoreau appeared on stage with a reputation, but as a recluse and a writer, not as a scientist. He used this reputation to his advantage, however, opening his address with a joke in reference to his own standing among the townspeople, but also a plea for recognizing the overlap between agricultural-scientific and literary-poetic interests: "Every man is entitled to come to Cattle-Show, even a transcendentalist." He continued, voicing the thoughts perhaps of some in the audience: "Why choose a man to do plain work who is distinguished for his oddity?" Thoreau then established the source of his authority, which was his role as a local land surveyor who, therefore, knew the forests well and was particularly posed, even more than farmers, to see the bigger picture of destruction caused by Concord's human inhabitants. The farmer may understand the land, but it was Thoreau who had "several times shown the proprietor the shortest way out of his woodlot." Of course, Thoreau does not address the fact that as a land surveyor he had helped map out and plan the spread of human settlement that was causing the very problems he now wished to address.

Still, he had established his authority as a speaker on the topic of managing the landscape and introduced the main question to be addressed: how forests could reproduce themselves, with different species sometimes replacing each other in one area, that is, how it was "that when a pine wood was cut down an oak one commonly sprang up, and *vice versa.*" Thoreau's research throughout the previous decade had led him to an answer: animals and wind carry seeds from one area to another and, although unable to sprout if overshadowed by other tree species, the transplanted seeds are free to grow once the forests have been cleared by humans. Thoreau's theories of tree growth and of "spontaneous generation" had been drawn from his studies in the late 1850s and, after delivering "The Succession of Forest Trees," he continued to research "the dispersion of seeds." Thoreau was the first 19th-century scientist to articulate these findings in such a thorough fashion, but he acknowledged that others had been developing similar conclusions. Thoreau owed a great intellectual debt to Charles DARWIN and to Alexander von HUMBOLDT, in particular, both of whom he was reading and modeling his own work and methods on at this time.

Henry David Thoreau's audience on that day, and many of his contemporaries, understood well his contribution to scientific knowledge. After the address was concluded, the president of the Agricultural Society, a former governor of Massachusetts, commended Thoreau on a presentation "so plain and practical, and at the same time showing such close and careful study of natural phenomena." In the 19th century, distinctions between the scientific and the literary were not so clear as in our own time, and history has remembered Thoreau not as a scientist at all but as one of America's most important writers and as a poet-naturalist. Of course, his conclusions about "the dispersion of seeds" did have philosophical as well as scientific impact and his address on "The Succession of Forest Trees" ended with one of his most well-recognized metaphors: "Though I do not believe that a plant will spring up where no seed has been, I have great faith in a seed . . . Convince me that you have a seed there, and I am prepared to expect wonders."

Bibliography

Berger, Michael Benjamin. *Thoreau's Later Career and The Dispersion of Seeds: The Saunterer's Synoptic Vision.* Rochester, N.Y.: Camden House, 2000.

Walls, Laura Dassow. *Seeing New Worlds: Henry David Thoreau and Nineteenth-Century Natural Science.* Madison: University of Wisconsin Press, 1995.

Summer on the Lakes, in 1843
Margaret Fuller
(1844)

Margaret FULLER's *Summer on the Lakes* is an account of an 1843 trip westward through New York, the Great Lakes, Illinois, and the Wisconsin Territory with her sometime companion, fellow Transcendentalist Sarah Freeman CLARKE, who also drew illustrations for the book. Clarke's brother, James Freeman CLARKE, financially sponsored Fuller's travels and also accompanied the women on some legs of the tour. Fuller recorded what she termed her "poetic impression of the country at large" based on her detailed journals of the people and places she encountered. The text that resulted, *Summer on the Lakes,* was Fuller's first original book-length work, as she had previously published only translations of German writers.

As with other 19th-century travel and nature writing—especially other Transcendentalist writing, such as that by Henry David THOREAU—Fuller's account in *Summer on the Lakes* is more a psychological or spiritual journey than just a physical one. She explicitly stated that "I have not been particularly anxious to give the geography of the scene," but instead sought to communicate the lessons she had learned from her experiences—lessons about history, politics, and moral life. Ultimately what was revealed was a voyage of discovery about herself, as a woman and a writer. Most scholarly critics of Fuller's text have noted that, particularly in the figure and story of "Mariana" within the book, Fuller offered up a semiautobiographical account of woman's struggle with the societal boundaries imposed upon her; or, as Fuller put it, "the defect in the position of woman" in American society.

Margaret Fuller's text went beyond the individual experience of the travel narrative or spiritual journey of self-development in offering a critique of American history and progress through an examination of the impact of westward expansion, particularly on the dispossessed native peoples and on white women as settlers and pioneers. Fuller's interest in Indian women began in her essay "THE GREAT LAWSUIT," published that same summer in the Transcendentalist journal, the DIAL, and in *Summer on the Lakes* she continued to compare Indians and white women in their lack of rights and subordinate social status.

Upon reading *Summer on the Lakes*, editor Horace GREELEY offered Fuller a job as a literary reviewer and critic for his NEW YORK TRIBUNE. Realizing the larger importance and appeal of Margaret Fuller's writings, it was Greeley who also suggested that she expand "The Great Lawsuit" essay into a full-length book, which she did with the 1845 WOMAN IN THE NINETEENTH CENTURY.

Bibliography

Fuller, Margaret. *Summer on the Lakes, in 1843.* Ed. Susan Belasco Smith. Urbana: University of Illinois Press, 1991.

Sumner, Charles
(1811–1874)

Charles Sumner was a graduate of Harvard College, a lawyer, and a Free Soil Senator from Massachusetts who moved within the same New England social reform and elite intellectual circles as many of the Transcendentalists, including Amos Bronson ALCOTT, the Reverend William Ellery CHANNING, Ralph Waldo EMERSON, Theodore PARKER, abolitionist Wendell PHILLIPS, and Henry David THOREAU. In 1845 Emerson heard Sumner speak at Harvard, where he invoked the antislavery commitment and example of Reverend Channing. That same year both Emerson and Sumner publicly announced that they would not speak at the New Bedford Lyceum because of its exclusionary practice of not allowing black members. Proponent of radical ABOLITIONISM William Lloyd GARRISON published the boycott letters from the two men in his paper, *The Liberator.*

Charles Sumner was well known for his powerful speaking skills, and this was what most attracted Ralph Waldo Emerson to him. Sumner spoke out vehemently against the FUGITIVE SLAVE LAW of 1850 and was elected to his U.S. Senate position on an antislavery platform. Emerson reached a turning point after 1850 as well and was motivated to give his "FUGITIVE SLAVE LAW ADDRESS" and enter the public arena on the issue. Sumner encouraged Emerson by writing to him and offering his comradeship and his confidence that "your judgment of the Fugitive Slave Bill posterity will adopt, even if the men of our day do not." Around that same time, in the summer of 1850, Sumner was linked with the Transcendentalists through a personal experience when it was discovered that Sumner's brother had drowned in the same shipwreck that claimed the life of Transcendentalist feminist and journalist Margaret FULLER. This event initiated a friendship between Sumner and Henry David Thoreau, who had been sent to the site of the wreckage to search for Fuller and her belongings, and in 1854 Thoreau sent Sumner a copy of his new book, WALDEN.

Sumner's outspoken and violent opposition to slavery and to the Kansas-Nebraska bill led to his May 1856 speech on "The Crime Against Kansas" in which he politically and personally attacked proslavery Southern Senators, in particular Senator Butler of South Carolina. Two days after the speech Sumner was physically attacked on the Senate floor by Butler's nephew and fellow congressman, Representative Preston Brooks of South Carolina. Although Sumner was unable to attend Senate sessions for over three years while recovering from serious injuries incurred in the beating, his antislavery supporters now saw him as a martyr to the cause and ensured his reelection for another Senate term, this time in the Republican Party. The attack on Sumner outraged Northern reformers and abolitionists, including the Transcendentalists, and was seen by many as evidence of the effect of a violent culture on the South. Just days after the attack a meeting was called in CONCORD, MASSACHUSETTS, which several Transcendentalists attended. Ralph Waldo Emerson gave an address on the "Assault upon Mr. Sumner" and declared "I think we must get rid of slavery, or we must get rid of freedom."

Charles Sumner continued his career in radical politics after the Civil War, aiding in the impeachment of Reconstruction President Johnson and supporting black civil rights. He remained a hero of New England reformers and intellectuals throughout his life. In 1874 Henry Wadsworth LONGFELLOW wrote a memorial to "Charles Sumner" upon his death, and former friends and colleagues Ralph Waldo Emerson and John Greenleaf WHITTIER served as pallbearers.

Bibliography

Gougeon, Len. *Virtue's Hero: Emerson, Antislavery, and Reform.* Athens: University of Georgia Press, 1990.

Swedenborg, Emanuel   *See* SWEDEN-
BORGIANISM.

"Swedenborg; or, The Mystic"   *See* REPRE-
SENTATIVE MEN.

Swedenborgianism

Swedenborgianism, or the ideas of Swedish mystic Emanuel Swedenborg, was one of the most important influences upon the development of Transcendentalist thought in the early 19th century and on Ralph Waldo EMERSON in particular. Swedenborg was a scientist who wrote on an eclectic range of scientific and metaphysical topics in the mid-18th century. In 1745 Swedenborg had a vision that shifted his philosophical focus toward a more metaphysical examination of the relationship between the spiritual and the natural worlds, a relationship he called a theory of "correspondence." The Swedenborgian idea of "correspondence" emphasized that nature itself was "purely symbolical of the spiritual world," and that language was the key to unlocking the "natural truth" around us, both ideas that formed the foundation of Transcendentalist philosophy as well. Swedenborg warned that nature's symbolism or "correspondence" could be interpreted wrongly to form the basis of religious dogma rather than spiritual truth. Emerson altered Swedenborg's

language but held to the same ideas when he discussed the "picture-language" of nature and the interpretation of nature's language into spiritual truths.

Before reading Swedenborg directly, Emerson was introduced to the ideas in the 1820s through the writings of the main American proponent of the philosophy, Sampson REED. Emerson read Reed's Swedenborgian ideas in the 1821 "Oration on Genius" as well as the 1826 *Observations on the Growth of the Mind.* In 1827 a Swedenborgian church in Boston began publishing the ideas in the NEW JERUSALEM MAGAZINE, a paper which Emerson also regularly read. Emerson's seminal work, NATURE, published in 1836, relied heavily and expanded upon the Swedenborgian concept of "correspondences" with its emphasis on decoding the language of nature. Many recognized the Swedenborgianian aspects of Emerson's early IDEALISM and associated the two thinkers, and Emerson himself continued to acknowledge Swedenborg directly as a "genius," along with Samuel Taylor COLERIDGE and Immanuel KANT, who influenced his own ideas.

Other Transcendentalists read and discussed Swedenborg with Ralph Waldo Emerson and applied Swedenborgian thought to their own philosophical and reform projects. Amos Bronson ALCOTT mused to Emerson that Swedenborg's writings "should be in the hands of every earnest student of the soul." Lydia Maria CHILD was attracted to Swedenborg's mysticism and, later, in the mid-1840s, Margaret FULLER wrote in her feminist manifesto, WOMAN IN THE NINETEENTH CENTURY, that Swedenborg should be considered one of three "prophets of the coming age," along with Charles Fourier (*see* FOURIERISM) and Johann Wolfgang von GOETHE, for their progressive ideas on relations between the sexes. Not all Transcendentalists were enthusiastic about Swedenborg's ideas, however. Early on Frederic Henry HEDGE, for example, had written an unfavorable review of Swedenborg's *The True Christian Religion* in the CHRISTIAN EXAMINER, the main journal of UNITARIANISM at that time. While acknowledging the "progressive spirit" of Swedenborgianism, which attracted many reformers and was practiced by Boston's New Church, Hedge ultimately rejected the attention given to Swedenborg himself as an "idolatry which can embrace a human tradition as if it were a revelation from God."

Ultimately it was as an individual thinker, a man of genius, that Ralph Waldo Emerson would honor Swedenborg "the Mystic" as one of his six REPRESENTATIVE MEN (1850) of history. Emerson first lectured on Swedenborg in 1845, and in the 1850 book Emerson reflects upon both the positive aspects and the faults with Swedenborgianism. He especially held up Swedenborg as an ideal scientist, one whose methods were "systematic" and comprehensive in taking the whole of the universe as his subject, but who, more importantly, "put science and soul, long estranged from each other, at one again." Still, Emerson felt that Swedenborg, as evidenced by the "New Church" devoted to his ideas, was too "exclusively theologic" in his reliance on Scripture. In the end, Swedenborgianism as a philosophy could not be universally applied because it was too attached "to the Christian symbol, instead of to the moral sentiment." Emerson's paradoxical debt to Swedenborg and his rejection of the Swedenborgians as an organized group brought criticism from members of the New Church, but he succeeded in distancing himself from that group and from the tinge of the "theologic," while acknowledging and retaining his debt to the philosophy. For Ralph Waldo Emerson, the true role of the prophet or "mystic" was as a messenger or interpreter of natural and spiritual laws, as an inspirer more than a leader.

Bibliography

Brock, Erland, ed. *Swedenborg and His Influence.* Bryn Athyn, Pa.: Academy of the New Church, 1988.

"Sympathy"
Henry David Thoreau
(1839)

Henry David THOREAU's poem "Sympathy" was recorded in his journal in the summer of 1839 and submitted for publication to Ralph Waldo EMERSON for the first issue of the Transcendentalist literary journal, the DIAL, in July 1840. Many of Thoreau's contemporaries and friends believed the poem to have been written to a neighbor girl in whom a young Thoreau had romantic interests. In "Sympathy," however, the object of his affection and attention is identified as a "boy," and it may have been the girl's younger brother who directly inspired the childlike in the young adult Thoreau. It is also possible to read the "gentle boy" of the poem, "Whose features all were cast in Virtue's mould," as in fact the young Thoreau himself. The poem is a celebration of childhood, including his own, as he describes some of his boyhood experiences from the perspective of the adult who now feels the loss but has also been changed by those experiences. The case that the "gentle boy" refers to a neighbor boy is further made by the fact that Thoreau wrote "Sympathy" just days after describing in his journal meeting a neighbor boy, Edmund Sewall, in whom Thoreau may have seen his own younger self: "this youth was glorious, / Himself a kingdom whereso'eer he came."

While this general theme describes the poem as a whole, it is in fact written in four separate and distinct parts. The first section sets up the theme of Thoreau's own lost childhood and describes the "gentle boy" from the perspective of an involved but separate adult observer: "Lately alas I knew a gentle boy." In the following stanzas Thoreau regrets that he could not appreciate the "boy" at the time, but only later upon reflection realizes that "Yet now am forced to know, though hard it is, / I might have loved him, had I loved him less." In some sense, however, it is too late and too difficult to reconnect with the vantage point of youth: "Each moment, as we nearer drew to each, / A stern respect withheld us farther yet, / So that we seemed beyond each other's reach, / And less acquainted than when first we met." Thoreau then moves beyond grieving the distance between the two, between youth and adulthood, to acceptance that "Eternity may not the chance repeat, / But I must tread my single way alone." Finally, in the final stanza, Thoreau rejoices that "If I but love that virtue which he is . . . Still shall we be truest acquaintances." That is, that in remembering and incorporating the "virtues" he admired in the "gentle boy" into his current Self, then they shall be one again, "Nor mortals know a sympathy more rare." Through opening himself up to what the child and the childlike has to teach, Thoreau can continue to grow as a person.

Henry David Thoreau's "Sympathy" is more than a love poem or a tribute to a childhood friend. In more spiritual terms, it is a Transcendentalist celebration of childhood and an acknowledgment of the struggle to return to the innocence and openness of childlike virtues, a recurring theme within the broader literature of ROMANTICISM in general.

Bibliography

Pitts, Mary E. "Thoreau's Poem 'Sympathy': His 'Gentle Boy' Identified," *The Concord Saunterer* 18:2 (December 1985): 20–27

T

Table-Talk
Amos Bronson Alcott
(1877)

Transcendentalist poet and reformer Amos Bronson ALCOTT gathered together more than 100 short verses he called "Philosophemes" into his 1877 book *Table-Talk*. The JOURNAL OF SPECULATIVE PHILOSOPHY, under the editorship of Alcott's friend and colleague William Torrey HARRIS, regularly published his "Philosophemes," a genre much like the "ORPHIC SAYINGS" that Alcott had published in the Transcendentalist literary journal, the DIAL, more than three decades before. In this particular format of short verse Alcott strove to provide spontaneous utterings or reflections on various spiritual or mystical themes. In its scope of topics and its presentation as more of a parlor discussion than a philosophical treatise (as indicated in the title, *Table-Talk*), the book was also in many ways an extension of Alcott's work through his CONVERSATIONS, at which he attempted to engage participants on some of the same mystical themes. It was also very similar in conversational format and in topics covered to his earlier works, TABLETS (1868) and CONCORD DAYS (1872). In all his works, Alcott sought to cover a range of subjects from his views on EDUCATION and child development to more provincial interests such as gardening and neighbors. Transcendentalist colleague and fellow reformer George RIPLEY reviewed *Table-Talk* in the NEW YORK TRIBUNE where he referred to Alcott as a seer who only suggested thoughts for his readers to develop. In Ripley's words, Alcott "lends a powerful aid to our aspirations after the highest, and supplies a refreshing cordial amidst the cares and perturbations of this working day world." *Table-Talk* received mostly positive reviews and was most influential in bringing attention to Alcott and to the town of CONCORD, MASSACHUSETTS, boosting the success of Alcott's next experiment, the CONCORD SCHOOL OF PHILOSOPHY AND LITERATURE summer program, which he initiated in 1879.

Bibliography
Dahlstrand, Frederick. *Amos Bronson Alcott: An Intellectual Biography.* East Brunswick, N.J.: Associated University Presses, 1982.

Tablets
Amos Bronson Alcott
(1868)

Tablets was a collection of essays published by Transcendentalist reformer and mystic poet Amos Bronson ALCOTT in 1868. The book was divided into two parts, "Practical" and "Speculative." The first part on "Practical" matters includes essays on "The Garden," "Books," "Counsels," "Friendship," and other topics. The "Speculative" essays include Transcendental reflections on "Instrumentalities," "Mind," "Genesis," and "Metamorphoses." Several of Alcott's poems were also included in each section. *Tablets* was essentially an edited volume of many writings Alcott had been working on over the previous two years, primarily in his journals.

Bronson Alcott published this book of reflections on various spiritual truths in 1868 as a contribution to the free religion (*see* FREE RELIGIOUS ASSOCIATION) or free thought movement then engaging many of the Transcendentalists and other religious reformers of the mid-19th century. The essays in *Tablets* were not tied together as part of any systematic philosophy. The lack of identifiable structure or theme itself was a deliberate attempt by Alcott, however, who, previously known primarily for his ambiguous mystical "ORPHIC SAYINGS," had cultivated a writing style based on the rejection of traditional forms and genres in favor of spontaneous utterings of the soul. In separating *Tablets* into the two sections, "Practical" and "Speculative," however, Alcott did guide the reader through the topics addressed as they concerned mundane daily aspects of life, such as "The Garden" and "Friendship," as well as loftier metaphysical concerns such as "Mind" and "Metamorpheses." If *Tablets* had one guiding theme, it was Alcott's Transcendentalist emphasis on the spiritual significance of all things.

As a Transcendentalist mediation, *Tablets* dealt extensively with the theme of nature; in particular, Alcott's own relationship to the land through gardening and farming, at home and at his short-lived communitarian experiment, FRUITLANDS. As he had believed in founding Fruitlands in the early 1840s, in *Tablets* Alcott praised the rural ideal of simple living as the route to spiritual awareness and criticized the dominant mid-19th century values of rampant commercialism, urbanization, and technological advances as leading humankind only to "covetousness and debasing cares." By contrast, agricultural life engendered virtues such as community with nature and family, and closer proximity to nature and thus God.

Tablets was one of Bronson Alcott's most popular and commercially successful books. He received many positive reviews from both within and outside of Transcendentalist circles. Philosopher of HEGELIANISM William Torrey HARRIS, who would later join Alcott as a lecturer at the CONCORD SCHOOL OF PHILOSOPHY AND LITERATURE, most clearly understood and appreciated Alcott's pro-

ject in *Tablets* when he concluded in his review that Alcott's "whole life and utterances have been one unceasing effort toward the emancipation of spiritual self-consciousness." Alcott's Transcendentalist friend and fellow reformer George RIPLEY reviewed *Tablets* in the NEW YORK TRIBUNE, promising readers that "From the serene heights of intuition he utters the burdens of his soul." The most negative review came from the *Nation* magazine where an anonymous critic declared that Alcott simply uttered what first came to mind, an "orphic" skill that even the "village idiot" could possess. While the book sold well and a variety of newspapers and magazines sought interviews and information on the author, his success and the interest in his work were no doubt aided by the coincidental rising fame of his daughter, Louisa May ALCOTT, whose immediately best-selling novel, *LITTLE WOMEN*, was published the same exact month as *Tablets*. Regardless, *Tablets* helped Bronson Alcott expand and strengthen his own connections within the world of religious studies and philosophical organizations as he answered invitations to speak and expand on his ideas for spiritual guidance.

Bibliography
Dahlstrand, Frederick. *Amos Bronson Alcott: An Intellectual Biography.* East Brunswick, N.J.: Associated University Presses, 1982.

Tappan, Caroline Sturgis
(1819–1888)

Transcendentalist poet Caroline Sturgis (later Tappan) was a close friend of both Ralph Waldo EMERSON and Margaret FULLER and published several of her poems in the main Transcendentalist literary journal, the *DIAL*. Fuller initially served as a mentor for the young Caroline, and the two became the closest of confidantes. In 1836 Fuller brought Sturgis to CONCORD, MASSACHUSETTS, where she met Emerson who would later characterize Sturgis as "the Ideal friend." Sturgis befriended others among the Transcendentalists in Concord including Amos Bronson ALCOTT, Sarah Freeman CLARKE, Elizabeth HOAR, and Henry David THOREAU. She had brief potentially romantic involvements with Charles NEWCOMB during his residency at BROOK FARM, and with fellow *Dial*-published poet William Ellery CHANNING II, who ultimately married Margaret Fuller's sister, Ellen. Caroline Sturgis also resided at the OLD MANSE for a while with Nathaniel HAWTHORNE and Sophia Peabody HAWTHORNE before her own 1847 marriage to William Tappan, to whom Caroline had been introduced by Emerson.

Caroline Sturgis was one of the most prolific of the *Dial* poets, publishing 25 poems in four different volumes of the journal, 11 of them in the October 1840 volume alone. As Margaret Fuller was the first editor of the *Dial,* she had solicited her friend's contributions and had sent several poems to Emerson to choose from as well. Sturgis's titles such as "From Goethe," "Art and Artist," "Life and Death," and "Betinna!" were all printed anonymously with only Emerson and Fuller knowing the identity of the author. Sturgis's poems continued to appear until she wrote to Emerson that she was not able to produce any new work. Her older sister, Ellen Sturgis HOOPER, also published poetry in the *Dial,* and the two were regarded as among the most talented of the early Transcendentalist poets whose verses, according to Emerson, served to "enrich & ensoul" the magazine. Although she remained friends and corresponded with Ralph Waldo Emerson, Caroline Sturgis Tappan's life after her marriage and the untimely death of her friend Margaret Fuller drew her away from Transcendentalist circles.

Bibliography

Myerson, Joel. *The New England Transcendentalists and the Dial: A History of the Magazine and Its Contributors.* London and Toronto: Associated University Presses, 1980.

Temple School

Transcendentalist educational reformer and philosopher Amos Bronson ALCOTT opened his Temple School for children in Boston in September 1834 with support from the Unitarian Reverend William Ellery CHANNING and assistance from Elizabeth Palmer PEABODY, who also helped him advertise for and set up the school. The Alcott family had been living in Philadelphia during an unsuccessful attempt to establish a school there and moved to Boston with encouragement that New England parents were more likely to send their children to an experimental school. Alcott's school was referred to as the Temple School because it met at the Tremont Street Masonic Temple in Boston, and in the fall of 1834 there were 30 young children enrolled, 15 boys and 15 girls. Alcott's primary teaching philosophy was to draw out the innate moral goodness of children with the goal of nurturing the self-development of the students, and he believed that the teacher's role was merely to guide children to recognize and develop their own spiritual natures. As a social reformer, Alcott also intended to provide a model of a new type of EDUCATION that other schools and parents could implement.

Elizabeth Palmer Peabody was herself a student of educational philosophy, teacher, and reformer when she enthusiastically agreed to assist Alcott in his school. Peabody taught Latin and recorded Alcott's daily sessions during his first year, noting his particular methods and teaching tools. Alcott furnished his classroom with objects intended to inspire intellectual and spiritual reflection, with portraits and busts of inspiring figures, and with as many books as he could afford to purchase. One of Alcott's signature methods was an emphasis on "CONVERSATION" with the students rather than authoritative instruction and rote learning. Through conversation, or discussion sessions, he attempted to draw out the students' own thoughts on various topics and guide them toward freer expression and relating general moral principles to their own lives. Although Alcott's goals and methods were idealistic, he also had to maintain authority as the teacher and implemented a system of rewards and punishments in order to get the students to participate on acceptable terms. Peabody recorded all of these aspects of the school experiment and published her account, along with her own introduction, in 1835 as RECORD OF A SCHOOL: *Exemplifying the General Principles of Spiritual Culture.* The book earned Alcott positive attention from other reformers for his efforts at the

Temple School and coincided with his meeting Ralph Waldo EMERSON (who praised the book) and becoming involved with many activities of the Transcendentalists.

Alcott began another year of the school in the fall of 1835 even more optimistic about his venture and his success inspired him to reinvigorate his own parenting methods with his two young daughters. Elizabeth Peabody's sister, Mary Peabody, joined the school as a French teacher and in October 1835 Alcott added a supplemental course on the gospels. Elizabeth Peabody again attended and recorded Alcott's meetings with children on broader spiritual themes related to Scripture and morality, again with the pedagogical purpose of drawing out the children's own innate virtues. The December 1836 publication of Peabody's second volume on Temple School, CONVERSATIONS WITH CHILDREN ON THE GOSPELS, however, brought unexpected criticism and charges of blasphemy for Alcott's uncensored discussions with students on subjects ranging from birth and marriage to heaven and hell. Elizabeth Peabody, concerned about the inevitable controversy, left Temple School before the book was published and Alcott had approached Margaret FULLER as a possible replacement. Although *Conversations* continued to influence Alcott's reformist educator friends, the negative publicity and religious controversy surrounding its publication led parents to withdraw their students, forcing Alcott to close the school permanently in June 1838.

Bibliography

Dahlstrand, Frederick. *Amos Bronson Alcott: An Intellectual Biography.* East Brunswick, N.J.: Associated University Presses, 1982.

"Terminus"
Ralph Waldo Emerson
(1867)

Ralph Waldo EMERSON began composing the poem "Terminus" as early as the mid-1840s, finalizing it sometime in the 1850s, but it was first published in 1867 in his second full collection of poems, MAY-DAY AND OTHER PIECES. "Terminus" deals with the question of dying and of how best to use one's time on Earth. Writing in the 1840s, Emerson was surrounded by the death of friends and loved ones, most notably, his first wife, Ellen Tucker EMERSON his brother, Charles Chauncy EMERSON, and his young son, Waldo, who died in 1842 at only five years old. While "THRENODY" is the poem that deals directly and heart-wrenchingly with the untimely death of Waldo, and to some degree "THE WORLD-SOUL" as well in that it also seeks to make sense of death, "Terminus" is usually read as a middle-aged Emerson's reflection on aging and opens with the modest declaration that "It is time to be old, / To take in sail," thus a reflection on the more natural course toward death than the unexplainable death of a child.

In "Terminus" Emerson seemed to recognize and accept his own physical limitations in comparing human life to that of a tree: "No more! No farther shoot Thy broad ambitious branches, and thy root." The image of a tree refers not only to an individual but to a family or genealogy, and perhaps Emerson was reflecting on the extent to which he himself had strayed from the ways of his ancestors. Emerson reflected on his decisions and his life accomplishments or, in his perception, his lack of accomplishments. In his eyes he had tried and failed in every realm, whether "Amid the gladiators" or powerful people of action in the world, or "Amid the Muses" in the world of literature and art. The last stanza moves from looking backward to thinking about the remainder of his life, about growing old, and concludes somewhat without emotion: "Lowly faithful, banish fear, Right onward drive unharmed; / The port, well worth the cruise, is near, And every wave is charmed."

Emerson biographer Gay Allen argues that "Terminus" is best read as an example of "Emerson trying to apply his philosophy of Fate to his own life." In the essay "FATE," Emerson attempted to balance the paradoxical viewpoints of individual will with the complete lack of control humans face as beings governed by the forces of nature, including aging. In "Terminus" he advises the reader to "Timely wise accept the terms," and to "Still plan and smile." In this sense, then, "Terminus" is not a poem about giving up or about regrets but about stoically facing the inevitable. Emerson retains a belief in individual choice and control, however, and concludes that he will remain the guiding force in his own life, for as long as the "storm" of nature will allow: "I trim myself to the storm of time, / I man the rudder, reef the sail." In the end, then, Emerson is less focused on death itself and remains interested in the quality of the life to be lived.

Bibliography

Allen, Gay Wilson. *Waldo Emerson: A Biography*. New York: Viking Press, 1981.

"Things and Thoughts in Europe"
Margaret Fuller
(1846–1850)

Margaret FULLER sailed for Europe in August 1846 and worked over the next several years as a foreign correspondent for Horace GREELEY at the NEW YORK TRIBUNE under the column title "Things and Thoughts in Europe." Fuller had previously written for the *Tribune* as a literary and social critic, and her columns on foreign affairs included commentary on European literary and artistic culture, as well as accounts of her travels and political issues. As in her earlier writings on American culture and society, Fuller's European dispatches emphasized her interest in reform of social and political institutions. She wrote a series of pieces on the condition of the poor and working classes in England, determining that the situation in England "has terrors of which I never dreamed at home." Again, as in her writings and travels throughout the United States, Fuller was particularly attuned to the condition of women working in English textile mills. From France she wrote of similar economic conditions and widespread unemployment and called for revolutionary change.

Her last set of dispatches to the *Tribune* came from Italy, where she observed firsthand the beginnings of a radical revolution that quickly engaged all of her attention and brought her together with her husband, Giovanni Ossoli, an Italian revolutionary. As to the political situation, she predicted the rise of socialism and that "All the more for what has happened in these sad days, will entire Europe, at the end of the century, be under Republican form of Government." Fuller sent her last dispatches to Greeley in early 1850 and set sail to return to the United States. Margaret Fuller died when her ship wrecked off the coast of New York in July 1850, killing her husband and young son as well. Her friends believed her to have a book-length manuscript history of the Italian revolution with her at the time of her death, but her papers were never recovered. Her articles for the *Tribune* became all the more interesting to the American public due to her untimely death, and her brother, Arthur Fuller, collected her writings together in the 1856 publication, *At Home and Abroad, or Things and Thoughts in America and Europe*.

Bibliography

Reynolds, Larry J., and Susan Belasco Smith, eds. *"These Sad but Glorious Days": Dispatches from Europe, 1846–1850*. New Haven, Conn.: Yale University Press, 1991.

"Thoreau"
Ralph Waldo Emerson
(1862)

Transcendentalist poet-naturalist Henry David THOREAU died on May 6, 1862, from tuberculosis, and friend and colleague Ralph Waldo EMERSON helped make the funeral arrangements in CONCORD, MASSACHUSETTS, and delivered the eulogy. Emerson's thoughts on "Thoreau" were expanded from a eulogy into more of a memoir and subsequently published in the ATLANTIC MONTHLY in August 1862 and, the following year, served as introduction to the collection of Thoreau's essays, *Excursions*, gathered together and published by Sophia THOREAU and William Ellery CHANNING II, in 1863. "Thoreau" was the most thorough and personal reminiscence by a contemporary and was, in fact, one of Ralph Waldo Emerson's last original essays.

Emerson had known Henry David Thoreau for 25 years, and in his eulogy provided an overview of the specifics and the peculiarities of his friend's character and lifestyle, remarking that Thoreau "was bred to no profession; he never married; he lived alone; he never went to church; he never voted; he refused to pay a tax to the State; he ate no flesh, he drank no wine, he never knew the use of tobacco; and though a naturalist, he used neither trap nor gun." These facts were used to explain the intense originality of Thoreau's character and personality, for Emerson pointed out the paradox of a man who had no regular income and no property but lived the life of "the only man of leisure in town," seeing "the material world as a means and a symbol" but never as an end. That is, Thoreau was free from the constraints of the material as well as the expectations of the social world, a fact that Emerson both admired and resented. He emphasized Thoreau's solitary lifestyle, referring to him variously as a "bachelor of thought and Nature," a "hermit and ascetic," a man for whom "the manners and talk of highly cultivated people, were all thrown away." The effect of this for Thoreau's literary career was, according to Emerson, most regrettable, and he admitted that "I cannot help counting it a fault in him that he had no ambition."

Thoreau did not define success, literary or otherwise, in the same terms as Emerson and, while Emerson undoubtedly meant that Thoreau had no economic or political ambition, like so many misguided men of their time, Emerson failed to fully acknowledge the publishing successes Thoreau did have, most notably the 1854 publication of WALDEN. Mentioning *Walden* briefly, and only the poems "SYMPATHY" and "SMOKE" by name, Emerson chose to focus on Thoreau's personality and his naturalist tendencies over his work as a writer, making only vague reference to Thoreau's impact on "reading Americans." Emerson recognized and admired that "Mr. Thoreau dedicated his genius with such entire love to the fields, hill and waters of his native town, that he made them known and interesting to all reading Americans, and to people over the sea." Glossing over the specifics of Thoreau's literary or scientific contributions, however, the result of Emerson's portrayal was that he helped create the image of the lone lover of the woods that we now associate with Henry David Thoreau: "He wore a straw hat, stout shoes, strong grey trousers to brave scrub-oaks and smilax, and to climb a tree for a hawk's or a squirrel's nest."

Ralph Waldo Emerson had a close personal and professional relationship with Henry David Thoreau, and his eulogy to his friend revealed the tensions of their interaction. When the two men met in 1837, Emerson was emerging as a controversial and prolific figure in the new Transcendentalist movement, having already published his manifesto on NATURE (1836). The elder Emerson served as a mentor to Thoreau and was responsible for introducing the younger man into literary and social circles. Emerson sought to nurture Thoreau as a promising young writer by publishing some of his early poetry in the Transcendentalist literary journal, the DIAL. Throughout their careers Emerson was frustrated that Thoreau had not reached his full potential, and his frank criticisms and minimizing of Thoreau's solitary time in nature come out in the final address: "with his energy and practical ability he seemed born for great enterprise and for command . . . Wanting this, instead of engineering for all America, he was the captain of a huckleberry party." Emerson spoke of Thoreau's "endless walks" and "miscellaneous studies" as if they were time-wasting hobbies rather than the basis of actual scientific studies and of Thoreau's philosophical quest to understand humanity's relationship to nature. While contemporaries assumed, rightly, that Emerson had much admiration for Thoreau—he praised him as "a truth-speaker" and a man of "robust common sense"—the overarching critique and even dismissal of Thoreau's life project did not go unnoticed by those in the audience. Louisa May ALCOTT, for example, privately felt that Emerson's comments were more critical than a eulogy should be and were ultimately "not appropriate to the time or place."

Despite some of his criticisms, Emerson recognized Thoreau's genius and lamented the unfinished work of a life cut short, "a kind of indignity to so noble a soul, that it should depart out of Nature before yet he has been really shown to his peers for what he is." Arguably, Emerson's eulogy, widely reprinted as it was, made it more difficult to understand what Thoreau was truly about, but Emerson ended the address with an emotional assessment of the great loss to both him and the nation by his friend's "sudden disappearance": "The country knows not yet, or in the least part, how great a son it has lost."

Bibliography

Sattelmeyer, Robert. "Thoreau and Emerson." In *Cambridge Companion to Henry David Thoreau*, ed. Joel Myerson. New York: Cambridge University Press, 1995, 25–39.

Smith, Harmon. *My Friend, My Friend: The Story of Thoreau's Relationship with Emerson*. Amherst: University of Massachusetts Press, 1999.

Thoreau, Henry David
(1817–1862)

Henry David Thoreau was a Transcendentalist naturalist and writer whose two seminal writings, WALDEN; OR, LIFE IN THE WOODS (1854) and the essay, "CIVIL DISOBEDIENCE" (1849), made him one of the most influential thinkers of his day and beyond. A graduate of Harvard, Henry David Thoreau lived in CONCORD, MASSACHUSETTS, almost his entire life near his senior colleague, philosopher Ralph Waldo EMERSON. The never-married Thoreau was intimate with Emerson's entire family, finding in Lidian EMERSON a confidante and taking pleasure in teaching and playing with the Emersons' young children. Other friends among the Transcendentalists included Amos Bronson ALCOTT, William Ellery CHANNING II, Margaret FULLER, and Nathaniel HAWTHORNE. While Emerson is usually regarded as the premier philosopher-poet of Transcendentalism, Henry David Thoreau is remembered for acting on his principles and pursuing a consistent lifelong purpose of self-reliance and self-government, living in harmony with nature and with the larger society. Indeed, Thoreau's writings on political philosophy directly influenced the work of some of the 20th-century's most important thinkers and activists, such as Mohandas K. GANDHI, Martin Luther King, Jr., and Leo Tolstoy.

Thoreau was born and raised in Concord, where he experienced the full range of benefits from an upbringing in close contact with nature. For young Thoreau, the importance of Concord was its ready access to river and forest. Thoreau learned from Indians who would camp near the river the art of paddling a canoe. In his 1862 elegy, "Thoreau," Emerson said, "He was a good swim-mer, runner, skater, boatman, and would probably out-walk most countrymen in a day's journey." At Harvard, Thoreau was thought to be outstanding neither scholastically nor socially, and he was not fond of athletics. Soon after his graduation from Harvard, Thoreau was introduced to Emerson, who had already expressed interest in the young man as a poet, and invited him to visit his home. Thoreau worked briefly as a schoolteacher, although, as he later recalled in *Walden*, "As I did not teach for the good of my fellow-men, but simply for a livelihood, this was a failure." In 1841 Emerson invited Thoreau to board with his family, where Thoreau ultimately resided for about two years. Thoreau was a skillful laborer, an expert handyman and gardener at the Emerson home, and the bond between the two men became closer. Early 1842 brought shocks through the household, however, when first Emerson's beloved five-year old son, Waldo, died from scarlet fever, and then Thoreau's brother John THOREAU, JR., died suddenly from lockjaw after cutting himself while shaving. Thoreau was heartbroken at the loss of his closest companion since childhood. In 1839 he had taken a trip with his brother John that would form the basis of his first book, A WEEK ON THE CONCORD AND MERRIMACK RIVERS, published 10 years later in 1849.

During this period, Henry David Thoreau became enmeshed in Transcendentalist activities swarming around Concord, and he attended meetings of the TRANSCENDENTAL CLUB and was published in every volume of the Transcendentalist quarterly magazine, the DIAL. His contributions included several poems, including "SYMPATHY," writings on "Friendship," the "Natural History of Massachusetts," selected sayings of Buddha and of Confucius, and other pieces. Thoreau spent some time in New York tutoring the children of Ralph Waldo Emerson's brother, William EMERSON, and he came into acquaintance with reformers of that city such as Horace GREELEY and Henry JAMES, SR.

By the 1840s Thoreau had returned to Concord and befriended many of the Transcendentalists who were interested in building communities based on social reform principles and simplified living. George RIPLEY's BROOK FARM and Bronson Alcott's FRUITLANDS were two short-lived attempts at sustainable communal living. Thoreau the individualist, however, was not interested in living in such a communal setting and was instead attracted to the ideal of a solitary life in nature, living according to his own philosophy. And so, in March of 1845, Thoreau began his preparations to build a cabin and live alone on a secluded spot at WALDEN POND, a mile from any neighbor. He later explained, "I wanted to live deep and suck out all the marrow of life . . . to drive life into a corner, and reduce it to its lowest terms . . . to get the whole and genuine meanness of it." Thoreau moved into his cabin on July 4, 1845, and lived there until September 1847. The account of his experience was published as *Walden* in 1854, one of only two books Thoreau published in his lifetime.

Walden is a series of essay-like chapters on living life simply and well, in touch with nature, aware of one's surroundings and one's self. The book recounts his two years spent at Walden Pond living alone in a cabin he constructed himself. In making a residence on the uninhabited shore of Walden Pond, a mile or two outside of the village of Concord, Thoreau declared in the opening pages of *Walden* that he "went to the woods because I wished to live deliberately, to front only the essential facts of life, and see if I could not learn what it had to teach, and not, when I came to die, discover that I had not lived." Although some criticized Thoreau for removing himself from society, of becoming a hermit philosopher, most of his Transcendentalist colleagues understood their friend to be enacting the virtues that their philosophy extolled. Emerson once said that "Thoreau gives me, in flesh & blood & pertinacious Saxon belief, my own ethics. He is far more real, & daily practically obeying them, than I; and fortifies my memory at all times with an affirmative experience which refuses to be set aside." In his desire to experience nature on its own terms and to sustain himself independently, while experiencing life in its fullness, Thoreau practiced the of ideas set forth in Emerson's "SELF-RELIANCE."

Thoreau's other seminal work, "Civil Disobedience," was also inspired by a personal experience: a single night spent in jail for refusing to pay a nine-dollar poll tax to a government that supported the Mexican War and the spread of slavery. It is this essay that 20th-century activists Gandhi and King studied and that influenced their own philosophy of nonviolent resistance to government. Thoreau argued, "let every man make known what kind of government would command his respect, and that will be one step toward obtaining it." Here lies the ideal that attracted Gandhi and King, that government should be improved and that it should be improved conscientiously, moved toward change by individual change. The essence of Thoreau's argument is that it is an individual's responsibility to decide as matter of his conscience what is right or wrong and that through individual change would come the widespread social and political change called for by reformers. Thoreau early on aligned himself with ABOLITIONISM, and some of his strongest political writings were inspired by his outrage over slavery. The question of a higher individual law based on conscience was at the center of his arguments in such writings as "A PLEA FOR CAPTAIN JOHN BROWN" (1859) and the posthumously published "LIFE WITHOUT PRINCIPLE" (1863).

The intertwining of his personal and political philosophies is the strain that ties together *Walden* and "Civil Disobedience" as well, in that Thoreau's work was vitally tied to his life experiences. *Walden* was an autobiographical account of Thoreau's experiment at self-sustenance and living in nature, a description of his philosophy in action. "Civil Disobedience" was also written as the result of an enactment of Thoreau's philosophy that a person should act according to his conscience. Both writings display Thoreau's own brand of Transcendentalist individualism. While Thoreau entreats his readers to act on their consciences, he does not tell them what their consciences should be telling them to do, for that would be a negation of individualism. Contrary to contemporary criticisms that Thoreau was a hermit intent on removing himself from society, he shared his experiments through his writings and sought to inspire readers themselves to "live deliberately."

After his death in 1862, Henry David Thoreau's sister, Sophia THOREAU, collected, edited, and published several additional volumes of his writings.

Bibliography

Richardson, Robert D. *Henry Thoreau: A Life of the Mind.* Berkeley: University of California Press, 1986.

Robinson, David M. *Natural Life: Thoreau's Worldly Transcendentalism.* Ithaca, N.Y.: Cornell University Press, 2004.

Salt, Henry S. *Life of Henry David Thoreau.* Edited by George Hendrick, et. al. Urbana: University of Illinois Press, 2000.

Thoreau, John, Jr.
(1815–1842)

John Thoreau, Jr., was the older brother and sometime traveling companion of Transcendentalist writer and naturalist Henry David THOREAU, who had two sisters as well, Helen and Sophia THOREAU. John Thoreau accompanied his brother on the 1839 excursion that would later form the basis of Henry David Thoreau's A WEEK ON THE CONCORD AND MERRIMACK RIVERS (1849). The book was in many ways a memorial to John, who died suddenly in 1842 at the age of only 26 from lockjaw, or tetanus, caused by a shaving cut. John Thoreau had worked as a schoolteacher to help pay for younger brother Henry's education at Harvard.

Thoreau, Sophia
(1819–1876)

Transcendentalist essayist and journalist Henry David THOREAU had three siblings: older brother John THOREAU (who died suddenly at age 26), sister Helen (who died at age 36), and Sophia, the youngest, who became the editor of Henry David Thoreau's unpublished papers after his death and was responsible for coordinating the publication of several posthumous volumes. In addition to managing the family business after her father's death and editing her brother's papers, Sophia Thoreau was a teacher, an antislavery activist, a naturalist like her brother, and an artist.

The entire Thoreau family was involved in ABOLITIONISM before the movement was widespread in New England. Sophia Thoreau, her mother, and sister were all members of the Women's Anti-Slavery Society in CONCORD, MASSACHUSETTS, which lent its support to radical abolitionists such as William Lloyd GARRISON in the late 1830s. Two decades later, Sophia was still at the center of Concord activism, and she coordinated a women's group to create memorial quilt for the widow of John BROWN, the radical antislavery crusader who was executed after his unsuccessful attempt to arm slaves at Harpers Ferry, Virginia.

Sophia shared with her brother, Henry, an interest in the natural world and, especially, in botany. Brother and sister regularly took walks together, gathering specimens, which Sophia sometimes sketched or painted. It is even reported that Sophia found a species of plant previously unknown in the Concord area, which was quickly identified by Henry. At home, Sophia cultivated flower gardens and pressed specimens. Sophia contributed one of the two drawings that appeared in Henry David Thoreau's 1854 book, WALDEN. The title page included Sophia's sketch of the cabin in which Thoreau lived alone at WALDEN POND; the only other artwork included in the book was a map of the area drawn by Henry.

Sophia Thoreau followed her famous brother's career closely, maintaining a scrapbook of newspaper clippings and reviews. Near the end of his life, plagued by months of ill health, Thoreau began dictating correspondence to Sophia, who remained by his side almost constantly. On the occasion of his death in 1862, Sophia reportedly said, "I feel as if something very beautiful happened—not death." *Walden* had made Henry David Thoreau popular, and Sophia helped arrange for mourners to buy copies of his portrait (painted by Samuel ROWSE) as souvenirs. After his death, Sophia worked with friend William Ellery CHANNING II to publish several of Thoreau's uncollected essays and journals. In 1864 they published THE MAINE WOODS, which included two previously published magazine articles and a third unpublished essay, all recounting Thoreau's excursions to Maine.

Bibliography

Harding, Walter. *The Days of Henry Thoreau.* New York: Dover, 1982.

Harding, Walter, ed. *Sophia Thoreau's Scrapbook*. Geneseo, N.Y.: Thoreau Society, 1964.

"Thoughts on Modern Literature"
Ralph Waldo Emerson
(1840)

Ralph Waldo EMERSON's essay "Thoughts on Modern Literature" was published in the Transcendentalist literary journal, the DIAL, in October 1840, but originated out of lectures given the previous year as part of "The Present Age" series. The essay was republished in 1893 as part of a posthumous collection of Emerson writings on the *Natural History of Intellect*. Much of Emerson's work was devoted not to discussion of specific texts in "modern literature" but to theorizing the role of literature in modern life and to encouraging the development of a distinctly American literature. He opened the essay by presenting literature as representative of human culture and society: "There is no better illustration of the laws by which the world is governed than Literature."

In "Thoughts on Modern Literature" Ralph Waldo Emerson identified a hierarchy of three classes of literature: "The highest class of books are those which express the moral element; the next, works of imagination; and the next, works of science;—all dealing in realities;—what ought to be, what is, and what appears." In considering these classes of literature, Emerson determined that Elizabethan dramatist William SHAKESPEARE was "the first literary genius of the world" but could not be considered representative of the "moral element" because of his reliance upon Christian ethics, that is, upon a specific religious doctrine, not a universal foundation for ethics. Shakespeare was therefore only "the highest in whom the moral is not the predominating element," for, in Emerson's view, Shakespeare's work "leans on the Bible: his poetry supposes it." The universality of Shakespeare's plays, as well as their limitations, would be a theme he returned to in other lectures on Shakespeare and, finally, in selecting Shakespeare as his representative "Poet" in the 1850 book, REPRESENTATIVE MEN.

Ralph Waldo Emerson was more of a literary theorist than a literary critic, as he rarely critiqued or analyzed specific books. Although he published some book reviews, written by himself and by others, during his editorship of the literary journal, the *Dial*, between 1840 and 1844, his primary concern was with the role and influence of the writer and poet in society, a theme addressed in other essays, such as "THE POET," as well as in several of his poems. The very purpose of the *Dial* was to nurture new literary forms and new writers, specifically those interested in the new Transcendentalist philosophy. In his own writings, however, Emerson was most interested in the role of the writer historically and within his own cultural and historical moment. In judging other writers and in presenting his own general "Thoughts on Modern Literature," Emerson emphasized that the critic must avoid the "intellectual selfishness" of simply offering up his biased opinion and instead seek himself to be "representative" of a broader human readership and not just responding as an individual. Emerson named many of modern literature's great thinkers and writers, but he generally avoided analysis of specific written works, other than commenting on their overall aesthetic or moral value, because, ultimately, the limitations of literature were too great: "There is somewhat in all life untranslatable into language."

"Threnody"
Ralph Waldo Emerson
(1847)

Ralph Waldo EMERSON wrote the poem "Threnody" as a eulogy to his son Waldo—who died of scarlet fever in 1842 at the age of only five years—and first published the piece in the collection POEMS (1847). This long narrative poem takes the reader, and Emerson, through various stages of grief, from the anger and shock of loss and separation from "The darling who shall not return," to joyful memories of the boy, to relinquishing the child to the claims of Nature and therein finding acceptance and some consolation.

The first half of the poem is a moving tribute to the "child of paradise, / Boy who made dear his father's home." Emerson recalls young Waldo's games—"And childhood's castles built or planned; /

His daily haunts I well discern,— / The poultry-yard, the shed, the barn,"—remembrances that are interrupted by the stark reality of the child's absence. Emerson's reluctance to accept this reality is represented in the poem in attempts by the father to find and understand where the boy has now gone: "And whither now, my truant wise and sweet, / O, whither tend thy feet? / I had the right, few days ago, / Thy steps to watch, thy place to know; / How have I forfeited the right? / Hast thou forgot me in a new delight?" Ultimately, not only the father, but "Nature, Fate, Men, him seek in vain."

The death of a child was a challenge to Emerson's Transcendentalist optimism in the eternal and divine purpose of life which helped him realize that even his own family life was not immune from the larger plan of the universe: "Would rushing life forget her laws, / Fate's glowing revolution pause?" In "Threnody," Emerson ultimately finds balance and reconciliation in humankind's inability, indeed the undesirability, of interfering in the cycle of nature: "Life is life which generates, / And many-seeming life is one,— / Wilt thou transfix and make it none?"

Ticknor, George
(1791–1871)

As a Harvard professor of languages and literature, George Ticknor had a direct influence on a generation that included many among the Transcendentalists, including Ralph Waldo EMERSON. Ticknor was born in Boston and was a graduate of Dartmouth, but eventually he studied in Germany with his colleague Edward EVERETT, the first American to receive a Ph.D. from the University of Göttingen. Everett and Ticknor were instrumental in bringing European ideas and actual books back to the United States and influencing a generation of young men at Harvard to learn European languages and travel to Europe to complete their studies. The emergence of Transcendentalism in the 1830s depended upon this widening interest in foreign literature, philosophy, and biblical criticism. These professors, along with Charles FOLLEN, Harvard's first professor of German literature, counted Ralph Waldo Emerson among their students and intro-

duced Emerson and others to many of the European, specifically German, writers and thinkers who would form the philosophical and literary foundations of the new Transcendentalist thought.

At Harvard, Ticknor was instrumental in establishing organizational reforms such as creating individual departments of study and instituting a system of student elective courses. Ticknor retired from Harvard in 1835 and was succeeded by Henry Wadsworth LONGFELLOW. Ticknor spent his postretirement years writing and traveling in Europe, where he met with such noteworthy literary figures as Johann Wolfgang von GOETHE, Madame de STAEL, and William WORDSWORTH. His primary scholarly interest was in Spanish literature and criticism, a new field of study at that time, and his most significant scholarly work, drawn from his years of teaching, was his three-volume *History of Spanish Literature*, first published in 1849. In the following decades, the work was translated into Spanish, German, and French and went through various editions in America as well.

Beyond his association with Harvard, Ticknor was involved in a variety of Boston intellectual and social activities, including serving on the board of the BOSTON ATHENEUM and eventually serving as its vice president, and partipating in the establishment of the Boston Public Library in the 1850s and becoming its president in 1865. He eventually donated many of his own Spanish and Portuguese literature and language books to the Boston Public Library.

George Ticknor's brother, William Davis Ticknor, was the founder of the prominent Boston publishing house, Ticknor and Fields, which produced the *ATLANTIC MONTHLY* as well as books by many of George Ticknor's intellectual friends, including Ralph Waldo Emerson, Nathaniel HAWTHORNE, James Russell LOWELL, and Henry David THOREAU.

Town and Country Club

Amos Bronson ALCOTT founded the Town and Country Club in 1849 "to establish better acquaintance between men of scientific, literary, and philanthropic pursuits," in particular bringing together

"Town" intellectuals with those living outside urban Boston-Cambridge in the "Country," such as Ralph Waldo EMERSON, who lived in CONCORD, MASSACHUSETTS, and aided Alcott in establishing the Club. Bronson Alcott had been inspired by his recent series of CONVERSATIONS to provide a more regular and permanent meeting place for discussing the "great questions" of the day. Many of the first attendees at the Town and Country Club had participated in Alcott's conversations as well as in the earlier TRANSCENDENTAL CLUB. The Town and Country Club was a more formal successor to these other gatherings, in its attempt to establish an organization with a constitution, formal rules, membership fees, and, hopefully, some control of membership. The Club was short-lived, lasting only one year, but attendees included most of the leading Transcendentalists as well as other Boston-area writers, artists, and community leaders. More than 100 people joined the Club and, in addition to Alcott and Emerson, James Freeman CLARKE, James Elliot CABOT, John Sullivan DWIGHT, Theodore PARKER, and Henry David THOREAU all attended at least one meeting.

Fellow Transcendentalist and movement historian Caroline DALL later accused the Town and Country Club of excluding women and, in fact, blamed this shortsightedness for the Club's brief existence. There was a controversy over the membership of women (and perhaps over the admission of blacks as well), and this did interfere with the Club's success. The male members were divided over the issue of whether to admit women, with more politically minded reformers such as William Lloyd GARRISON and Thomas Wentworth HIGGINSON demanding that membership be "broad and universal" in line with their current reform commitments, but other more conservative members, including even Emerson, fearing it would become a "ladies" club. Bronson Alcott was dismayed at the controversy as women had regularly attended his conversations, and he welcomed "the feminine element," but he was also concerned about the growing size of the meetings in general, which made the group more of a socialite gathering than a productive arena for thoughtful discussion. These tensions, along with the financial burden of holding regular meetings, resulted in the Town and Country Club's disbanding in May 1850.

Bibliography

Dahlstrand, Frederick. *Amos Bronson Alcott: An Intellectual Biography*. East Brunswick, N.J.: Associated University Presses, 1982.

"Transcendental Bible"
Lidian Emerson

At the height of what she called "the transcendental times" of the 1830s and 1840s, Lidian EMERSON, the wife of Ralph Waldo EMERSON, recorded in her journal some humorous but scathing reflections on the new Transcendentalist thought—reflections which their daughter, Ellen EMERSON, later characterized as "the Transcendental Bible." Lidian's comments were written as a satirical guide for aspiring Transcendentalists and declared "If you have refused all sympathy to the sorrowful, all pity and aid to the sick, all toleration to the infirm of character, if you have condemned the unintellectual," then you could rightfully call yourself a Transcendentalist because "you have done your whole duty to your noble self-sustained, impeccable, infallible Self" and are indeed "a perfect specimen of Humanity."

Lidian Emerson's "Transcendental Bible" highlighted the potential contradictions between spiritual ideals, such as the soul-searching of self-development, and such mundane earthly concerns as human relationships. Emerson's wife was a Christian and did not consider herself a Transcendentalist, although a number of friends left hints in their correspondences that they considered her a true Transcendentalist for her independence of thought and that Ralph Waldo Emerson was influenced by and incorporated her views into his own writings. Lidian Emerson's remarks were a critique of the worst tendencies of Transcendentalism, but her humor masked harsh words of some of the ideas promoted by certain individuals, including perhaps her own husband.

Ralph Waldo Emerson was aware of his wife's views and of this specific writing. He mentioned it in his own notebooks as "Queenie's Bible," referring to his nickname for his wife of 46 years. He regularly recorded some of her other thoughts and criticisms, indicating that they discussed such issues; for example, he noted that "Queenie says, 'Save me from magnificent souls. I like small common sized ones.'" Ultimately Ralph Waldo Emerson appreciated Lidian's criticism as a check on the potential extremes of his own philosophical tendencies.

Bibliography

Carpenter, Delores Bird. "Lidian Emerson's 'Transcendental Bible,'" *Studies in the American Renaissance* (1980): 91–95.

Transcendental Club

The Transcendental Club was formed in 1836 as one of the defining points of the new movement and met regularly for four years. In June 1836 Frederic Henry HEDGE wrote to Ralph Waldo EMERSON proposing the idea of a regular place "for the free discussion of theological and moral subjects." The first meeting gathered in Cambridge in September of that year. During the four years of its existence, the club steadily grew, and nearly every major early Transcendentalist attended a meeting of what was sometimes affectionately referred to as "Hedge's club." In addition to Emerson, Hedge, and cofounder George RIPLEY, who often held club meetings in his home, attendees at one time or another included Amos Bronson ALCOTT, Cyrus BARTOL, Orestes BROWNSON, William Ellery CHANNING II, William Henry CHANNING, James Freeman CLARKE, Christopher Pearse CRANCH, Margaret FULLER, Theodore PARKER, Elizabeth Palmer PEABODY, and Henry David THOREAU.

The Transcendental Club provided a point of gathering for what Hedge described as "like-minded men and women" and gave crucial form to the emerging Transcendentalist voice. The club was also instrumental in convincing these "like-minded" thinkers of the need for a more public voice for the movement, resulting in the creation of the *DIAL* magazine in 1840 after the club disbanded.

Bibliography

Myerson, Joel. "A Calendar of Transcendental Club Meetings," *American Literature* 44:2 (May 1972): 197–207.

Transcendentalism

Transcendentalism was a 19th-century literary, philosophical, and reform movement that emphasized the development of the individual as its primary subject of concern. As Ralph Waldo EMERSON, arguably the most significant spokesperson for the movement, stated in his 1841 essay "SELF-RELIANCE," the mid-19th century was "said to be the age of the first person singular." Transcendentalism emerged in America in the 1830s and 1840s as a critique of Boston UNITARIANISM. Transcendentalism thus emerged from within liberal Christianity but ultimately moved completely outside of Christian beliefs in doing away with the idea of the Bible as the source of spiritual knowledge and replacing the idea of a supernatural deity, or God, with a belief in the divinity of the human individual. Transcendentalism ultimately developed as an independent philosophy that synthesized several religious, philosophical, historical, and literary traditions.

The year 1836 is often identified as the single most important year marking the emergence of a Transcendentalist community and movement. In 1836 the TRANSCENDENTAL CLUB was formed, providing an identity and a meeting space for those individuals interested in "the new thought" and, that same year, several key texts were published, such as Ralph Waldo Emerson's seminal philosophical treatise, *NATURE*, religious reformer Orestes BROWNSON's *NEW VIEWS OF CHRISTIANITY, SOCIETY, AND THE CHURCH*, Unitarian minister and one of the founders of the Transcendental Club Convers FRANCIS's *Christianity as a Purely Internal Principle*, educational reformer and bookstore owner Elizabeth Palmer PEABODY's *RECORD OF A SCHOOL* (an account of Amos Bronson ALCOTT's educational experiment at TEMPLE SCHOOL, which he founded in 1834), and abolitionist and novelist Lydia Maria CHILD's *PHILOTHEA, A ROMANCE*, regarded as the first Transcendentalist novel. Many of these thinkers and writers published in the Unitarian press throughout the 1830s, but in 1841 the movement finally began its own periodical, the DIAL, with a more literary-philosophical rather than theological focus.

The controversy over Emerson's 1838 Harvard DIVINITY SCHOOL ADDRESS signaled for many the separation of Transcendentalist interests from its origins within the Unitarian church. Emerson not only questioned the scriptural basis of orthodox Christian beliefs but he shifted the terms of the debate from a purely theological issue to a more literary and public philosophical debate over the nature of the human soul. During this philosophical phase of the movement, a wider range of individual Transcendentalists published poetry, fiction, literary criticism, and philosophical treatises in the Unitarian and New England intellectual press and ultimately in their own journal, the Boston-based *Dial,* published between 1840 and 1844.

One of the most consistent and significant concepts that appears in much of Transcendentalist writing is that of "Nature." The Transcendentalists approached the natural world not empirically but subjectively, in that truths were perceived through one's own experience of the natural world, not through objective scientific information; through intuition, not formal learning. Transcendentalists believed that the world had meaning only as a reflection of the divine and that nature in fact provided a direct connection with the divine, thus any mediation between the individual and the divine, such as through churches, was no longer needed. As part of Nature, humanity and the human mind were thus a reflection of the divine; to understand human thoughts, feelings, and emotions was to understand God. As Emerson said, again referring to his own times, "the mind had become aware of itself." This self-awareness led to one other main concept used to define Transcendentalism in general: the emphasis on self-knowledge. The development of the individual self—what they termed *self-culture*—should be the goal of all EDUCATION and experience according to the Transcendentalists. One should approach whatever subject of study—

whether science, history, or languages—only for what can be learned or revealed about oneself.

Thus in all aspects of Transcendentalist thought, the individual was the source of and route to all knowledge. For the Transcendentalist, then, social conformity was the death of the soul, and anything that was anti-individualistic or that prohibited the growth of the self must be avoided or changed. One of the paradoxes of Transcendentalism was how a philosophy of the self could be translated into a social conscience, for Transcendentalists engaged with the numerous reform efforts that characterized their northern society in the antebellum era. Various reform associations proposed material or political solutions for what were, according to the Transcendentalists, spiritual problems. Thus they avoided involvement in organized reform for the most part while following their individual consciences in speaking and writing on ABOLITIONISM, labor rights, WOMEN'S RIGHTS, and utopian socialism. Like other mid-19th century reformers, the Transcendentalists had an optimistic view of human capabilities, a belief in innate human goodness and the capacity for individual and social PERFECTIONISM. Transcendentalist philosophy was inherently democratic in that it praised every individual, every mind, regardless of social status, and thus prompted the movement's main figures to become involved in social and moral reform efforts.

Some Transcendentalists looked to communal/social ways of perfecting themselves and society. One of the most well-known, well-publicized Transcendentalist reform efforts was the establishment of a utopian community at BROOK FARM, founded in April 1841 by George RIPLEY, another former Unitarian minister. Brook Farm was based upon French utopian socialist Charles Fourier's idea of a highly planned and organized community that would serve as an example to the rest of society. Fourier proposed a plan for reorganizing social roles and thus remedying a variety of social evils, such as poverty, ignorance, bad health, class tensions, and even sexual inequality. Transcendentalists, in particular, were attracted to FOURIERISM for its emphasis on the role of the individual and the belief that, in such a utopian community, people would be encouraged to develop their best selves by being allowed to do the work for which each one was best suited. The community at Brook Farm would allow them to be reformers perfecting society while also perfecting themselves. Another Transcendentalist attracted to the idea of such a utopian community was Amos Bronson Alcott, who established FRUITLANDS in 1843 with an even more radical critique of capitalist society as residents declared themselves "freed from the bondage of the cash nexus" by aspiring to be completely self-sufficient in their efforts.

Although the emergence and height of the movement was concentrated in the antebellum era, Transcendentalism continued to have a public presence in the post–Civil War era and to influence a new generation of reformers and thinkers. In the 1860s and 1870s Transcendentalists were involved in founding groups such as the FREE RELIGIOUS ASSOCIATION and the RADICAL CLUB where they continued to debate and discuss issues related to liberal theology and comparative religion. Others remained active as social reformers and at lecturers at experimental forums such as the CONCORD SCHOOL OF PHILOSOPHY AND LITERATURE.

Bibliography

Capper, Charles, and Conrad Edick Wright, eds. *Transient and Permanent: The Transcendentalist Movement and Its Contexts.* Boston: Massachusetts Historical Society, 1999.

Packer, Barbara. "The Transcendentalists." In *The Cambridge History of American Literature,* vol. 2: *1820–1865,* ed. Sacvan Bercovitch. New York: Cambridge University Press, 1995, 329–607.

Transcendentalism in New England
Caroline Dall
(1897)

Caroline DALL's *Transcendentalism in New England* is one of the only firsthand historical accounts of the 19th-century movement and a direct response and alternative history to Octavius Brooks FROTHINGHAM's more widely read and accepted *TRANSCENDENTALISM IN NEW ENGLAND: A HISTORY*

(1876). In May 1895, Caroline Dall, one of the last living of the self-identified Transcendentalists, presented a lecture before the Society for Philosophical Enquiry in Washington, D.C., which she subsequently published as *Transcendentalism in New England.*

When asked to speak on the history of this philosophical and literary movement that defined New England intellectual culture in the mid-19th century, Caroline Dall chose to tell a history framed by women. Her lecture traced a history of American Transcendentalist thought that began with colonist Anne HUTCHINSON's challenge to the orthodoxy of seventeenth-century PURITANISM and continued through to an analogy with the 19th-century feminist challenges of Margaret FULLER. Dall's lecture opened with an acknowledgment that this would be an alternative history with which her listeners or readers might not be familiar: "You will be surprised when you hear me say that the history of the Transcendental movement stretched along two hundred years, beginning with a woman's life and work in 1637, and ending with a woman's work and death in 1850. The arc, which we call transcendental, was subtended by a chord, held at first by Anne Hutchinson, and lost in the Atlantic waves with Margaret Fuller."

Dall singled out these particular women as Transcendentalists due to their intuitive approach to comprehending truth and knowledge. Anne Hutchinson was put on trial and banished by the Massachusetts colonial leadership for holding religious meetings in her home that, among other problems, were attended by men as well as women. Dall presented Hutchinson's 1637 trial as a struggle between conservative male leaders who were not "mystical enough" to understand Hutchinson's message and the "scores of women" who testified on her behalf. Interestingly, she also identified Hutchinson as a distinctly American source of Transcendentalism, de-emphasizing the influence of European IDEALISM and ROMANTICISM on 19th-century thinkers. Dall's lecture then moved forward 200 years to compare Hutchinson's meetings to Margaret Fuller's famous series of CONVERSATIONS FOR WOMEN, which Dall herself had attended. In Caroline Dall's account, then, women and feminism were central to the history of Transcendentalism. Of the 19th-century movement, Dall explicitly argued that "the characteristics of the Transcendental movement were shown in the temper of its agitation for the rights of woman and the enlargement of her duties . . . every Transcendentalist was ready, and indeed had good reason, to assert that there was 'no sex in souls.'" And, although framed around Hutchinson and Fuller, the bulk of her lecture was actually devoted to the lives and work of Dall's 19th-century contemporaries, the "distinguished" intellectual women and WOMEN'S RIGHTS activists whom Dall presented as living examples of the Transcendentalist legacies of Hutchinson and Fuller.

Bibliography

Deese, Helen. "Transcendentalism from the Margins: The Experience of Caroline Healey Dall." In *Transient and Permanent: The Transcendentalist Movement and Its Contexts,* eds. Charles Capper and Conrad Edick Wright. Boston: Massachusetts Historical Society, 1999, 527–547.

Wayne, Tiffany K. *Woman Thinking: Feminism and Transcendentalism in Nineteenth-Century America.* Lanham, Md.: Lexington Books, 2005.

Transcendentalism in New England: A History
Octavius Brooks Frothingham
(1876)

Octavius Brooks Frothingham's 1876 *Transcendentalism in New England* was the first comprehensive history of the movement by a contemporary. Frothingham was the son of Unitarian minister Nathaniel FROTHINGHAM and was active in the post–Civil War activities of many of the younger Transcendentalists, particular in his role as founding president of the FREE RELIGIOUS ASSOCIATION. Frothingham had previously written on the history of religion and turned his attention to the development of the "intuitive philosophy" of American Transcendentalism as it emerged from its European contexts to dominate mid-19th-century literary and intellectual culture. Frothingham sought to provide a comprehensive overview of the movement's influences as

well as its reach into and impact not only on American literary culture but on religious and social reform as well. Of transcendentalism Frothingham said "New England character received from it an impetus that never will be spent."

Frothingham identified five individuals as the most important figures of the movement, characterized for him by their representative intellectual contributions: he termed Amos Bronson ALCOTT "The Mystic," Ralph Waldo EMERSON "The Seer," Margaret FULLER "The Critic," Theodore PARKER "The Preacher," and George RIPLEY "The Man of Letters." Frothingham notably left Henry David THOREAU out of his history, even as he named several others associated with the movement as "Minor Prophets"—such as Cyrus BARTOL, William Henry CHANNING, James Freeman CLARKE, Thomas Wentworth HIGGINSON, Samuel JOHNSON, David WASSON, and John WEISS. He did not adequately address his own contribution, however, only establishing himself as a credible commentator on the movement by noting that "The writer was once a pure Transcendentalist . . . [and] still retains enough of his former faith to enable him to do it justice."

Octavius Brooks Frothingham was certainly not an unbiased historian as he had personal and philosophical connections to the movement that resulted in his overall praise and zeal for the influence of New England on American culture at large. He passionately concluded that "Transcendentalism was . . . an enthusiasm, a wave of sentiment, a breath of mind that caught up such as were prepared to receive it, elated them, transported them, and passed on,—no man knowing whither it went." The book garnered criticisms for such unabashed zeal. Most notably, fellow historian and intellectual Henry Adams reviewed Frothingham's work but was surprised at the significance Frothingham gave to most of the thinkers associated with the movement. Adams determined that of all those Frothingham named, only Ralph Waldo Emerson had a larger influence.

Bibliography

Caruthers, J. Wade. *Octavius Brooks Frothingham, Gentle Radical.* Tuscaloosa: University of Alabama Press, 1977.

"The Transcendentalist"
Ralph Waldo Emerson
(1842)

Ralph Waldo EMERSON delivered his lecture on "The Transcendentalist" in Boston in December 1841 as part of an eight-lecture series on "The Times," and it was subsequently published in the January 1842 issue of the movement's literary journal, the DIAL. Emerson opened the very first paragraph of "The Transcendentalist" by emphasizing that the new movement was, in fact, not new at all: "The first thing we have to say respecting what are called *new views* here in New England, at the present time, is, that they are not new, but the very oldest of thoughts cast into the mould of these new times." Emerson compared "The Transcendentalist" with his philosophical counterpart, the "Materialist," who believes in the lived experience of physical reality—who "insists on facts, on history, on the force of circumstances, and the animal wants of man"—and idealists, including the Transcendentalists, who insisted on higher forms of consciousness—"on the power of Thought and of Will, on inspiration, on miracle, on individual culture." Most important, the Transcendentalist believed in the ability of each individual to reach that higher state of consciousness and in "an invisible unsounded center in himself." For Emerson, IDEALISM must also be understood within particular historical circumstances, as he pointed out in defining the "new views" of Transcendentalism, first and foremost, as simply "Idealism as it appears in 1842."

Emerson explained Transcendentalism as a rejection of the Enlightenment-era philosophy of John LOCKE. Locke emphasized that all knowledge is empirical and sensual, that we only know that which we perceive with the physical senses, but Emerson presented the "intuitive thought" of Transcendentalism as an alternative way of understanding that sees all knowledge as based on "a subjective or relative existence," that is, reality and meaning determined by each individual mind, not by an outside preexisting set of "facts you call the world." The Transcendentalist, then, unlike the Materialist, "believes in inspiration, and in ecstasy."

As the title of his essay indicated, and as Transcendentalism itself was thus based on individual and subjective thought, Emerson was concerned not primarily with defining Transcendentalism, but with addressing and attempting to understand "The Transcendentalist" as a particular type of individual. Although Emerson was identified as the founder and spokesperson of the movement—partially explaining why he felt called to respond to and clarify misunderstandings about the philosophy—he argued that "there is no such thing as a Transcendental *party*" and "no pure Transcendentalist," and he referred to "the Transcendentalist" in the third person throughout the essay. It was not a term he regularly used, but which he now chose to accept and address, and it would seem that in addressing general criticisms about "the Transcendentalist," he was in fact responding to some of his own critics: "What right, cries the good world, has the man of genius to retreat from work, and indulge himself?" He readily admitted, however, that Transcendentalists in general "are not good citizens, not good members of society . . . do not even like to vote." Still, he hoped that society would at least concede that, in addition to "the farmers, sailors, and weavers," the productive members of society, "perhaps too there might be room for the exciters and monitors; collectors of the heavenly spark with power to convey the electricity to others," including perhaps himself.

Again speaking in the third person, he urged readers to consider not the immediately practical effect of these reformers, but the long-term spiritual and social effect of the idealism of "these seething brains, these admirable radicals, these unsocial worshippers, these talkers who talk the sun and moon away." Emerson passionately argued that his contemporaries take the Transcendentalists seriously, as "this heresy cannot pass away without leaving its mark." He went into great detail describing the character and actions of the Transcendentalists vis-à-vis their fellow Americans, their involvement (or not) in various reform movements, their solitary ways, their appreciation of and time spent in nature, and concluded that "by their unconcealed dissatisfaction they expose our poverty and the insignificance of man to man."

Emerson did not name his Transcendentalist colleagues, but one could easily think of the activities and public criticisms of figures such as Amos Bronson ALCOTT, Margaret FULLER, George RIPLEY, Henry David THOREAU, and Emerson himself at the time the essay was published in the early 1840s. Emerson considered the "labors" of such individuals in nonmaterial ways and challenged his readers to do the same, to consider writers, thinkers, and reformers, persons working "as gauges and meters of character," as just as important to society as the work of "farmers, sailors, and weavers." Emerson ended his essay with an appeal to recognize the valuable and unique contribution of intellectuals to the times, making a case for his own chosen VOCATION as a poet and thinker: "Amidst the downward tendency and proneness of things, when every voice is raised for a new road or another statute, or a subscription of stock, . . . will you not tolerate one or two solitary voices in the land, speaking for thoughts and principles not marketable or perishable?"

"Transcendental Wild Oats"
Louisa May Alcott
(1873)

Louisa May ALCOTT's short story "Transcendental Wild Oats" was a satirical account of the family's experience in 1843 at FRUITLANDS, the utopian community founded by her father, Transcendentalist reformer Amos Bronson ALCOTT. The story was first published in *The Independent* in 1873 and reprinted in *The Woman's Journal* in 1874. Louisa was only 10 years old at the time the family lived at the farm, but as an adult she criticized the impracticalities of the communal experiment and critiqued the gendered division of labor within Transcendentalist philosophy.

Alcott's fictional account of an aloof philosopher-reformer was a thinly veiled portrayal of her father Bronson Alcott's emotional and financial abuse of his family in pursuit of IDEALISM. In the story Fruitlands is called "Apple Slump," a community founded by Abel Lamb and Timon Lion, characters representing, respectively, Bronson Alcott

and Fruitlands cofounder Charles LANE. The men intended for the community to survive by farming, but by only disrupting and not assisting in domestic life, male thinkers such as Alcott and Lane ultimately depended not on themselves but on female domestic support at the community and thus made it impossible for women to pursue intellectual work as the men did.

Alcott acknowledged that the men may have had good intentions, but the main point of the story was that their ideals and their expectations were incompatible with the demands of daily life and survival. She wrote of the philosopher men trying unsuccessfully to turn themselves into farmers: "The band of brothers began by spading garden & field; but a few days of it lessened their ardor amazingly." The self-produced food was therefore somewhat limited in this scheme that went too far: "Unleavened bread, porridge, and water for breakfast; bread, fruit, and water for dinner. No teapot profaned that sacred stove, no gory steak cried aloud for vengeance from her chaste gridiron; and only a brave woman's taste, time, and temper were sacrificed on that domestic altar." This last comment was a reference to the character Hope Lamb, the fictional counterpart of Louisa's mother, Abigail May ALCOTT, who, according to Louisa May, was left with all of the cooking and domestic chores.

The story was not entirely fictitious as Louisa May Alcott followed closely the creation and demise of Fruitlands through the story of Apple Slump. She even drew upon actual letters and articles that her father had written about Fruitlands to create dialogue in the story. And although the fictional Abel Lamb is, as his name implies, a gentle-hearted radical, Louisa May Alcott is known to have harbored some resentment over her father's ventures, at Fruitlands and elsewhere, which mired her family in years of financial dependence on friends and relatives until she herself was able to support her family through her career as a writer. Interestingly, the title for this story may have come from Louisa May Alcott's own earlier work in *LITTLE WOMEN* (1868) where she wrote, "Boys will be boys, young men must sow their wild oats, and women must not expect miracles."

Bibliography

Johnson, Claudia Durst. "Transcendental Wild Oats" or "The Cost of an Idea," *ATQ* (1998) 12 (1): 45–65.

Petrulionis, Sandra Harbert. "By the Light of Her Mother's Lamp: Woman's Work versus Man's Philosophy in Louisa May Alcott's 'Transcendental Wild Oats,'" *Studies in the American Renaissance* (1995): 69–81.

Tribune   *See NEW YORK TRIBUNE.*

U

The Una
(1853–1855)

Published monthly between February 1853 and October 1855, *The Una* was the first paper devoted exclusively to the WOMEN'S RIGHTS cause and had ties to reform and Transcendentalist circles in both Boston and New York. The paper was founded by Paulina Wright DAVIS, coedited by Caroline DALL, and listed Ednah Dow CHENEY and Elizabeth Palmer PEABODY as regular contributors. Some Transcendentalist men as well contributed regularly to its pages, including well-known supporters of woman's cause such as Unitarian minister Theodore PARKER and literary biographer and abolitionist Thomas Wentworth HIGGINSON. The tone, purpose, and content of *The Una*—including its masthead: *"Out of the great heart of Nature seek we Truth"*—all reflected the influence of Transcendentalism.

Paulina Wright Davis began plans for the paper immediately following the 1850 national women's rights convention. Caroline Dall had corresponded with Davis about plans for the paper from the beginning, and Dall contributed writings for nearly every issue before eventually taking over as primary editor in 1855. In addition to Cheney, Dall, and Davis, other major 19th-century feminists also wrote for its pages, including Frances Dana Gage, Elizabeth Oakes SMITH, and Elizabeth Cady Stanton. Paulina Davis envisioned the paper as a general organ for the movement at large. In 1853 Davis complained to Caroline Dall that "the Conventions have become unwieldy" and clearly articulated her plan that the paper serve as an alternative strategy which could set "the tone for the movement." Davis felt that women needed "stronger nourishment" than provided by other "Ladies' magazines."

Other periodicals of the time acknowledged *The Una* as having a different purpose and catering to a different audience, whether they praised or criticized its pages. For example, the *Woman's Advocate* (a labor rights paper published between 1855 and 1860) urged their "most transcendental sisters" of *The Una* to take a more practical approach to acknowledging woman's wrongs rather than "talking of abstract questions of rights." *The Una*'s discussion of rights was "abstract" in that it did not explicitly demand specific rights but was instead more concerned with woman's subordination that allowed the denial of rights in the first place. In the pages of *The Una* feminist writers translated the Transcendentalist philosophy and rhetoric of self-culture into a reform agenda to promote women's EDUCATION and "right to think." These writers shared the Transcendentalist feminist viewpoint of Margaret FULLER, whom many of them had known personally, and they promoted Fuller's ideas in *The Una* and elsewhere. In the July 1855 issue Caroline Dall reviewed for her readers Fuller's WOMAN IN THE NINETEENTH CENTURY, which had been published 10 years earlier, calling upon the women's rights movement to use this text as the basis for their work. Editor Davis desired "to make women think," and each issue contained a mix of poetry, news, and statistics about women's lives internationally; fiction, political commentary, book reviews, biographical and historical sketches of women, and excerpts and commentary on the key inspirers of Transcendentalist thought, such as William BLAKE, Thomas CARLYLE, Charles Fourier (*see* FOURIERISM), Johann Wolfgang von GOETHE, and Emanuel Swedenborg (*see* SWEDENBORGIANISM).

Bibliography

Tonn, Mari Boor. *"The Una, 1853–1855: The Premiere of the Woman's Rights Press."* In *A Voice of Their Own: The Woman Suffrage Press, 1840–1910,* ed. Martha M. Solomon. Tuscaloosa: University of Alabama, 1991, 48–70.

Wayne, Tiffany K. *Woman Thinking: Feminism and Transcendentalism in Nineteenth-Century America.* Lanham, Md.: Lexington Books, 2005.

"Unitarian Christianity"
William Ellery Channing
(1819)

Reverend William Ellery CHANNING's sermon, "Unitarian Christianity" marked the beginning of UNITARIANISM as a separate denomination in the United States with Channing as its spiritual and intellectual leader. His 1819 address was published under the full title *A Sermon Delivered at the Ordination of the Rev. Jared Sparks, to the Pastoral Care of the First Independent Church in Baltimore, May 5, 1819,* but commonly referred to simply as "Unitarian Christianity." Unitarianism had begun in England as a critique of orthodox Calvinist beliefs in the innate depravity of humankind and in predestination, or the preselection by God of the saved and unsaved. Influenced by Enlightenment rationalism of the late 18th century, Unitarians began to preach instead a humanistic emphasis on the individual soul, free will, and the role of reason in religious experience. When Channing preached on "Unitarian Christianity" in 1819 he created a sense of community among other Boston liberal congregations who then joined together as part of this new denomination, the Unitarians. Throughout all of his orations and writings Channing sought to moderate the split off into a new denom-

ination by focusing on the positive approach to a spiritual life offered through Unitarianism, rather than defining the split solely in negative terms of a critique of Calvinism.

Whereas conservative Unitarians such as Andrews NORTON rejected the idea that the Bible was anything other than divine revelation, Channing established as mainstream Unitarian doctrine the idea that the Bible, in fact, should be read and interpreted "in the same manner as that of other books"—that is, using the full faculty of human "reason" as well as "comparison and inference" with other books—and not taken by faith only. He argued that God did not intend for the Bible to be difficult for common men to understand and that "the Bible is a book written for men, in the language of men." Beyond differences of opinion on interpretation, however, Unitarians had serious problems with fundamental doctrines of Calvinism, such as innate depravity and predestination. With these beliefs Channing clearly disagreed on the grounds that a loving God would not create such a tortuous situation in which "the rest of mankind, though left without that special grace which their conversion requires, are commanded to repent, under penalty of aggravated woe"; a system which leaves an unknown portion of humanity "born under a blighting curse" and which, to believers such as Channing, seemed "a horror which we want words to express." Other liberal clergymen had been voicing such critiques of Calvinism in the years leading up to his sermon, but through his eloquent words and respected position he was able to give voice to the liberal movement and move such critiques toward the positive development of a new denomination. William Ellery Channing's "Unitarian Christianity" influenced the development of Unitarianism in both the United States and England and established him as 19th-century liberal Christianity's leading spokesperson.

Unitarianism

American Unitarianism was a form of liberal Christianity that arose in the early 19th century and formed the spiritual foundation for the Transcendentalist movement. Many of the early adherents of Transcendentalism began their careers as Unitarian ministers but soon took its legacy of questioning orthodoxy and inquiries into the divine nature of human beings to radical spiritual extremes. Many intellectual elites of the era believed that Unitarianism would eventually become the dominant religion in America. Although this was not to be the case, the ideas began during the mid-18th century, and Unitarianism was formally organized and grew through the 1820s.

Influenced by 18th-century rationalists such as John LOCKE, Unitarians (initially referred to simply as "liberal Christians") got their name from the belief in "unifying" the concept of God as an overarching Divine Nature, rather than as three distinct entities as in the "trinity" of Father, Son, and Holy Ghost in traditional Christianity. Unitarians also questioned Calvinist beliefs in predestination and original sin, ideas dependent upon a belief in humanity's innately depraved nature and the subsequent inability to do anything about it other than hope for God's grace. Young men trained at HARVARD DIVINITY SCHOOL in the late 18th and early 19th centuries had been steeped in Enlightenment ideas about empiricism and rationalism that emphasized that humans could know and understand universal systems not only of nature but of religion and, furthermore, that this knowledge could be gained through empirical or external observation and experience.

Unitarianism was in many ways the religion of the elite classes, and Unitarian intellectuals coined terms like *self-culture* and *active mind* in their quest for the perfection of individual character as humankind's spiritual destiny. Ministers, including Ralph Waldo EMERSON in his early career as a Unitarian preacher, sought to inspire congregants more than teach them and encouraged the cultivation of the intellect as a large part of Unitarian religious practice. Churchgoers were introduced to a wide range of knowledge in history, biblical criticism, poetry, the arts and sciences. Boston Unitarians of the early 19th century formed lecture and literary societies and published many theological periodicals and literary magazines such as the *CHRISTIAN EXAMINER,* the *CHRISTIAN REGISTER,* and the *WESTERN MESSENGER.* By the late 1830s

and early 1840s, these concepts and forums for writing and discussing were identified not solely with Unitarianism but with the "new school" of Transcendentalism, whose adherents were made up of Boston's elite class of ministers, poets, teachers, lecturers, and critics.

The leading Unitarian minister who most influenced the Transcendentalists personally was the Reverend William Ellery CHANNING of Boston. Channing preached of God not as the benevolent but stern father figure of Calvinist PURITANISM but as a model of perfection for human beings to emulate. Although Unitarians essentially rejected the divinity of Jesus Christ, they retained the Christian belief in the Bible as a divinely inspired revelation to humankind and the belief in the historical figure of Jesus Christ as a moral example of human perfection. The debate over whether Unitarians should, in fact, even claim the name of "Christian" became heated in the much-publicized MIRACLES CONTROVERSY of the 1830s. Conservative Unitarians attempted to create an empirical model to explain Jesus' actions, his earthly activities, for clues about his divine nature. Rather than accept Christ's divinity based on scriptural assertion alone, it was important to rationalist Unitarians to "prove" that he was divine based on some outward sign, in this case believing the miracles to be that sign. Radical Unitarians such as Ralph Waldo Emerson and George RIPLEY asserted that the miracles were provable natural phenomena, only symbolic of spiritual and moral truths, but not the work of a supernatural being. Emerson, Ripley, and others eventually broke all ties with the organized Unitarian church and pursued a humanistic philosophy that moved beyond this debate to look inward to individual subjective beliefs as the basis of truth and to the divine within human beings themselves. Thus Transcendentalism emerged in part as the logical extension Unitarianism to a point where many rejected the very foundations of Christian belief.

Some Transcendentalists, such as Frederic Henry HEDGE and even radical Theodore PARKER, maintained their Unitarian connections, but others found their perspectives and beliefs meant that formal ties with the church were compromised by their changing beliefs. Ralph Waldo Emerson left his position as a Unitarian minister in 1832 over disagreements about the offering of the LORD'S SUPPER, which was, in Emerson's view, an act that constituted blind obedience to the traditions of historical Christianity but a ritual devoid of spiritual meaning for most participants. Emerson's final break from the church did not come until his 1838 DIVINITY SCHOOL ADDRESS when he created controversy by urging his audience of emerging Unitarian ministers to ignore tradition and even the scriptures and to be "a divine man," believing only in themselves. Likewise, minister Theodore Parker found himself shut out of most congregations, even as a visiting guest preacher, after his controversial 1841 ordination sermon, later published as *A DISCOURSE ON THE TRANSIENT AND PERMANENT IN CHRISTIANITY.*

Transcendentalism was ultimately more than a theological break with Unitarianism, but then again, Unitarianism was more than a religion. It was the basis of an identity for New England's intellectual and social elite in the first decades of the 19th century, and the split between Unitarianism and Transcendentalism ultimately signaled a new era in American philosophical and literary culture as well.

Bibliography

Wright, Conrad Edick, ed. *American Unitarianism, 1805–1865.* Boston: Massachusetts Historical Society and Northeastern University Press, 1989.

"Uriel"
Ralph Waldo Emerson
(1846)

Published in *POEMS* (1847), Transcendentalist Ralph Waldo EMERSON's "Uriel" was once declared by fellow poet Robert Frost to be the "greatest Western poem yet." One modern biographer sees it, at least, as Emerson's "most pointed satire." Like other Emerson poems, such as "BRAHMA," "Uriel" used religious and mythological symbolism to address the theme of balance and reconciliation between the human and spiritual realms. Taken from the allegorical figure in Milton's *Paradise Lost,* Uriel

is an archangel, "the sharpest-sighted Spirit of all in Heav'n," but one misunderstood in his rebellion against God. Although Emerson sets his poem in the distant but unspecified past—"It fell in the ancient periods"—the poem is another allegory, this time one which casts Emerson himself in the role of Uriel and HARVARD DIVINITY SCHOOL as "Paradise" in what amounted to a belated response to the unexpected criticisms of his 1838 DIVINITY SCHOOL ADDRESS. "In vain produced, all rays return; Evil will bless, and ice will burn." The image of Uriel invoked not just rebellion but a particular perspective on God. Uriel the angel saw God in everything, in nature, and in turning to nature as symbol and teacher, rejected the laws and traditions set forth by God. This was the philosophical foundation of Emerson's Transcendentalism and, in his hands, Uriel recognizes that even without religion, truth and knowledge "Still floats upon the morning wind, / Still whispers to the willing mind." Of course, this was the message he had attempted to convey to the young men embarking upon careers as ministers in his address at Harvard.

Emerson had initially refrained from responding to the controversy generated by the Divinity School Address. If Emerson himself is "Uriel," a misunderstood speaker of a "rash word," the conservative Unitarian Harvard faculty, including Henry WARE and Andrews NORTON, are "The stern old war-gods" who "shook their heads" at his message. Uriel is not interested in "repentance," however, but accepts his position as one who brings word of change and resistance to orthodoxy. This liminal and maligned position is a difficult one for any individual to occupy, however, and so it is that Uriel withdraws into a "sad self-knowledge, withering," recognizing that he has been abandoned once-and-for-all by the community of Harvard and of the Unitarian church. In the poem, however, he is vindicated in that his critics would eventually be moved by his message: "a blush tinged the upper sky, / And the gods shook, they knew not why."

Ultimately "the gods shook" over more than just Emerson's ideas, as Transcendentalism in general was an act of rebellion against the forms and traditions of New England religious and literary culture. Other Transcendentalists would be criticized for their religious and social views as well—the Unitarian church attempted to banish Theodore PARKER from the pulpit after the sermon he later published as *A DISCOURSE ON THE TRANSIENT AND PERMANENT IN CHRISTIANITY;* and Amos Bronson ALCOTT, Margaret FULLER, and Henry David THOREAU were all criticized and persecuted in various ways for their radical social and political views. In "Uriel," perhaps, they found sympathy.

Bibliography
Allen, Gay Wilson. *Waldo Emerson: A Biography.* New York: Viking Press, 1981.

"Uses of Great Men"   *See* REPRESENTATIVE MEN.

utopianism   *See* BROOK FARM; FOURIERISM, FRUITLANDS.

V

Very, Jones
(1813–1880)

Jones Very was the most prolific and visionary of the Transcendentalist poets. Very befriended Transcendentalist reformer and publisher Elizabeth Palmer PEABODY after she heard him give an 1837 lecture on "Why There Cannot Be Another Epic Poem." Peabody told Ralph Waldo EMERSON about Very, and Emerson invited Very to lecture in CONCORD, MASSACHUSETTS. Very began to accompany Emerson to meetings of the TRANSCENDENTAL CLUB, but soon after becoming involved in the Transcendentalist circle, Very underwent an intense religious conversion experience that culminated in a psychological crisis. His mental instability, particularly an apocalyptic religious enthusiasm that frightened some of his students, resulted in his dismissal from his post as a Greek tutor at Harvard and a one-month institutionalization at an asylum. He emerged with a new excitement and vision for poetry, and the months and years following this incident were his most prolific and inspired.

Very sent some of his writings to Emerson, who was impressed with Very's creativity, his theory of poetry, and, in particular, his essay analyzing the poetry of William SHAKESPEARE. Emerson volunteered to edit a collection of Very's writings, which were published in 1839 as *Essays and Poems*. Very understood his poetry as utterances of the Holy Spirit whom he believed to be speaking through him and, in several poems, he even adopted the persona of the divine. Editor Emerson excluded many of Very's most radical poems from the published volume and struggled to change others against Very's insistence that the words could not be tampered with since they were not even his own but those of the Holy Spirit. Emerson convinced Very, however, that the "Spirit should be a better speller" and not have such "bad grammar."

Throughout his life Jones Very's friends and acquaintances, including those among the Transcendentalists, debated his mental health. Emerson appears to have tolerated Very's emotional outbursts without concern and remained his most steadfast supporter. Emerson remarked to Elizabeth Palmer Peabody that he would like it if "the whole world was as mad as he," and he wrote of Very in his essay on "FRIENDSHIP": "To stand in true relations with men in a false age is worth a fit of insanity, is it not?" Others, such as Peabody, were increasingly convinced that Very was mentally unstable and urged Emerson to avoid too close an association. In the pages of the *WESTERN MESSENGER*, editor James Freeman CLARKE vouched for Very by declaring that "the charge of insanity is almost always brought against any man who endeavours to introduce to the common mind any very original ideas." Clarke described Very as "a genuine mystic" and worked after Very's death to produce a more complete edition of his poems.

Regardless of such differing opinions about the man, all recognized and appreciated Very's talents as a poet, although, as historian Joel Myerson points out, Jones Very was caught in a dilemma whereby he was "judged insane when the quality and quantity of his writing were greatest, when they declined he was thought quite competent."

Jones Very eventually wrote more than 900 poems in his lifetime. Most of his best ones were produced during the early years of the Transcendentalist movement, and many of them were published in various religious as well as Transcendentalist periodicals, such as the DIAL and the *Western Messenger*. After 1840 he wrote very few poems. His primary occupation for the last half of his life was as a regular and surprisingly moderate Unitarian preacher in Salem, Massachusetts.

Bibliography

Myerson, Joel. *The New England Transcendentalists and the Dial: A History of the Magazine and Its Contributors*. London and Toronto: Associated University Presses, 1980.

Deese, Helen, ed. *Jones Very: The Complete Poems*. Athens: University of Georgia Press, 1993.

vocation

The idea of vocation was a central part of the Transcendentalist philosophy of self-culture or self-knowledge, for to know oneself was to know one's true calling. Transcendentalism itself began, in one sense, due to Ralph Waldo EMERSON's own vocational crisis. Emerson had initially pursued the ministry as his father and generations before him had done and as was certainly expected of a well-educated and talented young man such as himself. After a few short years as a Unitarian minister, however, he resigned his post, ostensibly over theological disagreements about the LORD'S SUPPER, but also triggered by a personal crisis over what was to be his true "nature and vocation." He determined that instead of a preacher he was meant to be a writer—what he termed a poet—and embarked upon a new career as a lecturer and essayist, emerging in fact as America's first public intellectual. In his 1837 address, "THE AMERICAN SCHOLAR," Emerson presented his ideal vocation as one which combined various intellectual roles. A true "scholar" combined the functions of "the

Naturalist, the Teacher, the Poet, and the Thinker." Emerson's own vocational crisis had culminated in the idea presented in "The American Scholar" of "Man Thinking," which was not so much a job as a "right state" of being in the world. Emerson rejected the idea of the formally trained or institutionally affiliated intellectual and pursued a more idealized vision of vocation as a calling, a cultivation of natural talents and self-discipline.

The Transcendentalists in general rejected traditional and institutional forms of knowledge and therefore many rejected the established professions as too tied into economic and political interests to allow for individual freedom and growth. Many Transcendentalists pursued alternative careers as artists, writers, poets, and, eventually, public lecturers, even as they found it difficult to balance the pursuit of philosophical ideals with real material or financial needs. Amos Bronson ALCOTT struggled throughout his lifetime to make a living through such experimental vocations as founder of a utopian community at FRUITLANDS, leader of CONVERSATIONS, or founder of alternative EDUCATION institutions such as his TEMPLE SCHOOL or the CONCORD SCHOOL OF PHILOSOPHY AND LITERATURE. Christopher Pearse CRANCH struggled as an artist, and Henry David THOREAU gave up school-teaching in favor of more meaningful work as a naturalist-poet.

Margaret FULLER and Elizabeth Palmer PEABODY faced special obstacles as women, barred from many of the professional pursuits that were at least options for their male colleagues. Peabody created a career as an educational reformer, but she later lamented that her true calling would have been as a minister, if only women could have been ordained. School-teaching was one of the few options available to educated women of their time, but Margaret Fuller was more interested in teaching adults and hoped that her CONVERSATIONS FOR WOMEN would "prove at last my vocation." Fuller is credited with ultimately opening up vocational opportunities for other women by becoming a prominent journalist, working at the *NEW YORK TRIBUNE* as one of the country's first literary critics and its first foreign correspondent.

Bibliography

Field, Peter S. *Ralph Waldo Emerson: The Making of a Democratic Intellectual.* Lanham, Md.: Rowman and Littlefield, 2002.

"Voluntaries"
Ralph Waldo Emerson
(1863)

Ralph Waldo EMERSON wrote the poem "Voluntaries" in the summer of 1863 in response to the death of Colonel Robert Gould Shaw, leader of the Union army's all-black Massachusetts 54th regiment. Shaw and several of his men were killed in an attack on Fort Wagner in South Carolina in July 1863. Like other Emerson poems, such as "ODE, INSCRIBED TO W. H. CHANNING" (published in *POEMS* in 1847) and "BOSTON HYMN" (also written in 1863, to celebrate the Emancipation Proclamation), "Voluntaries" was one of his few poems addressing specific social and political issues of the day, as most of his poetry dealt with more idealistic and mystical themes related to Transcendentalism. Emerson was a supporter of the Union cause against slavery, as discussed in the poem, and was also personally acquainted with Shaw and his family, to whom Emerson first submitted the poem. "Voluntaries" was published in the *ATLANTIC MONTHLY* of October 1863, appeared in a Shaw memorial volume the following year, and was included in Emerson's collection of poems, *MAY-DAY AND OTHER PIECES* in 1867.

"Voluntaries" is a five-part poem in praise of volunteers for the Union army, the "heroic boys" willing "To hazard all in Freedom's fight." The first part of the poem provides background by commenting on the history of slavery in the United States, going back to the capture of slaves from Africa, "Where a captive sits in chains." The poet wonders "What his fault, or what his crime?" and uses images of the family, of a child "Dragged from his mother's arms and breast," to emphasize the separation from Africa. Emerson then moves from this scene to the starkly different perspective on the celebrated events surrounding the founding of the United States and the Constitution. Again in the language of family and, more specifically, of paternity, the African is a "Hapless sire to hapless son," compared to the founding fathers, the "Great men in the Senate sate, / Sage and hero, side by side, / Building for their sons the State." Emerson compares the decisions of the founding fathers not only to the practice of kidnapping slaves in Africa, but to the recent events leading the nation to Civil War. Emerson finds then, as now, that the "great men" were "Lured by 'Union' as the bribe" in allowing slavery to continue.

In the next section of the poem, however, Emerson provides hope for Africans and for the nation, since "Freedom all winged expands" and "loves a poor and virtuous race." Although not naming him directly, Emerson honors heroes such as Colonel Shaw, "the generous chief" who led those "willing to be led," the black soldiers, in their fight for their own freedom.

In the third part of the poem, Emerson addresses directly those "voluntaries" who were willing to "quit proud homes and youthful dames" and consider the future of their race and their nation. In this section is one of the most famous passages from the poem, honoring military sacrifice: "So near is God to man, / When duty whispers low, *Thou must,* / The youth replies, *I can.*" Part four of the poem mourns the deaths of Shaw and the others lost while recognizing that regardless of "whoever fights, whoever falls," the cause is still worthy and their side is still right since "justice conquers evermore." And it is justice who will be the final "Victor over death and pain." The final section of the poem continues this theme of praising not the men themselves but "Lauding the Eternal Rights" and asserting here in 1863, in the middle of the war, much-needed confidence in the final victory of the Union.

Walden; or, Life in the Woods
Henry David Thoreau
(1854)

On July 4, 1845, Henry David THOREAU moved into a cabin near WALDEN POND, on land owned by Ralph Waldo EMERSON, as an experiment in Transcendentalist self-reliance and he published his account of *Walden* a few years later in 1854. He explained: "I went to the woods because I wished to live deliberately, to front only the essential facts of life, and see if I could learn what it had to teach, and not, when I came to die, discover that I had not lived." He also intended to use the solitude to write another book, *A WEEK ON THE CONCORD AND MERRIMACK RIVERS* (published in 1849), an account of a trip he had taken with his brother, John THOREAU, who died tragically just a few years earlier at the age of 27. While Henry David Thoreau did complete the manuscript for *A Week*, his most lasting literary legacy would in fact be the account of his stay at *Walden*, an account that has come to represent the core of a Transcendentalist perspective on self-reliance, frugality and economy, humanity's relationship with nature, and environmentalism. In going to Walden to live alone in a one-room cabin, Henry David Thoreau sought to separate himself from what he and other Transcendentalists saw as the increasing materialism and commercialism guiding antebellum American life. Thoreau wanted to get back to the basics and live in the simplest manner possible so as not only to remove himself from those negative values he associated with a capitalist economy but to look within himself and to nature for his physical as well as spiritual and intellectual needs.

Thoreau's concern with the material aspects of his society was indicated by the focus of his first chapter in *Walden* on "Economy." This chapter served as a how-to guide explaining how he simplified his life of excess and unnecessary material goods and provided details of how he built his cabin with the smallest and cheapest materials available, in the end the construction costing him a mere \$28.12½. Thoreau obviously, as a self-reliant individual, did the work of building the cabin himself, but his was not a moral of industrious hard labor; his goal was to emphasize that, with such minimal necessary expenses, one did not need to work hard every day; he argued that if he first reduced his material needs to as little as possible ("Simplify, simplify" as he urges his readers), he would need to work for wages or trade only six weeks out of the year to provide the basic needs of clothing, food, shelter, and fuel. Thus the "economy" of *Walden* also critiqued the way that the Puritan work ethic had been pulled into the service of a 19th-century capitalist economy in convincing people that they must be wage laborers and, as such, had no time for other pursuits.

Thoreau, of course, intended to spend his free nonworking hours and days in bettering himself through study and through spiritual communion with nature. It was as a poet, one who drew his inspiration from self-sufficiency and from nature, that Thoreau was most effective in presenting the main theme of *Walden*. As with his other naturalist and "travel" writings, such as *A Week on the Concord and Merrimack Rivers,* Thoreau ultimately presented not merely an account of his physical experiment or a guide to local wildlife but a road map for an individual spiritual journey. Thoreau used nature's rhythms, the days and weeks and seasons, to symbolize the change and growth of the human spirit, the death and rebirth of humanity necessary to move forward. Although he lived there more than two full years, *Walden* the book takes us through only a year of seasons. Thoreau moved into his cabin in the summer, symbolically on Independence Day. He takes his reader through the productive summer of "Sounds" and "Solitude," into the bountiful fall in "House-Warming," the cold icy winter of "Winter Animals" and "The Pond in Winter," which changes nature so drastically and requires him to see and understand it in new ways, and finally the rebirth that comes with "Spring" in the last full chapter in which he declared "Walden was dead and is alive again."

Thoreau was a botanist-naturalist who was interested in recording and understanding every aspect of nature for its own sake. Thus he differed from other Transcendentalists, such as Ralph Waldo Emerson, who sought to learn about nature, but not necessarily by living and communing with it. Ultimately, however, Thoreau's approach to nature as symbolic was the same as other Transcendentalists in that he believed that in particular microcosms of nature one could find larger universal truths. His in-depth study of one hillside, for example, in the chapter "Spring," led him to remark that just "this one hillside illustrated the principle of all the operations of Nature." Thoreau the naturalist also accepted that not all of nature could be explained; that there remain mysteries unknown and therefore unusable, in the Transcendentalist sense, to humankind.

Walden Pond itself served as the best example of Henry David Thoreau's dual perspective of nature as having both physical and spiritual aspects, but also of having both knowable and unknown qualities. The pond itself is the symbolic center of the text, a place that Thoreau had known as a child and thus was, in a sense, part of his own self that he had come to learn about in new ways. The pond symbolized for Thoreau the human spirit or soul. Local legend was that the pond was bottomless, but Thoreau had set out first to measure the pond's depth—which he found to be more than 100 feet—and then to see that not as a limitation but as representative of holding specific identifiable truths that just have not yet been fully comprehended or mined. The fact that these truths remained unseen, in this case literally underwater, was the source of their mystery.

Contrary to contemporary criticisms of Thoreau that he removed himself from society to live as a hermit during his "two years and two months" stay at the pond, Thoreau had no desire to live completely apart from human society. He did seek solitude for contemplation and for writing, but he was ever observant of his neighbors, visited or dined with family or friends in nearby CONCORD, MASSACHUSETTS, and took trips into town for supplies. One such interaction in 1846, in fact, led to an attempt by local officials to collect a poll tax from Thoreau. He refused to pay on grounds of objection to the government's use of his money, in particular in pursuit of slavery and expansionism through the Mexican War, and was arrested and spent one night in jail, an experience that formed the basis for his most enduring political message in "CIVIL DISOBEDIENCE." Ultimately Thoreau's was not a solitary or selfish experiment in that he presented his work publicly, in part as a response to his neighbors' and friends' curiosity and criticisms about his lonely stay at the pond, but also in hopes that the ideas and conclusions he drew there would cure some of the evils of the society he cared about, or, as he put it "wake my neighbors up." In the opening paragraph of *Walden* he noted that his stay had only been temporary and that "At present I am a sojourner in civilized life again."

Bibliography

Thoreau, Henry David. *Walden: A Fully Annotated Edition.* Edited by Jeffrey S. Cramer. New Haven, Conn.: Yale University Press, 2004.

Walden Pond

Located just outside of the village of CONCORD, MASSACHUSETTS, Walden Pond was the site of Henry David THOREAU's extended wilderness excursion that resulted in the writing of his most famous work, WALDEN (1854). Due to Thoreau's work, the pond itself has become synonymous with Transcendentalist nature philosophy. The best physical descriptions of the pond come from the book *Walden*. On July 4, 1845, Thoreau went to the woods by the pond to live in a cabin, as he later wrote in *Walden*, near "a small pond, about a mile and a half south of the village of Concord and somewhat higher than it, in the midst of an extensive wood. . . . It is a clear and deep green well, half a mile long and a mile and three quarters in circumference, and contains about sixty-one and a half acres; a perennial spring in the midst of pine and oak woods, without any visible inlet or outlet except by the clouds and evaporation." Although Thoreau carefully recorded such facts about the pond, his appreciation of nature was a spiritual journey, and his two-year and two-month stay at the pond provided him with deeper meaning about life and human existence. The pond was, for Thoreau, the site of "perennial spring," or rebirth and revitalization, of nature as well as of humankind.

Other Transcendentalists visited the nearby pond as well, such as Ralph Waldo EMERSON, who owned much of the property around the pond, including the site where Henry David Thoreau built his cabin. Emerson took weekly walks to Walden Pond and often brought visitors with him to show off what he believed to be Concord's greatest attraction. At one time or another friends such as Christopher Pearse CRANCH, Margaret FULLER, and Nathaniel HAWTHORNE all accompanied Emerson to Walden Pond. Franklin Benjamin SANBORN even jokingly named Emerson's regular tours the Walden Pond Society.

Walden Pond remains an important site for U.S. history, and travelers regularly make the journey to see what Thoreau and Emerson saw and feel what they felt. In 1965 the pond was named the first National Literary Landmark, and numerous individuals and organizations work today to preserve the natural beauty of the pond from overuse due to fishing, swimming, and more than half a million visitors each year.

Bibliography

Maynard, W. Barksdale. *Walden Pond: A History.* Oxford and New York: Oxford University Press, 2004.

Walden Woods Project. Available online. URL: http://www.walden.org. Accessed August 2005.

Walden Woods

Walden Woods is a 2,680-acre area near CONCORD, MASSACHUSETTS, that encompasses WALDEN POND, the site where Henry David THOREAU lived alone in his cabin between 1845 and 1847. Thoreau resided near the pond, but he enveloped himself in the woods as a whole, as he declared his intentions in his 1854 book, WALDEN, "I went to the woods because I wished to live deliberately, to front only the essential facts of life, and see if I could learn what it had to teach, and not, when I came to die, discover that I had not lived." His meanderings and his observations took him on walks to locations throughout the woods as a whole, so that his experiences were not limited to Walden Pond, the site that most people associate with his experiment. While the pond garnered the attention of conservationists throughout the 20th-century, it was not until 1989 that the entire Walden Woods region seemed threatened by commercial and residential development plans. In 1990 the Walden Woods Project was founded by recording artist Don Henley to purchase and protect the area by identifying its larger cultural and historical as well as environmental significance.

Bibliography

Henley, Don, and David Marsh, eds. *Heaven Is under Our Feet: A Book for Walden Woods.* Stamford, Conn.: Longmeadow Press, 1991.

Maynard, W. Barksdale. *Walden Pond: A History.* Oxford and New York: Oxford University Press, 2004.

Walden Woods Project. Available online. URL: http://www.walden.org. Accessed August 2005.

Walker, James
(1794–1874)

James Walker influenced the Transcendentalist movement as a Unitarian minister and as the editor of the CHRISTIAN EXAMINER between 1831 and 1839, a periodical in which many of the emerging Transcendentalist figures published their early views. Walker attended HARVARD DIVINITY SCHOOL and after preaching for 20 years returned as a professor and eventually president of the university between 1853 and 1860. He was also one of the founders of the AMERICAN UNITARIAN ASSOCIATION, which sought to unify Unitarian doctrine and organize the congregations.

Walker served as editor of the *Christian Examiner* during the crucial years of a split within UNITARIANISM that resulted in the formation of a separate Transcendentalist philosophy and movement. Walker changed the emphasis of the periodical from the primary forum for Unitarian theological debate, as had been the purpose of the paper under the editorship of Henry WARE, JR., to a forum for more wide-ranging topics and viewpoints. In the interest of promoting "free inquiry" Walker extended the paper's list of contributors as well as its audience by moving beyond strictly mainstream Unitarian views and publishing the radical views of emerging Transcendentalists such as Orestes BROWNSON, Frederic Henry HEDGE, and George RIPLEY. This editorial decision invited controversy into Walker's *Christian Examiner*, however. An 1836 article by George Ripley sparked one of the defining controversies of early Transcendentalism by provoking the criticism of prominent conservative Unitarian Andrews NORTON in a published debate with Ripley and the Transcendentalists over the divinity of Christ known as the "MIRACLES CONTROVERSY." Beyond the theological differences, Norton also felt that by publishing such pieces in the *Christian Examiner*, Walker had let the paper stray from accurately representing the Unitarian faith.

James Walker himself was initially associated with the "infidel" philosophy of Transcendentalism in publishing his own 1834 essay on "The Philosophy of Man's Spiritual Nature in Regard to the Foundation of Faith," in which he emphasized the importance of intuition over logic in religious or spiritual experience. Beyond providing an early forum for Transcendentalist thought, however, he had no further connections with the movement.

"Walking"
Henry David Thoreau
(1862)

Henry David THOREAU's essay "Walking" was published in the ATLANTIC MONTHLY in June 1862, one month after Thoreau's death. The essay originated from writings in his journal in the 1850s, and he delivered sections of it as two separate public lectures, "Walking" and "The Wild" (thus the essay is still sometimes referred to by the combined title "Walking, or the Wild"). The final published version retained these two distinct parts. The first part of the essay is a reflection on the physical act of walking through the natural landscape. He provided descriptions of the area surrounding CONCORD, MASSACHUSETTS, and mused that, in subconsciously always setting out on his walks toward the southwest, he was following the destiny of America as a whole as "Westward the star of empire takes its way." The second part of the essay, based on the lecture on "The Wild," is a more abstract philosophical discussion of the restorative aspect of nature, walking through which humans can gain "nourishment and vigor." As he emphasized in his other writings, humanity's relationship to nature cannot be based solely on the selfish needs of humans but must be reciprocal. Thoreau's conservationist statement in "Walking," that "in Wildness is the preservation of the World," has become one of his most often remembered quotes, an urgent call repeated by environmentalists since his own time and ultimately adopted by the Sierra Club as its official motto.

As in his other writings, such as "LIFE WITHOUT PRINCIPLE," as well as in the themes explored at length in "CIVIL DISOBEDIENCE" and *WALDEN*, Thoreau's overall philosophy of nature and of humanity's place within it may be gleaned from his description of the simple act of "walking." Henry David Thoreau was, of course, Concord's most famous walker, preferring to spend the extra time it took to get from one place to another by foot, walking and communing with nature, rather than rushing past it. He was regularly accompanied on walks in the woods by his siblings, John THOREAU and Sophia THOREAU, or by friends such as Amos Bronson ALCOTT, Ralph Waldo EMERSON, or William Henry CHANNING. The "Walking" essay itself may have been inspired by William WORDSWORTH's *Guide to the Lakes*, intended as a walking guide or tour of the Lake District of England, with Thoreau envisioning doing the same for Massachusetts. Thoreau was not interested in global traveling, explaining in *Walden* that he "traveled a good deal in Concord."

"Walking" about was Thoreau's primary activity and method of conducting his scientific and spiritual quests. Around the time he was writing this essay, he wrote to friend Harrison Gray Otis BLAKE, explaining that he preferred to "live at home like a traveler . . . Is not each withered leaf that I see in my walks something which I have traveled to find?—traveled, who can tell how far?" Thoreau walked as a process of discovering the natural world, of discovering something about himself, and as a route to understanding humanity's place in nature. The goal, in his words, was "to regard man as an inhabitant, or a part and parcel of Nature, rather than a member of society." Henry David Thoreau did not walk for the reasons others might engage in such activity, that is, either for the sake of reaching a particular destination or for exercise. He explicitly stated that "the walking of which I speak has nothing in it akin to taking exercise, as it is called . . . but is itself the enterprise and adventure of the day."

Bibliography

Walls, Laura Dassow. *Seeing New Worlds: Henry David Thoreau and Nineteenth-Century Natural Science*. Madison: University of Wisconsin Press, 1995.

Ward, Anna Hazard Barker
(1813–unknown)

Anna Hazard Barker was introduced to the circle of Transcendentalists through her cousin Eliza Far-rar. Initially Anna lived in New York and only visited her cousin and her Boston-Cambridge friends occasionally, but after moving to Boston, Anna regularly attended Margaret FULLER's CONVERSATIONS FOR WOMEN and became one of the young protégés surrounding Fuller whom Elizabeth HOAR characterized disparagingly as "diamonds" worn around Fuller's neck simply for display. Fuller's relationship with Anna Barker was more complex, however, as Barker came to hold a special place in Fuller's heart; she once declared "If I write a novel I shall take Anna for my heroine." The two women traveled together on New England holidays, and Fuller dedicated many of her poems to Barker whom she described as "my heart's sister and my fancy's love." In 1835–36 Fuller wrote a series of poems to Anna that reflected the emotional intensity of their relationship. Fuller's poem, "To A.H.B. On our meeting, on my return from New York to Boston, August 1835," celebrated the beauty and strength of a female friendship removed "from the haunts of men." "To the Same. A Feverish Vision," however, reveals a more disturbed unstable aspect of that relationship as it details a nightmare Fuller had about drowning in blood and being rescued by Anna: "When with soft eyes, beaming the tenderest love, / I see thy dear face, Anna! Far above." Here is introduced a recurrent theme in Fuller's writing, that of a female savior but, in this case, the savior is not just a reference to a spiritual savior, or a mythological reference to the strength of womankind, but manifests literally in the figure of Anna Barker, whom Fuller looked to for personal fulfillment and emotional completeness at this time. Barker's marriage to Samuel Gray WARD in October 1840 was an emotional crisis for Fuller who not only felt her intense emotional relationship with Anna would be damaged but had by that time developed feelings for Samuel as well.

Bibliography

Steele, Jeffrey. *Transfiguring America: Myth, Ideology, and Mourning in Margaret Fuller's Writing*. Columbia: University of Missouri Press, 2001.

Tilton, Eleanor M. "The True Romance of Anna Hazard Barker and Samuel Gray Ward." *Studies in the American Renaissance* (1987): 53–72.

Ward, Samuel Gray
(1817–1907)

Samuel Gray Ward was friends with several Transcendentalists, from his Harvard schoolmates William Ellery CHANNING II, to Jones VERY, to Margaret FULLER, with whom he shared a close intellectual and emotional relationship. It was through Fuller that he first met Ralph Waldo EMERSON and was brought into the growing circle of Transcendentalists in the late 1830s. Ward eventually contributed several pieces to the DIAL magazine, including four of his poems chosen by editor Fuller to appear in the first issue of July 1840. In later issues he published essays on themes such as "Notes on Art and Architecture" and "Translation of Dante."

Samuel Ward married Anna Hazard Barker (WARD) in October 1840. Their engagement was a shock and personal disappointment to their mutual friend, Margaret Fuller, who felt not only that her long friendship with Anna would be interrupted by the marriage, but who herself had become attached to Samuel. The fact that he had chosen Anna, a close mutual friend, over her made the news of his marriage even worse to take, Fuller saw Samuel Ward's marriage not only as a personal crisis but as a crisis of VOCATION for a scholarly mind. In order to prove his ability to support her and thus marry Anna, Samuel Ward had chosen to pursue business rather than literature and this choice at such a young age was seen by some of his friends as stunting his intellectual growth. As Margaret Fuller put it in a letter to Ward, "I had longed to see you a painter . . . when I learned you were to become a merchant, to sit at the dead wood of the desk, and calculate figures, I was betrayed into unbelief."

Besides his *Dial* contributions, Samuel Ward did not pursue a literary career but instead, as the wealthiest member of the Transcendentalist community due to the inheritance of his father's sizable estate as well as his own business dealings, lived the life of a gentleman. Emerson did choose three of Ward's poems for his 1874 collection of favorites, PARNASSUS. The Wards eventually moved to New York where Samuel used his influence and money as a patron of the arts, most notably as a founder of the Metropolitan Museum of Art. Despite their distance from Boston, Samuel Ward maintained correspondences with his Transcendentalist friends throughout his life.

Bibliography

Myerson, Joel. *The New England Transcendentalists and the Dial: A History of the Magazine and Its Contributors.* London and Toronto: Associated University Presses, 1980.

Tilton, Eleanor M. "The True Romance of Anna Hazard Barker and Samuel Gray Ward," *Studies in the American Renaissance* (1987): 53–72.

Ware, Henry, Jr.
(1794–1843)

Ralph Waldo EMERSON took Henry Ware's place as minister of Boston's Second Church and, even after he left the Unitarian church, the influence of Ware had an impact on Emerson's rhetorical style and intellectual development as a Transcendentalist. Emerson initially assisted Ware, but took over when Ware accepted a position as professor at HARVARD DIVINITY SCHOOL in 1830. Ware was one of the most important Unitarian ministers of the early 19th century and had a direct influence on the Transcendentalists in establishing the liberal model that would be taught at the Divinity School during that time, with its emphasis on self-culture and the spiritual development of the individual. The appointment of Ware's father, Henry Ware, Sr., to a professorship at Harvard's Divinity School in 1805 was one of the defining moments of the Unitarian controversy that led to the organization of the new liberal denomination promoted by Ware, Jr., during his ministry. Ware, Jr., was one of the most articulate defenders of UNITARIANISM and had as his forum the CHRISTIAN EXAMINER, a periodical for which he served as editor at one time. Although he influenced Emerson and a generation of young Unitarian men at Harvard, Ware did not espouse the Transcendentalist philosophy and theological critique that emerged from that liberal religious atmosphere. His 1838 *The Personality of the Deity* was a response to and critique of Emerson's controversial DIVINITY SCHOOL ADDRESS of that year, in which Ware defended the concept of a personal God against Emerson's rejection of both the supernatural aspects and the literalness of the Bible.

Wasson, David
(1823–1887)

David Wasson was a younger Transcendentalist minister and writer involved in most of the major post–Civil War activities of the movement, such as the FREE RELIGIOUS ASSOCIATION and the RADICAL CLUB. He was a minister but had difficulty holding a regular position. He was dismissed in 1852 by the first Congregational Church he served due to unorthodox views, apparently having been influenced by the Transcendentalist critiques of radical Unitarians Ralph Waldo EMERSON and Theodore PARKER. Wasson instead founded his own liberal church and occasionally served as a guest preacher in the pulpits of friends such as Parker or Thomas Wentworth HIGGINSON. Like Higginson, Wasson was increasingly drawn into the controversy, over ABOLITIONISM and in 1860 he wrote "A Letter to William Lloyd GARRISON," in which he put forth his own perspective on the course the movement should take, mainly through a focus on human rights and justice.

Wasson began to pursue writing more fully and published many essays on religious and social themes in periodicals such as the ATLANTIC MONTHLY and the NORTH AMERICAN REVIEW. His essays and reviews of other writers and thinkers serve as the clearest statement of his own interpretation of Transcendentalist ideas. At one time he lived in the former CONCORD, MASSACHUSETTS, home of Henry David THOREAU, and several of Wasson's essays on Thoreau showed him engaging with Thoreau's ideas but not convinced of his methods. He was more likely to praise Ralph Waldo Emerson as the model of self-reliance in essays such as the 1858 "The New World and the New Man." Emerson in turn praised Wasson and Theodore Parker so admired his independence of thought that the radical Twenty-Eighth Congregational Society chose Wasson to replace the venerable Parker after his death. In this position he delivered and published a sermon on *The Radical Creed* (1865), which established him as a free religious proponent. Wasson preached there briefly, however, due to ill health. He would contribute to the *Life of Theodore Parker* (1864) edited by friend John WEISS.

After leaving Parker's congregation David Wasson never held a regular ministerial position again, but as a religious radical not tied to any one denomination, Wasson was central to the founding of the Free Religious Association in 1867 and contributed to movement's paper, *The Radical*. The Free Religious Association and the Radical Club, of which Wasson was also a participant, attracted many of the Transcendentalists during the post-Civil War years, and through these clubs Wasson maintained contact with figures such as Amos Bronson ALCOTT and Ednah Dow CHENEY. He would join with Alcott and Cheney in the 1870s as a lecturer at the CONCORD SCHOOL OF PHILOSOPHY AND LITERATURE. David Wasson was also a prolific Transcendentalist poet among the younger generation, although his poems have received little attention from scholars of the movement. Several of Wasson's poems were collected and published by Ednah Dow Cheney in 1888, the year after his death.

Webster, Daniel
(1782–1852)

Daniel Webster was one of the most admired and remembered lawyers and senators of the 19th century and admired especially by the first generation of American Transcendentalists for his noted powers of speaking, memorializing the Revolutionary generation in his famous 1826 eulogies for John Adams and Thomas Jefferson, and his impassioned defense of freedom and of a strong central government. Although associated with the elite of Boston due to his two terms as a senator from Massachusetts in 1827–41 and 1845–50, Webster actually hailed from an ordinary New Hampshire background and had begun his political career as a New Hampshire representative to Congress in the 1810s. He went on to become a representative from Massachusetts and then a senator. Bracketing his time as senator, Webster also served as one of the country's most notable secretaries of state between 1841 and 1843 and again during the last two years of his life, 1850–52.

It was at the end of his term as a senator, however, that the Massachusetts-based Transcendentalists were among those particularly disappointed by what they perceived as the "fall" of Daniel Webster when the statesman defended the FUGITIVE SLAVE LAW as part of the Compromise of 1850 made with southern states to avoid secession. While Webster's position was technically consistent with his belief in preserving the Union, many New England abolitionists, reformers, and intellectuals denounced Webster from then forward for preserving and even strengthening southerner's control over their slaves and possibly endangering the freedom of non-slaves.

Ralph Waldo EMERSON, in particular, had held up Daniel Webster as a representative of the ideal intellect and speaker and modeled his own rhetorical and oratory skills after Webster. Even before 1850, however, Emerson had reservations about such a man putting his talents to use within the world of political interests and toward the attainment of personal power. When Webster supported the Fugitive Slave Law, however, Emerson lost all respect for Webster and criticized him publicly in the "FUGITIVE SLAVE LAW ADDRESS" as having "no moral sentiment." Even after Webster's death just two years later, Emerson lamented that Webster had once been the "completest man" but ended up "the victim of his ambition." Theodore PARKER agreed that "Never was there such a fall" and concluded that "No man has done so much to debauch the conscience of the nation." Unlike some of his colleagues, Henry David THOREAU seems not to have been impressed with Webster even before the 1850s. Thoreau was particularly harsh after Webster's death and referred to him as a "dirt-bug" in the 1854 address "SLAVERY IN MASSACHUSETTS." For men such as Ralph Waldo Emerson and Theodore Parker, however, the greater the man, the harder the fall, and the fall of such a man as Webster was especially difficult to understand or ignore. For all of the attention, both positive and negative, that the Transcendentalists paid to Daniel Webster as a political figure, he seems to have had little interest in them in turn.

Bibliography
Gougeon, Len. *Virtue's Hero: Emerson, Antislavery, and Reform.* Athens: University of Georgia Press, 1990.

A Week on the Concord and Merrimack Rivers
Henry David Thoreau
(1849)

Henry David THOREAU's first book, *A Week on the Concord and Merrimack Rivers,* sold only 219 copies and cost the author several hundred dollars of his own money to have it printed. The book was first drafted during his stay at WALDEN POND in 1845–47. In fact, he had originally sought out the solitary time at Walden Pond with a plan to write this book. The trip described in the account was a two-week boat voyage he had taken with his brother, John THOREAU, JR., in 1839. The book itself was intended as a tribute to John, who died of tetanus in 1842 at the age of only 27. Henry David Thoreau had only a few journal notes from this outing with his brother but eventually expanded those notes into an essay for the Transcendentalist journal, the DIAL (where Thoreau was first published), and finally into more than a 400-page book. The book ultimately incorporated many other writings by Thoreau, unrelated to this trip, including many of his other *Dial* essays on various topics and thus provided an account not just of the boat journey but of a larger metaphorical life journey. He incorporated earlier writings and reflections on mythology, religion, and literature, as well as several of his poems into the final work.

Thoreau's *A Week on the Concord and Merrimack Rivers* was also part of the nature and travel writing genre explored by other Transcendentalists such as in Ralph Waldo EMERSON's NATURE (1836) and Margaret FULLER's SUMMER ON THE LAKES (1844), both of which influenced Thoreau. As part of his own literary legacy, *A Week* is often overshadowed by the more commercial and literary accomplishment of WALDEN published five years later.

Contemporary literary critic, and Thoreau's eventual editor at the ATLANTIC MONTHLY, James Russell LOWELL reviewed *A Week on the Concord and Merrimack Rivers* as part of this travel-nature genre when he characterized the book as a "river-party," an invitation by Thoreau for the reader to join him on his travels. The book is organized as such a journey with its organization into separate essays taking the reader through the days of the week: "Sunday," "Monday," "Tuesday," etc. Each "daily" section is an exploration of the physical journey and the natural surroundings, but each also examines a larger spiritual or literary theme that engages Thoreau on his quest. As scholar Linck Johnson characterizes it, the book is ultimately much more than just Lowell's lighthearted "river-party," as it is a "voyage of discovery" of the self and of the meaning of life and death. As his companion on the original trip that inspired the book, John Thoreau, Jr. appeared in the text as coauthor as well as muse or inspiration for Thoreau's ability to grasp the larger life and death lessons to be drawn from nature: the passage of time (also emphasized by the days of the week as chapter titles), the seasons, the inevitable flow of the river.

A Week also reflects the influence of Ralph Waldo Emerson on the young Henry David Thoreau. His time at Walden and his literary production while there were efforts to live the idealized self-reliant life of engagement that Emerson promoted in his essays and lectures and, indeed, many of Emerson's ideas echo in *A Week*. Beyond philosophical inspiration, Thoreau's relationship with Emerson at the time of writing the book was guided by professional concerns as well. Emerson helped Thoreau negotiate a contract with the publisher James Munroe for the book, a deal that left Thoreau in debt and the Emerson-Thoreau friendship fractured. Thoreau wrote of how the book came between him and Emerson in his journal shortly after the publication of *A Week*: "I had a friend, I wrote a book, I asked my friend's criticism, I never got but praise for what was good in it—my friend became estranged from me and then I got blame for all that was bad,—& so I got at last the criticism which I wanted."

A Week on the Concord and Merrimack Rivers is ultimately part an account of his actual trip and part a reflection on humanity's relationship with nature, part history (literary, social, and natural), part elegy to his brother, and part social and political critique, although, again, *Walden* and Thoreau's lecture "CIVIL DISOBEDIENCE" are the better known and fuller representations of this latter category of his writings.

Bibliography

Johnson, Linck. "*A Week on the Concord and Merrimack Rivers.*" In *The Cambridge Companion to Henry David Thoreau*, ed. Joel Myerson. New York: Cambridge University Press, 1995, 40–56.

Thoreau, Henry David. *A Week on the Concord and Merrimack Rivers.* Edited by Carl F. Hovde et al. Princeton, N.J.: Princeton University Press, 2004.

Weiss, John, Jr.
(1818–1879)

Essayist and Unitarian minister John Weiss, Jr., was a Harvard colleague of Henry David THOREAU. Through his friendship with Unitarian minister Convers FRANCIS, whose pulpit the younger Weiss would eventually take over, he became involved in many activities of the Transcendentalist circle in the 1830s and 1840s. He was a member of the TOWN AND COUNTRY CLUB and, in his hometown of Worcester, Massachusetts, he was part of the intellectual literary circle of Thoreau friend and disciple Harrison Gray Otis BLAKE. As a member of the younger generation, Weiss was particularly influential in post-Civil War Transcendentalist activities as a member of the RADICAL CLUB and founding member of the FREE RELIGIOUS ASSOCIATION. Weiss maintained a prolific literary life as the author of numerous essays and published sermons and lectures, but he is most well known for his two-volume biographical study of fellow Transcendentalist and radical Unitarian minister Theodore PARKER: *The Life and Correspondence of Theodore Parker* (1864).

Western Messenger
(1835–1841)

The *Western Messenger* was the first published journal to feature the writings and thoughts of the emerging American Transcendentalist movement and, printed between 1835 and 1841, was the longest-running of the movement's antebellum publications. The paper was not New England based, however, as its original purpose was as a forum for UNITARIANISM in the western United States. It was established in Cincinnati and subsequently published out of Kentucky, with the Western Unitarian Association and later the AMERICAN UNITARIAN ASSOCIATION providing financial support at different times for its publication. James Freeman CLARKE was one of the founders of the magazine and served as its first editor. Transcendentalist colleagues William Henry CHANNING and Christopher Pearce CRANCH joined Clarke as coeditors beginning in 1839 and, finally, in May 1840, Channing took over as sole editor. Many Transcendentalist writers and thinkers who would later contribute to the Boston DIAL were first published in the *Western Messenger*—John Sullivan DWIGHT, Ralph Waldo EMERSON, Margaret FULLER, Frederic Henry HEDGE, and Elizabeth Palmer PEABODY, as well as the core of *Messenger* editors themselves, Channing, Clarke, and Cranch.

The paper combined Unitarian religious themes with attention to literary culture during the first several years, but when Henry Channing took over as editor and brought the magazine to New England he maintained a stricter focus on literature and philosophy, primarily Transcendentalism. A contemporary literary critic asserted that the *Western Messenger* was "essentially an eastern messenger, the organ of New England liberalism in the Valley of the Ohio," and another quipped that its primary purpose was even more specific: to provide a forum for the words of Ralph Waldo Emerson. The paper boasted many New England subscribers, and it was an important site for early articulation of Emersonian Transcendentalism—what writer and editor Cranch characterized as the "purer elements struggling to the surface of the stream of society," or simply as "the New School." The *Western Messenger*'s publication of reviews or excerpts of Emerson's early work such as NATURE, published in 1836, and the DIVINITY SCHOOL ADDRESS given in 1838, helped to disseminate early ideas that would be more fully developed by the time Boston Transcendentalists established the *Dial* in 1840.

Although the Boston *Dial* is most often referred to as the first Transcendentalist journal, the *Western Messenger* was published earlier with a similar purpose and philosophical perspective. It initiated the idea of a journalistic forum for the Transcendentalist movement and provided a model for how such a paper should be organized and what its themes should be with its attention to literary criticism, religious themes, and reflections on European ROMANTICISM and IDEALISM. Historian Clarence Gohdes determined in his analysis of Transcendentalist periodicals that "The reader of *The Dial* and *The Western Messenger* finds scarcely any type of material which is not common to both journals." The two papers briefly overlapped in their publication dates during 1840 and 1841 before the *Dial* became the main periodical for New England Transcendentalism.

Bibliography

Gohdes, Clarence L. F. *The Periodicals of American Transcendentalism.* Durham, N.C.: Duke University Press, 1931.

Habich, Robert. *Transcendentalism and the Western Messenger: A History of the Magazine and Its Contributors, 1835–1841.* London and Cranbury, N.J.: Associated University Presses, 1985.

West Roxbury, Massachusetts   *See* BROOK FARM.

Wheeler, Charles Stearns
(1816–1843)

Charles Stearns Wheeler was a childhood friend of Henry David THOREAU and a prolific younger Transcendentalist writer whose life and promising career were cut short by his death at the age of 26. After graduation from Harvard in 1837 Wheeler spent the summer with Thoreau in a cabin, a trip believed to be the inspiration for Thoreau's later experiment at WALDEN POND. Wheeler served as a Greek tutor at Harvard for four years during which time he befriended others of the Transcendentalists, including Ralph Waldo EMERSON. Wheeler worked with Emerson on an early publication of the work of Thomas CARLYLE, and Wheeler himself was central to introducing Carlyle to the Transcendentalists by editing a multivolume series of Carlyle's writings published in 1838–39. In addition to other publications during this prolific period of writing, he also put out an edition of *Herodotus* that became the standard Harvard textbook.

In 1842 Charles Stearns Wheeler sailed to Europe where he traveled with friends James Elliot CABOT and John WEISS and planned to complete his studies of German and English ROMANTICISM. In the next several months he sent at least two reports, or "intelligences," from Europe to Ralph Waldo Emerson, who published them in two separate 1843 issues of the Transcendentalist literary journal, the DIAL. After less than a year in Germany, however, Wheeler died of what his friends called either a "gastric" or "consumptive" fever.

Whipple, Edwin Percy
(1819–1886)

Edwin Whipple was a lyceum lecturer and literary critic who reviewed the work of some of the Transcendentalists and, in particular, had a personal influence on the publication of Nathaniel HAWTHORNE's stories and novels. Whipple helped change the way Americans thought about literary criticism and about their role as readers of literature by emphasizing that a book reveals as much about the author as about the subject matter. In seeing a book as a conversation between the author and the reader, Whipple also established a new role for the critic in negotiating that relationship by revealing the author to the readers. Like many of the Transcendentalists, such as Ralph Waldo EMERSON and George RIPLEY, Whipple promoted the creation of a distinctly American literature and American authors, breaking from dependence upon Europe as the arbiter of taste and culture. It was perhaps a great compliment, then, in the posthumous publication *Recollections of Emi-*

nent Men (1890), for Whipple to have referred to Emerson perceptively as a "Hindoo-Yankee,—a cross between Brahma and Poor Richard."

Toward this purpose of appreciating new forms and styles of literature, Edwin Percy Whipple argued that the critic or reviewer should discard outdated rules of criticism and instead begin from a more natural or "organic" relationship to the text and the author. Whipple had influence on the developing careers on a range of authors during the American Renaissance of the 1850s, including Edgar Allan POE and walt WHITMAN, but his most significant input was in regards to the work of Nathaniel Hawthorne. He consistently praised Hawthorne's work in reviews for the ATLANTIC MONTHLY and other periodicals, pointing out both the "dark passions" and "the humor" that set Hawthorne apart from other writers. As a consultant to publisher James Fields, of Ticknor and Fields, Whipple helped select the title for *House of the Seven Gables*, and Hawthorne personally sought Whipple's advice on the manuscript for THE BLITHEDALE ROMANCE, wanting it "looked over by a keen, yet not unfriendly eye, like yours." Hawthorne looked to Whipple for advice on a title for this book as well as for *The Marble Faun*.

Edwin Percy Whipple wrote articles and reviews for a number of newspapers and published his lectures and critical reviews in such collections as the two-volume *Essays and Reviews* (1848–49), *Lectures on Subjects Connected with Literature and Life* (1850), and *Character and Characteristic Men* (1866).

Whitman, Walt
(1819–1892)

Walt Whitman, perhaps the singularly most significant American poet of the 19th century, was of the same generation as many of the Boston Transcendentalists and shared certain social and literary connections to the movement. Whitman was based in New York, however, and worked for many years as a newspaper journalist before emerging as a poet, but he certainly knew several of the Transcendentalists, including Ralph Waldo EMERSON, and in some ways each influenced the work of the other. Most famously, in 1860 Walt Whitman told a correspondent: "I was simmering, simmering, simmering; Emerson brought me to a boil." Scholars have been most interested in Whitman's personal as well as literary connections with the Transcendentalists, and with Emerson in particular. In addition to at least minimal acquaintance with Amos Bronson ALCOTT and Henry David THOREAU, whom he met in New York, Whitman had met Emerson a few times, and a letter from Emerson was published in the second edition of *Leaves of Grass*. Whitman saw himself in many ways as the fulfillment of Emerson's call for an "American poet," but the two did not necessarily share the same vision of his poetry. In 1860 Emerson had urged Whitman to remove some of the sexually themed poems from the next edition of the volume, probably because his name was attached as an endorser of the volume, but Whitman took Emerson's larger philosophy to heart in remaining true to himself and left the poems in.

For his part, Ralph Waldo Emerson was enthusiastic about *Leaves of Grass* when Whitman sent him a copy and he responded to Whitman that the poems were "the most extraordinary piece of wit and wisdom that America has yet contributed," praise that Whitman included in future editions of the poems. However, Emerson failed to respond to *Leaves of Grass* after that or to continue to give Whitman the praise and encouragement he had hoped for. By the 1860s Whitman had become critical of the Emerson he once referred to as "Master" and was permanently insulted when Emerson published his anthology of favorite poems, PARNASSUS, in 1874 and chose not to include any of Whitman's verses. Although scholars point out the unmistakable connections between specific Emersonian works and Whitman's later writing, primarily the echoes of "SELF-RELIANCE" in "SONG OF MYSELF," for his part, Whitman declared until his death that Emerson was not, in the end, a major literary influence on the writing of *Leaves of Grass* and that he had not even read Emerson before composing the work.

Regardless of the nature of the relationship between Emerson and Whitman, or the influence of one upon the other, "Song of Myself" has been regarded by many as Whitman's most clearly

Transcendental poetry, with its emphasis on the development and celebration of the individual self, the symbolic use of nature and natural themes to illuminate human life and thought, and self-consciousness about the role of the poet, a theme characteristic of Emerson's poetry and prose. Like Emerson, Whitman, in *Leaves of Grass*, presented the poet in a spiritual, not just literary, role. He also called for new forms, or a rejection of traditional forms, and experimented with longer unstructured lines of prose-poetry and a wider range of subject matter than poets before him. Whitman took as his subject all of America and presented poetry as reflective of the democratic spirit in the United States. In "Song of Myself" and other poems in *Leaves of Grass*, Whitman gave voice to a cross section of American life, cataloging the everyday lives of people, black and white, young and old, and men and women, celebrating American cities, farms, occupations, ideals, and landscapes. Like the Transcendentalists, Whitman promoted what he termed a "new theology," a belief that divine truths and principles could be found in ordinary life and ordinary people.

While Walt Whitman may or may not have been directly influenced by Ralph Waldo Emerson or other Transcendentalists, his writing was characteristic of the spirit of their times in its celebration of democracy and optimism about the progress of human society. Although Whitman himself realized "that I have not gained acceptance in my own times," he is remembered now as one of the most important poets ever produced by the United States.

Bibliography

Loving, Jerome. *Emerson, Whitman, and the American Muse*. Chapel Hill: University of North Carolina Press, 1982.

Reynolds, David S. *Walt Whitman*. New York: Oxford University Press, 2005.

Whittier, John Greenleaf
(1807–1892)

Quaker poet and reformer John Greenleaf Whittier was one of the central figures in American

ABOLITIONISM and was influenced by the same social and literary circles of the Transcendentalists of his generation. Whittier admired both Ralph Waldo EMERSON and Henry David THOREAU, and knew Emerson personally, but never considered himself among the Transcendentalists. His energies were toward the abolition of slavery and, after reports of Emerson's controversial August 1844 speech on "EMANCIPATION IN THE BRITISH WEST INDIES," Whittier became particularly interested in Emerson and the following month invited him to speak at an antislavery convention. Although Emerson declined that particular invitation, Whittier reviewed Emerson's address in the September 1844 issue of the *Middlesex Standard* and praised the philosopher for lending his voice to the cause. Like Emerson and many other Northern liberal reformers, Whittier was outraged when Massachusetts Senator Daniel WEBSTER voted to appease southern slaveholders by supporting the Compromise of 1850, including the notoriously harsh FUGITIVE SLAVE LAW. Whittier wrote a poem, "Ichabod," lamenting Webster's fall. After the Civil War, Whittier remained active in the struggle for black civil rights and periodically came into contact with Emerson through reform organizations. In 1874 the two men served together as pallbearers at the funeral of abolitionist Senator Charles SUMNER.

John Greenleaf Whittier is more likely remembered for his poetry than for his direct activism as a reformer and within national politics. He briefly served in the Massachusetts legislature in the mid-1830s and was one of the founders of the Republican party after an unsuccessful Congressional bid as the Liberty party candidate in 1842. After the 1840s, poor health forced him into semiretirement and he turned his attention to writing and editing. Between 1847 and 1859 he was an editor for the Washington-based abolitionist paper, the *National Era*. He also published a volume of poetry approximately every two years. His most famous poem, "Snow-Bound" (1866), a tribute to his New England boyhood and home, drew its imagery and influence directly from Ralph Waldo Emerson's "THE SNOW-STORM" (1841). Whittier was one of the most popular poets of his time, writing many other verses as well as nearly 100 hymns.

Bibliography

Gougeon, Len. *Virtue's Hero: Emerson, Antislavery, and Reform.* Athens: University of Georgia Press, 1990.

Woodell, Roland H. *John Greenleaf Whittier: A Biography.* Haverhill, Mass.: Trustees of the John Greenleaf Whittier Homestead, 1985.

"Wild Apples"
Henry David Thoreau
(1862)

"Wild Apples" was first presented as an 1860 CONCORD LYCEUM lecture by Henry David THOREAU, but it was not published until after his death, appearing first in the November 1862 issue of the ATLANTIC MONTHLY, and then in an 1863 collection of his essays, *Excursions*. "Wild Apples" is considered by some scholars to be one of Thoreau's most successful and popular essays. The essay is a somewhat humorous natural history of the fruit, tracing its origins in the Garden of Eden up to the current species available to him right in CONCORD, MASSACHUSETTS, and its struggle for survival in the face of the wildlife and the humans who would make it one of their favorite foods. For Thoreau, the environmentalist, however, the history and the fate of the apple was quite serious and paralleled that of humanity: "It is remarkable how closely the history of the Apple-tree is connected with that of man. The geologist tells us that the order of the Rosaceæ, which includes the Apple, also the true Grasses, and the Labiatæ, or mints, were introduced only a short time previous to the appearance of man on the globe." And, like New Englanders, the apples eventually migrated across the globe in search of new fertile ground in which to flourish: "What a lesson to man! . . . browsed on by fate; and only the most persistent and strongest genius defends itself and prevails, sends a tender scion upward at last, and drops its perfect fruit on the ungrateful earth. . . . Such is always the pursuit of knowledge."

More than the basic facts of the apple's beginnings and travels, as described by Thoreau, there is something spiritual about the fruit as well that few humans truly appreciate: "There is thus about all natural products a certain volatile and ethereal quality which represents their highest value, and which cannot be vulgarized, or bought and sold. No mortal has ever enjoyed the perfect flavor of any fruit, and only the god-like among men begin to taste its ambrosial qualities." Thoreau's fruit are not just apples but wild apples and, like them, he would rather be independent and free than be tamed for domestic use: "I would have my thoughts, like wild apples, to be food for walkers, and will not warrant them to be palatable, if tasted in the house." As in his other writings, Thoreau is not interested in the natural world purely for its own sake, although its appreciation and preservation are central to his arguments. He was using a lesson from nature to reveal insights about human life as well. Through close observation of what nature had to offer, in this case a beautiful but limited supply of wild apples, it is revealed to humans something of their own tenuous place on earth, as well as the beauty and spontaneity of human creation and ideas: "But our wild apple is wild perchance like myself who belong not to the original race here—but have strayed into the woods from the cultivated stock—where the birds were winged thoughts or agents have planted or are planting me. Even these at length furnish hardy stocks for the orchard."

Henry David Thoreau concluded his analysis with a warning of the potential spiritual costs of America's burgeoning market economy. If humans did not learn to respect the wildness of the apple (treating them as only a commodity to be purchased and consumed), as well as the connection between the apple and their own fate, something would eventually be lost for both plant and animal: "The era of the Wild Apple will soon be past. It is a fruit which will probably become extinct in New England . . . and the end of it all will be that we shall be compelled to look for our apples in a barrel."

Bibliography

Walls, Laura Dassow. *Seeing New Worlds: Henry David Thoreau and Nineteenth-Century Natural Science.* Madison: University of Wisconsin Press, 1995.

"Woman" Ralph Waldo Emerson *See* "ADDRESS AT THE WOMAN'S RIGHTS CONVENTION."

"Woman"
Sophia Ripley
(1841)

Sophia RIPLEY's essay on "Woman" was an extension of a piece she wrote as an attendee at Margaret FULLER's CONVERSATIONS FOR WOMEN and was published in the January 1841 issue of the Transcendentalist movement's periodical, the DIAL. It was to Ripley that Fuller first suggested the idea for the Conversations as a place for Boston's thinking women to discuss Transcendentalist literary, philosophical, and social reform themes, including WOMEN'S RIGHTS. Fuller frequently suggested that participants write about a topic in preparation for the next meeting. Prompted by Fuller to consider the intellectual differences, if any, between the sexes, Ripley produced this essay. In "Woman" Ripley argued against the idea that there were separate spheres of influence and activity for men and women, stating that "all adjusting of the whole sex to a sphere is in vain," and, instead, "what is individual and peculiar to each" individual should determine one's sphere. She pointed to women's inferior educations as the explanation for women's lack of greatness in literary and cultural life. Women themselves, therefore, did not yet know of what they were capable: "Very few of her sex suspect even how noble and beautiful is that which they legitimately occupy, for they are early deprived of the privilege of seeing things as they are."

In her thoughts on woman's sphere and nature, and in looking to women's EDUCATION as the key to reform, Sophia Ripley essentially echoed many of the same arguments that Margaret Fuller had presented at the Conversations. Ripley asserted that women should be "encouraged to question the opinions of others, calmly contemplating beauty in all its forms, studying the harmony of life . . . gradually forming her own ideal." This was the language used in Fuller's feminist perspective in her own essay, "THE GREAT LAWSUIT," published in the *Dial* two years later. Sophia Ripley went on to publish two other pieces in the *Dial* and in 1841, the same year that "Woman" appeared, joined her husband George RIPLEY in establishing the utopian community at BROOK FARM. She did not, however, write further on the "woman question," which is surprising given the influence of having attended Fuller's Conversations and the radical themes Ripley so forcefully argued in this one essay.

Woman and Her Needs
Elizabeth Oakes Smith
(1851)

Writer and reformer Elizabeth Oakes SMITH's 1851 feminist book, *Woman and Her Needs*, was rhetorically and philosophically influenced by Margaret FULLER's *WOMAN IN THE NINETEENTH CENTURY*, published six years earlier. Just months after Fuller's untimely death in July 1850, Smith became a regular contributor to the *NEW YORK TRIBUNE* where Fuller had been employed as a foreign correspondent. In November 1850, just following the first national WOMEN'S RIGHTS convention, Smith began a series for the paper on "Woman and Her Needs," which ultimately included 10 articles subsequently gathered together and published in book form with only slight modifications.

In *Woman and Her Needs* Smith addressed a problem facing many Transcendentalists: how to reconcile a philosophy of individual conscience with participation in organized reform efforts. In regards to the emerging women's rights movement, in particular, Smith acknowledged the effectiveness of the convention as a strategy, the benefit of "many converging lights of many minds all bent upon the same point, even although I myself peer about with my solitary lantern." Smith's "solitary lantern," her preference to arrive at her own personal truth, expressed the Transcendentalist desire to pursue reform as an individual. Smith had to concede, however, that, although not ideal, organized efforts may be necessary in some circumstances. While in the past women "have been content with individual influence," Smith understood that a more public and more organized effort was now under way, and while such "movement as yet may not be altogether the best or wisest," they "truly and solemnly point to a step higher in the scale of influence."

Beyond the question of participation in the organized movement, the self-development of the intellectual woman was a theme taken up by Smith. This theme as well as that of how to achieve harmony between the sexes aligned Smith with Margaret Fuller, as well as with Caroline DALL and other feminist Transcendentalists. Smith's text was especially similar to Fuller's *Woman in the Nineteenth Century* in its emphasis on the nature of genius in woman and its many historical examples of independent and strong-minded women. For Smith the goal of contemporary reform was that woman "be recognized as an intelligence." Smith argued that woman's current condition denied her full humanity and thus society as a whole could not progress to its full potential. Only when women were whole would society move toward "a higher and freer humanity" and realize the ultimate Transcendentalist goal of "a better identification of the individual with his species." In particular, Smith articulated a Transcendentalist ideal of "feminine" qualities in opposition to the negative "masculine" qualities associated with the material world, as woman's "mind . . . has in it more of aspiration, more of the subtle and intuitive character, that links it to the spiritual; . . . Would that women . . . out of their own souls, reject the hardness of materialism which the masculine mind engenders from its own elements." Echoing Fuller's androgynous vision, Smith also argued for essential differences between the sexes and for a need to combine the strengths of each into one complete humanity. Smith did not see women's rights as a separate reform issue affecting only half of humanity but, like Fuller and even Ralph Waldo EMERSON, envisioned a society that valued feminine qualities and allowed women to reach their full potential as one in which full human rights would be finally achieved.

Bibliography
Wayne, Tiffany K. *Woman Thinking: Feminism and Transcendentalism in Nineteenth-Century America.* Lanham, Md.: Lexington Books, 2005.

Woman in the Nineteenth Century
Margaret Fuller
(1845)

Margaret FULLER's *Woman in the Nineteenth Century* was the clearest expression of a Transcendentalist feminist ethos and one of the starting points for the emergence of a WOMEN'S RIGHTS movement in the United States. The text was, in fact, the first full-length work of feminist theory in the United States and was radical in its declaration that women were individuals and its call for cultural and social change to fully acknowledge that fact. The book was a revised and expanded form of Fuller's July 1843 essay, "THE GREAT LAWSUIT. Man *versus* Men. Woman *versus* Women," published in the Transcendentalist literary journal, the *DIAL* under Fuller's editorship. Fuller explained the title change from essay to book in the preface to *Woman in the Nineteenth Century:* "Objections having been made to the former title, as not sufficiently easy to be understood, the present has been substituted as expressive of the main purpose of the essay." This change in title was accompanied by clarification and expansion of the text itself and facilitated Fuller's ability to reach a wider audience beyond her immediate circle of Transcendentalist friends.

The book had a stronger emphasis on political and social reform than the original essay. By the time the book was published, Fuller herself had gone from *Dial* editor to journalist at Horace GREELEY'S *NEW YORK TRIBUNE* and had taken a tour of the western territories that had resulted in the publication of her 1844 book, SUMMER ON THE LAKES, IN 1843. It was Horace Greeley who, after offering her a job as a reviewer for the *New York Tribune,* suggested that Fuller expand her essay into a book. During these years of writing for the broader and more popular audience of the *Tribune* and traveling beyond New England, Fuller had the opportunity to expand her own vision not only on women's rights but on a wider range of reform issues, including the plight of native Americans, and the economics and politics of westward expansion.

Fuller's text was not just outward-looking in terms of a call to social reform; it also included semiautobiographical information and, not surprisingly, emphasized the self-development of the individual as a main theme. The book was an attempt by Fuller to work out the dilemmas of 19th-century womanhood in her own life—the struggle between the private relations and public aspirations of woman, and women's need for access to EDUCATION and meaningful VOCATIONs. In *Woman in the Nineteenth Century,* Margaret Fuller herself appeared in a section which purported to introduce the reader to a character named "Miranda," detailing Miranda's youth, the education provided by her father, and the eventual obstacles for a 19th-century woman without any outlets for her education and talents. Another theme expanded upon in *Woman in the Nineteenth Century* was that of marriage as an obstacle to women's self-development. Fuller detailed multiple levels or types of marriage, culminating in the "ideal" type of marriage between intellectual equals. The final theme that emerged was that of how to go about affecting the reforms necessary for woman's pursuit of self-culture and the elevation of humanity in its entirety.

Here Fuller engaged many of the reform theories then circulating among her Transcendentalist friends, in particular the social theories of French socialist Charles Fourier (*see* FOURIERISM). Fuller characterized Fourier as one of the "three prophets of the coming age," along with Johann Wolfgang von GOETHE (the German poet-philosopher from whom Fuller's Transcendentalist understanding of self-culture came and from whose writings she, in particular, found excellent examples of idealized and individualized womanhood), and Emanuel Swedenborg (*see* SWEDENBORGIANISM), the Swedish mystic who influenced Ralph Waldo EMERSON as well and from whom Fuller in particular found support for her ideas about social and intellectual equality between the sexes.

Woman in the Nineteenth Century was heavily infused with ancient, mythological, religious, and literary allusions, displaying Fuller's own far-reaching knowledge and her Transcendentalist sensibilities. Despite early warnings by critics of the text's difficulties for the common reader (criticisms made of the essay "The Great Lawsuit," to which Fuller responded in the introduction), the book became a theoretical and rhetorical foundation for an emerging woman's rights movement. The next generation or two of feminist activists and writers held up the text as a historically important document in their own movement—a foundation for their demands for woman's independence and cultural reform—and held up the example of Margaret Fuller herself, her life and career, as a personal role model.

Bibliography

Reynolds, Larry J. "From *Dial* Essay to New York Book: The Making of *Woman in the Nineteenth Century.*" In *Periodical Literature in Nineteenth-Century America,* eds. Susan Belasco Smith and Kenneth M. Price. Charlottesville: University of Virginia, 1995, 17–34.

woman suffrage   *See* WOMEN'S RIGHTS.

women's rights

Transcendentalists were involved with most major reforms of the antebellum period: ABOLITIONISM, UTOPIANISM, industrial or labor reform, EDUCATION, and women's rights. Although Margaret FULLER is recognized as the central feminist Transcendentalist, other Transcendentalist women also applied the philosophical ideals of self-culture and individualism to woman's situation. In an 1895 retrospective lecture on *TRANSCENDENTALISM IN NEW ENGLAND,* Caroline DALL explicitly identified the "idealism made practical" of the movement as one of the historical and theoretical underpinnings of 19th-century reform in general and, in particular, of women's rights activism: "The characteristics of the Transcendental movement were shown in the temper of its agitation for the rights of woman and the enlargement of her duties."

Besides actively working to improve the social and political conditions of their time, Transcendentalists also valued certain perceptions that were recognized as "feminine" ways of knowing. The Transcendentalist emphasis on intuition and their critique of traditional social and religious authorities appealed to female thinkers. Margaret Fuller's primary contribution to women's rights ideas was a refusal to discuss the idea of a separate "woman's sphere." In her CONVERSATIONS FOR WOMEN, held in Boston between 1839 and 1844, she spoke to women directly, as individuals, and encouraged them to consider as part of their "sphere" any activity that they deemed themselves capable of or which interested them. As recorded by Elizabeth Palmer PEABODY, an attendee of Fuller's Conversations, which were often held in Peabody's bookstore parlor, Fuller asserted "that we should hear no more of repressing or subduing faculties because they were not fit for women to cultivate. She desired that whatever faculty we felt to be moving within us, that we should consider a principle of our perfection, & cultivate it accordingly."

Margaret Fuller further developed her ideas in print, first in the essay "THE GREAT LAWSUIT. Man *versus* Men. Woman *versus* Women," published in the July 1843 issue of the *DIAL,* the Transcendentalist literary journal for which she was the founding editor, and in the essay's expanded book-length form, *WOMAN IN THE NINETEENTH CENTURY.* In this work Fuller radically called for acknowledging woman's ability to pursue her own individual talents and interests: "What Woman needs is not as a woman to act or rule, but as a nature to grow, as an intellect to discern, as a soul to live freely and unimpeded, to unfold such powers as were given her when we left our common home." One of Fuller's most radical critiques was against the institution of marriage, which, she argued, prevented women from developing fully as individuals by channeling their own talents and intellect into their roles as wives and mothers. Inspired by the more mystical conception of marriage put forth by Swedish philosopher Emanuel Swedenborg (*see* SWEDENBORGIANISM), Fuller did not call for the abolition of marriage but, instead, saw the symbolic importance of marriage as a union of the male and female energies. Marriage, for Fuller, was a spiritual, not a legal or economic, union—a coming together of souls, of individuals.

Margaret Fuller's reform goal was not just individual development but larger social progress, although, unfortunately, she died prematurely in July 1850, just as a national women's rights movement was beginning, and so she did not live to participate in a greater way. The president of the first national convention, Paulina Wright DAVIS, was a follower and reader of Fuller and expressed her regret that Fuller was not there to lead the movement, as many of the women had expected. The influence of Transcendentalist philosophical ideals, and of the works of Margaret Fuller in particular, can be traced in the major theoretical works of other prolific feminist writers and activists such as Paulina Davis, Ednah Dow CHENEY, Caroline

DALL, and Elizabeth Oakes SMITH throughout the 1850s and 1860s. Transcendentalist women were involved in both the first national woman's rights convention held in Worcester, Massachusetts, in 1850 and the founding of the first paper dedicated specifically to the cause of woman, THE UNA, established in 1852.

Like Margaret Fuller, many feminists and other Transcendentalists were particularly interested in experiments aimed at reforming the family and relations between the sexes. The utopian communities of BROOK FARM and of Amos Bronson ALCOTT's FRUITLANDS attracted the attention, as well as the criticism, of some women's rights activists. Brook Farm, in particular, sought to have equality for women within its community through including women's voices and votes in official community matters and encouraging shared domestic duties and women's participation in intellectual and speaking engagements at the community.

Some prominent Transcendentalist men, such as Bronson Alcott, Thomas Wentworth HIGGINSON, and Theodore PARKER, spoke out publicly on behalf of women's rights. Although Ralph Waldo EMERSON lent his voice to the cause with an 1855 "ADDRESS AT THE WOMAN'S RIGHTS CONVENTION," he was ultimately much more reluctant to embrace the idea of the desirability of women's full political equality in the United States.

Bibliography

Cole, Phyllis. "The Nineteenth-Century Women's Rights Movement and the Canonization of Margaret Fuller," *ESQ: A Journal of the American Renaissance* 44 (1998): 1–33.

Garvey, T. Gregory, ed. *The Emerson Dilemma: Essays on Emerson and Social Reform.* Athens: University of Georgia Press, 2001.

Wayne, Tiffany K. *Woman Thinking: Feminism and Transcendentalism in Nineteenth-Century America.* Lanham, Md.: Lexington Books, 2005.

"Woodnotes"
Ralph Waldo Emerson
(1840–1841)

Ralph Waldo EMERSON's prose-poem "Woodnotes" was published in the Transcendentalist literary journal, the DIAL, in two parts, in the October 1840 and October 1841 issues, and subsequently included in his 1847 collection of POEMS. "Woodnotes" is a long two-part prose poem, totaling more than 400 lines, that has been termed Emerson's "great comprehensive nature poem," the verse counterpart to his philosophical treatise in NATURE (1836). Indeed, much of Emerson's poetry of this period had nature as a primary theme, including several others from the volume of *Poems,* such as "THE SNOW-STORM," "THE HUMBLE-BEE," and "THE RHODORA."

In describing the Transcendentalist ideal relationship to nature, the primary symbol used in both parts of the poem is the pine tree, an abundant and common tree, even taken for granted in Emerson's own Massachusetts, but of significant importance to the New England landscape: "So waved the pine-tree through my thought, And fanned the dreams it never brought." For those who seek it, salvation itself is found in nature, in the woods: "Into that forester shall pass . . . power and grace." Finding the divine in the universal language of nature invoked the nature-religion or PANTHEISM feared by Emerson's critics. While the poem acknowledges God as creator—"God said, 'Throb!'"—Emerson also invokes the "eternal Pan." The poem ultimately focuses not on worshipping a specific deity but on finding the divine all around, "in pure transparency": "Thou askest in fountains and in fires . . . He is the axis of the star . . . He is the heart of every creature; He is the meaning of each feature; And his mind is the sky. Than all it holds more deep, more high." The poem presented the general Transcendentalist philosophy of humanity seeking a spiritual relationship with nature. Emerson evoked a musical metaphor of poetry as song of nature, and the tree as the one singing the song "which knits the world in music." "Nature beats in perfect tune," while humanity is the "poor child! unbound, unrhymed." In the end, mankind would be wise to remember that "The wood is wiser far than thou."

In describing the Transcendentalist relationship to nature Emerson identified the ideal human role as that of "forest seer." Some scholars have seen in Emerson's "minstrel of the natural year, Foreteller of the vernal ides" a potential reference to Henry David THOREAU, the poet-naturalist. If not Thoreau specifically, the poem is at least a reference to the ideal relationship with nature that Thoreau perhaps represented. This interpretation is supported by Emerson's own reference to "Woodnotes" as his "Waldenic poem." As in other poems and essays, "Woodnotes," not only highlighted but directly addressed the role of the poet in interpreting the message and significance of nature for the reader. The poet's place is in the forest, not as an objective student of nature or as a scientist, but as a "seer," and Emerson's poet is a romantic "philosopher," a "Lover of all things alive," and a "Wonderer at all he meets." On the other side of celebrating mankind's relationship with nature, however, is Emerson's critique of the danger to this relationship posed by human society, including industrialization and urbanization, the "city's poisoning spleen." Humanity risks being "divorced, deceived and left," "an exile from the wilderness." Emerson, though, remains optimistic and assures us that, in the right relationship to nature, humankind will come to a Transcendentalist epiphany in which he becomes not only a "wonderer" of nature, but a "Wonderer chiefly at himself."

Wordsworth, William
(1770–1850)

English poet William Wordsworth was one of the originators of European ROMANTICISM, a literary and philosophical movement that directly influenced the American Transcendentalists. Wordsworth's romantic aesthetic, like that of his colleague Samuel Taylor COLERIDGE, was a rejection of the rationalist legacy of Enlightenment thought and a rejection of formal poetic and literary structure in favor of an emphasis on imagination as inspiration and emotional response as the goal of poetry. In addition, Wordsworth, like Ralph Waldo EMERSON after him, advocated that poetry be for the common people and that it be written in the language and symbolism of everyday life, in particular the language and symbolism of nature. With themes of moral and spiritual lessons to be derived from the simplest aspects of the natural world, Wordsworth's model influenced the Transcendentalist ethos of

the next generation. In 1798 Wordsworth collaborated with Coleridge in publishing *Lyrical Ballads,* one of the markers of the beginning of romanticism. This and other works were read by a young Emerson and helped develop his ideas about nature, self-reliance, and individualism, including the belief that individuals must rely upon their own definitions of morality rather than arbitrary social rules that may, in fact, work against the individual.

Wordsworth influenced Ralph Waldo Emerson and American romanticism even more significantly, perhaps, in his emphasis on the role of the poet as interpreter of nature and as a "representative" or ideal man in his relationship to nature and to the life of the mind. Emerson adopted Wordsworth's model of poetry as a revelation and a spiritual, not merely literary, event, with significance to the development of the individual soul and its relationship to the universe. Wordsworth used the term *World Soul* to describe the universal force that brought humanity and nature, indeed the force of the entire world, together as one, a phrase that Emerson returned to for the title of his own poem on "THE WORLD-SOUL." Emerson also modeled himself as a romantic poet after Wordsworth in style and imagery, reading and rereading Wordsworth as he began to create himself as the ideal poet. As Emerson's most recent biographer, Robert Richardson, notes, "From 1828, he went back to Wordsworth every year," and Emerson eventually met Wordsworth in England in the early 1830s. It was Wordsworth, the man and the poetry, that Emerson had in mind as he wrote his essay on "THE POET," which would be published in 1841. He again met Wordsworth during an 1847 tour of England and in 1856 discussed Wordsworth along with other British writers in his ENGLISH TRAITS. In this account, Emerson declared Wordsworth's "Immortality Ode" to be "the high water mark which the intellect has reached in this age." Emerson included his friend and inspiration among the poets he selected for his 1874 anthology PARNASSUS.

William Wordsworth had an impact on other Transcendentalists as well. Henry David THOREAU read Wordsworth from a young age and regularly quoted Wordsworth poems in his journals. Like Emerson, Thoreau was influenced by Wordsworth's conception of the poet as a representative of the romantic age in his relationship to nature but also in his individualism and nonconformity. Thoreau's observations at WALDEN POND and around CONCORD, MASSACHUSETTS, and his written accounts of his experiences in the natural surroundings, relied upon a Wordsworthian respect for nature as humanity's greatest teacher and muse. Emerson and Thoreau, as well as other Transcendentalist-inspired 19th-century poets, such as Emily DICKINSON and Walt WHITMAN, ultimately created a uniquely American response to the romantic philosophy and model of William Wordsworth.

Bibliography

Weisbuch, Robert. *Atlantic Double-Cross: American Literature and British Influence in the Age of Emerson.* Chicago: University of Chicago Press, 1986.

Work: A Story of Experience
Louisa May Alcott
(1873)

The primary theme of Louisa May ALCOTT's semi-autobiographical novel is a woman's life and work. *Work: A Story of Experience* was first serialized in 1872–73 as "Work; or Christie's Experiment" in the magazine *The Christian Union* before appearing as a book. The heroine of "Work," Christie Devon, is representative of the options available to a 19th-century American woman who has made a "new Declaration of Independence" from her family. Christie embarks upon a series of jobs in her quest for independence and, in the process, Alcott revealed the economic as well as social obstacles to female "self-knowledge, self control, self-help," or, in Transcendentalist terms, "SELF-RELIANCE." Christie, like Louisa May Alcott herself, attempts to support herself through nearly every employment opportunity that would have been available to a white woman of that time, from seamstress and household servant to nursing to the more unconventional actress. Christie ultimately finds herself unsuited to the demands of each particular job, but, importantly, in the process she learns at each stage something important about herself. Alcott's message

then, was twofold; first, that the opportunities for women to pursue a VOCATION were too limited, but second, that through paid work women, like men, would learn to understand and define themselves. Although Christie is in search of her self, part of the lesson learned at each job is that one cannot seek self-satisfaction merely for its own sake but must learn about oneself through interaction with others. For example, although Christie does not like nursing as a profession, she learns through her work as a nurse about sympathy and caring for others. In this, as in other writings, Alcott provided a check on what she perceived as some of the flaws or shortcomings of Transcendentalist philosophy, particularly as it applied to women.

In fact, the character Christie's individualistic pursuits in the first part of the novel lead her at one point to contemplate suicide. It is in society and, in particular, in the society of reformers in which she finds herself, that she ultimately finds her purpose as well as a husband. In depicting the world of reformers Alcott provided characterizations of many of her family's Transcendentalist friends of her childhood. In her satirical short story published the same year, "TRANSCENDENTAL WILD OATS," Louisa May Alcott had biting criticism for the shortsightedness, the selfishness, and the chauvinism of male Transcendentalists, including her own father, Amos Bronson ALCOTT, but in *Work*, the Transcendentalists received gentler treatment through sympathetic characters such as the wise Reverend Power (modeled on radical Unitarian minister and abolitionist Theodore PARKER) and the gentle David Sterling (who bears resemblance to Henry David THOREAU), to whom Christie is briefly married. David Sterling becomes a martyr for ABOLITIONISM and the Union cause, as he dies during the Civil War in an attempt to save a slave woman and her child. Significantly, Christie is able to be with him at his death because she is working as a nurse during the war, rather than waiting at home. Thus Alcott shows us a woman whose "work" allowed her to fulfill her emotional duties and caretaking obligations as a wife, balancing the commitments of work and family and taking the self-interestedness aspect out of Christie's search for meaningful work.

Work was a successful book for Alcott, although not as successful as the enormously popular *LITTLE WOMEN* (1868) and its spin-off novels. Lousia May Alcott remained best known for her children's fiction, which, although they contained strong independent females (such as Jo March, the character modeled most closely on Alcott herself), were not quite as nontraditional or even controversial as Christie Devon. Perhaps fans of Alcott's children's books were also not interested in or put off by the overtly feminist message of Christie's life, including her continued independence as a result of her short-lived marriage. Even more explicitly delivering her message, in the novel Alcott refashions Christie after the Civil War as a WOMEN'S RIGHTS lecturer. In the end, Christie's life "experience" is defined by work and independence, not through marriage and family. The novel was dedicated to Alcott's mother, however, and invoked the family history of hardship endured by Abigail May ALCOTT, a reformer, a worker, in her own right despite the demands of her large family: to "My Mother, whose life had been a long labor of love."

"The World-Soul"
Ralph Waldo Emerson
(1847)

Ralph Waldo EMERSON wrote the poem "The World-Soul" in 1843, just a year after the death of his young son, Waldo, and first published it in the collection *POEMS*. The poem is, in some sense, an attempt to explore any defenses that mankind might have against death and to celebrate the possibility of self-renewal and reconciliation within the limitations imposed by nature: "Spring still makes spring in the mind." It is not only nature that puts limits on human existence but human society as well, which restrains the full development of the individual soul. "The World-Soul," a term Emerson got from reading William WORDSWORTH, is an extensive critique of the degenerative aspects of human society and the dangers posed to the soul by the forces of urbanization, commercialization, politics, and technology. These aspects of human society cater to our basest desires and are impediments to the soul. In the end, however, even in recognizing the negative forces we have brought upon ourselves and our powerlessness against such natural forces as death and aging, "The World-Soul" retains Emerson's characteristic Transcendental optimism in the triumph of the soul: "He will from wrecks and sediment / The fairer world complete," and "He forbids to despair."

On his 69th birthday, in May 1872, Ralph Waldo Emerson reflected on the history of Boston and on the fact that his greatest teacher, his aunt Mary Moody EMERSON, had been born nearly 100 years earlier. Emerson was inspired then to reflect upon his own mortality, and he wrote in his journal: "If I live another year, I think I shall cite still the last stanza of my own poem, 'The World-Soul.'" The last stanza to which he referred reads: "Spring still makes spring in the mind / When sixty years are told; / Love wakes anew this throbbing heart, / And we are never old. / Over the winter glaciers / I see the summer glow, / And through the wild-piled snowdrift / The warm rosebuds below." The imagery of the poem invokes for Emerson the cycles of life, the seasons, youth and old age. Emerson had originally composed "The World-Soul" in reflecting on the death of his five-year-old son, but nearly 30 years later, invoked the poem yet again in reference to his own mortality, a theme he addresses as well in the poem, "TERMINUS."

Bibliography
Allen, Gay Wilson. *Waldo Emerson: A Biography*. New York: Viking Press, 1981.

A Yankee in Canada
Henry David Thoreau
(1866)

A Yankee in Canada is an account of a one-week excursion to Canada made by Henry David THOREAU and his friend William Ellery CHANNING II in the fall of 1850. Thoreau originally intended to present the short account of their journey as a lecture, but he submitted it for publication instead and portions of it were published by editor George William CURTIS in *PUTNAM'S MONTHLY MAGAZINE* beginning in January 1853. Curtis and Thoreau soon came to disagreement over Curtis's attempts to edit specific anti-Catholic statements, or what he termed "heresies," from the essay. An angered Thoreau pulled the manuscript from *Putnam's* after only three of the five planned installments. The full text of what he had written was not published until 1866, four years after Thoreau's death, under the complete title, *A Yankee in Canada, with Anti-Slavery and Reform Papers.* This collection was put together by Ellery Channing and Thoreau's sister, Sophia THOREAU, and included several other pieces culled from Thoreau's papers.

A *Yankee in Canada* is Thoreau's shortest and least informative travel or nature piece, partly because the trip itself was so brief and was concentrated in a primarily urban area. Thoreau himself counted it as among his least memorable trips, declaring Canada's French citizens as "a nation of peasants" and concluding that "what I got by going to Canada was a cold." The essay does, however, provide insight into his social and political concerns, particularly in his criticism of the Catholic church and the military in Canada, criticisms which editor George Curtis deemed unacceptable for publication in his magazine.

"The Young American"
Ralph Waldo Emerson
(1844)

"The Young American" was a lecture given by Ralph Waldo EMERSON in Boston in February 1844 and published in the April 1844 issue of the Transcendentalist literary journal, the *DIAL*. One of the main themes of the essay was the recent enthusiasm of the expansion westward of the nation, "this rage of road building," and the youth of the nation itself. Emerson often invoked the importance of the land to national and personal identity, a theme addressed in the poem "HAMATREYA," for example. Part of his rejection of offers to join the Utopian community at BROOK FARM, established by his Unitarian colleague, George RIPLEY just a few years earlier in 1841, was that he did not want to give up the idea of private property and its role in his own independence. In "The Young American" he moved from interest in his own land to interest in the role of land in the larger national identity and in national progress.

He wrote, "The land is the appointed remedy for whatever is false and fantastic in our culture. The continent we inhabit is to be physic and food for our mind, as well as our body." In this viewpoint, "the land" is considered as a physical part of nature and as such, in terms of Transcendentalist philosophy, it provided not only physical support for humans but spiritual and even intellectual support as well, but "the land" did not contribute to national growth and consciousness in its untamed or "natural" state; the land must be developed and cultivated by humans in a way that other aspects of nature need not, even should not, be. Emerson saw that the potential for identification with the land could be cultivated by encouraging American cultural improvements on the land such as public spaces, gardens, parks, even architecture: "I look on such improvements also as directly tending to endear the land to the inhabitants."

Despite his warnings in other contexts about the negative effects of population growth and technological developments, in "The Young American" Emerson's tone is optimistic. He not only encourages development and changes in the land but welcomes the inevitable population growth and spread westward as a positive step for America. He welcomes the "heterogeneous population crowding on all ships from all corners of the world," as the promise of the spread not only of people but of ideas and liberty. In this sense, then, Emerson was completely in agreement with the idealistic promotion of "Manifest Destiny" circulating at that time—the belief that it was America's destiny to fill the continent and grow as a people called for a special purpose in the world: "It seems so easy for America to inspire and express the most expansive and humane spirit; new-born, free, healthful, strong, the land of the laborer, of the democrat, of the philanthropist, of the believer, of the saint, she should speak for the human race. It is the country of the future." Emerson was speaking here not so much to "The Young American" as an individual but to the fact that America itself was still young, full of promise and hope not only for itself but also for the world.

Emerson's argument took him down a path in which he had to look at commercialism—trade and business—as the driving force behind expansion. He declared that "The history of commerce is the record of . . . beneficent tendency." While many of his reformer friends and colleagues around him, including, most notably, Amos Bronson ALCOTT (whose utopian experiments existed primarily as alternatives to a commerce, and therefore slavery, oriented society), Orestes BROWNSON (whose 1840 essay on "THE LABORING CLASSES" was one of the most searing critiques of the antebellum northern system of wage labor), and Henry David THOREAU (who sought to live a philosophy of self-reliance apart from the demands and control of wage labor and the political system), were developing stringent critics of American capitalism and commercialism, Emerson remained not merely optimistic about the importance of what he termed "trade" but, in fact, suggested that we look to the spirit of trade or business for the answers to those reformers' concerns. Perhaps in direct response to criticisms such friends might have made, he confidently declared that "the historian of the world will see that trade was the principle of liberty, that trade planted America and destroyed feudalism, that is makes peace and keeps peace, and it will abolish slavery," and that it is, in fact, "a very intellectual force." Emerson was not, of course, naïve to the negative aspects of a world in which commerce becomes the most important defining aspect of a society: "This is the good and evil of trade, that it would put everything into market; talent, beauty, virtue, and man himself." In "The Young American," however, Emerson's optimism about the expansion of the population and of trade ignored some of the most pernicious aspects of American commercialism, such as the issues of slavery and war. In particular, in his private journals he was much more critical of events such as the annexation of Texas, the Mexican War, and, increasingly, the spread of slavery into the western territories.

In "The Young American" he glided over those events in favor of a belief that these issues would eventually be worked out in the natural progress of things, in favor of believing in "a sublime and friendly Destiny by which the human race is guided."

Bibliography

Allen, Gay Wilson. *Waldo Emerson: A Biography.* New York: Viking Press, 1981.

MAJOR TRANSCENDENTALIST AUTHORS AND WORKS

Note: Works in **boldface** have entries in the text of this book.

BRONSON ALCOTT

Observations on the Principles and Methods of Infant Instruction (1830)
***Record of a School* (1835–36)**
***Conversations with Children on the Gospels* (1836)**
"Orphic Sayings" (1840–41)
Tablets (1868)
Concord Days (1872)
Table-Talk (1877)
New Connecticut: An Autobiographical Poem (1881)
Sonnets and Canzonets (1882)

LOUISA MAY ALCOTT

Moods (1864)
Little Women (1868–69)
***Work: A Story of Experience* (1873)**
"Transcendental Wild Oats" (1873)

CYRUS BARTOL

Discourse on the Christian Spirit and Life (1850)
Radical Problems (1872)
The Rising Faith (1874)

ORESTES BROWNSON

***New Views of Christianity, Society, and the Church* (1836)**

The Laboring Classes (1840)
"Transcendentalism, or the Latest Form of Infidelity" (1845)

WILLIAM ELLERY CHANNING

"Unitarian Christianity" (1819)
"The Moral Argument Against Calvinism" (1820)
"Evidences of Revealed Religion" (1821)
"Likeness to God" (1828)
"The Importance and Means of a National Literature" (1830)
Slavery (1835)
"Self-Culture" (1838)

LYDIA MARIA CHILD

The Biographies of Madame de Staël and Madame Roland (1832)
An Appeal in Favor of That Class of Americans Called Africans (1833)
History of the Condition of Women, in Various Ages and Nations (1835)
***Philothea, a Romance* (1836)**
***Letters from New York* (1843–45)**
***The Progress of Religious Ideas, Through Successive Ages* (1855)**

CAROLINE DALL

Essays and Sketches (1849)
"Woman's Right to Labor": or, Low Wages and Hard Work (1860)
***Historical Pictures Retouched* (1860)**

The College, the Market, and the Court; or, Woman's Relation to Education, Labor, and Law (1867)
What We Really Know about Shakespeare (1885)
Margaret and Her Friends: or Ten Conversations with Margaret Fuller (1895)
Transcendentalism in New England (1897)

RALPH WALDO EMERSON

"The Lord's Supper" (1832)
Nature (1836)
"The American Scholar" (1837)
"The Divinity School Address" (1838)
"Thoughts on Modern Literature" (1840)
"Man the Reformer" (1841)
Essays: First Series (1841)
    "History"
    "Self-Reliance"
    "Compensation"
    "Spiritual Laws"
    "Love"
    "Friendship"
    "Heroism"
    "The Over-Soul"
    "Circles"
    "Intellect"
    "Art"
"The Transcendentalist" (1843)
Essays: Second Series (1844)
    "The Poet"
    "Experience"
    "Character"
    "Politics"
    "New England Reformers"
"Emancipation in the British West Indies" (1844)
"The Young American" (1844)
Poems (1847)
    "The Sphinx"
    "Each and All"
    "Uriel"
    "Hamatreya"
    "The Rhodora"
    "The Humble-Bee"
    "The Snow-Storm"
    "Ode, Inscribed to W. H. Channing"
    "Give All to Love"
    "Merlin"
    "Bacchus"
    "Blight"

    "Threnody"
    "Concord Hymn"
    "Saadi"
Representative Men (1850)
"Fugitive Slave Law Address" (1851)
Memoirs of Margaret Fuller Ossoli (coeditor) (1852)
"Address at the Woman's Rights Convention" (1855)
"American Slavery" (1855)
English Traits (1856)
The Conduct of Life (1860)
    "Fate"
"Thoreau" (1862)
May-Day and Other Pieces (1867)
    "Brahma"
    "Boston Hymn"
    "Voluntaries"
    "Days"
    "Terminus"
    "Woodnotes"
    "World-Soul"
Society and Solitude (1870)
Parnassus (1874)
Letters and Social Aims (1876)

OCTAVIUS BROOKS FROTHINGHAM

The Religion of Humanity (1873)
Transcendentalism in New England: A History (1876)

MARGARET FULLER

Conversations with Goethe (translated) (1839)
"The Great Lawsuit. Man versus Men. Woman versus Women." (1843)
"Double Triangle, Serpent and Rays" (1844)
Summer on the Lakes (1844)
"The Sacred Marriage" (1845)
Woman in the Nineteenth Century (1845)
Papers on Literature and Art (1846)

NATHANIEL HAWTHORNE

Mosses from an Old Manse (1846)
    "The Old Manse"
    "Rappaccini's Daughter"

The Scarlet Letter (1850)
The Blithedale Romance (1852)

FREDERIC HENRY HEDGE

"Coleridge's Literary Character" (1833)
Prose Writers of Germany (1848)
Recent Inquiries in Theology (1860)
Reason in Religion (1865)

THEODORE PARKER

A Discourse on the Transient and Permanent in Christianity (1842)
A Discourse of Matters Pertaining to Religion (1842)
The Relation of Jesus to His Age and the Ages (1845)
Sermons of Theism, Atheism, and the Popular Theology (1853)
A Sermon of the Public Function of Woman (1853)
The Revival of Religion Which We Need (1858)

ELIZABETH PALMER PEABODY

Record of a School (1835–36)
"A Glimpse of Christ's Idea of Society" (1841)
"Fourierism" (1844)
Aesthetic Papers (1849)
Kindergarten Culture (1870)
Reminiscences of Rev. Wm. Ellery Channing, D. D. (1880)
Last Evening with Allston, and Other Papers (1886)

GEORGE RIPLEY

The Divinity of Jesus Christ (1831)
Discourses on the Philosophy of Religion (1836)
Specimens of Foreign Standard Literature (1838–42)
"The Latest Form of Infidelity" Examined. A Letter to Mr. Andrews Norton (1839–40)
New American Cyclopedia (1858–63)

HENRY DAVID THOREAU

"Sympathy" (1840)
"Fog" (1849)
A Week on the Concord and Merrimack Rivers (1849)
"Resistance to Civil Government" ("Civil Disobedience") (1849)
Walden; or, Life in the Woods (1854)
"Slavery in Massachusetts" (1854)
"A Plea for Captain John Brown" (1860)
"The Succession of Forest Trees" (1860)
"Autumnal Tints" (1862)
"Walking" (1862)
"Wild Apples" (1862)
"Life Without Principle" (1863)
The Maine Woods (1864)
Cape Cod (1865)
A Yankee in Canada, with Anti-Slavery and Reform Papers (1866)

CHRONOLOGY

1780
William Ellery Channing born (April 4)

1799
Amos Bronson Alcott born (November 29)

1802
Lydia Maria Child born (February 11)

1803
Ralph Waldo Emerson born (May 25)
The Monthly Anthology founded

1804
Elizabeth Palmer Peabody born (May 16)
Nathaniel Hawthorne born (July 4)

1807
Boston Athenaeum founded

1810
Margaret Fuller born (May 23)
Theodore Parker born (August 24)

1813
Christian Disciple (later *Christian Examiner*) founded

1815
North American Review founded

1817
Henry David Thoreau born (July 12)

1819
William Ellery Channing preaches on "Unitarian Christianity"

1820
William Ellery Channing preaches on "The Moral Argument Against Calvinism"

1821
Christian Register founded

1823
Louisa May Alcott born (November 29)

1825
American Unitarian Association formed

1826
First American lyceum established in Millbury, Massachusetts

1827
New Jerusalem Magazine founded

1828
William Ellery Channing preaches on "Likeness to God"

1829

Concord Lyceum founded

Ralph Waldo Emerson ordained as pastor of Second Church in Boston

James Marsh publishes American edition of Coleridge's *Aids to Reflection*

1831

The Liberator founded by William Lloyd Garrison

George Ripley publishes *The Divinity of Jesus Christ*

1832

Ralph Waldo Emerson preaches on "The Lord's Supper"

Emerson resigns as pastor of Second Church

Lydia Maria Child publishes *The Biographies of Madame de Staël and Madame Roland*

1833

Frederic Henry Hedge publishes review of Samuel Taylor Coleridge ("Coleridge's Literary Character") in *Christian Examiner*

Lydia Maria Child publishes *An Appeal in Favor of That Class of Americans Called Africans*

1834

Bronson Alcott opens Temple School in Boston

1835

The *Western Messenger* founded

William Ellery Channing publishes *Slavery*

Bronson Alcott and Elizabeth Palmer Peabody publish *Record of a School*

1836

Transcendental Club founded

Ralph Waldo Emerson arranges for American edition of Thomas Carlyle's *Sartor Resartus*

Bronson Alcott and Elizabeth Palmer Peabody publish *Conversations with Children on the Gospels*

Orestes Brownson publishes *New Views of Christianity, Society, and the Church*

Lydia Maria Child publishes *Philothea, a Romance*

Ralph Waldo Emerson publishes *Nature*

Convers Francis publishes *Christianity as a Purely Internal Principle*

William Henry Furness publishes *Remarks on the Four Gospels*

James Martineau publishes *The Rationale of Religious Inquiry*

George Ripley publishes *Discourses on the Philosophy of Religion*

1837

Ralph Waldo Emerson lectures on "The American Scholar" at Harvard

Andrews Norton publishes *Evidences of the Genuineness of the Gospels*

Harriet Martineau publishes *Society in America*

1838

Bronson Alcott's Temple School is closed

Alcott House established in England

Abner Kneeland put on trial for blasphemy

New England Non-Resistance Society formed

Boston Quarterly Review is founded by Orestes Brownson

William Ellery Channing lectures on "Self-Culture"

Ralph Waldo Emerson delivers "Divinity School Address" at Harvard

George Ripley publishes first volumes of *Specimens of Foreign Standard Literature*

Andrews Norton publishes "The New School in Literature and Religion" in the Boston *Daily Advertiser*

1839

Elizabeth Palmer Peabody opens bookstore on West Street in Boston

Margaret Fuller holds first series of Conversations for women

Margaret Fuller translates Eckermann's *Conversations with Goethe*

Orestes Brownson responds to "Norton's Evidence" in the *Boston Quarterly Review*

Andrews Norton publishes *A Discourse on the Latest Form of Infidelity*

George Ripley responds to Norton with *"The Latest Form of Infidelity Examined"*

Jones Very publishes *Essays and Poems*

Henry David Thoreau writes poem "Sympathy"

1840

The *Dial* is founded

Bronson Alcott publishes "Orphic Sayings" in the *Dial*

Ralph Waldo Emerson lectures on "Thoughts on Modern Literature"

Orestes Brownson publishes *The Laboring Classes*

Chardon Street Convention meets

1841

Brook Farm community established

New York Tribune founded by Horace Greeley

Sophia Ripley publishes "Woman" in the *Dial*

Elizabeth Palmer Peabody publishes "A Glimpse of Christ's Idea of Society" in the *Dial*

Ralph Waldo Emerson lectures on "Man the Reformer"

Emerson publishes *Essays: First Series*

Theodore Parker delivers South Boston Sermon, subsequently published as *A Discourse on the Transient and Permanent in Christianity*

1842

Theodore Parker publishes *A Discourse of Matters Pertaining to Religion*

William Ellery Channing dies (October 2)

1843

Fruitlands community established

The Present founded by William Henry Channing

Ralph Waldo Emerson publishes "The Transcendentalist" in the *Dial*

Margaret Fuller publishes "The Great Lawsuit" in the *Dial*

Lydia Maria Child publishes first volume of *Letters from New York*

1844

Fruitlands community ends

Brownson's Quarterly Review founded by Orestes Brownson

Ralph Waldo Emerson lectures on "Emancipation in the British West Indies"

Emerson lectures on "The Young American"

Emerson publishes *Essays: Second Series*

Margaret Fuller publishes *Summer on the Lakes*

Elizabeth Palmer Peabody publishes "Fourierism" in the *Dial*

1845

The Harbinger founded

Henry David Thoreau moves into cabin at Walden Pond

Margaret Fuller publishes *Woman in the Nineteenth Century*

Sylvester Judd publishes *Margaret*

1846

Margaret Fuller leaves for Europe and becomes foreign correspondent for the *New York Tribune*

Henry David Thoreau jailed for refusal to pay tax

American Union of Associationists formed

Margaret Fuller publishes *Papers on Literature and Art*

Nathaniel Hawthorne publishes *Mosses from an Old Manse*

1847

Brook Farm community ends

Henry David Thoreau leaves Walden Pond

Massachusetts Quarterly Review founded by Theodore Parker

Ralph Waldo Emerson publishes *Poems*

1848

James Russell Lowell publishes *A Fable for Critics*

Frederic Henry Hedge publishes *Prose Writers of Germany*

1849

Elizabeth Palmer Peabody publishes *Aesthetic Papers*, which includes first printing of Henry

David Thoreau's "Resistance to Civil
   Government"
Thoreau writes poem "Fog"
Town and Country Club established
Spirit of the Age founded by William Henry
   Channing
Thoreau publishes *A Week on the Concord and
   Merrimack Rivers*
Ralph Waldo Emerson publishes *Nature: Addresses,
   and Lectures*

1850

Fugitive Slave Law passed by U.S. Congress
Margaret Fuller dies in shipwreck returning from
   Europe (July 19)
First national women's rights convention held in
   Worcester, Massachusetts
Ralph Waldo Emerson publishes *Representative
   Men*
Nathaniel Hawthorne publishes *The Scarlet Letter*

1851

Ralph Waldo Emerson delivers "Fugitive Slave
   Law Address"
Elizabeth Oakes Smith publishes *Woman and Her
   Needs*
Herman Melville publishes *Moby-Dick*

1852

Dwight's Journal of Music founded by John Sullivan
   Dwight
Nathaniel Hawthorne publishes *The Blithedale
   Romance*
William Henry Channing, James Freeman Clarke,
   and Ralph Waldo Emerson edit and publish
   the *Memoirs of Margaret Fuller Ossoli*

1853

Putnam's Monthly Magazine founded
The Una founded

1854

Saturday Club established
Fugitive slave trial of Anthony Burns in Boston

Henry David Thoreau lectures on "Slavery in
   Massachusetts"
Thoreau publishes *Walden: or, Life in the Woods*

1855

Ralph Waldo Emerson lectures on "American
   Slavery"
Emerson delivers address at women's rights
   convention in Boston ("Woman")
Walt Whitman publishes *Leaves of Grass*
Lydia Maria Child publishes *The Progress of
   Religious Ideas, Through Successive Ages*

1856

Ralph Waldo Emerson publishes *English Traits*

1857

Atlantic Monthly founded

1858

Adirondack Club established
Cyrus Bartol publishes *Church and Congregation: A
   Plea for Unity*
Theodore Parker publishes *The Revival of Religion
   Which We Need*
George Ripley publishes first volume of *New
   American Cyclopaedia*

1859

Secret Six organized
John Brown raids federal arsenal at Harpers Ferry,
   Virginia, and is subsequently captured and
   executed
Charles Darwin publishes *On the Origin of Species*

1860

Elizabeth Palmer Peabody establishes first U.S.
   kindergarten in Boston
The Cincinnati *Dial* founded by Moncure
   Conway
Henry David Thoreau delivers "A Plea for Captain
   John Brown"
Thoreau lectures on "The Succession of Forest
   Trees"

Ralph Waldo Emerson publishes *The Conduct of Life*

James Redpath publishes *Echoes of Harper's Ferry*

Caroline Dall publishes *Historical Pictures Retouched*

Frederic Henry Hedge publishes *Recent Inquiries in Theology*

Theodore Parker dies (May 10)

1861
American Civil War begins

1862
Julia Ward Howe publishes "Battle Hymn of the Republic" in *Atlantic Monthly*

Henry David Thoreau dies (May 6)

Thoreau's essays, "Autumnal Tints," "Walking," and "Wild Apples" published posthumously in *Atlantic Monthly*

Ralph Waldo Emerson eulogizes "Thoreau"

1863
Ralph Waldo Emerson publicly reads "Boston Hymn" to celebrate Emancipation Proclamation

Henry David Thoreau's essay "Life Without Principle" published posthumously in *Atlantic Monthly*

1864
Henry David Thoreau's *The Maine Woods* published posthumously

Louisa May Alcott publishes *Moods*

Nathaniel Hawthorne dies (May 19)

1865
The Radical founded

American Social Science Association founded

Frederic Henry Hedge publishes *Reason in Religion*

Henry David Thoreau's *Cape Cod* published posthumously

1866
St. Louis Philosophical Society established

Henry David Thoreau's *A Yankee in Canada* published posthumously

Frederic Henry Hedge publishes *Reason in Religion*

David Wasson publishes *The Radical Creed*

1867
Radical Club established

Free Religious Association established

Journal of Speculative Philosophy founded by William Torrey Harris

Ralph Waldo Emerson publishes *May-Day and Other Pieces*

1868
Louisa May Alcott publishes *Little Women*

Bronson Alcott publishes *Tablets*

1870
Ralph Waldo Emerson publishes *Society and Solitude*

1871
James Freeman Clarke publishes *Ten Great Religions*

1872
Bronson Alcott publishes *Concord Days*

Cyrus Bartol publishes *Radical Problems*

1873
The Kindergarten Messenger founded by Elizabeth Palmer Peabody

Louisa May Alcott publishes *Work: A Story of Experience*

Louisa May Alcott publishes "Transcendental Wild Oats"

Octavius Brooks Frothingham publishes *The Religion of Humanity*

1874
Ralph Waldo Emerson publishes *Parnassus*

Cyrus Bartol publishes *The Rising Faith*
James Freeman Clarke publishes *Common-Sense in Religion*

1875
Christopher Pearse Cranch publishes *The Bird and the Bell with Other Poems*

1876
Ralph Waldo Emerson publishes *Letters and Social Aims*
Octavius Brooks Frothingham publishes *Transcendentalism in New England: A History*

1877
Bronson Alcott publishes *Table-Talk*
Harriet Martineau publishes *Autobiography*

1879
Concord School of Philosophy and Literature established

1880
Elizabeth Palmer Peabody publishes *Reminiscences of Rev. Wm. Ellery Channing*
Lydia Maria Child dies (October 20)

1881
Bronson Alcott publishes *New Connecticut: An Autobiographical Poem*
James Freeman Clarke publishes *Events and Epochs in Religious History*
Ednah Dow Cheney publishes *Gleanings in the Fields of Art*

1882
Ralph Waldo Emerson dies (April 27)
Bronson Alcott publishes *Sonnets and Canzonets*
Moncure Conway publishes *Emerson at Home and Abroad*
Franklin Benjamin Sanborn publishes biography of *Henry D. Thoreau*

1883
Julia Ward Howe publishes biography of *Margaret Fuller*
Concord Lectures on Philosophy published

1884
Thomas Wentworth Higginson publishes biography of *Margaret Fuller Ossoli*
Julian Hawthorne publishes *Nathaniel Hawthorne and His Wife*
Oliver Wendell Holmes publishes biography of *Ralph Waldo Emerson*

1886
Octavius Brooks Frothingham publishes *Memoir of William Henry Channing*
Franklin Benjamin Sanborn edits and publishes Concord School of Philosophy lectures on *The Life and Genius of Goethe*
Henry James publishes *The Bostonians*

1887
James Elliot Cabot publishes *A Memoir of Ralph Waldo Emerson*

1888
Bronson Alcott dies (March 4)
Louisa May Alcott dies (March 6)
Concord School of Philosophy holds final sessions

1890
Henry Salt publishes *The Life of Henry David Thoreau*

1892
Franklin Benjamin Sanborn and William Torrey Harris publish *A. Bronson Alcott: His Life and Philosophy*

1894
Elizabeth Palmer Peabody dies (January 3)

1895
Caroline Dall publishes *Margaret and Her Friends*

1897
Caroline Dall publishes *Transcendentalism in New England*

1898
Thomas Wentworth Higginson publishes *Cheerful Yesterdays*
Franklin Benjamin Sanborn edits and publishes Concord School of Philosophy lectures on *The Genius and Character of Emerson*

1899
Julia Ward Howe publishes *Reminiscences, 1819–1899*

1902
Ednah Dow Cheney publishes *Reminiscences*

1909
Franklin Benjamin Sanborn publishes *Recollections of Seventy Years*

BIBLIOGRAPHY

COLLECTIONS OF PRIMARY SOURCES

Transcendentalism

Miller, Perry, ed. *The Transcendentalists: An Anthology.* Cambridge, Mass.: Harvard University Press, 1950.

———. *The American Transcendentalists: Their Prose and Poetry.* New York: Doubleday, 1957.

Myerson, Joel, ed. *Transcendentalism: A Reader.* New York: Oxford University Press, 2000.

Bronson Alcott

The Journal of Bronson Alcott. Edited by Odell Shepard. Boston: Little, Brown, 1938.

The Letters of A. Bronson Alcott. Edited by Richard L. Herrnstadt. Ames: Iowa State University Press, 1969.

Ralph Waldo Emerson

The Journals and Miscellaneous Notebooks of Ralph Waldo Emerson, 16 volumes. Edited by William H. Gilman et al. Cambridge, Mass.: Harvard University Press, 1960–82.

The Poetry Notebooks of Ralph Waldo Emerson. Edited by Ralph H. Orth et al. Columbia: University of Missouri Press, 1986.

The Complete Sermons of Ralph Waldo Emerson, 4 volumes. Edited by Albert J. von Frank et al. Columbia: University of Missouri Press, 1989–92.

The Topical Notebooks of Ralph Waldo Emerson, 3 volumes. Edited by Ralph H. Orth et al. Columbia: University of Missouri Press, 1990–94.

English Traits. Edited by Robert E. Burkholder, Philip Nicoloff, Douglas Emory Wilson. Cambridge, Mass.: Harvard University Press, 1994.

Gougeon, Len, and Joel Myerson, eds. *Emerson's Anti-Slavery Writings.* New Haven, Conn.: Yale University Press, 1995.

Representative Men: Seven Lectures. Edited by Douglas Emory Wilson, with introduction by Andrew Delbarco. London: Belknap Press, 1996.

The Selected Letters of Ralph Waldo Emerson. Edited by Joel Myerson. New York: Columbia University Press, 1997.

The Later Lectures of Ralph Waldo Emerson, 1843–1871. Edited by Ronald Bosco and Joel Myerson. Athens: University of Georgia Press, 2001

Emerson's Prose and Poetry. Edited by Joel Porte and Saundra Morris. New York: Norton, 2001.

The Conduct of Life. Introduction by Barbara L. Packer. Cambridge, Mass.: Harvard University Press, 2003.

Margaret Fuller

The Letters of Margaret Fuller, 6 volumes. Edited by Robert Hudspeth. Ithaca, N.Y.: Cornell University Press, 1983–94.

Summer on the Lakes, in 1843. Edited by Susan Belasco Smith. Urbana: University of Illinois Press, 1991.

"These Sad but Glorious Days": Dispatches from Europe, 1846–1850. Edited by Larry J. Reynolds and Susan Belasco Smith. New Haven, Conn.: Yale University Press, 1992.

The Essential Margaret Fuller. Edited by Jeffrey Steele. New Brunswick, N.J.: Rutgers University Press, 1992.

The Portable Margaret Fuller. Edited by Mary Kelley. New York: Penguin, 1994.

Margaret Fuller's New York Journalism: A Biographical Essay and Key Writings. Edited by Catherine C. Mitchell. Knoxville: University of Tennessee Press, 1995.

Margaret Fuller, Critic, Writings from the New York Tribune. Edited by Judith Mattson Bean and Joel Myerson. New York: Columbia University Press, 2000.

Elizabeth Palmer Peabody

Ronda, Bruce, ed. *The Letters of Elizabeth Palmer Peabody, American Renaissance Woman.* Middletown, Conn.: Wesleyan University Press, 1984.

Henry David Thoreau

The Writings of Henry David Thoreau. 12 vols. to date. Edited by Walter Harding, Elizabeth Hall Witherall et. al. Princeton: Princeton N.J.: University Press, 1971–.

Faith in a Seed: The Dispersion of Seeds and Other Late Natural History Writings. Edited by Bradley P. Dean. Washington, D.C.: Island Press, 1993.

Wild Fruits: Thoreau's Rediscovered Last Manuscript. Edited by Bradley P. Dean. New York: Norton, 1999.

Cape Cod. Edited by Joseph J. Moldenhauer. Princeton, N.J.: Princeton University Press, 2004.

The Maine Woods. Edited by Joseph J. Moldenhauer. Princeton, N.J.: Princeton University Press, 2004.

Walden: A Fully Annotated Edition. Edited by Jeffrey S. Cramer. New Haven, Conn.: Yale University Press, 2004.

A Week on the Concord and Merrimack Rivers. Edited by Carl F. Hovde et al. Princeton, N.J.: Princeton University Press, 2004.

SECONDARY SOURCES

Abzug, Robert H. *Cosmos Crumbling: American Reform and the Religious Imagination.* New York: Oxford, 1994.

Ackroyd, Peter. *Blake: A Biography.* New York: Knopf, 1996.

Adams, John R. *Edward Everett Hale.* Boston: Twayne, 1977.

Allen, Gay Wilson. *Waldo Emerson: A Biography.* New York: Viking Press, 1981.

Ashton, Rosemary. *The Life of Samuel Taylor Coleridge.* Cambridge, Mass.: Blackwell Publishing, 1996.

Bartlett, Elizabeth Ann. *Liberty, Equality, Sorority: The Origins and Interpretation of American Feminist Thought: Frances Wright, Sarah Grimké, and Margaret Fuller.* New York: Carlson, 1994.

Bartlett, Irving H. "The Philosopher and the Activist," *New England Quarterly* 62 (June 1989): 280–296.

Barton, Cynthia H. *Transcendental Wife: The Life of Abigail May Alcott.* Lanham, Md.: University Press of America, 1996.

Bassan, Maurice. *Hawthorne's Son: The Life and Literary Career of Julian Hawthorne.* Columbus: Ohio State University Press, 1970.

Batchelor, John. *John Ruskin: A Life.* New York: Carroll and Graf, 2000.

Bean, Judith Mattson. "Texts from Conversation: Margaret Fuller's Influence on Emerson," *Studies in the American Renaissance* (1994): 227–244.

———. "'A Presence among Us': Fuller's Place in Nineteenth-Century Oral Culture," *ESQ: A Journal of the American Renaissance* 44 (1998): 79–123.

———. "Margaret Fuller and Julia Ward Howe: A Woman-to-Woman Influence." In *Margaret Fuller's Cultural Critique: Her Age and Legacy,* edited by Fritz Fleischmann. New York: Peter Lang, 2000, 91–108.

Beecher, Jonathan. *Charles Fourier: The Visionary and His World.* Berkeley: University of California Press, 1986.

Bennett, Fordyce Richard. "Bronson Alcott and Free Religion," *Studies in the American Renaissance.* Boston: Twayne, 1981, 407–421.

Bercovitch, Sacvan, ed. *The Cambridge History of American Literature, vol. 2. 1820–1865.* New York: Cambridge University Press, 1995.

Berger, Michael Benjamin. *Thoreau's Later Career and The Dispersion of Seeds: The Saunterer's Synoptic Vision.* Rochester, N.Y.: Camden House, 2000.

Birch, Dinah, ed. *John Ruskin: Selected Writings.* New York: Oxford University Press, 2004.

Biswas, Robindra. *Arthur Hugh Clough.* Oxford: Clarendon Press, 1972.

Bjelajac, David. *Washington Allston, Secret Societies, and the Alchemy of Anglo-American Painting.* New York: Cambridge University Press, 1997.

Bolles, Edmund Blair. *The Ice Finders: How a Poet, a Professor, and a Politician Discovered the Ice Age.* Washington, D.C.: Counterpoint, 1999.

Bosco, Ronald A. "Poetry for the World of Readers" and "Poetry for Bards Proper: Poetic Theory and Textual Integrity in Emerson's *Parnassus*." In *Studies in the American Renaissance* (1989): 257–312.

Braude, Ann. *Radical Spirits: Spiritualism and Women's Rights in Nineteenth-Century America*. Bloomington: Indiana University Press, 2001.

Brock, Erland, ed. *Swedenborg and His Influence*. Bryn Athyn, Pa.: Academy of the New Church, 1988.

Brooks, Paul. *The People of Concord: One Year in the Flowering of New England*. Chester, Conn.: Globe Pequot Press, 1990.

Brown, Florence Whiting. "Alcott and the Concord School of Philosophy." (August 1926). Reprinted in *Concord Harvest: Volume II*, edited by Kenneth Cameron. Hartford, Conn.: Transcendental Books, 1970.

Buell, Lawrence. *Literary Transcendentalism: Style and Vision in the American Renaissance*. Ithaca, N.Y.: Cornell University Press, 1973.

———. "The American Transcendentalist Poets." In *The Columbia History of American Poetry: The 19th Century*, edited by Jay Parini, 1993, 97–119.

———. "Transcendentalist Literary Legacies." In *Transient and Permanent: The Transcendentalist Movement and Its Contexts*, edited by Charles Capper and Conrad Edick Wright. Boston: Massachusetts Historical Society, 1999, 605–619.

———. *Emerson*. Cambridge, Mass.: Harvard University Press, 2003.

Burkholder, Robert E. "Emerson, Kneeland, and the Divinity School Address," *American Literature* 58 (March 1986): 1–14.

———. "(Re)Visiting 'The Adirondacs': Emerson's Confrontation with Wild Nature" (paper presented, Massachusetts Historical Society, April 2003).

Burkholder, Robert E., and Wesley T. Mott, eds. *Emersonian Circles: Essays in Honor of Joel Myerson*. Rochester, N.Y.: University of Rochester Press, 1997.

Cain, William E., ed. *A Historical Guide to Henry David Thoreau*. New York: Oxford University Press, 2000.

Calhoun, Charles C. *Longfellow: A Rediscovered Life*. Boston: Beacon Press, 2004.

Cameron, Kenneth Walter. "The Rowse Drawings of the Emersons," *ATQ* 13:2 (winter 1972): 49–52.

Capper, Charles. "Margaret Fuller as Cultural Reformer: The Conversations in Boston," *American Quarterly* 39:4 (winter 1987): 509–528.

———. *Margaret Fuller: An American Romantic Life*. Vol. 1, *The Private Years*. New York: Oxford University Press, 1992.

———. "Comments on 'Discovering Women's Intellectual History,'" *Intellectual History Newsletter* 15 (1993): 45–47.

———. "'A Little Beyond': The Problem of the Transcendentalist Movement in American History," *Journal of American History* 85:2 (September 1998): 502–539.

Capper, Charles, and Conrad Edick Wright, eds. *Transient and Permanent: The Transcendentalist Movement and Its Contexts*. Boston: Massachusetts Historical Society, 1999.

Carafiol, Peter. *Transcendent Reason: James Marsh and the Forms of Romantic Thought*. Tallahassee: University Presses of Florida, 1982.

Carpenter, Delores Bird. "Lidian Emerson's 'Transcendental Bible,'" *Studies in the American Renaissance* (1980): 91–95.

———. *The Selected Letters of Lidian Jackson Emerson*. Columbia: University of Missouri Press, 1987.

Caruthers, J. Wade. *Octavius Brooks Frothingham, Gentle Radical*. Tuscaloosa: University of Alabama Press, 1977.

Chernus, Ira. *American Nonviolence: The History of an Idea*. Maryknoll, N.Y.: Orbis Books, 2004.

Colbert, Charles. *A Measure of Perfection: Phrenology and the Fine Arts in America*. Chapel Hill: University of North Carolina Press, 1997.

Cole, Phyllis. *Mary Moody Emerson and the Origins of Transcendentalism: A Family History*. New York: Oxford University Press, 1998.

———. "The Nineteenth-Century Women's Rights Movement and the Canonization of Margaret Fuller," *ESQ: A Journal of the American Renaissance* 44 (1998): 1–33.

———. "Woman Questions: Emerson, Fuller, and New England Reform." In *Transient and Permanent: The Transcendentalist Movement and Its Contexts*, edited by Charles Capper and Conrad Edick Wright. Boston: Massachusetts Historical Society, 1999, 408–446.

———. "Stanton, Fuller, and the Grammar of Romanticism," *New England Quarterly* (December 2000): 533–559.

———. "Pain and Protest in the Emerson Family." In *The Emerson Dilemma: Essays on Emerson and Social*

Reform, edited by T. Gregory Garvey. Athens: University of Georgia Press, 2001, 67–92.

———. "The New Movement's Tide: Emerson and Women's Rights." In *Emerson Bicentennial Essays,* edited by Ronald Bosco and Joel Myerson. Boston: Massachusetts Historical Society and Northeastern University Press, forthcoming.

Collison, Gary. "A True Toleration: Harvard Divinity School Students and Unitarianism, 1830–1859." In *American Unitarianism, 1805–1865,* edited by Conrad Edick Wright. Boston: Northeastern University Press, 1989, 209–237.

Cromphout, Gustaaf Van. *Emerson's Modernity and the Example of Goethe.* Columbia: University of Missouri Press, 1990.

Crowe, Charles. *George Ripley: Transcendentalist and Utopian Socialist.* Athens: University of Georgia Press, 1967.

Dahlstrand, Frederick. *Amos Bronson Alcott: An Intellectual Biography.* East Brunswick, N.J.: Associated University Presses, 1982.

———. "Science, Religion, and the Transcendentalist Response to a Changing America," *Studies in the American Renaissance* (1988): 1–25.

Delano, Sterling. *The Harbinger and New England Transcendentalism: A Portrait of Associationism in America.* London: Associated University Presses, 1983.

———. *Brook Farm: The Dark Side of Utopia.* Cambridge, Mass.: Harvard University Press, 2004.

Delbanco, Andrew. *William Ellery Channing: An Essay on the Liberal Spirit in America.* Cambridge, Mass.: Harvard University Press, 1981.

d'Entremont, John. *Southern Emancipator: Moncure Conway, The American Years, 1832–1865.* New York: Oxford University Press, 1987.

Deese, Helen R. "Alcott's Conversations on the Transcendentalists: The Record of Caroline Dall," *American Literature* 60 (1988): 17–25.

———. "A New England Women's Network: Elizabeth Palmer Peabody, Caroline Healey Dall, and Delia S. Bacon," *Legacy* 8:2 (1991): 77–91.

———. "Tending the 'Sacred Fires': Theodore Parker and Caroline Healey Dall," *Unitarian Universalist Historical Society* 23 (1995): 22–38.

———. "'A Liberal Education': Caroline Healey Dall and Emerson." In *Emersonian Circles: Essays in Honor of Joel Myerson,* edited by Robert E. Burkholder and Wesley T. Mott. Rochester, N.Y.: University of Rochester Press, 1997, 237–260.

———. "Transcendentalism from the Margins: The Experience of Caroline Healey Dall." In *Transient and Permanent: The Transcendentalist Movement and Its Contexts,* edited by Charles Capper and Conrad Edick Wright. Boston: Massachusetts Historical Society, 1999, 527–547.

De Groot, Jean, ed. *Nature in American Philosophy.* Washington, D.C.: Catholic University of America Press, 2004.

Duberman, Martin. *James Russell Lowell.* Boston: Houghton Mifflin, 1966.

Duffy, Timothy. "The Gender of Letters: Charles Eliot Norton and the Decline of the Amateur Intellectual Tradition," *New England Quarterly* 69:1 (March 1996): 91–109.

Dykeman, Therese B. "Ednah Dow Cheney's American Aesthetics." In *Presenting Women Philosophers,* edited by Sara Ebenreck and Cecile T. Tougas. Philadelphia: Temple University Press, 2000, 41–50.

Elfe, Wolfgang, James Hardin, and Gunther Holst, eds. *The Fortunes of German Writers in America: Studies in Literary Reception.* Columbia: University of South Carolina Press, 1992.

Eiselein, Gregory, and Anne K. Phillips, eds. *The Louisa May Alcott Encyclopedia.* Westport, Conn.: Greenwood Press, 2001.

Emerson, Ellen Tucker. *The Life of Lidian Jackson Emerson,* ed. Delores Bird Carpenter. Boston: Twayne, 1980.

Fahrney, Ralph Ray. *Horace Greeley and the Tribune in the Civil War.* New York: Da Capo Press, 1970.

Field, Peter S. *Ralph Waldo Emerson: The Making of a Democratic Intellectual.* Lanham, Md.: Rowman & Littlefield, 2002.

Fisher, Benjamin Franklin, ed. *Poe and His Times: The Artist and His Milieu.* Baltimore: Edgar Allan Poe Society, 1990.

Fleck, Richard. "John Muir's Homage to Henry David Thoreau," *Pacific Historian* 29 (summer–fall 1985): 55–64.

Fleischmann, Fritz, ed. *Margaret Fuller's Cultural Critique: Her Age and Legacy.* New York: Peter Lang, 2000.

Francis, Richard. *Transcendental Utopias: Individual and Community at Brook Farm, Fruitlands, and Walden.* Ithaca, N.Y.: Cornell University Press, 1997.

Gabriel, Ralph Henry. *The Course of American Democratic Thought.* Westport, Conn.: Greenwood Press, 1986.

Gale, Richard. *The Philosophy of William James.* New York: Cambridge University Press, 2005.

Garvey, T. Gregory. "Margaret Fuller's *Woman in the Nineteenth Century* and the Rhetoric of Social Reform in the 1840s," *ESQ: A Journal of the American Renaissance* 47:2 (2001): 113–133.

Garvey, T. Gregory, ed. *The Emerson Dilemma: Essays on Emerson and Social Reform.* Athens: University of Georgia Press, 2001.

Glick, Wendell, ed. *The Higher Law: Thoreau on Civil Disobedience and Reform.* Princeton, N.J.: Princeton University Press, 2004.

Goetzmann, William, ed. *The American Hegelians: An Intellectual Episode in the History of Western America.* New York: Knopf, 1973.

Gohdes, Clarence. *The Periodicals of American Transcendentalism.* Durham, N.C.: Duke University Press, 1931.

Golemba, Henry. *George Ripley.* Boston: Twayne, 1977.

Goodwin, Joan W. *The Remarkable Mrs. Ripley: The Life of Sarah Alden Bradford Ripley.* Boston: Northeastern University Press, 1998.

Gougeon, Len. *Virtue's Hero: Emerson, Antislavery, and Reform.* Athens: University of Georgia Press, 1990.

———. "Emerson and the Woman Question: The Evolution of His Thought," *New England Quarterly* 71:4 (December 1998): 570–592.

Green, Judith Kent. "A Tentative Transcendentalist in the Ohio Valley: Samuel Osgood and the *Western Messenger,*" *Studies in the American Renaissance* (1987): 79–92.

Greenspan, Ezra. "Evert Duyckinck and the History of Wiley and Putnam's Library of American Books, 1845–1847," *American Literature* 64 (December 1992): 677–693.

Grodzins, Dean David. *American Heretic: Theodore Parker and Transcendentalism.* Chapel Hill: University of North Carolina Press, 2002.

Guarneri, Carl. *The Utopian Alternative: Fourierism in Nineteenth Century America.* Ithaca, N.Y.: Cornell University Press, 1991.

Gura, Philip. *The Wisdom of Words: Language, Theology, and Literature in the New England Renaissance.* Middletown, Conn.: Wesleyan University Press, 1981.

Gura, Philip F. "A wild, rank place: Thoreau's *Cape Cod.*" In *The Cambridge Companion to Henry David Thoreau,* edited by Joel Myerson. New York: Cambridge University Press, 1995, 142–151.

———. "Essaying Antebellum Prose," *Reviews in American History* 24:1 (1996): 21–28.

Gura, Philip F., and Joel Myerson, eds. *Critical Essays on American Transcendentalism.* Boston: G. K. Hall, 1982.

Habich, Robert D. *Transcendentalism and the Western Messenger: A History of the Magazine and Its Contributors, 1835–1841.* Rutherford, N.J.: Fairleigh Dickinson University Press, 1985.

———. "Emerson's Reluctant Foe: Andrews Norton and the Transcendentalist Controversy," *NEQ* 65 (June 1992): 208–237.

Handlin, Lillian. *George Bancroft: The Intellectual as Democrat.* New York: Harper and Row, 1984.

Harding, Walter, ed. *Sophia Thoreau's Scrapbook.* Geneseo, N.Y.: Thoreau Society, 1964.

Harding, Walter. *The Days of Henry Thoreau.* New York: Dover, 1982.

Harding, Walter Roy, and Michael Meyer. *The New Thoreau Handbook.* New York: New York University Press, 1980.

Hardwick, Elizabeth. *Herman Melville.* New York: Viking, 2000.

Harris, Kenneth Marc. *Carlyle and Emerson: Their Long Debate.* Cambridge, Mass.: Harvard University Press, 1978.

Harris, Mark W. *Historical Dictionary of Unitarian Universalism.* Lanham, Md.: Scarecrow Press, 2004.

Haskell, Thomas L. *The Emergence of Professional Social Science: The American Social Science Association and the Nineteenth-Century Crisis of Authority.* Urbana: University of Illinois Press, 1977.

Hathaway, Richard D. *Sylvester Judd's New England.* University Park: Pennsylvania State University Press, 1981.

Heath, William G. "Cyrus Bartol's Transcendentalism," *Studies in the American Renaissance* (1979): 399–408.

Hendrick, George. *Henry Salt: Humanitarian Reformer and Man of Letters.* Urbana: University of Illinois Press, 1977.

Hendrick, George et al., eds. *The Life of Henry David Thoreau, by Henry Salt.* Urbana: University of Illinois, 2000.

Henley, Don, and David Marsh, eds. *Heaven Is under Our Feet: A Book for Walden Woods.* Stamford, Conn.: Longmeadow Press, 1991.

Hoag, Ronald Wesley. "Thoreau's Later Natural History Writings." In *The Cambridge Companion to Henry*

David Thoreau, edited by Joel Myerson. New York: Cambridge University Press, 1995.

Hoecker-Drysdale, Susan E. *Harriet Martineau: First Woman Sociologist.* New York: St. Martin's Press, 1992.

Hoffman, R. Joseph, "William Henry Furness: The Transcendentalist Defense of the Gospels," *NEQ* 56 (1983): 236–260.

Horner, Charles F. *The Life of James Redpath and the Development of the Modern Lyceum.* New York: Barse and Hopkins, 1926.

Howe, Daniel Walker. *The Unitarian Conscience: Harvard Moral Philosophy, 1805–1861.* Cambridge, Mass.: Harvard University Press, 1970.

———. *Making the American Self: Jonathan Edwards to Abraham Lincoln.* Cambridge, Mass.: Harvard University Press, 1997.

Hudspeth, Robert N. *Ellery Channing.* New York: Twayne, 1973.

———. " 'A Higher Standard in Thought and Action': Margaret Fuller and the Idea of Criticism." In *American Unitarianism, 1805–1865,* edited by Conrad Edick Wright. Boston: Massachusetts Historical Society, 1989, 145–160.

Irie, Yukio. *Emerson and Quakerism.* Tokyo: Kenkyusha, 1967.

Irons, Susan. "Channing's Influence on Peabody: Self-Culture and the Danger of Egoism," *Studies in the American Renaissance* (1992): 121–135.

Jackson, Carl T. *The Oriental Religions and American Thought: 19th-century Explorations.* Westport, Conn.: Greenwood Press, 1981.

Johnson, Claudia Durst. "Transcendental Wild Oats" or "The Cost of an Idea," *ATQ* 1998 12(1): 45–65.

Jones Very: The Complete Poems. Edited by Helen Deese. Athens: University of Georgia Press, 1993.

Kamp, Jim, ed. *Reference Guide to American Literature,* 3rd ed. Detroit: St. James Press, 1994.

Karcher, Carolyn. *The First Woman of the Republic: A Cultural Biography of Lydia Maria Child.* Durham, N.C.: Duke University Press, 1994.

———. "Margaret Fuller and Lydia Maria Child: Intersecting Careers, Reciprocal Influences." In *Margaret Fuller's Cultural Critique: Her Age and Legacy,* edited by Fritz Fleischmann. New York: Peter Lang, 2000, 75–87.

Karcher, Carolyn L., ed. *A Lydia Maria Child Reader.* Durham, N.C.: Duke University Press, 1997.

Kaur, Harpinder. *Gandhi's Concept of Civil Disobedience: A Study with Special Reference to Thoreau's Influence on Gandhi.* New Delhi: Intellectual, 1986.

Kearns, Francis E. "Margaret Fuller and the Abolition Movement." In *Race, Class, and Gender in Nineteenth-Century Culture,* edited by Maryanne Cline Horowitz. Rochester, N.Y.: University of Rochester Press, 1991, 187–194.

Lang, Amy Schrager. *Prophetic Woman: Anne Hutchinson and the Problem of Dissent in the Literature of New England.* Berkeley: University of California Press, 1987.

Lapati, Americo D. *Orestes A. Brownson.* New York: Twayne, 1965.

LeBeau, Bryan F. *Frederic Henry Hedge: Nineteenth Century American Transcendentalist.* Allison Park, Pa.: Pickwick Publications, 1985.

Leidecker, Kurt F. "Amos Bronson Alcott and the Concord School of Philosophy," *The Personalist* (summer 1952): 242–256.

———. *Yankee Teacher: The Life of William Torrey Harris.* New York: Kraus, 1971.

Leighton, Walter L. *French Philosophers and New England Transcendentalism.* New York: Greenwood Press, 1968.

The Life and Letters of Christopher Pearse Cranch, by his Daughter Leonora Scott Cranch. Brooklyn, N.Y.: AMS Press, 1969.

Lopez, Michael. "*The Conduct of Life:* Emerson's Anatomy of Power." In *The Cambridge Companion to Ralph Waldo Emerson,* edited by Joel Porte and Saundra Morris. New York: Cambridge University Press, 1999, 243–366.

Loving, Jerome. *Emerson, Whitman, and the American Muse.* Chapel Hill: University of North Carolina Press, 1982.

Lunde, Erik S. *Horace Greeley.* Boston: Twayne, 1981.

Marovitz, Sanford E. "Emerson's Shakespeare: From Scorn to Apotheosis." In *Emerson Centenary Essays,* edited by Joel Myerson. Carbondale: Southern Illinois University Press, 1982.

Marshall, Megan. *The Peabody Sisters: Three Women Who Ignited American Romanticism.* Boston: Houghton Mifflin, 2005.

Mathews, James W. "George Partridge Bradford: Friend of Transcendentalists," *Studies in the American Renaissance* (1981): 133–156.

Maxfield-Miller, Elizabeth. "Elizabeth of Concord: Selected Letters of Elizabeth Sherman Hoar to the

Emerson Family and the Emerson Circle," *Studies in the American Renaissance* (1984, 1985, 1986).

Maynard, W. Barksdale. *Walden Pond: A History.* Oxford and New York: Oxford University Press, 2004.

McFarland, Philip. *Hawthorne in Concord.* New York: Grove Press, 2004.

McLoughlin, Michael. *Dead Letters to the New World: Melville, Emerson, and American Transcendentalism.* New York: Routledge, 2003.

Menand, Louis. *The Metaphysical Club: A Story of Ideas in America.* New York: Farrar, Straus, and Giroux, 2001.

Messerli, Jonathan. *Horace Mann: A Biography.* New York: Knopf, 1972.

Metzger, Charles R. *Emerson and Greenough: Transcendental Pioneers of an American Esthetic.* Berkeley: University of California Press, 1954.

Meyer, Howard N. *The Magnificent Activist: The Writings of Thomas Wentworth Higginson.* Cambridge, Mass.: Da Capo Press, 2000.

Meyers, Jeffrey. *Edgar Allan Poe: His Life and Legacy.* New York: Cooper Square Press, 2000.

Mikics, David. *The Romance of Individualism in Emerson and Nietzsche.* Athens: Ohio University Press, 2003.

Miller, F. DeWolfe. *Christopher Pearse Cranch and his Caricatures of New England Transcendentalism.* Cambridge, Mass.: Harvard University Press, 1951.

Miller, Perry. *Errand into the Wilderness.* Cambridge, Mass.: Harvard University Press, 1956.

Milne, Gordon. *George William Curtis and the Genteel Tradition.* Bloomington: Indiana University Press, 1956.

Mitchell, Thomas R. *Hawthorne's Fuller Mystery.* Amherst: University of Massachusetts Press, 1998.

Moldenhauer, Joseph J. *"The Maine Woods."* In *The Cambridge Companion to Henry David Thoreau,* edited by Joel Myerson. New York: Cambridge University Press, 1995, 124–141.

Mott, Wesley T., ed. *Biographical Dictionary of Transcendentalism.* Westport, Conn.: Greenwood Press, 1996.

———. *Encyclopedia of Transcendentalism.* Westport, Conn.: Greenwood Press, 1996.

Myerson, Joel. "A Calendar of Transcendental Club Meetings," *American Literature* 44:2 (May 1972): 197–207.

———. "'A True & High Minded Person': Transcendentalist Sarah Clarke," *Southwest Review* (spring 1974): 163–172.

———. "Caroline Dall's Reminiscences of Margaret Fuller," *Harvard Library Bulletin* 22:4 (October 1974): 414–428.

———. "Mrs. Dall Edits Miss Fuller: The Story of *Margaret and Her Friends*," *Papers of the Bibliographical Society of America* 72:2 (1978): 187–200.

———. *Brook Farm: An Annotated Bibliography and Resources Guide.* New York: Garland, 1978.

———. *The New England Transcendentalists and the* Dial: *A History of the Magazine and Its Contributors.* London and Toronto: Associated University Presses, 1980.

———. "The Women of Transcendentalism and the New Biography," *New England Quarterly* (December 1999): 625–645.

Myerson, Joel, ed. *The Transcendentalists: A Review of Research and Criticism.* New York: Modern Language Association, 1984.

———. *Emerson and Thoreau: The Contemporary Reviews.* New York: Cambridge University Press, 1992.

———. *The Cambridge Companion to Henry David Thoreau.* New York: Cambridge University Press, 1995.

Norko, Julie. "Christopher Cranch's Struggle with the Muses." *Studies in the American Renaissance* (1992): 209–227.

Packer, Barbara. "The Transcendentalists." In *The Cambridge History of American Literature,* vol. 2: *1820–1865,* edited by Sacvan Bercovitch. New York: Cambridge University Press, 1995, 329–607.

Petrulionis, Sandra Harbert. "By the Light of Her Mother's Lamp: Woman's Work versus Man's Philosophy in Louisa May Alcott's 'Transcendental Wild Oats,'" *Studies in the American Renaissance* (1995): 69–81.

Pfaelzer, Jean. "The Sentimental Promise and the Utopian Myth: Rebecca Harding Davis's 'The Harmonists' and Louisa May Alcott's 'Transcendental Wild Oats,'" *American Transcendental Quarterly* 3:1 (March 1989): 85–99.

Pitts, Mary E. "Thoreau's Poem 'Sympathy': His 'Gentle Boy' Identified," *The Concord Saunterer* 18:2 (December 1985): 20–27.

Pochmann, Henry A. *New England Transcendentalism and St. Louis Hegelianism.* New York: Haskell House, 1970.

Porte, Joel, and Saundra Morris, eds. *The Cambridge Companion to Ralph Waldo Emerson.* New York: Cambridge University Press, 1999.

Power, Edward J. *Religion and the Public Schools in Nineteenth-Century America: The Contribution of Orestes A. Brownson.* New York: Paulist Press, 1996.

Ray, Angela. *The Lyceum and Public Culture in the 19th-Century U.S.* East Lansing: Michigan State University, 2005.

Raymond, Henrietta Dana. *Sophia Dana Willard Ripley.* Portsmouth, N.H.: Peter E. Randall, 1994.

Renehan, Edward J., Jr. *The Secret Six: The True Tale of the Men Who Conspired with John Brown.* New York: Crown, 1995.

Reynolds, David S. *Walt Whitman.* New York: Oxford University Press, 2005.

Reynolds, Larry J. "From *Dial* Essay to New York Book: The Making of *Woman in the Nineteenth Century.*" In *Periodical Literature in Nineteenth-Century America*, edited by Susan Belasco Smith and Kenneth M. Price. Charlottesville: University of Virginia Press, 1995, 17–34.

Richardson, Robert, Jr. *Emerson: The Mind on Fire.* Berkeley: University of California Press, 1995.

———. *Henry Thoreau: A Life of the Mind.* Berkeley: University of California Press, 1986.

Richman, Michael. *Daniel Chester French: An American Sculptor.* Washington, D.C.: Preservation Press, 1983.

Ritchie, Amanda. "Margaret Fuller's First Conversation Series: A Discovery in the Archives," *Legacy: A Journal of American Women Writers* 18:2 (June 2001): 216–232.

Robbins, Paula I. *The Royal Family of Concord: Samuel, Elizabeth, and Rockwood Hoar and Their Friendship with Ralph Waldo Emerson.* Philadelphia: Xlibris, 2003.

Robinson, David M. "Margaret Fuller and the Transcendental Ethos: *Woman in the Nineteenth Century,*" *PMLA* 97 (1982): 83–98.

———. *Emerson and The Conduct of Life: Pragmatism and Ethical Purpose in the Later Work.* New York: Cambridge University Press, 1993.

———. *Natural Life: Thoreau's Worldly Transcendentalism.* Ithaca, N.Y.: Cornell University Press, 2004.

Ronda, Bruce. *Elizabeth Palmer Peabody: A Reformer on Her Own Terms.* Cambridge, Mass.: Harvard University Press, 1999.

Rose, Anne C. *Transcendentalism as a Social Movement, 1830–1850.* New Haven, Conn.: Yale University Press, 1981.

Rosenthal, Bernard. "Thoreau's Book of Leaves," *ESQ* 56 (1969): 7–11.

Rossi, William. "Poetry and Progress: Thoreau, Lyell, and the Geological Principles of *A Week,*" *American Literature* 66 (June 1994): 275–300.

Sablosky, Irving. *What They Heard: Music in America, 1852–1881, from the Pages of "Dwight's Journal of Music."* London and Baton Rouge: Louisiana State University Press, 1986.

Sacks, Kenneth. *Understanding Emerson: "The American Scholar" and His Struggle for Self-Reliance.* Princeton, N.J.: Princeton University Press, 2003.

Saloman, Ora Frishberg. *Beethoven's Symphonies and J. S. Dwight: The Birth of American Music Criticism.* Boston: Northeastern University Press, 1995.

Sayre, Robert F. *Thoreau and the American Indians.* Princeton, N.J.: Princeton University Press, 1977.

Sealts, Merton M., Jr. *Emerson on the Scholar.* Columbia: University of Missouri Press, 1992.

Sebouhian, George. "A Dialogue with Death: An Examination of Emerson's 'Friendship,'" *Studies in the American Renaissance* (1989), 219–239.

Sedgwick, Ellery. *The Atlantic Monthly, 1857–1909: Yankee Humanism at High Tide and Ebb.* Amherst: University of Massachusetts Press, 1994.

Shakir, Evelyn. "Ednah Dow Cheney: 'Jack at all trades,'" *American Transcendental Quarterly* 47–48 (summer–fall 1980): 95–115.

Shepard, Odell. *Pedlar's Progress: The Life of Bronson Alcott.* Boston: Little, Brown, 1937.

Simmons, Nancy Craig. "Arranging the Sibylline Leaves: James Elliot Cabot's Work as Emerson's Literary Executor." *Studies in the American Renaissance* (1983): 335–389.

Smith, Harmon L. *My Friend, My Friend: The Story of Thoreau's Relationship with Emerson.* Amherst: University of Massachusetts Press, 1999.

Spevack, Edmund. *Charles Follen's Search for Nationality and Freedom: Germany and America, 1796–1840.* Cambridge, Mass.: Harvard University Press, 1997.

Stack, George J. *Nietzsche and Emerson: An Elective Affinity.* Athens: Ohio University Press, 1992.

Steele, Janet E. *The Sun Shines for All: Journalism and Ideology in the Life of Charles A. Dana.* New York: Syracuse University Press, 1993.

Steele, Jeffrey. "Transcendental Friendship: Emerson, Fuller, and Thoreau." In *The Cambridge Companion to Ralph Waldo Emerson,* edited by Joel Porte and

Saundra Morris. New York: Cambridge University Press, 1999, 121–139.

———. *Transfiguring America: Myth, Ideology, and Mourning in Margaret Fuller's Writing.* Columbia: University of Missouri Press, 2001.

Stern, Madeleine B. *Heads and Headlines: The Phrenological Fowlers.* Norman: University of Oklahoma Press, 1971.

———. "Emerson and Phrenology," *Studies in the American Renaissance* (1984): 213–228.

———. *Louisa May Alcott.* New York: Random House, 1996.

Stewart, James Brewer. *Wendell Phillips: Liberty's Hero.* Baton Rouge: Louisiana State University Press, 1986.

Strickland, Charles. "A Transcendentalist Father: The Child-Rearing Practices of Bronson Alcott," *Perspectives in American History,* 3 (1969): 5–73.

Tharp, Louisa Hall. *The Peabody Sisters of Salem.* Boston: Little, Brown, 1950.

Tilton, Eleanor M. "The True Romance of Anna Hazard Barker and Samuel Gray Ward," *Studies in the American Renaissance* (1987): 53–72.

Tomlinson, Stephen. *Head Masters: Phrenology, Secular Education, and 19th-Century Social Thought.* Tuscaloosa: University of Alabama Press, 2005.

Tonn, Mari Boor. "The *Una,* 1853–1855: The Premiere of the Woman's Rights Press." In *A Voice of Their Own: The Woman Suffrage Press, 1840–1910,* edited by Martha M. Solomon. Tuscaloosa: University of Alabama Press, 1991, 48–70.

Tufariello, Catherine. "'The Remembering Wine': Emerson's Influence on Whitman and Dickinson." In *The Cambridge Companion to Ralph Waldo Emerson,* edited by Joel Porte and Saundra Morris. New York: Cambridge University Press, 1999, 162–191.

Turner, Frederick. *John Muir: Rediscovering America.* Cambridge, Mass.: Perseus, 2000.

Turner, James. *The Liberal Education of Charles Eliot Norton.* London and Baltimore: Johns Hopkins University Press, 1999.

Tuttleton, James W. *Thomas Wentworth Higginson.* Boston: Twayne, 1978.

Valenti, Patricia Dunlavy. *Sophia Peabody Hawthorne. A Life, Volume 1, 1809–1847.* Columbia: University of Missouri Press, 2004.

Varg, Paul A. *Edward Everett: The Intellectual in the Turmoil of Politics.* Selinsgrove, Pa.: Susquehanna University Press, 1992.

Vogel, Stanley M. *German Literary Influences on the American Transcendentalists.* New Haven, Conn.: Yale University Press, 1955.

Von Frank, Albert J. *The Trials of Anthony Burns: Freedom and Slavery in Emerson's Boston.* Cambridge, Mass.: Harvard University Press, 1998.

———. "Essays: First Series (1841)," Joel Porte and Saundra Morris, eds. *The Cambridge Companion to Ralph Waldo Emerson.* New York: Cambridge University Press, 1999, 106–120.

Von Mehren, Joan. *Minerva and the Muse: A Life of Margaret Fuller.* Amherst: University of Massachusetts Press, 1994.

Walls, Laura Dassow. "'The Napoleon of Science': Humboldt in Antebellum America," *19th-Century Contexts* 14:1 (1990): 71–98.

———. *Seeing New Worlds: Henry David Thoreau and Nineteenth-Century Natural Science.* Madison: University of Wisconsin Press, 1995.

Wayne, Tiffany K. *Woman Thinking: Feminism and Transcendentalism in Nineteenth-Century America.* Lanham, Md.: Lexington Books, 2005.

Weisbuch, Robert. *Atlantic Double-Cross: American Literature and British Influence in the Age of Emerson.* Chicago: University of Chicago Press, 1986.

Wells, Ronald Vale. *Three Christian Transcendentalists: James Marsh, Caleb Sprague Henry, and Frederic Henry Hedge.* New York: Octagon Books, 1972.

White, Michael, and John Gribbin. *Darwin: A Life in Science.* New York: Dutton, 1995.

Williams, Gary. *Hungry Heart: The Literary Emergence of Julia Ward Howe.* Amherst: University of Massachusetts Press, 1999.

Wineapple, Brenda. *Hawthorne: A Life.* New York: Knopf, 2003.

Woodell, Roland H. *John Greenleaf Whittier: A Biography.* Haverhill, Mass.: Trustees of the John Greenleaf Whittier Homestead, 1985.

Wright, Conrad Edick, ed. *American Unitarianism: 1805–1865.* Boston: Northeastern University Press, 1989.

Wunder, Richard P. *Hiram Powers: Vermont Sculptor, 1805–1873.* Cranbury, N.J.: Associated University Presses, 1991.

Wynkoop, William M. *Three Children of the Universe: Emerson's View of Shakespeare, Bacon, and Milton.* The Hague: Mouton, 1966.

Yacovone, Donald. *Samuel Joseph May and the Dilemmas of the Liberal Persuasion.* Philadelphia: Temple University Press, 1991.

Yannella, Donald. *Ralph Waldo Emerson.* Boston: Twayne, 1982.

Zwarg, Christina. *Feminist Conversations: Fuller, Emerson, and the Play of Reading.* Ithaca, N.Y.: Cornell University Press, 1995.

Note: **Boldface** page numbers indicate main entries.